205328

THE RANDOM HOUSE

Health and
Medicine

DICTIONARY

THE RANDOM HOUSE

Health and Medicine

DICTIONARY

DICTIONARY

RANDOM HOUSE

NEW YORK

Library of Congress Cataloging-in-Publication Data

The Random House dictionary of health and medicine

    p.   cm.
  ISBN 0-679-41590-4 : $7.00
  1. Medicine—Dictionaries.   2. Health—Dictionaries.   I. Random House (Firm)   II. Title:
Dictionary of health and medicine.
R121.R214 1992
610'.3—dc20   92-25714
                                      CIP

vided into syllables to show end-of-line hy-phenation. Every entry word is either followed by a parenthesized pronunciation (see the Pronunciation Key on page ix) or given stress marks to indicate relative differences in emphasis between syllables or words. Most entries are provided with part-of-speech labels (as *n., v.t., adj.,* etc.) and, where appropriate, irregular plural forms (as those for **adenoma**) and irregular inflected forms of verbs (as those for **intubate**) are indicated. In addition, many derivative forms are run on to main entries (as **bariatric** and **bariatrician** under the main entry **bariatrics**), and certain entries, such as abbreviations of Latin phrases used in prescriptions, are given brief etymologies.

It is hoped that this book, with its large selection of entries and clear, concise definitions, will serve as a practical reference guide for anyone interested in health and well-being.

Preface

The Random House Health and Medicine Dictionary is a handy, portable reference book designed to help lay people better understand the language of health and medicine. Familiarity with this specialized language will lead to better communication with one's doctor, nurse, or other health professional. Over 8,000 terms have been carefully selected and defined to cover the most important areas of health and medicine. The vocabulary includes major diseases and disorders; treatments, tests, and therapies; bodily parts and functions; diagnostic tools and techniques; medical and surgical equipment; drugs and medicines; and medical disciplines, theories, and specialties.

Based on Random House's constantly updated "Living Dictionary" database, the book's hundreds of new terms and meanings reflect the most recent advances and discoveries in such fields as immunology, genetics, molecular biology, pharmacology, and biotechnology, making this the most up-to-date pocket-size medical dictionary available.

All the entries are listed in convenient alphabetical order. Each boldface entry is di-

Staff

Enid Pearsons, *Editor*
Sol Steinmetz, *Executive Editor*
Mia McCroskey, *Managing Editor*

Constance Baboukis Padakis, *Associate Editor*
Judy Kaplan Johnson, *Supervising Copyeditor*
Sasan Doroudian, Lani Mysak, Maria Padilla,
  Editorial Assistants
Stephen Weinstein, *Research Assistant*

Patricia W. Ehresmann, *Production Director*
Rita E. Rubin, *Production Associate*
Charlotte Staub, *Designer*

Publisher, Michael Mellin
Associate Publishers, Catherine Fowler,
  John L. Hornor III

Contents

Pronunciation Key

STRESS

Pronunciations are marked for stress to reveal the relative differences in emphasis between syllables. In words of two or more syllables, a primary stress mark (ʹ), as in **mother** (muth′ər), follows the syllable having greatest stress. A secondary stress mark (ʹ), as in **grandmother** (grand′ muth′ər), follows a syllable having slightly less stress than primary but more stress than an unmarked syllable.

ENGLISH SOUNDS

a	act, bat, marry
ā	age, paid, say
â(r)	air, dare, Mary
ä	ah, part, balm
b	back, cabin, cab
ch	child, beach
d	do, madder, bed
e	edge, set, merry
ē	equal, bee, pretty
ēr	ear, mere
f	fit, differ, puff
g	give, trigger, beg
h	hit, behave
hw	which, nowhere
i	if, big, mirror
ī	ice, bite, deny
j	just, tragic, fudge
k	keep, token, make
l	low, mellow, bottle (bot′l)
m	my, summer, him
n	now, sinner, button (but′n)
ng	sing, Washington
o	ox, bomb, wasp
ō	over, boat, no
ô	order, ball, raw

oi	oil, joint, joy
o͝o	book, tour
o͞o	ooze, fool, too
ou	out, loud, cow
p	pot, supper, stop
r	read, hurry, near
s	see, passing, miss
sh	shoe, fashion, push
t	ten, matter, bit
th	thin, ether, path
th	that, either, smooth
u	up, sun
û(r)	urge, burn, cur
v	voice, river, live
w	witch, away
y	yes, onion
z	zoo, lazy, those
zh	treasure, mirage
ə	used in unaccented syllables to indicate the sound of the reduced vowel in *a*lone, syst*e*m, eas*i*ly, gall*o*p, circ*u*s
ᵊ	used between i and r and between ou and r to show triphthongal quality, as in fire(fīᵊr), hour (ouᵊr)

NON-ENGLISH SOUNDS

A	as in French *ami* (A mē′)
KH	as in Scottish *loch* (lôKH)
N	as in French *bon* (bôN) [used to indicate that the preceding vowel is nasalized.]
Œ	as in French *feu* (fŒ)
R	[a symbol for any non-English *r*, including a trill or flap in Italian and Spanish and a sound in French and German similar to KH but pronounced with voice]
Y	as in French *tu* (tY)
ᵊ	as in French *Bastogne* (bA stôn′yᵊ)

Abbreviations
Used in This Book

adj.	adjective
adv.	adverb
Anat.	Anatomy
at. no.	atomic number
at. wt.	atomic weight
Biochem.	Biochemistry
Biol.	Biology
disting.	distinguished
Embryol.	Embryology
esp.	especially
lit.	literally
Gr.	Greek
L.	Latin
n.	noun
Pathol.	Pathology
Pharm.	Pharmacology
Physiol.	Physiology
pl.	plural
Psychoanal.	Psychoanalysis
Psychol.	Psychology
sp. gr.	specific gravity
Surg.	Surgery
usu.	usually
v.	verb
v.i.	intransitive verb
v.t.	transitive verb

A, *Symbol.* **1.** a major blood group. Compare ABO SYSTEM. **2.** adenine. **3.** alanine.

AB, *Symbol.* a major blood group. Compare ABO SYSTEM.

ab·do·men (ab′də mən, ab dō′-), *n.* **1.** (in mammals) **a.** the part of the body between the thorax and the pelvis; belly. **b.** the cavity of this part of the body containing the stomach, intestines, etc. **2.** (in nonmammalian vertebrates) a region of the body corresponding to, but not coincident with, this part or cavity. —**ab·dom′i·nal** (-dom′ə nl), *adj.*

ab·dom·i·no·plas·ty (ab dom′ə nə plas′tē), *n., pl.* **-ties.** excision of abdominal fat and skin for cosmetic purposes.

ab·du·cens (ab dōō′senz, -sənz, -dyōō′-), *n., pl.* **ab·du·cen·tes** (ab′dōō sen′tēz, -dyōō-). ABDUCENS NERVE.

abdu′cens nerve′, *n.* either one of the sixth pair of cranial nerves, composed of motor fibers that innervate the lateral rectus muscle of the eye.

ab·du·cent (ab dōō′sənt, -dyōō′-), *adj.* drawing away, as by the action of a muscle; abducting.

ab·duct (ab dukt′), *v.t.* to move or draw away from the axis of the body or a limb (opposed to *adduct*).

ab·duc′tor, *n.* any muscle that abducts (opposed to *adductor*).

ab·er·ra·tion (ab′ə rā′shən), *n.* **1.** any disturbance of the rays of a pencil of light such that they can no longer be brought to a sharp focus or form a clear image. **2.** mental unsoundness or disorder, esp. of a minor or temporary nature; mental lapse. —**ab′er·ra′tion·al,** *adj.*

ab·la·tion (a blā′shən), *n.* the removal of organs, abnormal growths, or harmful substances from the body by mechanical means, as by surgery.

abnor′mal psychol′ogy, *n.* the branch of psychology that deals with modes of behavior, mental phenomena, etc., that deviate markedly from the standards believed to characterize a well-adjusted personality.

ABO, ABO SYSTEM.

a·bort (ə bôrt′), *v.i.* **1.** to bring forth a fetus before it is viable. —*v.t.* **2.** to cause to bring forth (a fetus) before it is viable. **3.** to cause (a pregnant female) to be delivered of a nonviable fetus.

a·bor·ti·fa·cient (ə bôr′tə fā′shənt), *adj.* **1.** causing abortion. —*n.* **2.** a drug or device for inducing abortion.

a·bor·tion (-shən), *n.* **1.** the removal of an embryo or fetus from the uterus in order to end a pregnancy. **2.** any of various procedures for terminating a pregnancy. **3.** Also called **spontaneous abortion.** MISCARRIAGE. **4.** an immature and nonviable fetus. **5.** a malformed or monstrous person or thing. **6.** the arrested development of an embryo or an organ at a more or less early stage. **7.** the stopping of an illness, infection, etc., at a very early stage.

abor'tion-on-demand', *n.* the right of a woman to have an abortion during the first six months of a pregnancy.

abor'tion pill', *n.* an antigestational drug, such as RU 486.

a·bor·tive (-tiv), *adj.* acting to halt progress of a disease.

a·bor·tus (-təs), *n., pl.* **-tus·es.** a miscarriage.

ABO system, *n.* a classification of human blood into four major groups, A, B, AB, and O, based on the presence on the surface of red blood cells of either of two antigens, A or B, or their absence, O: used in determining compatibility for transfusions.

a·bou·li·a (ə bōō′lē ə), *n.* ABULIA. —**a·bou′lic,** *adj.*

a·bra·sion (ə brā′zhən), *n.* a scraped spot or area; the result of rubbing or scraping: *abrasions on the leg.*

ab·re·ac·tion (ab′rē ak′shən), *n.* the release of emotional tension achieved through recalling a repressed traumatic experience, esp. during psychoanalysis. —**ab′re·act′,** *v.t.* —**ab′re·ac′tive,** *adj.*

ab·scess (ab′ses), *n.* a localized accumulation of pus in a body tissue. —**ab′scessed,** *adj.*

ab·sti·nence (ab′stə nəns) also **ab′sti·nen·cy,** *n.* abstention from a drug, as alcohol or heroin, esp. a drug on which one is dependent: *total abstinence.* —**ab′sti·nent,** *adj.* —**ab′sti·nent·ly,** *adv.*

a·bu·li·a (ə byōō′lē ə, ə bōō′-) also **aboulia,** *n.* a symptom of mental disorder involving impairment or loss of volition. —**a·bu′lic,** *adj.*

a.c., (in prescriptions) before meals. [Latin, *ante cibum*]

ac·a·ri·a·sis (ak′ə rī′ə sis), *n., pl.* **-ses** (-sēz′). **1.** infestation with acarids, esp. mites. **2.** a skin disease caused by such infestation, as scabies.

ac·cept (ak sept′), *v.t.* to receive (a transplanted organ or tissue) without adverse reaction. Compare REJECT.

ac·couche·ment (ə kōōsh′mənt, ak′ōōsh mäN′), *n.* the confinement of childbirth; lying-in.

ac·cou·cheur (ak′ōō shûr′), *n.* a person who assists during childbirth, esp. an obstetrician.

Ace′ band′age (ās), *Trademark.* an elasticized bandage, usu. in a continuous strip, for securely binding an injured wrist, knee, or other joint.

a·cen·tric (ā sen′trik), *adj.* (of a chromosome) lacking a centromere.

a·cet·a·min·o·phen (ə sē′tə min′ə fən, as′ī tə-), *n.* a crystalline substance, $C_8H_9NO_2$, used as a headache and pain reliever and to reduce fever.

a·ce·tyl·cho·line (ə sēt′l kō′lēn, ə set′-), *n.* a short-acting neurotransmitter, widely distributed in the body, that functions as a nervous system stimulant, a vasodilator, and a cardiac depressant. *Abbr.:* ACh —**a·ce′tyl·cho·lin′ic** (-lin′ik), *adj.*

a·ce′tyl·cho·lin·es′ter·ase′ (-kō′lə nes′tə rās′, -rāz′), *n.* an enzyme that counteracts the effects of acetylcholine by hydrolyzing it to choline and acetate.

a·ce′tyl·cys′te·ine (-sis′tē ēn′, -in), *n.* a substance,

$C_9H_9NO_3S$, used in solution as an inhalant, esp. in treating asthma and bronchitis.

a·ce/tyl·sal/i·cyl/ic ac/id (-sal/ə sil/ik), *n.* ASPIRIN (def. 1).

ACh, acetylcholine.

ach·a·la·sia (ak/ə lā/zhə, -zhē ə, -zē ə), *n.* inability of a circular muscle, esp. of the esophagus or rectum, to relax, resulting in widening of the structure above the muscular constriction.

Achil/les (or Achil/les') ten/don (ə kil/ēz), *n.* the tendon joining the calf muscles to the heel bone.

a·chon·dro·pla·sia (ā kon/drə plā/zhə, -zhē ə), *n.* a defect of fetal bone development, resulting in a type of dwarfism characterized by a large head and short limbs. —**a·chon/dro·plas/tic** (-plas/tik), *adj.*

ach·ro·mat·ic (ak/rə mat/ik, ā/krə-), *adj.* (of a cell structure) difficult to stain. —**ach/ro·mat/i·cal·ly,** *adv.* —**a·chro·ma·tism** (ā krō/mə tiz/əm), **a·chro/ma·tic/i·ty** (-tis/ə tē), *n.*

ac·id (as/id), *n.* **1.** a compound usu. having a sour taste and capable of neutralizing alkalis and turning blue litmus paper red, containing hydrogen that can be replaced by a metal or an electropositive group to form a salt, or containing an atom that can accept a pair of electrons from a base. —*adj.* **2.** having a pH value of less than 7. Compare ALKALINE.

ac/id-fast/, *adj.* resistant to decolorizing by acidified alcohol after staining. —**ac/id-fast/ness,** *n.*

ac/id·head/, *n. Slang.* a person who habitually takes the drug LSD.

a·cid·i·ty (ə sid/i tē), *n.* excessive acid quality.

a·cid·o·phil·ic (ə sid/ə fil/ik, as/i də-) also **ac·i·doph·i·lous** (as/i dof/ə ləs), *adj.* **1.** having an affinity for acid stains; eosinophilic. **2.** thriving in or requiring an acid environment.

ac·i·doph/i·lus milk/ (as/i dof/ə ləs), *n.* milk cultured with the bacterium *Lactobacillus acidophilus,* used in medicine for modifying bacterial content of the intestine.

ac·i·do·sis (as/i dō/sis), *n.* a blood condition in which the bicarbonate concentration is below normal. —**ac/i·dot/ic** (-dot/ik), *adj.*

ac/id rain/, *n.* precipitation containing acid-forming chemicals, chiefly industrial pollutants, that have been released into the atmosphere and combined with water vapor: ecologically harmful.

ac·i·nus (as/ə nəs), *n., pl.* **-ni** (-nī/). the smallest secreting portion of a gland. —**ac/i·nar** (-nər, -när/), **a·cin·ic** (ə sin/ik), *adj.*

ac·ne (ak/nē), *n.* any of various inflammatory skin eruptions involving breakdown of sebum from the sebaceous glands and characterized by pimples on the face, neck, and upper back. —**ac/ned,** *adj.*

ac/ne rosa/cea, *n.* ROSACEA.

acquired/ char/acter, *n.* a noninheritable trait that results from certain environmental influences.

acquired/ immune/ defi/ciency syn/drome, *n.* See AIDS. Also called **acquired/ immunodefi/ciency syn/-drome.**

ac·ri·fla·vine (ak/rə flā/vin, -vēn), *n.* an orange-brown, granular solid, $C_{14}H_{14}N_3Cl$, formerly used as an antiseptic.

ac·ro·cen·tric (ak/rō sen/trik), *adj.* (of a chromosome) having the centromere closer to one end than the other, resulting in two arms of unequal length.

ac·ro·ceph·a·ly (-sef/ə lē), *n.* OXYCEPHALY. —**ac/ro·ce·phal/ic** (-sə fal/ik), *adj.* —**ac/ro·ceph/a·lous,** *adj.*

ac·ro·meg·a·ly (-meg/ə lē), *n.* a disorder of the pituitary gland involving excessive production of growth hormone and resulting in enlargement of the head, hands, and feet. —**ac·ro·me·gal·ic** (ak/rō mə gal/ik), *adj.*

ac·ro·pho·bi·a (-fō/bē ə), *n.* a pathological fear of heights. —**ac/ro·phobe/,** *n.* —**ac/ro·pho/bic,** *adj., n.*

ACTH, a hormone of the anterior pituitary that stimulates the production of steroids in the cortex of the adrenal glands. Also called **adrenocorticotropic hormone, adrenocorticotropin.**

ac·tin (ak/tin), *n.* a protein that functions in muscular contraction by combining with myosin. Compare ACTOMYOSIN.

ac·tin·o·my·ces (ak tin/ō mi/sēz, ak/tə nō-), *n., pl.* **-ces.** any of several filamentous, anaerobic bacteria of the genus *Actinomyces,* certain species of which are pathogenic for humans and animals. —**ac/tin·o·my·ce/tal,** *adj.*

ac·tin·o·my·cete (-mi/sēt, -mi sēt/), *n.* any of several rod-shaped or filamentous, aerobic or anaerobic bacteria of the phylum Chlamydobacteriae, or in some classification schemes, the order Actinomycetales, certain species of which are pathogenic for humans and animals. —**ac·tin/o·my·ce/tous,** *adj.*

ac·tin·o·my·cin (-mi/sin), *n.* any of a group of related antibiotics derived from streptomyces bacteria, used against susceptible bacteria and fungi and in the treatment of various cancers.

ac·tin·o·my·co·sis (-mi kō/sis), *n.* an infectious, inflammatory disease caused by *Actinomyces israelii* in humans and *A. bovis* in domestic animals, and characterized by lumpy, often suppurating tumors, esp. about the jaws; lumpy jaw. —**ac·tin/o·my·cot/ic** (-kot/ik), *adj.*

ac/tion poten/tial, *n.* the change in electrical potential that occurs between the inside and outside of a nerve or muscle fiber when it is stimulated, serving to transmit nerve signals. Compare NERVE IMPULSE.

ac/tive immu/nity, *n.* immunity resulting from one's own production of antibody or white blood cells.

ac/tive trans/port, *n.* the movement of ions or molecules across a cellular membrane from a lower to a higher concentration.

ac·to·my·o·sin (ak/tə mi/ə sin), *n.* a complex of the proteins actin and myosin that is a major constituent of muscle tissue and that interacts with ATP to cause muscular contraction.

ac·u·pres·sure (ak'yŏŏ presh'ər), *n.* **1.** a type of massage therapy using finger pressure on the bodily sites used in acupuncture. **2.** a procedure for stopping blood flow from an injured blood vessel by inserting needles into adjacent tissue.

ac'u·punc'ture, *n.* Chinese medical practice that treats illness or provides local anesthesia by the insertion of needles at specified sites of the body. —**ac'u·punc'tur·ist**, *n.*

a·cute (ə kyōōt'), *adj.* (of disease) brief and severe (disting. from *chronic*). —**a·cute'ly**, *adv.* —**a·cute'ness**, *n.*

acute' nec'rotizing gingivi'tis, *n.* TRENCH MOUTH. *Abbr.:* ANG

a·cy·clo·vir (ā sī'klō vēr', -klə-), *n.* a synthetic crystalline compound, $C_{18}H_{11}N_5O_3$, used as an antiviral drug in the treatment of herpes infections.

Ad'am's ap'ple, *n.* a projection of the thyroid cartilage at the front of the neck.

ad·ap·ta·tion (ad'əp tā'shən), *n.* **1.** the decrease in response of sensory receptor organs, as those of vision or touch, to changed, constantly applied environmental conditions. **2.** the regulating for the pupil of the quantity of light entering the eye.

ADD, attention deficit disorder.

ad·dic·tion (ə dik'shən), *n.* dependence on or commitment to a habit, practice, or habit-forming substance to the extent that its cessation causes trauma.

ad·dic·tive (-tiv), *adj.* producing or tending to cause addiction: *an addictive drug.* —**ad·dic'tive·ness**, *n.*

Ad'di·son's disease' (ad'ə sənz), *n.* diminished function of the adrenal glands, resulting in low blood pressure, weight loss, anxiety, darkened skin, and other disturbances.

ad·di·tive (ad'i tiv), *n.* **1.** a substance added directly to food during processing, as for preservation, coloring, or stabilization. **2.** something that becomes part of food or affects it as a result of packaging or processing, as debris or radiation. —**ad'di·tive·ly**, *adv.*

ad·du·cent (ə dōō'sənt, ə dyōō'-), *adj.* drawing toward, as by the action of a muscle; adducting.

ad·duct (ə dukt'), *v.t.* to move or draw toward the axis of the body or one of its parts (opposed to *abduct*). —**ad·duc'tive**, *adj.*

ad·duc'tion, *n.* the action of an adducent muscle.

ad·duc'tor, *n.* any muscle that adducts (opposed to *abductor*).

ad·e·nine (ad'n in, -ēn', -in'), *n.* a purine base, $C_5H_5N_5$, one of the fundamental components of nucleic acids, forming a base pair with thymine in DNA and pairing with uracil in RNA. *Symbol:* A

ad·e·ni·tis (ad'n ī'tis), *n.* LYMPHADENITIS.

ad·e·no·car·ci·no·ma (ad'n ō kär'sə nō'mə), *n., pl.*

-mas, -ma·ta (-mə tə). **1.** a malignant tumor arising from secretory epithelium. **2.** a malignant tumor of glandlike structure. —**ad′e·no·car′ci·nom′a·tous** (-nom′ə təs, -nō′mə-), *adj.*

ad′e·no·hy·poph′y·sis (-hi pof′ə sis), *n., pl.* **-ses** (-sēz′). ANTERIOR PITUITARY. —**ad′e·no·hy·poph′y·se′al** (-sē′əl, -zē′-), *adj.*

ad·e·noid (ad′n oid′), *n.* Usu., **adenoids.** growths of lymphoid tissue in the upper throat: when enlarged, they can block the back of the throat and cause the voice to have a nasal quality.

ad′e·noi′dal (-oid′l), *adj.* **1.** ADENOID. **2.** characteristic of a person having the adenoids enlarged, esp. to a degree that interferes with normal breathing.

ad′e·noid·ec′to·my (-oi dek′tə mē), *n., pl.* **-mies.** surgical removal of the adenoids.

ad′e·noid·i′tis (-oi di′tis), *n.* inflammation of the adenoid tissue.

ad·e·no·ma (ad′n ō′mə), *n., pl.* **-mas, -ma·ta** (-mə tə). **1.** a benign tumor originating in a secretory gland. **2.** a benign tumor of glandlike structure. —**ad′e·nom′a·tous** (-om′ə təs, -ō′mə-), *adj.*

a·den·o·sine (ə den′ə sēn′, -sin), *n.* a white, crystalline, water-soluble nucleoside, $C_{10}H_{13}N_5O_4$, of adenine and ribose.

aden′osine di·phos′phate (di fos′fāt), *n.* See ADP.

aden′osine mon·o·phos′phate (mon′ə fos′fāt), *n.* See AMP.

aden′osine tri·phos′phate (tri fos′fāt), *n.* See ATP.

ad·e·no·vi·rus (ad′n ō vī′rəs), *n., pl.* **-rus·es.** any of a group of DNA-containing viruses that cause eye and respiratory diseases. —**ad′e·no·vi′ral,** *adj.*

ad′e·nyl′ic ac′id (ad′n il′ik, ad′-), *n.* See AMP.

ADH, antidiuretic hormone. Compare VASOPRESSIN.

ad·he·sion (ad hē′zhən), *n.* **1.** the abnormal union of adjacent tissues. **2.** the tissue involved. —**ad·he′sion·al,** *adj.*

ad·i·po·cyte (ad′ə pō sit′), *n.* FAT CELL.

ad′i·pose (-pōs′), *adj.* **1.** consisting of, resembling, or pertaining to fat; fatty. —*n.* **2.** animal fat stored in the fatty tissue of the body. —**ad′i·pose′ness, ad′i·pos′i·ty** (-pos′-i tē), *n.*

ad′ipose tis′sue, *n.* loose connective tissue in which fat cells accumulate.

ad·just·ment (ə just′mənt), *n.* therapeutic manipulation of the vertebrae or joints to bring them into alignment.

ad·ju·vant (aj′ə vənt), *adj.* **1.** utilizing drugs, radiation therapy, or other means of supplementary treatment following cancer surgery. —*n.* **2.** anything that aids in removing or preventing a disease, esp. a substance added to a prescription to aid the effect of the main ingredient. **3.** a substance admixed with an immunogen in order to elicit a more marked immune response.

Ad·le·ri·an (ad lēr′ē ən), *adj.* of or pertaining to Alfred Adler or his psychoanalytic theories, esp. the belief that behavior is determined by compensation for feelings of inferiority.

ADP, adenosine diphosphate: a nucleotide that functions in the transfer of energy during the catabolism of glucose, formed by the removal of a phosphate from adenosine triphosphate and composed of adenine, ribose, and two phosphate groups. Compare ATP.

ad·re·nal (ə drēn′l), *adj.* **1.** of or produced by the adrenal glands. **2.** situated near or on the kidneys; suprarenal. —*n.* **3.** ADRENAL GLAND.

adre′nal gland′, *n.* one of a pair of ductless glands, located above the kidneys, consisting of a cortex, which produces steroidal hormones, and a medulla, which produces epinephrine and norepinephrine.

A·dren·al·in (ə dren′l in), *Trademark.* EPINEPHRINE (def. 2).

a·dren·a·line (ə dren′l in, -ēn′), *n.* EPINEPHRINE.

ad·ren·er·gic (ad′rə nûr′jik), *adj.* **1.** resembling epinephrine in physiological effect: *an adrenergic drug.* **2.** releasing epinephrine: *adrenergic neurons.* **3.** activated by epinephrine or a substance with a similar effect: *adrenergic receptor.* —*n.* **4.** a drug or other agent having an epinephrinelike effect.

a·dre·no·cor·ti·co·ster·oid (ə drē′nō kôr′ti kō ster′oid, -stēr′-), *n.* any of a group of steroid hormones produced by the cortex of the adrenal gland.

a·dre·no·cor·ti·co·trop·ic (-trop′ik, -trō′pik) also **a·dre·no·cor·ti·co·troph·ic** (-trof′ik, -trō′fik), *adj.* stimulating the adrenal cortex.

adre′nocor′ticotrop′ic hor′mone, *n.* See ACTH. Also called **a·dre·no·cor·ti·co·tro·pin** (-trō′pin).

adult′-on′set diabe′tes, *n.* See under DIABETES MELLITUS.

aer·obe (âr′ōb), *n.* an organism, esp. a bacterium, that requires air or free oxygen to sustain life (opposed to *anaerobe*).

aer·o·bic (â rō′bik), *adj.* **1.** (of an organism or tissue) requiring the presence of air or free oxygen to sustain life. **2.** pertaining to or caused by the presence of oxygen. **3.** of or pertaining to aerobics: *aerobic dancing.* —**aer·o′bi·cal·ly,** *adv.*

aer·o′bics, *n.* (*used with a pl. v.*) any of various sustained exercises, as jogging, calisthenics, and vigorous dancing, designed esp. to stimulate and strengthen the heart.

aer·o·em·bo·lism (âr′ō em′bə liz′əm), *n.* **1.** an obstruction of the circulatory system caused by one or more air bubbles, as may arise during surgery. **2.** DECOMPRESSION SICKNESS.

aer·o·med·i·cine (âr′ə med′ə sən), *n.* AVIATION MEDICINE.

aer·o·pho·bi·a (âr′ə fō′bē ə), *n.* an abnormal fear of drafts of air, gases, or airborne matter. —**aer′o·pho′bic** (-fō′bik), *adj.*

aer·o·phore (âr′ə fôr′, -fōr′), *n.* a portable breathing apparatus filled with compressed air.

a·fe·brile (ā fē′brəl, ā feb′rəl), *adj.* without fever.

af·fect (af′ekt), *n. Psychiatry.* an expressed or observed emotional response: *the blunted affect of schizophrenia.*

af′fective disor′der, *n.* any of several mental disorders in which a major disturbance of emotions is predominant, as depression or bipolar disorder.

af·fer·ent (af′ər ənt), *adj.* **1.** bringing to or leading toward an organ or part, as a nerve or arteriole (opposed to *efferent*). —*n.* **2.** an afferent part, as a nerve that conveys an impulse toward the central nervous system. —**af′fer·ent·ly,** *adv.*

AFP, alpha-fetoprotein.

af′ter·birth′, *n.* the placenta and fetal membranes expelled from the uterus after childbirth.

af′ter·care′, *n.* the care and treatment of a convalescent patient.

af′ter·im′age, *n.* a visual image that persists after the stimulus that caused it is no longer operative.

a·gar (ä′gär, ag′ər), *n.* **1.** Also, **a′gar·a′gar.** a gel prepared from the cell walls of various red algae, used in laboratories as a culture medium, in food processing as a thickener and stabilizer, and in industry as a filler, adhesive, etc. **2.** a culture medium having an agar base.

a·gen·e·sis (ā jen′ə sis) also **a·ge·ne·sia** (ā jə nē′zhə), *n.* absence or failed development of a body part. —**a′ge·net′ic** (-net′ik), *adj.*

a·gent (ā′jənt), *n.* **1.** a drug or chemical capable of eliciting a biological response. **2.** an organism that is a cause or vector of disease. —**a·gen′tial** (ā jen′shəl), *adj.*

ag·glu·ti·nate (ə glōōt′n āt′), *v.t.,* **-nat·ed, -nat·ing.** to cause (bacteria or cells) to undergo agglutination.

ag·glu′ti·na′tion, *n.* the clumping of bacteria, red blood cells, or other cells, due to the introduction of an antibody.

ag·glu′ti·nin (-in), *n.* an antibody that causes agglutination.

ag·glu·tin·o·gen (ag′lōō tin′ə jən, -jen′, ə glōōt′nə-), *n.* an antigen that causes the production of agglutinins.

ag·i·ta·tion (aj′i tā′shən), *n.* psychomotor restlessness, manifested by pacing, hand-wringing, or similar activity. —**ag′i·ta′tion·al,** *adj.*

a·glos·si·a (ə glō′sē ə, ā glô′-, ə glos′ē ə, ā glos′-), *n.* absence of the tongue, esp. when congenital.

ag·nail (ag′nāl′) *n.* FELON.

ag·no·sia (ag nō′zhə, -zhē ə, -zē ə), *n. Psychiatry.* partial or total inability to recognize objects by use of the senses.

ag·o·nist (ag′ə nist), *n.* **1.** a contracting muscle whose action is opposed by another muscle. Compare ANTAGONIST (def. 1). **2.** a chemical substance capable of activating a receptor to induce a full or partial pharmacological response.

ag′o·nis′tic also **ag′o·nis′ti·cal,** *adj.* pertaining to a behavioral response to an aggressive encounter, as attack or appeasement. —**ag′o·nis′ti·cal·ly,** *adv.*

ag·o·ra·pho·bi·a (ag′ər ə fō′bē ə), *n.* an abnormal fear of being in crowds, public places, or open areas. —**ag′o·ra·pho′bic,** *adj., n.*

a·gran·u·lo·cy·to·sis (ə gran′yə lō si tō′sis), *n.* an acute blood disorder characterized by a loss of circulating granulocytes, leading to fever and ulcerations of the mucous membranes.

a·graph·i·a (ā graf′ē ə, ə graf′-), *n.* a cerebral disorder characterized by total or partial inability to write. —**a·graph′ic,** *adj.*

a·gue (ā′gyoō), *n.* **1.** chills, fever, and sweating associated with an active episode of malaria. **2.** any fever marked by fits of shivering.

aid·man (ād′man′, -mən), *n., pl.* -**men** (-men′, -mən). a military medical corpsman trained to provide initial emergency treatment.

AIDS (ādz), *n.* a disease of the immune system characterized by increased susceptibility to opportunistic infections, to certain cancers, and to neurological disorders: caused by a retrovirus and transmitted chiefly through blood or blood products that enter the body's bloodstream, esp. by sexual contact or contaminated hypodermic needles. [*a(cquired) i(mmune) d(eficiency) s(yndrome)*]

AIDS′-relat′ed com′plex, a syndrome caused by the AIDS virus and characterized primarily by chronically swollen lymph nodes and persistent fever: sometimes a precursor of AIDS. *Abbr.:* ARC

AIDS′ vi′rus, *n.* a variable retrovirus that invades and inactivates helper T cells of the immune system and is a cause of AIDS and AIDS-related complex; HIV.

ail·ment (āl′mənt), *n.* a physical disorder or illness, esp. of a minor or chronic nature.

ai·lu·ro·phobe (ī lŏŏr′ə fōb′, ā lŏŏr′-), *n.* a person who has an abnormal fear of cats. —**ai·lu·ro·pho′bi·a,** *n.* —**ai·lu′ro·pho′bic,** *adj.*

air·sick′ness, *n.* motion sickness induced by travel in an aircraft. —**air′sick′,** *adj.*

air′way′, *n.* a tubelike device used to maintain adequate, unobstructed respiration, as during general anesthesia.

Ala, alanine.

al·a·nine (al′ə nēn′, -nin), *n.* any of several isomers of a colorless, crystalline, water-soluble amino acid, $CH_3CH(NH_2)COOH$, found in many proteins and produced synthetically: used chiefly in biochemical research. *Abbr.:* Ala; *Symbol:* A

al·bi·no (al bī′nō; *esp. Brit.* -bē′-), *n., pl.* -**nos.** a person with pale skin, white hair, pinkish eyes, and visual abnormalities resulting from a hereditary inability to produce the pigment melanin.

al·bu·men (al byoō′mən), *n.* **1.** the white of an egg. **2.** ALBUMIN.

al·bu·min or **al·bu·men** (al byoō′mən), *n.* any of a class of simple, sulfur-containing, water-soluble proteins that coagulate when heated, occurring in egg white, milk, blood, and other animal and vegetable tissues and secretions.

al·bu'mi·nous also **al·bu'mi·nose'** (-nōs'), *adj.* of, containing, or resembling albumen or albumin.

al·bu'mi·nu·ri·a (-nŏŏr'ē ə, -nyŏŏr'-), *n.* the presence of albumin in the urine. —**al·bu'mi·nu'ric,** *adj.*

al·co·hol·ism (al'kə hô liz'əm, -ho-), *n.* a chronic disorder characterized by dependence on alcohol, repeated excessive use of alcoholic beverages, and decreased ability to function socially and vocationally.

al·do·ster·one (al'də sti rōn', al'dō sti rōn', al dos'tə-rōn'), *n.* a hormone produced by the cortex of the adrenal gland, instrumental in the regulation of sodium and potassium reabsorption by the cells of the tubular portion of the kidney.

al·do·ster·on·ism (al'dō ster'ə niz'əm, al dos'tə rō-), *n.* an abnormality of the body's electrolyte balance, caused by excessive secretion of aldosterone by the adrenal cortex and characterized by hypertension, low serum potassium, excessive urination, and alkalosis.

a·lex·i·a (ə lek'sē ə), *n.* a neurologic disorder marked by loss of the ability to understand written or printed language, usu. resulting from a brain lesion or a congenital defect. Also called **word blindness.**

a·lex·i·phar·mic (ə lek'sə fär'mik), *adj.* **1.** warding off poisoning or infection; antidotal; prophylactic. —*n.* **2.** an alexipharmic agent, esp. an internal antidote.

al·go·lag·ni·a (al'gə lag'nē ə), *n.* sexual pleasure derived from enduring or inflicting pain, as in masochism or sadism.

al·gom·e·ter (al gom'i tər), *n.* a device for determining sensitiveness to pain caused by pressure. —**al·go·met·ric** (al'gə me'trik), **al'go·met'ri·cal,** *adj.* —**al'go·met'ri·cal·ly,** *adv.* —**al·gom'e·try,** *n.*

al·ien·ist (āl'yə nist, ā'lē ə-), *n.* (formerly) a physician specializing in the treatment of mental illness; psychiatrist.

al·i·men·ta·ry (al'ə men'tə rē), *adj.* **1.** concerned with the function of nutrition; nutritive. **2.** pertaining to food.

alimen'tary canal', *n.* a tubular passage functioning in the digestion and absorption of food and the elimination of food residue, beginning at the mouth and terminating at the anus.

al'i·men·ta'tion, *n.* nourishment; nutrition.

al·ka·li (al'kə li'), *n., pl.* **-lis, -lies,** *adj.* —*n.* **1.** any of various bases, the hydroxides of the alkali metals and of ammonium, that neutralize acids to form salts and turn red litmus paper blue. —*adj.* **2.** ALKALINE.

al·ka·line (al'kə lin', -lin), *adj.* of, containing, or like an alkali, esp. in having a pH greater than 7. Compare ACID (def. 2). —**al'ka·lin'i·ty** (-lin'-), *n.*

al'ka·loid' (-loid'), *n.* any of a large class of bitter-tasting, nitrogen-containing, alkaline ring compounds common in plants and including caffeine, morphine, nicotine, quinine, and strychnine. —**al'ka·loi'dal,** *adj.*

al·ka·lo·sis (-lō′sis), *n.* a condition of the blood and other body fluids in which the bicarbonate concentration is above normal, tending toward alkalinity. —**al′ka·lot′ic** (-lot′ik), *adj.*

al·lan·toid (ə lan′toid), *adj.* **1.** Also, **al·lan·toi·dal** (al′ən-toid′l), of or pertaining to the allantois. —*n.* **2.** the allantois.

al·lan·to·in (-tō in), *n.* a white powder, $C_4H_6N_4O_3$, produced by oxidation of uric acid: used as an emollient.

al·lan′to·is (-tō is, -tois), *n., pl.* **al·lan·to·i·des** (al′ən tō′i-dēz′). a nourishing membrane surrounding the embryo, between the amnion and chorion, in birds and reptiles developing as a sac from the hindgut and in mammals developing as an inner layer of the placenta. —**al′lan·to′ic**, *adj.*

al·lele (ə lēl′), *n.* one of two or more alternative forms of a gene occupying the same position on matching chromosomes: an individual normally has two alleles for each trait, one from either parent. —**al·lel·ic** (ə lē′lik, ə lel′ik), *adj.*

al·le·lo·morph (ə lē′lə môrf′, ə lel′ə-), *n.* ALLELE. —**al·le·lo·mor′phic**, *adj.*

al·ler·gen (al′ər jən, -jen′), *n.* any substance, usu. a protein, that induces an allergic reaction in a particular individual.

aller′gic rhini′tis, *n.* a condition characterized by head congestion, sneezing, tearing, and swelling of the nasal mucous membranes, caused by an allergic reaction. Compare HAY FEVER.

al·ler·gist (al′ər jist), *n.* a physician specializing in the diagnosis and treatment of allergies.

al′ler·gy, *n., pl.* **-gies.** an overreaction of the immune system to a previously encountered, ordinarily harmless substance, resulting in skin rash, swelling of mucous membranes, sneezing or wheezing, or other abnormal conditions. —**al·ler·gic** (ə lûr′jik), *adj.*

al·lo·graft (al′ə graft′, -gräft′), *n.* a tissue or organ obtained from one member of a species and grafted to a genetically dissimilar member of the same species. Also called **homograft.** Compare AUTOGRAFT, XENOGRAFT.

al·lo·path (al′ə path′) also **al·lop·a·thist** (ə lop′ə thist), *n.* a person who practices or favors allopathy.

al·lop′a·thy, *n.* the method of treating disease by the use of agents that produce effects different from those of the disease treated (opposed to *homeopathy*). —**al·lo·path·ic** (al′ə path′ik), *adj.* —**al′lo·path′i·cal·ly,** *adv.*

al·lo·pol·y·ploid (al′ə pol′ə ploid′), *adj.* **1.** having more than two haploid sets of chromosomes that are dissimilar and derived from different species. —*n.* **2.** an allopolyploid cell or organism.

al·lo·ster·ic (al′ə ster′ik, -stēr′-), *adj.* of or pertaining to a change in the activity of an enzyme at a site other than the binding site of the substrate. —**al′lo·ster′i·cal·ly,** *adv.* —**al′lo·ster′ism, al′lo·ster′y** (-ster′ē), *n.*

al·lo·trans·plant (al′ō trans′plant′, -plänt′), *n.* ALLOGRAFT.

al·o·pe·ci·a (al/ə pē/shē ə, -sē ə), *n.* loss of hair; baldness. —**al/o·pe/cic** (-pē/sik), *adj.*

al/pha-ad·ren·er·gic (al/fə ad/rə nûr/jik), *adj.* of, pertaining to, or designating an alpha receptor.

al/pha block/er or **al/pha-block/er,** *n.* any of various substances that interfere with the action of the alpha receptors. —**al/pha-block/ing,** *adj.*

al/pha-fe/to·pro/tein (fē/tō prō/tēn, -tē in), *n.* a serum protein produced during pregnancy, useful in the prenatal diagnosis of multiple births or birth defects. *Abbr.:* AFP

al/pha he/lix, *n.* the rodlike spatial configuration of many protein molecules in which the polypeptide backbone is stabilized by hydrogen bonds between amino acids in successive helical turns.

al/pha recep/tor or **al/pha-recep/tor,** *n.* a site on a cell that, upon interaction with epinephrine or norepinephrine, controls vasoconstriction, intestinal relaxation, pupil dilation, and other physiological processes. Compare BETA RECEPTOR.

al/pha rhythm/, *n.* a pattern of slow brain waves (**al/pha waves/**) in normal persons at rest with closed eyes, thought by some to be associated with an alert but daydreaming mind.

ALS, amyotrophic lateral sclerosis.

al/titude sick/ness, *n.* a disorder associated with the low oxygen content of the atmosphere at high altitudes, in acute conditions resulting in prostration, shortness of breath, and cardiac disturbances, and in chronic conditions resulting in thickened and poorly circulating blood.

al·ve·o·lar (al vē/ə lər), *adj.* of or pertaining to an alveolus or to alveoli. —**al·ve/o·lar·ly,** *adv.*

al·ve·o·lus (-ləs), *n., pl.* **-li** (-lī/). **1.** any of the tiny bunched air sacs at the ends of the bronchioles of the lungs. **2.** the socket within the jawbone in which the root or roots of a tooth are set.

Alz/hei·mer's disease/ (älts/hī mərz, alts/-, ölts/-), *n.* a common form of dementia of unknown cause, usu. beginning in late middle age, characterized by progressive memory loss and mental deterioration associated with brain damage.

A.M.A., American Medical Association.

a·man·ta·dine (ə man/tə dēn/), *n.* a water-soluble crystalline substance, $C_{10}H_{17}NHCl$, that inhibits penetration of viruses into cells and is used against certain types of influenza and in the treatment of Parkinson's disease.

am·au·ro·sis (am/ô rō/sis), *n.* partial or total loss of sight, esp. in the absence of a gross lesion or injury. —**am/au·rot/ic** (-rot/ik), *adj.*

am·bi·dex·trous (am/bi dek/strəs), *adj.* able to use both hands equally well. —**am/bi·dex/trous·ly,** *adv.* —**am/bi·dex/trous·ness,** *n.*

am·bi·sex·u·al (am/bi sek/shōō əl), *adj., n.* BISEXUAL (defs. 1, 2). —**am/bi·sex/u·al/i·ty,** *n.*

am·bly·o·pi·a (am'blē ō'pē ə), *n.* dimness of sight without apparent organic defect. —**am'bly·op'ic** (-op'ik), *adj.*

am·bu·lant (am'byə lənt), *adj.* AMBULATORY.

am'bu·la·to·ry (-lə tôr'ē, -tōr'ē) also **ambulant**, *adj.* **1.** not confined to bed; able or strong enough to walk: *an ambulatory patient.* **2.** serving patients who are able to walk: *an ambulatory care center.*

a·me·ba or **a·moe·ba** (ə mē'bə), *n., pl.* **-bas, -bae** (-bē). **1.** any of numerous one-celled aquatic or parasitic protozoans of the order Amoebida, having a jellylike mass of cytoplasm that forms temporary pseudopodia, by which the organism moves and engulfs food particles. **2.** a protozoan of the genus *Amoeba,* inhabiting bottom vegetation of freshwater ponds and streams: used widely in laboratory studies.

am·e·bi·a·sis (am'ə bī'ə sis), *n.* **1.** infection with a pathogenic ameba. **2.** AMEBIC DYSENTERY.

a·me·bic (ə mē'bik), *adj.* **1.** of, pertaining to, or resembling an ameba. **2.** characterized by or due to the presence of amebas, as certain diseases.

ame'bic dys'entery, *n.* a type of dysentery caused by the protozoan *Entamoeba histolytica,* characterized esp. by ulceration of the large intestine. Also called **amebiasis, ame'bic coli'tis.**

a·men·or·rhe·a (ā men'ə rē'ə, ə men'-), *n.* absence of the menses. —**a·men'or·rhe'al, a·men'or·rhe'ic,** *adj.*

a·men·tia (ā men'shə, ə men'-), *n.* lack of intellectual development; severe mental retardation.

Ames' test' (āmz), *n.* a test that exposes a strain of bacteria to a chemical compound in order to determine the potential of the compound for causing cancer.

am·e·tro·pi·a (am'i trō'pē ə), *n.* faulty refraction of light rays by the eye, as in astigmatism or myopia. —**am'e·trop'ic** (-trop'ik, -trō'pik), *adj.*

a·mi·no (ə mē'nō, am'ə nō'), *adj.* containing or pertaining to the univalent group –NH₂.

ami'no ac'id, *n.* any of a class of organic compounds that contains at least one amino group, –NH₂, and one carboxyl group, –COOH: the alpha-amino acids, RCH(NH₂)COOH, are the building blocks from which proteins are constructed. See also ESSENTIAL AMINO ACID.

a·mi·noph·yl·line (-fil'in, -ēn), *n.* a theophylline derivative, $C_{16}H_{24}N_{10}O_4$, used chiefly to relieve bronchial spasm in asthma, in the treatment of certain heart conditions, and as a diuretic.

am·i·to·sis (am'i tō'sis, ā'mi-), *n.* the direct method of cell division, characterized by simple cleavage of the nucleus without the formation of chromosomes. —**am'i·tot'ic** (-tot'ik), *adj.* —**am'i·tot'i·cal·ly,** *adv.*

am·i·trip·ty·line (am'i trip'tə lēn', -lin', -lin), *n.* a white crystalline powder, $C_{20}H_{23}N$, used to treat depression and enuresis.

am·ne·sia (am nē'zhə), *n.* loss of a large block of interrelated memories; complete or partial loss of memory caused by brain injury, shock, etc.

am·ne·si·ac (-zhē ak′, -zē-), n. **1.** a person affected by amnesia. —adj. **2.** Also, **am·ne·sic** (-sik, -zik). displaying the symptoms of amnesia.

am·ni·o (am′nē ō′), n., pl. **-ni·os.** Informal. amniocentesis.

am·ni·o·cen·te′sis (-sen tē′sis), n., pl. **-ses** (-sēz) the surgical procedure of guiding a hollow needle through the abdomen of a pregnant woman into the uterus and withdrawing a sample of amniotic fluid for genetic diagnosis of the fetus.

am′ni·on (-ən), n., pl. **-ni·ons, -ni·a** (-nē ə) the innermost membrane of the sac surrounding the embryo in reptiles, birds, and mammals, enclosing the amniotic fluid. —**am′·ni·ot′ic** (-ot′ik), **am′ni·on′ic,** adj.

am′niot′ic flu′id, n. the watery fluid in the amnion, in which the embryo is suspended.

am·o·bar·bi·tal (am′ō bär′bi tal′, -tôl′), n. a colorless, crystalline barbiturate, $C_{11}H_{18}N_2O_3$, used chiefly as a sedative.

a·moe·ba (ə mē′bə), n., pl. **-bas, -bae** (-bē). AMEBA.

a·moe·bi·a·sis (am′ə bī′ə sis), n. AMEBIASIS.

a·moe·bic (ə mē′bik), adj. AMEBIC.

am·ox·i·cil·lin (am ok′sə sil′in, ə mok′-), n. a semisynthetic penicillin, $C_{16}H_{19}N_3O_5S$, taken orally as a broad-spectrum antibiotic.

AMP, adenosine monophosphate: a nucleotide composed of adenine, ribose, and one phosphate group, formed by the partial breakdown of adenosine triphosphate, usu. at an end point in the metabolic pathway; adenylic acid. Compare ADP, ATP.

am·phet·a·mine (am fet′ə mēn′, -min), n. a drug, $C_9H_{13}N$, that stimulates the central nervous system: used in medicine chiefly to counteract depression and misused illegally as a stimulant.

am·phi·ploid (am′fə ploid′), n. a hybrid organism having a diploid set of chromosomes from each parental species.

am·pi·cil·lin (am′pə sil′in), n. a broad-spectrum semisynthetic penicillin, $C_{16}H_{19}N_3O_4S$, effective against certain susceptible Gram-positive and Gram-negative bacteria.

am·pule or **am·pul** or **am·poule** (am′pyōōl, -pōōl), n. a sealed glass or plastic bulb containing solutions for hypodermic injection.

am·pu·tate (am′pyōō tāt′), v.t., **-tat·ed, -tat·ing.** to cut off (all or part of a limb or digit of the body), as by surgery. —**am′pu·ta′tion,** n.

am′pu·tee′ (-tē′), n. a person who has lost all or part of an arm, hand, leg, etc., by amputation.

a·myg·da·la (ə mig′də lə), n., pl. **-lae** (-lē′). any of various almond-shaped anatomical parts, as a brain structure of the limbic system that is involved in emotions of fear and aggression.

a·myg′da·lin (-lin), n. a white, bitter-tasting, water-soluble, glycosidic powder, $C_{20}H_{27}NO_{11}$, used chiefly as an expectorant.

am·yl·ase (am′ə lās′, -lāz′), *n.* any of several digestive enzymes that break down starches.

am′yl ni′trite (am′əl), *n.* a yellowish, fragrant, flammable liquid, $C_5H_{11}NO_2$, used as an inhalant to dilate blood vessels, esp. for treating angina pectoris.

am′y·loid′ (-ə loid′), *n.* **1.** a waxy, translucent substance, composed primarily of protein fibers, that is deposited in various organs of animals in certain diseases. **2.** a nonnitrogenous food consisting esp. of starch.

am′y·lol′y·sis (-lol′ə sis), *n.* the chemical conversion of starch into sugar. —**am′y·lo·lyt′ic** (-lō lit′ik), *adj.*

a·my·o·troph′ic lat′eral sclero′sis (ā′mī ə trof′ik, -trō′fik, ā mī′ə-), *n.* a nervous system disease in which degeneration of motor neurons in the brain stem and spinal cord leads to atrophy and paralysis of the voluntary muscles. *Abbr.:* ALS Also called **Lou Gehrig's disease.**

Am·y·tal (am′i tôl′, -tal′), *Trademark.* a brand of amobarbital.

an′abol′ic ster′oid, *n.* any of a class of steroid hormones, esp. testosterone, that promote growth of muscle tissue.

a·nab·o·lism (ə nab′ə liz′əm), *n.* constructive metabolism; the synthesis in living organisms of more complex substances from simpler ones (opposed to *catabolism*). —**an·a·bol′ic** (-ə bol′ik), *adj.*

an·a·cli·sis (an′ə kli′sis), *n.* libidinal attachment or emotional dependency, esp. on the basis of the love object's resemblance to early childhood parental or protective figures. —**an′a·clit′ic** (-klit′ik), *adj.*

a·nae·mi·a (ə nē′mē ə), *n.* ANEMIA.

a·nae′mic, *adj.* ANEMIC.

an·aer·obe (an′ə rōb′, an âr′ōb), *n.* an organism, esp. a bacterium, that does not require air or free oxygen to live (opposed to *aerobe*).

an·aer·o·bic (an′ə rō′bik, an′â-), *adj.* **1.** (of an organism or tissue) living in the absence of air or free oxygen. **2.** pertaining to or caused by the absence of oxygen. —**an′aer·o′bi·cal·ly,** *adv.*

an·aes·the·sia (an′əs thē′zhə), *n.* ANESTHESIA. —**an′aes·thet′ic** (-thet′ik), *n., adj.* —**an·aes·the·tist** (ə nes′thi tist), *n.*

an·aes·the·si·ol·o·gy (-zē ol′ə jē), *n.* ANESTHESIOLOGY.

an·aes·the·tize (ə nes′thi tiz′; *esp. Brit.* ə nēs′-), *v.t.*, **-tized, -tiz·ing.** ANESTHETIZE.

a·nal (ān′l), *adj.* **1.** of, pertaining to, or near the anus. **2.** *Psychoanal.* **a.** of or pertaining to the second stage of psychosexual development, during which gratification is derived from the retention or expulsion of feces. **b.** of or pertaining to a group of adult behaviors and personality traits that include being meticulous, rigid, and ungenerous. —**a′nal·ly,** *adv.*

an·a·lep·tic (an′l ep′tik), *adj.* **1.** restoring; invigorating;

giving strength after disease. **2.** awakening, esp. from drug stupor. —*n.* **3.** a nervous system stimulant.

an·al·ge·si·a (an/l jē/zē ə, -sē ə), *n.* absence of sense of pain.

an·al·ge/sic, *n.* **1.** a remedy that relieves or allays pain. —*adj.* **2.** of, pertaining to, or causing analgesia.

a·nal·y·sand (ə nal/ə sand/, -zand/), *n.* a person undergoing psychoanalysis.

a·nal/y·sis (-sis), *n., pl.* **-ses** (-sēz/). PSYCHOANALYSIS.

an·a·lyze (an/l īz/), *v.t.* **-lyzed, -lyz·ing.** PSYCHOANALYZE.

an·am·ne·sis (an/am nē/sis), *n., pl.* **-ses** (-sēz). **1.** the medical history of a patient. **2.** a prompt immune response to a previously encountered antigen, as after a booster shot in a previously immunized person. —**an/am·nes/tic** (-nes/tik), *adj.* —**an/am·nes/ti·cal·ly,** *adv.*

an·a·phase (an/ə fāz/), *n.* the stage in mitosis or meiosis following metaphase in which the daughter chromosomes move away from each other to opposite ends of the cell. —**an/a·pha/sic,** *adj.*

an·a·phy·lax·is (an/ə fə lak/sis), *n.* a hypersensitive reaction to an allergen, as a severe bout of hay fever, the rapid appearance of wheals, or profound physiological changes and shock (**an/aphylac/tic shock/**). —**an/a·phy·lac/tic** (-lak/tik), *adj.*

an·a·pla·sia (an/ə plā/zhə, -zhē ə), *n.* the loss of structural differentiation within a cell or group of cells. —**an/a·plas/tic** (-plas/tik), *adj.*

an·a·sar·ca (an/ə sär/kə), *n.* a pronounced, generalized edema. —**an/a·sar/cous,** *adj.*

an·as·tig·mat (ə nas/tig mat/, an/ə stig/mat), *n.* a compound lens corrected for the aberrations of astigmatism and curvature of field.

an·as·tig·mat·ic (an/ə stig mat/ik, a nas/tig-), *adj.* (of a lens) not having astigmatism; forming point images of a point object located off the axis of the lens.

a·nas·to·mo·sis (ə nas/tə mō/sis), *n., pl.* **-ses** (-sēz). a joining of or opening between two organs or spaces normally not connected. —**a·nas/to·mose/,** *v.t., v.i.,* **-mosed, -mos·ing.** —**a·nas/to·mot/ic** (-mot/ik), *adj.*

an·a·tom·i·cal (an/ə tom/i kəl) also **an/a·tom/ic,** *adj.* of or pertaining to anatomy. —**an/a·tom/i·cal·ly,** *adv.*

a·nat·o·my (ə nat/ə mē), *n., pl.* **-mies. 1.** the science dealing with the structure of animals and plants. **2.** the structure of an animal or plant, or of any of its parts. **3.** dissection of all or part of an animal or plant in order to study its structure.

an·dro·gen (an/drə jən, -jen/), *n.* any substance, as testosterone or androsterone, that promotes male characteristics. —**an/dro·gen/ic,** *adj.*

an·drog·e·nous (an droj/ə nəs), *adj.* pertaining to the production of or tending to produce male offspring.

an·drog/y·nous (-ə nəs), *adj.* **1.** hermaphroditic. **2.** having both masculine and feminine characteristics. —**an/dro·gyne/** (-drə jīn/), *n.* —**an·drog/y·ny,** *n.*

An·drom′e·da strain′ (an drom′i də), *n.* an infectious pathogen that mutates unpredictably into new forms and shows extreme resistance to destruction by conventional means.

an·dros·ter·one (an dros′tə rōn′), *n.* an androgenic sex hormone that is a metabolite of testosterone and has much less effect.

a·ne·mi·a (ə nē′mē ə), *n.* a reduction in the hemoglobin of red blood cells with consequent deficiency of oxygen in the blood, leading to weakness and pallor.

a·ne′mic, *adj.* suffering from anemia. —**a·ne′mi·cal·ly,** *adv.*

an·en·ceph·a·ly (an′en sef′ə lē), *n.* the absence at birth of a portion of the skull and brain, caused by a failure of the embryonic upper neural tube to close and the consequent erosion of tissue. —**an′en·ce·phal′ic** (-sə fal′ik), *adj.*

an·es·the·sia or **an·aes·the·sia** (an′əs thē′zhə), *n.* **1.** general or localized insensibility, induced by drugs or other intervention and used in surgery or other painful procedures. **2.** general loss of the senses of feeling, as pain, temperature, and touch.

an′es·the·si·ol′o·gy (-zē ol′ə jē), *n.* the science of administering anesthetics. —**an′es·the′si·ol′o·gist,** *n.*

an′es·thet′ic (-thet′ik), *n.* **1.** a substance that produces anesthesia, as halothane, procaine, or ether. —*adj.* **2.** pertaining to or causing physical insensibility. **3.** physically insensitive: *an anesthetic state.* —**an′es·thet′i·cal·ly,** *adv.*

an·es·the·tist (ə nes′thi tist), *n.* a person who administers anesthetics, usu. a specially trained doctor or nurse.

an·es·the·tize (ə nes′thi tīz′), *v.t.,* **-tized, -tiz·ing.** to render physically insensible, as by an anesthetic. —**an·es′the·ti·za′tion,** *n.*

an·es·trous (an es′trəs), *adj.* **1.** not showing estrus. **2.** of or pertaining to anestrus.

an·es·trus (an es′trəs), *n.* the interval of sexual inactivity in a female mammal between two periods of heat or rut.

an·eu·rysm or **an·eu·rism** (an′yə riz′əm), *n.* a permanent cardiac or arterial dilatation usu. caused by weakening of the vessel wall.

ANF, atrial natriuretic factor.

ANG, acute necrotizing gingivitis; trench mouth.

an′gel dust′, *n. Slang.* PHENCYCLIDINE.

an·gi·na (an jī′nə; *in Med. often* an′jə nə), *n.* **1.** any attack of painful spasms or crushing pressure accompanied by a sensation of suffocating. **2.** ANGINA PECTORIS. —**an·gi′nal,** *adj.*

angi·na pec′to·ris (pek′tə ris), *n.* a sensation of crushing pressure in the chest, usu. at the sternum and sometimes radiating to the back or arm, caused by ischemia of the heart muscle.

an·gi·o·car·di·og·ra·phy (an′jē ō kär′dē og′rə fē), *n., pl.* **-phies.** x-ray examination of the heart and its blood vessels following intravenous injection of radiopaque fluid. —**an′gi·o·car′di·o·graph′ic** (-ə graf′ik), *adj.*

an·gi·o·gram′ (-ə gram′), *n.* an x-ray produced by angiography.

an·gi·og′ra·phy (-og′rə fē), *n., pl.* **-phies.** x-ray examination of blood vessels or lymphatics following injection of a radiopaque substance. —**an′gi·o·graph′ic** (-ə graf′ik), *adj.*

an·gi·ol′o·gy (-ol′ə jē), *n.* the branch of anatomy dealing with blood vessels and lymph vessels.

an·gi·o·ma (-ō′mə), *n., pl.* **-mas, -ma·ta** (-mə tə). a benign tumor consisting chiefly of dilated or newly formed blood vessels (**hemangioma**) or lymph vessels (**lymphangioma**). —**an′gi·om′a·tous** (-om′ə təs, -ō′mə-), *adj.*

an′gi·o·plas′ty (-ə plas′tē), *n., pl.* **-ties.** the surgical repair of a blood vessel, as by inserting a balloon-tipped catheter to unclog it or by replacing part of the vessel.

an′gi·o·ten′sin (-ō ten′sin), *n.* a plasma protein that elevates blood pressure and stimulates the adrenal cortex to produce the hormone aldosterone.

an·he·do·ni·a (an′hē dō′nē ə), *n. Psychol.* lack of pleasure or of the capacity to experience it. —**an′he·don′ic** (-don′ik), *adj.*

an·i·ma (an′ə mə), *n., pl.* **-mas. 1.** (in the psychology of C. G. Jung) the inner personality (contrasted with *persona*). **2.** the feminine principle, esp. as present in men (contrasted with *animus*).

an·i·mal·cule (an′ə mal′kyōōl), *n.* a minute or microscopic animal.

an′imal heat′, *n.* heat produced in a living animal by any of various metabolic activities.

an′imal pole′, *n.* the formative part of an ovum, opposite the vegetal pole, that contains the nucleus and has the most cytoplasm.

an·i·mus (an′ə məs), *n.* (in the psychology of C. G. Jung) the masculine principle, esp. as present in women (contrasted with *anima*).

an·i·sog·a·mous (an′i sog′ə məs) also **an·i/so·gam′ic** (-sə gam′ik), *adj.* reproducing by the fusion of dissimilar gametes or individuals, usu. differing in size. —**an′i·sog′a·my,** *n.*

an·ky·lose (ang′kə lōs′), *v.t., v.i.,* **-losed, -los·ing.** to unite, as the bones of a joint.

an′kylosing spondyli′tis, *n.* a degenerative inflammatory disease characterized by impaired mobility of the spinal column, in some cases leading to fusion of joints.

an·ky·lo·sis, *n., pl.* **-lo·ses** (-lō′sēz). abnormal adhesion of the bones of a joint. —**an′ky·lot′ic** (-lot′ik), *adj.*

an′ky·lo·sto·mi′a·sis (-lō stə mī′ə sis, -los tə-), *n.* HOOKWORM (def. 2).

an·la·ge (än′lä gə), *n., pl.* **-gen** (-gən), **-ges.** (*sometimes cap.*) an embryonic area capable of forming a structure: the primordium, germ, or bud.

an·neal (ə nēl′), *v.t.,* **-nealed, -neal·ing.** to recombine (nucleic acid strands) at low temperature after separating by heat. —**an·neal′er,** *n.*

an·oes·trous (an es′trəs, -ē′strəs), *adj.* ANESTROUS.

an·oes′trus (-es′trəs, -ē′strəs), *n.* ANESTRUS.

a·no·mi·a (ə nō′mē ə), *n.* the inability to name objects or to recognize the written or spoken names of objects.

a·noph·e·les (ə nof′ə lēz′), *n., pl.* **-les.** any of several mosquitoes of the genus *Anopheles*, certain species of which are vectors of the parasite causing malaria in humans. —**a·noph′e·line′** (-lin′, -lin), *adj., n.*

an·o·rec·tic (an′ə rek′tik) also **an′o·ret′ic** (-ret′ik), *adj.* **1.** having no appetite. **2.** causing a loss of appetite. —*n.* **3.** a substance, as a drug, causing loss of appetite.

an′o·rex′i·a (-rek′sē ə), *n.* **1.** loss of appetite and inability to eat. **2.** ANOREXIA NERVOSA.

anorex′ia ner·vo′sa (nûr vō′sə), *n.* an eating disorder characterized by a fear of becoming fat, a distorted body image, and excessive dieting leading to emaciation.

an′o·rex′ic, *n.* **1.** a person suffering from anorexia or esp. anorexia nervosa. —*adj.* **2.** ANORECTIC.

an·os·mi·a (an oz′mē ə, -os′-), *n.* absence or loss of the sense of smell. —**an′os·mat′ic** (-əz mat′ik), **an·os′mic,** *adj.*

an·ov·u·lant (an ov′yə lənt, -ō′vyə-), *adj.* **1.** of, pertaining to, or characterized by a lack of or suppression of ovulation. —*n.* **2.** a substance that suppresses ovulation.

an·ov′u·la′tion, *n.* the absence of ovulation.

an·ov′u·la·to′ry (-lə tôr′ē, -tōr′ē) also **an·ov′u·lar** (-lər), *adj.* **1.** not associated with, caused by, or exhibiting ovulation. **2.** inhibiting ovulation.

an·ox·e·mi·a (an′ok sē′mē ə), *n.* a deficiency of oxygen in the arterial blood. —**an′ox·e′mic,** *adj.*

an·ox·i·a (an ok′sē ə, ə nok′-), *n.* **1.** lack of oxygen, as in suffocation. **2.** the mental and physical disturbances that occur as a result of hypoxia. —**an·ox′ic,** *adj.*

ant·ac·id (ant as′id), *adj.* **1.** preventing, neutralizing, or counteracting acidity, as of the stomach. —*n.* **2.** an antacid agent.

an·tag·o·nism (an tag′ə niz′əm), *n.* **1.** an opposing physiological action, as by one muscle in relation to another. **2.** the opposing action of substances, as drugs, that when taken together decrease the effectiveness of at least one of them (contrasted with *synergism*).

an·tag′o·nist, *n.* **1.** a muscle that acts in opposition to another. Compare AGONIST (def. 1). **2.** a drug that counteracts the effects of another drug.

an·te·na·tal (an′tē nāt′l), *adj.* prenatal: *an antenatal clinic.* —**an′te·na′tal·ly,** *adv.*

ante′rior pitu′itary, *n.* the mostly glandular anterior region of the pituitary gland. Also called **adenohypophysis.**

ant·hel·min·tic (ant′hel min′tik, an′thel-), *adj.* **1.** of or pertaining to a substance capable of destroying or eliminating parasitic worms, esp. human intestinal worms. —*n.* **2.** an anthelmintic substance.

an·thra·co·sis (an′thrə kō′sis), *n. Pathol.* the deposition of coal dust in the lungs; asymptomatic pneumoconiosis. —**an′thra·cot′ic** (-kot′ik), *adj.*

an·thrax (an′thraks), *n., pl.* **-thra·ces** (-thrə sēz′). **1.** an infectious disease of cattle, sheep, and other mammals caused by the bacterium *Bacillus anthracis*, transmitted to humans through wool and other animal products. **2.** any of the characteristic dark boils that erupt on the skin of humans infected with this.

an·ti·ad·ren·er·gic (an′tē ad′rə nûr′jik, an′ti-), *adj.* **1.** of or pertaining to a substance that opposes the physiological effects of epinephrine. —*n.* **2.** an antiadrenergic substance.

an′ti·anx·i·e′ty, *adj.* tending to prevent or relieve anxiety: *an antianxiety drug.*

an′ti·bac·te′ri·al, *adj.* destructive to or inhibiting the growth of bacteria.

an·ti·bi·ot·ic (an′ti bi ot′ik, -bē-, an′tē-, -ti-), *n.* **1.** any of a large group of chemical substances, as penicillin and streptomycin, that are produced by various microorganisms and fungi, have the capacity in dilute solutions to inhibit the growth of or to destroy bacteria and other microorganisms, and are used in the treatment of infectious diseases. —*adj.* **2.** of or involving antibiotics. —**an′ti·bi·ot′i·cal·ly,** *adv.*

an·ti·bod·y (an′ti bod′ē), *n., pl.* **-bod·ies. 1.** any of numerous protein molecules produced by B cells as a primary immune defense, each kind having a uniquely shaped site that combines with a foreign antigen, as of a virus, and disables it. **2.** antibodies of a particular type collectively. Also called **immunoglobulin.**

an′tibody-me′diated immu′nity, *n.* immunity conferred to an individual through the activity of B cells and circulating antibodies. Compare CELL-MEDIATED IMMUNITY.

an′ti·can′cer, *adj.* used or effective in the prevention or treatment of cancer.

an·ti·cho·lin·er·gic (an′tē kō′lə nûr′jik, -kol′ə-), *adj.* **1.** of or pertaining to a substance that opposes the effects of acetylcholine; interfering with the passage of parasympathetic nerve impulses. —*n.* **2.** an anticholinergic substance, as a drug.

an·ti·cho·lin·es·ter·ase (an′tē kō′lə nes′tə rās′, -rāz′, -kol′ə-, an′ti-), *n.* an enzyme or drug that blocks the action of acetylcholinesterase, thereby increasing the stimulating effect of acetylcholine on the muscles.

an′ti·co·ag′u·lant, *adj.* **1.** Also, **an′ti·co·ag′u·la′tive** (-lā′tiv, -lə tiv). preventing coagulation, esp. of blood. —*n.* **2.** an anticoagulant agent, as heparin.

an′ti·co′don (-kō′don), *n.* a set of three nucleotide bases at the loop end of tRNA that forms base pairs with the codon of messenger RNA.

an′ti·de·pres′sant also **an′ti·de·pres′sive,** *adj.* **1.** used to relieve or treat mental depression. —*n.* **2.** an antidepressant drug.

an′ti·di·u·ret′ic (an′tē-), *adj.* **1.** of or pertaining to a substance that suppresses the formation of urine. —*n.* **2.** an antidiuretic substance.

an′ti·di·uret′ic hor′mone, *n.* VASOPRESSIN. *Abbr.:* ADH

an·ti·dote (an′ti dōt′), *n., v.,* **-dot·ed, -dot·ing.** —*n.* **1.** a medicine or other remedy for counteracting the effects of poison, disease, etc. —*v.t.* **2.** to counteract with an antidote. —**an′ti·dot′al,** *adj.*

an·ti·drom·ic (an′ti drom′ik), *adj.* conducting nerve impulses in a direction opposite to the usual one. —**an′ti·drom′i·cal·ly,** *adv.*

an·ti·fer·til·i·ty (an′tē far til′i tē, an′ti-), *adj.* of or being a substance that inhibits the ability to produce offspring; contraceptive.

an·ti·gen (an′ti jən, -jen′), *n.* **1.** any substance that can stimulate the production of antibodies and combine specifically with them. **2.** any commercial substance that, when injected or absorbed into animal tissues, stimulates the production of antibodies. **3.** antigens of a particular type collectively. —**an′ti·gen′ic,** *adj.* —**an′ti·gen′i·cal·ly,** *adv.* —**an′ti·ge·nic′i·ty** (-jə nis′i tē), *n.*

antigen′ic deter′minant, *n.* EPITOPE.

an′ti·ges·ta′tion·al drug′ (an′tē je stā′shə nl, an′ti-), *n.* a drug that averts a pregnancy by preventing the fertilized egg from becoming implanted in the uterine wall.

an′ti·his′ta·mine′, *n.* any of various synthetic compounds capable of blocking the action of histamines, used esp. for treating allergies and gastric ulcers. —**an′ti·his′ta·min′ic** (-min′ik), *adj.*

an′ti·hy′per·ten′sive, *adj.* **1.** acting to reduce hypertension. —*n.* **2.** a drug, as a diuretic, used to treat hypertension.

an′ti·in·flam′ma·to′ry, *adj., n., pl.* **-ries.** —*adj.* **1.** acting to reduce certain signs of inflammation, as swelling, tenderness, fever, and pain. —*n.* **2.** a medication, as aspirin, used to reduce inflammation.

an′ti·me·tab′o·lite′, *n.* any substance that interferes with growth by competing with a nutrient metabolite for receptors or enzymes in the body, used esp. for treating certain cancers. —**an′ti·met′a·bol′ic,** *adj.*

an′ti·mi·tot′ic, *adj.* **1.** of or pertaining to a substance capable of arresting the process of cell division. —*n.* **2.** an antimitotic substance, as a drug used to destroy cancer cells.

an′ti·ne′o·plas′tic, *adj.* **1.** destroying, inhibiting, or preventing the growth or spread of tumors. —*n.* **2.** an antineoplastic substance.

an′ti·ox′i·dant (-ok′si dənt), *n.* an enzyme or other organic substance, as vitamin E or beta carotene, capable of counteracting the damaging effects of oxidation in animal tissues.

an′ti·phlo·gis′tic, *adj.* **1.** acting against inflammation or fever. —*n.* **2.** an antiphlogistic agent.

an′ti·psy·chot′ic, *adj.* **1.** of or pertaining to any of various drugs used in the treatment of psychosis, esp. schizophrenia, and acute or severe states of mania, depression, or paranoia; neuroleptic. —*n.* **2.** Also called **neuroleptic.** an antipsychotic drug, as a phenothiazine.

an·ti·py·ret·ic, *adj.* **1.** checking or preventing fever. —*n.* **2.** an antipyretic agent. —**an/ti·py·re/sis,** *n.*

an·ti·scor·bu/tic, *adj.* **1.** efficacious against scurvy. —*n.* **2.** an antiscorbutic agent, as ascorbic acid.

an/ti·sense/, *adj.* of or pertaining to a gene that is derived from RNA or complementary DNA, and is inserted in reverse orientation into a strand of DNA, and is used in genetic regulation to regulate genetic expression of a trait.

an·ti·sep·sis (an/tə sep/sis), *n.* destruction of the microorganisms that produce sepsis or septic disease.

an/ti·sep/tic, *adj.* **1.** pertaining to or effecting antisepsis. **2.** free from or cleaned of germs and other microorganisms. —*n.* **3.** an antiseptic agent. —**an/ti·sep/ti·cal·ly,** *adv.*

an/ti·se/rum, *n., pl.* **-se·rums, -se·ra** (-sēr/ə). animal or human serum that contains antibodies to a specific disease, used for injections to confer passive immunity to that disease.

an·ti·tox·ic (an/ti tok/sik, an/tē-), *adj.* **1.** counteracting toxic influences. **2.** of or serving as an antitoxin.

an/ti·tox/in, *n.* **1.** a substance formed in the body that counteracts a specific toxin. **2.** the antibody formed in immunization with a given toxin, used in treating certain infectious diseases or in immunizing against them.

an·ti·tus·sive (an/tē tus/iv, an/ti-), *adj.* **1.** of or pertaining to a substance used to suppress coughing. —*n.* **2.** an antitussive substance.

an/ti·ven/in also **an/ti·ven/om,** *n.* an antitoxin that counteracts venom, as from snakebite, obtained from the serum of a large animal that has had a series of controlled venom injections: used for treating victims of severe venomous bites.

an·u·re·sis (an/yə rē/sis), *n.* retention of urine in the bladder. —**an/u·ret/ic** (-ret/ik), *adj.*

an·u·ri·a (ə nŏŏr/ē ə, ə nyŏŏr/-, ə yŏŏr/-), *n.* the absence or suppression of urine. —**an/u/ric,** *adj.*

a·nus (ā/nəs), *n., pl.* **a·nus·es.** the excretory opening at the lower end of the alimentary canal.

an·vil (an/vil), *n.* **INCUS.**

anx·i·e·ty (ang zī/i tē), *n., pl.* **-ties.** a state of apprehension and psychic tension occurring in some forms of mental disorder.

anx·i·o·lyt·ic (ang/zē ə lit/ik), *adj.* **1.** relieving anxiety. —*n.* **2.** **TRANQUILIZER** (def. 1).

a·or·ta (ā ôr/tə), *n., pl.* **-tas, -tae** (-tē). the main artery of the mammalian circulatory system, conveying blood from the left ventricle of the heart to all the other arteries except the pulmonary artery. —**a·or/tic, a·or/tal,** *adj.*

APC, aspirin, phenacetin, and caffeine: a compound formerly used in headache and cold remedies.

a·per·i·ent (ə pēr/ē ənt), *adj.* **1.** having a mild purgative or laxative effect. —*n.* **2.** a substance that acts as a mild laxative.

Ap·gar score (ap′gär), *n.* a quantitative evaluation of the health of a newborn, rating breathing, heart rate, muscle tone, etc., on a scale of 1 to 10.

a·pha·sia (ə fā′zhə), *n.* the loss of a previously held ability to speak or understand spoken or written language, due to disease or injury of the brain. —**a·pha′sic**, *adj., n.*

a·pher·e·sis or **a·phaer·e·sis** (ə fer′ə sis), *n.* the withdrawal of whole blood from the body, separation of one or more components, and return by transfusion of the remaining blood to the donor. —**aph·e·ret·ic** (af′ə ret′ik), *adj.*

a·pho·ni·a (ā fō′nē ə), *n.* loss of voice, esp. due to an organic or functional disturbance of the vocal organs. —**a·phon·ic** (ā fon′ik), *adj., adv., n.*

aph·ro·dis·i·ac (af′rə dē′zē ak′, -diz′ē ak′), *adj.* **1.** Also, **aph′ro·di·si′a·cal** (-də zīʹē kəl, -sī′-). arousing sexual desire. —*n.* **2.** a food, drug, or other agent that arouses or is reputed to arouse sexual desire.

a·plas·tic ane·mia (ā plas′tik), *n.* severe anemia due to destruction or depressed functioning of the bone marrow, usu. resulting from bone cancer, radiation, or the toxic effects of drugs or chemicals.

ap·ne·a (ap′nē ə, ap nē′ə), *n.* suspension of breathing. Compare SLEEP APNEA. —**ap·ne′ic**, *adj.*

ap·o·crine (ap′ə krin, -krin′, -krēn′), *adj.* **1.** of or pertaining to certain glands whose secretions are acted upon by bacteria to produce the characteristic odor of perspiration (distinguished from *eccrine*). **2.** of or pertaining to such secretions.

ap·o·en·zyme (ap′ō en′zīm), *n.* the protein component that with a coenzyme forms a complete enzyme.

a·pog·a·my (ə pog′ə mē), *n.* PARTHENOGENESIS. —**ap·o·gam·ic** (ap′ə gam′ik), **a·pog′a·mous**, *adj.*

ap·o·mict (ap′ə mikt), *n.* an organism produced by apomixis.

ap′o·mix′is (-mik′sis), *n., pl.* **-mix·es** (-mik′sēz). any of several types of asexual reproduction, as parthenogenesis. —**ap′o·mic′tic** (-mik′tik), *adj.* —**ap′o·mic′ti·cal·ly**, *adv.*

ap·o·mor·phine (ap′ə môr′fēn, -fin) also **ap·o·mor·phin** (-fin), *n.* an alkaloid, $C_{17}H_{17}NO_2$, derived from morphine and used as a fast-acting emetic.

ap·o·plec·tic (ap′ə plek′tik), *adj.* Also, **ap′o·plec′ti·cal.** **1.** of or pertaining to apoplexy. **2.** having or inclined to apoplexy. —*n.* **3.** a person having or predisposed to apoplexy. —**ap′o·plec′ti·cal·ly**, *adv.*

ap·o·plex·y (ap′ə plek′sē), *n.* **1.** STROKE. **2.** a sudden, usu. marked, loss of bodily function due to rupture or occlusion of a blood vessel. **3.** a hemorrhage into an organ cavity or tissue.

a·poth·e·car·y (ə poth′ə ker′ē), *n., pl.* **-car·ies.** **1.** a druggist; pharmacist. **2.** a pharmacy; drugstore.

ap·pen·dec·to·my (ap/ən dek/tə mē), *n., pl.* **-mies.** surgical removal of the vermiform appendix.

ap·pen·di·ci·tis (ə pen/də sī/tis), *n.* inflammation of the vermiform appendix.

ap·pen·dic·u·lar (ap/ən dik/yə lər), *adj.* of or pertaining to an appendage or limb.

ap·pen·dix (ə pen/diks), *n., pl.* **-dix·es, -di·ces** (-də sēz/). VERMIFORM APPENDIX.

ap·pe·stat (ap/ə stat/), *n.* a presumed region in the human brain, possibly the hypothalamus, that functions to regulate appetite.

ap·pli·ca·tion (ap/li kā/shən), *n.* a salve, ointment, or the like, applied as a soothing or healing agent.

a·prax·i·a (ə prak/sē ə, ā prak/-), *n.* a disorder of the nervous system characterized by an inability to perform purposeful movements but not with paralysis or a loss of feeling. —**a·prac/tic** (-tik), **a·prax/ic,** *adj.*

a/queous hu/mor, *n.* the watery fluid between the cornea and the lens of the eye.

a·rab·i·nose (ə rab/ə nōs/), *n.* a white, crystalline solid, C₅H₁₀O₅, used esp. as a culture medium in bacteriology. —**a·rab/i·nos/ic** (-nos/ik), *adj.*

a·rab·i·no·side (ar/ə bin/ə sid/, ə rab/ə nə-), *n.* a glycoside of arabinose, esp. any of those used in antiviral therapy.

a·rach·noid (ə rak/noid), *n.* the serous membrane forming the middle of the three coverings of the brain and spinal cord. Compare DURA MATER, MENINGES, PIA MATER.

a·ra·ro·ba (ar/ə rō/bə), *n., pl.* **-bas.** **1.** GOA POWDER. **2.** the Brazilian tree from which Goa powder is obtained.

ar·bo·vi·rus (är/bə vī/rəs), *n., pl.* **-rus·es.** any of several togaviruses that are transmitted by bloodsucking arthropods, as ticks, fleas, or mosquitoes, and may cause encephalitis, yellow fever, or dengue fever.

ARC (ärk), *n.* AIDS-RELATED COMPLEX.

ar/chae·bac·te/ri·a (är/kē-) also **ar/chae·o·bac·te/ri·a** (är/kē ō-), *n.pl., sing.* **-te·ri·um.** a group of microorganisms, including methanogens and halobacteria, that are genetically and functionally different from all other living forms, thrive in oxygen-poor environments, and are sometimes classified as a separate kingdom.

arch·en·ceph·a·lon (är/ken sef/ə lon/), *n., pl.* **-lons, -la** (-lə). the primitive forebrain region of the embryo that is anterior to the notochord and gives rise to the midbrain and forebrain.

arch·en·ter·on (är ken/tə ron/), *n., pl.* **-ter·a** (-tər ə). the primitive enteron or digestive cavity of a gastrula. —**arch/en·ter/ic** (-ter/ik), *adj.*

ar·che·type (är/ki tīp/), *n.* (in Jungian psychology) an inherited unconscious idea, pattern of thought, image, etc., universally present in individual psyches. —**ar/che·typ/al** (-tī/pəl), **ar/che·typ/i·cal** (-tip/i kəl), *adj.*

ARDS, adult respiratory distress syndrome. See RESPIRATORY DISTRESS SYNDROME (def. 2).

ar·en·a·vi·rus (âr′en ā′vī/rəs), *n.*, *pl.* **-rus·es.** any of various RNA-containing viruses of the family Arenaviridae, usually transmitted to humans by contact with excreta of infected rodents.

Arg, arginine.

ar·gi·nase (är′jə nās′, -nāz′), *n.* a liver enzyme that converts arginine to urea.

ar′gi·nine′ (-nēn′, -nin′, -nin), *n.* an essential amino acid, $C_6H_{14}N_4O_2$: the free amino acid increases insulin secretion. *Abbr.:* Arg; *Symbol:* R

a·ro·ma·ther′a·py, *n.* the use of fragrances to affect or alter a person's mood or behavior.

ar·rhyth·mi·a (ə rith′mē ə, ā rith′-), *n.* any disturbance in the rhythm of the heartbeat. —**ar·rhyth′mic, ar·rhyth′mi·cal,** *adj.* —**ar·rhyth′mi·cal·ly,** *adv.*

ar·se·nic (är′sə nik, ärs′nik), *n.* a grayish white element having a metallic luster, vaporizing when heated, and forming poisonous compounds. *Symbol:* As; *at. wt.:* 74.92; *at. no.:* 33.

ar·te·ri·al (är tēr′ē əl), *adj.* pertaining to the blood in the arteries and pulmonary veins, richer in oxygen and redder than venous blood. —**ar·te′ri·al·ly,** *adv.*

ar·te′ri·o·gram′ (-ə gram′), *n.* an x-ray produced by arteriography.

ar·te′ri·og′ra·phy (-og′rə fē), *n.*, *pl.* **-phies.** x-ray examination of an artery or arteries following injection of a radiopaque substance. Compare ANGIOCARDIOGRAPHY. —**ar·te′ri·o·graph′ic** (-ə graf′ik), *adj.*

ar·te·ri·ole (är tēr′ē ōl′), *n.* any of the smallest branches of an artery. —**ar·te′ri·o′lar,** *adj.*

ar·te′ri·o·scle·ro′sis (är tēr′ē ō-), *n.* abnormal thickening and loss of elasticity in the arterial walls. —**ar·te′ri·o·scle·rot′ic,** *adj.*

ar·te′ri·o·ve′nous, *adj.* of, pertaining to, or affecting both arteries and veins.

ar·te·ri·tis (är′tə rī′tis), *n.* inflammation of an artery.

ar·ter·y (är′tə rē), *n.*, *pl.* **-ter·ies.** a blood vessel that conveys blood from the heart to any part of the body.

ar·thral·gia (är thral′jə), *n.* pain in a joint. —**ar·thral′gic,** *adj.*

ar·thrit·ic (är thrit′ik), *adj.* **1.** of, pertaining to, or afflicted with arthritis. —*n.* **2.** a person afflicted with arthritis. —**ar·thrit′i·cal·ly,** *adv.*

ar·thri·tis (är thrī′tis), *n.* inflammation of one or more joints. Compare BURSITIS, OSTEOARTHRITIS, RHEUMATOID ARTHRITIS.

ar·throd·e·sis (är throd′ə sis), *n.*, *pl.* **-ses** (-sēz′). permanent surgical immobilization of a joint.

ar·throp·a·thy (är throp′ə thē), *n.* disease of the joints. —**ar′thro·path′ic** (-thrə path′ik), *adj.*

ar·thro·scope (är′thrə skōp′), *n.* an endoscope specialized for use in the diagnosis and surgical treatment of diseased or injured joints. —**ar·thros′co·py** (-thros′kə pē), *n.* —**ar′thro·scop′ic** (-skop′ik), *adj.*

artic'ulated joint', *n.* an artificial appendage, limb, or the like, esp. one activated and controlled by a computer, as the mechanical arm of a robot.

ar·tic·u·la·tion (är tik/yə lā/shən), *n.* **1.** the union of a joint or joints. **2.** a joint between bones. —**ar·tic/u·la·to·ry** (-lə tôr/ē, -tōr/ē), *adj.*

ar·ti·fact or **ar·te·fact** (är/tə fakt/), *n.* a substance or structure not naturally present in the matter being observed but formed by artificial means, as during preparation of a microscope slide. —**ar/ti·fac·ti/tious** (-faktish/əs), *adj.* —**ar/ti·fac/tu·al** (-fak/chōō əl), *adj.*

ar'tifi'cial gene', *n.* a duplicate gene synthesized in the laboratory by combining nucleotides in a sequence characteristic of the copied gene.

artifi'cial insemina'tion, *n.* the injection of semen into the vagina or uterus by means of a syringe or the like.

artifi'cial respira'tion, *n.* the stimulation of natural respiratory functions in a person whose breathing has failed by forcing air into and out of the lungs.

as·bes·to·sis (as/be stō/sis, az/-), *n.* a lung disease caused by the inhalation of asbestos dust.

as·ca·ri·a·sis (as/kə rī/ə sis), *n.* infestation with ascarids, esp. *Ascaris lumbricoides.*

as·ca·rid (as/kə rid), *n.* any parasitic roundworm of the family Ascaridae.

as·ca·ris (-ris), *n., pl.* **as·car·i·des** (a skar/i dēz/). any intestinal parasitic roundworm of the genus *Ascaris,* esp. the species causing colic and diarrhea in humans.

ascend'ing co'lon (kō/lən), *n.* the first portion of the large intestine, extending from the small intestine upward.

as·ci·tes (ə sī/tēz), *n.* accumulation of serous fluid in the peritoneal cavity. —**as·cit·ic** (ə sit/ik), *adj.*

a·scor·bate (ə skôr/bāt, -bit), *n.* a salt or other derivative of ascorbic acid.

a·scor/bic ac/id (-bik), *n.* a white, crystalline, water-soluble vitamin, $C_6H_8O_6$, occurring naturally in citrus fruits, green vegetables, etc., and also produced synthetically, essential for normal metabolism: used in the prevention and treatment of scurvy, and in wound-healing and tissue repair. Also called **vitamin C.**

a·sep·sis (ə sep/sis, ā sep/-), *n.* **1.** absence of the microorganisms that produce sepsis or septic disease. **2.** methods, such as sterile surgical techniques, used to assure asepsis.

a·sep/tic, *adj.* free from the living germs of disease, fermentation, or putrefaction. —**a·sep/ti·cal·ly**, *adv.*

a·sex·u·al (ā sek/shōō əl), *adj.* **1.** having no sex or sexual organs. **2.** independent of sexual processes, esp. not involving the union of male and female germ cells. —**a·sex/u·al/i·ty**, *n.* —**a·sex/u·al·ly**, *adv.*

Asn, asparagine.

Asp, aspartic acid.

as·par·a·gine (ə spar/ə jēn/, -jin), *n.* an essential amino acid, $NH_2COCH_2CH(NH_2)COOH$, abundant in legumes. *Abbr.:* Asn; *Symbol:* Ν

as·par·tame (ə spär′tām, a spär′-, as′pər tām′), *n.* a white crystalline powder, $C_{14}H_{18}N_2O_5$, synthesized from amino acids, that is many times sweeter than sucrose and is used as a low-calorie sugar substitute.

as·par′tic ac′id (ə spär′tik) *n.* a nonessential amino acid, $C_4H_7NO_4$, found in molasses. *Abbr.:* Asp; *Symbol:* D

as·per·gil·lo·sis (as′pər jə lō′sis), *n., pl.* **-ses** (-sēz) an infection or disease caused by a mold of the genus *Aspergillus*, characterized by granulomatous lesions, as of the lungs and skin.

as·phyx·i·a (as fik′sē ə), *n.* an extreme condition usu. involving loss of consciousness caused by lack of oxygen and excess of carbon dioxide in the blood, as from suffocation. —**as·phyx′i·a′tion,** *n.*

as·pi·rate (*v.* as′pə rāt′; *n.* -pər it), *v.,* **-rat·ed, -rat·ing,** *n.* —*v.t.* **1.** to remove (a fluid) from a body cavity by aspiration. **2.** to inhale (fluid or a foreign body). **3.** to draw or remove by suction. —*n.* **4.** the substance or contents inhaled in aspiration. —**as·pi·ra·to·ry** (ə spīr′r/ə tôr/ē, -tôr/ē), *adj.*

as·pi·ra′tion, *n.* **1.** the act of removing a fluid, as pus or serum, from a cavity of the body by a hollow needle and tro-car connected with a suction syringe. **2.** the act of inhaling fluid or a foreign body into the bronchi and lungs, often after vomiting. —**as·pi·ra′tion·al,** *adj.*

as·pi·ra′tor, *n.* a medical suction instrument used in aspirating fluids from the body.

as·pi·rin (as′pər in, -prin), *n., pl.* **-rin, -rins. 1.** a white, crystalline substance, $C_9H_8O_4$, derivative of salicylic acid, used as an anti-inflammatory agent and to relieve pain and fever; acetylsalicylic acid. **2.** a tablet of this.

as·say (a sā′), *v.t.,* **-sayed, -say·ing.** to analyze (a drug) to determine potency or composition. —**as·say′a·ble,** *adj.* —**as·say′er,** *n.*

asser′tiveness train′ing, *n.* behavior therapy in which one is taught how to assert oneself constructively through direct expression of both positive and negative feelings.

as·sim·i·late (ə sim′ə lāt′), *v.,* **-lat·ed, -lat·ing.** —*v.t.* **1.** to convert (ingested food) to substances suitable for incorporation into the body and its tissues. —*v.i.* **2.** (of ingested food) to be converted into the substance of the body.

as·sim′i·la′tion, *n.* **1.** the conversion of absorbed food into the substance of the body. **2.** the process of plant nutrition, including photosynthesis and the absorption of nutrient matter.

as·so·ci·a·tion·ism (ə sō′sē ā′shə niz′əm, -shē ā′-), *n.* any theory that explains complex psychological phenomena as being built up from combinations of simple sensory and behavioral elements. —**as·so′ci·a′tion·ist,** *adj., n.* —**as·so′ci·a′tion·is′tic,** *adj.*

as·the·ni·a (as thē′nē ə), *n.* lack or loss of strength; weakness.

as·then′ic (-then′ik), *adj.* of, pertaining to, or characterized by asthenia; weak.

asth·ma (az′mə, as′-), *n.* a paroxysmal, often allergic disorder of respiration characterized by bronchospasm, wheezing, and difficulty in expiration. Also called **bronchial asthma.**

as·tig·mat·ic (as′tig mat′ik), *adj.* pertaining to, exhibiting, or correcting astigmatism. —**as′tig·mat′i·cal·ly,** *adv.*

a·stig·ma·tism (ə stig′mə tiz′əm), *n.* **1.** Also called **a·stig·mi·a** (ə stig′mē ə). a refractive error of the eye in which parallel rays of light from an external source do not converge on a single focal point on the retina. **2.** an aberration of a lens or other optical system in which the image of a point is spread out along the axis of the system.

as·trin·gent (ə strin′jənt), *adj.* **1.** causing contraction or constriction of soft tissue; styptic. —*n.* **2.** a substance that contracts the tissues or canals of the body. —**as·trin′gen·cy,** *n.* —**as·trin′gent·ly,** *adv.*

as·tro·cyte (as′trə sīt′), *n.* a star-shaped neuroglial cell of ectodermal origin. —**as′tro·cyt′ic** (-sit′ik), *adj.*

a·sy·lum (ə sī′ləm), *n.* (esp. formerly) an institution for the maintenance and care of the mentally ill, orphans, or other persons requiring specialized assistance.

a·symp·to·mat·ic (ā simp′tə mat′ik, ā′simp-), *adj.* showing no evidence of disease. —**a·symp′to·mat′i·cal·ly,** *adv.*

a·syn·ap·sis (ā′si nap′sis), *n., pl.* **-ses** (-sēz). failure of the pairing of homologous chromosomes during meiosis.

At·a·brine (at′ə brin, -brēn′), *Trademark.* a brand of quinacrine.

a·tax·i·a (ə tak′sē ə), *n.* loss of coordination of the muscles, esp. of the extremities. —**a·tax′ic,** *adj.*

at·e·lec·ta·sis (at′l ek′tə sis), *n.* **1.** incomplete expansion of the lungs at birth, as from lack of breathing force. **2.** collapse of the lungs, as from bronchial obstruction. —**at′e·lec·tat′ic** (-tat′ik), *adj.*

ath·er·ec·to·my (ath′ə rek′tə mē), *n., pl.* **-mies.** the removal of plaque from an artery by means of a tiny rotating cutting blade inserted through a catheter.

ath′er·o·gen′ic (-rō jen′ik), *adj.* capable of producing atheromatous plaques in arteries.

ath′er·o′ma (-rō′mə), *n., pl.* **-mas, -ma·ta** (-mə tə). **1.** a sebaceous cyst. **2.** an abnormal deposition of plaque and fibrous matter on the inner wall of an artery. —**ath′er·om′a·tous** (-rom′ə təs, -rō′mə-), *adj.*

ath′er·o·scle·ro′sis, *n.* a common form of arteriosclerosis in which fatty substances form a deposit of plaque on the inner lining of arterial walls. —**ath′er·o·scle·rot′ic** (-rot′ik), *adj.* —**ath′er·o·scle·rot′i·cal·ly,** *adv.*

ath′lete's foot′, *n.* a contagious disease of the feet, caused by a fungus that thrives on moist surfaces; ringworm of the feet.

a·ton·ic (ə ton′ik, ā ton′-), *adj.* characterized by atony.

at·o·ny (at′n ē) also **a·to·ni·a** (ə tō′nē ə, ā tō′-), *n.* lack of tone or energy; muscular weakness, esp. in a contractile organ.

ATP, adenosine triphosphate: a nucleotide that is the primary source of energy in all living cells because of its function in donating a phosphate group during biochemical activities; composed of adenosine, ribose, and three phosphate groups and formed by enzymatic reaction from adenosine diphosphate and an orthophosphate. Compare ADP.

ATPase (ā′tē/pē′ās, -āz), *n.* adenosine triphosphatase: any of several enzymes that catalyze the hydrolysis of ATP to ADP and phosphate.

a·tre·sia (ə trē′zhə, -zhē ə), *n.* the absence, or failure to develop, of a normal body opening or duct, as the ear canal. —**a·tre′sic** (-zik, -sik), **a·tret·ic** (ə tret′ik), *adj.*

a′trial na′triuret′ic fac′tor, *n.* a hormone of the heart's atrial muscles that helps to regulate blood pressure and electrolyte balance. *Abbr:* ANF

a·tri·o·ven·tric·u·lar (ā′trē ō ven trik′yə lər), *adj.* of or pertaining to the atria and ventricles of the heart. *Abbr.:* AV, A-V

a′trioventric′ular bun′dle, *n.* a bundle of conducting muscle fibers in the heart leading from the atrioventricular node to the ventricles. Also called **bundle of His.**

a′trioventric′ular node′, *n.* a small mass of conducting muscle fibers in the heart, at the base of the right atrium, that transmits heartbeat impulses to the ventricles.

a·tri·um (ā′trē əm), *n., pl.* **a·tri·a** (ā′trē ə), **a·tri·ums. 1.** a cavity of the body. **2.** Also called **auricle.** either of the two thin-walled upper chambers of the heart that receive blood from the veins and force it into the ventricles. —**a′tri·al,** *adj.*

at·ro·phy (a′trə fē) also **a·tro·phi·a** (ə trō′fē ə), *n.* a wasting away of the body or of an organ or part, as from defective nutrition or nerve damage. —**a·troph·ic** (ə trof′ik, ə trō′fik), *adj.*

at·ro·pine (a′trə pēn′, -pin), *n.* a poisonous crystalline alkaloid, $C_{17}H_{23}NO_3$, obtained from belladonna or other nightshade plants, used chiefly to relieve spasms or, topically, to dilate the pupil of the eye.

at·tend·ing (ə ten′ding), *adj.* (of a physician) **1.** having primary responsibility for a patient. **2.** holding a staff position in an accredited hospital: *an attending physician.*

atten′tion def′icit disor′der, *n.* a developmental disorder of children characterized by inattention, impulsiveness, distractibility, and often hyperactivity.

at·ten·u·ate (ə ten′yōō āt′), *v.t.* **-at·ed, -at·ing.** to render less virulent, as a strain of pathogenic virus or bacterium.

at·ten·u·a·tion, *n.* the process by which a virus, bacterium, etc., changes under laboratory conditions to become harmless or less virulent.

au·dile (ô′dil, -dīl), *adj.* **1.** of, pertaining to, or affecting the auditory nerves or the sense of hearing. **2.** oriented to or relying heavily on the faculty of hearing for information or for creating mental images.

au·di·o·gram (ô′dē ə gram′), *n.* the graphic record produced by an audiometer.

au·di·ol·o·gy (-ol′ə jē), *n.* the study of hearing disorders, including evaluation of hearing function and rehabilitation of patients with hearing impairments. —**au′di·o·log′i·cal** (-ə loj′i kəl), **au′di·o·log′ic,** *adj.* —**au′di·ol′o·gist,** *n.*

au·di·om′e·ter (-om′i tər), *n.* an instrument for gauging and recording acuity of hearing.

au′di·om′e·try, *n.* the testing of hearing by means of an audiometer. —**au′di·o·met′ric** (-me′trik), *adj.* —**au′di·o·met′ri·cal·ly,** *adv.*

au·di·to·ry (ô′di tôr′ē, -tōr′ē-), *adj.* pertaining to hearing, to the sense of hearing, or to the organs of hearing. —**au′di·to′ri·ly, au′di·to′ri·al·ly,** *adv.*

au·ra (ôr′ə), *n., pl.* **au·ras** or, for 2, **au·rae** (ôr′ē). **1.** a light or radiance claimed to emanate from the body and to be visible to certain individuals with psychic or spiritual powers. **2.** a sensation, as of a glowing light or an aroma, preceding an attack of migraine or epilepsy.

au·ral (ôr′əl), *adj.* of or pertaining to the ear or to the sense of hearing. —**au′ral·ly,** *adv.*

Au·re·o·my·cin (ôr′ē ō mī′sin), *Trademark.* a brand of chlortetracycline.

au·ri·cle (ôr′i kəl), *n.* **1.** the outer ear; pinna. **2.** (loosely) the atrium of the heart. —**au′ri·cled,** *adj.*

au·ric·u·lar (ô rik′yə lər), *adj.* pertaining to the ear or to hearing; aural. s —**au·ric′u·lar·ly,** *adv.*

aus·cul·tate (ô′skəl tāt′), *v.t., v.i.,* **-tat·ed, -tat·ing.** to examine by auscultation. —**aus·cul·ta·tive** (ô′skəl tā′tiv, ô skul′tə-), **aus·cul·ta·to·ry** (ô skul′tə tôr′ē, -tōr′ē), *adj.* —**aus′cul·ta′tor,** *n.*

aus′cul·ta′tion, *n.* the act of listening, either directly or through a stethoscope or other instrument, to sounds within the body as a method of diagnosis.

au·ta·coid (ô′tə koid′), *n.* any physiologically active internal secretion, esp. one of uncertain classification. —**au′ta·coi′dal,** *adj.*

au·tism (ô′tiz əm), *n.* a pervasive developmental disorder characterized by impaired communication, extreme self-absorption, and detachment from reality. —**au′tist,** *n.* —**au·tis′tic,** *adj.* —**au·tis′ti·cal·ly,** *adv.*

au′to·a·nal′y·sis (ô′tō-), *n. Psychoanal.* self-analysis.

au′to·an′ti·bod′y, *n., pl.* **-bod·ies.** an antibody that an organism produces against any of its own components.

au′to·an′ti·gen, *n.* an antigen of one's own cells or cell products. Also called **self-antigen.**

au′to·ca·tal′y·sis, *n., pl.* **-ses.** catalysis caused by a catalytic agent formed during a chemical reaction. —**au′to·cat′a·lyt′ic** (-kat′l it′ik), *adj.* —**au′to·cat′a·lyt′i·cal·ly,** *adv.*

au·toch·tho·nous (ô tok′thə nəs) also **au·toch′tho·nal,** *adj.* **1.** *Pathol.* located in a part of the body in which it originated, as a cancer or infection. **2.** *Psychol.* of or pertaining to ideas that originate independently of normal modes of thought or influences, as an obsession or schizophrenic construct. —**au·toch'tho·nism, au·toch'tho·ny,** *n.* —**au·toch'tho·nous·ly,** *adv.*

au·to·clave (ô'tə klāv'), *n.* a heavy vessel for sterilizing or cooking by means of steam under pressure.

au·to·ga·my (ô tog'ə mē), *n.* conjugation in an individual organism by division of its nucleus into two parts that in turn reunite to form a zygote. —**au·tog'a·mous, au·to·gam·ic** (ô'tō gam'ik), *adj.*

au·to·ge·nous (ô toj'ə nəs) also **au·to·gen·ic** (ô'tə jen'ik), *adj.* self-produced, as substances generated in the body; self-generated. —**au·tog'e·nous·ly,** *adv.*

au·to·graft (ô'tə graft', -gräft'), *n.* a tissue or organ that is grafted into a new position on the body of the individual from whom it was removed. Compare ALLOGRAFT, XENOGRAFT.

au·to·hyp·no·sis (ô'tō hip nō'sis), *n.* self-induced hypnosis or hypnotic state. —**au'to·hyp·not'ic** (-not'ik), *adj.* —**au'to·hyp·not'i·cal·ly,** *adv.*

au'to·im·mune', *adj.* of or pertaining to the immune response of an organism against any of its own components. —**au'to·im·mu'ni·ty,** *n.*

autoimmune' disease', *n.* a disease resulting from a disordered immune reaction in which antibodies are produced that damage components of one's own body.

au'to·in·fec'tion, *n.* infection caused by a pathogen that is already in one's own body.

au'to·in·oc'u·la'tion, *n.* inoculation with a vaccine prepared from a pathogen within a person's own body.

au'to·in·tox'i·ca'tion, *n.* poisoning with toxic substances formed within the body, as during intestinal digestion. Also called **autotoxemia.**

au'to·ki·ne'sis, *n.* spontaneous or voluntary movement. —**au'to·ki·net'ic,** *adj.*

au·tol·o·gous (ô tol'ə gəs), *adj.* from the same organism: *an autologous graft.*

au'to·ly·sin (ôt'l ī'sin, ô tol'ə-), *n.* any agent producing autolysis.

au·tol·y·sis (ô tol'ə sis), *n.* the breakdown of tissue by the action of enzymes contained in the tissue affected; self-digestion. —**au'to·lyt'ic** (ôt'l it'ik), *adj.*

au·to·lyze (ôt'l īz'), *v.,* **-lyzed, -lyz·ing.** —*v.t.* **1.** to cause to undergo autolysis. —*v.i.* **2.** to undergo autolysis.

au·to·mat·ic (ô'tə mat'ik), *adj.* occurring independently of volition, as certain muscular actions; involuntary; reflex. —**au·to·mat'i·cal·ly,** *adv.* —**au·to·ma·tic'i·ty** (-mə tis'i·tē), *n.*

au'tomat'ic writ'ing, *n.* writing performed without apparent intent or conscious control, esp. to achieve spontaneity or uncensored expression.

au·tom·a·tism (ô tom'ə tiz'əm), *n.* **1.** the involuntary functioning of an organic process, esp. muscular, without apparent neural stimulation. **2.** *Psychol.* the performance of an act or actions without the performer's awareness or conscious volition. —**au·tom′a·tist**, *n., adj.*

au·to·nom·ic (ô′tə nom′ik), *adj.* of, pertaining to, or controlled by the autonomic nervous system. —**au′to·nom′i·cal·ly**, *adv.*

au′to·nom′ic nerv′ous sys′tem, *n.* the system of nerves and ganglia that innervates the blood vessels, heart, smooth muscles, viscera, and glands and controls their involuntary functions and consists of sympathetic and parasympathetic portions.

au·top·sy (ô′top sē, ô′təp-), *n., pl.* **-sies**, *v.,* **-sied, -sy·ing.** —*n.* **1.** the inspection and dissection of a body after death, as for determination of the cause of death; post-mortem examination. —*v.t.* **2.** to perform an autopsy on. —**au′top·sist**, *n.*

au·to·some (ô′tə sōm′), *n.* any chromosome other than a sex chromosome. —**au′to·so′mal**, *adj.* —**au′to·so′mal·ly**, *adv.*

au·to·sug·ges·tion (ô′tō-), *n.* suggestion arising from oneself, as the repetition of verbal messages as a means of changing behavior. —**au′to·sug·gest′i·ble**, *adj.* —**au′to·sug·gest′i·bil′i·ty**, *n.*

au′to·tox·e′mi·a, *n.* AUTOINTOXICATION.

au′to·tox′in, *n.* a poisonous chemical formed within the body and acting against it. —**au′to·tox′ic**, *adj.*

au′to·trans·fu′sion, *n.* a blood transfusion using the recipient's own blood, either from a previously stored supply or from blood recovered during surgery.

aux·e·sis (ôg zē′sis, ôk sē′-), *n.* growth, esp. that resulting from an increase in cell size. —**aux·et·ic** (ôg zet′ik, ôk set′-), *adj.*

AV or **A-V,** atrioventricular.

a·ver·sion ther′apy, *n.* AVERSIVE CONDITIONING.

a·ver·sive (ə vûr′siv, -ziv), *adj.* **1.** of or pertaining to aversive conditioning. —*n.* **2.** a reprimand, punishment, or agent used in aversive conditioning.

aver′sive condi′tioning, *n.* conditioning by linking an unpleasant or noxious stimulus with the performance of undesirable behavior. Also called **aversion therapy.**

avia′tion med′icine, *n.* the branch of medicine dealing with the psychological, physiological, and pathological effects of flying in airplanes. Also called **aeromedicine.**

av·i·din (av′i din, ə vid′in), *n.* a protein of raw egg white that combines with the vitamin biotin and prevents its absorption.

a·vir·u·lent (ā vir′yə lənt, ā vir′ə-), *adj.* (of microorganisms) having lost virulence; no longer pathogenic. —**a·vir′u·lence**, *n.*

a·vi·ta·min·o·sis (ā vī′tə mə nō′sis), *n.* any disease caused by a lack of vitamins. —**a·vi′ta·min·ot′ic** (-not′ik), *adj.*

a·vulse (ə vuls′), *v.t.,* **a·vulsed, a·vuls·ing.** to pull off or tear away forcibly: *to avulse a ligament.*

a·xen·ic (ā zen′ik, ā zē′nik), *adj.* **1.** (of an experimental animal) raised under sterile conditions; germfree. **2.** (of a laboratory culture) uncontaminated. —**a·xen′i·cal·ly,** *adv.*

ax·i·al skel′eton (ak′sē əl), *n.* the skeleton of the head and trunk.

ax·il·la (ak sil′ə), *n., pl.* **ax·il·lae** (ak sil′ē). the armpit.

ax·il·lar (ak′sə lər), *adj.* of or pertaining to an axilla.

ax·il·lar·y (ak′sə ler′ē), *adj.* of or pertaining to the axilla.

ax·on (ak′son), *n.* the appendage of a neuron that transmits impulses away from the cell body. —**ax′on·al** (-sə nl, -son′l), *adj.*

a·zi·do·thy·mi·dine (ə zi′dō thi′mi dēn′, -zē′-, az′i-), *n.* See AZT.

az·o·te·mi·a (az′ə tē′mē ə, ā′zə-), *n.* the accumulation of abnormally large amounts of nitrogenous waste products in the blood, as in kidney failure. —**az′o·te′mic,** *adj.*

az·o·tu′ri·a (-tŏor′ē ə, -tyŏor′-), *n.* an elevated level of nitrogenous compounds in the urine.

AZT, *Trademark.* azidothymidine: an antiviral drug, manufactured from genetic materials in fish sperm or produced synthetically, used in the treatment of AIDS. Compare ZIDOVUDINE.

B

B, *Symbol.* a major blood group. See ABO SYSTEM.

B., bacillus.

ba·be·sia (bə bē′zhə, -zhē ə, -zē ə), *n., pl.* **-sias.** any protozoan of the genus *Babesia*, certain species of which are parasitic and pathogenic for warm-blooded animals.

BAC, blood-alcohol concentration: the percentage of alcohol in the bloodstream: in most U.S. states, a BAC of 0.10 is the legal definition of intoxication.

bac·il·lar·y (bas′ə ler′ē, bə sil′ə rē) also **ba·cil·lar** (bə sil′ər, bas′ə lər), *adj.* characterized by bacilli.

ba·cil·lus (bə sil′əs), *n., pl.* **-cil·li** (-sil′ī). **1.** any rod-shaped or cylindrical bacterium of the genus *Bacillus*, comprising spore-producing bacteria. **2.** (formerly) any bacterium.

bacil′lus Cal·mette′-Gué·rin′ (kal met′gā raN′, -raN′), *n.* a weakened strain of the tubercle bacillus *Mycobacterium bovis*, used in the preparation of BCG vaccine.

bac·i·tra·cin (bas′i trā′sin), *n.* an antibiotic polypeptide derived by the hydrolytic action of *Bacillus subtilis* on protein, primarily used topically in the treatment of superficial infections.

back′ache′, *n.* a pain or ache in the back, usu. in the lumbar region.

back′bone′, *n.* the spinal column; spine.

bact., **1.** bacteriology. **2.** bacterium.

bac·te·re·mi·a (bak′tə rē′mē ə), *n.* the presence of bacteria in the blood. —**bac′te·re′mic** (-mik), *adj.*

bac·te·ri·a (bak tēr′ē ə), *n.pl., sing.* **-te·ri·um** (-tēr′ē əm). any of numerous groups of microscopic one-celled organisms constituting the phylum Schizomycota, of the kingdom Monera, various species of which are involved in infectious diseases, fermentation, or putrefaction. —**bac·te′ri·al,** *adj.* —**bac·te′ri·al·ly,** *adv.*

bac·te′ri·cide′ (-ə sid′), *n.* any substance capable of killing bacteria. —**bac·te′ri·cid′al,** *adj.* —**bac·te′ri·cid′al·ly,** *adv.*

bacteriol., bacteriology.

bac·te′ri·ol′o·gy (-ē ol′ə jē), *n.* a branch of microbiology dealing with bacteria. —**bac·te′ri·o·log′i·cal** (-ə loj′i kəl), **bac·te′ri·o·log′ic,** *adj.* —**bac·te′ri·o·log′i·cal·ly,** *adv.* —**bac·te′ri·ol′o·gist,** *n.*

bac·te′ri·ol′y·sis (-ol′ə sis), *n.* disintegration or dissolution of bacteria. —**bac·te′ri·o·lyt′ic** (-ə lit′ik), *n., adj.*

bac·te′ri·o·phage′ (-ə fāj′), *n.* any of a group of viruses that infect specific bacteria, usu. causing their disintegration or dissolution. Also called **phage.** —**bac·te′ri·o·phag′ic** (-faj′ik, -fā′jik), **bac·te′ri·oph′a·gous** (-of′ə gəs), *adj.* —**bac·te′ri·oph′a·gy** (-jē), *n.*

bac·te′ri·o·sta·sis (-ə stā′sis), *n.* the prevention of the further growth of bacteria. —**bac·te'ri·o·stat'ic** (-stat'ik), adj. —**bac·te'ri·o·stat'i·cal·ly**, adv.

bac·te'ri·o·stat' (-stat'), n. a substance or preparation that inhibits the further growth of bacteria.

bac·te'ri·um (-əm), n. sing. of BACTERIA.

bac·te'ri·u·ria (-tēr'ē yŏŏr'ē ə) also **bac'ter·u·ria** (-tə rŏŏr'ē ə, -tər yŏŏr'-), n. the presence of bacteria in the urine.

bac'te·rize (-tə rīz'), v.t., **-rized, -riz·ing.** to change in composition by means of bacteria. —**bac'te·ri·za'tion**, n.

bac'te·roid (-roid') also **bac'te·roi'dal**, adj. resembling bacteria.

bag' of wa'ters, n. AMNION.

bak'ing so'da, n. SODIUM BICARBONATE.

ball'-and-sock'et joint', n. an anatomical joint in which the rounded end of one bone fits into a cuplike end of the other bone, as at the hip or shoulder. Also called **enarthrosis.**

bal·lis'to·car'di·o·gram' (bə lis'tō-), n. the graphic record produced by a ballistocardiograph.

bal·lis'to·car'di·o·graph', n. a device that measures the volume of blood ejected by the heart by recording the movements of the body in response to heart contraction. —**bal·lis'to·car'di·og'ra·phy**, n.

bal·lotte·ment (bə lot'mənt), n. a medical diagnostic technique of palpating an organ or floating mass by pushing it forcefully and feeling it rebound.

bal·ne·ol'o·gy (bal'nē ol'ə jē), n. the study of the therapeutic effects of baths and bathing. —**bal'ne·o·log'ic** (-loj'ik), **bal'ne·o·log'i·cal**, adj. —**bal'ne·ol'o·gist**, n.

band·age (ban'dij), n., v., **-aged, -ag·ing.** —n. **1.** a strip of cloth or other material used to bind up a wound, sore, sprain, etc. —v.t. **2.** to bind or cover with a bandage.

Band-Aid, n. Trademark. an adhesive bandage with a gauze pad in the center, used to cover minor abrasions and cuts.

barb (bärb), n. Slang. a barbiturate.

bar'ber's itch', n. inflammation of hair follicles in a shaved area of the skin, usu. caused by a fungal or staphylococcal infection; sycosis barbae.

bar·bi·tal (bär'bi tôl', -tal'), n. a barbiturate compound, $C_7O_3N_2H_{12}$, formerly used as a hypnotic.

bar·bi·tu·rate (bär bich'ər it, -ə rāt'; bär'bi tŏŏr'it, -āt, -tyŏŏr'-), n. any of a group of barbituric acid derivatives, used in medicine as sedatives and hypnotics.

bar'bitu'ric ac'id (bär'bi tŏŏr'ik, -tyŏŏr'-, bär'-), n. a white, crystalline, slightly water-soluble powder, $C_4H_4N_2O_3$, used chiefly in the synthesis of barbiturates.

bar·bi'tur·ism (-bich'ə riz'əm), n. Pathol. chronic poisoning caused by the excessive use of phenobarbital, secobarbital, or other derivative of barbituric acid.

bar·i·at·rics (bar'ē a'triks), n. (used with a sing. v.) a branch of medicine that deals with the control and treat-

ment of obesity and allied diseases. —**bar/i·at/ric**, adj.
—**bar/i·a·tri/cian** (-ə trish/ən), n.

bar/i·um sul/fate/ (bâr/ē əm, bar/-), n. a white, crystalline, water-insoluble powder, BaSO₄, used chiefly in the
synthesis of pigments and as a contrast medium in x-ray
diagnosis.

barium x-ray, n. an x-ray given as part of a GI series.

bar·o·re·cep·tor (bar/ō ri sep/tər), n. a nerve ending
that responds to changes in pressure.

Barr/ bod/y (bär), n. an inactive X chromosome present
in the nuclear membrane of female somatic cells, used for
verifying the sex of an individual.

Bar·tho·lin's gland (bär tō/linz, bär/tl inz), n. either of
a pair of small lubricating glands at the base of the vagina.

ba·sal (bā/səl, -zəl), adj. 1. indicating a standard low level
of activity of an organism, as during total rest. 2. of an
amount required to maintain this level. —**ba/sal·ly**, adv.

ba/sal cell/, n. any cell situated at the base of a multilay-
ered tissue, as at the lowest layer of the epidermis.

ba/sal cell/ carcino/ma, n. a common and usu. curable skin cancer that arises from basal cells of the epithelium.

ba/sal gang/lion, n. any of several masses of gray matter in the cerebral cortex, involved in the control of movement.

ba/sal metabol/ic rate/, n. the rate at which energy is
expended while fasting and at rest, calculated as calories
per hour per square meter of body surface. Abbr.: BMR

ba/sal metab/olism, n. the minimal amount of energy
necessary to maintain respiration, circulation, and other vital body functions while fasting and at total rest.

base (bās), n. 1. a chemical compound that reacts with an
acid to form a salt. 2. Genetics. any of the purine or pyrimidine compounds that constitute a portion of the nucleotide molecule of DNA or RNA: adenine, guanine, cytosine,
thymine, or uracil.

base/ pair/, n. any two of the nucleotide bases that readily form weak bonds with each other, bringing together
strands of DNA or RNA and linking codons with anticodons
during translation of the genetic code: adenine pairs with
thymine or uracil, and guanine pairs with cytosine.

base/-pair/ing, n. the process of bringing together separate sequences of DNA or RNA by the bonding of base
pairs.

bas·i·lar (bas/ə lər) also **bas·i·lar·y** (-ler/ē), adj. pertaining to or situated at the base, esp. the base of the skull.

ba·so·phil (bā/sə fil) also **ba·so·phile** (-fīl/, -fil), n. 1. a
basophilic cell, tissue, organism, or substance. 2. a white
blood cell having a two-lobed nucleus and basophilic granules in its cytoplasm. —adj. 3. BASOPHILIC.

ba·so·phil·ic (bā/sə fil/ik) also **ba·soph·i·lous** (bā sof/ə-
ləs), adj. (of a cell, cytoplasm, etc.) having an affinity for
basic stains.

ba·trach·o·tox·in (bə trak/ə tok/sin, ba/trə kō-), n. a

powerful neurotoxic venom, $C_{31}H_{42}N_2O_6$, secreted through the skin by South American frogs of the genus *Phyllobates*: used on arrow tips to paralyze prey.

bat/tle fatigue/, *n.* a posttraumatic stress disorder occurring among soldiers engaged in active and usu. prolonged combat. Also called **combat fatigue.**

B cell, *n.* **1.** Also called **B lymphocyte.** a type of white blood cell that circulates in the blood and lymph and produces antibody upon encountering any antigen that has a molecular arrangement complementary to the antibody. **2.** BETA CELL.

BCG vaccine, *n.* a vaccine made from weakened strains of tubercle bacilli, used to produce immunity against tuberculosis. [B(ACILLUS) C(ALMETTE-)G(UÉRIN)]

bed/sore/, *n.* a skin ulcer over a bony part of the body, caused by immobility and prolonged pressure, as in bedridden persons; decubitus ulcer. Also called **pressure sore.**

be·hav·ior (bi hāv/yər), *n. Psychol., Animal Behav.* **1.** observable activity in a human or animal. **2.** the aggregate of responses to internal and external stimuli. **3.** a stereotyped species-specific activity, as a courtship dance or startle reflex. —**be·hav/ior·al,** *adj.* —**be·hav/ior·al·ly,** *adv.*

be·hav·ior·ism, *n.* the theory or doctrine that human or animal psychology can be accurately studied only through the examination and analysis of objectively observable and quantifiable behavioral events, in contrast with subjective mental states. —**be·hav/ior·ist,** *n., adj.* —**be·hav/ior·is/tic,** *adj.* —**be·hav/ior·is/ti·cal·ly,** *adv.*

behav/ior modifica/tion, *n.* the direct changing of unwanted behavior by means of biofeedback or conditioning.

behav/ior ther/apy, *n.* a form of therapy emphasizing techniques for changing behavioral patterns that are maladaptive.

bej·el (bej/əl), *n.* a nonvenereal syphilis occurring mainly among children in certain subtropical areas of S Africa and SE Asia, caused by the spirochete strain *Treponema pallidum endemicum.*

bel·la·don·na (bel/ə don/ə), *n.* ATROPINE.

Bell's/ pal/sy (belz), *n.* suddenly occurring paralysis that distorts one side of the face, caused by a lesion of the facial nerve.

bend (bend), *n.* **the bends,** DECOMPRESSION SICKNESS.

be·nign (bi nīn/), *adj.* not cancerous or malignant; self-limiting: *a benign tumor.*

ben·ny (ben/ē), *n., pl.* **-nies.** *Slang.* a Benzedrine tablet.

Ben·ze·drine (ben/zi drēn/, -drin), *Trademark.* a brand of amphetamine.

ben·zo·di·az·e·pine (ben/zō di az/ə pēn/, -ā/zə-), *n.* any of a family of minor tranquilizers that act against anxiety and convulsions and produce sedation and muscle relaxation.

ben·zo/ic ac/id (ben zō/ik), *n.* a white, crystalline,

slightly water-soluble powder, $C_7H_6O_2$, used chiefly as a preservative and in medicine as a germicide.

ber·be·rine (bûr′bə rēn′), *n.* a white or yellow, crystalline, water-soluble alkaloid, $C_{20}H_{19}NO_5$, derived from barberry or goldenseal and used for treating burns and as an antibacterial agent and stomachic.

ber·i·ber·i (ber′ē ber′ē), *n.* a disease of the peripheral nerves caused by a deficiency of vitamin B_1, leading to paralysis and congestive heart failure. —**ber′i·ber′ic,** *adj.*

be·ta·dren·er·gic (bā′tə ad′rə nûr′jik; *esp. Brit.* bē′-), *adj.* of or pertaining to a beta receptor.

be′ta block′er or **be′ta-block′er,** *n.* any of a group of drugs that interfere with the ability of adrenaline to stimulate the beta receptors of the heart, thereby slowing heart rate and lessening the force of blood flow. —**be′ta-block′ing,** *adj.*

be′ta car′otene, *n.* the most abundant of various isomers of carotene, $C_{40}H_{56}$, that can be converted by the body to vitamin A.

be′ta cell′, *n.* a cell in the islets of Langerhans that produces and secretes insulin.

be·ta·ine (bēt′ə ēn′, -in; bi tā′ēn, -in), *n.* a colorless crystalline alkaloid, $C_5H_{11}NO_2$, usu. obtained from sugar beets or synthesized from glycine and used in medicine.

be′ta recep′tor or **be′ta-recep′tor,** *n.* a site on a cell, as of the heart, that upon interaction with epinephrine or norepinephrine controls heartbeat and heart contractibility, vasodilation, and other physiological processes.

be′ta rhythm′, *n.* a pattern of high-frequency brain waves **(beta waves)** observed in normal persons upon sensory stimulation, esp. with light, or when they are engaging in purposeful mental activity.

be′ta waves′, *n.pl.* See under BETA RHYTHM.

BFT, biofeedback training.

bGH, bovine growth hormone.

BHA, butylated hydroxyanisole: the antioxidant $C_{11}H_{16}O_2$, used to retard rancidity in products containing fat or oil.

bhang (bang), *n.* a mild preparation of cannabis, drunk as a fermented brew or smoked for its intoxicant or hallucinogenic effects.

BHT, butylated hydroxytoluene: the antioxidant $C_{15}H_{24}O$, used to retard rancidity in products containing fat or oil.

bib·li·o·ther·a·py (bib′lē ō ther′ə pē), *n.* the use of books and other reading materials as an enhancing adjunct to therapy. —**bib′li·o·ther′a·peu′tic,** *adj.*

bi·car′bo·nate of so′da (bī kär′bə nit, -nāt′), *n.* SODIUM BICARBONATE.

bi·ceps (bī′seps), *n., pl.* **-ceps, -ceps·es** (-sep siz). a muscle with two points of origin, as the flexor at the front of the upper arm and the similar flexor at the back of the thigh.

bi·cus·pid (bī kus′pid), *adj.* **1.** Also, **bi·cus′pi·date′** (-pi-dāt′). having or terminating in two cusps or points, as certain teeth. —*n.* **2.** PREMOLAR (def. 3).

bicus′pid valve′, *n.* MITRAL VALVE.

b.i.d., (in prescriptions) twice a day. [Latin, *bis in diē*]

bi·fo·cal (bī fō′kəl, bī′fō′-), *adj.* (of an eyeglass or contact lens) having two portions, one for near and one for far vision.

bi·gem·i·ny (bī jem′ə nē), *n.* the occurrence of premature atrial or ventricular heartbeats in pairs. —**bi·gem′i·nal,** *adj.*

bilat′eral sym′metry, *n.* a basic body plan in which the left and right sides of the organism can be divided into approximate mirror images of each other along the midline. Compare RADIAL SYMMETRY.

bi·lay·er (bī′lā′ər), *n.* a structure composed of two molecular layers, esp. of phospholipids in cellular membranes.

bile (bīl), *n.* a bitter, alkaline, yellow or greenish liquid, secreted by the liver, that aids in absorption and digestion, esp. of fats.

bile′ ac′id, *n.* any of various steroid acids, produced in the liver and stored with bile, that emulsify fats during digestion.

bile′ salt′, *n.* a product of a bile acid and a base, functioning as an emulsifier of lipids and fatty acids for absorption in the duodenum.

bil·har·zi·a (bil här′zē ə), *n.,* *pl.* **-zi·as.** SCHISTOSOME.

bil·har·zi·a·sis (-zī′ə sis) also **bil·har·zi·o′sis** (-zē ō′sis), *n.* SCHISTOSOMIASIS.

bil·i·ar·y (bil′ē er′ē, bil′yə rē), *adj.* **1.** of bile. **2.** conveying bile: *a biliary duct.*

bil′ious (-yəs), *adj.* **1.** pertaining to bile or to excess secretion of bile. **2.** suffering from or caused or attended by trouble with the bile or liver. —**bil′ious·ly,** *adv.* —**bil′ious·ness,** *n.*

bil·i·ru·bin (bil′ə rōō′bin, bil′ə rōō′bin), *n.* a reddish bile pigment, $C_{33}H_{36}O_6N_4$, resulting from the degradation of heme by reticuloendothelial cells in the liver and at a high level in the blood producing the yellow skin symptomatic of jaundice.

bi·lo·bate (bī lō′bāt) also **bi·lo·bat·ed, bi′lobed′,** *adj.* consisting of or divided into two lobes.

bi·loc·u·lar (bī lok′yə lər) also **bi·loc·u·late** (-lit, -lāt′), *adj.* Biol. divided into two chambers or compartments.

bi·man′u·al, *adj.* involving or requiring the use of both hands. —**bi·man′u·al·ly,** *adv.*

bin·au·ral (bī nôr′əl, bin ôr′əl), *adj.* **1.** having two ears. **2.** of, with, or for both ears.

Bi·net′-Si′mon scale′ (or **test′**) (bi nā′si′mən), *n.* a test for determining the relative development of intelligence, esp. of children, consisting of a series of questions and tasks graded with reference to the ability of the normal child at successive age levels. Compare STANFORD-BINET TEST.

binge′-purge′ syn′drome, *n.* BULIMIA (def.1).

bi·o·a·cous′tics (bī′ō-), *n.* (*used with a sing. v.*) a science dealing with the sounds produced by or affecting living organisms. —**bi·o·a·cous'ti·cal**, *adj.*

bi·o·ac·tiv'i·ty, *n.* any effect on, interaction with, or response from living tissue. —**bi·o·ac'tive,** *adj.*

bi·o·as·say' (*n.* -ə sā', -as/ā; *v.* -ə sā'), *n., v.,* **-sayed, -say·ing.** —*n.* **1.** determination of the biological activity or potency of a substance, as a vitamin or hormone, by testing its effect on the growth of an organism. —*v.t.* **2.** to subject to a bioassay.

bi·o·au·tog'ra·phy (-ô tog'rə fē), *n.* an analytical technique in which organic compounds are separated by chromatography and identified by studying their effects on microorganisms. —**bi·o·au'to·graph** (-ô'tə graf', -gräf'), *n.* —**bi·o·au'to·graph'ic,** *adj.*

bi·o·a·vail·a·bil'i·ty, *n.* the extent to which a nutrient or medication can be used by the body. —**bi·o·a·vail'a·ble,** *adj.*

bi·o·chem'i·cal ox'y·gen demand', *n.* the oxygen required by aerobic organisms, as those in sewage, for metabolism. *Abbr.:* BOD Also called **biological oxygen demand.**

bi·o·chem'is·try, *n.* **1.** the scientific study of the chemical substances and processes of living matter. **2.** biochemical substances or processes. —**bi·o·chem'i·cal,** *adj., n.* —**bi·o·chem'i·cal·ly,** *adv.* —**bi·o·chem'ist,** *n.*

bi·o·chip', *n.* an experimental integrated circuit composed of biochemical substances or organic molecules.

bi·o·clean', *adj.* free or almost free from harmful microorganisms.

bi·o·com·pat'i·bil'i·ty, *n.* the capability of coexistence with living tissues or organisms without causing harm. —**bi·o·com·pat'i·ble,** *adj.*

bi·o·con·trol', BIOLOGICAL CONTROL.

bi·o·cor·ro'sion, *n.* corrosion caused by or enhanced by bacteria or other microorganisms; biologically induced corrosion.

bi·o·e·lec'tric also **bi·o·e·lec'tri·cal,** *adj.* of or pertaining to electric phenomena occurring in living organisms. —**bi·o·e·lec·tric'i·ty,** *n.*

bi·o·e·lec·tron'ics, *n.* (*used with a sing. v.*) the application of electronic devices to living organisms for clinical testing, diagnosis, and therapy. —**bi·o·e·lec·tron'ic,** *adj.*

bi·o·en·er·get'ics, *n.* (*used with a sing. v.*) the study of energy transformation in living systems.

bi·o·en·gi·neer'ing, *n.* the application of engineering principles and techniques to problems in medicine and biology, as the design and production of artificial limbs and organs. —**bi·o·en·gi·neer',** *n.*

bi·o·e·quiv·a·lence also **bi·o·e·quiv·a·len·cy,** *n.* equality of absorption rate between different formulations of the same drug or chemical when taken into the body. —**bi·o·e·quiv'a·lent,** *adj.*

bi·o·eth'ics, *n.* (*used with a sing. v.*) a field of study and counsel concerned with the implications of certain medical procedures, as organ transplants, genetic engineering, and care of the terminally ill. —**bi/o·eth/i·cal**, *adj.* —**bi/o·eth/i·cist**, *n.*

bi/o·feed/back/, *n.* **1.** a method of learning to modify a particular body function, as temperature, blood pressure, or muscle tension, by monitoring it with the aid of an electronic device. **2.** the feedback thus obtained.

bi/o·fla/vo·noid/ (-flā/və noid/), *n.* any of a group of water-soluble yellow compounds, present in citrus fruits, rose hips, and other plants, that in mammals maintain the resistance of capillary walls to permeation and change of pressure. Also called **vitamin P.**

bi/o·gen·e·sis (bī/ō jen/ə sis) also **bi·og/e·ny** (-oj/ə nē), *n.* the production of living organisms from other living organisms. —**bi/o·ge·net/ic**, *adj.* —**bi/o·ge·net/i·cal·ly**, *adv.*

bi/o·ge·net/ics, *n.* (*used with a sing. v.*) GENETIC ENGINEERING. —**bi/o·ge·net/ic**, *adj.* —**bi/o·ge·net/i·cist**, *n.*

bi/o·gen/ic, *adj.* **1.** resulting from the activity of living organisms, as fermentation. **2.** necessary for the life process, as food and water.

bi/o·ge/o·chem/is·try, *n.* the science dealing with the relationship between the geological and chemical characteristics of a given region and its flora and fauna, including the circulation of such elements as carbon and nitrogen between the environment and the cells of living organisms. —**bi/o·ge/o·chem/i·cal**, *adj.*

bi/o·haz/ard, *n.* **1.** any hazard to living things, as environmental pollution. **2. a.** a pathogen, esp. one used in or produced by biological research. **b.** the health risk posed by the possible release of such a pathogen into the environment. —**bi/o·haz/ard·ous**, *adj.*

bi/o·in/stru·men·ta/tion, *n.* **1.** the use of sensors and other instruments to record and transmit physiological data from persons or other living things, as in space flight. **2.** such instruments collectively.

bi·o·log·i·cal (bī/ə loj/i kəl) also **bi/o·log/ic**, *adj.* **1.** of or pertaining to biology. **2.** of or pertaining to the products and operations of applied biology: *a biological test.* **3.** related by blood rather than by adoption: *the biological father.* —*n.* **4.** a medical product that is derived from biological sources. —**bi/o·log/i·cal·ly**, *adv.*

biolog/ical clock/, *n.* **1.** an innate mechanism of the body that regulates its rhythmic and periodic cycles, as that of sleeping and waking. **2.** such a mechanism perceived as inexorably marking the passage of one's youth and esp. one's ability to bear children.

biolog/ical control/, *n.* the control of pests by interference with their ecological status, as by introducing a natural enemy or a pathogen into the environment. Also called **biocontrol.**

biolog/ical ox/ygen demand/, *n.* BIOCHEMICAL OXYGEN DEMAND.

biolog/ical par/ent, *n.* BIRTH PARENT.

biolog′ical rhythm′, *n.* BIORHYTHM.

bi·ol·o·gy (bī ol′ə jē) *n.* **1.** the scientific study of life or living matter in all its forms and processes. **2.** the living organisms of a region: *the biology of Montana.* **3.** the biological phenomena characteristic of an organ or other body part, or of an organism: *the biology of a cell; the biology of a worm.* —**bi·ol′o·gist,** *n.*

bi·ol·y·sis (-ə sis), *n.* disintegration of organic matter by the action of living microorganisms.

bi·o·ma·te·ri·al (bī′ō mə tēr′ē əl, bī′ō mə tēr′-), *n.* a natural or synthetic material that is compatible with living tissue and is suitable for surgical implanting.

bi·o·me·chan·ics, *n.* (*used with a sing. v.*) **1. a.** the study of the action of external and internal forces on the living body, esp. on the skeletal system. **b.** the development of prostheses. **2.** the study of the mechanical nature of biological processes, as heart action and muscle movement. —**bi′o·me·chan′i·cal,** *adj.* —**bi′o·me·chan′i·cal·ly,** *adv.*

bi′o·med′i·cine, *n.* the application of the natural sciences, esp. the biological and physiological sciences, to clinical medicine. —**bi′o·med′i·cal,** *adj.*

bi·om·e·ter (bī om′i tər), *n.* an instrument for measuring the amount of carbon dioxide given off by an organism, tissue, etc.

bi·o·me·tri·cian (bī′ō mi trish′ən) also **bi·o·met′ri·cist** (-mē′trə sist), *n.* a person skilled in biometrics.

bi·o·met·rics (bī′ə me′triks), *n.* (*used with a sing. v.*) **1.** BIOSTATISTICS. **2.** BIOMETRY (def. 1). —**bi′o·met′ric,** *adj.* —**bi′o·met′ri·cal·ly,** *adv.*

bi·om·e·try (bī om′i trē), *n.* **1.** the calculation of the probable duration of human life. **2.** BIOSTATISTICS.

bi·on·ic (bī on′ik), *adj.* **1.** having normal functions enhanced by electronic devices and mechanical parts for dangerous or intricate tasks: *a bionic hand.* **2.** of or pertaining to bionics. —**bi·on′i·cal·ly,** *adv.*

bi·on·ics, *n.* (*used with a sing. v.*) the study of the means by which humans and animals perform tasks and solve problems, and of the application of the findings to the design of electronic devices and mechanical parts.

bi′o·pol′y·mer, *n.* **1.** any polymeric chemical manufactured by a living organism, as a protein or polysaccharide. **2.** such a chemical prepared by laboratory synthesis.

bi′o·proc′ess, *n.* **1.** a method or procedure for preparing biological material, esp. a product of genetic engineering, for commercial use. —*v.t.* **2.** to treat or prepare through bioprocess.

bi·op·sy (bī′op sē), *n., pl.* **-sies,** *v.,* **-sied, -sy·ing.** —*n.* **1.** the removal for diagnostic study of a piece of tissue from a living body. **2.** a specimen obtained from a biopsy. —*v.t.* **3.** to remove (living tissue) for diagnostic evaluation.

bi′o·re·ac′tor, *n.* a fermentation vat for the production of living organisms, as bacteria or yeast.

bi′o·rhythm, *n.* an innate periodicity in an organism's physiological processes, as sleep and wake cycles. —**bi/o·rhyth/mic**, *adj.* —**bi/o·rhyth·mic/i·ty**, *n.*

bi/o·safe/ty, *n.* the maintenance of safe conditions in biological research to prevent harm to workers, nonlaboratory organisms, or the environment.

bi/o·sta·tis/tics, *n.* (*used with a sing. v.*) the application of statistics to biological and medical data. —**bi/o·stat/is·ti/cian**, *n.*

bi/o·syn/the·sis, *n.* **1.** the formation of chemical compounds by the action of living organisms. **2.** the laboratory preparation of biological molecules.

bi/o·syn·thet/ic, *adj.* **1.** of or pertaining to biosynthesis. **2.** of or pertaining to a substance produced by a biosynthetic process. —*n.* **3.** such a substance.

bi/o·tech·nol/o·gy, *n.* the use of living organisms or other biological systems in the manufacture of drugs or other products or for environmental management. —**bi/o·tech/ni·cal, bi/o·tech/no·log/i·cal**, *adj.* —**bi/o·tech·nol/o·gist**, *n.*

bi/o·te·lem/e·try, *n.* the tracking or monitoring of a human being or animal at a distance with the use of a telemeter. —**bi/o·te·lem/e·ter**, *n.* —**bi/o·tel/e·met/ric**, *adj.*

bi·ot·ic (bi ot/ik) also **bi·ot/i·cal**, *adj.* pertaining to life or living beings.

bi·o·tin (bi/ə tin), *n.* a crystalline, water-soluble vitamin, $C_{10}H_{16}O_3N_2S$, of the vitamin B complex, present in all living cells. Also called **vitamin H.**

bi/o·trans·for·ma/tion, *n.* the series of chemical changes occurring in a compound, esp. a drug, as a result of enzymatic or other activity by a living organism.

bi·o·tron (bi/ə tron/), *n.* a controlled laboratory environment designed to produce uniform organisms for use in experiments.

bi·o·type (bi/ə tip/), *n.* **1.** a group of organisms having the same genotype. **2.** a distinguishing feature of the genotype. —**bi/o·typ/ic** (-tip/ik), *adj.*

bip·a·rous (bip/ər əs), *adj.* bringing forth offspring in pairs.

bi·ped (bi/ped), *n.* **1.** a two-footed animal. —*adj.* **2.** Also, **bi·ped/al.** having two feet.

bi·po·lar disor/der (bi pō/lər), *n.* an affective disorder characterized by periods of mania alternating with depression, usu. interspersed with relatively long intervals of normal mood; manic-depressive illness.

birth/ canal/, *n.* the passage through which the young of mammals pass during birth, formed by the cervix, vagina, and vulva.

birth/ certif/icate, *n.* an official form recording the birth of a baby and containing pertinent data, as name, sex, date, place, and parents.

birth/ control/, *n.* regulation of the number of children born through control or prevention of conception.

birth/-control/ pill/, *n.* an oral contraceptive for women, usu. containing estrogen and progesterone or progesterone alone, that inhibits ovulation, fertilization, or implantation of a fertilized ovum, causing temporary infertility.

birth′ defect′, *n.* any physical, mental, or biochemical abnormality present at birth.

birth′ing, *n.* an act or instance of giving birth, esp. by natural childbirth.

birth′mark′, *n.* a minor disfigurement or blemish on a person's skin at birth; nevus.

birth′ par′ent, *n.* a parent who has conceived or sired rather than adopted a child and whose genes are therefore transmitted to the child. Also called **biological parent.**

birth′weight′, *n.* the weight of an infant at birth.

bi·sex·u·al (bī-), *adj.* **1.** sexually responsive to both sexes. —*n.* **2.** a person sexually responsive to both sexes. —**bi′sex·u·al′i·ty, bi·sex′u·al·ism,** *n.* —**bi·sex′u·al·ly,** *adv.*

bis·muth (biz′məth), *n.* a brittle, grayish white, red-tinged, metallic element used in the manufacture of fusible alloys and in medicine. *Symbol:* Bi; *at. wt.:* 208.980; *at. no.:* 83. —**bis′muth·al,** *adj.*

bit·ters (bit′ərz), *n. (used with a pl. v.)* **1.** a usu. alcoholic liquid impregnated with a bitter medicine, as gentian or quassia, used to increase the appetite or as a tonic. **2.** bitter medicinal substances in general, as quinine.

bi·va·lent (bī vā′lənt, biv′ə-), *adj.* pertaining to associations of two homologous chromosomes. —**bi·va′lence, bi·va′len·cy,** *n.*

Black′ Death′, *n.* an outbreak of bubonic plague that spread over Europe and Asia in the 14th century and killed an estimated quarter of the population.

black′head′, *n.* a small, black-tipped fatty mass in a skin follicle, esp. of the face; comedo.

black′ lung′, *n.* pneumoconiosis of coal miners caused by coal dust.

black′out′, *n.* **1. a.** temporary loss of consciousness or vision. **b.** a period of total memory loss, as one induced by an accident or prolonged alcoholic drinking. **2.** a brief, passing lapse of memory.

black′wa′ter, *n.* **1.** any of several diseases characterized by the production of dark urine as a result of the rapid breakdown of red blood cells. **2.** BLACKWATER FEVER.

black′water fe′ver, *n.* a severe form of malaria characterized by kidney damage and hemoglobinuria resulting in urine that is dark red or black.

blad·der (blad′ər), *n.* **1.** a distensible saclike organ serving as a receptacle for liquids or gases. **2.** URINARY BLADDER.

blad′der worm′, *n.* a cysticercus.

blain (blān), *n.* an inflammatory swelling or sore.

blast′ cell′, *n.* any undifferentiated or immature cell.

blas·te·ma (bla stē′mə), *n., pl.* **-mas, -ma·ta** (-mə tə) an aggregation of cells in an early embryo capable of differentiation into specialized tissue and organs. —**blas·te·mat·ic** (blas′tə mat′ik), **blas·te′mic** (-stē′mik, -stem′ik), *adj.*

blas·to·coel (blas′tə sēl′), *n.* the cavity of a blastula arising in the course of cleavage. —**blas′to·coel′ic**, *adj.*

blas·to·cyst (-sist′), *n.* the blastula of the mammalian embryo consisting of an inner cell mass, a cavity, and the trophoblast.

blas·to·derm′ (-dûrm′), *n.* **1.** the primitive layer of cells that results from the segmentation of the ovum. **2.** the layer of cells forming the wall of the blastula and in most vertebrates enclosing a cavity or a yolk mass. —**blas′to·der′mic**, *adj.*

blas·to·gen·e·sis, *n.* the theory that hereditary characteristics are transmitted by germ plasm.

blas·to·mere (-mēr′), *n.* any cell produced during cleavage. —**blas·to·mer′ic** (-mer′ik, -mēr′-), *adj.*

blas·to·my′cete (-mī′sēt, -mi sēt′), *n.* any yeastlike fungus of the genus *Blastomyces*, whose members are pathogenic to humans and other animals.

blas·to·my·co·sis (blas′tō-), *n.* any of several diseases caused by certain yeastlike fungi, esp. blastomycetes. —**blas·to·my·cot′ic**, *adj.*

blas·to·pore (blas′tə pôr′, -pōr′), *n.* the opening of the archenteron in the early embryo.

blas·to·sphere′, *n.* a blastula, esp. a blastocyst.

blas·tu·la (blas′chə lə), *n., pl.* **-las, -lae** (-lē′), the early developmental stage of an animal, following the morula stage and consisting of a single spherical layer of cells enclosing a hollow, central cavity. —**blas′tu·lar**, *adj.* —**blas′tu·la′tion** (-lā′shən), *n.*

bleb (bleb), *n.* a blister or vesicle. —**bleb′by**, *adj.*

bleed′er, *n.* a hemophiliac.

blend′ing inher′itance, *n.* inheritance in which contrasting parental characters appear as a blend in the offspring.

bleph·a·ri·tis (blef′ə rī′tis), *n.* inflammation of the eyelids. —**bleph·a·rit′ic** (-rit′ik), *adj.*

bleph·a·ro·plas·ty (blef′ər ə plas′tē), *n., pl.* **-ties.** plastic surgery of the eyelid.

blind (blīnd), *adj.,* **1.** unable to see; lacking the sense of sight. **2.** of or pertaining to an experimental design that prevents investigators or subjects from knowing the hypotheses or conditions being tested. —**blind′ly**, *adv.* —**blind′ness**, *n.*

blind′sight′, *n.* the ability of a blind person to sense accurately a light source or other visual stimulus.

blind′ spot′, *n.* a small area of the retina, where it continues to the optic nerve, that is insensitive to light.

blis·ter (blis′tər), *n.* **1.** a thin vesicle on the skin containing watery matter or serum, as from a burn or other injury. —*v.t.* **2.** to raise a blister on. —*v.i.* **3.** to become blistered. —**blis′ter·y**, *adj.*

bloat (blōt), *n.* a gassy distension of the abdomen or other part of the digestive system.

block·ade (blo kād′), *n.* interruption or inhibition of a normal physiological signal, as a nerve impulse.

block′er, *n.* a substance that inhibits the physiological action of another substance.

blood (blud), *n.* the red fluid that circulates through the heart, arteries, and veins of vertebrates, consisting of plasma in which red blood cells, white blood cells, and platelets are suspended.

blood′ bank′, *n.* **1.** a place where blood or blood plasma is collected, processed, stored, and distributed. **2.** the supply of blood or blood plasma at such a place.

blood′-brain′ bar′rier, *n.* a layer of tightly packed cells that make up the walls of brain capillaries and prevent many substances in the blood from diffusing into the brain.

blood′ cell′, *n.* any of the cellular elements of the blood, as white blood cells or red blood cells. Also called **blood′ cor′puscle.**

blood′ count′, *n.* the count of the number of red and white blood cells and platelets in a specific volume of blood.

blood′ dop′ing, *n.* a procedure in which an athlete is injected with his or her own previously drawn and stored red blood cells to increase the body's oxygen-carrying capacity before a competition.

blood′ fluke′, *n.* a schistosome.

blood′ group′, *n.* any of various classes into which human blood can be divided according to immunological compatibility based on the presence or absence of specific antigens on red blood cells. Also called **blood type.** Compare ABO SYSTEM, RH FACTOR.

blood′ heat′, *n.* the normal temperature of human blood, being about 98.6°F (37°C).

blood′let′ting, *n.* the act of letting blood by opening a vein; phlebotomy. —**blood′let′ter,** *n.*

blood′mo•bile′ (-mə bēl′), *n.* a small truck with medical equipment for receiving blood donations.

blood′ plas′ma, *n.* the liquid portion of vertebrate blood.

blood′ plate′let, *n.* any of the minute, nonnucleated cellular elements in mammalian blood essential for coagulation.

blood′ poi′soning, *n.* invasion of the blood by toxic matter or microorganisms, characterized by chills, sweating, fever, and prostration; toxemia; septicemia; pyemia.

blood′ pres′sure, *n.* the pressure of the blood against the inner walls of the blood vessels, esp. of the arteries during different phases of contraction of the heart. Compare DIASTOLE, SYSTOLE.

blood′ se′rum, *n.* SERUM (def. 1).

blood′shot′, *adj.* (of the eyes) red because of dilated blood vessels.

blood′stream′, *n.* the blood flowing through the circulatory system.

blood′ sug′ar, *n.* **1.** glucose in the blood. **2.** the quantity or percentage of glucose in the blood.

blood′ test′, *n.* a test of blood sample, as to determine blood group, presence of infection or other pathology, or parentage.

blood′ transfu′sion, *n.* the injection of blood from one person or animal into the bloodstream of another.

blood′ type′, *n.* BLOOD GROUP.

blood′ typ′ing, *n.* the process of classifying blood into blood groups through laboratory tests for particular antigens on the surface of red blood cells.

blood′ ves′sel, *n.* any channel through which the blood normally circulates; an artery, vein, or capillary.

blue′ ba′by, *n.* an infant born with cyanosis resulting from a congenital heart or lung defect.

blue′ dev′ils, *n.pl.* DELIRIUM TREMENS.

B lymphocyte, *n.* B CELL (def 1).

BMR, basal metabolic rate.

BOD, biochemical oxygen demand.

bod′y lan′guage, *n.* nonverbal, usu. unconscious, communication through the use of gestures, facial expressions, etc.

boil (boil), *n.* a painful circumscribed inflammation of the skin with a pus-filled inner core, usu. caused by a local infection; furuncle.

bo·lus (bō′ləs), *n., pl.* **-lus·es.** a round mass of medicinal material, larger than an ordinary pill.

bond·ing (bon′ding), *n.* a relationship that usu. begins at the time of birth between a parent and offspring and that establishes the basis for an ongoing mutual attachment.

bone (bōn), *n.* **1.** one of the structures composing the skeleton of a vertebrate. **2.** the hard connective tissue forming these structures, composed of cells enclosed in a calcified matrix.

bone′set′ter, *n.* a person, usu. not a licensed physician, skilled at setting broken or dislocated bones.

boost·er (bōōs′tər), *n.* **1.** Also called **boost′er dose′, boost′er shot′.** a dose of an immunizing substance given to maintain or renew the effect of a previous one. **2.** a drug, medicine, etc., that serves as a synergist.

bor·bo·ryg·mus (bôr′bə rig′məs), *n., pl.* **-mi** (-mī). intestinal rumbling caused by the movement of gas.

bo′ric ac′id, *n.* a white, crystalline acid, H_3BO_3, used as an antiseptic.

bo·tan·i·cal (bə tan′i kəl), *n.* a drug made from part of a plant, as from roots or bark.

bot·u·lin (boch′ə lin), *n.* the toxin formed by botulinus and causing botulism.

bot·u·li·nus (boch′ə lī′nəs) also **bot′u·li′num** (-nəm), *n., pl.* **-nus·es** also **-nums.** a soil bacterium, *Clostridium botulinum,* that thrives and forms botulin under anaerobic conditions. **—bot′u·li′nal,** *adj.*

bot′u·lism (-liz′əm), *n.* a sometimes fatal disease of the nervous system acquired from spoiled foods in which botulin is present, esp. improperly canned or marinated foods.

bou·gie (bōō′jē, -zhē, bōō zhē′), *n.* **1.** a slender, flexible instrument introduced into passages of the body, esp. the urethra, for dilating, examining, medicating, etc. **2.** a suppository.

bo′vine growth′ hor′mone, *n.* a growth hormone of cattle, harvested from genetically engineered bacteria for administering to cows to increase milk production. *Abbr.:* bGH

bow·el (bou′əl, boul), *n.* **1.** Usu., **bowels.** the intestine. **2.** a part of the intestine. —**bow′el·less,** *adj.*

bow′el move′ment, *n.* the evacuation of the bowels; defecation.

bow′leg′ (bō′-), *n.* **1.** outward curvature of the legs. **2.** a leg so curved, as by rickets. —**bow′leg′ged,** *adj.* —**bow′-leg′ged·ness,** *n.*

Bow′man's cap′sule (bō′mənz), *n.* a membranous, double-walled capsule surrounding a glomerulus of a nephron.

BP, blood pressure.

brace (brās), *n.* an orthopedic appliance for supporting a weak joint or joints.

bra·chi·al (brā′kē əl, brak′ē-), *adj.* **1.** belonging or pertaining to the arm, foreleg, wing, or pectoral fin of a vertebrate. **2.** armlike, as an appendage.

bra·chi·um (brā′kē əm, brak′ē-), *n., pl.* **bra·chi·a** (brā′-kē ə, brak′ē ə). **1.** the part of the arm from the shoulder to the elbow. **2.** an armlike part or process.

brach·y·ce·phal·ic (brak′ē sə fal′ik) also **brach′y-ceph′a·lous** (-sef′ə ləs), *adj.* short-headed; having a cephalic index of 81.0–85.4. —**brach′y·ceph′a·ly,** *n.*

brad·y·car·di·a (brad′i kär′dē ə), *n.* a slow heartbeat rate, usu. less than 60 beats per minute. —**brad′y·car′-dic,** *adj.*

brad′y·kin′in (-kin′in, -ki′nin), *n.* a peptide hormone that dilates peripheral blood vessels and increases capillary permeability.

brain (brān), *n.* the anterior part of the central nervous system enclosed in the cranium of vertebrates, consisting of a mass of nerve tissue organized for the perception of sensory impulses, the regulation of motor impulses, and the production of memory, learning, and consciousness.

brain′-dead′ or **brain′ dead′,** *adj.* having undergone brain death.

brain′ death′, *n.* complete cessation of brain function as evidenced by absence of brain-wave activity on an electroencephalogram: sometimes used as a legal definition of death.

brain′ fe′ver, *n.* MENINGITIS.

brain′stem′ or **brain′ stem′,** *n.* the portion of the brain that is continuous with the spinal cord and in mammals comprises the medulla oblongata and parts of the midbrain.

brain′ wave′, *n.* Usu., **brain waves.** electrical potentials or impulses given off by brain tissue. Compare ALPHA RHYTHM, BETA RHYTHM, DELTA RHYTHM.

break′bone fe′ver (brāk′bōn′), *n.* DENGUE.

break′down′, *n.* a loss of mental or physical health; collapse. Compare NERVOUS BREAKDOWN.

breast′bone′, *n.* the sternum.

breast′-feed′, *v.t.,* **-fed, -feed·ing.** to nurse (a baby) at the breast; suckle.

breath (breth), *n.* **1.** the air inhaled and exhaled in respiration. **2.** respiration, esp. as necessary to life.

Breath·a·lyz·er (breth′ə lī′zər), *Trademark.* a breath analyzer.

breath′ an′alyzer, *n.* an instrument consisting of a small bag or tube filled with chemically treated crystals, into which a sample of a motorist's breath is taken as a test for intoxication.

breathe (brēth), *v.,* **breathed, breath·ing.** —*v.i.* **1.** to take air, oxygen, etc., into the lungs and expel it; inhale and exhale; respire. **2.** (of the skin) to absorb oxygen and give off perspiration. —*v.t.* **3.** to inhale and exhale in respiration.

breath′ test′, *n.* a test by breath analyzer.

breech′ deliv′ery, *n.* the delivery of an infant with the feet or buttocks appearing first.

breg·ma (breg′mə), *n., pl.* **-ma·ta** (-mə tə). the place on the top of the skull where the frontal bone and parietal bones join. —**breg·mat′ic** (-mat′ik), **breg′mate** (-māt), *adj.*

brei (brī), *n.* a suspension of finely divided tissue in an isotonic medium, used chiefly as a culture for certain viruses.

bridge (brij), *n.* **1.** the ridge or upper line of the nose. **2.** an artificial replacement, fixed or removable, of a missing tooth or teeth, supported by adjacent or natural teeth or roots.

Bright′s′ disease′ (brīts), *n.* any kidney disease characterized by albuminuria and heightened blood pressure.

Brill′s′ disease′ (brilz), *n.* a relatively mild form of typhus.

Brit′ish ther′mal u′nit, *n.* the amount of heat required to raise the temperature of 1 lb. (0.4 kg) of water 1°F. *Abbr.:* Btu, BTU

broad′-spec′trum, *adj.* (of an antibiotic) effective against a wide range of organisms.

bro·mide (brō′mīd), *n.* potassium bromide, formerly used as a sedative.

bro′mism (-miz əm) also **bro′min·ism** (-mə niz′əm), *n.* a poisoned condition caused by the overuse of bromides, characterized by skin eruptions and lethargy.

bron·chi·al (brong′kē əl), *adj.* of or pertaining to the bronchi. —**bron′chi·al·ly,** *adv.*

bron′chial asth′ma, *n.* ASTHMA.

bron′chial pneumo′nia, *n.* BRONCHOPNEUMONIA.

bron′chial tube′, *n.* a bronchus or any of its ramifications or branches.

bron·chi·ec·ta·sis (-ek′tə sis), *n.* a chronic disease of the bronchial tubes characterized by distention and paroxysmal coughing.

bron'chi·ole' (-ōl'), *n.* a small branch of a bronchus. —**bron'chi·o·lar**, *adj.*

bron·chi'tis (-kī'tis), *n.* acute or chronic inflammation of the membrane lining of the bronchial tubes, caused by infection or inhalation of irritants. —**bron·chit'ic** (-kit'ik), *adj.*

bron'cho·di·la'tor (brong'kō-), *n.* a substance that acts to dilate constricted bronchial tubes to aid breathing, used esp. for relief of asthma.

bron'cho·pneu·mo'nia, *n.* a form of pneumonia centering on bronchial passages.

bron·cho·scope (brong'kə skōp'), *n.* a lighted, flexible tubular instrument that is inserted into the trachea for diagnosis and for removing inhaled objects. —**bron'cho·scop'ic** (-skop'ik), *adj.* —**bron·chos'co·pist** (-kos'kə-pist), *n.* —**bron·chos'co·py**, *n., pl.* **-pies.**

bron'cho·spasm, *n.* spasmodic contraction of the muscular lining of the bronchi, as in asthma, causing difficulty in breathing. —**bron'cho·spas'tic**, *adj.*

bron'chus (-kəs), *n., pl.* **-chi** (-kē, -kī). either of the two branches of the trachea that extend into the lungs.

bronze' diabe'tes, *n.* HEMOCHROMATOSIS.

broth (brôth, broth), *n.* a liquid medium containing nutrients suitable for culturing microorganisms. —**broth'y**, *adj.*

brown' fat', *n.* brownish yellow adipose tissue that accumulates in hibernating mammals, producing heat if the body becomes too cold.

brown' lung', *n.* a chronic lung disease of textile workers caused by inhalation of cotton dust and other fine fibers. Also called **byssinosis.**

bru·cel·lo·sis (broo'sə lō'sis), *n.* infection with bacteria of the *Brucella* genus, frequently causing spontaneous abortions in animals and remittent fever in humans. Also called **undulant fever.**

bruit (broot), *n.* any generally abnormal sound or murmur heard on auscultation.

brux·ism (bruk'siz əm), *n.* habitual, purposeless clenching and grinding of the teeth, esp. during sleep.

Btu or **BTU,** British thermal unit.

bu·bo (byoo'bō, boo'-), *n., pl.* **-boes.** an inflammatory swelling of a lymphatic gland, esp. in the groin or armpit. —**bu'boed,** *adj.*

bu·bon·ic (byoo bon'ik, boo-), *adj.* **1.** of or pertaining to a bubo. **2.** accompanied by or affected with buboes.

bubon'ic plague', *n.* a severe infection caused by the bacterium *Yersinia pestis,* transmitted by the bite of fleas from infected rats, characterized by the formation of buboes at the armpits and groin. Compare BLACK DEATH.

buc·cal (buk'əl), *adj.* **1.** of or pertaining to the cheek. **2.** pertaining to the mouth or the sides of the mouth. **3.** of or designating the surface of a tooth facing the cheek. Compare LABIAL (def. 3), LINGUAL (def. 2). —**buc'cal·ly,** *adv.*

buff·er (buf′ər), *n.* **1.** any substance capable of neutralizing both acids and bases in a solution without appreciably changing the solution's original acidity or alkalinity. **2.** Also called **buff′er solu′tion.** a solution containing such a substance.

bu·fo·tox·in (byōō′fə tok′sin), *n.* a toxin obtained from the skin glands of a European toad, *Bufa vulgaris.*

build′ing sick′ness, *n.* SICK BUILDING SYNDROME.

bul·bar (bul′bər, -bär), *adj.* of or pertaining to a bulb, esp. to the medulla oblongata.

bu·lim·a·rex·i·a (byōō lim′ə rek′sē ə, -lē′mə-, bōō-, bə-), *n.* BULIMIA (def. 1). —**bu·lim′a·rex′ic,** *adj., n.*

bu·lim·i·a (byōō lim′ē ə, -lē′mē ə, bōō-, bə-), *n.* **1.** Also called **bulim′ia ner·vo′sa** (nûr vō′sə) a habitual disturbance in eating behavior characterized by bouts of excessive eating followed by self-induced vomiting, purging with laxatives, strenuous exercise, or fasting. **2.** Also called **hyperphagia.** abnormally voracious appetite or unnaturally constant hunger. —**bu·lim′ic,** *adj., n.*

bulk (bulk), *n.* FIBER (def. 2).

bul·la (bŏŏl′ə, bul′ə), *n., pl.* **bul·lae** (bŏŏl′ē, bul′ē). a large blister or vesicle. —**bul′lous** (bul′əs), *adj.*

bun′dle of His′ (his), *n.* ATRIOVENTRICULAR BUNDLE.

bun·ion (bun′yən), *n.* an inflammation of the synovial bursa of the great toe, usu. resulting in enlargement of the joint and lateral displacement of the toe.

bur (bûr), *n.* **1.** a rotary cutting tool for removing carious material from teeth and preparing cavities for filling. **2.** a surgical cutting tool resembling this, used for the excavation of bone.

bu·rette or **bu·ret** (byŏŏ ret′), *n.* a graduated glass tube with a stopcock at the bottom, used in a laboratory to measure or dispense liquids.

Bur′kitt's lympho′ma (bûr′kits), *n.* a cancer of the lymphatic system characterized by lesions of the jaw or abdomen, mainly affecting children in central Africa.

burn (bûrn), *n.* an injury caused by heat, abnormal cold, chemicals, poison gas, or electricity, and characterized by a painful reddening and swelling of the epidermis (**first-degree burn**), damage extending into the dermis, usu. with blistering (**second-degree burn**), or destruction of the epidermis and dermis extending into the deeper tissue (**third-degree burn**).

burn′out′, *n.* fatigue, frustration, or apathy resulting from prolonged stress, overwork, or intense activity.

bur·sa (bûr′sə), *n., pl.* **-sae** (-sē) **-sas.** a pouch, sac, or vesicle, esp. a sac containing synovia, to facilitate motion, as between a tendon and a bone.

bur·si·tis (bər sī′tis), *n.* inflammation of a bursa.

bute (byōōt), *n. Slang.* phenylbutazone.

but′terfly band′age, *n.* a butterfly-shaped bandage for holding a cut together.

bu·tyl·at·ed hy·drox·y·an·i·sole (byōō′tl ā′tid hi drok′-sē an′ə sōl′), *n.* See BHA.

bu′tylated hy·drox·y·tol′u·ene (hi drok′sē tol′yo͞o-ēn′), *n.* See BHT.

by′pass′ or **by′-pass′,** *n.* a surgical procedure in which a diseased or obstructed hollow organ is temporarily or permanently circumvented. Compare CORONARY BYPASS.

bys·si·no·sis (bis′ə nō′sis), *n.* BROWN LUNG.

m. } min.	a minim (L. *minimum*).
mist.	a mixture (L. *mistura*).
no.	number (L. *numero*).
noct.	at night (L. *nocte*).
non rep.	do not repeat (L. *non repetatur*).
omn. hor.	every hour (L. *omni hora*).
omni nocte	every night (L. *omni nocte*).
p.c.	after food (L. *post cibum*).
	after meals (L. *post cibos*).
pil.	pill (L. *pilula*).
p.o.	by mouth (L. *per os*).
p.r.n.	as occasion arises; given when necessary (L. *pro re nata*).
pulv.	powder (L. *pulvis*).
q.h.	every hour (L. *quaque hora*).
q. 2 h.	every 2 hours (L. *quaque secunda hora*).
q.i.d.	four times a day (L. *quater in die*).
q.s.	as much as will suffice (L. *quantum sufficit*).
S. } sig.	write or label (L. *signa*): indicating directions to be written on a package or label.
sine, s̄	without (L. *sine*).
sol.	solution (L. *solutio*).
sp.	spirit (L. *spiritus*).
s̄s̄, ss	one half (L. *semis*).
stat.	immediately (L. *statim*).
suppos.	a suppository (L. *suppositorium*).
syr.	syrup (L. *syrupus*).
tabel.	a lozenge (L. *tabella*).
talis.	such; like this (L. *talis*).
t.d.	three times a day (L. *ter die*).
t.i.d.	three times a day (L. *ter in die*).
tinct. } tr.	a tincture (L. *tinctura*).
ung.	ointment (L. *unguentum*).
ut dict.	as directed (L. *ut dictum*).

C

C, *Symbol.* **1.** cysteine. **2.** cytosine.

Ca, *Chem. Symbol.* calcium.

ca·chet (ka shāʹ, kashʹā), *n.* a hollow wafer for enclosing an ill-tasting medicine.

ca·chex·i·a (kə kekʹsē ə) also **ca·chex·y** (-sē), *n.* general ill health with emaciation, usu. occurring in association with a disease. **—ca·checʹtic** (-tik), **ca·checʹti·cal, ca·chexʹic,** *adj.*

ca·chou (kə shōōʹ, ka-, kashʹōō), *n., pl.* **-chous.** a lozenge for sweetening the breath.

ca·dav·er (kə davʹər), *n.* a dead body, esp. a human body to be dissected; corpse.

ca·dav·er·ine (-ə rēnʹ), *n.* a colorless, viscous, toxic ptomaine, $C_5H_{14}N_2$, having an offensive odor, formed by the action of bacilli on meat, fish, and other protein.

ca·du·ce·us (kə dōōʹsē əs, -syōōs, -shəs, -dyōōʹ-), *n., pl.* **-ce·i** (-sē iʹ). a usu. winged staff around which one or two serpents are coiled, used as a symbol of the medical profession. **—ca·duʹce·an,** *adj.*

cae·cum (sēʹkəm), *n., pl.* **-ca** (-kə). CECUM.

Cae·sar·e·an or **Cae·sar·i·an** (si zârʹē ən), *n., adj.* CESAREAN.

caf·fe·ine (ka fēnʹ, kafʹēn), *n.* a white, crystalline, bitter alkaloid, $C_8H_{10}N_4O_2$, usu. derived from coffee or tea, used medicinally as a stimulant. **—caf·feinʹic** (ka fēʹnik, kaf·fēin'ik), *adj.*

caisʹson diseaseʹ, *n.* DECOMPRESSION SICKNESS.

Cal, kilocalorie.

cal, calorie.

cal·a·mine (kalʹə minʹ, -min), *n.* a pink, water-insoluble powder consisting of zinc oxide and about 0.5 percent ferric oxide, used in ointments, lotions, or the like, for the treatment of skin eruptions.

cal·ca·ne·um (kal kāʹnē əm), *n., pl.* **-ne·a** (-nē ə). CALCANEUS.

cal·ca·ne·us (-nē əs), *n., pl.* **-ne·i** (-nē iʹ). the largest tarsal bone, forming the prominence of the heel. **—cal·caʹne·al, cal·caʹne·an,** *adj.*

cal·car·e·ous (kal kârʹē əs) *adj.* of, containing, or like calcium carbonate; chalky. **—cal·carʹe·ous·ly,** *adv.* **—cal·carʹe·ous·ness,** *n.*

cal·cif·er·ol (kal sifʹə rôlʹ, -rolʹ), *n.* a fat-soluble, crystalline, unsaturated alcohol, $C_{28}H_{43}OH$, occurring in milk, fish-liver oils, etc., produced by ultraviolet irradiation of ergosterol and used as a dietary supplement, as in fortified milk. Also called **vitamin D₂.**

cal·cif·ic (kal sifʹik), *adj.* of or pertaining to calcification.

calʹci·fi·caʹtion, *n.* the deposition of lime or insoluble salts of calcium and magnesium, as in a tissue.

cal·ci·fy', *v.t.*, *v.i.*, **-fied**, **-fy·ing**. to make or become calcareous or bony; harden by the deposit of calcium salts.

cal·ci·no·sis (-nō'sis), *n.* an abnormal condition characterized by the deposit of calcium salts in various tissues of the body.

cal·ci·to·nin (-tō'nin), *n.* a thyroid hormone involved in regulating calcium levels in the blood.

cal·cit/ri·ol' (-si'trē ôl', -ol'), *n.* **1.** a vitamin D compound derived from cholesterol, involved in the regulating and absorption of calcium. **2.** a preparation of this compound, used in the treatment of osteoporosis and bone fracture.

cal·ci·um (-sē əm), *n.* a silver-white divalent metal, combined in limestone, chalk, etc., occurring also in animals in bone, shell, etc. Symbol: Ca; *at. wt.*: 40.08; *at. no.*: 20; *sp. gr.*: 1.55 at 20°C.

cal'cium block'er, *n.* a drug that prevents the influx of calcium into the smooth muscle of the heart or arterioles, used in the treatment of angina, hypertension, and certain arrhythmias. Also called **cal'cium chan'nel block'er.**

cal'cium phos'phate, *n.* a phosphate of calcium, used as a fertilizer, food additive, and in baking powder.

cal'cium pro'pionate, *n.* a white, water-soluble powder, $CaC_6H_{10}O_4$, used in bakery products to inhibit the growth of fungi.

cal·cu·lous (kal'kyə ləs), *adj.* characterized by the presence of a calculus or calculi.

cal·cu·lus (-ləs), *n.*, *pl.* **-li** (-lī'), **-lus·es.** a stone, or concretion, formed in the gallbladder, kidney, or other part of the body.

cal·en·ture (kal'ən chər, -chŏŏr'), *n.* a violent fever with delirium, affecting persons in the tropics.

cal·i·brate (kal'ə brāt'), *v.t.*, **-brat·ed**, **-brat·ing**. **1.** to set or check the graduation of (a quantitative measuring instrument). **2.** to mark (a thermometer or other instrument) with indexes of degree or quantity. —**cal/i·bra'tion**, *n.*

cal·i·per or **cal·li·per** (kal'ə pər), *n.* Usu., **calipers.** an instrument for measuring thicknesses and diameters, consisting usu. of a pair of adjustable pivoted legs.

cal·is·then·ics or **cal·lis·then·ics** (kal'əs then'iks), *n.* **1.** (*used with a pl. v.*) gymnastic exercises designed to develop physical health and vigor. **2.** (*used with a sing. v.*) the art, practice, or a session of such exercises.

cal·los·i·ty (kə los'i tē), *n.*, *pl.* **-ties.** CALLUS (def. 1).

cal·lous (kal'əs), *adj.* **1.** having a callus; indurated, as parts of the skin exposed to friction. —*v.t.*, *v.i.* **2.** to make or become hard or callous.

cal'lus (-əs), *n.*, *pl.* **-lus·es.** **1.** a hardened or thickened part of the skin; callosity. **2.** a new growth of osseous matter at the ends of a fractured bone, serving to unite them.

calm·a·tive (kä'mə tiv, kal'mə-), *adj.* **1.** having a soothing or sedative effect. —*n.* **2.** a calmative drug or agent.

cal·mod·u·lin (kal moj'ə lin), *n.* a protein, present in most cells, that binds calcium and participates in many physiological functions.

cal·o·mel (kal′ə mel′, -məl), *n.* a white, tasteless powder, Hg₂Cl₂, used chiefly as a purgative and fungicide. Also called **mercurous chloride**.

cal·o·rie or **cal·o·ry** (kal′ə rē), *n., pl.* **-ries. 1. a.** Also called **gram calorie, small calorie.** an amount of heat exactly equal to 4,1840 joules. *Abbr.:* cal **b.** (*usu. cap.*) KIL-OCALORIE. *Abbr.:* Cal **2. a.** a unit equal to the kilocalorie, used to express the heat output of an organism and the energy value of food. **b.** the quantity of food capable of producing such an amount of energy.

cal·o·rif·ic (-rif′ik), *adj.* pertaining to conversion into heat. —**cal′o·rif′i·cal·ly,** *adv.*

cal′o·rim′e·ter (-rim′i tər), *n.* an apparatus for measuring quantities of heat.

cAMP (kamp), *n.* CYCLIC AMP.

cam·phor (kam′fər), *n.* a white, pleasant-smelling terpene ketone, C₁₀H₁₆O, used as a counterirritant.

cam′phor ice′, *n.* a salve for mild skin eruptions, made of camphor, spermaceti, white beeswax, and a vegetable oil.

ca·nal (kə nal′), *n.* a tubular passage for food, air, etc., in an animal or plant; duct.

can·cel·late (kan′sə lāt′, -lit) also **can·cel·lat·ed** (-lā′-tid), *adj.* of spongy or porous structure, as at the ends of long bones.

can′cel·lous, *adj.* CANCELLATE.

can·cer (kan′sər), *n.* **1.** a malignant and invasive growth or tumor, esp. one originating in epithelium, tending to recur after excision and to metastasize to other sites. **2.** any disease characterized by such growths. —**can′cer·ous,** *adj.*

can′cer gene′, *n.* ONCOGENE.

can·di·di·a·sis (kan/di di′ə sis), *n., pl.* **-ses** (-sēz′). any of a variety of infections caused by fungi of the genus *Candida,* occurring most often in the mouth, respiratory tract, or vagina. Compare THRUSH.

can′dy strip′er, *n.* a volunteer worker at a hospital, esp. a teenager.

ca·nine (kā′nīn), *adj.* of or pertaining to any of the four single-cusped, pointed teeth, esp. prominent in dogs, situated in the upper and lower jaws next to the incisors.

can·ker (kang′kər), *n.* a gangrenous or ulcerous sore, esp. in the mouth. Also called **can′ker sore′.** —**can′ker·ous,** *adj.*

can·nab·i·noid (kə nab′ə noid′, kan′ə bə-), *n.* any of the chemical compounds that are the active principles of marijuana.

can·na·bis (kan′ə bis), *n.* **1.** the flowering tops of the hemp plant, *Cannabis sativa.* **2.** ny of the various parts of the plant from which hashish, marijuana, bhang, and similar drugs are prepared. —**can′na·bic,** *adj.*

can·nu·la or **can·u·la** (kan′yə lə), *n., pl.* **-las, -lae** (-lē′)

a metal tube for insertion into the body to draw off fluid or to introduce medication. —**can/nu·lar, can/nu·late** (-lit, -lāt/), adj. —**can/nu·la/tion,** n.

can·thus (kan/thəs), n., pl. **-thi** (-thī). the angle or corner on each side of the eye, formed by the junction of the upper and lower lids. —**can/thal,** adj.

can·u·la (kan/yə lə), n., pl. **-las, -lae** (-lē/). CANNULA.

cap·il·lar·y (kap/ə ler/ē), n., pl. **-lar·ies,** adj. —n. one of the minute blood vessels between the terminations of the arteries and the beginnings of the veins.

cap·let (kap/lit), n. an oval-shaped tablet that is coated to facilitate swallowing.

cap·sid (kap/sid), n. the coiled or polyhedral structure, composed of proteins, that encloses the nucleic acid of a virus. Also called **protein coat.**

cap·so·mere/ (-sə mēr/), n. any of the protein subunits of a capsid.

cap·sule (kap/səl, -sool, -syool), n. a gelatinous case enclosing a dose of medicine.

cap·to·pril (kap/tə pril), n. a white, crystalline powder, $C_9H_{15}NO_3S$, used as an antihypertensive.

car·bo (kär/bō), n., pl. **-bos. 1.** carbohydrate. **2.** a food having a high carbohydrate content.

car·bo·hy·drate (kär/bō hī/drāt, -bə-), n. any of a class of organic compounds composed of carbon, hydrogen, and oxygen, including starches and sugars, produced in green plants by photosynthesis: important source of food for animals and people.

car·bo·load/ing, n. the practice of eating large amounts of carbohydrates for a few days before competing in a strenuous athletic event, as a marathon, to provide energy reserves in the form of glycogen. —**car/bo·load/,** v.i.

car·bon cy/cle, n. the biological cycle by which atmospheric carbon dioxide is converted to carbohydrates by plants and other photosynthesizers, consumed and metabolized by organisms, and returned to the atmosphere through respiration, decomposition, and the combustion of fossil fuels.

car·bon diox/ide, n. a colorless, odorless, incombustible gas, CO_2, present in the atmosphere and formed during respiration.

car·box·yl (kär bok/sil), n. the univalent group COOH, characteristic of organic acids. —**car/box·yl/ic,** adj.

car·box/yl·ase/ (-sə lās/, -lāz/), n. any of the class of enzymes that catalyze the release of carbon dioxide from the carboxyl group of certain organic acids.

car·bun·cle (kär/bung kəl), n. a local skin inflammation of deep interconnected boils. —**car/bun·cled,** adj. —**car·bun/cu·lar,** adj.

car·cin·o·gen (kär sin/ə jən, -jen/, kär/sə nə jen/). any substance or agent that tends to produce a cancer. —**car/cin·o·gen/ic,** adj. —**car/ci·no·ge·nic/i·ty** (-jə nis/i·tē), n.

car·ci·no·gen·e·sis (kär'sə nə jen'ə sis, -nō-), *n.* the development of a cancer.

car'ci·noid' (-noid'), *n.* a small, yellowish amino-acid- and peptide-secreting tumor usu. found in the gastrointestinal tract and the lungs.

car·ci·no·ma (-nō'mə), *n., pl.* **-mas, -ma·ta** (-mə tə). a malignant tumor composed of epithelial tissue. —**car'ci·no'ma·toid'**, *adj.* —**car·ci·no'ma·tous**, *adj.*

car'ci·no·ma·to'sis (-tō'sis), *n.* a condition marked by the production of carcinomas throughout the body.

car·di·a (kär'dē ə), *n., pl.* **-di·ae** (-dē ē'), **-di·as.** an opening that connects the esophagus and the upper part of the stomach.

car·di·ac', *adj.* **1.** of, of or pertaining to the heart: *cardiac disease.* **2.** of or pertaining to the esophageal portion of the stomach. —*n.* **3.** a person suffering from heart disease.

car'diac arrest', *n.* abrupt cessation of heartbeat.

car'diac mus'cle, *n.* **1.** a specialized form of striated muscle in the hearts of vertebrates. **2.** the myocardium.

car'di·al·gi·a (-al'jē ə, -jə), *n.* **1.** HEARTBURN. **2.** pain in the heart region.

car'di·o·gen'ic (-ə jen'ik), *adj.* originating in the heart; caused by a disorder of the heart.

car'di·o·gram', *n.* ELECTROCARDIOGRAM.

car'di·o·graph', *n.* ELECTROCARDIOGRAPH. —**car'di·o·graph'ic**, *adj.* —**car·di·og'ra·phy** (-og'rə fē), *n.*

car'di·o·lip'in (-ō lip'in), *n.* a lipid purified from bovine heart and used as an antigen for reacting with reagin, the Wassermann antibody, in the Wassermann diagnostic test for syphilis.

car·di·ol'o·gy (-ol'ə jē), *n.* the study of the heart and its functions. —**car'di·o·log'ic** (-ə loj'ik), **car'di·o·log'i·cal**, *adj.* —**car·di·ol'o·gist**, *n.*

car'di·o·my·op'a·thy (kär'dē ō-), *n.* any disease of the myocardium.

car'di·op'a·thy (-op'ə thē), *n.* any disease or disorder of the heart.

car'di·o·pul'mo·nar'y (kär'dē ō-), *adj.* of, pertaining to, or affecting the heart and lungs.

cardiopul'monary resuscita'tion, *n.* an emergency procedure for reviving heart and lung function, consisting of mouth-to-mouth resuscitation combined with chest compression. *Abbr.:* CPR

car'di·o·res'pi·ra·to'ry, *adj.* of or affecting the heart and respiratory system.

car'di·o·vas'cu·lar, *adj.* of, pertaining to, or affecting the heart and blood vessels.

car'di·o·ver'sion (-vûr'zhən, -shən), *n.* restoration of the normal heart rhythm by applying direct-current electrical shock.

car·di'tis (-dī'tis), *n.* inflammation of the pericardium, myocardium, or endocardium. —**car·dit'ic** (-dit'ik), *adj.*

care·giv'er, *n.* an adult who cares for a child.

car·ies (kâr′ēz, -ē ēz′), *n., pl.* **-ies. 1.** decay, as of bone. **2.** DENTAL CARIES. —**car′i·ous,** *adj.*

car·min·a·tive (kär min′ə tiv, kär′mə nā′-), *adj.* **1.** expelling gas from the stomach and bowel. —*n.* **2.** a carminative medicine.

car·o·tene (kar′ə tēn′) also **car′o·tin** (-tin), *n.* any of three yellow or orange fat-soluble pigments having the formula $C_{40}H_{56}$, found in many plants, esp. carrots, and transformed into vitamin A in the liver; provitamin A.

ca·rot·e·noid or **ca·rot·i·noid** (kə rot′n oid′), *n.* **1.** any of a group of red and yellow pigments, chemically similar to carotene, contained in animal fat and some plants. —*adj.* **2.** similar to carotene. **3.** pertaining to carotenoids.

ca·rot·id (kə rot′id), *n.* **1.** Also called **carot′id ar′tery.** either of two large arteries, one on each side of the neck, that carry blood from the aorta to the head. —*adj.* **2.** pertaining to a carotid artery. —**ca·rot′id·al,** *adj.*

car·pal (kär′pəl), *adj.* **1.** pertaining to the carpus: *the carpal joint.* —*n.* **2.** any of the bones of the carpus; a wrist bone.

car′pal tun′nel syn′drome, *n.* a disorder of the hand characterized by pain, weakness, and numbness in the thumb and other fingers, caused by an inflamed ligament that presses on a nerve in the wrist.

car·pus (-pəs), *n., pl.* **-pi** (-pī). **1.** the wrist. **2.** the wrist bones collectively.

car·ra·gee·nan or **car·ra·gee·nin** (kar′ə gē′nən), *n.* a colloidal substance extracted from seaweed used chiefly as an emulsifying and stabilizing ingredient in foods and pharmaceuticals.

car·ri·er (kar′ē ər), *n.* **1.** an individual harboring a disease who may be immune to the disease but transmits it to others. **2. a.** an individual with an unexpressed recessive genetic trait. **b.** the bearer of a defective gene.

car·ti·lage (kär′tl ij), *n.* **1.** a firm, elastic, whitish type of connective tissue; gristle. **2.** a part or structure composed of cartilage.

car′ti·lag′i·nous (-aj′ə nəs), *adj.* pertaining to, composed of, or resembling cartilage.

cas·cade (kas kād′), *n.* a series of reactions catalyzed by enzymes that are activated sequentially by successive products of the reactions, resulting in an amplification of the initial response.

case (kās), *n.* an instance of disease, injury, etc., requiring medical or surgical attention.

ca·se·ate (kā′sē āt′), *v.i.,* **-at·ed, -at·ing.** to undergo caseation.

ca′se·a′tion, *n.* **1.** transformation of tissue into a soft cheeselike mass, as in tuberculosis. **2.** the formation of cheese from casein during the coagulation of milk.

ca·sein (kā′sēn, -sē in, kā sēn′), *n.* a protein precipitated from milk, as by rennet, and forming the basis of cheese.

cast (kast, käst), *n.* **1.** a rigid surgical dressing, usu. made of bandage treated with plaster of Paris. **2.** effused plastic matter produced in the hollow parts of various diseased organs.

cas·tor oil′ (kas′tər), *n.* a colorless or pale oil expressed from the bean of the castor-oil plant, *Ricinus comunis,* used as a lubricant and cathartic.

cas·trate (kas′trāt), *v.*, **-trat·ed, -trat·ing.** *n.* —*v.t.* **1.** to remove the testes of; emasculate. **2.** to remove the ovaries of. **3.** to render impotent by psychological means, as disparagement. —*n.* **4.** a castrated person or animal. —**cas·tra′tion,** *n.* —**cas′tra·tor,** *n.*

CAT, computerized axial tomography. Compare CAT SCAN, CAT SCANNER.

ca·tab·o·lism (kə tab′ə liz′əm), *n.* destructive metabolism; the breaking down in living organisms of more complex substances into simpler ones, with the release of energy (opposed to *anabolism*). —**cat·a·bol·ic** (kat′ə bol′ik), *adj.* —**cat′a·bol′i·cal·ly,** *adv.*

ca·tab′o·lite (-līt′), *n.* a product of catabolism.

cat·a·lase (kat′l ās′, -āz′), *n.* an enzyme that decomposes hydrogen peroxide into oxygen and water. —**cat′a·lat′ic** (-at′ik), *adj.*

cat′a·lep′sy (-ep′sē) also **cat′a·lep′sis,** *n.* a seizure or abnormal condition characterized by postural rigidity and mental stupor, associated with certain brain disorders. —**cat′a·lep′tic,** *adj., n.* —**cat′a·lep′ti·cal·ly,** *adv.*

ca·tal·y·sis (kə tal′ə sis), *n., pl.* **-ses** (-sēz′). the causing or accelerating of a chemical change by the addition of a catalyst. —**cat·a·lyt·ic** (kat′l it′ik), *adj., n.*

cat·a·lyst (kat′l ist), *n.* a substance that causes or speeds a chemical reaction without itself being affected.

cat·a·me·ni·a (kat′ə mē′nē ə), *n.* (*used with a sing. or pl. v.*) MENSES. —**cat′a·me′ni·al,** *adj.*

cat·a·plasm (kat′ə plaz′əm), *n.* a poultice.

cat·a·ract (kat′ə rakt′), *n.* **1.** an abnormality of the eye characterized by opacity of the lens. **2.** the opaque area.

ca·tarrh (kə tär′), *n.* inflammation of a mucous membrane, esp. of the respiratory tract, causing excessive secretions. —**ca·tarrh′al, ca·tarrh′ous,** *adj.*

cat·a·to·ni·a (kat′ə tō′nē ə), *n.* a psychotic syndrome, esp. in schizophrenia, characterized by muscular rigidity and mental stupor, sometimes alternating with excitability and confusion. —**cat′a·ton′ic** (-ton′ik), *adj., n.*

cat′ box′, *n.* a region of DNA containing the base sequence GCCAAT, associated with a family of DNA-binding proteins that affect the expression of genes.

cat·e·chol·a·mine (kat′i kōl′ə mēn′, -kō′lə-), *n.* any of a group of chemically related neurotransmitters, as epinephrine and dopamine, that have similar effects on the sympathetic nervous system.

ca·ten·u·late (kə ten′yə lit, -lāt′), *adj.* having a chainlike form.

ca·thar·sis (kə thär′sis), *n., pl.* **-ses** (-sēz). **1.** *Med.* PURGATION. **2.** *Psychiatry.* a discharge of repressed or pent-up emotions resulting in the alleviation of symptoms or the elimination of the condition.

ca·thar·tic, *adj.* **1.** of or pertaining to catharsis. **2.** Also, **ca·thar'ti·cal.** evacuating the bowels; purgative. —*n.* **3.** a purgative.

ca·thect (kə thekt', ka-), *v.t. Psychoanal.* to invest emotion or feeling in (an idea, object, or another person).

ca·thep·sin (kə thep'sin), *n.* any of a class of intracellular enzymes that break down protein in certain abnormal conditions and after death. —**ca·thep'tic** (-tik), *adj.*

cath·e·ter (kath'i tər), *n.* a thin flexible tube inserted into a bodily passage, vessel, or cavity to allow fluids to pass into or out of it, to distend it, or to convey diagnostic or other instruments through it.

cath'e·ter·ize', *v.t.,* **-ized, -iz·ing.** to introduce a catheter into. —**cath'e·ter·i·za'tion,** *n.*

ca·thex·is (kə thek'sis), *n., pl.* **-thex·es** (-thek'sēz). *Psychoanal.* **1.** the investment of emotional significance in an activity, object, or idea. **2.** the charge of psychic energy so invested.

CAT' scan' (kat), *n.* **1.** an examination performed with a CAT scanner. **2.** an x-ray image obtained by examination with a CAT scanner. Also called **CT scan.**

CAT' scan'ner, *n.* a tomographic device employing narrow beams of x-rays in two planes at various angles to produce computerized cross-sectional images of the body, including soft tissue. Also called **CT scanner.**

cau·dal (kôd'l), *adj.* **1.** of, at, or near the tail end of the body. **2.** taillike: *caudal appendages.* —**cau'dal·ly,** *adv.*

caul (kôl), *n.* **1.** a part of the amnion sometimes covering the head of a child at birth. **2.** GREATER OMENTUM.

cau'liflower ear', *n.* an ear that has been deformed by repeated injury, resulting in an irregular thickening of scar tissue.

cau·sal·gi·a (kô zal'jē ə, -jə), *n.* a neuralgia distinguished by a burning pain along certain nerves, usu. of the upper extremities. —**cau·sal'gic,** *adj.*

cau·ter·ize (kô'tə rīz'), *v.t.,* **-ized, -iz·ing.** to burn with a hot iron, electric current, fire, or a caustic, esp. for curative purposes; treat with a cautery. —**cau'ter·i·za'tion,** *n.*

cau'ter·y, *n., pl.* **-ter·ies. 1.** any substance or instrument, as an electric current or hot iron, used to destroy tissue. **2.** the process of destroying tissue with a cautery.

CCK, cholecystokinin.

CCU, coronary-care unit.

CD4, *n.* a protein on the surface of T cells and other cells, functioning as a receptor for the AIDS virus antigen.

CDC, Centers for Disease Control.

cDNA, complementary DNA: a DNA molecule that is complementary to a specific messenger RNA.

ce·cum or **cae·cum** (sē'kəm), *n., pl.* **-ca** (-kə). an anatomical cul-de-sac, esp. that in which the large intestine begins. —**ce'cal,** *adj.*

ce·li·ac or **coe·li·ac** (sē/lē ak/), *adj.* of, pertaining to, or located in the cavity of the abdomen.

ce/liac disease/, *n.* a hereditary digestive disorder involving intolerance to gluten, characterized by malnutrition and fatty stools.

cell (sel), *n.* a usu. microscopic structure containing nuclear and cytoplasmic material enclosed by a semipermeable membrane and, in plants, a cell wall; the basic structural unit of all organisms. —**cel/lu·lar** (-yə lər), *adj.*

cell/ biol/ogy, *n.* the branch of biology dealing with the study of cells, esp. their formation, structure, and function.

cell/ cy/cle, *n.* the cycle of growth and asexual reproduction of a cell, consisting of interphase followed in actively dividing cells by prophase, metaphase, anaphase, and telophase.

cell/ fu/sion, *n.* the fusion of the nuclei of two types of cells in the laboratory to form a new and genetically distinct cell.

cell/-me/di·ated immu/nity, *n.* immunity conferred to an individual through the activity of T cells, involving the direct destruction of viruses, foreign particles, etc. Compare ANTIBODY-MEDIATED IMMUNITY.

cel·loi·din (sə loi/din), *n.* a concentrated form of pyroxylin used to embed tissues for cutting and microscopic examination.

cel/lular respira/tion, *n.* the oxidation of organic compounds that occurs within cells, producing energy for cellular processes.

cel/lu·lite/ (-lit/, -lēt/), *n.* (not used scientifically) lumpy fat deposits, esp. in the thighs and buttocks.

cel/lu·li/tis (-li/tis), *n.* inflammation of cellular tissue.

Cel·si·us (sel/sē əs), *adj.* pertaining to or noting a temperature scale (**Cel/sius scale/**) in which 0° represents the ice point and 100° the steam point; Centigrade. *Symbol:* C

cent., centigrade

cen·ti·grade (sen/ti grād/), *adj.* **1.** divided into 100 degrees, as a scale. **2.** (*cap.*) CELSIUS. *Abbr.:* cent. *Symbol:* C

cen/tral nerv/ous sys/tem, *n.* the part of the nervous system comprising the brain and spinal cord.

cen·trif·u·gal (sen trif/yə gəl, -ə gəl), *adj. Physiol.* efferent. —**cen·trif/u·gal·ly,** *adv.*

cen·tri·ole (sen/trē ōl/), *n.* a small cylindrical cell organelle, seen near the nucleus in the cytoplasm of most eukaryotic cells, that divides perpendicularly during mitosis.

cen·trip·e·tal (sen trip/i tl), *adj. Physiol.* afferent. —**cen·trip/e·tal·ly,** *adv.*

cen·tro·mere (sen/trə mēr/), *n.* a structure appearing on the chromosome during mitosis or meiosis, at the place where the chromatids remain joined as they form an X shape. —**cen/tro·mer/ic** (-mer/ik, -mēr/-), *adj.*

cen/tro·some/ (-sōm/), *n.* a small region near the nucleus in the cytoplasm of a cell, containing the centrioles. —**cen/tro·som/ic** (-som/ik), *adj.*

cen/tro·sphere/, *n.* the protoplasm around a centrosome; the central portion of an aster, containing the centrosome.

ceph·a·lex·in (sef′ə lek′sin), *n.* an oral antibiotic of the cephalosporin group, used chiefly for treating minor respiratory and urinary tract infections.

ce·phal·ic (sə fal′ik), *adj.* of or pertaining to the head. —**ce·phal′i·cal·ly,** *adv.*

cephal′ic in′dex, *n.* the ratio of the greatest breadth of the head to its greatest length from front to back, multiplied by 100.

ceph·a·lin (sef′ə lin), *n.* a phospholipid of the cell membrane, abundant esp. in the brain.

ceph′a·lo·spo′rin (-lō spôr′in, -spōr′-), *n.* any of a group of widely used broad-spectrum antibiotics, derived from the fungus *Cephalosporium acremonium.*

ce·rate (sēr′āt), *n.* an unctuous, often medicated, preparation for external application, consisting of lard or oil mixed with wax, rosin, or the like.

cer·car·i·a (sər kâr′ē ə), *n., pl.* **-i·ae** (-ē ē′). the free-swimming, tailed larva of parasitic trematodes. —**cer·car′i·al,** *adj.* —**cer·car′i·an,** *adj., n.*

cer·e·bel·lum (ser′ə bel′əm), *n., pl.* **-bel·lums, -bel·la** (-bel′ə). the rounded portion of the cerebrum in birds and mammals, directly behind the cerebrum in birds and mammals, that serves mainly to coordinate movement, posture, and balance. —**cer′e·bel′lar,** *adj.*

ce·re·bral (sə rē′brəl, ser′ə-), *adj.* of or pertaining to the cerebrum or the brain. —**ce·re·bral·ly,** *adv.*

cere′bral cor′tex, *n.* the outer layer of gray matter in the cerebrum associated with the higher brain functions, as voluntary movement, sensory perception, and learning.

cere′bral hem′isphere, *n.* either of the rounded halves of the cerebrum connected by the corpus callosum. Compare LEFT BRAIN, RIGHT BRAIN.

cere′bral pal′sy, *n.* a condition of muscular weakness and difficulty in coordinating voluntary movement owing to developmental or congenital damage to the brain. —**cere′bral pal′sied,** *adj.*

ce·re·bro·side (′-brə sid′), *n.* any of a class of glycolipids that occur in the myelin sheath of cerebrospinal neurons.

ce·re·bro·spi·nal (-brō-), *adj.* **1.** pertaining to or affecting the brain and the spinal cord. **2.** of or pertaining to the central nervous system.

cerebrospi′nal flu′id, *n.* a fluid, rich in glucose, that circulates in the brain and spinal column. *Abbr.:* CSF

cerebrospi′nal meningi′tis, *n.* MENINGITIS.

ce·re·bro·vas·cu·lar (-brō-), *adj.* of or pertaining to the cerebrum and its associated blood vessels.

cere′brovas′cular ac′cident, *n.* STROKE. *Abbr.:* CVA

ce·re·brum (-brəm), *n., pl.* **-brums, -bra** (-brə). the forward and upper part of the brain, involved with voluntary movement and conscious processes, in mammals and birds being greatly enlarged. Compare CEREBRAL HEMISPHERE.

ce·ru·men (si rōō′mən), *n.* EARWAX. —**ce·ru′mi·nous,** *adj.*

cer·vi·cal (sûr′vi kəl), *adj.* of or pertaining to the cervix or neck.

cer′vical cap′, *n.* a contraceptive device made of rubberlike plastic and fitted over the cervix, where it may be kept for long periods without removal.

cer·vi·ci·tis (-sī′tis), *n.* inflammation of the cervix.

cer·vix (sûr′viks), *n., pl.* **cer·vix·es, cer·vi·ces** (sûr′və-sēz′, sər vī′sēz). **1.** the neck, esp. the back part. **2.** any necklike part, esp. the constricted lower end of the uterus.

Ce·sar·e·an or **Cae·sar·e·an** or **Ce·sar·i·an** (si zâr′ē-ən), *n.* (*sometimes l.c.*) **1.** Also called **Cesar′ean sec′tion.** an operation by which a fetus is taken from the uterus by cutting through the walls of the abdomen and uterus. —*adj.* **2.** (*sometimes l.c.*) of or pertaining to a Cesarean.

CF, cystic fibrosis.

CFS, chronic fatigue syndrome.

cGMP, cyclic GMP.

Cha·gas′ disease′ (shä′gəs), *n.* an infectious disease caused by the protozoan *Trypanosoma cruzi,* occurring chiefly in tropical America and characterized by irregular fever, palpable lymph nodes, and often heart damage.

chalk′stone′, *n.* a chalklike concretion in the tissues or small joints of a person with gout.

chal·lenge (chal′inj), *n., v.,* **-lenged, -leng·ing.** —*n.* **1.** the assessment of a specific function in an organism by exposing it to a provocative substance or activity. —*v.t.* **2.** to inject (an organism) with a specific substance in order to assess its physiological or immunological activity.

chal·one (kal′ōn), *n.* an endocrine secretion that depresses or inhibits physiological activity.

chan·cre (shang′kər), *n.* the initial lesion of syphilis and certain other infectious diseases, commonly a more or less distinct ulcer or sore with a hard base. —**chan′crous,** *adj.*

chan′croid (-kroid), *n.* an infectious venereal ulcer with a soft base. Also called **soft chancre.** —**chan·croi′dal,** *adj.*

change′ of life′, *n.* MENOPAUSE.

char·ac·ter (kar′ik tər), *n.* any trait, function, structure, or substance of an organism resulting from the effect of one or more genes.

char′ley horse′ (chär′lē), *n.* a cramp or a sore muscle, esp. in the leg, resulting from overuse or strain.

check′up′, *n.* a comprehensive physical examination.

che·la·tion (kē lā′shən), *n.* **1.** a method of removing certain heavy metals from the bloodstream, used esp. in treating lead or mercury poisoning. **2.** a controversial treatment for arteriosclerosis that attempts to remove calcium deposits from the inner walls of the coronary arteries.

che·mo·pro·phy·lax·is (kē′mō-, kem′ō-), *n.* prevention of disease by means of chemical agents or drugs or by food nutrients. Also called **che·mo·pre·ven′tion.** —**che·mo·pro·phy·lac′tic,** *adj.*

che·mo·re·cep'tion, *n.* the physiological response to chemical stimuli. —**che'mo·re·cep'tive,** *adj.*

che·mo·re·cep'tor, *n.* a receptor stimulated by chemical means.

che·mo·sen'so·ry, *adj.* sensitive to chemical stimuli, as the nerve endings that mediate taste and smell.

che·mos·mo·sis (kē'moz mō'sis, -mos-, kem'oz-, -os-), *n.* chemical action between substances that occurs through an intervening, semipermeable membrane. —**che'mos·mot'ic** (-mot'ik), *adj.*

che'mo·sur'ger·y, *n.* the use of chemical substances to destroy diseased or unwanted tissue. —**che'mo·sur'gi·cal,** *adj.*

che'mo·syn'the·sis, *n.* the synthesis of organic compounds within an organism, with chemical reactions providing the energy source. —**che'mo·syn·thet'ic,** *adj.* —**che'mo·syn·thet'i·cal·ly,** *adv.*

che'mo·tax·on'o·my, *n.* the identification and classification of organisms by comparative analysis of their biochemical composition. —**che'mo·tax'o·nom'ic,** *adj.* —**che'mo·tax'o·nom'i·cal·ly,** *adv.* —**che'mo·tax·on'o·mist,** *n.*

che'mo·ther'a·py, *n.* the treatment of disease by means of chemicals that have a specific toxic effect upon the disease-producing microorganisms or that selectively destroy cancerous tissue. —**che'mo·ther'a·peu'tic,** *adj.* —**che'mo·ther'a·pist,** *n.*

che·mo·troph (kē'mə trof', -trōf', kem'ə-), *n.* any organism that oxidizes inorganic or organic compounds as its principal energy source. —**che'mo·troph'ic,** *adj.*

chi·as·ma (kī az'mə) also **chi'asm** (-az əm), *n., pl.* **-as·mas, -as·ma·ta** (-az'mə tə) also **-asms.** **1.** *Anat.* a crossing or decussation. Compare OPTIC CHIASMA. **2.** a point of overlap of paired chromatids at which fusion and exchange of genetic material take place during prophase of meiosis.

chi·as'ma·typ'y (-ti'pē), *n.* the process of chiasma formation, which is the basis for crossing over. Compare CROSSING OVER. —**chi·as'ma·type',** *adj., n.*

chick'en breast', *n.* a congenital or acquired malformation of the chest in which there is abnormal projection of the sternum and the sternal region, often associated with rickets. Also called **pigeon breast.** —**chick'en-breast'ed,** *adj.* —**chick'en-breast'ed·ness,** *n.*

chick'en·pox' or **chick'en pox',** *n.* a disease, commonly of children, caused by a herpesvirus and characterized by fever and the eruption of blisters. Also called **varicella.**

chil·blain (chil'blān), *n.* Usu., **chilblains.** an inflammation of the hands and feet caused by exposure to cold and moisture. Also called **pernio.** —**chil'blained,** *adj.*

child'bed fe'ver, *n.* PUERPERAL FEVER.

child'birth', *n.* an act or instance of bringing forth a child; parturition.

chi·me·ra or **chi·mae·ra** (ki mēr'ə, kī-), *n., pl.* **-ras.** an organism composed of two or more genetically distinct tissues.

Chi/nese-res/taurant syn/drome, *n.* a reaction, as headache or sweating, to monosodium glutamate, sometimes added to food in Chinese restaurants.

chin/-up/, *n.* an exercise in which a person grasps an overhead bar and pulls the body upward until the chin is above or level with the bar.

chi·rop·o·dist (ki rop′ə dist, ki- *or, often,* shə-), *n.* PODIATRIST.

chi·rop/o·dy, *n.* PODIATRY.

chi·ro·prac·tic (ki′rə prak′tik), *n.* a therapeutic system based upon the interactions of the spine and nervous system, the method of treatment usu. being to adjust the segments of the spinal column. —**chi/ro·prac/tor,** *n.*

chla·myd·i·a (klə mid′ē ə), *n., pl.* **-myd·i·ae** (-mid′ē ē′). **1.** any coccoid rickettsia of the genus *Chlamydia*, parasitic in birds and mammals, including humans, and causing various infections. **2.** a widespread, often asymptomatic sexually transmitted disease caused by *Chlamydia trachomatis*, a major cause of nongonococcal urethritis in men and pelvic inflammatory disease and ectopic pregnancy in women.

chlo·as·ma (klō az′mə), *n.* a condition in which light brown spots occur on the skin, caused by exposure to sun, dyspepsia, or certain specific diseases.

chlor·ac·ne (klôr ak′nē, klōr-), *n.* acne caused by exposure to chlorine compounds.

chlo·ral (klôr′əl, klōr′-), *n.* Also called **chlo/ral hy/drate.** a white crystalline solid, $C_2H_3Cl_3O_2$, used as a hypnotic.

chlo·ram·phen·i·col (klôr′am fen′i kôl′, -kol′, klōr′-), *n.* an antibiotic obtained from cultures of *Streptomyces venezuelae* or synthesized, used chiefly for treating rickettsial infections.

chlor/di·az/e·pox/ide (-di az′ə pok/sid), *n.* a compound, $C_{16}H_{14}ClN_3O$, used as a tranquilizer.

chlo·ride (klôr′id, -id, klōr′-), *n.* a salt of hydrochloric acid consisting of two elements, one of which is chlorine, as sodium chloride, NaCl.

chlo·ri·nate (klôr′ə nāt′, klōr′-), *v.t.,* **-nat·ed, -nat·ing.** to combine or treat with chlorine, esp. for disinfecting. —**chlo/ri·na/tion,** *n.* —**chlo/ri·na/tor,** *n.*

chlo·rine (klôr′ēn, -in, klōr′-), *n.* a halogen element, a heavy, greenish yellow poisonous gas: used to purify water and to make bleaching powder and various chemicals. Symbol: Cl; *at. wt.:* 35.453; *at. no.:* 17.

chlo·ro·form (klôr′ə fôrm′, klōr′-), *n.* **1.** a colorless volatile liquid, $CHCl_3$, used chiefly in medicine as a solvent and formerly as an anesthetic. —*v.t.* **2.** to administer chloroform to, esp. in order to anesthetize. —**chlo/ro·for/mic,** *adj.*

chlo/ro·phyll or **chlo/ro·phyl** (-fil) *n.* the green pigment of plant leaves and algae, essential to their production of carbohydrates by photosynthesis.

chlo·ro·quine (-kwin) *n.* a synthetic drug, $C_{18}H_{26}ClN_3$, used chiefly to control malaria attacks.

chlo·ro·sis (klô rō′sis, klō-) *n.* Also called **greensickness**. a benign iron-deficiency anemia in adolescent girls, marked by a pale yellow-green complexion. —**chlo·rot′ic** (-rot′ik), *adj.* —**chlo·rot′i·cal·ly**, *adv.*

chlo′ro·thi′a·zide′ (klôr′ə-, klōr′-), *n.* a white, crystalline, slightly water-soluble powder, $C_7H_6ClN_3O_4S_2$, used as a diuretic and in the treatment of hypertension.

chlor·prom′a·zine′ (-prom′ə zēn′), *n.* a crystalline powder derived from phenothiazine, used chiefly as an antipsychotic and antinauseant.

chlor·tet′ra·cy′cline (-tet′rə-), *n.* a yellow, crystalline, antibiotic powder, $C_{22}H_{23}N_2O_8Cl$, produced by *Streptomyces aureofaciens*, used in the treatment of infections.

cho·lan·gi·og·ra·phy (kə lan′jē og′rə fē, kō-), *n.* x-ray examination of the bile ducts using a radiopaque contrast medium.

cho·late (kō′lāt), *n.* the salt form of cholic acid.

cho·le·cal·cif′er·ol (kō/lə-, kol′ə-), *n.* VITAMIN D_3.

cho′le·cys·tec′to·my, *n.*, *pl.* **-mies**. surgical removal of the gallbladder.

cho′le·cys·ti′tis, *n.* inflammation of the gallbladder.

cho′le·cys′to·ki′nin (-sis/tə ki′nin), *n.* a hormone secreted by the upper intestine that stimulates contraction of the gallbladder and increases secretion of pancreatic juice. *Abbr.:* CCK

cho′le·cys·tot′o·my (-si stot′ə mē), *n.*, *pl.* **-mies**. surgical incision of the gallbladder.

cho′le·li·thi′a·sis, *n.* the presence of gallstones.

chol·er·a (kol′ər ə), *n.* a severe contagious infection of the small intestine characterized by profuse watery diarrhea and dehydration, caused by *Vibrio cholerae* bacteria, and commonly transmitted through contaminated drinking water. —**chol·e·ra′ic** (-rā′ik), *adj.*

cho′le·sta·sis (kō/lə-, kol′ə-), *n.* impairment of the flow of bile. —**cho′le·stat′ic**, *adj.*

cho·les·ter·ol (kə les/tə rōl′, -rôl′), *n.* a sterol, $C_{27}H_{46}O$, abundant in animal fats, brain and nerve tissue, meat, and eggs, that functions in the body as a membrane constituent and as a precursor to steroid hormones and bile acids: high levels in the blood are associated with arteriosclerosis and gallstones. Compare HDL, LDL.

cho′lic ac′id (kō′lik, kol′ik), *n.* a bile acid, $C_{24}H_{40}O_5$, related to cholesterol.

cho·line (kō′lēn, kol′ēn), *n.* a viscous fluid, $C_5H_{14}N^+O$, that is a constituent of lecithin and a primary component of the neurotransmitter acetylcholine: one of the B complex vitamins.

cho·lin·er·gic (kō/lə nûr′jik, kol′ə-), *adj.* **1.** resembling acetylcholine in physiological effect: *a cholinergic drug.* **2.** releasing acetylcholine: *a cholinergic neuron.* Compare **adrenergic** (-rā′ik), *adj.*

cho·lin·es·ter·ase (kō/lə nes′tə rās′, -rāz′, kol′ə-), *n.* an enzyme, found esp. in the heart, brain, and blood, that hydrolyzes acetylcholine to acetic acid and choline.

cho·li·no·lyt·ic (kō/lə nl it/ik), *adj.* **1.** capable of blocking the action of acetylcholine and related compounds. —*n.* **2.** a cholinolytic drug or other substance.

chon·dro·ma (kon drō/mə), *n., pl.* **-mas, -ma·ta** (-mə tə). a benign cartilaginous tumor or growth. —**chon·dro/ma·tous,** *adj.*

cho·re·a (kə rē/ə, kô-, kō-), *n.* **1.** any of several diseases of the nervous system characterized by jerky, involuntary movements, esp. of the face and extremities. **2.** Also called **St. Vitus's dance.** such a disease occurring chiefly in children and associated with rheumatic fever. —**cho·re/al, cho·re/ic, cho·re·at/ic** (kôr/ē at/ik, kōr/-), *adj.*

cho·ri·o·al·lan·to·is (kôr/ē ō- al/ən tō/is), *n.* a vascular membrane surrounding the embryo, formed by the fusion of the walls of the chorion and allantois. —**cho/ri·o·al/lan·to/ic,** *adj.*

cho·ri·on/ (-on/), *n.* the outermost of the membranes enclosing the embryo, developing into part of the placenta. —**cho/ri·on/ic, cho/ri·al,** *adj.*

chorion/ic gonadotro/pin, *n.* gonadotropin produced and secreted by the chorion. Compare HUMAN CHORIONIC GONADOTROPIN.

chorion/ic vil/lus (vil/əs), *n.* one of the branching outgrowths of the chorion that together with maternal tissue form the placenta.

chorion/ic vil/lus sam/pling, *n.* a test for detecting birth defects in early pregnancy involving examination of cells obtained from the chorionic villus. *Abbr.:* CVS

cho·roid (kôr/oid, kōr/-), *adj.* **1.** Also, **cho·roi/dal.** like the chorion; membranous. —*n.* **2.** CHOROID COAT.

cho/roid coat/, *n.* a pigmented, highly vascular membrane of the eye that is continuous with the iris and lies between the sclera and the retina, functioning to nourish the retina and absorb scattered light. Also called **choroid, cho/roid mem/brane.**

chro·maf·fin (krō/mə fin), *adj.* staining with chromium salts: indicates the presence of epinephrine or norepinephrine.

chromat/ic aberra/tion, *n.* the variation of either the focal length or the magnification of a lens system with different wavelengths of light.

chro·ma·tid (krō/mə tid), *n.* either of two identical chromosomal strands into which a chromosome splits before cell division.

chro·ma·tin (-tin), *n.* the readily stainable substance of a cell nucleus that consists of DNA, RNA, and various proteins, and forms chromosomes during cell division. —**chro/ma·tin/ic,** *adj.* —**chro/ma·toid/,** *adj.*

chro·mat·o·phil (krə mat/ə fil), *adj., n.* CHROMOPHIL.

chro·mo·gen (krō/mə jən, -jen/), *n.* a chromogenic bacterium.

chro·mo·gen/ic, *adj.* (of bacteria) producing some characteristic color or pigment that is useful as a means of identification.

chro·mo·mere′ (-mēr′), *n.* one of the beadlike granules arranged in a linear series in a chromonema. —**chro′mo·mer′ic** (-mer′ik, -mēr′-), *adj.*

chro·mo·ne·ma (-nē′mə), *n.*, *pl.* **-ma·ta** (-mə tə). a chromosome thread that is relatively uncoiled at early prophase but assumes a spiral form at metaphase. —**chro′mo·ne·mat′ic** (-nə mat′ik, -nē-), *adj.*

chro′mo·phil (-fil), *adj.* **1.** staining readily with dye in the laboratory. —*n.* **2.** a chromophil cell or cell part.

chro′mo·phobe′ (-fōb′) also **chro′mo·pho′bic**, *adj.* not staining readily: *chromophobe cells.*

chro′mo·pro′tein, *n.* a protein, as hemoglobin or rhodopsin, containing a pigmented nonprotein group, as heme, riboflavin, or retinal.

chro′mo·some′ (-sōm′), *n.* one of a set of threadlike structures, composed of DNA and a protein, that form in the nucleus when the cell begins to divide and that carry the genes which determine an individual's hereditary traits. —**chro′mo·so′mal**, *adj.*

chro·nax·ie or **chro·nax·y** (krō′nak sē, kron′ak-), *n.* the minimum time that an electric current of twice the threshold strength must flow in order to excite a muscle or nerve tissue.

chron·ic (kron′ik), *adj.* (of a disease) having long duration (disting. from *acute*). —**chron′i·cal·ly**, *adv.* —**chro·nic·i·ty** (kro nis′i tē), *n.*

chron′ic fatigue′ syn′drome, *n.* a viral disease of the immune system, usu. characterized by debilitating fatigue and flu-like symptoms.

chron′ic obstruc′tive pul′monary disease′, *n.* any of various lung diseases, as emphysema, that lead to poor pulmonary aeration.

chron·o·bi·ol·o·gy (kron′ō-), *n.* the science or study of the effect of time, esp. rhythms, on living systems. —**chron′o·bi·o·log′i·cal**, *adj.* —**chron′o·bi·ol′o·gist**, *n.*

chron·o·trop·ic (kron′ə trop′ik, -trō′pik), *adj.* affecting the rate or timing of a physiologic process, as the heart rate.

chrys·a·ro·bin (kris′ə rō′bin), *n.* a mixture of compounds obtained from Goa powder and used in the treatment of psoriasis and other skin conditions.

chyle (kīl), *n.* a milky fluid containing emulsified fat and other products of digestion, that forms from chyme in the small intestine, is absorbed by the lacteals, and reaches the bloodstream through the thoracic duct. —**chy′lous**, *adj.*

chy·lo·mi·cron (kī′lə mī′kron), *n.* a lipoprotein droplet that forms in the small intestine and conveys fat through the lymph to the blood.

chyme (kīm), *n.* the semifluid mass into which food is converted by gastric secretion and which passes from the stomach into the small intestine. —**chy′mous**, *adj.*

chy′mo·pa·pa′in (ki′mō-), *n.* an enzyme of the papaya that is capable of breaking down protein: used to dissolve cartilage in the treatment of herniated disks.

chy′mo·tryp′sin, *n.* an enzyme of the pancreatic juice that breaks down food protein in the small intestines. —**chy′mo·tryp′tic**, *adj.*

Ci, curie.

cic·a·trix (sik′ə triks, si kā′triks) also **cic′a·trice** (-tris), *n., pl.* **cic·a·tri·ces** (sik′ə trī′sēz). new tissue that forms over a wound and later contracts into a scar. —**cic·a·tri′cial** (-trish′əl), *adj.* —**ci·cat·ri·cose** (si ka′tri kōs′, sik′ə-), *adj.*

cil·i·a (sil′ē ə), *n.pl., sing.* **-i·um** (-ē əm). **1.** short, hairlike, rhythmically beating organelles on the surface of certain cells that provide mobility, as in protozoans, or move fluids and particles along ducts in multicellular forms. **2.** the eyelashes.

cil′i·ar′y (-er′ē-), *adj.* **1.** pertaining to various anatomical structures in or about the eye, as in the ciliary body. **2.** pertaining to cilia.

cil′iary bod′y, *n.* the part of the eye between the choroid coat and the iris, consisting of the ciliary muscle and ciliary processes.

cil′iary mus′cle, *n.* the smooth muscle in the ciliary body, which affects lens shape and accommodation.

cil′iary proc′ess, *n.* one of the folds on the ciliary body, connected with the suspensory ligament of the lens.

ci·met·i·dine (si met′i dēn′), *n.* a substance, $C_{10}H_{16}N_6S$, used for inhibiting gastric secretion in the treatment of duodenal ulcers.

cin·e·mi·cro·graph (sin′ə mi′krə graf′, -gräf′), *n.* a motion picture filmed through a microscope. —**cin′e·mi·cro·graph′ic,** *adj.*

cin·e·mi·crog′ra·phy (-krog′rə fē), *n.* the cinematographic recording of microscopic pictures, as for the study of bacterial motion. —**cin′e·mi·crog′ra·pher,** *n.*

cir·ca·di·an (sûr kā′dē ən, sûr′kə dē′ən), *adj.* of or pertaining to rhythmic cycles recurring at approximately 24-hour intervals: *the circadian biological clock.* —**cir·ca′di·an·ly,** *adv.*

circ·an·nu·al (sûr kan′yoo əl), *adj.* of or pertaining to any activity or cycle that recurs yearly.

cir·cu·la·tion (sûr′kyə lā′shən), *n.* the continuous movement of blood through the heart and blood vessels, maintained chiefly by the action of the heart. —**cir′cu·la·to·ry** (-lə tôr′ē, -tōr′ē), *adj.*

cir′culatory sys′tem, *n.* the system of organs and tissues, including the heart, blood, blood vessels, lymph, lymphatic vessels, and lymph glands, involved in circulating blood and lymph through the body.

cir·cum·cise (sûr′kəm sīz′), *v.t.,* **-cised, -cis·ing. 1.** to remove the prepuce of (a male). **2.** to remove the clitoris, prepuce, or labia of (a female). —**cir′cum·cis′er,** *n.* —**cir′cum·ci′sion** (-sizh′ən), *n.*

cir·cum·flex (sûr′kəm fleks′), *adj.* (of a nerve, blood vessel, etc.) bending or winding around.

cir·rho·sis (si rō′sis), *n.* a chronic disease of the liver in which fibrous tissue invades and replaces normal tissue, disrupting important functions, as digestion and detoxification. —**cir·rhot′ic** (-rot′ik), *adj.* —**cir·rhosed′**, *adj.*

cis·tern (sis′tərn), *n.* a reservoir or receptacle of some natural fluid of the body.

cis·ter·na (si stûr′nə), *n., pl.* **-nae** (-nē). CISTERN. —**cis·ter′nal**, *adj.*

cis·tron (sis′tron), *n.* a segment of DNA that codes for the formation of a specific protein; a structural gene. —**cis·tron′ic**, *adj.*

cit·ric ac·id, *n.* a white powder, $C_6H_8O_7 \cdot H_2O$, an intermediate in the metabolism of carbohydrates, occurring esp. in citrus fruits: used chiefly in flavorings and pharmaceuticals.

cit′ric ac′id cy′cle, *n.* KREBS CYCLE.

cit·rul·line (si′trə lēn′), *n.* an amino acid, $C_6H_{13}N_3O_3$, abundant in watermelons and an intermediate compound in the urea cycle.

Cl, *Symbol.* chlorine.

clair·au·di·ence (klâr ô′dē əns), *n.* the power to hear sounds said to exist beyond the reach of ordinary experience or capacity, as the voices of the dead. —**clair·au′di·ent**, *n., adj.* —**clair·au·di·ent·ly**, *adv.*

clap (klap), *n. Slang (vulgar).* gonorrhea (often prec. by *the*).

clas′sical condi′tioning, *n.* CONDITIONING (def. 2).

clas·tic (klas′tik), *adj.* pertaining to an anatomical model made up of detachable pieces.

clau·di·ca·tion (klô′di kā′shən), *n.* a limp or a lameness.

claus·tro·pho·bi·a (klô′strə fō′bē ə), *n.* an abnormal fear of being in enclosed or narrow places. —**claus′tro·phobe′**, *n.* —**claus·tro·pho·bic**, *adj.*

clav·i·cle (klav′i kəl), *n.* either of two slender bones of the pectoral girdle that connect the sternum and the scapula; collarbone.

cleav·age (klē′vij), *n.* the series of cell divisions in mitosis that converts the fertilized egg into blastomeres.

cleft′ lip′, *n.* a congenital defect of the upper lip in which a longitudinal fissure extends into one or both nostrils.

cleft′ pal′ate, *n.* a congenital defect of the palate in which a longitudinal fissure exists in the roof of the mouth.

cli·mac·ter·ic (klī mak′tər ik, klī′mak ter′ik), *n.* a period of decrease of reproductive capacity in men and women, culminating, in women, in the menopause. —**cli′mac·ter′i·cal·ly**, *adv.*

cli·max (klī′maks), *n.* an orgasm.

clin·ic (klin′ik), *n.* **1.** a place for the medical treatment of nonresident patients, sometimes at reduced cost. **2.** a group of physicians, dentists, or the like, working in cooperation and sharing facilities. **3.** the instruction of medical students by examining or treating patients in their presence or by their examining or treating patients under supervision. **4.** a class of students assembled for such instruction. —*adj.* **5.** of a clinic; clinical.

clin′i·cal, *adj.* **1.** pertaining to a clinic. **2.** concerned with or based on actual observation and treatment of disease in patients rather than experimentation or theory: *clinical medicine.* **3.** pertaining to or used in a sickroom: *a clinical bandage.* —**clin′i·cal·ly,** *adv.*

clin′ical psychol′ogy, *n.* the branch of psychology dealing with the diagnosis and treatment of behavioral and personality disorders. —**clin′ical psychol′ogist,** *n.*

clin′ical thermom′eter, *n.* a small thermometer used to measure body temperature.

cli·ni·cian (kli nish′ən), *n.* a physician or other qualified person who is involved in the treatment and observation of living patients, as distinguished from one engaged in research.

clit·o·ris (klit′ər is, kli tôr′is, -tôr′-), *n., pl.* **clit·o·ris·es, cli·to·ri·des** (kli tôr′i dēz′, -tôr′-). the small erectile organ of the vulva.

clo·a·ca (klō ā′kə), *n., pl.* **-cae** (-sē). the common cavity into which the intestinal, urinary, and generative canals open in certain mammals.

clone (klōn), *n., v.,* **cloned, clon·ing.** —*n.* **1.** a cell, cell product, or organism that is genetically identical to the unit or individual from which it was asexually derived. **2.** a population of identical units, cells, or individuals that derive a sexually from the same ancestral line. —*v.t.* **3.** to cause to grow as a clone. **4.** separate (a batch of cells or cell products) so that each portion produces only its own kind. —**clon′al,** *adj.*

clon·i·dine (klon′i dēn′, klō′ni-), *n.* a synthetic white crystalline substance, $C_9H_9Cl_2N_3$, used in the treatment of high blood pressure.

clo·nus (klō′nəs), *n., pl.* **-nus·es.** a rapid succession of flexions and extensions of a muscle group during movement, often symptomatic of a nervous system disorder. —**clon·ic** (klon′ik), *adj.* —**clo·nic·i·ty** (klō nis′i tē, klo-), *n.*

closed′-an′gle glauco′ma, *n.* See under GLAUCOMA.

clos·trid·i·um (klo strid′ē əm), *n., pl.* **-i·a** (-ē ə) any of several rod-shaped, spore-forming, anaerobic bacteria of the genus *Clostridium,* found in soil and in the intestinal tract. —**clos·trid′i·al, clos·trid′i·an,** *adj.*

clot (klot), *n., v.,* **clot·ted, clot·ting.** —*n.* **1.** a semisolid mass, as of coagulated blood. —*v.i.* **2.** to form into clots; coagulate.

club·foot′, *n., pl.* **-feet. 1.** a congenitally deformed or distorted foot. **2.** the condition of having such a foot; talipes. —**club′foot′ed,** *adj.*

clump (klump), *n.* **1.** a cluster of agglutinated bacteria, red blood cells, etc. —*v.i.* **2.** to gather or be gathered into clumps; agglutinate.

clus′ter head′ache, *n.* a type of recurrent headache characterized by sudden attacks of intense pain on one side of the head.

clys·ter (klis′tər), *n.* an enema.

CMV, cytomegalovirus.

Co, *Chem. Symbol.* cobalt.

co·ad·ap·ta′tion (kō′-), *n.* Also called **integration.** the accumulation in a population's gene pool of genes that interact by harmonious epistasis in the development of an organism. —**co′ad·ap·ta′tion·al,** *adj.* —**co′ad·ap·ta′tion·al·ly,** *adv.*

co′a·dapt′ed, *adj.* having undergone coadaptation; mutually accommodating.

co·ag·u·lant (kō ag′yə lənt), *n.* a substance that produces or aids coagulation.

co·ag·u·late′ (-lāt′), *v.i., v.t.* **-lat·ed, -lat·ing.** (of blood) to form or cause to form a clot. —**co·ag′u·la′tion,** *n.* —**co·ag′u·la·to·ry** (-lə tôr′ē, -tōr′ē), **co·ag′u·la′tive** (-lā′tiv, -lə tiv), *adj.*

co·apt (kō apt′), *v.t.* to join or adjust (separate parts) to one another: *to coapt the edges of a wound.* —**co′ap·ta′tion,** *n.*

co·arc·ta·tion (kō′ärk tā′shən), *n.* a narrowing or constriction, as of a blood vessel. —**co·arc′tate,** *adj.*

coat′ pro′tein, *n.* any protein that is a constituent of the capsid of a virus.

co·bal·a·min (kō bal′ə min) also **co·bal′a·mine′** (-mēn′), *n.* VITAMIN B₁₂.

co·balt (kō′bôlt), *n.* a hard, ductile element occurring in compounds; esp. nickel and iron. Symbol: Co; *at. wt.:* 58. 933; *at. no.:* 27; *sp. gr.:* 8.9 at 20°C.

cobalt 60, *n.* a radioisotope of cobalt having a mass number of 60 and a half-life of 5.2 years, used chiefly in radiotherapy.

co·caine (kō kān′, kō′kān), *n.* a bitter, white, crystalline alkaloid, C₁₇H₂₁NO₄, obtained from coca leaves, used as a local anesthetic and also widely used as an illicit drug for its stimulant and euphorigenic properties.

co·cain·ism (kō kā′niz əm, kō′kə niz′əm), *n.* an abnormal condition due to excessive or habitual use of cocaine.

co·cain·ize, *v.t.,* **-ized, -iz·ing.** to treat with or affect by cocaine. —**co·cain′i·za′tion,** *n.*

coc·ci (kok′sī, -sē), *n.* **1.** pl. of coccus. **2.** coccidioidomycosis.

coc·cid·i·oi·do·my·co·sis (kok sid′ē oi′dō mī kō′sis), *n.* a respiratory infection, often with a skin rash, caused by inhaling spores of *Coccidioides* fungi, common in semiarid regions. Also called **desert fever.**

coc·coid (kok′oid) also **coc·coi′dal,** *adj.* resembling a coccus; globular.

coc·cus (kok′əs), *n., pl.* **-ci** (-sī, -sē). a spherical bacterium, as a streptococcus. —**coc′cal, coc′cic** (-sik), *adj.* —**coc′cous,** *adj.*

coc·cyx (kok′siks), *n., pl.* **coc·cy·ges** (kok si′jēz, kok′si·jēz′). a triangular bone at the lower end of the spinal column; tailbone. —**coc·cyg′e·al** (-sijē əl), *adj.*

coch·le·a (kok′lē ə), *n., pl.* **-le·ae** (-lē ē′, -lē ī′), **-le·as.**

the fluid-filled, spiral-shaped part of the inner ear in mammals. —**coch′le·ar**, *adj.*

coch′lear im′plant, *n.* a surgically implanted hearing aid that converts sound reaching the cochlea into electrical impulses that are transmitted by wire to the auditory nerve.

cock′tail′, *n.* a beverage or solution concocted of various ingredients.

code (kōd), *n., v.,* **cod·ed, cod·ing.** —*n.* **1.** a directive or alert to a hospital team assigned to emergency resuscitation of patients. Compare CODE BLUE. **2.** GENETIC CODE. —*v.i.* **3.** to specify the amino acid sequence of a protein by the sequence of nucleotides comprising the gene for that protein: *a gene that codes for the production of insulin.* —**cod′er,** *n.*

code′ blue′, *n.* (*often caps.*) a medical emergency in which paramedics are dispatched to aid a person undergoing cardiac arrest.

co·deine (kō′dēn), *n.* a white, crystalline alkaloid, $C_{18}H_{21}NO_3$, obtained from opium, used chiefly as an analgesic and cough suppressant.

co′de·pend′ent, *adj.* **1.** of or pertaining to a relationship in which one person is physically or psychologically addicted, as to alcohol or gambling, and the other person is psychologically dependent on the first in an unhealthy way. —*n.* **2.** one who is codependent or in a codependent relationship. —**co′de·pend′en·cy, co′de·pend′ence,** *n.*

cod′-liv′er oil′, *n.* an oil extracted from the liver of cod and related fishes, used chiefly as a source of vitamins A and D.

co·dom′i·nant, *adj.* of or pertaining to two different alleles that are fully expressed in a heterozygous individual. —**co·dom′i·nance,** *n.*

co·don (kō′don), *n.* a triplet of adjacent nucleotides in the messenger RNA chain that codes for a specific amino acid in the synthesis of a protein molecule. Compare ANTICODON.

coe·no·cyte (sē′nə sit′, sen′ə-), *n.* a syncytium, esp. one formed by repeated division of the cell nucleus rather than by cellular fission. —**coe′no·cyt′ic** (-sit′ik), *adj.*

co·en′zyme, *n.* a molecule that provides the transfer site for biochemical reactions catalyzed by an enzyme. —**co·en′zy·mat′ic,** *adj.* —**co·en′zy·mat′i·cal·ly,** *adv.*

co′fac′tor, *n.* any of various organic or inorganic substances necessary to the function of an enzyme.

cog·ni·tive (kog′ni tiv), *adj.* of or pertaining to the mental processes of perception, memory, judgment, and reasoning, as contrasted with emotional and volitional processes. —**cog′ni·tive·ly,** *adv.* —**cog′ni·tiv′i·ty,** *n.*

cog′nitive dis′sonance, *n.* anxiety that results from simultaneously holding contradictory or incompatible attitudes, beliefs, or the like, as when one likes a person but disapproves of one of his or her habits.

cog′nitive ther′apy, *n.* a form of psychotherapy that

emphasizes the correction of distorted thinking associated with faulty self-perception and unrealistic expectations.

coil (koil), *n*. INTRAUTERINE DEVICE.

co·i·tion (kō ish′ən), *n*. COITUS. —**co·i′tion·al**, *adj*.

co·i·tus (kō′i təs), *n*. sexual intercourse, esp. between a man and a woman. —**co′i·tal**, *adj*.

co′itus in·ter·rup′tus (in′tə rup′təs), *n*. coitus that is intentionally interrupted by withdrawal before ejaculation of semen into the vagina.

coke (kōk), *n*., *v*., **coked, cok·ing.** *Slang.* —*n.* **1.** cocaine. —*v.t.* **2.** to affect with a narcotic drug, esp. with cocaine (usu. fol. by *up*).

col·chi·cine (kol′chə sēn′, -sin, kol′kə-), *n*. a pale yellow, crystalline alkaloid, $C_{22}H_{25}NO_6$, the active principle of colchicum.

col′chi·cum (-kəm), *n*. **1.** the dried seeds or corms of an Old World plant of the genus *Colchicum*, of the lily family. **2.** a medicine or drug prepared from these, used chiefly in the treatment of gout.

cold (kōld), *n*. Also called **common cold.** a respiratory disorder characterized by sneezing, sore throat, coughing, etc., caused by any of various viruses of the rhinovirus group.

cold′-blood′ed or **cold′blood′ed**, *adj*. of or designating animals, as fishes and reptiles, whose blood temperature ranges from the freezing point upward, in accordance with the temperature of the surrounding medium. —**cold′-blood′ed·ly**, *adv*. —**cold′-blood′ed·ness**, *n*.

cold′ sore′, *n*. See under ORAL HERPES. Also called **fever blister.**

co·lec·to·my (kə lek′tə mē), *n., pl.* **-mies.** the removal of all or part of the colon or large intestine.

col·ic (kol′ik), *n*. **1.** paroxysmal pain in the abdomen or bowels. **2.** a condition in young infants characterized by loud and prolonged crying, for which no physiological or other cause has been found. —*adj.* **3.** pertaining to or affecting the colon or the bowels. —**col′icky**, *adj*.

col·i·form (kol′ə fôrm′, kō′lə-), *adj*. of or pertaining to any of several bacilli, esp. *Escherichia coli* and members of the genus *Aerobacter*, that are normally present in the colon and that indicate fecal contamination when found in a water supply.

col·i·phage (kol′ə fāj′), *n*. any bacteriophage that specifically infects the *Escherichia coli* bacterium.

co·lis·tin (kə lis′tin), *n*. a broad-spectrum antibiotic derived from the soil bacterium *Bacillus colistinus*, used esp. for treating gastroenteritis.

co·li·tis (kə lī′tis, kō-), *n*. inflammation of the colon. —**co·lit′ic** (-lit′ik), *adj*.

col·la·gen (kol′ə jən), *n*. a strongly fibrous protein that is abundant in bone, tendons, cartilage, and connective tissue, yielding gelatin when denatured by boiling. —**col·lag·e·nous** (kə laj′ə nəs), *adj*.

col·lapse (kə laps′), *v.i.*, **-lapsed, -laps·ing. 1.** to fall unconscious or fall down, as from a heart attack or exhaustion. **2.** (of lungs) to come into an airless state. —**col·laps'i·ble,** *adj.*

col'lar·bone', *n.* the clavicle.

collat'eral circula'tion, *n.* circulation of blood through a network of minor vessels that become enlarged and joined with adjacent vessels when a major vein or artery is impaired, as by obstruction.

collec'tive uncon'scious, *n.* (in Jungian psychology) inborn unconscious psychic material common to humankind, accumulated by the experience of all preceding generations. Compare ARCHETYPE.

col·loid (kol'oid), *n.* **1.** a substance made up of a system of particles with linear dimensions in the range of about 10^{-7} to 5×10^{-5} cm dispersed in a continuous gaseous, liquid, or solid medium. **2.** a colloidal substance in the body, as a stored secretion.

col·loi·dal (kə loid'l), *adj.* pertaining to or of the nature of a colloid: *colloidal gold and silver.*

col·lyr·i·um (kə lēr'ē əm), *n., pl.* **-i·a** (-ē ə), **-i·ums.** EYEWASH.

co·lon (kō'lən), *n., pl.* **-lons, -la** (-lə). the part of the large intestine extending from the cecum to the rectum.

co·lon·ic (kō lon'ik, kə-), *n.* an enema.

col·o·ny (kol'ə nē), *n., pl.* **-nies.** an aggregation of bacteria growing together as the descendants of a single cell.

col'or-blind', *adj.* **1.** unable to distinguish one or more chromatic colors. **2.** unable to distinguish colors, seeing only shades of gray, black, and white. —**col'or blind'·ness,** *n.*

co·los·to·my (kə los'tə mē), *n., pl.* **-mies. 1.** the surgical construction of an artificial opening from the colon to the outside of the body, permitting passage of intestinal contents. **2.** the opening so constructed.

co·los·trum (kə los'trəm), *n.* a yellow fluid rich in protein and immune factors, secreted by the mammary glands during the first few days of lactation.

col·pi·tis (kol pī'tis), *n.* VAGINITIS.

col·po·da (kol pō'də), *n., pl.* **-das.** any ciliated protozoan of the genus *Colpoda,* common in fresh water.

col·po·scope (kol'pə skōp'), *n.* a magnifying instrument used for examining the vagina and cervix, esp. to detect cancer cells. —**col'po·scop'ic** (-skop'ik), *adj.* —**col·pos'·co·py** (-pos'kə pē), *n., pl.* **-pies.**

co·ma (kō'mə), *n., pl.* **-mas.** a state of prolonged unconsciousness, including a lack of response to stimuli.

com·a·tose (kom'ə tōs', kō'mə-), *adj.* affected with or characterized by coma. —**com'a·tose'ly,** *adv.*

com'bat fatigue', *n.* BATTLE FATIGUE.

com·e·do (kom'i dō'), *n., pl.* **com·e·dos, com·e·do·nes** (kom'i dō'nēz). BLACKHEAD.

com'mon cold', *n.* COLD.

com·mu·ni·ca·ble (kə myōō'ni kə bəl), *adj.* capable of being easily communicated or transmitted: *a communica-*

ble disease. **—com·mu′ni·ca·bil′i·ty, com·mu′ni·ca·ble·ness,** n. **—com·mu′ni·ca·bly,** adv.

com·pat·i·ble (kəm pat′ə bəl), adj. able to be mixed or blended without rejection, antagonism, etc.: compatible blood; compatible drugs. **—com·pat′i·bil′i·ty,** n.

com·pen·sate (kom′pən sāt′), v.i., **-sat·ed, -sat·ing.** to develop or employ mechanisms of psychological compensation. **—com′pen·sa′tor,** n. **—com·pen·sa·to·ry** (kəm-pen′sə tôr′ē, -tōr′ē), **com·pen·sa·tive** (kom′pən sā′tiv, kəm pen′sə-), adj.

com′pen·sa′tion, n. **1.** the improvement of any defect by the excessive development or action of another part of the same structure. **2.** a psychological mechanism by which an individual attempts to make up for some personal deficiency by developing or stressing another aspect of personality or ability. **—com′pen·sa′tion·al,** adj.

com·pe·tence (kom′pi təns), n. the sum total of possible developmental responses of any group of blastematic cells under varied external conditions.

com·ple·ment (kom′plə mənt), n. **1.** a set of about 20 proteins that circulate in the blood and react in various combinations to promote the destruction of any cell displaying foreign surfaces or immune complexes. **2.** any of the proteins in the complement system, designated C1, C2, etc.

com·ple·men·ta·ry (kom′plə men′tə rē, -trē), adj. designating or consisting of a strand of DNA or RNA that can serve as a template for another strand. **—com′ple·men′ta·ri·ness,** n.

com′plement fixa′tion, n. the binding of complement to immune complexes or to certain foreign surfaces, as those of invading microorganisms.

complete′ blood′ count′, n. a diagnostic test that determines the exact numbers of each type of blood cell in a fixed quantity of blood.

com·plex (kom′pleks), n. **1.** a cluster of interrelated, emotion-charged ideas, desires, and impulses that may be wholly or partly suppressed but influence attitudes, associations, and behavior. **2.** an entity composed of molecules in which the constituents maintain much of their chemical identity: a receptor-hormone complex. **—com·plex′ly,** adv. **—com·plex′ness,** n.

com·plex·ion (kəm plek′shən), n. the natural color, texture, and appearance of the skin, esp. of the face.

com·pli·ca·tion (kom′pli kā′shən), n. a concurrent disease, accident, or adverse reaction that aggravates the original disease. **—com′pli·ca·tive,** adj.

com′pound frac′ture, n. a fracture in which the broken bone is exposed through a wound in the skin.

compound Q, trichosanthin: an antiviral drug derived from the root of a Chinese cucumber plant, used in the treatment of AIDS.

com·press (kom′pres), n. a soft pad or cloth held or secured on the body to provide pressure or to supply moisture, cold, heat, or medication.

com·pro·mised (kom′prə mizd′), *adj.* unable to function optimally, esp. with regard to immune response, owing to underlying disease, harmful environmental exposure, or the side effects of a course of treatment.

com·pul·sion (kəm pul′shən), *n.* a strong, usu. irresistible impulse to perform an act, esp. one that is irrational or contrary to one's will.

com·pul·sive (-siv), *adj.* **1.** characterized by perfectionism, rigidity, conscientiousness, and an obsessive concern with order and detail. —*n.* **2.** a compulsive person. —**com·pul′sive·ly**, *adv.* —**com·pul′sive·ness**, *n.*

comput′er-assist′ed tomog′raphy, *n.* COMPUTERIZED AXIAL TOMOGRAPHY.

comput′erized ax′ial tomog′raphy, *n.* the process of producing a CAT scan. Compare CAT SCANNER.

co·na·tion (kō nā′shən), *n.* the aspect of mental life having to do with purposive behavior, including desiring, resolving, and striving. —**con·a·tive** (kon′ə tiv, kō′nə-), *adj.*

con·cep·tus (kən sep′təs), *n., pl.* **-tus·es.** an embryo or fetus and all its associated membranes.

con·cord·ance (kon kôr′dns, kən-), *n.* (in genetic studies) the degree of similarity in a pair of twins with respect to the presence or absence of a particular disease or trait.

con·cres·cence (kon kres′əns, kən-), *n.* a growing together, as of tissue or embryonic parts. —**con·cres′cent**, *adj.*

con·cre·tion (kon krē′shən, kong-), *n.* a solid or calcified mass in the body formed by a disease process. —**con·cre′tion·ar·y**, *adj.*

con·cus·sion (kən kush′ən), *n.* injury to the brain or spinal cord due to jarring from a blow, fall, or the like. —**con·cus′sive**, *adj.*

con·di·tion (kən dish′ən), *n.* **1.** state of health: *a patient in critical condition.* **2.** an abnormal or diseased state of part of the body: *a heart condition; a skin condition.* —*v.t.* **3.** to establish a conditioned response in (a subject).

condi′tioned response′, *n. Psychol.* a response that becomes associated with a previously unrelated stimulus as a result of pairing the stimulus with another stimulus normally yielding the response. Also called **condi′tioned re′flex.**

con·di·tion·ing, *n.* **1.** a process of changing behavior by rewarding or punishing a subject each time an action is performed. **2.** Also called **classical conditioning.** a process in which a previously neutral stimulus comes to evoke a specific response by being repeatedly paired with another stimulus that evokes the response.

con·dom (kon′dəm, kun′-), *n.* a thin sheath, usu. of rubber, worn over the penis during sexual intercourse to prevent conception or sexually transmitted disease.

con·duc·tion (kən duk′shən), *n.* the carrying of sound

waves, electrons, heat, or nerve impulses by a nerve or other tissue. —**con·duc′tion·al,** adj.

con·dy·lo·ma (kon/dl ō′mə), n., pl. **-mas, -ma·ta** (-mə·tə). a wartlike growth on the skin, usu. in the region of the anus or genitals. —**con′dy·lom′a·tous** (-om′ə təs, -ō′mə-), adj.

cone (kōn), n. one of the cone-shaped cells in the retina of the eye, sensitive to bright light and color. Compare ROD.

con·fab·u·late (kən fab′yə lāt′), v.i., **-lat·ed, -lat·ing.** Psychiatry. to fill a gap in memory with a falsification that the falsifier believes to be true. —**con·fab′u·la′tion,** n. —**con·fab′u·la′tor,** n.

con·fec·tion (kən fek′shən), n. a medicinal preparation made with sugar, honey, or syrup.

con·fig·u·ra·tion (kən fig/yə rā′shən), n. GESTALT. —**con·fig′u·ra′tion·al, con·fig′u·ra·tive** (-yər ə tiv, -yə rā′tiv), adj. —**con·fig′u·ra′tion·al·ly,** adv.

con·flict (kon′flikt), n. a mental struggle arising from opposing demands or impulses.

cong., gallon. [Latin congius]

con·gen·i·tal (kən jen′i tl), adj. present or existing at the time of birth: a congenital abnormality. —**con·gen′i·tal·ly,** adv.

con·gest (kən jest′), v.t. to cause an unnatural accumulation of mucus, blood, or other fluid in (a body part or blood vessel). —**con·gest′i·ble,** adj. —**con·ges′tive,** adj.

con·ges·tion (kən jes′chən), n. clogging in a duct, blood vessel, or other body part due to an accumulation of fluid, mucus, etc.: nasal congestion.

conges′tive heart′ fail′ure, n. HEART FAILURE (def. 2).

con·gi·us (kon′jē əs), n., pl. **-gi·i** (-jē ī′) (in prescriptions) a gallon (3.7853 liters).

con·ju·gant (kon′jə gənt), n. either of two organisms participating in the process of conjugation.

con′ju·gate′ (-gāt′), v.i., **-gat·ed, -gat·ing.** Biol. to unite; to undergo conjugation. —**con′ju·ga·ble** (-gə bəl), adj. —**con′ju·ga·bly,** adv. —**con′ju·ga′tive,** adj. —**con′ju·ga′tor,** n.

con′jugated pro′tein, n. a complex protein, as a lipoprotein, combining amino acids with other substances.

con′ju·ga′tion, n. **1.** (in bacteria, protozoans, etc.) the temporary fusion of two organisms with an exchange of nuclear material. **2.** (in certain algae and fungi) the fusion of a male and female gamete as a form of sexual reproduction.

con·junc·ti·va (kon/jungk ti′və), n., pl. **-vas, -vae** (-vē). the mucous membrane that covers the exposed portion of the eyeball and lines the inner surface of the eyelids.

con·junc·ti·vi·tis (kən jungk/tə vi′tis), n. inflammation of the conjunctiva.

connec′tive tis′sue, n. a kind of tissue, usu. of mesoblastic origin, that connects, supports, or surrounds other tissues and organs, including tendons, bone, cartilage, and fatty tissue.

con·san·guin·e·ous (kon/sang gwin/ē əs) also **con·san/guine** (-gwin), *adj.* having the same ancestry or descent; related by blood. —**con/san·guin/e·ous·ly,** *adv.*

con/san·guin/i·ty, *n.* **1.** relationship by descent from a common ancestor; kinship. **2.** close relationship or connection.

con·scious (kon/shəs), *n.* **the conscious,** *Psychoanal.* the part of the mind comprising psychic material of which the individual is aware.

con/scious·ness, *n.* the mental activity of which a person is aware, as contrasted with unconscious mental processes.

con/scious·ness-rais/ing, *n.* the process of learning to recognize, esp. through group discussion, one's own needs, goals, and problems or those of a group to which one or someone else belongs.

con·sen·su·al (kən sen/shōō əl), *adj.* involuntarily correlative with a voluntary action, as the contraction of the iris when the eye is opened. —**con·sen/su·al·ly,** *adv.*

con·sol·i·da·tion (kən sol/i dā/shən), *n.* the process of becoming solid, as the changing of lung tissue from aerated and elastic to firm in certain diseases. —**con·sol/i·da/tive,** *adj.*

con·sti·pa·tion (kon/stə pā/shən), *n.* a condition of the bowels in which the feces are dry and hardened and evacuation is difficult and infrequent.

con·sti·tu·tion (kon/sti tōō/shən, -tyōō/-), *n.* the aggregate of a person's physical and psychological characteristics.

con·sump·tion (kən sump/shən), *n.* **1.** *Older Use.* tuberculosis of the lungs. **2.** progressive wasting of the body.

con·sump/tive (-tiv), *n. Older Use.* a person suffering from tuberculosis.

con·tact (kon/takt), *n.* **1.** a person who has lately been exposed to an infected person. —*adj.* **2.** involving or produced by touching or proximity: *a contact allergy.* —**con/tact·ee/,** *n.* —**con·tac/tu·al,** (-tak/chōō əl), *adj.* —**con·tac/tu·al·ly,** *adv.*

con·tac·tant (kən tak/tənt), *n.* any substance that induces an allergy on coming in contact with the skin or a mucous membrane.

con/tact lens/, *n.* either of a pair of small plastic disks that are held in place over the cornea by surface tension and correct vision defects inconspicuously.

con·ta·gion (kən tā/jən), *n.* **1.** the communication of disease by direct or indirect contact. **2.** a disease so communicated. **3.** the medium by which a contagious disease is transmitted.

con·ta/gious, *adj.* **1.** capable of being transmitted by bodily contact with an infected person or object: *contagious diseases.* **2.** carrying or spreading a contagious disease. —**con·ta/gious·ly,** *adv.* —**con·ta/gious·ness,** *n.*

con·ta′gium (-jəm, -jē əm), *n., pl.* **-gia** (-jə, -jē ə). the causative agent of a contagious or infectious disease, as a virus.

con·ti·nence (kon′tn əns) also **con′ti·nen·cy,** *n.* the ability to voluntarily control urinary and fecal discharge.

con′ti·nent, *adj.* able to control urinary and fecal discharge. —**con′ti·nent·ly,** *adv.*

con·tra·cep·tion (kon′trə sep′shən), *n.* the deliberate prevention of conception or impregnation by any of various drugs, techniques, or devices; birth control.

con′tra·cep′tive, *adj.* **1.** tending or serving to prevent conception or impregnation. **2.** pertaining to contraception. —*n.* **3.** a contraceptive device, drug, foam, etc.

con·trac·tion (kən trak′shən), *n.* the change in a muscle by which it becomes thickened and shortened. —**con·trac′tion·al,** *adj.* —**con·trac′tive** (-tiv), *adj.* —**con·trac′tive·ly,** *adv.* —**con·trac′tive·ness,** *n.*

con·trac·ture (-chər), *n.* an abnormal persistent flexing of a muscle or tendon at a joint, usu. caused by a shortening or scarring of tissue. —**con·trac′tured,** *adj.*

con·tra·in·di·cate (kon′trə in′di kāt′), *v.t.,* **-cat·ed, -cat·ing.** to make (a procedure or treatment) inadvisable: *The patient's lung congestion contraindicated general anesthesia.* —**con′tra·in·di·cant** (-kənt), *n.* —**con′tra·in·di·ca′tion,** *n.*

con′trast me′dium, *n.* a radiopaque substance introduced into a part of the body to produce a contrasting background for the tissues in an x-ray examination.

con·tre·coup (kon′trə kōō′), *n.* an injury of one point of an organ or part resulting from a blow on the opposite point.

con·trol (kən trōl′), *v.,* **-trolled, -trol·ling.** *n.* —*v.t.* **1.** to test or verify (a scientific experiment) by a parallel experiment or other standard of comparison. —*n.* **2.** a standard of comparison in scientific experimentation. **3.** a person or subject that serves in such a comparison. —**con·trol′la·ble,** *adj.*

control′ group′, *n.* (in an experiment or clinical trial) a group that closely resembles an experimental group but does not receive the active medication or factor under study, thereby serving as a comparison for evaluation of results.

controlled′ exper′iment, *n.* an experiment in which the variables are controlled so that the effects of varying one factor at a time may be observed.

controlled′-release′, *adj.* (of a substance) released or activated at predetermined intervals or gradually over a period of time.

controlled′ sub′stance, *n.* any of a category of behavior-altering or addictive drugs, as heroin or cocaine, whose possession and use are restricted by law.

con·tuse (kən tōōz′, -tyōōz′), *v.t.,* **-tused, -tus·ing.** to injure (tissue), esp. without breaking the skin; bruise. —**con·tu′sive** (-tōō′siv, -tyōō′-), *adj.*

con·tu'sion (-zhən), *n.* an injury to the subsurface tissue without the skin being broken; bruise. —**con·tu'sioned,** *adj.*

con·va·lesce (kon'və les'), *v.i.,* **-lesced, -lesc·ing.** to recover health and strength after illness.

con·va·les'cence, *n.* **1.** the gradual recovery of health and strength after illness. **2.** the period during which one is convalescing.

con·va·les'cent, *adj.* **1.** convalescing. **2.** of or pertaining to convalescence or convalescing persons. —*n.* **3.** a person who is convalescing.

con·ver'gence (kən vûr'jəns), *n.* a coordinated turning of the eyes to bear upon a near point. Also, **con·ver'gen·cy.**

con·ver'sion (kən vûr'zhən, -shən), *n. Psychoanal.* the process by which a repressed psychic event, idea, feeling, memory, or impulse is represented by a bodily change or symptom. —**con·ver'sion·al, con·ver'sion·ar'y** (-zhə-ner'ē, -shə-), *adj.*

con'voluted tu'bule (tōō'byōōl, tyōō'-), *n.* the portion of a kidney nephron that concentrates urine and maintains salt and water balance.

con·vo·lu'tion (kon'və lōō'shən), *n.* one of the sinuous folds or ridges of the surface of the brain.

con·vul'sant (kən vul'sənt), *adj.* **1.** causing convulsions; convulsive. —*n.* **2.** a convulsant agent.

con·vulse (kən vuls'), *v.t.,* **-vulsed, -vuls·ing.** to cause to suffer violent, spasmodic contractions of the muscles. —**con·vuls'ed·ly,** *adv.*

con·vul'sion (-vul'shən), *n.* contortion of the body caused by violent, involuntary muscular contractions. —**con·vul'sive** (-siv), *adj.*

con·vul'sion·ar'y (-shə ner'ē), *adj.* of or affected with convulsions.

Coo'ley's ane'mia (kōō'lēz), *n.* THALASSEMIA.

COPD, chronic obstructive pulmonary disease.

cop·ro·phil·i·a (kop'rə fil'ē ə), *n. Psychiatry.* an obsessive interest in feces. —**cop'ro·phil'i·ac,** *n.* —**cop'ro·phil'ic,** *adj.* —**co·proph·i·lism** (kə prof'ə liz'əm), *n.*

cop·u·late (kop'yə lāt'), *v.i.,* **-lat·ed, -lat·ing.** to engage in sexual intercourse. —**cop'u·la'tion,** *n.*

cor·don sa·ni·taire (Fr. kôr dôn sa nē ter'), *n., pl.* **cordons sa·ni·taires** (Fr. kôr dôn sa nē ter'). a line around a quarantined area guarded to prevent the spread of a disease by restricting passage into or out of the area.

co·ri·um (kôr'ē əm, kōr'-), *n., pl.* **co·ri·a** (kôr'ē ə, kōr'-). DERMIS.

corn (kôrn), *n.* a horny growth of tissue with a tender core, formed over a bone, esp. on the toes, as a result of pressure or friction.

cor·ne·a (kôr'nē ə), *n., pl.* **-ne·as.** the transparent anterior part of the external coat of the eye covering the iris and the pupil and continuous with the sclera. —**cor'ne·al,** *adj.*

cor·ni·fi·ca·tion (kôr′nə fi kā′shən), *n.* the formation of a horny layer of skin, or horny skin structures, as hair, nails, or scales, from squamous epithelial cells.

corn′ sug′ar, *n.* DEXTROSE.

cor·o·nar·y (kôr′ə ner′ē, kor′-), *adj., n., pl.* **-nar·ies.** —*adj.* **1.** of or pertaining to the heart. **2. a.** pertaining to the coronary arteries. **b.** encircling like a crown, as certain blood vessels. —*n.* **3.** a heart attack, esp. a coronary thrombosis. **4.** a coronary artery.

cor′onary ar′tery, *n.* either of two arteries that originate in the aorta and supply the heart muscle with blood.

cor′onary by′pass, *n.* the surgical revascularization of the heart, using healthy blood vessels of the patient, performed to circumvent obstructed coronary vessels.

cor′onary-care′ u′nit, *n.* a specialized hospital unit for the early care and treatment of heart-attack patients. *Abbr.:* CCU

cor′onary occlu′sion, *n.* partial or total obstruction of a coronary artery.

cor′onary si′nus, *n.* a large venous channel in the heart wall that receives blood via the coronary veins and empties into the right atrium.

cor′onary thrombo′sis, *n.* a coronary occlusion in which there is blockage of a coronary arterial branch by a blood clot within the vessel.

cor′onary vein′, *n.* any of several veins that receive blood from the heart wall and empty into the coronary sinus.

co·ro·na·vi·rus (kə rō′nə vī′rəs), *n., pl.* **-rus·es.** any of various RNA-containing spherical viruses of the family Coronaviridae, including several that cause acute respiratory illnesses.

cor·o·ner (kôr′ə nər, kor′-), *n.* an officer, as of a county or municipality, whose chief function is to investigate by inquest, as before a jury, any death not clearly resulting from natural causes. —**cor′o·ner·ship′,** *n.*

cor·pus (kôr′pəs), *n., pl.* **-po·ra** (-pər ə). the body of a person or animal, esp. when dead.

cor′pus cal·lo′sum (kə lō′səm), *n., pl.* **cor·po·ra cal·lo·sa** (kə lō′sə). the thick band of transverse nerve fibers between the two halves of the cerebrum in placental mammals.

cor′pus lu′te·um (lōō′tē əm), *n., pl.* **cor·po·ra lu·te·a** (lōō′tē ə). a yellowish structure that develops in the ovary on the site where an ovum is released and that secretes progesterone if fertilization occurs.

cor′pus stri·a′tum (strī ā′təm), *n., pl.* **cor·po·ra stri·a·ta** (strī ā′tə). a mass of banded gray and white matter in front of the thalamus in each cerebral hemisphere.

cor·tex (kôr′teks), *n., pl.* **-ti·ces** (-tə sēz′). **1.** the outer region of a body organ or structure, as the outer portion of the kidney. **2.** CEREBRAL CORTEX.

cor·ti·cal (-ti kəl), *adj.* resulting from the function or condition of the cerebral cortex. —**cor′ti·cal·ly,** *adv.*

cor·ti·co·ster·oid (kôr′ti kō-), *n.* any of a class of steroid hormones formed in the cortex of the adrenal gland and having antiinflammatory properties. Also called **cor′ti·coid′** (-koid′).

cor·ti·cos′ter·one′ (-kos′tə rōn′, -kō stə rōn′), *n.* a corticosteroid that is involved in water and electrolyte balance.

cor·ti·co·tro′pin (-kō trō′pin), *n.* See ACTH.

corticotro′pin releas′ing fac′tor, *n.* a hormonelike substance of the hypothalamus that increases the production of ACTH in response to stress. *Abbr.:* CRF

cor·ti·sol (-sôl′, -sōl′), *n.* one of several steroid hormones produced by the adrenal cortex and resembling cortisone in its action.

cor·ti·sone (-zōn′, -sōn′), *n.* a corticosteroid, $C_{21}H_{28}O_5$, used chiefly in the treatment of autoimmune and inflammatory diseases and certain cancers.

co·ry·za (kə rī′zə), *n.* acute nasal congestion due to secretion of mucus; cold in the head. —**co·ry′zal,** *adj.*

cos·met·ic (koz met′ik), *adj.* serving to impart or improve beauty, esp. of the face: *cosmetic surgery.* —**cos·met′i·cal·ly,** *adv.*

cos·tive (kos′tiv, kô′stiv), *adj.* affected with or causing constipation. —**cos′tive·ly,** *adv.* —**cos′tive·ness,** *n.*

cough′ drop′, *n.* a small medicinal lozenge for relieving a cough, sore throat, hoarseness, etc.

cough′ syr′up, *n.* a medicated, syruplike fluid, usu. flavored and nonnarcotic or mildly narcotic, for relieving coughs or soothing irritated throats. Also called **cough′ med′icine.**

Cou·ma·din (kōō′mə din), *Trademark.* a brand name for warfarin.

coun·sel·ing (koun′sə ling), *n.* professional guidance in resolving personal conflicts and emotional problems.

coun·ter·con·di′tion·ing (koun′tər-), *n.* the extinction of an undesirable response to a stimulus through the introduction of a more desirable, often incompatible, response.

coun·ter·ir′ri·tant, *n.* **1.** an agent for producing inflammation in superficial tissues to relieve pain or inflammation in deeper structures. —*adj.* **2.** of or acting as a counterirritant.

coun′ter·stain′, *n.* **1.** a second stain applied to a microscopic specimen for contrast. —*v.t.* **2.** to treat (a microscopic specimen) with a counterstain. —*v.i.* **3.** to become counterstained; take a counterstain.

court′ plas′ter, *n.* a fine fabric coated with an adhesive preparation of isinglass or glycerin, formerly used for medicinal and cosmetic purposes.

Cow′per's gland′ (kou′pərz, kōō′-), *n.* either of two small glands that secrete a mucous substance onto the male urethra during sexual excitement.

cow·pox′, *n.* a mild disease of cattle, now rare, characterized by a pustular rash on the teats and udder, caused by a poxvirus that was formerly used for smallpox vaccinations.

cox·a (kok′sə), *n., pl.* **cox·ae** (kok′sē). **1.** INNOMINATE BONE. **2.** the joint of the hip. —**cox′al,** *adj.*

cox·al·gi·a (kok sal′jē ə, -jə) also **cox′al·gy,** *n.* pain in the hip. —**cox·al′gic,** *adj.*

cox·sack·ie vi′rus or **Cox·sack′ie vi′rus** (kok sak′ē-, kōōk sä′kē-), *n., pl.* **-rus·es.** any of a group of enteroviruses that may infect the intestinal tract, esp. in the summer months.

CPR, cardiopulmonary resuscitation.

crab (krab), *n.* **1.** CRAB LOUSE. **2. crabs,** PEDICULOSIS.

crab′ louse′, *n.* a crablike louse, *Phthirus pubis,* that infests pubic hair and other body hair in humans.

crack (krak), *n.* highly addictive, purified cocaine in the form of pellets prepared for smoking.

cra·dle (krād′l), *n.* a frame that prevents the bedclothes from touching an injured part of a bedridden patient.

cra′dle cap′, *n.* an inflammation of the scalp, occurring in infants and characterized by greasy, yellowish scales.

cramp (kramp), *n.* **1.** Often, **cramps. a.** an involuntary, usu. painful contraction or spasm of a muscle or muscles. **b.** a painful contraction of involuntary muscle in the wall of the abdomen, uterus, or other organ. —*v.t.* **2.** to affect with or as if with a cramp.

cra·ni·al (krā′nē əl), *adj.* of or pertaining to the cranium or skull.

cra′nial in′dex, *n.* CEPHALIC INDEX.

cra′nial nerve′, *n.* any of the paired nerves arising from the brainstem and reaching the periphery through skull openings.

cra·ni·ol·o·gy (-ol′ə jē), *n.* a science that deals with the size, shape, and other characteristics of human skulls. —**cra·ni·o·log′i·cal** (-ə loj′i kəl), *adj.* —**cra·ni·o·log′i·cal·ly,** *adv.* —**cra·ni·ol′o·gist,** *n.*

cra·ni·om′e·ter (-om′i tər), *n.* an instrument for measuring external dimensions of skulls.

cra·ni·om′e·try, *n.* the science of measuring skulls, chiefly to determine their characteristic relationship to sex, body type, or genetic population. —**cra·ni·o·met′ric** (-ə me′trik), **cra·ni·o·met′ri·cal,** *adj.* —**cra·ni·o·met′ri·cal·ly,** *adv.* —**cra·ni·om′e·trist,** *n.*

cra·ni·o·sa′cral (-ō sā′krəl, -sak′rəl), *adj.* parasympathetic.

cra·ni·ot′o·my (-ot′ə mē), *n., pl.* **-mies.** the surgical opening of the skull, usu. for operations on the brain.

cra·ni·um (-əm), *n., pl.* **-ni·ums, -ni·a** (-nē ə). **1.** the skull of a vertebrate. **2.** the part of the skull that encloses the brain.

crash (krash), *v.i. Slang.* to experience unpleasant sensations, as sudden exhaustion or depression, when a drug, esp. an amphetamine, wears off.

C-re·ac′tive protein (sē′rē ak′tiv), *n.* a globulin that increases in concentration in the bloodstream during infectious states and other abnormal conditions. *Abbr.:* CRP

cre·a·tine (krē′ə tēn′, -tin), *n.* an amino acid, $C_4H_9N_3O_2$, that is a constituent of the muscles of vertebrates and is phosphorylated to store energy used for muscular contraction.

cre′atine phos′phate, *n.* PHOSPHOCREATINE.

cre·tin·ism (krēt′n iz′əm; *esp. Brit.* kret′-), *n.* a congenital deficiency of thyroid secretion, resulting in stunted growth, deformity, and mental retardation.

Creutz′feldt-Ja′kob disease′ (kroits′felt yä′kôp), *n.* a rare, normally fatal degenerative disease of the human brain that resembles scrapie in sheep.

CRF, corticotropin releasing factor.

crib′ death′, *n.* SUDDEN INFANT DEATH SYNDROME.

crick (krik), *n.* **1.** a sharp, painful spasm of the muscles, as of the neck or back. —*v.t.* **2.** to give a crick or wrench to (the neck, back, etc.).

cri·sis (krī′sis), *n., pl.* **-ses** (-sēz). **1.** the point in the course of a serious disease at which a decisive change occurs, leading either to recovery or to death. **2.** the change itself.

crit·i·cal (krit′i kəl), *adj.* (of a patient's condition) having unstable and abnormal vital signs and one or more unfavorable indicators. —**crit′i·cal·ly,** *adv.*

Crohn′s′ disease′ (krōnz), *n.* a chronic inflammatory bowel disease that causes scarring and thickening of the intestinal walls and frequently leads to obstruction. Also called **ileitis.**

cross′-eye′, *n.* strabismus, esp. the form in which one or both eyes turn inward. —**cross′-eyed′,** *adj.*

cross′-fer′tile, *adj.* capable of cross-fertilization.

cross′-fertiliza′tion, *n.* the fertilization of an organism by the fusion of an egg from one individual with a sperm or male gamete from a different individual. —**cross′-fer′tilize,** *v.i., v.t.,* **-lized, -liz·ing.**

cross′ing o′ver, *n.* the exchange of segments of chromatids between pairs of chromosomes during meiosis, resulting in a recombination of linked genes.

cross′ match′ing, *n.* the testing for compatibility of a donor's and a recipient's blood prior to transfusion, in which serum of each is mixed with red blood cells of the other and observed for hemagglutination.

cross′o′ver, *n.* **1.** *Genetics.* CROSSING OVER **2.** a genotype resulting from crossing over.

cross′-ster′ile, *adj.* incapable of reproducing due to hybridization. —**cross′-steril′i·ty,** *n.*

cross′-tol′erance, *n.* resistance or low reaction to the effects of a drug, poison, etc., because of tolerance to a pharmacologically similar substance.

cro′ton oil′ (krōt′n), *n.* an oil, expressed from the seeds of the croton, *Croton tiglium,* that is a drastic purgative and counterirritant.

croup (krōōp), *n.* any condition of the larynx or trachea characterized by a hoarse cough and difficult breathing. —**croup′y,** *adj.,* **-i·er, -i·est.**

CRP, C-reactive protein.

crutch (kruch), *n.* a staff or support to assist a lame or infirm person in walking, usu. having a crosspiece at one end to fit under the armpit.

cry·o·bi·ol·o·gy (krī′ō-), *n.* the study of the effects of low temperatures on living organisms and biological systems. —**cry·o·bi·o·log′i·cal,** *adj.* —**cry·o·bi·ol′o·gist,** *n.*

cry·o·gen·ic (krī′ə jen′ik), *adj.* **1.** of or pertaining to the production or use of extremely low temperatures. **2.** of or pertaining to cryogenics. —**cry·o·gen′i·cal·ly,** *adv.* —**cry·og′e·nist** (-oj′ə nist), *n.*

cry·o·gen·ics, *n.* (*used with a sing. v.*) the scientific study of extremely low temperatures.

cry·on·ics (krī on′iks), *n.* (*used with a sing. v.*) the deep-freezing of human bodies at death for preservation and possible revival in the future. —**cry·on′ic,** *adj.*

cry·o·probe (krī′ə prōb′), *n.* an instrument used in cryo-surgery, having a supercooled tip for applying extreme cold to diseased tissue in order to remove or destroy it.

cry′o·scope (-skōp′), *n.* an instrument for determining the freezing point of a liquid or solution.

cry·os′co·py (-os′kə pē), *n.* the determination of the freezing points of certain bodily fluids, as urine, for diagnosis. —**cry′o·scop′ic** (-ə skop′ik), *adj.*

cry·o·sur·ger·y (krī′ō-), *n.* the use of extreme cold to destroy tissue for therapeutic purposes. —**cry·o·sur′gi·cal,** *adj.*

cry·o·ther·a·py, *n.* medical treatment by means of applications of cold.

crypt·es·the·sia (krip′təs thē′zhə, -zhē ə, -zē ə), *n.* paranormal perception.

cryp·to·coc·co·sis (krip′tō ko kō′sis), *n.* a disease caused by the fungus *Cryptococcus neoformans,* characterized by lesions, esp. of the nervous system and lungs.

cryp·tor·chi·dism (krip tôr′ki diz′əm) also **cryp·tor·chism** (-kiz əm), *n.* failure of one or both testes to descend into the scrotum. —**cryp·tor′chid,** *adj.*

crys·tal (kris′tl), *n. Slang.* any stimulant drug in solid form, as methamphetamine.

crys′talline lens′, *n.* see LENS.

C-sec·tion (sē′sek′shən), *n. Informal.* CESAREAN.

CSF, cerebrospinal fluid.

CT scan, *n.* CAT SCAN.

CT scanner, *n.* CAT SCANNER.

cu·bi·tal (kyōō′bi tl), *adj.* pertaining to, involving, or situated near the forearm.

cu′bi·tus (-təs), *n., pl.* **-ti** (-tī′). the forearm.

cu′boid (-boid), *adj.* **1.** Also, **cu·boi′dal.** of or pertaining to the tarsal bone above the fourth metatarsal in mammals. —*n.* **2.** the cuboid bone.

cue (kyōō), *n.* a sensory signal that serves to elicit a behavioral response.

cuff (kuf), *n.* an inflatable wrap placed around the upper arm and used in conjunction with a device for recording blood pressure.

cul-de-sac (kul/də sak/, -sak/, kōōl/-), n., pl. **culs-de-sac.** a saclike anatomical cavity or tube open at only one end, as the cecum.

cul·ture (kul/chər), n. **1.** the cultivation of microorganisms, as bacteria, or of tissues, for scientific study, medicinal use, etc. **2.** the product or growth resulting from such cultivation.

cul/ture me/dium, n. MEDIUM.

cun·ni·lin·gus (kun/l ing/gəs) also **cun/ni·linc/tus** (-ingk/təs), n. oral stimulation of the female genitals, esp. to orgasm.

cup·ping (kup/ing), n. the process of drawing blood to the surface of the body by the application of a cupping glass, as for relieving internal congestion.

cup/ping glass/, n. a glass vessel, used in cupping, in which a partial vacuum is created, as by heat.

cu·ra·re or **cu·ra·ri** (kyōō rär/ē, kōō-), n. a blackish, resinlike substance derived chiefly from tropical plants belonging to the genus *Strychnos*, of the logania family, esp. *S. toxifera*, forms of which are used to relax or paralyze muscles.

cu·ra/rize, v.t., **-rized, -riz·ing.** to administer curare to. —**cu·ra/ri·za/tion,** n.

cure (kyōōr), n., v., **cured, cur·ing.** —n. **1.** a means of healing or restoring to health; remedy. **2.** a method or course of remedial treatment, as for disease. **3.** successful remedial treatment; restoration to health. —v.t. **4.** to restore to health.

cu·ret·tage (kyōōr/i täzh/, kyōō ret/ij), n. the process of curetting. Compare D AND C.

cu·rette or **cu·ret** (kyōō ret/), n., v., **-ret·ted, -ret·ting.** —n. **1.** a scoop-shaped surgical instrument for removing tissue from body cavities, as the uterus. —v.t. **2.** to scrape with a curette.

cu·rie (kyōōr/ē, kyōō rē/), n. a unit of activity of radioactive substances equivalent to 3.70×10^{10} disintegrations per second. *Abbr.:* Ci

Cush/ing's disease/ (kōōsh/ingz), n. a disorder of metabolism caused by overproduction of the hormone ACTH, resulting in hypertension, striated skin, accumulations of fat on the face and other areas, and various other disturbances.

cu·ta·ne·ous (kyōō tā/nē əs), adj. of, pertaining to, or affecting the skin. —**cu·ta/ne·ous·ly,** adv.

cut/down/, n. the incision of a superficial vein in order to insert a catheter.

cu·ti·cle (kyōō/ti kəl), n. **1.** the hardened skin that surrounds the edges of a fingernail or toenail. **2.** the epidermis. —**cu·tic/u·lar** (-tik/yə lər), adj.

CVA, cerebrovascular accident. STROKE.

CVS, chorionic villus sampling.

cy·a·nide (si/ə nid/, -nid) also **cy/a·nid** (-nid), n. a salt of hydrocyanic acid, as potassium cyanide, KCN.

cy·a·no·co·bal·a·min (si′ə nō kō bal′ə min, si an′ō-), *n.*
VITAMIN B$_{12}$.

cy·a·no′sis (-sis), *n.* blueness or lividness of the skin,
caused by a deficiency of oxygen or defective hemoglobin
in the blood. —**cy′a·not′ic** (-not′ik), *adj.*

cy·ber·net·ics (si′bər net′iks), *n. (used with a sing. v.)*
the comparative study of organic control and communication systems, as the brain and its neurons, and mechanical
or electronic systems analogous to them, as robots or
computers. —**cy′ber·net′ic**, *adj.* —**cy′ber·net′i·cist** (-ə-
sist), *n.*

cy·clic (si′klik, sik′lik), *adj.* of or pertaining to a chemical
compound containing a closed chain or ring of atoms.
—**cy·clic′i·ty** (-klis′i tē), *n.*

cyclic AMP, *n.* a small molecule, a cyclic anhydride of
AMP, that activates enzymes, amplifies the effects of hormones and neurotransmitters, and performs other vital
functions within the cell. Also called **cAMP.**

cyclic GMP, *n.* a small molecule, a cyclic anhydride of
GMP, that acts in cellular metabolism to increase cell division and growth. Also called **cGMP.**

cy′cloid (-kloid), *adj. Psychiatry.* of or denoting a personality type characterized by wide fluctuations in mood within
the normal range. —**cy·cloi′dal,** *adj.* —**cy·cloi′dal·ly,**
adv.

cy·clo·ple·gi·a (si′klə plē′jē ə, -jə, sik′lə-), *n.* paralysis of
the intraocular muscles. —**cy′clo·ple′gic,** *adj., n.*

cy·clo·pro·pane, *n.* a colorless, flammable gas, C$_3$H$_6$,
used in organic synthesis and as an anesthetic.

cy·clo·spo′rine (-spôr′ēn, -in, -spōr′-) also **cy·clo·
spo′rin** (-in), *n.* a product of certain soil fungi that suppresses immune reactions by disabling helper T cells, used
for minimizing rejection of transplants and for treating certain autoimmune diseases.

cy·clo·thy′mi·a (-thī′mē ə), *n.* a mild bipolar disorder
characterized by mood swings between elation and depression. —**cy′clo·thy′mic,** *adj.*

cy·mo·graph (si′mə graf′, -gräf′), *n.* KYMOGRAPH.

Cys, cysteine.

cyst (sist), *n.* **1.** any abnormal saclike growth of the body
in which matter is retained. **2.** a bladder, sac, or vesicle.
3. a protective capsule or spore surrounding an inactive or
resting organism or enclosing a reproductive body.

cys·tec·to·my (si stek′tə mē), *n., pl.* **-mies. 1.** the surgical removal of a cyst. **2.** the surgical removal of the urinary
bladder.

cys·te·ine (sis′tē ēn′, -in), *n.* a crystalline amino acid,
C$_3$H$_7$O$_2$NS, a component of nearly all proteins, obtained by
the reduction of cystine. *Abbr.:* Cys; *Symbol:* C —**cys′te·
in′ic,** *adj.*

cys′tic, *adj.* **1.** pertaining to, of the nature of, or having a
cyst or cysts; encysted. **2.** belonging or pertaining to the
urinary bladder or gallbladder.

cys·ti·cer·co·sis (sis′tə sər kō′sis), *n.* infestation with larvae of the pork or beef tapeworm that have migrated from the intestines to other body parts.

cys·ti·cer·cus (-sûr′kəs), *n., pl.* **-ci** (-sī). the larva of certain tapeworms, having the head retracted into a bladder-like structure; bladder worm.

cys·tic fibro′sis, *n.* a hereditary disease of the exocrine glands, characterized by the production of thickened mucus that chronically clogs the bronchi and pancreatic ducts, leading to breathing difficulties, infection, and fibrosis.

cys′tine (-tēn, -tin), *n.* a crystalline amino acid, $C_6H_{12}O_4N_2S_2$, occurring in most proteins, esp. the keratins.

cys·ti·tis (si stī′tis), *n.* inflammation of the urinary bladder.

cys·to·cele (sis′tə sēl′), *n.* a herniation of the urinary bladder into the vagina.

cyst′oid (-toid), *adj.* **1.** resembling a cyst. —*n.* **2.** a cyst-like structure.

cys·to·scope (sis′tə skōp′), *n.* a slender tubular instrument for visually examining and treating the interior of the urinary bladder. —**cys′to·scop′ic** (-skop′ik), *adj.* —**cys·tos·co·py** (si stos′kə pē), *n.*

cys·tos·to·my (si stos′tə mē), *n., pl.* **-mies.** the surgical construction of an artificial opening from the bladder through the abdominal wall, permitting the drainage of urine.

cy·to·chem·is·try (sī′tə-), *n.* the branch of cell biology dealing with the detection of cell constituents by means of biochemical analysis and visualization techniques. —**cy′to·chem′i·cal,** *adj.*

cy′to·chrome′ (-krōm′), *n.* any of a series of compound molecules, consisting of a protein and a porphyrin ring, that participate in cell respiration by the stepwise transfer of electrons, each cytochrome alternately accepting and releasing an electron at a lower energy level.

cy′to·ge·net·ics (sī′tō-), *n.* (*used with a sing. v.*) the branch of biology linking the study of genetic inheritance with the study of cell structure. —**cy′to·ge·net′ic, cy′to·ge·net′i·cal,** *adj.* —**cy′to·ge·net′i·cal·ly,** *adv.* —**cy′to·ge·net′i·cist,** *n.*

cy·to·ki·ne·sis, *n.* the division of the cell cytoplasm that usu. follows mitotic or meiotic division of the nucleus. —**cy′to·ki·net′ic,** *adj.*

cy·tol·y·sis (sī tol′ə sis), *n.* the dissolution or degeneration of cells. —**cy·to·lyt·ic** (sīt′l it′ik), *adj.*

cy·to·meg·a·lo·vi·rus (sī′tō meg′ə lō vī′rəs), *n., pl.* **-rus·es.** a herpesvirus that produces cytomegaly of epithelial cells, usu. mildly infectious but a cause of pneumonia in immunodeficient persons and more systemic damage in the newborn. *Abbr.:* CMV

cy′to·meg′a·ly, also **cy′to·me·ga′li·a** (-mi gā′lē ə), *n.* an abnormal enlargement of cells in the body. —**cy′to·me·gal′ic** (-mi gal′ik), *adj.*

cy·to·path·ic (sī′tə path′ik), *adj.* of, pertaining to, or characterized by a pathological change in the function or form of a cell, leading to its death.

cy′to·pe′ni·a (-pē′nē ə), *n.* the condition of having a decreased number of cellular elements in the blood.

cy′to·plasm (-plaz′əm), *n.* the cell substance between the cell membrane and the nucleus, containing the cytosol, organelles, cytoskeleton, and various particles. —**cy′to·plas′mic,** *adj.*

cy′to·plast (-plast′), *n.* the intact cytoplasmic content of a cell. —**cy′to·plas′tic,** *adj.*

cy′to·sine′ (-sēn′, -zēn′, -sin), *n.* a pyrimidine base, $C_4H_5N_3O$, that is one of the fundamental components of DNA and RNA, in which it forms a base pair with guanine. *Symbol:* C

cy′to·skel′e·ton, *n.* a shifting lattice arrangement of structural and contractile components distributed throughout the cell cytoplasm, composed of microtubules, microfilaments, and larger filaments. —**cy′to·skel′e·tal,** *adj.*

cy′to·sol′ (-sôl′, -sol′), *n.* the water-soluble components of cell cytoplasm, constituting the fluid portion that remains after removal of the organelles and other intracellular structures. —**cy′to·sol′ic** (-sol′ik), *adj.*

cy′to·some′ (-sōm′), *n.* the cytoplasmic part of a cell.

cy′to·stat′ic (-stat′ik), *adj.* **1.** inhibiting cell growth and division. —*n.* **2.** any substance that inhibits cell growth and division.

cy′to·tox·ic′i·ty (si′tō-), *n.* cell destruction caused by a cytotoxin.

cytotoxic T cell, *n.* KILLER T CELL. Also called **cytotoxic T lymphocyte.**

cy′to·tox′in (si′tə-), *n.* a substance that has a toxic effect on certain cells. —**cy′to·tox′ic,** *adj.*

cy·tot·ro·pism (si tot′rə piz′əm), *n.* the tendency of certain cells to grow or move toward or away from each other. —**cy′to·trop′ic** (-tə trop′ik, -trō′pik), *adj.*

D

D, *Symbol.* aspartic acid.

d-, *Symbol.* dextrorotatory.

dal·ton·ism (dôl′tn iz′əm), *n.* (*sometimes cap.*) color blindness, esp. the inability to distinguish red from green. —**dal·ton′ic** (-ton′ik), *adj.*

D and C, *n.* dilatation and curettage: a surgical method for the removal of diseased tissue or an early embryo from the lining of the uterus by means of scraping.

dan·druff (dan′drəf), *n.* a seborrheic scurf that forms on the scalp and comes off in small scales. —**dan′druff·y,** *adj.*

dap·sone (dap′sōn), *n.* an antibacterial substance, $C_{12}H_{12}N_2O_2S$, used to treat leprosy and certain forms of dermatitis.

dark′ adapta′tion, *n.* the reflex adjustment of the eye to dim light or darkness, consisting of a dilation of the pupil, an increase in the number of functioning rods, and a decrease in the number of functioning cones. —**dark′-a·dapt′ed,** *adj.*

Dar·von (där′von), *Trademark.* a brand of propoxyphene.

daugh·ter (dô′tər), *adj.* pertaining to a cell or other structure arising from division or replication: *daughter cell; daughter DNA.*

day′ blind′ness, *n.* HEMERALOPIA.

D.D.S., 1. Doctor of Dental Science. **2.** Doctor of Dental Surgery.

death′ ben′efit, *n.* the amount of money payable to a beneficiary upon the death of the insured.

death′ certif′icate, *n.* a certificate signed by a physician, giving information about the time, place, and cause of a person's death.

death′ in′stinct, *n. Psychoanal.* an impulse to withdraw or destroy, working in opposition to forces urging survival and creation **(life instinct).**

death′ rat′tle, *n.* a sound produced by a person immediately preceding death, resulting from the passage of air through the mucus in the throat.

death′ wish′, *n. Psychiatry.* an unconscious desire for one's own death.

de·bride·ment (di brēd′mənt, dā-), *n.* surgical removal of foreign matter and dead tissue from a wound. —**de·bride′,** *v.t.,* -**brid·ed,** -**brid·ing.**

de·cal·ci·fy (dē kal′sə fī′), *v.,* -**fied,** -**fy·ing.** —*v.t.* **1.** to deprive of lime or calcareous matter, as a bone. —*v.i.* **2.** to become decalcified. —**de·cal′ci·fi·ca′tion,** *n.* —**de·cal′ci·fi′er,** *n.*

de·cer·e·brate (dē ser′ə brāt′), *v.t.,* -**brat·ed,** -**brat·ing.** to remove the cerebrum from. —**de·cer′e·bra′tion,** *n.*

de·cid·u·a (di sij′ōō ə), *n., pl.* -**u·as,** -**u·ae** (-ōō ē′), the endometrium of a pregnant uterus, cast off at parturition. —**de·cid′u·al,** *adj.*

de′com·pen·sa′tion, *n.* **1.** the inability of a diseased heart to compensate for its defect. **2.** inability to maintain normal or appropriate psychological defenses, resulting in neurotic or psychotic symptoms. —**de·com′pen·sate′,** *v.i.,* **-sat·ed, -sat·ing.**

de′com·pres′sion, *n.* **1.** the gradual reduction in atmospheric pressure experienced after working in deep water or breathing compressed air. **2.** a surgical procedure for relieving increased cranial, cardiac, or orbital pressure.

decompres′sion cham′ber, *n.* HYPERBARIC CHAMBER.

decompres′sion sick′ness, *n.* an acute disorder involving the formation of nitrogen bubbles in the body fluids, caused by a sudden drop in external pressure, as during a too-rapid ascent from diving, and resulting in pain in the lungs and joints and faintness; the bends; caisson disease.

de′con·di′tion, *v.t.,* **-tioned, -tion·ing.** to diminish or eliminate the conditioned responses or behavior patterns of.

de·con·ges·tant (dē′kən jes′tənt), *adj.* **1.** relieving mucus congestion of the upper respiratory tract. —*n.* **2.** a decongestant agent.

de·cor·ti·cate (dē kôr′ti kāt′), *v.t.,* **-cat·ed, -cat·ing.** to remove the cortex from surgically, as an organ or structure. —**de·cor′ti·ca′tion,** *n.* —**de·cor′ti·ca′tor,** *n.*

de·cu′bi·tus ul′cer (di kyōō′bi təs), *n.* BEDSORE.

def·e·cate (def′i kāt′), *v.i.,* **-cat·ed, -cat·ing.** to void excrement from the bowels through the anus. —**def′e·ca′tion,** *n.*

de·fense (di fens′), *n.* DEFENSE MECHANISM.

defense′ mech′anism, *n.* an unconscious process that protects an individual from unacceptable or painful ideas or impulses.

de·fen′sive, *adj.* sensitive to the threat of criticism or injury to one's ego. —**de·fen′sive·ly,** *adv.* —**de·fen′sive·ness,** *n.*

de·fer·ves·cence (dē′fər ves′əns, def′ər-), *n.* abatement of fever. —**de·fer·ves′cent,** *adj.*

de·fi′bril·late′, *v.t.,* **-lat·ed, -lat·ing.** to arrest the fibrillation of (cardiac muscle) by applying electric shock across the chest. —**de·fi′bril·la′tion,** *n.*

de·fi′bril·la′tor, *n.* an agent or device for arresting fibrillation of the cardiac muscle.

de·fi·bri·nate (dē fi′brə nāt′), *v.t.,* **-nat·ed, -nat·ing.** to remove fibrin from (blood). —**de·fi′bri·na′tion,** *n.*

defi′ciency disease′, *n.* any illness associated with an insufficient supply of one or more essential dietary constituents.

de·form·i·ty (di fôr′mi tē), *n., pl.* **-ties.** an abnormally formed part of the body.

de·gen·er·ate (*v.* di jen′ə rāt′; *n.* -ər it), *v.,* **-at·ed, -at·ing,** *n.* —*v.i.* **1.** (of an organ or tissue) to lose structure or function. **2.** (of a species or any of its traits or structures) to lose function or structural organization in the course of evolution, as the vestigial wings of a flightless bird. —*n*. **3.** a person or thing that reverts to an earlier stage of culture, development, or evolution. —**de·gen′er·a′tion,** *n*.

de·gen′er·a·tive (-ər ə tiv, -ə rā′tiv), *adj*. **1.** tending to degenerate. **2.** characterized by degeneration.

degen′erative joint′ disease′, *n*. OSTEOARTHRITIS.

de·glu·ti·tion (dē′glōō tish′ən), *n*. the act or process of swallowing. —**de/glu·ti/tious,** *adj*.

deg·ra·da·tion (deg′ri dā′shən), *n*. the breakdown of an organic compound. —**deg/ra·da/tion·al,** *adj*. —**deg/ra·da/tive,** *adj*.

de·hy·drate (dē hī′drāt), *v.t*. **-drat·ed, -drat·ing. 1.** to lose an abnormal amount of water from the body: *Infants are easily dehydrated by diarrhea* **2.** to free (fruit, vegetables, etc.) from moisture for preservation; dry. —**de/hy·dra/tion,** *n*. —**de/hy·dra/tor,** *n*.

de·hy·dro·gen·ase (dē hī′drə jə nās′, -nāz′), *n*. an oxidoreductase enzyme that catalyzes the removal of hydrogen.

dé·jà vu (dā′zhä vōō′, vyōō′), *n*. the illusion of having previously experienced something actually being encountered for the first time.

de·jec·ta (di jek′tə), *n.pl*. EXCREMENT.

de·lam·i·na·tion (dē lam′ə nā′shən), *n*. the separation of a primordial cell layer into two layers by a process of cell migration.

de·le·tion (di lē′shən), *n*. **1.** a type of chromosomal aberration in which a segment of the chromosome is removed or lost. **2. a.** the removal or loss of a segment of DNA or RNA. **b.** the segment removed or lost.

de·lir·i·ous (di lēr′ē əs), *adj*. affected with or characterized by delirium: *a delirious patient or fever*. —**de·lir/i·ous·ly,** *adv*. —**de·lir/i·ous·ness,** *n*.

de·lir/i·um (-əm), *n., pl*. **-i·ums, -i·a** (-ē ə) a temporary disturbance of consciousness characterized by restlessness, excitement, and delusions or hallucinations.

delir/ium tre/mens (trē′mənz, -menz), *n*. a withdrawal syndrome occurring in persons who have developed physiological dependence on alcohol, characterized by tremor, visual hallucinations, and autonomic instability. Also called **the d.t.'s.**

de·liv·er (di liv′ər), *v.t*. **1.** to give birth to. —*v.i*. **2.** to give birth.

de·liv/er·y, *n., pl*. **-ies.** the state of being delivered of or giving birth to a child; parturition.

de·louse (dē lous′, -louz′), *v.t.*, **-loused, -lous·ing.** to free of lice; remove lice from.

del′ta hepati′tis, (del′tə), *n*. HEPATITIS DELTA.

del′ta rhythm′, *n*. a pattern of slow brain waves, less than 6 cycles per second, associated with the deepest phase of slow-wave sleep.

del′ta vi′rus, *n*. See under HEPATITIS DELTA.

del·ta wave′, *n.* any of the slow brain waves constituting delta rhythm.

del·toid (del′toid), *n.* a large, triangular muscle covering the joint of the shoulder, the action of which raises the arm away from the side of the body.

delts (delts), *n.pl. Informal.* deltoid muscles.

de·lu·sion (di lōō′zhən), *n.* a false belief that is resistant to reason or confrontation with actual fact: *a paranoid delusion.* —**de·lu′sion·al, de·lu′sion·ar′y,** *adj.*

de·men·tia (di men′shə, -shē ə), *n.* severely impaired memory and reasoning ability, usu. with disturbed behavior, associated with damaged brain tissue. —**de·men′tial,** *adj.*

demen′tia prae′cox (prē′koks), *n.* SCHIZOPHRENIA.

Dem·e·rol (dem′ə rôl′, -rol′), *Trademark.* a brand of meperidine.

de·mul·cent (di mul′sənt), *adj.* **1.** soothing or mollifying, as a medicinal substance. —*n.* **2.** a demulcent substance or agent, often mucilaginous, as for use on irritated mucous membrane.

de·my·e·li·nate (di mī′ə lə nāt′), *v.t.,* **-nat·ed, -nat·ing.** to obliterate or remove the myelin sheath from (a nerve or nerves).

de′my·e·li·na′tion, *n.* loss of myelin from the nerve sheaths.

de·na·ture (dē nā′chər), *v.t.,* **-tured, -tur·ing.** to treat (a protein or the like) by chemical or physical means so as to alter its original state. —**de·na′tur·ant,** *n.* —**de·na′tur·a′tion,** *n.*

den·drite (den′drīt), *n.* any branching process of a neuron that conducts impulses toward the cell body.

de·ner·vate (dē nûr′vāt), *v.t.,* **-vat·ed, -vat·ing.** to cut off the nerve supply from (an organ or body part) by surgery or anesthetic block. —**de′ner·va′tion,** *n.*

den·gue (deng′gā, -gē), *n.* an infectious, eruptive fever of warm climates, usu. epidemic, caused by a togavirus and characterized esp. by severe pains in the joints and muscles. Also called **den′gue fe′ver, breakbone fever.**

de·ni·al (di nī′əl), *n. Psychol.* the reduction of anxiety by the unconscious exclusion from the mind of intolerable thoughts, feelings, or facts.

den·tal (den′tl), *adj.* **1.** of or pertaining to the teeth. **2.** of or pertaining to dentistry or a dentist. —**den·tal′i·ty,** *n.* —**den′tal·ly,** *adv.*

den′tal car′ies, *n.* decay in teeth caused by bacteria that form acids in the presence of sucrose, other sugars, and refined starches.

den′tal floss′, *n.* a soft, strong thread used to dislodge food particles from between the teeth.

den′tal hygien′ist, *n.* a person who is trained and licensed to clean teeth, take dental x-rays, and otherwise assist a dentist.

den′tal pulp′, *n.* PULP (def. 3).

den·tal techni·cian, *n.* a person who makes dentures, bridges, etc.

den·tin (den′tn, -tin) also **den·tine** (-tēn), *n.* the hard, calcareous tissue, similar to but denser than bone, that forms the major portion of a tooth, surrounds the pulp cavity, and is situated beneath the enamel and cementum. —**den′tin·al,** *adj.*

den·tist (den′tist), *n.* a person whose profession is dentistry.

den′tist·ry, *n.* the science or profession dealing with the prevention or treatment of diseases of the teeth, gums, and oral cavity, the correction or removal of decayed, damaged, or malformed parts, and the replacement of lost structures.

den·ti′tion (-tish′ən), *n.* **1.** the makeup of a set of teeth including their kind, number, and arrangement. **2.** the cutting of the teeth.

den′ture (-chər, -chŏŏr), *n.* **1.** an artificial replacement of one or more teeth. **2.** Often **dentures.** a replacement of all the teeth of one or both jaws.

de·ox′y·cor′ti·cos′ter·one′ (dē ok′si-), *n.* a steroid hormone, $C_{21}H_{30}O_3$, secreted by the adrenal cortex, related to corticosterone, and involved in water and electrolyte balance.

de·ox′y·ri·bo·nu·cle·ase′, *n.* See DNASE.

de·ox′y·ri·bo·nu·cle′ic ac′id, *n.* See DNA.

de·ox′y·ri·bo·nu·cle·o·pro′tein, *n.* any of a class of nucleoproteins that yield DNA upon partial hydrolysis.

de·ox′y·ri·bo·nu·cle·o·side′, *n.* a compound composed of deoxyribose and either a purine or a pyrimidine.

de·ox′y·ri·bo·nu·cle·o·tide′, *n.* an ester of a deoxyribonucleoside and phosphoric acid; a constituent of DNA.

de·ox′y·ri′bose, *n.* **1.** any of certain carbohydrates derived from ribose by the replacement of a hydroxyl group with a hydrogen atom. **2.** the sugar, $HOCH_2(CHOH)_2CH_2CHO$, obtained from DNA by hydrolysis.

de·pend·ence (di pen′dəns), *n.* the state of being psychologically or physiologically dependent on a drug.

de·phos·pho·ryl·a·tion (dē fos′fər ə lā′shən), *n.* **1.** the removal of a phosphate group from an organic compound, as in the changing of ATP to ADP. **2.** the resulting state or condition.

de·pig′men·ta′tion, *n.* loss of pigment.

de·pil·a·to·ry (di pil′ə tôr′ē, -tōr′ē), *adj., n., pl.* **-ries.** —*adj.* **1.** capable of removing hair. —*n.* **2.** a depilatory agent, esp. in a mild liquid or cream form for temporarily removing unwanted hair from the body.

de·pres·sant (di pres′ənt), *adj.* **1.** tending to slow the activity of one or more bodily systems. —*n.* **2.** a drug or other agent that reduces irritability or excitement; sedative.

de·pressed′, *adj.* suffering from depression.

de·pres′sion, *n.* Psychiatry. a condition of general emotional dejection and withdrawal; dejection greater and more prolonged than that warranted by any objective reason.

de·pres·sive (-iv), *adj.* **1.** characterized by depression. —*n.* **2.** a person suffering from a depressive illness. —**de·pres'sive·ly,** *adv.* —**de·pres'sive·ness,** *n.*

de·pres·sor, *n.* **1.** a device for pressing down a protruding part: *a tongue depressor.* **2.** any muscle that draws down a part of the body. Compare LEVATOR. **3.** a nerve that induces a decrease in activity when stimulated.

depth′ percep′tion, *n.* the ability to judge the dimensions and spatial relationships of objects.

depth′ psychol′ogy, *n.* any approach to psychology that explains personality in terms of unconscious processes.

derm·a·bra·sion (dûr′mə brā′zhən), *n.* the removal of acne scars, dermal nevi, or the like, by scraping or rubbing.

der′ma·ti′tis (-tī′tis), *n.* inflammation of the skin.

der·mat·o·glyph·ics (dər mat′ə glif′iks, dûr′mə tə-), *n.* **1.** (*used with a pl. v.*) the ridged patterns on the fingers, palms of the hands, toes, and soles of the feet. **2.** (*used with a sing. v.*) the study of these patterns. —**der·mat′o·glyph′ic,** *adj.*

der·ma·tol·o·gy (dûr′mə tol′ə jē), *n.* the branch of medicine dealing with the skin and its diseases. —**der′ma·to·log′i·cal** (-tl oj′i kəl), **der′ma·to·log′ic,** *adj.* —**der′ma·tol′o·gist,** *n.*

der′ma·tome′ (-tōm′), *n.* the portion of a mesodermal somite in an embryo that develops into dermis. —**der′ma·tom′ic** (-tom′ik), **der′ma·to·mal,** *adj.*

der·mat·o·phyte (dər mat′ə fīt′, dûr′mə tə-), *n.* any fungus parasitic on the skin and causing a skin disease, as ringworm. —**der·mat′o·phyt′ic** (-fit′ik), *adj.* —**der·mat′o·phy·to′sis,** *n.*

der·mat′o·plas′ty (-plas′tē), *n., pl.* **-ties.** SKIN GRAFTING. —**der·mat′o·plas′tic,** *adj.*

der·ma·to·sis (dûr′mə tō′sis), *n., pl.* **-to·ses** (-tō′sēz). any disease of the skin.

der·mis (dûr′mis), *n.* the thick layer of skin beneath the epidermis. —**der′mal,** *adj.*

DES, diethylstilbestrol.

descend′ing co′lon, *n.* the last portion of the colon.

de·sen·si·ti·za·tion (dē sen′si tə zā′shən), *n.* the reduction or elimination of an allergic reaction or psychological oversensitivity to an external stimulus by controlled repeated exposure to the stimulus.

des′ert fe′ver, *n.* COCCIDIOIDOMYCOSIS.

des·ic·cant (des′i kənt), *adj.* **1.** desiccating or drying. —*n.* **2.** a desiccant substance or agent.

des′ic·cate′, *v.t.,* **-cat·ed, -cat·ing.** to preserve (food) by removing moisture; dehydrate. —**des′ic·ca′tion,** *n.* —**des′ic·ca′tive,** *adj.*

design′er drug′, *n.* a drug produced by a minor modification in the chemical structure of an existing drug, result-

di·a·lyze′ (-līz′), v., **-lyzed, -lyz·ing.** —v.t. **1.** to subject to dialysis; separate or procure by dialysis. —v.i. **2.** to undergo dialysis. —**di′a·lyz′a·ble,** adj. —**di′a·lyz·a·bil′i·ty,** n. —**di′a·ly·za′tion,** n.

di·a·lyz′er also **di·al′y·za′tor** (-al′i zā′tər), n. an apparatus containing a semipermeable membrane for dialysis.

di·a·pe·de·sis (dī′ə pi dē′sis), n. the passage of blood cells, esp. white blood cells, through intact blood vessel walls into the tissues. —**di′a·pe·det′ic** (-det′ik), adj.

di·a·pho·re·sis (dī′ə fə rē′sis), n. perspiration, esp. when artificially induced. —**di′a·pho·ret′ic** (-ret′ik), adj., n.

di·a·phragm (dī′ə fram′), n. **1.** a wall of muscle and connective tissue separating two cavities, esp. the partition separating the thoracic cavity from the abdominal cavity in mammals. **2. a.** a porous plate separating two liquids, as in a galvanic cell. **b.** a semipermeable membrane. **3.** a thin, dome-shaped device usu. of rubber for wearing over the uterine cervix during sexual intercourse to prevent conception; pessary.

di·ar·rhe·a (dī′ə rē′ə), n. an intestinal disorder characterized by frequent and fluid fecal evacuations. —**di′ar·rhe′al,** **di′ar·rhe′ic,** **di′ar·rhet′ic** (-ret′ik), adj.

di·ar·thro·sis (dī′är thrō′sis), n., pl. **-ses** (-sēz) a form of joint articulation that permits free movement, as at the shoulder. —**di′ar·thro′di·al** (-dē əl), adj.

di·a·stase (dī′ə stās′, -stāz′), n. an enzyme that breaks down starch into maltose and dextrose and is present in malt.

di′a·stat′ic (-stat′ik) also **di·a·sta·sic** (-stā′sik), adj. **1.** **2.** having the properties of diastase: *diastatic action.*

di·a·ste·ma (dī′ə stē′mə), n., pl. **-ma·ta** (-mə tə). a gap between two adjacent teeth.

di·as·to·le (dī as′tl ē′, -tl ē), n. the normal rhythmical dilatation of the heart during which the chambers are filling with blood. Compare **SYSTOLE.** —**di′as·tol′ic** (-ə stol′ik), adj.

di·a·ther·my (dī′ə thûr′mē) also **di′a·ther′mi·a,** n. the therapeutic generation of heat in body tissues by electric currents. —**di′a·ther′mic,** adj.

di·ath·e·sis (dī ath′ə sis), n., pl. **-ses** (-sēz′). a predisposition, as to a disease. —**di′a·thet′ic** (-ə thet′ik), adj.

di·az·e·pam (dī az′ə pam′), n. a benzodiazepine, $C_{16}H_{13}ClN_2O$, used chiefly as a muscle relaxant and to alleviate anxiety.

di·cen·tric (dī sen′trik), adj. (of a chromosome or chromatid) having two centromeres.

di·chro·ma·tism (dī krō′mə tiz′əm), n. a defect of vision in which the retina responds to only two of the three primary colors. Also called **di·chro′ma·top′si·a** (-top′sē ə).

di·chro′mic, adj. pertaining to or involving two colors only: *dichromic vision.*

Dick′ test′ (dik), n. a test for determining immunity or susceptibility to scarlet fever in which scarlet fever toxin is injected into the skin.

di·crot·ic (di krot′ik), *adj.* pertaining to or having a double beat of the pulse for each beat of the heart. —**di′cro·tism** (-krə tiz′əm), *n.*

di·cu·ma·rol or **di·cou·ma·rol** (di koo̅′mə rôl′, -rol′, -kyoo̅′-), *n.* a synthetic drug, $C_{19}H_{12}O_6$, used chiefly to prevent blood clots.

di·el (dī′əl, dē′-), *adj.* of or pertaining to a 24-hour period, esp. a regular daily cycle, as of the physiology or behavior of an organism.

di·en·ceph·a·lon (dī′en sef′ə lon′), *n., pl.* **-lons, -la** (-lə). the posterior portion of the forebrain including the thalami and hypothalamus. —**di′en·ce·phal′ic** (-sə fal′ik), *adj.*

di·es·trus (di es′trəs), *n.* an interval of sexual inactivity between periods of estrus. —**di·es′trous,** *adj.*

di·et (dī′it), *n.* **1.** food and drink considered in terms of qualities, composition, and effects on health. **2.** a particular selection of food, esp. for improving a person's physical condition or to prevent or treat disease: *a low-fat diet.* **3.** such a selection or a limitation on the amount a person eats for reducing weight: *to go on a diet.* **4.** the foods habitually eaten by a particular person, animal, or group.

di·e·tar·y (-i ter′ē), *adj., n., pl.* **-tar·ies.** —*adj.* **1.** of or pertaining to diet. —*n.* **2.** an allowance of food. —**di·e·tar′i·ly,** *adv.*

di·e·tet·ic (-tet′ik), *adj.* Also, **di·e·tet′i·cal. 1.** pertaining to diet or to regulation of the use of food. **2.** prepared or suitable for special diets, esp. those requiring a restricted sugar, salt, or caloric intake. —*n.* **3.** dietetics, (*used with a sing. v.*) the science concerned with nutrition and food preparation. —**di·e·tet′i·cal·ly,** *adv.*

di·eth·yl·stil·bes·trol (di eth′əl stil bes′trôl, -trol), *n.* a synthetic estrogen, $C_{18}H_{20}O_2$, found to be carcinogenic to offspring when used to support pregnancy and now restricted in use. *Abbr.:* DES

di·e·ti′tian or **di·e·ti′cian** (-tish′ən), *n.* a person who is an expert in nutrition or dietetics.

differen′tial associa′tion, *n.* a theory that criminal and deviant behavior is learned through close and frequent association with criminal or deviant behavior patterns, norms, and values.

di·gest (di jest′, di-), *v.t.* **1.** to convert (food) in the alimentary canal into a form that can be assimilated by the body. **2.** to promote the digestion of (food). —*v.i.* **3.** to digest food. **4.** to undergo digestion. —**di·gest′ed·ly,** *adv.* —**di·gest′ed·ness,** *n.*

di·gest′ant (-jes′tənt), *n.* a substance that promotes digestion.

di·gest′i·ble, *adj.* capable of being readily digested. —**di·gest′i·bil′i·ty,** *n.* —**di·gest′i·bly,** *adv.*

di·ges·tion (-chən), *n.* **1.** the process in the alimentary canal by which food is broken up physically, as by the action of the teeth, and chemically, as by the action of enzymes, and converted into a substance suitable for absorption and assimilation into the body. **2.** the function or power of digesting food. **3.** the act of digesting or the state of being digested. —**di·ges′tion·al**, *adj.*

di·ges′tive (-tiv), *adj.* **1.** serving for or pertaining to digestion; having the function of digesting food: *the digestive tract.* —*n.* **2.** a substance promoting digestion. —**di·ges′tive·ly**, *adv.*

diges′tive gland′, *n.* any gland that secretes enzymes serving to promote digestion.

diges′tive sys′tem, *n.* the system by which ingested food is acted upon by physical and chemical means to provide the body with absorbable nutrients and to excrete waste products: in mammals the system includes the alimentary canal extending from the mouth to the anus and the hormones and enzymes assisting in digestion.

dig·it (dij′it), *n.* a finger or toe.

dig·it·al (dij′i tl), *adj.* of, pertaining to, or resembling a digit or finger. —**dig′it·al·ly**, *adv.*

dig·i·tal·in (dij′i tal′in, -tā′lin), *n.* **1.** a glucoside obtained from digitalis. **2.** any of several extracts of mixtures of glucosides obtained from digitalis.

dig·i·tal·is (-tal′is, -tā′lis), *n.* the dried leaves of the foxglove used as a heart stimulant.

dig·i·tal·ize (dij′i tl iz′, dij′i tal′iz), *v.t.,* **-ized, -iz·ing.** to treat with a regimen of digitalis so as to achieve or maintain adequate pumping action of the heart. —**dig′i·tali·za′tion**, *n.*

dig′i·tox′in, *n.* a glycoside extract of digitalis used in the treatment of congestive heart failure.

dig·ox·in (dij ok′sin), *n.* a glycoside of purified digitalis, relatively mild in action and widely used in the treatment of congestive heart failure.

di·hy·brid (di hi′brid), *n.* **1.** the offspring of parents differing in two specific pairs of genes. —*adj.* **2.** of or pertaining to such an offspring. —**di·hy′brid·ism**, *n.*

di·hy·dro·mor·phi·none (di hi′drō môr′fə nōn′), *n.* a narcotic compound, $C_{17}H_{19}O_3N$, prepared from morphine and used as an analgesic.

Di·lan·tin (di lan′tn, -tin, di-), *Trademark.* a brand of phenytoin.

dil·a·ta·tion (dil′ə tā′shən, dīl′ə-) also **di·la·tion** (di lā′shən, di-), *n.* **1.** an abnormal enlargement of an organ, aperture, or canal of the body. **2. a.** an enlargement made in a body aperture or canal for surgical or medical treatment. **b.** a restoration to normal patency of an abnormally small body opening or passageway.

di·la·tor (di lā′tər, di-, di′lā-), *n.* a surgical instrument for performing a dilatation.

di·men·hy·dri·nate (di′men hi′drə nāt′), *n.* a synthetic antihistamine in powder form, used for treating allergic disorders and preventing motion sickness.

di·meth·yl sulf·ox·ide (di meth′əl sul fok′sid), *n.* See DMSO.

di·op·tom·e·ter (di′op tom′i tər), *n.* an instrument for measuring the refraction of the eye.

di·op·tric (di op′trik), *adj.* of or pertaining to refraction or refracted light. Also, **di·op′tri·cal.** —**di·op′tri·cal·ly**, *adv.*

di·ox·in (di ok′sin), *n.* a general name for a family of chlorinated hydrocarbons, $C_{12}H_4Cl_4O_2$, esp. the isomer TCDD, a toxic by-product of pesticide manufacture.

di·phen·yl·hy·dan·to·in (di fen′l hi dan′tō in, -fēn′-), *n.* PHENYTOIN.

diph·the·ri·a (dif thēr′ē ə, dip-), *n.* a febrile infectious disease caused by the bacillus *Corynebacterium diphtheriae*, and characterized by the formation of a false membrane in the air passages, esp. the throat. —**diph·the′ri·al, diph·the·rit′ic** (-thə rit′ik), *adj.*

diph′the·roid (-thə roid′), *adj.* **1.** resembling diphtheria, esp. in the formation of a false membrane in the throat. —*n.* **2.** any bacterium, esp. of the genus *Corynebacterium*, that resembles the diphtheria bacillus but does not produce diphtheria toxin.

di·ple·gia (di plē′jə, -jē ə), *n.* paralysis of the identical part on both sides of the body. —**di·ple′gic**, *adj.*

dip·lo·coc·cus (dip′lə kok′əs), *n., pl.* **-coc·ci.** any of several spherical bacteria occurring in pairs, as *Diplococcus pneumoniae*. —**dip·lo·coc′cal, dip·lo·coc′cic**, *adj.*

dip·loid (dip′loid), *adj.* **1.** having two similar complements of chromosomes. —*n.* **2.** an organism or cell having double the basic haploid number of chromosomes. —**dip·loi′dic**, *adj.*

dip·lont (dip′lont), *n.* **1.** the diploid individual in a life cycle that has a diploid and a haploid phase. **2.** an organism having two sets of chromosomes in its somatic cells and a single haploid set of chromosomes in its gametes. —**di·plo′pi·a** (di plō′pē ə), *n.* a pathological condition of vision in which a single object appears double. Also called **double vision.** —**di·plop′ic** (-plop′ik, -plō′pik), *adj.*

dip·so·ma·ni·a (dip′sə mā′nē ə, -sō-), *n.* an irresistible, typically periodic craving for alcoholic drink.

dip′so·ma′ni·ac′, *n.* an alcoholic. **dip′so·ma·ni′a·cal**, *adj.*

di·sac·cha·ride (di sak′ə rid′, -rid), *n.* any of a group of carbohydrates, as sucrose or lactose, that yield monosaccharides on hydrolysis.

dis·cis·sion (di sish′ən), *n.* an incision of the lens of the eye.

dis·ease (di zēz′), *n.* a disordered or abnormal condition of an organ or other part of an organism resulting from the effect of genetic or developmental errors, infection, nutritional deficiency, toxicity, or unfavorable environmental factors; illness; sickness. —**dis·eased′**, *adj.*

dis·func·tion (dis fungk′shən), *n.* DYSFUNCTION.

dis·in·hi·bi·tion (dis in′i bish′ən, -in′hi-, dis′in-), *n.* a temporary loss of inhibition caused by an outside stimulus.

disk (disk), *n.* INTERVERTEBRAL DISK. —**disk′like′**, *adj.*

dis·lo·cate (dis′lō kāt′, dis lō′kāt), *v.t.*, **-cat·ed, -cat·ing.** to put out of joint or out of position, as a limb or an organ. —**dis′lo·ca′tion**, *n.*

dis·o·ri·ent (dis ôr′ē ent′, -ōr′-), *v.t.* to cause to lose perception of time, place, or one's personal identity. —**dis·o′·ri·en·ta′tion,** *n.*

dis·pen·sa·ry (di spen′sə rē), *n., pl.* **-ries. 1.** a place where something is dispensed, esp. medicines. **2.** a charitable or public facility where medicines are furnished and free or inexpensive medical advice is available.

dis·pen·sa·to·ry (di spen′sə tôr′ē, -tōr′ē), *n., pl.* **-ries.** a book in which the composition, preparation, and uses of medicinal substances are described.

dis·pense′, *v.t.,* **-pensed, -pens·ing.** to make up and distribute (medicine), esp. on prescription.

dis·place·ment (dis plās′mənt), *n.* the transfer of an emotion from its original focus to another object, person, or situation; transference.

dis·sep·i·ment (di sep′ə mənt), *n.* SEPTUM. —**dis·sep′i·men′tal,** *adj.*

dis·so·ci·a·tion (di sō′sē ā′shən, -shē ā′-), *n.* the splitting off of a group of mental processes from the main body of consciousness, as in amnesia or certain forms of hysteria.

dis·tem·per (dis tem′pər), *n.* **1.** Also called **canine distemper.** an infectious disease chiefly of young dogs, caused by an unidentified virus and characterized by lethargy, fever, catarrh, photophobia, and vomiting. **2.** Also called **strangles.** an infectious disease of horses, caused by the bacillus *Streptococcus equi* and characterized by catarrh of the upper air passages and the formation of pus in the submaxillary and other lymphatic glands. **3.** Also called **feline distemper.** a usu. fatal viral disease of cats, characterized by fever, vomiting, and diarrhea, leading to severe dehydration.

di·u·re·sis (dī′ə rē′sis), *n.* increased discharge of urine.

di·u·ret·ic (-ret′ik), *adj.* **1.** increasing the volume of the urine excreted. —*n.* **2.** a diuretic medicine or agent, as a thiazide.

di·ver·gence (di vûr′jəns, dī-), *n.* a turning of the eyes outward from each other.

di·ver·tic·u·li·tis (dī′vər tik′yə lī′tis), *n.* inflammation of one or more diverticula.

di·ver·tic·u·lo·sis (-lō′sis), *n.* the presence of saclike herniations of the mucosal layer of the colon through the muscular wall.

di·ver·tic·u·lum (-ləm), *n., pl.* **-la** (-lə). a blind, tubular sac or process branching off from a canal or cavity, esp. an abnormal, saclike herniation of the mucosal layer through the muscular wall of the colon. —**di′ver·tic′u·lar,** *adj.*

di·vulse (di vuls′, dī-), *v.t.,* **-vulsed, -vuls·ing.** *Surg.* to tear away or apart, as distinguished from cut or dissect. —**di·vul′sion** (-vul′shən), *n.*

di·zy·got·ic (dī′zī got′ik) also **di·zy′gous** (-gəs), *adj.* developed from two fertilized ova, as fraternal twins. —**di′zy·gos′i·ty** (-gos′i tē), *n.*

DMSO, dimethyl sulfoxide: a liquid industrial solvent,

C_2H_6OS, approved for topical use to reduce inflammation and diffuse drugs into the bloodstream.

DNA, deoxyribonucleic acid: an extremely long, double-stranded nucleic acid molecule arranged as a double helix that is the main constituent of the chromosome and that carries the genes as segments along its strands: found chiefly in the chromatin of cells and in many viruses.

DNA fingerprinting, *n.* the use of a DNA probe for the purpose of identifying an individual, as for the matching of genes from a forensic sample with those of a criminal suspect. Also called **genetic fingerprinting.** —**DNA fingerprint,** *n.*

DNA polymerase, *n.* any of a class of enzymes involved in synthesizing DNA from precursor molecules.

DNA probe, *n.* **1.** a laboratory-produced quantity of a known segment of labeled DNA that is used for finding matching DNA in a biological sample, as blood or hair, by the base-pairing of strands from both sources. **2.** a search or examination with such a DNA segment.

DNase (dē/en/ās, -āz) also **DNAase** (dē/en/ā/ās, -āz), *n.* deoxyribonuclease: any of several enzymes that break down the DNA molecule into its component nucleotides.

DNA virus, *n.* any virus containing DNA.

DNR, do not resuscitate: used in hospitals to indicate a prior decision by the patient or the patient's family to avoid extraordinary means of prolonging life.

DOA or **D.O.A.,** dead on arrival.

doc/o·sa·hex·a·e·no/ic ac/id (dok/ə sə hek/sə i nō/ik, dok/-), *n.* See DHA.

dom·i·nance (dom/ə nəns) *n.* **1.** *Psychol.* the disposition of an individual to assert control in dealing with others. **2.** the normal tendency for one side of the brain to be more important than the other in controlling certain functions. Sometimes, **dom/i·nan·cy.**

dom/i·nant, *Genetics.* —*adj.* **1. a.** of or pertaining to that allele of a gene pair that masks the effect of the other when both are present in the same cell or organism. **b.** of or pertaining to the hereditary trait determined by such an allele. —*n.* **2. a.** the dominant allele of a gene pair. **b.** the individual carrying such an allele. **c.** a dominant trait. Compare RECESSIVE.

Don Juan·ism (don wä/niz əm), *n.* SATYRIASIS.

do·nor (dō/nər), *n.* a provider of blood, an organ, or other biological tissue for transfusion or transplantation. —**do/·nor·ship/,** *n.*

do·pa (dō/pə), *n.* an amino acid, $C_9H_{11}NO_4$, formed from tyrosine in the liver during melanin and epinephrine biosynthesis. Compare L-DOPA.

do/pa·mine/ (-mēn/), *n.* a monoamine neurotransmitter that acts within certain brain cells to help regulate movement and emotion.

do/pa·mi·ner/gic (-mi nûr/jik), *adj.* activated by or sensitive to dopamine.

dop/ing, *n.* the use of a substance foreign to the body, or the use of a natural physiological substance taken in an abnormal quantity or by unnatural route of entry into the body, with the sole intention of artificially increasing performance in a competition.

dor·mant (dôr′mənt), *adj.* being in a state of minimal metabolic activity with cessation of growth, often as a reaction to adverse conditions. —**dor′man·cy,** *n.*

dor·sal (dôr′səl), *adj.* **1.** of, pertaining to, or situated at the back, or dorsum. **2.** situated on or toward the upper side of the body, equivalent to the back, or posterior, in humans. —**dor′sal·ly,** *adv.*

dor′sal lip′, *n.* the dorsal marginal region of the blastopore, which acts as a center of differentiation.

dor·so·lum·bar (dôr′sō lum′bər, -bär), *adj.* pertaining to or affecting the back in the region of the lumbar vertebrae.

dor′sum (-səm), *n., pl.* **-sa** (-sə). **1.** the back, as of the body. **2.** the back or outer surface of an organ, part, etc.

dos·age (dō′sij), *n.* **1.** the administration of medicine in doses. **2.** the amount of medicine to be given. **3.** DOSE (def. 1).

dose (dōs), *n., v.,* **dosed, dos·ing.** —*n.* **1.** a quantity of medicine prescribed to be taken at one time. **2.** the amount of radiation to which something has been exposed or the amount that has been absorbed by a given mass of material, esp. living tissue. —*v.t.* **3.** to give a dose of medicine to. —*v.i.* **4.** to take a dose of medicine.

dose′-response′ curve′, *n.* a curve plotting the relationship between the dose of a drug given and its pharmacological effect.

dou′ble bind′, *n.* a situation in which a person is faced with contradictory demands such that to obey one is to disobey the other.

dou′ble-blind′, *adj.* of or pertaining to an experiment or clinical trial in which neither the researchers nor the subjects know which subjects are receiving the active treatment, medication, etc., so as to eliminate bias.

dou′ble he′lix, *n.* the spiral arrangement of the two complementary strands of DNA.

dou′ble-joint′ed, *adj.* having especially flexible joints that can bend in unusual ways or to an unusually great extent.

dou′ble vi′sion, *n.* DIPLOPIA.

douche (dōōsh), *n., v.,* **douched, douch·ing.** —*n.* **1.** a jet or current of water, sometimes with a dissolved medicating or cleansing agent, applied to a body part, organ, or cavity for medicinal or hygienic purposes. **2.** the application of such a jet. **3.** an instrument, such as a syringe, for administering it. —*v.t.* **4.** to apply a douche to. —*v.i.* **5.** to use a douche.

douche′ bag′, *n.* a small syringe having detachable nozzles for fluid injections, used chiefly for vaginal lavage and for enemas.

down·er (dou′nər), *n. Slang.* a depressant or sedative drug, esp. a barbiturate.

Down's/ syn/drome, *n.* DOWN SYNDROME.

down/stream/, *adv.* with or in the direction of transcription, translation, or synthesis of a DNA, RNA, or protein molecule.

Down/ (or **Down's/**) **syn/drome**, *n.* a genetic disorder associated with the presence of an extra chromosome 21, characterized by mental retardation, weak muscle tone, and epicanthic folds at the eyelids. Formerly, **mongolism.** Also called **trisomy 21.**

D.P.H., Doctor of Public Health.

DPT or **DTP,** diphtheria, tetanus, pertussis: a mixed vaccine of inactivated diphtheria and tetanus toxoids and pertussis vaccine, used for primary immunization.

Dram·a·mine (dram/ə mēn/), *Trademark.* a brand of dimenhydrinate.

draw (drô), *v.,* **drew, drawn, draw·ing.** *Med.* —*v.t.* **1.** to cause to discharge: *to draw an abscess by a poultice.* —*v.i.* **2. a.** to act as an irritant; cause blisters. **b.** to cause blood, pus, or the like to gather at a specific point. —**draw/a·ble,** *adj.*

dress (dres), *v.t.* to apply medication or a dressing to (a wound or sore).

drip (drip), *n.* the continuous, slow introduction of a fluid into the body, usu. intravenously.

drop (drop), *n.* Usu., **drops. 1.** liquid medicine given in a dose or form of globules from a medicine dropper. **2.** a solution for dilating the pupils of the eyes, administered to the eyes in this manner.

drop·per (drop/ər), *n.* a glass tube with a hollow rubber bulb at one end and a small opening at the other for drawing in a liquid and expelling it in drops; eyedropper.

drop/sy, *n.* (formerly) edema. —**drop/si·cal,** *adj.* —**drop/si·cal·ly,** *adv.* —**drop/sied,** *adj.*

drug (drug), *n., v.,* **drugged, drug·ging.** —*n.* **1.** a chemical substance used in the treatment, cure, prevention, or diagnosis of disease or to otherwise enhance physical or mental well-being. **2.** a habit-forming medicinal or illicit substance, esp. a narcotic. —*v.t.* **3.** to administer a drug to.

dry/ eye/, *n.* an abnormal eye condition caused by an inadequate tear film.

DSR, dynamic spatial reconstructor: an x-ray machine that displays bodily organs in three-dimensional moving images.

DTP, diphtheria, tetanus, and pertussis. See DPT.

d.t.'s or **D.T.'s** (dē/tēz/), *n.* DELIRIUM TREMENS.

duct (dukt), *n.* a tube conveying bodily secretions or excretions. —**duct/less,** *adj.*

duct/less gland/, *n.* ENDOCRINE GLAND.

duc·tus ar·te·ri·o·sis (duk/təs är tēr/ē ō/sis), *n.* a fetal blood vessel that connects the left pulmonary artery to the descending aorta.

du/ode/nal ul/cer, *n.* a peptic ulcer located in the duodenum.

du·o·de·num (dŏŏ′ə dē′nəm, dyŏŏ′-; dŏŏ od′n əm, dyŏŏ-), *n., pl.* **du·o·de·na** (dŏŏ′ə dē′nə, dyŏŏ′-; dŏŏ od′-n ə, dyŏŏ-), **du·o·de·nums.** the first portion of the small intestine, from the stomach to the jejunum. —**du′o·de′nal,** *adj.*

du·plex (dŏŏ′pleks, dyŏŏ′-), *n.* a double-stranded region of DNA.

du·ral (dŏŏr′əl, dyŏŏr′əl), *adj.* of or pertaining to the dura mater.

du·ra ma·ter (dŏŏr′ə mā′tər), *n.* the tough, fibrous membrane forming the outermost of the three coverings of the brain and spinal cord. Also called **du′ra.** Compare ARACHNOID, MENINGES, PIA MATER.

dwarf (dwôrf), *n., pl.* **dwarfs, dwarves.** a person of abnormally small stature owing to a pathological condition, esp. a condition that produces short limbs or anatomical deformation. —**dwarf′ness,** *n.*

dwarf′ism, *n.* the condition of being a dwarf.

dy·nam·ics (dī nam′iks), *n.* (*used with a sing. or pl. v.*) PSYCHODYNAMICS.

dynam′ic spa′tial reconstruc′tor, *n.* See DSR.

dys·ar·thri·a (dis är′thrē ə), *n.* difficulty in speech articulation due to poor muscular control, usu. related to nerve damage. —**dys·ar′thric,** *adj.*

dys·cra·sia (dis krā′zhə, -zhē ə, -zē ə), *n.* an imbalance of the constituents of the blood or bone marrow. —**dys·cra′sial, dys·cras′ic** (-kraz′ik, -kras′-), **dys·crat′ic,** *adj.*

dys·en·ter·y (dis′ən ter′ē), *n.* any infectious disease of the large intestines marked by hemorrhagic diarrhea with mucus and often blood in the feces. —**dys·en·ter′ic,** *adj.*

dys·func·tion (dis fungk′shən), *n.* impairment of function or malfunctioning, as of an organ or structure of the body. —**dys·func′tion·al,** *adj.*

dys·gen·ic (dis jen′ik), *adj.* pertaining to or causing degeneration in the type of offspring produced. Compare EUGENIC.

dys·gen′ics, *n.* (*used with a sing. v.*) the study of factors causing genetic deterioration in a population or species.

dys·ki·ne·si·a (dis′ki nē′zhə, -zhē ə, -zē ə, -ki-), *n.* difficulty or abnormality in performing voluntary muscular movements. Compare TARDIVE DYSKINESIA. —**dys·ki·net′ic** (-net′ik), *adj.*

dys·la·li·a (dis lā′lē ə, -lal′ē ə), *n.* difficulty in speech articulation due to an abnormality in one or more organs of speech.

dys·lex·i·a (dis lek′sē ə), *n.* any of various reading disorders associated with impairment of the ability to interpret spatial relationships or to integrate auditory and visual information.

dys·lex′ic, *n.* **1.** a person subject to or having dyslexia. —*adj.* **2.** of or pertaining to dyslexia.

dys·men·or·rhe·a or **dys·men·or·rhoe·a** (dis′men ə-rē′ə), *n.* painful menstruation. —**dys·men·or·rhe′al,** *adj.*

dys·pep·sia (dis pep′shə, -sē ə) also **dys·pep′sy,** *n.*

deranged or impaired digestion; indigestion (opposed to *eupepsia*).

dys•pep•tic (-tik), *adj.* Also, **dys•pep/ti•cal.** **1.** pertaining to, subject to, or suffering from dyspepsia. —*n.* **2.** a person subject to or suffering from dyspepsia. —**dys•pep/ti•cal•ly,** *adv.*

dys•pha•gia (dis fā/jə, -jē ə), *n.* difficulty in swallowing. —**dys•phag/ic** (-faj/ik, -fā/jik), *adj.*

dys•pha•sia (dis fā/zhə, -zhē ə, -zē ə), *n.* inability to speak or understand words because of a brain lesion. —**dys•pha/sic** (-fā/zik, -sik), *adj.*

dys•phe•mi•a (dis fē/mē ə), *n.* any impairment in the ability to speak.

dys•pho•ni•a (dis fō/nē ə), *n.* any disturbance of normal vocal function. —**dys•phon/ic** (-fon/ik), *adj.*

dys•pho•ri•a (dis fôr/ē ə, -fōr/-), *n.* a state of dissatisfaction, anxiety, restlessness, or fidgeting. —**dys•phor/ic** (-fôr/ik, -for/-), *adj.*

dys•pla•sia (dis plā/zhə, -zhē ə, -zē ə), *n.* abnormal growth or development of cells, tissue, bone, or an organ. —**dys•plas/tic** (-plas/tik), *adj.*

dysp•ne•a (disp nē/ə), *n.* difficult or labored breathing. —**dysp•ne/al, dysp•ne/ic,** *adj.*

dys•rhyth•mi•a (dis rith/mē ə), *n.* a disturbance of rhythm, as of speech patterns or brain waves.

dys•to•ni•a (dis tō/nē ə), *n.* a neurological disorder marked by strong involuntary muscle spasms that cause painful and disabling twisting of the body. —**dys•ton•ic** (-ton/ik), *adj.*

dys•troph•ic (di strof/ik, -strō/fik), *adj.* pertaining to or caused by dystrophy.

dys•tro•phy (dis/trə fē) also **dys•tro•phi•a** (di strō/fē ə), *n.* **1.** faulty or inadequate nutrition or development. **2.** any of a number of disorders characterized by weakening, degeneration, or abnormal development of muscle.

dys•u•ri•a (dis/yŏŏ rē/ə, dis yŏŏr/ē ə), *n.* difficult or painful urination. —**dys•u/ric,** *adj.*

E

E, *Symbol.* glutamic acid.

ead., (in prescriptions) the same. [Latin, *eādem*]

ear (ēr), *n.* **1.** the organ of hearing and equilibrium in vertebrates, in mammals consisting of an external ear and ear canal ending at the tympanic membrane, a middle ear with three ossicles for amplifying vibrations, and a liquid-filled inner ear with sensory nerve endings for hearing and balance. **2.** the external ear alone.

ear′ache′, *n.* a pain or ache in the ear; otalgia.

ear′ drops′, *n.pl.* medicinal drops for use in the ears.

ear′drum′, *n.* a membrane in the ear canal between the external ear and the middle ear; tympanic membrane.

ear′wax′, *n.* a yellowish, waxlike secretion from certain glands in the external auditory canal; cerumen.

EBV, Epstein-Barr virus.

ec·bol·ic (ek bol′ik), *adj.* **1.** promoting birth or abortion by increasing uterine contractions. —*n.* **2.** a drug that promotes birth or abortion.

ec·chy·mo·sis (ek/ə mō′sis), *n., pl.* **-ses** (-sēz). a discoloration of the skin due to extravasation of blood, as in a bruise. —**ec′chy·mot′ic** (-mot′ik), *adj.*

ec·crine (ek′rin, -rīn, -rēn), *adj.* of or pertaining to certain sweat glands, distributed over the entire body, that secrete a type of sweat important for regulating body heat (disting. from *apocrine*).

ECF, extended-care facility.

ECG, 1. electrocardiogram. **2.** electrocardiograph.

ech′o·car′di·o·gram′ (ek/ō-), *n.* a graphic record produced by an echocardiograph.

ech′o·car′di·o·graph′, *n.* an instrument using reflected ultrasonic waves to show the structures and functioning of the heart: for diagnosing heart abnormalities.

ech′o·en·ceph′a·lo·gram′, *n.* a graphic record produced by an echoenchephalograph.

ech′o·en·ceph′a·lo·graph′, *n.* an instrument employing reflected ultrasonic waves to show the position of brain structures: used in diagnosing brain abnormalities. —**ech′o·en·ceph′a·lo·graph′ic,** *adj.* —**ech′o·en·ceph′a·log′ra·phy,** *n.*

ech′o·gram′, *n.* SONOGRAM.

ech·o·la·li·a (ek/ō lā′lē ə), *n.* the uncontrollable and immediate repetition of words spoken by another person, esp. as associated with mental disorder. —**ech′o·lal′ic** (-lal′ik, -lā′lik), *adj.*

ech′o·vi′rus, *n., pl.* **-rus·es.** any of numerous retroviruses of the picornavirus group, some harmless and others associated with various human disorders, as aseptic meningitis.

ec·lamp·si·a (i klamp′sē ə), *n.* a form of toxemia of

pregnancy, characterized by albuminuria, hypertension, and convulsions. —**ec·lamp′tic,** *adj.*

E. co·li (ē′ kō′li), *n.* ESCHERICHIA COLI.

ec·sta·sy (ek′stə sē), *n.,* *pl.* **-sies.** *Slang.* See MDMA.

ECT, electroconvulsive therapy.

ec·to·derm (ek′tə dûrm′), *n.* the outer germ layer in an embryo. —**ec′to·der′mal, ec′to·der′mic,** *adj.* —**ec′to·der·moi′dal** (-dər moid′l), *adj.*

ec·tog·e·nous (ek toj′ə nəs) also **ec′to·gen′ic** (-tə·jen′ik), *adj.* growing outside the body of the host, as certain bacteria and other parasites.

ec·to·mere (ek′tə mēr′), *n.* any of the blastomeres that participate in the development of the ectoderm. —**ec′to·mer′ic** (-mer′ik), *adj.*

ec·to·morph (ek′tə môrf′), *n.* a person of the ectomorphic type.

ec·to·mor·phic, *adj.* having a thin body build, roughly characterized by the relative prominence of structures developed from the embryonic ectoderm (contrasted with *endomorphic, mesomorphic*). —**ec′to·morph′y,** *n.*

ec·to·par·a·site (ek′tō-), *n.* an external parasite (opposed to *endoparasite*). —**ec′to·par′a·sit′ic,** *adj.*

ec·to·pi·a (ek tō′pē ə), *n.* the usu. congenital displacement of an organ or part. —**ec·top′ic** (-top′ik), *adj.* —**ec·top′i·cal·ly,** *adv.*

ectop′ic preg′nancy, *n.* the development of a fertilized ovum outside the uterus, as in a Fallopian tube.

ec·ze·ma (ek′sə mə, eg′zə-, ig zē′-), *n.* an inflammatory condition of the skin accompanied by itching and the exudation of serous matter. —**ec·zem′a·tous** (ig zem′ə təs, -zē′mə-), *adj.*

ED, effective dose.

e·de·ma (i dē′mə), *n.,* *pl.* **-mas, -ma·ta** (-mə tə). an abnormal accumulation of fluid in the tissue spaces, cavities, or joint capsules of the body, causing swelling of the area. —**e·dem·a·tous** (i dem′ə təs, i dē′mə-), *adj.*

EDTA, ethylenediaminetetraacetic acid: a colorless compound, $C_{10}H_{16}N_2O_8$, capable of chelating a variety of divalent metal cations: used in food preservation, as an anticoagulant, and in the treatment of heavy-metal poisonings.

EEG, 1. electroencephalogram. **2.** electroencephalograph.

EENT, eye, ear, nose, and throat.

effec′tive dose′, *n.* the amount of a drug, or level of radiation exposure, that is sufficient to achieve the desired clinical improvement.

ef·fec·tor (i fek′tər), *n.* **1.** an organ, cell, etc. that reacts to a nerve impulse, as a muscle by contracting or a gland by secreting. **2.** the part of a nerve that conveys such an impulse.

ef·fer·ent (ef′ər ənt), *adj.* **1.** conveying or conducting away from an organ or part (opposed to *afferent*). —*n.* **2.** an efferent part, as a nerve or blood vessel. —**ef′fer·ent·ly,** *adv.*

ef·flo·res·cence (ef′lə res′əns), *n.* a rash or eruption of the skin. —**ef′flo·res′cent,** *adj.*

ef·fu·sion (i fyo͞o′zhən), *n.* **1.** the escape of a fluid, as blood, from its natural vessels into a body cavity. **2.** the fluid that escapes.

e·gest (ē jest′, i jest′), *v.t.* to discharge from the body; excrete (opposed to *ingest*). —**e·ges′tion,** *n.* —**e·ges′tive,** *adj.*

e·ges·ta (ē jes′tə, i jes′-), *n.* (*used with a sing. or pl. v.*) matter egested from the body, as excrement or other waste.

egg (eg), *n.* the female gamete; ovum. Also called **egg′ cell′.**

e·go (ē′gō, eg′ō), *n., pl.* **e·gos.** *Psychoanal.* the conscious, rational component of the psyche that experiences and reacts to the outside world and mediates between the demands of the id and superego.

e′go ide·al′, *n. Psychoanal.* an ideal of personal excellence based on positive identification with parent figures.

e′go·ma′ni·a, *n.* psychologically abnormal egotism; extreme egocentrism. —**e′go·ma′ni·ac′,** *n.* —**e′go·ma·ni′a·cal,** *adj.*

ei′co·sa·pen′ta·e·no′ic ac′id (i′kō sə pen′tə i nō′ik, i′kō sə pen′-), *n.* See EPA.

e·jac·u·late (*v.* i jak′yə lāt′; *n.* -lit), *v.,* **-lat·ed, -lat·ing,** *n.* —*v.t., v.i.* **1.** to eject or discharge, esp. semen. —*n.* **2.** the semen emitted in an ejaculation.

e·jac·u·la′tion, *n.* **1.** the act or process of ejaculating, esp. the discharge of semen by the male reproductive organs. **2.** the semen emitted in an ejaculation; ejaculate.

ejac′ulatory duct′, *n.* a duct through which semen is ejaculated, esp. the duct in human males that passes from the seminal vesicle and vas deferens to the urethra.

EKG, 1. electrocardiogram. **2.** electrocardiograph.

e·las·tin (i las′tin), *n.* a protein constituting the basic substance of elastic tissue.

Elec′tra com′plex (i lek′trə), *n. Psychoanal.* an unresolved, unconscious libidinous desire of a daughter for her father: designation based on the Greek myth of Electra and Agamemnon. Compare OEDIPUS COMPLEX.

e·lec′tro·car′di·o·gram′, *n.* the graphic record produced by an electrocardiograph. *Abbr.:* EKG, ECG Also called **cardiogram.**

e·lec′tro·car′di·o·graph′, *n.* a galvanometric device that detects variations in the electric potential that triggers the heartbeat, used to evaluate the heart's health. *Abbr.:* EKG, ECG Also called **cardiograph.** —**e·lec′tro·car′di·o·graph′ic,** *adj.* —**e·lec′tro·car′di·og′ra·phy,** *n.*

e·lec′tro·cau′ter·y, *n., pl.* **-ter·ies. 1.** a hand-held, needlelike cautery heated by an electric current. **2.** Also, **e·lec′tro·cau′ter·i·za′tion,** the process of cutting and cauterizing skin simultaneously, or coagulating blood from vessels around a surgical incision, by means of an electrocautery.

e·lec/tro·con·vul/sive ther/apy, *n.* the application of electric current to the head in order to induce a seizure, used to treat serious mental illnesses. *Abbr.:* ECT Also called **electroshock.**

e·lec/tro·en·ceph/a·lo·gram/, *n.* a graphic record produced by an electroencephalograph. *Abbr.:* EEG

e·lec/tro·en·ceph/a·lo·graph/, *n.* an instrument for measuring and recording the electric activity of the brain. *Abbr.:* EEG —**e·lec/tro·en·ceph/a·lo·graph/ic,** *adj.* —**e·lec/tro·en·ceph/a·log/ra·phy,** *n.*

e·lec·trol·o·gist (i lek trol/ə jist), *n.* a person trained in the use of electrolysis for removing moles, warts, or unwanted hair. —**e·lec·trol/o·gy,** *n.*

e·lec·trol/y·sis (-ə sis), *n.* the destruction of hair roots, tumors, etc., by an electric current.

e·lec·tro·lyte/ (-trə līt/), *n.* **1.** any substance, as sodium or potassium, that dissociates into ions when melted or dissolved in a suitable medium and thus forms a conductor of electricity. **2.** a conducting medium in which the flow of current is accompanied by the movement of ions.

e·lec·tro·my·o·gram (i lek/trō mī/ə gram/), *n.* a graphic record of the electric currents associated with muscular action.

e·lec·tro·my/o·graph/, *n.* a device for recording electric currents from an active muscle to produce an electromyogram. *Abbr.:* EMG —**e·lec/tro·my/o·graph/ic,** *adj.* —**e·lec/tro·my/o·graph/i·cal·ly,** *adv.* —**e·lec/tro·my·og/ra·phy,** *n.*

elec/tron mi/croscope, *n.* a microscope of extremely high power that uses beams of electrons focused by magnetic lenses instead of rays of light, the magnified image being formed on a fluorescent screen or recorded on a photographic plate.

elec/tron trans/port, *n.* the stepwise transfer of electrons from one carrier molecule, as a flavoprotein or a cytochrome, to another and ultimately to oxygen during the aerobic production of ATP.

e·lec·tro·pho·re·sis (i lek/trō fə rē/sis), *n.* the motion of colloidal particles suspended in a fluid medium that is due to the influence of an electric field on the medium. —**e·lec/tro·pho·ret/ic** (-ret/ik), *adj.*

e·lec·tro·phys/i·ol·o·gy, *n.* the branch of physiology dealing with the electric phenomena associated with the body and its functions. —**e·lec/tro·phys/i·o·log/i·cal,** *adj.* —**e·lec/tro·phys/i·ol/o·gist,** *n.*

e·lec·tro·ret/i·no·gram/ (-ret/ə nə gram/), *n.* the graphic record obtained by an electroretinograph.

e·lec·tro·ret/i·no·graph/ (-graf/, -gräf/), *n.* an instrument that measures the electrical response of the retina to light stimulation. —**e·lec/tro·ret/i·no·graph/ic** (-graf/ik), *adj.* —**e·lec/tro·ret/i·nog/ra·phy** (-og/rə fē), *n.*

e·lec/tro·shock/ (i lek/trə-), *n.* ELECTROCONVULSIVE THERAPY.

e·lec·tro·ther′a·py (i lek′trō-), *n.* treatment of diseases by means of electricity.

e·lec·trot·o·nus (i lek trot′n əs, ē′lek-), *n.* the altered state of a nerve during the passage of an electric current through it. —**e·lec′tro·ton′ic** (-trə ton′ik), *adj.*

el·e·phan·ti·a·sis (el′ə fən tī′ə sis, -fan-), *n.* a chronic disease characterized by marked enlargement of the legs, scrotum, and other parts due to obstruction of the lymphatic vessels, usu. caused by filariasis.

el′ephant man′s′ disease′, *n.* a variant, extreme form of neurofibromatosis.

e·lim·i·nate (i lim′ə nāt′), *v.t.,* **-nat·ed, -nat·ing.** *Physiol.* to void or expel, as waste, from the body.

ELISA (i lī′zə, -sə), *n.* a diagnostic test for detecting exposure to an infectious agent, as the AIDS virus, by combining a blood sample with antigen of the agent and probing with an enzyme that causes a color change when antibody to the infection is present in the sample.

e·lix·ir (i lik′sər), *n.* a sweetened aromatic solution of alcohol and water containing or used as a vehicle for medicinal substances.

em·balm (em bäm′), *v.t.* to treat (a dead body) so as to preserve it, as with chemicals, drugs, or balsams. —**em·balm′er,** *n.* —**em·balm′ment,** *n.*

em·bar·rass·ment (em bar′əs mənt), *n.* impairment of functioning associated with disease: *respiratory embarrassment.*

em·bol·ic (em bol′ik), *adj.* **1.** pertaining to an embolus or to embolism. **2.** of, pertaining to, or resulting from emboly.

em·bo·lism (-bə liz′əm), *n.* the occlusion of a blood vessel by an embolus. —**em′bo·lis′mic,** *adj.*

em·bo·lus (-ləs), *n., pl.* **-li** (-lī′). a formerly circulating clump of tissue, gas bubble, fat globule, etc., that has lodged in a blood vessel.

em·bo·ly (-lē) *n., pl.* **-lies.** the pushing or growth of one embryonic part into another, as in the formation of certain gastrulas.

em·bro·cate (em′brō kāt′, -brə-), *v.t.,* **-cat·ed, -cat·ing.** to moisten and rub with a liniment or lotion.

em·bro·ca′tion, *n.* the act of embrocating a bruised or diseased part of the body.

em·bry·o (em′brē ō′), *n., pl.* **-os.** an animal in the early stages of development in the womb or egg; in humans, the stage approximately from attachment of the fertilized egg to the uterine wall until about the eighth week of pregnancy. Compare FETUS, ZYGOTE.

em·bry·og′e·ny (-oj′ə nē) also **em′bry·o·gen′e·sis** (-ō jen′ə sis), *n.* the formation and development of the embryo. —**em′bry·o·gen′ic, em′bry·o·ge·net′ic,** *adj.*

em·bry·ol′o·gy (-ol′ə jē), *n., pl.* **-gies. 1.** the study of embryonic formation and development. **2.** the origin, growth, and development of an embryo. —**em′bry·o·log′-**

i·cal (-ə loj′i kəl), *adj.* —**em′bry·o·log′ic**, *adj.* —**em′bry·o·log′- i·cal·ly**, *adv.* —**em′bry·ol′o·gist**, *n.*

em′bry·on′ic (-on′ik), *adj.* pertaining to or being in the state of an embryo. —**em′bry·on′i·cal·ly**, *adv.*

em′bryon′ic disk′, *n.* in the early embryo of mammals, the flattened inner cell mass that arises at the end of the blastocyst stage and from which the embryo begins to differentiate.

em′bryo mem′brane, *n.* EXTRAEMBRYONIC MEMBRANE.

em′bryo trans′fer, *n.* the transfer of a developing embryo to or from the uterus of a surrogate mother. Also called **em′bryo trans′plant.**

emer′gency room′, *n.* a hospital area equipped and staffed for the prompt treatment of acute illness, trauma, or other medical emergencies. *Abbr.:* ER

e·mer·gi·cen·ter (i mûr′jə sen′tər), *n.* a walk-in facility for treatment of minor medical emergencies.

em·e·sis (em′ə sis), *n.* VOMITUS.

e·met·ic (i met′ik), *adj.* **1.** causing vomiting, as a medicinal substance. —*n.* **2.** an emetic medicine or agent. —**e·met′i·cal·ly**, *adv.*

em·i·gra·tion (em′i grā′shən), *n.* DIAPEDESIS. —**em′i·gra′tion·al**, *adj.*

e·mis·sion (i mish′ən), *n.* an ejection or discharge of semen or other fluid from the body.

em·me·tro·pi·a (em′i trō′pē ə), *n.* the normal refractive condition of the eye in which the rays of light are accurately focused on the retina. —**em′me·trope′,** *n.* —**em′- me·trop′ic** (-trop′ik, -trō′pik), *adj.*

e·mol·lient (i mol′yənt), *adj.* **1.** having the power to soften or soothe: *an emollient lotion for the skin.* —*n.* **2.** an emollient substance. —**e·mol′lience,** *n.*

em·phy·se·ma (em′fə sē′mə, -zē′-), *n.* **1.** a chronic disease of the lungs characterized by difficulty in breathing due to abnormal enlargement and loss of elasticity of the air spaces. **2.** any abnormal distention of an organ or part of the body with air or other gas. —**em′phy·sem′a·tous** (-sem′ə təs, -sē′mə-, -zem′ə-, -zē′mə-), *adj.* —**em′phy·se′mic,** *adj.*

em·pir·i·cal (em pir′i kəl), *adj.* depending upon experience or observation alone, without using scientific method or theory, esp. in medicine. —**em·pir′i·cal·ly**, *adv.*

emp′ty cal′orie, *n.* a calorie whose food source has little or no nutritional value.

emp′ty nest′ syn′drome, *n.* a depressed state felt by some parents after their children have grown up and left home.

em·py·e·ma (em′pē ē′mə, -pi-), *n.* a collection of pus in a body cavity, esp. the pleural cavity. —**em′py·e′mic,** *adj.*

EMS, emergency medical service.

EMT, emergency medical technician.

e·mul·sion (i mul′shən), *n.* any liquid mixture containing medicine suspended in minute globules. —**e·mul′sive,** *adj.*

en·ar·thro·sis (en′är thrō′sis), *n.*, *pl.* **-ses** (-sēz). BALL-AND-SOCKET JOINT. —**en·ar·thro′di·al** (-dē əl), *adj.*

en·ceph·a·li·tis (en sef′ə lī′tis), *n.* inflammation of the substance of the brain. 2. SLEEPING SICKNESS (def. 2). —**en·ceph′a·lit′ic** (-lit′ik), *adj.*

en·ceph′a·lo·gram (en sef′ə lə gram′), *n.* an x-ray of the brain, using replacement of some cerebrospinal fluid by air or other gas that circulates to the brain's ventricular spaces and acts as a contrast medium.

en·ceph′a·lo·graph′ (-graf′, -gräf′), *n.* **1.** an encephalogram. **2.** an electroencephalograph. —**en·ceph′a·lo·graph′ic** (-graf′ik), *adj.* —**en·ceph′a·log′ra·phy** (-log′rə-fē), *n.*

en·ceph′a·lo·my′e·li′tis (en sef′ə lō-), *n.* inflammation of the brain and spinal cord. —**en·ceph′a·lo·my′e·lit′ic**, *adj.*

en·ceph′a·lop′a·thy (-lop′ə thē), *n.* any disease of the brain.

encoun′ter group′, *n.* a group of people who meet, usu. with a trained leader, to increase self-awareness and social sensitivity, and to change behavior through interpersonal confrontation, self-disclosure, and strong emotional expression.

en·cyst (en sist′), *v.t.*, *v.i.* to enclose or become enclosed in a cyst. —**en·cyst′ment, en′cys·ta′tion,** *n.*

end·ar·ter·ec·to·my (en där′tə rek′tə mē), *n.*, *pl.* **-mies.** the surgical stripping of a fat-encrusted, thickened arterial lining so as to open or widen the artery for improved blood circulation.

end·er·gon·ic (en′dər gon′ik), *adj.* (of a biochemical reaction) requiring energy. Compare EXERGONIC.

en·der·mic (en dûr′mik), *adj.* acting through the skin, as a medicine, by absorption. —**en·der′mi·cal·ly,** *adv.*

en·do·blast (en′də blast′), *n.* **1.** ENDODERM. **2.** HYPOBLAST (def. 2). —**en′do·blas′tic,** *adj.*

en′do·car·di′tis (en′dō-), *n.* inflammation of the endocardium. —**en′do·car·di′tis,** *adj.*

en′do·car′di·um (-kär′dē əm), *n.*, *pl.* **-di·a** (-dē ə). the serous membrane that lines the cavities of the heart.

en·do·crine (en′də krin, -krin′, -krēn′), *adj.* Also, **en′do·cri′nal** (-krin′l, -krēn′l). **1.** secreting internally into the blood or lymph. **2.** of or pertaining to an endocrine gland or its secretion. —*n.* **3.** ENDOCRINE GLAND. Compare EXOCRINE.

en′docrine gland′, *n.* any gland, as the thyroid, adrenal, or pituitary gland, that secretes hormones into the blood or lymph; ductless gland.

en·do·cy·to·sis (en′dō si tō′sis), *n.* the transport of particles into a living cell by the movement of a filled vacuole that has formed from the folding inward of the part of the cell membrane on which the particles rest (disting. from *exocytosis*). Compare PHAGOCYTOSIS. —**en·do·cyt′ic** (-sit′ik), **en′do·cy·tot′ic** (-si tot′ik), *adj.*

en·do·derm (en′də dûrm′) also **entoderm,** *n.* the innermost cell layer of the embryo in its gastrula stage. Also called **endoblast.** —**en'do·der'mal, en'do·der'mic,** *adj.*

en·do·don·tics (en'dō don'tiks), *n.* (*used with a sing. v.*) the branch of dentistry dealing with the prevention, diagnosis, and treatment of diseases of the dental pulp and associated structures and tissues. Compare ROOT CANAL THERAPY (def. 1).

en·dog·e·nous (en doj'ə nəs) also **en'do·gen'ic** (-dō-jen'ik), *adj.* of or pertaining to anabolic metabolism within cells. —**en'do·ge·nic'i·ty** (-jə nis'i tē), *n.* —**en·dog'e·nous·ly,** *adv.*

en·dog·e·ny (en doj'ə nē) also **en'do·gen'e·sis** (-dō-jen'ə sis), *n.* development or growth from within.

en·do·lymph (en'də limf'), *n.* the fluid contained within the inner ear. —**en'do·lym·phat'ic** (en'dō-), *adj.*

en·do·me·tri·o·sis (en'dō mē'trē ō'sis), *n.* the presence of uterine lining in other pelvic organs, esp. the ovaries, characterized by cyst formation, adhesions, and menstrual pains.

en·do·me·tri·tis (-mi trī'tis), *n.* inflammation of the lining of the uterus.

en·do·me·tri·um (-mē'trē əm), *n.,* *pl.* **-tri·a** (-trē ə). the membrane lining the uterus. —**en'do·me'tri·al,** *adj.*

en·do·mor·phic (en'də môr'fik), *adj.* having a heavy body build roughly characterized by the relative prominence of structures developed from the embryonic endoderm (contrasted with *ectomorphic, mesomorphic*). —**en'do·mor'phy,** *n.*

en·do·nu·cle·ase (en'dō nōō'klē ās', -āz', -nyōō'-), *n.* any of a group of enzymes that degrade DNA or RNA molecules by breaking linkages within the polynucleotide chains.

en·do·par·a·site (en'dō par'ə sīt'), *n.* an internal parasite (opposed to *ectoparasite*). —**en'do·par'a·sit'ic,** *adj.*

end' or'gan, *n.* one of several specialized structures at the peripheral end of sensory or motor nerve fibers.

en·dor·phin (en dôr'fin), *n.* any of a group of peptides, resembling opiates, that are released in the body in response to stress or trauma and that react with the brain's opiate receptors to reduce the sensation of pain. Compare ENKEPHALIN.

en·do·scope (en'də skōp'), *n.* a slender, tubular optical instrument used for examining the interior of a body cavity or hollow organ. —**en'do·scop'ic** (-skop'ik), *adj.* —**en·dos'co·pist** (-dos'kə pist), *n.* —**en·dos'co·py,** *n.*

en·dos·mo·sis (en'doz mō'sis, -dos-), *n.* osmosis toward the inside of a cell or vessel. —**en'dos·mot'ic** (-mot'ik), *adj.* —**en'dos·mot'i·cal·ly,** *adv.*

en·do·the·li·um (en'dō thē'lē əm), *n.,* *pl.* **-li·a** (-lē ə). a single layer of smooth tissue that lines the heart, blood vessels, lymphatic vessels, and serous cavities. —**en'do·the'li·al,** *adj.*

en'do·tox'in (en'dō-), *n.* a toxin that is released from certain bacteria as they disintegrate in the body, causing fever, toxic shock, etc. —**en′do·tox′ic,** *adj.*

en·do·tra·che·al (-trā′kē əl), *adj.* placed or passing within the trachea: *an endotracheal tube.*

en·e·ma (en′ə mə), *n., pl.* **-mas. 1.** the injection of a fluid into the rectum. **2.** the fluid injected. Also called **en′- ema bag′.** a baglike device for administering an enema.

en·graft (en graft′, -gräft′), *v.t.* to implant surgically. —**en′graf·ta′tion, en·graft′ment,** *n.*

en·gram (en′gram), *n.* a presumed encoding in neural tissue that provides a physical basis for the persistence of memory; a memory trace. —**en·gram′mic,** *adj.*

en·keph·a·lin (en kef′ə lin), *n.* either of two polypeptides that bind to morphine receptors in the central nervous system and have opioid properties of relatively short duration. Compare ENDORPHIN.

En·o·vid (en ov′id), *Trademark.* a brand name for a hormonal compound used in medicine for ovulation control, adjustment of the menses, and control of uterine bleeding.

en·rich (en rich′), *v.t.,* **1.** to restore to (a food) a nutrient lost in processing. **2.** to add vitamins and minerals to (food) to enhance its nutritive value. —**en·rich′ment,** *n.*

ENT, ear, nose, and throat.

ent·a·me·ba or **ent·a·moe·ba** (en′tə mē′bə), *n., pl.* **-bae** (-bē), **-bas.** any protozoan of the genus *Entamoeba,* members of which are parasitic in vertebrates, including the human pathogens *E. gingivalis,* found in dental plaque, and *E. histolytica,* the cause of amebic dysentery.

en·ter·ic (en ter′ik), *adj.* **1.** of or pertaining to the enteron; intestinal. —*n.* **2.** enterics, ENTEROBACTERIA.

enter′ic fe′ver, *n.* TYPHOID (def. 1).

en′ter·i′tis (-tə rī′tis), *n.* inflammation of the intestines, esp. the small intestine.

en′ter·o·bac·te′ri·a (en′tə rō-), *n.pl., sing.* **-te·ri·um.** rod-shaped Gram-negative bacteria of the family Enterobacteriaceae, as those of the genera *Escherichia, Salmonella,* and *Shigella,* occurring normally or pathogenically in the intestines. —**en′ter·o·bac·te′ri·al,** *adj.*

en′ter·o·bi′a·sis (-bī′ə sis), *n.* infestation with pinworms.

en′ter·o·co·li′tis, *n.* inflammation of the small intestine and the colon.

en′ter·o·gas′trone (-gas′trōn), *n.* a hormone of the intestinal mucosa that retards gastric secretion and movement.

en′ter·o·ki′nase, *n.* an enzyme of the intestinal mucosa that promotes the conversion of trypsinogen into trypsin.

en·ter·on (en′tə ron′, -tər ən), *n., pl.* **-ter·a** (-tər ə). ALIMENTARY CANAL.

en′ter·os′to·my (-ros′tə mē), *n., pl.* **-mies.** the making of an artificial opening into the intestine through the abdominal wall, leaving an open passage for drainage. —**en′ter·os′to·mal,** *adj.*

en′ter·o·tox·e′mi·a (en′tə rō-), *n.* systemic toxemia caused by an enterotoxin.

en·ter·o·tox′in, *n.* a toxic substance produced by certain bacteria that on ingestion causes violent vomiting and diarrhea.

en′ter·o·vi′rus, *n.*, *pl.* **-rus·es.** any of several picornaviruses of the genus *Enterovirus*, including poliovirus, that infect the human gastrointestinal tract and cause diseases of the nervous system. —**en′ter·o·vi′ral,** *adj.*

en·to·derm (en′tə dûrm′), *n.* ENDODERM.

en·to·zo·ic (en′tə zō′ik), *adj.* (of a parasitic animal) living within the body of its host.

en′to·zo′on (-zō′on, -ən), *n.*, *pl.* **-zo·a** (-zō′ə). any animal parasite, as an intestinal worm, that lives within the body of its host.

e·nu·cle·ate (*v.* i nōō′klē āt′, i nyōō′-; *adj.* -it, -āt′), *v.*, **-at·ed, -at·ing,** *adj.* —*v.t.* **1.** to deprive (a cell) of the nucleus. **2.** to remove (a kernel, tumor, eyeball, etc.) from its enveloping cover. —*adj.* **3.** having no nucleus. —**e·nu′cle·a′tion,** *n.*

en·u·re·sis (en′yə rē′sis), *n.* lack of control of urination; bedwetting; urinary incontinence. —**en′u·ret′ic** (-ret′ik), *adj.*

en·zy·mat·ic (en′zī mat′ik, -zi-) also **en·zy′mic** (-zī′mik, -zim′ik), *adj.* of or pertaining to an enzyme. —**en′zy·mat′i·cal·ly, en·zy′mi·cal·ly,** *adv.*

en′zyme, *n.* any of various proteins, as pepsin and amylase, originating from living cells and capable of producing certain chemical changes in organic substances by catalytic action, as in digestion.

en′zy·mol′o·gy (-mol′ə jē), *n.* the branch of biology that deals with the chemistry, biochemistry, and effects of enzymes. —**en′zy·mol′o·gist,** *n.*

e·o·sin (ē′ə sin) also **e′o·sine** (-sin, -sēn′), *n.* a red, crystalline, water-insoluble solid, $C_{20}H_8Br_4O_5$, used chiefly as an acid dye and as a histological stain. —**e′o·sin′ic,** *adj.*

e′o·sin′o·phil (-ə fil) also **e′o·sin′o·phile** (-fil′), *n.* **1.** any biological tissue or substance that stains when exposed to eosin. —*adj.* **2.** EOSINOPHILIC.

e′o·sin′o·phil′i·a (-fil′ē ə, -fēl′yə), *n.* the presence of an abnormally increased number of eosinophils in the blood.

e′o·sin′o·phil′ic (-fil′ik) also **e′o·si·noph′i·lous** (-si·nof′ə ləs), **eosinophil,** *adj.* having an affinity for eosin and other acid dyes; acidophilic.

EPA, eicosapentaenoic acid: an omega-3 fatty acid present in fish oils.

e·phed·rine (i fed′rin, ef′i drēn′, -drin), *n.* a white, crystalline alkaloid, $C_{10}H_{15}N$, obtained from a species of *Ephedra* or synthesized: used in medicine chiefly for the treatment of asthma, hay fever, and colds.

ep·i·blast (ep′ə blast′), *n.* the primordial outer layer of a young embryo. —**ep′i·blas′tic,** *adj.*

e·pib·o·ly (i pib′ə lē), *n.*, *pl.* **-lies.** the movement of a group of cells over a more slowly dividing group, resulting in an outer and inner layer, as in a gastrula. —**ep·i·bol′ic** (ep′ə bol′ik), *adj.*

ep·i·can·thus (ep/i kan/thəs), *n.*, *pl.* **-thi** (-thi, -thē). a fold of skin extending from the upper eyelid to or over the inner canthus of the eye, especially well developed in Asian peoples. Also called **ep/ican/thic fold/.** —**ep/i·can/thic,** *adj.*

ep·i·crit·ic (ep/i krit/ik), *adj.* of or pertaining to neurons that are responsive to fine variations in touch or temperature.

ep·i·dem·ic (ep/i dem/ik), *adj.* Also, **ep/i·dem/i·cal.** **1.** (of a disease) affecting many individuals at the same time, and spreading from person to person in a locality where the disease is not permanently prevalent. —*n.* **2.** a temporary prevalence of a disease. —**ep/i·dem/i·cal·ly,** *adv.* —**ep/i·de·mic/i·ty** (-də mis/i tē), *n.*

ep/i·de·mi·ol·o·gy (-dē/mē ol/ə jē, -dem/ē-), *n.* **1.** the branch of medicine dealing with the incidence and prevalence of disease in large populations and with detection of the source and cause of epidemics. **2.** the factors contributing to the presence or absence of a disease. —**ep/i·de/mi·o·log/i·cal** (-ə loj/i kəl), *adj.* —**ep/i·de/mi·o·log/i·cal·ly,** *adv.* —**ep/i·de·mi·ol/o·gist,** *n.*

ep·i·der·mis (ep/i dûr/mis), *n.* the outermost, nonvascular, nonsensitive layer of the skin, covering the dermis. —**ep/i·der/mal, ep/i·der/mic,** *adj.* —**ep/i·der/mi·cal·ly,** *adv.*

ep·i·did·y·mis (-did/ə mis), *n.*, *pl.* **-di·dym·i·des** (-di·dim/i dēz/, -did/ə mi-). an oval structure at the upper surface of each testicle, consisting of tightly convoluted sperm ducts. —**ep/i·did/y·mal,** *adj.*

ep·i·du·ral (ep/i dŏŏr/əl, -dyŏŏr/-), *adj.* **1.** situated on or outside the dura mater. **2.** of or pertaining to the insertion of an anesthetic into the lumbar spine in the space between the spinal cord and dura mater, which blocks sensation in the body from that point downward: *epidural anesthesia.* —*n.* **3.** an epidural injection of anesthesia; spinal anesthesia.

ep/i·gas/tric, *adj.* lying upon, distributed over, or pertaining to the epigastrium.

ep/i·gas/tri·um (-trē əm), *n.*, *pl.* **-tri·a** (-trē ə). the upper and median part of the abdomen, lying over the stomach.

ep·i·gen·e·sis, *n.* **1.** the approximately stepwise process by which genetic information, as modified by environmental influences, is translated into the substance and behaviour of an organism. **2.** the theory that an embryo develops from the successive differentiation of an originally undifferentiated structure (opposed to *preformation*). —**ep/i·gen/e·sist, e·pig/e·nist** (i pij/ə nist), *n.* —**ep/i·ge·net/ic,** *adj.* —**ep/i·ge·net/i·cal·ly,** *adv.*

ep/i·glot/tis, *n.*, *pl.* **-glot/tis·es, -glot/ti·des.** a flap of cartilage behind the tongue that helps close the opening to the windpipe during swallowing. —**ep/i·glot/tal,** *adj.*

ep·i·late (ep/ə lāt/), *v.t.,* **-lat·ed, -lat·ing.** to remove (hair) from by means of physical, chemical, or radiological agents; depilate. —**ep/i·la/tion,** *n.* —**ep/i·la/tor,** *n.*

ep·i·lep·sy (ep′ə lep′sē), *n.* a disorder of the nervous system, characterized either by mild, episodic loss of attention or sleepiness **(petit mal)** or by severe convulsions with loss of consciousness **(grand mal).**

ep·i·lep·tic (-tik), *adj.* **1.** pertaining to, symptomatic of, or affected with epilepsy. —*n.* **2.** a person affected with epilepsy. —**ep′i·lep′ti·cal·ly,** *adv.*

ep·i·neph·rine or **ep·i·neph·rin** (ep′ə nef′rin), *n.* **1.** a hormone secreted by the adrenal medulla upon stimulation by the central nervous system in response to stress, as anger or fear, and acting to increase heart rate, blood pressure, cardiac output, and carbohydrate metabolism. **2.** a commercial preparation of this substance, used chiefly as a heart stimulant and antiasthmatic. Also called **adrenaline.**

ep·i·phe·nom·e·non (ep′ə fə nom′ə non′, -nən), *n., pl.* **-na** (-nə), **-nons.** a secondary or additional symptom or complication arising during the course of a disease. —**ep′i·phe·nom′e·nal,** *adj.* —**ep′i·phe·nom′e·nal·ly,** *adv.*

e·piph·y·sis (i pif′ə sis), *n., pl.* **-ses** (-sēz′). **1.** either of the ends of a long bone separated from the shaft by cartilage but later ossifying with it. **2.** PINEAL GLAND. —**e·piph′y·se′al** (-sē′əl, -zē′-), **e·piph′y·si·al** (-fiz′ē əl), *adj.*

e·pis·i·ot·o·my (ə pē′zē ot′ə mē, ep′ə si-), *n., pl.* **-mies.** a surgical incision into the perineum and vagina to allow sufficient clearance for childbirth.

ep·i·some (ep′ə sōm′), *n.* a strand of DNA that is extrachromosomal, as a bacterial plasmid. —**ep′i·so′mal,** *adj.* —**ep′i·so′mal·ly,** *adv.*

e·pis·ta·sis (i pis′tə sis), *n., pl.* **-ses** (-sēz′). a form of interaction between nonallelic genes in which one combination of such genes has a dominant effect over other combinations. —**ep·i·stat·ic** (ep′ə stat′ik), *adj.*

ep·i·stax·is (ep′ə stak′sis), *n.* NOSEBLEED.

ep·i·the·li·al (ep′ə thē′lē əl), *adj.* of the epithelium.

ep′i·the′li·o′ma (-ō′mə), *n., pl.* **-mas, -ma·ta** (-mə tə). a growth or tumor consisting chiefly of epithelial cells.

ep·i·the·li·um (-lē əm), *n., pl.* **-li·ums, -li·a** (-lē ə). any tissue layer covering body surfaces or lining the internal surfaces of body cavities, tubes, or hollow organs.

ep·i·tope (ep′i tōp′), *n.* a site on an antigen at which an antibody can bind, the molecular arrangement of the site determining the specific combining antibody. Also called **antigenic determinant.**

ep·i·trich·i·um (ep′i trik′ē əm), *n., pl.* **-ums.** PERIDERM. —**ep′i·trich′i·al,** *adj.*

Ep′som salt′ (ep′səm), *n.* Often, **Epsom salts.** hydrated magnesium sulfate, $MgSO_4 \cdot 7H_2O$, occurring as small colorless crystals: used as a cathartic.

Ep′stein-Barr′ vi′rus (ep′stin bär′), *n.* a type of herpesvirus that causes infectious mononucleosis. *Abbr.:* EBV

e′quine encephali′tis, *n.* a viral disease of horses and mules that is communicable to humans, marked by inflammation of the brain and spinal cord.

ER, emergency room.

e·rec·tile (i rek′tl, -til, -tīl), *adj.* capable of being distended with blood and becoming rigid, as tissue. —**e·rec·til·i·ty** (i rek til′i tē, ē′rek-), *n.*

e·rec′tion (-shən), *n.* a distended and rigid state of an organ or part containing erectile tissue, esp. the penis.

e·rec′tor, *n.* a muscle that erects a part of the body.

er·e·thism (er′ə thiz′əm), *n.* an unusual or excessive degree of irritability or stimulation in an organ or tissue. —**er′e·this′mic**, **er′e·this′tic** (-this′tik), **er′e·thit′ic** (-thit′ik), **e·reth·ic** (ə reth′ik, e reth′-), *adj.*

er·go·graph (ûr′gə graf′, -gräf′), *n.* an instrument that measures and records the force of a muscular contraction. —**er′go·graph′ic** (-graf′ik), *adj.*

er·gom·e·ter (ûr gom′i tər), *n.* a device for measuring the physiological effects of a period of work or exercise, as calories expended while bicycling. —**er′go·met′ric** (-gə-me′trik), *adj.*

er·go·no·vine (ûr′gə nō′vēn, -vin), *n.* an alkaloid, $C_{23}H_{27}N_3O_2$, obtained from ergot or produced synthetically, used chiefly in obstetrics to induce uterine contractions or control uterine bleeding.

er·gos·ter·ol (ûr gos′tə rōl′, -rōl), *n.* a colorless, crystalline, water-insoluble sterol, $C_{28}H_{43}OH$, that occurs in ergot and yeast and that, when irradiated with ultraviolet light, is converted into vitamin D.

er·got (ûr′gət, -got), *n.* the dried sclerotium of *C. purpurea*, developed on rye plants, from which various medicinal alkaloids are derived.

er·got′a·mine′ (-got′ə mēn′, -min), *n.* a crystalline, water-soluble polypeptide, $C_{33}H_{35}N_5O_5$, obtained from ergot, used to stimulate uterine contractions during labor and in the treatment of migraine.

er′got·ism (-gə tiz′əm), *n.* poisoning from excessive medication with ergot or from eating grain contaminated with ergot fungus.

E·ros (ēr′os, er′os), *n. Psychoanal.* the libido.

e·ro·to·ma·ni·a (i rō′tə mā′nē ə, i rot′ə-), *n.* abnormally strong or persistent sexual desire; obsession with sexual thoughts and fantasies. —**e·ro′to·ma′ni·ac′**, *n.* —**e·ro′to·man′ic** (-man′ik), *adj.*

ERT, estrogen replacement therapy.

e·ruct (i rukt′), *v.t., v.i.* to belch. —**e·ruc·ta·tion** (i ruk-tā′shən, ē′ruk-), *n.*

e·rup·tion (i rup′shən), *n.* **1. a.** the breaking out of a rash or the like. **b.** the rash itself. **2.** the emergence of a growing tooth through the gum tissue.

e·rup·tive (-tiv), *adj.* causing or accompanied by a rash. —**e·rup′tive·ly**, *adv.* —**e·rup·tiv′i·ty**, *n.*

er·y·sip·e·las (er′ə sip′ə ləs, ēr′ə-), *n.* a deep-red rash of the skin and mucous membranes accompanied by fever and pain, caused by any of a group of hemolytic streptococci. —**er′y·si·pel′a·tous** (-si pel′ə təs), *adj.*

er′y·the·ma (-thē′mə), *n.* abnormal redness of the skin due to local congestion, as in inflammation. —**er′y·them/a·tous** (-them′ə təs, -thē′mə-), **er′y·the/mic**, *adj.*

e·ryth·rism (i rith′riz əm, er′ə thriz′əm), *n.* abnormal redness, as of plumage or hair. —**er′y·thris/mal, er′y·thris/tic** (-thris′tik), *adj.*

e·ryth·ro·blast (i rith′rə blast′), *n.* a nucleated cell in the bone marrow from which a red blood cell develops. —**e·ryth/ro·blas/tic,** *adj.*

e·ryth·ro·bla·to·sis (-rō bla stō′sis), *n.* the abnormal presence of erythroblasts in the blood, esp. in the fetus or newborn as a result of an Rh incompatibility between mother and baby. —**e·ryth/ro·blas·tot/ic** (-stot′ik), *adj.*

e·ryth′ro·cyte′ (-rə sīt′), *n.* RED BLOOD CELL. —**e·ryth/ro·cyt/ic** (-sit′ik), *adj.*

e·ryth′ro·my/cin (-mī′sin), *n.* an antibiotic, $C_{37}H_{67}NO_{13}$, produced by an actinomycete, *Streptomyces erythraeus,* used in the treatment of diseases caused by many Gram-positive and some Gram-negative organisms.

e·ryth′ro·poi·e/sis (-rō poi ē′sis), *n.* the production of red blood cells. —**e·ryth/ro·poi·et/ic** (-et′ik), *adj.*

e·ryth′ro·poi/e·tin (-poi′i tn, -poi ēt′n), *n.* a hormone that stimulates production of red blood cells and hemoglobin in the bone marrow.

escape′ mech/anism, *n.* a means of avoiding an unpleasant life situation, as daydreaming.

es·char (es′kär, -kər), *n.* a hard crust or scab, as from a burn.

es/cha·rot/ic (-rot′ik), *adj.* **1.** producing an eschar, as a medicinal substance; caustic. —*n.* **2.** an escharotic agent.

Esch·e·rich·i·a co·li (esh/ə rik′ē ə kō′li), *n.* a species of rod-shaped, facultatively anaerobic bacteria in the large intestine of humans and other animals, sometimes pathogenic.

es·er·ine (es′ə rēn′, -rin), *n.* PHYSOSTIGMINE.

e·soph·a·ge·al (i sof/ə jē′əl, ē′sə faj′ē əl), *adj.* pertaining to the esophagus.

e·soph·a·gus (i sof/ə gəs, ē sof/ə-), *n., pl.* **-gi** (-jī′, gī′), a muscular tube for the passage of food from the pharynx to the stomach; gullet.

ESP, extrasensory perception: perception or communication outside of normal sensory capability, as in telepathy and clairvoyance.

es·sen·tial (ə sen/shəl), *adj.* not associated with an underlying disease: *essential hypertension.*

essen/tial ami/no ac/id, *n.* any amino acid that is required for life and growth but is not produced in the body, or is produced in insufficient amounts, and must be supplied by protein in the diet.

es·ter (es′tər), *n.* a chemical compound produced by the reaction between an acid and an alcohol with the elimination of a molecule of water, as ethyl acetate, $C_4H_8O_2$, or methyl methacrylate, $C_5H_8O_2$.

es·tra·di·ol (es′trə dī′ōl, -ol), *n.* an estrogenic hormone, $C_{18}H_{24}O_2$, produced by the maturing Graafian follicle, that causes proliferation and thickening of the tissues and blood vessels of the endometrium, used medically in the treatment of estrogen deficiency and certain menopausal conditions.

es·tri·ol/ (-trē ôl′, -ol′, -trī-), *n.* an estrogenic hormone, $C_{18}H_{21}(OH)_3$, occurring in urine during pregnancy.

es·tro·gen (-trə jən), *n.* any of several major female sex hormones produced primarily by ovarian follicles, capable of inducing estrus, producing secondary female sex characteristics, and preparing the uterus for the reception of a fertilized egg: synthesized and used in oral contraceptives and in various therapies.

es·tro·gen·ic, *adj.* **1.** promoting or producing estrus. **2.** of, pertaining to, or caused by estrogen. —**es′tro·gen′i·cal·ly,** *adv.*

es′trogen replace′ment ther′apy, *n.* the administration of estrogen, esp. in postmenopausal women, to reduce the chance of osteoporosis and sometimes to lower cholesterol levels. *Abbr.:* ERT

es·trone (es′trōn), *n.* an estrogenic hormone, $C_{18}H_{22}O_2$, produced by the ovarian follicles and found during pregnancy in urine and placental tissue.

e·ther (ē′thər), *n.* Also called **ethyl ether.** a colorless, highly volatile, flammable liquid, $C_{18}H_{22}O_2$, having an aromatic odor and sweet burning taste, used as a solvent and formerly as an inhalant anesthetic. —**e·ther·ic** (i ther′ik, i thēr′-), *adj.*

e/ther·ize/, *v.t.* **-ized, -iz·ing.** to anesthetize with vaporized ether. —**e/ther·i·za/tion,** *n.*

eth·i·cal (eth′i kəl), *adj.* (of drugs) sold only upon medical prescription.

eth·moid (eth′moid), *adj.* **1.** Also, **eth·moi·dal.** of or pertaining to a cranial bone at the back of the nasal cavity, through which olfactory nerve processes pass into the nose. —*n.* **2.** the ethmoid bone.

eth·no·phar·ma·col·o·gy (eth′nō fär′mə kol′ə jē), *n.* the scientific study of substances used medicinally, esp. folk remedies, by different ethnic or cultural groups. —**eth/no·phar/ma·co·log/i·cal,** **eth/no·phar/ma·co·log/ic,** *adj.*

eth/yl·ene·di/a·mine·tet/ra·a·ce/tic ac/id (eth′ə lēn·dī′ə mēn te/trə ə sē′tik, -set/ik, -min-, eth′ə lēn dī/ə mēn·te/trə-), *n.* See EDTA.

e·ti·ol·o·gy (ē′tē ol′ə jē), *n., pl.* **-gies. 1.** the study of the causes of diseases. **2.** the cause or origin of a disease. —**e′ti·o·log/ic** (-ə loj′ik), **e′ti·o·log/i·cal,** *adj.* —**e′ti·ol/o·gist,** *n.*

eu·chro·ma·tin (yōō krō′mə tin), *n.* the part of a chromosome that condenses maximally during metaphase and contains most of the genetically active material. —**eu/chro·mat/ic** (-krə mat′ik), *adj.*

eu·gen·ic (yōō jen′ik), *adj.* **1.** pertaining to or causing improvement in the type of offspring produced. Compare

DYSGENIC. **2.** of or pertaining to eugenics. —**eu·gen′i·cal·ly,** *adv.*

eu·gen′ics, *n.* (*used with a sing. v.*) a science concerned with improving a breed or species, esp. the human species, by such means as influencing or encouraging reproduction by persons presumed to have desirable genetic traits. —**eu·gen′i·cist** (-ə sist), *n.*

eu·ge·nol (yōō′jə nôl′, -nōl′), *n.* an oily aromatic liquid, $C_{16}H_{12}O_2$, used in perfumes and as a dental antiseptic.

eu·gle·na (yōō glē′nə), *n., pl.* **-nas.** any freshwater protozoan of the genus *Euglena,* having a reddish eyespot and a single flagellum.

eu·gle′noid (-noid) also **eu·gle′nid** (-nid), *adj.* **1.** of, pertaining to, or resembling euglenas. —*n.* **2.** a euglena or euglenoid organism.

eu·kar·y·ote or **eu·car·y·ote** (yōō kar′ē ōt′, -ē ət), *n.* any organism with a fundamental cell type containing a distinct membrane-bound nucleus. —**eu·kar′y·ot′ic** (-ot′ik), *adj.*

eu·nuch·oid (yōō′nə koid′), *adj.* **1.** lacking fully developed male genitalia or other sex characteristics. —*n.* **2.** a eunuchoid male.

eu·pep·sia (yōō pep′shə, -sē ə), *n.* good digestion (opposed to *dyspepsia*). —**eu·pep′tic** (-tik), *adj.*

eu·pho·ri·a (yōō fôr′ē ə, -fōr′-), *n.* a strong feeling of happiness, confidence, or well-being. —**eu·phor′ic** (-fôr′ik, -for′-), *adj.* —**eu·phor′i·cal·ly,** *adv.*

eu·pho′ri·ant (-ənt), *adj.* **1.** tending to induce euphoria. —*n.* **2.** a euphoriant drug or other substance.

eu·pho·ri·gen·ic (-i jen′ik), *adj.* giving rise to euphoria: *the euphorigenic properties of some drugs.*

Eu·sta′chian tube′ (yōō stā′shən, -stā′kē ən), *n.* (*often l.c.*) a canal extending from the middle ear to the pharynx.

eu·tha·na·sia (yōō′thə nā′zhə, -zhē ə, -zē ə), *n.* Also called **mercy killing.** the act of putting to death painlessly or allowing to die, as by withholding medical measures from a person or animal suffering from an incurable, esp. a painful, disease or condition. —**eu·tha·na′si·ast** (-zē-ast′), *n.* —**eu′tha·na′sic** (-zik), *adj.*

eu′tha·nize′, *v.t.,* **-nized, -niz·ing.** to subject to euthanasia.

e·vac·u·ant (i vak′yōō ənt), *adj.* **1.** promoting evacuation from the bowels. —*n.* **2.** an evacuant medicine.

e·vac′u·ate′, *v.t., v.i.,* **-at·ed, -at·ing.** to discharge or eject (waste matter), esp. from the bowels. —**e·vac′u·a′tor,** *n.*

e·vac′u·a′tion, *n.* discharge, as of waste matter, esp. from the bowels.

e·vag·i·nate (i vaj′ə nāt′), *v.t.,* **-nat·ed, -nat·ing.** to turn inside out, or cause to protrude by eversion, as a tubular organ. Compare INVAGINATE. —**e·vag′i·na·ble** (-nə bəl), *adj.* —**e·vag′i·na′tion,** *n.*

e·val·u·a·tion (i val′yōō ā′shən), *n.* a diagnosis or diagnostic study of a physical or mental condition.

e·vis·cer·ate (i vis′ə rāt′), *v.t.,* **-at·ed, -at·ing.** to remove the contents of (a body organ) by surgery. —**e·vis′cer·a′-tion,** *n.*

evoked′ poten′tial, *n.* an electrical response of a neuron to externally induced stimulation, used esp. for measuring speed of sensory-nerve impulses along pathways to the brain.

ex·am·ine (ig zam′in), *v.t.,* **-ined, -in·ing.** to observe, test, or investigate (a person's body or any part of it), esp. in order to evaluate general health or determine the cause of illness. —**ex·am′i·na′tion,** *n.*

ex·an·them (eg zan′thəm, ig-, ek san′-), *n.* an eruptive disease, esp. one attended with fever, as smallpox or measles. —**ex·an′the·mat′ic, ex′an·them′a·tous** (-them′ə-təs), *adj.*

ex′an·the·ma (-thē′mə), *n., pl.* **-the·ma·ta** (-them′ə tə, -thē′mə-), **-the·mas.** EXANTHEM.

ex·cip·i·ent (ik sip′ē ənt), *n.* any pharmacologically inert substance used for combining with a drug for the desired bulk, consistency, etc.

ex·cise (ik sīz′), *v.t.,* **-cised, -cis·ing.** to cut out or off, as a tumor. —**ex·cis′a·ble,** *adj.*

ex·ci·sion (ek sizh′ən, ik-), *n.* the surgical removal of a foreign body or of tissue. —**ex·ci′sion·al,** *adj.*

ex·cit·a·ble (ik sī′tə bəl), *adj.* Physiol. capable of responding to a stimulus; irritable. —**ex·cit′a·bil′i·ty, ex·cit′a·ble·ness,** *n.* —**ex·cit′a·bly,** *adv.*

ex·cit·ant (ik sīt′nt, ek′si tənt), *n.* Physiol. something that excites; stimulant.

ex·cite′, *v.t.,* **-cit·ed, -cit·ing.** Physiol. to stimulate: *to excite a nerve.*

ex·ci′tor (-sī′tər, -tôr), *n.* a nerve that increases the intensity of an action when stimulated.

ex·clu·sion (ik sklōō′zhən), *n.* Physiol. a keeping apart; blocking of an entrance. —**ex·clu′sion·ar′y,** *adj.*

ex·cre·ment (ek′skrə mənt), *n.* waste matter discharged from the body, esp. feces. —**ex′cre·men′tous** (-men′təs), *adj.*

ex·cres·cence (ik skres′əns), *n.* **1.** an abnormal outgrowth, usu. harmless, on an animal or vegetable body. **2.** abnormal growth or increase.

ex·cres·cent (ik skres′ənt), *adj.* growing abnormally out of something else. —**ex·cres′cent·ly,** *adv.*

ex·cre·ta (ik skrē′tə), *n.pl.* excreted matter, as urine, feces, or sweat. —**ex·cre′tal,** *adj.*

ex·crete′, *v.t.,* **-cret·ed, -cret·ing.** to separate and eliminate from an organic body; separate and expel from the blood or tissues, as waste or harmful matter. —**ex·cre′-tive,** *adj.*

ex·cre′tion, *n.* **1.** the act of excreting. **2.** a substance excreted, as urine or sweat.

ex·cre·to·ry (ek′skri tôr′ē, -tōr′ē), *adj.* pertaining to or concerned in excretion; having the function of excreting: *excretory organs.*

ex·er·gon·ic (ek/sər gon/ik), *adj.* (of a biochemical reaction) liberating energy.

ex·fo·li·ate (eks fō/lē āt/), *v.*, **-at·ed, -at·ing.** —*v.t.* to remove the surface of (a bone, the skin, etc.) in scales or laminae. —**ex·fo/li·a/tive** (-ā/tiv, -ə tiv), *adj.*

ex·fo/li·a/tion, *n.* **1.** the act or process of exfoliating. **2.** the state of being exfoliated.

ex·hal·ant (eks hāl/ənt, ek sā/-), *adj.* exhaling; emitting.

ex·ha·la·tion (eks/hə lā/shən, ek/sə-), *n.* **1.** the act of exhaling. **2.** something that is exhaled; vapor; emanation.

ex·hale (eks hāl/, ek sāl/), *v.*, **-haled, -hal·ing.** —*v.i.* **1.** to emit breath or vapor; breathe out. —*v.t.* **2.** to breathe out; emit (air, vapor, etc.).

ex·hi·bi·tion·ism (ek/sə bish/ə niz/əm), *n.* a psychiatric disorder characterized by a compulsion to exhibit the genitals. —**ex/hi·bi/tion·ist,** *n., adj.* —**ex/hi·bi/tion·is/tic,** *adj.*

ex·o·crine (ek/sə krin, -krin/, -krēn/), *adj.* **1.** secreting to an epithelial surface. **2.** of or pertaining to an exocrine gland or its secretion. —*n.* **3. EXOCRINE GLAND.**

ex/ocrine gland/, *n.* any gland, as a sweat gland or salivary gland, that secretes externally through a duct.

ex·o·cy·to·sis (ek/sō si tō/sis), *n.* the transport of matter out of a living cell by the movement of a filled vacuole to the cell membrane and the extrusion of its contents (distinct from *endocytosis*). —**ex/o·cy·tot/ic** (-tot/ik), **ex/o·cyt/ic** (-sit/ik), *adj.*

ex·og·a·my (ek sog/ə mē), *n.* the union of gametes from parental organisms that are not closely related. —**ex·og/a·mous, ex/o·gam/ic** (-sə gam/ik), *adj.*

ex·on (ek/son), *n.* a segment of DNA that is transcribed to RNA and specifies the sequence of a portion of protein. Compare **INTRON.**

ex·oph·thal·mos or **ex·oph·thal·mus** (ek/sof thal/məs), also **ex/oph·thal/mi·a,** *n.* protrusion of the eyeball from the orbit, caused by disease, esp. hyperthyroidism, or injury. —**ex/oph·thal/mic,** *adj.*

ex·os·mo·sis (ek/sos mō/sis, ek/soz-), *n.* osmosis toward the outside of a cell or vessel. —**ex/os·mot/ic** (-mot/ik), *adj.* —**ex/os·mot/i·cal·ly,** *adv.*

ex·o·tox·in (ek/sō tok/sin), *n.* a soluble toxin excreted by a microorganism. —**ex/o·tox/ic,** *adj.*

ex·o·tro·pi·a (ek/sə trō/pē ə), *n.* a condition in which the eyes are turned outward in relation to each other, as in divergent strabismus. Also called **walleye.** —**ex/o·trop/ic** (-trop/ik), *adj.*

ex·pec·to·rant (ik spek/tər ənt), *adj.* **1.** promoting the discharge of phlegm or other fluid from the respiratory tract. —*n.* **2.** an expectorant medicine.

ex·pec/to·rate/ (-rāt/), *v.i., v.t.* **-rat·ed, -rat·ing.** to expel (phlegm, etc.) from the throat or lungs by coughing or hawking and spitting. —**ex·pec/to·ra/tor,** *n.*

ex·plant (*v.* eks plant/, -plänt/; *n.* eks/plant/, -plänt/), *v.t.* **1.** to take (living material) from an animal or plant for placement in a culture medium. —n. **2.** a piece of explanted tissue. —**ex/plan·ta/tion,** n.

ex·plore (ik splōr′, -splôr′), v.t., **-plored, -plor·ing.** to examine, esp. mechanically, as with a surgical probe: to explore a wound. —**ex·plor/a·ble,** adj. —**ex·plor/a·bil/i·ty,** n. —**ex·plo·ra·tion** (eks/plə rā/shən), n. —**ex·plor/ing·ly,** adv.

ex·press (ik spres′), v.t. (of a gene) to be active in the production of a protein or a phenotype.

ex·pres/sion, n. **1.** the action of a gene in the production of a protein or a phenotype. **2.** EXPRESSIVITY.

ex·pres·siv·i·ty (ek/spres siv′i tē), n. the degree to which a particular gene produces its effect in an organism. Compare PENETRANCE.

ex·san·gui·nate (eks sang′gwə nāt′), v.t., **-nat·ed, -nat·ing.** to drain of blood. —**ex·san/gui·na/tion,** n.

ex·san/guine (-gwin), adj. anemic; bloodless. —**ex/san·guin/i·ty,** n.

ex·scind (ek sind′), v.t. to cut out or off.

extend/ed care/, n. generalized health or nursing care for convalescents or the disabled, when hospitalization is not required.

ex·tend·er (ik sten′dər), n. a substance added to another substance, as to food, to increase its volume or bulk.

ex·ten·si·ty (-si tē), n. the sensation that underlies the perception of space and size.

ex·ten·sor (-sər, -sôr), n. a muscle that serves to extend or straighten a part of the body.

ex·te·ri·or·ize (ik stēr′ē ə rīz′), v.t., **-ized, -iz·ing.** Surg. to expose (an internal part) to the outside. —**ex·te/ri·or·i·za/tion,** n.

ex·tern (ek′stûrn), n. a person connected with an institution but not residing in it, as a doctor or medical student at a hospital.

ex·ter·nal (ik stûr′nl), adj. to be applied to the outside of a body. —**ex·ter/nal·ly,** adv.

ex·ter·o·cep·tor (ek′stər ə sep′tər), n. a sensory receptor responding to stimuli originating outside the body. —**ex/ter·o·cep/tive,** adj.

ex·tinc·tion (ik stingk′shən), n. the reduction or loss of a conditioned response as a result of the absence or withdrawal of reinforcement.

ex·tir·pate (ek′stər pāt′, ik stûr′pāt), v.t., **-pat·ed, -pat·ing.** to pull up by or as if by the roots. —**ex/tir·pa/tion,** n.

ex·tra·cor·po·re·al (ek/strə kôr pôr′ē əl, -pōr′-), adj. occurring or situated outside the body. —**ex/tra·cor·po/re·al·ly,** adv.

ex/tra·em·bry·on/ic, adj. **1.** situated outside the embryo. **2.** pertaining to structures that lie outside the embryo.

ex/traembryon/ic mem/brane, n. any of the membranes derived from embryonic tissue that lie outside the embryo, as the allantois, amnion, chorion, and yolk sac.

ex/tra·py·ram/i·dal, adj. **1.** pertaining to nerve tracts other than the pyramidal tracts, esp. the corpora striata and their associated structures. **2.** located outside the pyramidal tracts.

ex′trasen′sory percep′tion, *n.* See ESP.

ex·tra·sys·to·le (ek′strə sis′tə lē′), *n.,* *pl.* **-les.** a premature contraction of the heart, resulting in momentary interruption of the normal heartbeat. —**ex′tra·sys·tol′ic,** *adj.*

ex′tra·u′ter·ine, *adj.* situated, developing, or occurring outside the uterus.

ex·trav·a·sate (ik strav′ə sāt′), *v.,* **-sat·ed, -sat·ing,** *n.* —*v.t.* **1.** to force out, as blood, from the proper vessels, esp. so as to diffuse through the surrounding tissues. —*v.i.* **2.** to become extravasated. —*n.* **3.** extravasated material; extravasation.

ex·trav′a·sa′tion, *n.* **1.** the act of extravasating. **2.** EXTRAVASATE.

ex·tra·ver·sion (ek′strə vûr′zhən, -shən, ek′strə vûr′-), *n.* EXTROVERSION.

ex′tra·vert′ (-vûrt′), *n., adj.* EXTROVERT.

extrin′sic fac′tor, *n.* VITAMIN B₁₂.

ex·tro·ver·sion (ek′strə vûr′zhən, -shən, ek′strə vûr′-), *n.* the act or state of being concerned primarily with the external environment rather than with one's own thoughts and feelings. Compare INTROVERSION. —**ex′tro·ver′sive, ex′tro·ver′tive,** *adj.*

ex′tro·vert′ (-vûrt′), *n.* **1.** a person who exhibits extroversion. —*adj.* **2.** Also, **ex′tro·vert′ed.** marked by extroversion; outgoing.

ex·u·da·tion (eks′yŏŏ dā′shən, ek′sə-, eg′zə-), *n.* **1.** the act of exuding. **2.** something that is exuded. **3.** a discharge exuded by the body, as sweat. —**ex·u·da·tive** (ig-zōō′də tiv, ik sōō′-), *adj.*

ex·ude (ig zōōd′, ik sōōd′), *v.,* **-ud·ed, -ud·ing.** —*v.i.* **1.** to come out gradually in drops; ooze out. —*v.t.* **2.** to emit through small openings.

eye (ī), *n.* **1.** the organ of sight; in vertebrates, one of a pair of spherical bodies contained in an orbit of the skull, along with its associated structures. **2.** the visible parts of this organ, as the cornea, iris, and pupil, and the surrounding eyebrows, eyelids, and eyelashes.

eye′ chart′, *n.* a chart for testing vision, usu. containing letters in rows of decreasing size that are to be read at a fixed distance.

eye′cup′, *n.* a device for applying eyewash to the eye, consisting of a cup or glass with a rim shaped to fit snugly around the orbit of the eye.

eye′ doc′tor, *n.* **1.** OPHTHALMOLOGIST. **2.** OPTOMETRIST.

eye′drop′per, *n.* DROPPER.

eye′lift′, *n.* cosmetic blepharoplasty.

eye′ lock′, *n.* EYELIFT.

eye′wash′, *n.* a soothing solution applied locally to the eye. Also called **collyrium.**

eye′wear′, *n.* any of various devices, as spectacles or goggles, for aiding the vision or protecting the eyes.

F

F, filial.

F, *Symbol.* **1.** Fahrenheit. **2.** fluorine. **3.** phenylalanine.

face′-lift′ or **face′lift′,** *n.* **1.** plastic surgery on the face to eliminate sagging and wrinkles. —*v.t.* **2.** to perform a face-lift upon.

fa′cial nerve′, *n.* either one of the seventh pair of cranial nerves, in mammals supplying facial muscles, the taste buds at the front of the tongue, the tear glands, and the salivary glands.

fa·ci·es (fā′shē ēz′, -shēz), *n., pl.* **fa·ci·es.** a facial expression characteristic of a pathological condition.

fa·cil·i·ta·tion (fə sil′i tā′shən), *n.* the lowering of resistance in a neural pathway to an impulse resulting from previous or simultaneous stimulation.

FACS, fluorescence-activated cell sorter: a machine that sorts cells according to whether or not they have been tagged with antibodies carrying a fluorescent dye.

fac·tor (fak′tər), *n.* any of certain substances necessary to a biochemical or physiological process, esp. those whose exact nature and function are unknown.

factor VIII, *n.* an enzyme of blood plasma that is essential to normal blood clotting: lacking or deficient in hemophiliacs.

fac·ul·ta·tive (fak′əl tā′tiv), *adj.* having the capacity to live under more than one specific set of environmental conditions, as an organism that can lead either a parasitic or a nonparasitic life (opposed to *obligate*). —**fac′ul·ta′tive·ly,** *adv.*

fae·ces (fē′sēz), *n.* (*used with a pl. v.*) Chiefly Brit. FECES. —**fae′cal** (-kəl), *adj.*

Fahr·en·heit (far′ən hīt′), *adj.* noting, pertaining to, or measured according to a temperature scale (**Fahr′enheit scale′**) in which 32° represents the ice point and 212° the steam point. *Symbol:* F

fal·lo′pi·an (or **Fal·lo′pi·an**) **tube′** (fə lō′pē ən), *n.* either of a pair of long slender ducts in the female abdomen that transport ova from the ovary to the uterus and in fertilization transport sperm cells from the uterus to the released ova.

false′ preg′nancy, *n.* the appearance of physiological signs of pregnancy without conception; pseudocyesis.

fam′ily plan′ning, *n.* **1.** a program for determining the size of families through the spacing or prevention of pregnancies. **2.** (loosely) birth control.

fam′ily prac′tice, *n.* medical specialization in general practice that requires additional training and leads to board certification. Also called **fam′ily med′icine.** —**fam′ily practi′tioner,** *n.*

fam′ily ther′apy, *n.* the psychotherapeutic treatment of more than one member of a family, esp. at the same session.

fan·ta·sy or **phan·ta·sy** (fan/tə sē, -zē), *n., pl.* **-sies. 1.** an imagined or conjured up sequence of events, esp. one provoked by an unfulfilled psychological need. **2.** an abnormal or bizarre sequence of mental images, as a hallucination.

far·a·dize (far/ə dīz/), *v.t.,* **-dized, -diz·ing.** to stimulate or treat (muscles or nerves) with induced alternating electric current. **—far/a·di·za/tion,** *n.* **—far/a·diz/er,** *n.* **—far/a·dism,** *n.*

far'-point', *n.* the point farthest from the eye at which an object is clearly focused on the retina when accommodation of the eye is completely relaxed. Compare NEAR-POINT.

far/sight·ed, *adj.* seeing objects at a distance more clearly than those near at hand; hyperopic. **—far/sight/ed·ness,** *n.*

FAS, fetal alcohol syndrome.

fas·ci·a (fash/ē ə), *n., pl.* **fas·ci·ae** (fash/ē ē/). **1.** a band or sheath of connective tissue covering, supporting, or connecting the muscles or internal organs of the body. **2.** tissue of this kind.

fas·ci·i·tis (fash/ē ī/tis, fas/-), *n.* inflammation of the fascia.

fas·tig·i·um (fa stij/ē əm), *n., pl.* **-i·ums, -i·a** (-ē ə). the highest point of a fever or disease.

fat' cell', *n.* a cell in loose connective tissue that is specialized for the synthesis and storage of fat. Also called **adipocyte.**

fate' map', *n.* a diagram or series of diagrams indicating the structures that later develop from specific regions of an embryo.

fa·tigue (fə tēg/), *n.* **1.** weariness from bodily or mental exertion. **2.** temporary diminution of the irritability or functioning of organs, tissues, or cells after excessive exertion or stimulation.

fat/-sol/uble, *adj.* capable of dissolving in oil or fats.

fat/ty ac/id, *n.* any of a class of organic acids consisting of a long hydrocarbon chain ending in a carboxyl group that bonds to glycerol to form a fat.

fa·vus (fā/vəs), *n., pl.* **fa·vus·es.** a skin infection characterized by itching and crusting at the hair follicles, usu. caused by the fungus *Trichophyton schoenleinii.*

FDA, Food and Drug Administration.

fe·brif·ic (fi brif/ik), *adj.* producing or marked by fever.

feb·ri·fuge (feb/rə fyōōj/), *adj.* **1.** serving to dispel or reduce fever, as a medicine. **—n. 2.** such a medicine or agent.

fe·brile (fē/brəl, feb/rəl; *esp. Brit.* fē/brīl), *adj.* pertaining to, affected with, or marked by fever; feverish. **—fe·bril·i·ty** (fi bril/i tē), *n.*

fe·cal (fē/kəl), *adj.* of, pertaining to, or consisting of feces.

fe·ces (fē/sēz), *n.* (*used with a pl. v.*) waste matter discharged from the intestines through the anus; excrement. Also, *esp. Brit.*, **faeces.**

feed/back/, *n.* a self-regulatory biological system, as in the synthesis of some hormones, in which the output or response affects the input, either positively or negatively.

fel·la·ti·o (fə lā/shē ō′, -lä/tē ō′, fe-) *n.* oral stimulation of the penis, esp. to orgasm.

fel·on (fel/ən), *n.* an acute and painful inflammation of the tissues of a finger or toe, usu. near the nail. Also called **agnail, whitlow.**

fe·male (fē/māl), *n.* **1.** a person of the sex whose cell nuclei contain two X chromosomes and who is normally able to conceive and bear young. **2.** any organism of the sex or sexual phase that normally produces egg cells.

fe·mur (fē/mər), *n., pl.* **fe·murs, fem·o·ra** (fem/ər ə). the long upper bone of the hind leg of vertebrates, extending from the pelvis to the knee; thighbone.

fe·nes·tra (fi nes/trə), *n., pl.* **-trae** (-trē) a small opening or perforation, as in a bone, esp. either of the two oval openings between the middle and inner ears. **—fe·nes/-tral,** *adj.*

fen·es·tra·tion (fen/ə strā/shən), *n.* **1.** an opening or perforation in an anatomical structure. **2.** surgery to effect such an opening. **3.** the creation of an artificial opening into the labyrinth of the ear to restore hearing loss from otosclerosis.

fer·ment (fûr/ment), *n.* **1.** any of a group of living organisms, as yeasts, molds, and certain bacteria, that cause fermentation. **2.** an enzyme that catalyzes the anaerobic breakdown of molecules that yield energy.

fer/men·ta/tion, *n.* a chemical change brought about by a ferment, as the conversion of grape sugar into ethyl alcohol by yeast enzymes.

fer·ri·tin (fer/i tn), *n.* a protein of the liver, spleen, and bone marrow that stores iron for use in metabolism.

fer·tile (fûr/tl; *esp. Brit.* -til), *adj.* bearing or capable of bearing offspring. **—fer/tile·ly,** *adv.* **—fer/tile·ness,** *n.*

fer·til·i·ty (fər til/i tē), *n.* the ability to produce offspring; power of reproduction.

fer·ti·li·za·tion (fûr/tl ə zā/shən), *n.* **1.** an act, process, or instance of fertilizing. **2.** the state of being fertilized. **3.** the union of male and female gametic nuclei.

fer/ti·lize/, *v.t.* **-lized, -liz·ing. 1.** to render (the female gamete) capable of development by uniting it with the male gamete. **2.** to fecundate or impregnate (an animal, plant, or other organism).

fe·tal or **foe·tal** (fēt/l), *adj.* of, pertaining to, or having the character of a fetus.

fe/tal al/cohol syn/drome, *n.* a variable cluster of birth defects that may include facial abnormalities, growth deficiency, mental retardation, and other impairments, caused by the mother's consumption of alcohol during pregnancy. *Abbr.:* FAS

fe/tal posi/tion, *n.* a posture resembling that of the fetus in the uterus, in which the body is curled with head and limbs drawn in.

fe·ti·cide (fē′ti-sīd′), *n.* the act of destroying a fetus. —**fe′·ti·cid′al**, *adj.*

fet·ish (fet′ish, fē′tish), *n.* an object or nongenital part of the body, as a shoe, undergarment, or hank of hair, that is repeatedly preferred or exclusively used for achieving sexual excitement.

fe·tol·o·gy (fē tol′ə jē), *n.* a field of medicine involving the study, diagnosis, and treatment of the fetus. —**fe·tol′·o·gist**, *n.*

fe′to·scope′ (-tə skōp′), *n.* a tubular fiberoptic instrument used to examine the fetus and interior of the uterus. —**fe′to·scop′ic** (-skop′ik), *adj.* —**fe·tos′co·py** (-tos′kə pē), *n.*

fe·tus or **foe·tus**, *n., pl.* **-tus·es.** (used chiefly of viviparous mammals) the young of an animal in the womb or egg, esp. in the later stages of development, in humans being after the end of the second month of gestation. Compare EMBRYO.

fe·ver (fē′vər), *n.* **1.** an abnormally high body temperature. **2.** any of various diseases in which high temperature is a prominent symptom, as scarlet fever or rheumatic fever. —**fe′ver·ish**, *adj.*

fe′ver blis′ter, *n.* a cold sore.

fi·ber (fī′bər), *n.* **1.** any of the filaments or elongated cells or structures that are combined in a bundle of tissue: *nerve fiber.* Also called **bulk, roughage.** the structural parts of plants, as cellulose, pectin, and lignin, that are wholly or partly indigestible, acting to increase intestinal bulk and peristalsis. Also, *esp. Brit.,* **fi′bre.**

fi·bril·late (fī′brə lāt′, fib′rə-), *v.i., v.t.* **-lat·ed, -lat·ing.** to undergo or cause to undergo fibrillation.

fi′bril·la′tion, *n.* chaotic contractions across the atrium of the heart, causing fast and irregular ventricular activity; arrhythmia.

fi·brin (fī′brin), *n.* the insoluble protein end product of blood coagulation, formed from fibrinogen by the action of thrombin. —**fi·brin·ous**, *adj.*

fi·brin′o·gen (-ə jən), *n.* a globulin occurring in blood and yielding fibrin in blood coagulation.

fi·bri·noid (fī′brə noid′, fib′rə-), *adj.* having the characteristics of fibrin.

fi·bri·nol·y·sin (fī′brə nol′ə sin), *n.* PLASMIN.

fi′bri·nol′y·sis, *n., pl.* **-ses** (-sēz′). the disintegration or dissolution of fibrin, esp. by enzymatic action. —**fi′bri·no·lyt′ic** (-nl it′ik), *adj.*

fi·bro·ad·e·no·ma (fī′brō ad′n ō′mə), *n., pl.* **-mas, -ma·ta** (-mə tə). a benign tumor originating from glandular tissue.

fi′bro·car′ti·lage, *n.* **1.** a type of cartilage having a large number of fibers. **2.** a part or structure composed of such cartilage. —**fi′bro·car′ti·lag′i·nous**, *adj.*

fi′bro·cys′tic, *adj.* showing or having the increased fibrosis associated with dilated glandular structure, as in benign breast cysts.

fi′broid, *adj.* **1.** resembling fiber or fibrous tissue. —*n.* **2.** FIBROMA. **3.** LEIOMYOMA.

fi·bro·ma (-brō′mə), *n., pl.* **-mas, -ma·ta** (-mə tə). a tumor consisting essentially of fibrous tissue. —**fi·brom′a·tous,** (-brōm′ə təs), *adj.*

fi′bro·my·al′gia, *n.* FIBROSITIS.

fi·bro·pla·sia (-brə plā′zhə, -zhē ə), *n.* the formation of new fibrous tissue, as in wound healing. —**fi′bro·plas′tic** (-plas′tik), *adj.*

fi·bro′sis (-brō′sis), *n.* the development in an organ of excess fibrous connective tissue. —**fi·brot′ic** (-brot′ik), *adj.*

fi′bro·si′tis (-brə sī′tis), *n.* a chronic disease syndrome marked by debilitating fatigue, widespread muscular pain, and tenderness at specific points on the body.

fi′brous (-brəs), *adj.* containing, consisting of, or resembling fibers. —**fi′brous·ly,** *adv.* —**fi′brous·ness,** *n.*

fib·u·la (fib′yə lə), *n., pl.* **-lae** (-lē′), **-las.** the outer and thinner of the two bones extending from the knee to the ankle in primates. —**fib′u·lar,** *adj.*

field′ of vi′sion, *n.* the entire view encompassed by the eye when it is trained in any particular direction. Also called **visual field.**

fi·lar·i·a (fi lâr′ē ə), *n., pl.* **-lar·i·ae** (-lâr′ē ē′). any small threadlike roundworm of the superfamily Filarioidea, carried by mosquitoes and parasitic when adult in the blood or tissues of vertebrates. —**fi·lar′i·al,** *adj.*

fil·a·ri·a·sis (fil′ə rī′ə sis), *n.* infestation with filarial worms in the blood, lymphatic tissue, etc.

fil·i·al (fil′ē əl), *adj. Genetics.* pertaining to the sequence of generations following the parental generation, each generation being designated by an *F* followed by a subscript number indicating its place in the sequence.

fil·ter·a·ble (fil′tər ə bəl), *adj.* capable of passing through bacteria-retaining filters. —**fil′ter·a·bil′i·ty, fil′ter·a·ble·ness,** *n.*

fil′terable vi′rus, *n.* a virus small enough to pass through a bacteria-retaining filter: a rough indicator of size, as recent filters can hold back the smallest viruses.

fin′ger·print′, *n.* any unique or distinctive pattern that presents unambiguous evidence of a specific person, substance, disease, etc.

fin′ger·print′ing, *n.* the use of a DNA probe for the unique identification of an individual, as for the matching of genes from a forensic sample with those of a criminal suspect.

first′-degree′ burn′, *n.* See under BURN.

fis·sion (fish′ən), *n.* the division of a biological organism into new organisms as a process of reproduction.

fis·sip·a·rous (fi sip′ər əs), *adj.* reproducing by fission.

fis·tu·la (fis′chŏŏ lə), *n., pl.* **-las, -lae** (-lē′). **1.** a narrow passage or duct formed by disease or injury. **2.** a surgical opening into a hollow organ for drainage.

fis·tu·lous, also **fis·tu·lar**, **fis·tu·late** (-lit), *adj.* pertaining to or resembling a fistula.

fix·a·tion (fik sā′shən), *n. Psychoanal.* a partial arrest of libidinal expression at an early stage of psychosexual development.

fixed′ ide′a, *n.* IDÉE FIXE.

fla·gel·lum (flə jel′əm), *n.*, *pl.* **-gel·la** (-jel′ə), **-gel·lums**. a long hairlike appendage serving as an organ of locomotion in protozoa, sperm cells, etc.

flash′back′, *n.* Also called **flash′back hallucino′sis.** *Psychiatry.* an abnormally vivid, often recurrent recollection of a disturbing past event, sometimes accompanied by hallucinations.

flat′foot′ (-fŏŏt′, -fŏŏt′), *n.*, *pl.* **-feet. 1.** a condition in which the arch of the foot is flattened so that the entire sole rests upon the ground. **2.** Also, **flat′ foot′.** a foot with such an arch.

flat·u·lent (flach′ə lənt), *adj.* having or chronically tending to have an accumulation of gas in the intestinal tract. —**flat′u·lence**, **flat′u·len·cy**, *n.*

fla·tus (flā′təs), *n.*, *pl.* **-tus·es.** intestinal gas.

fla·vin (flā′vin), *n.* any of a group of yellow nitrogen-containing pigments, as riboflavin, that function as coenzymes.

fla·vine (flā′vēn), *n.* FLAVIN.

fla·vo·pro·tein (flā′vō prō′tēn, -tē ən), *n.* any of a class of flavin-linked yellow enzymes that participate in cell respiration.

flesh′ wound′ (wŏŏnd), *n.* a wound that does not penetrate beyond the flesh; a slight or superficial wound.

flex (fleks), *v.t.* to tighten (a muscle) by contraction.

float·ing (flō′ting), *adj.* (of a body part or organ) away from its proper position, esp. in a downward direction: *a floating kidney.*

floc·cil·la·tion (flok′sə lā′shən), *n.* a purposeless compulsive picking at one's clothing or bedding, as in delirium.

flo·ra (flôr′ə, flōr′ə), *n.*, *pl.* **flo·ras, flo·rae** (flôr′ē, flōr′ē) . the aggregate of bacteria, fungi, and other microorganisms occurring on or within the body: *intestinal flora.*

flu (flŏŏ), *n.* **1.** influenza. **2.** a specific variety of influenza, usu. marked by its point of dissemination or its animal vector: *Hong Kong flu; swine flu.*

flu′id·ex′tract, *n.* a liquid preparation of a drug with alcohol as a solvent or preservative, containing in each cubic centimeter the medicinal activity of one gram of the powdered drug.

fluke (flŏŏk), *n.* TREMATODE.

fluo·res′cence-ac′tivated cell′ sort′er (flŏŏ res′əns, flô-, flō-), *n.* See FACS.

fluor·ine (flŏŏr′ēn, -in, flôr′-, flōr′-), *n.* the most reactive nonmetallic element, a pale yellow, corrosive, toxic gas that occurs combined in minerals and is found naturally in bones and teeth. *Symbol:* F; *at. wt.:* 18.9984; *at. no.:* 9.

fluor·o·chrome (flŏŏr′ə krōm′, flôr′-, flōr′-), *n.* any of a group of fluorescent dyes used to label biological material.

fluo·rog·ra·phy (flŏŏ rog′rə fē, flô-, flō-), *n.* PHOTOFLUOROGRAPHY.

fluor·o·scope (flŏŏr′ə skōp′, flôr′-, flōr′-), *n., v.,* **-scoped, -scop·ing.** *—n.* **1.** a tube or box fitted with a screen coated with a fluorescent substance, used for viewing objects, esp. deep body structures, by means of x-ray or other radiation. *—v.t.* **2.** to examine by means of a fluoroscope. **—fluor′o·scop′ic** (-skop′ik), *adj.* **—fluor′o·scop′i·cal·ly,** *adv.* **—fluo·ros·co·py** (flŏŏ ros′kə pē, flô-, flō-), *n.*

fluo·ro·sis (flŏŏ rō′sis, flô-, flō-), *n.* **1.** an abnormal condition caused by excessive intake of fluorides, characterized in children by discoloration and pitting of the teeth and in adults by pathological bone changes. **2.** Also called **mottled enamel.** the changes in tooth enamel symptomatic of fluorosis.

fluor·o·u·ra·cil (flŏŏr′ə yŏŏr′ə sil, flôr′-, flōr′-), *n.* a pyrimidine analog, $C_4H_3FN_2O_2$, used in the treatment of certain cancers.

flux (fluks), *n.* an abnormal discharge of liquid matter from the bowels.

fo·cus (fō′kəs), *n., pl.* **-cus·es, -ci** (-sī, -kī). the primary center from which a disease develops or in which it localizes.

foe·tus (fē′təs), *n., pl.* **-tus·es.** FETUS. **—foe′tal,** *adj.*

fo·late (fō′lāt, fol′āt), *n.* FOLIC ACID.

fo·lic ac·id (fō′lik, fol′ik), *n.* a water-soluble vitamin that is converted to a coenzyme essential to purine and thymine biosynthesis: deficiency causes a form of anemia.

fo·lie à deux (*Fr.* fô lē A dœ′), *n., pl.* **fo·lies à deux** (*Fr.* fô lē ZA dœ′). the sharing of delusional ideas by two people who are closely associated.

fo·lie de gran·deur (*Fr.* fô lēd° grän dœ̃R′), *n., pl.* **fo·lies de grandeur** (*Fr.* fô lēd°). a delusion of grandeur; megalomania.

folk′ med′icine, *n.* health practices arising from cultural traditions, from empirical use of native remedies, esp. food substances, or from superstition.

fol′licle mite′, *n.* any mite of the family Demodicidae, parasitic in hair follicles of various mammals, including humans.

fol′licle-stim′ulating hor′mone, *n.* See FSH.

fon·ta·nel or **fon·ta·nelle** (fon′tn el′), *n.* any of the spaces, covered by membrane, between the bones of a fetal or young skull.

food′ poi′soning, *n.* **1.** any illness, as salmonellosis or botulism, caused by eating food contaminated with bacterial toxins and typically marked by severe intestinal symptoms, as diarrhea, vomiting, and cramps. **2.** any illness caused by eating poisonous mushrooms, plants, fish, etc., or food containing chemical contaminants.

fora′men mag′num (mag′nəm), *n.* the large opening in the base of the skull through which the spinal cord merges with the brain.

for·ceps (fôr′səps, -seps), *n., pl.* **-ceps, -ci·pes** (-sə pēz′). an instrument, as pincers or tongs, for seizing and holding objects firmly, as in surgical operations. —**for·cip·i·al** (-sip′ē əl), *adj.*

fore·brain (fôr′brān′, fōr′-), *n.* **1.** Also called **prosen·cephalon.** the anterior of the three embryonic divisions of the vertebrate brain, or the part of the adult brain derived from this tissue including the diencephalon and telenceph·alon. **2.** TELENCEPHALON.

fore·gut′, *n.* the upper portion of the embryonic verte·brate alimentary canal from which the pharynx, esophagus, lungs, stomach, duodenum, liver, and pancreas develop. Compare HINDGUT, MIDGUT.

fore·milk′, *n.* COLOSTRUM.

fo·ren·sic (fə ren′sik), *adj.* **1.** of, pertaining to, or in·volved with forensic medicine or forensic anthropology: *fo·rensic laboratories.* —*n.* (*used with a sing. v.*) **2.** **forensics,** a department of forensic medicine, as in a po·lice laboratory.

foren′sic anthropol′ogy, *n.* the branch of physical an·thropology concerned with identifying or characterizing skeletal or biological remains in questions of civil or crimi·nal law.

foren′sic med′icine, *n.* the application of medical knowledge to questions of civil and criminal law, esp. in court proceedings.

fore′play′, *n.* sexual stimulation intended as a prelude to sexual intercourse.

fore′skin′, *n.* the prepuce of the penis.

form·a·tive (fôr′mə tiv), *adj.* **1.** capable of developing new cells or tissue by cell division and differentiation: *formative tissue.* **2.** concerned with the formation of an embryo, organ, or the like. —**form′a·tive·ly,** *adv.* —**form′a·tive·ness,** *n.*

for′mic ac′id (fôr′mik), *n.* a colorless, irritating, fuming liquid, CH_2O_2, orig. obtained from ants and now made syn·thetically, used as a counterirritant and astringent.

for·mu·la (fôr′myə lə), *n., pl.* **-las, -lae** (-lē′). **1.** a recipe or prescription. **2.** a special nutritive mixture, esp. of milk or milk substitute with other ingredients, in prescribed proportions for feeding a baby.

for′mu·lar′y (-ler′ē), *n., pl.* **-lar·ies.** a book listing phar·maceutical substances and medicinal formulas.

for·nix (fôr′niks), *n., pl.* **-ni·ces** (-nə sēz′). any of various arched or vaulted anatomical structures, as the triangular bands of white fibers beneath the corpus callosum of the mammalian brain. —**for′ni·cal,** *adj.*

fos·sa (fos′ə), *n., pl.* **fos·sae** (fos′ē). a pit, cavity, or de·pression, as in a bone.

fou·droy·ant (fōō droi′ənt; *Fr.* fōō drwA yäN′), *adj.* (of disease) beginning in a sudden and severe form.

four·chette (foor shet/), *n.* the fold of skin that forms the posterior margin of the vulva.

fo·ve·a (fō/vē ə), *n., pl.* **-ve·ae** (-vē ē/). **1.** a small pit or depression, as in a bone. **2.** FOVEA CENTRALIS. —**fo/ve·al,** *adj.*

fo/vea cen·tra/lis (sen trā/lis), *n.* a small rodless area near the center of the retina in some vertebrates that allows particularly acute vision.

frac·ture (frak/chər), *n., v.,* **-tured, -tur·ing.** —*n.* **1.** the breaking of a bone, cartilage, or the like, or the resulting condition. Compare COMPOUND FRACTURE. —*v.t.* **2.** to cause or to suffer a fracture in. —**frac/tur·a·ble,** *adj.* —**frac/-tur·al,** *adj.*

fragile X syndrome, *n.* a widespread form of mental retardation caused by a faulty gene on the X chromosome.

fram·be·sia (fram bē/zhə), *n.* YAWS.

frame/shift/, *n.* the addition or deletion of one or more nucleotides in a strand of DNA, which shifts the codon triplets of the genetic code of messenger RNA, resulting in a mutation.

frater/nal twin/, *n.* one of a pair of twins, not necessarily resembling each other or of the same sex, that develop from two separately fertilized ova. Compare IDENTICAL TWIN.

free/ associa/tion, *n. Psychoanal.* the uncensored expression of the ideas, impressions, etc., passing through the mind of an analysand, used to facilitate access to the unconscious. —**free/-asso/ciate,** *v.i.,* **-at·ed, -at·ing.**

free/base/ or **free/-base/,** *v.,* **-based, -bas·ing,** *n.* —*v.t.* **1.** to purify (cocaine) by dissolving under heat with ether to remove salts and impurities. **2.** to smoke or inhale (freebased cocaine). —*v.i.* **3.** to freebase cocaine. —*n.* **4.** freebased cocaine. —**free/bas/er,** *n.*

free/ rad/ical, *n.* a molecular fragment that bears one or more unpaired electrons and is therefore highly reactive, being capable of rapid oxidizing reactions that destabilize other molecules.

frem·i·tus (frem/i təs), *n., pl.* **-tus.** palpable vibration, as of the walls of the chest.

fre·num (frē/nəm), *n., pl.* **-na** (-nə) a fold of membrane, as on the underside of the tongue, that checks or restrains motion.

Freud·i·an (froi/dē ən), *adj.* **1.** of or pertaining to Sigmund Freud or his theories. —*n.* **2.** a person, esp. a psychoanalyst, who adheres to the basic theories or practices of Freud. —**Freud/i·an·ism,** *n.*

Freud/ian slip/, *n.* an inadvertent mistake in speech or writing that supposedly reveals an unconscious motive, wish, attitude, etc.

frig·id (frij/id), *adj.* (of a woman) unable to experience an orgasm or sexual excitement during sexual intercourse. —**fri·gid/i·ty,** *n.*

fron·tal (frun/tl), *adj.* of, pertaining to, or situated near the forehead or the frontal bone. —**front/al·ly,** *adv.*

fron'tal bone', *n.* the broad front part of the skull, forming the forehead.

fron'tal lobe', *n.* the anterior part of each cerebral hemisphere, in front of the central sulcus.

frost'bite', *n.* injury to any part of the body after excessive exposure to extreme cold.

frost'bit'ten, *adj.* injured by frost or extreme cold.

frot·tage (frô täzh'), *n.* sexual stimulation through rubbing the genitals against another person.

fruc·tose (fruk'tōs, frŏŏk'-, frŏŏk'-), *n.* a crystalline, water-soluble, levorotatory ketose sugar, $C_6H_{12}O_6$, sweeter than sucrose, occurring in invert sugar, honey, and many fruits: chiefly used in foodstuffs.

FSH, follicle-stimulating hormone: an anterior pituitary peptide that stimulates the development of Graafian follicles in the female and spermatozoa in the male.

ful·gu·rate (ful'gyə rāt'), *v.t.* **-rat·ed, -rat·ing.** to destroy (esp. an abnormal growth) by electricity. —**ful'gu·ra'tion,** *n.*

ful·mi·nant (ful'mə nənt), *adj. Pathol.* developing or progressing suddenly.

fu·ma·rate (fyŏŏ'mə rāt'), *n.* the salt of fumaric acid, a key chemical intermediate in the Krebs cycle.

func·tion·al (fungk'shə nl), *adj.* of or pertaining to impaired function without known organic or structural cause: *a functional disorder.* —**func'tion·al'i·ty,** *n.* —**func'tion·al·ly,** *adv.*

func'tion·al·ism', *n.* a school of psychology that emphasizes the adaptiveness of mental and behavioral processes. —**func'tion·al·ist,** *n., adj.* —**func'tion·al·is'tic,** *adj.*

fun·gi·cide (fun'jə sīd', fung'gə-), *n.* a substance or agent used for destroying fungi. —**fun'gi·cid'al,** *adj.* —**fun'gi·cid'al·ly,** *adv.*

fun·goid (fung'goid), *n.* a growth having the characteristics of a fungus.

fun'gous (-gəs), *adj.* **1.** of, pertaining to, or caused by fungi; fungal. **2.** of the nature of or resembling a fungus.

fun'gus (-gəs), *n., pl.* **fun·gi** (fun'jī, fung'gī), **fun·gus·es,** *adj.* —*n.* **1.** any member of the kingdom Fungi (or division Thallophyta of the kingdom Plantae), comprising single-celled or multinucleate organisms that live by decomposing and absorbing the organic material in which they grow: includes the mushrooms, molds, mildews, smuts, rusts, and yeasts. —*adj.* **2.** fungous.

fun'ny bone', *n.* the part of the elbow where the ulnar nerve passes close to the surface and which, when struck, causes a peculiar tingling sensation in the arm and hand.

fu·run·cle (fyŏŏr'ung kəl), *n.* BOIL. —**fu·run'cu·lar** (-kyə-lər), **fu·run'cu·lous,** *adj.*

fu·run·cu·lo·sis (-kyə lō'sis), *n.* a condition or disease characterized by the presence of boils.

G

G, *Symbol.* **1.** glycine. **2.** guanine.

g or **g.,** gram.

GABA (gab'ə), *n.* gamma-aminobutyric acid: a neurotransmitter that inhibits excitatory responses.

gag (gag), *v.,* **gagged, gag·ging,** *n.* —*v.t.* **1.** to hold open the jaws of, as in surgical operations. —*n.* **2.** a surgical instrument for holding the jaws open.

ga·lac·tic (gə lak'tik), *adj.* pertaining to or stimulating the secretion of milk.

ga·lac·tor·rhe·a (-tə rē'ə), *n.* **1.** an abnormally persistent flow of milk. **2.** secretion of milk from the breast of a nonlactating person.

ga·lac'tose (-tōs), *n.* a white sugar, $C_6H_{12}O_6$, obtained from milk sugar and vegetable mucilage.

ga·lac'to·se·mi·a (-tə sē'mē ə), *n.* an inherited disorder characterized by the inability to metabolize galactose and necessitating a galactose-free diet. —**ga·lac'to·se'mic,** *adj.*

ga·len·i·cal (gā len'i kəl, gə-), *n.* a standard medical preparation containing one or more organic ingredients, as herbs, rather than having a purely chemical content.

gall'blad·der or **gall' blad'der** (gôl'-), *n.* a membranous sac attached by ducts to the liver, in which bile is stored and concentrated.

gall'stone', *n.* an abnormal stony mass in the gallbladder or the bile passages, usu. composed of cholesterol.

gal·va·nism (gal'və niz/əm), *n.* the therapeutic application of electricity to the body.

gam·ete (gam'ēt, gə mēt'), *n.* a mature sexual reproductive cell, as a sperm or egg, that unites with another cell to form a new organism. —**ga·met·ic** (gə met'ik), **ga·met·al** (-mēt'l), *adj.* —**ga·met'i·cal·ly,** *adv.*

ga·me·to·cyte (gə mē'tə sit', gam'i-), *n.* a cell that produces gametes.

gam·e·to·gen·e·sis, *n.* the development of gametes. —**ga·me'to·gen'ic, gam'e·tog'e·nous** (-toj'ə nəs), *adj.*

gam·ic (gam'ik), *adj.* **1.** requiring fertilization for reproduction; sexual. **2.** capable of developing only after fertilization.

gam'ma-a·mi·no·bu·tyr'ic ac'id (gam'ə ə mē'nō-byoo tir'ik, -am'ə nō-), *n.* See GABA.

gam·o·gen·e·sis (gam'ə jen'ə sis), *n.* sexual reproduction. —**gam'o·ge·net'ic** (-ō jə net'ik), **gam'o·ge·net'i·cal,** *adj.*

gan·gli·ate (gang'glē āt', -it) also **gan'gli·at'ed,** *adj.* having ganglia.

gan'gli·on (-glē ən), *n., pl.* **-gli·a** (-glē ə), **-gli·ons.** **1.** a concentrated mass of interconnected nerve cells. **2.** a cystic tumor formed on the sheath of a tendon. —**gan'gli·al, gan'gli·ar,** *adj.* —**gan'gli·on'ic** (-on'ik), *adj.*

gan·gli·o·side (-ə sīd′), *n.* any of a group of glycolipids abundant in nerve ganglia.

gan·grene (gang′grēn, gang grēn′), *n., v.,* **-grened, -gren·ing. —n. 1.** necrosis or death of soft tissue due to obstructed circulation, usu. followed by decomposition and putrefaction. —*v.t., v.i.* **2.** to affect or become affected with gangrene. —**gan′gre·nous** (-grə nəs), *adj.*

gan·ja or **gan·jah** (gän′jə, gan′-), *n.* marijuana, esp. in the form of a potent preparation used chiefly for smoking.

gas (gas), *n.* FLATUS.

gas′ gan′grene, *n.* a gangrenous infection developing in wounds, esp. deep wounds with closed spaces, caused by bacteria that form gases in the subcutaneous tissues.

gas·trec·to·my (ga strek′tə mē), *n., pl.* **-mies.** partial or total surgical removal of the stomach.

gas·tric (gas′trik), *adj.* pertaining to the stomach.

gas′tric juice′, *n.* the digestive fluid, containing pepsin and other enzymes, secreted by the glands of the stomach.

gas′tric ul′cer, *n.* an ulcer in the inner wall of the stomach.

gas·trin (-trin), *n.* a hormone that stimulates the secretion of gastric juice.

gas·tri·tis (ga strī′tis), *n.* inflammation of the stomach, esp. of its mucous membrane. —**gas·trit′ic** (-strit′ik), *adj.*

gas·troc·ne·mi·us (gas′trok nē′mē əs, gas′trə nē′-), *n., pl.* **-mi·i** (-mē ī′). the largest muscle of the calf of the leg, arising on the femur and merging with the Achilles tendon. —**gas·troc·ne′mi·al, gas·troc·ne′mi·an,** *adj.*

gas·tro·en·ter·i·tis (gas′trō en′tə rī′tis), *n.* inflammation of the stomach and intestines. —**gas·tro·en·ter·it′ic** (-rit′ik), *adj.*

gas·tro·en·ter·ol·o·gy (-en′tə rol′ə jē), *n.* the study of the structure, functions, and diseases of digestive organs. —**gas·tro·en·ter·o·log′ic** (-tər ə loj′ik), **gas·tro·en·ter·o·log′i·cal,** *adj.* —**gas·tro·en·te·rol′o·gist,** *n.*

gas·tro·in·tes·ti·nal, *adj.* of, pertaining to, or affecting the stomach and intestines.

gas·tro·lith (gas′trə lith), *n.* a calculous concretion in the stomach.

gas·tro·scope′ (-skōp′), *n.* an endoscope passed through the mouth for examining and treating the stomach. —**gas·tro·scop′ic** (-skop′ik), *adj.* —**gas·tros·co·py** (ga stros′kə pē), *n., pl.* **-pies.**

gas·trot·o·my (ga strot′ə mē), *n., pl.* **-mies.** the surgical operation of cutting into the stomach. —**gas·tro·tom·ic** (gas′trə tom′ik), *adj.*

gas·tru·la (gas′trŏŏ lə), *n., pl.* **-las, -lae** (-lē′). an embryo in an early stage of development during which the blastula differentiates into two cell layers and the central cavity becomes the archenteron. —**gas′tru·lar,** *adj.* —**gas′tru·late′,** *v.i.,* **-lat·ed, -lat·ing.** —**gas′tru·la′tion,** *n.*

gate′way drug′, *n.* any mood-altering drug, as a stimulant or tranquilizer, that does not cause physical dependence but may lead to the use of addictive drugs, as heroin.

gauze (gôz), *n.* a surgical dressing of loosely woven cotton.

gDNA, genomic DNA.

gel′ electrophore′sis, *n.* a technique for separating proteins in a mixture by drawing the mixture through a block of gel with an electric field, each protein thereby traveling a specific distance according to its size.

gen′der-specif′ic, *adj.* for, characteristic of, or limited to either males or females: *gender-specific roles.*

gene (jēn), *n.* the basic physical unit of heredity; a linear sequence of nucleotides along a segment of DNA that provides the coded instructions for synthesis of RNA, which, when translated into protein, leads to the expression of hereditary character.

gene′ amplifica′tion, *n.* **1.** an increase in the frequency of replication of a DNA segment. **2.** such an increase induced by a polymerase chain reaction.

gene′ flow′, *n.* changes in the frequency of alleles within a gene pool that occur as a result of interbreeding. Compare GENETIC DRIFT.

gene′ fre′quency, *n.* the frequency of occurrence or proportions of different alleles of a particular gene in a given population.

gene′ map′, *n.* GENETIC MAP.

gene′ map′ping, *n.* the act or process of determining the precise location of a gene or genes on a particular chromosome.

gene′ pool′, *n.* the total genetic information in the gametes of all the individuals in a population.

gen·er·al·i·za·tion (jen′ər ə lə zā′shən), *n.* the act or process of responding to a stimulus similar to but distinct from a conditioned stimulus.

gen′eral practi′tioner, *n.* a medical practitioner whose practice is not limited to any specific branch of medicine or class of diseases. *Abbr.:* G.P.

gen·er·a′tion (-ə rā′shən), *n.* the term of years, about 30 among human beings, accepted as the average period between the birth of parents and the birth of their offspring. —**gen′er·a′tion·al,** *adj.* —**gen·er·a′tion·al·ly,** *adv.*

ge·ner·ic (jə ner′ik), *adj.* **1.** not protected by trademark registration; nonproprietary: *a generic drug.* —*n.* **2.** any product, as a food, drug, or cosmetic, that can be sold without a brand name. —**ge·ner′i·cal·ly,** *adv.*

gene′ splic′ing, *n.* the act or process of recombining genes from different sources to form new genetic combinations.

gene′ ther′apy, *n.* the treatment of a disease by replacing aberrant genes with normal ones, esp. through the use of viruses to transport the desired genes into the nuclei of blood cells.

ge·net·ic (jə net′ik) also **ge·net′i·cal,** *adj.* **1.** pertaining or according to genetics. **2.** of, pertaining to, or produced by genes; genic. —**ge·net/i·cal·ly,** *adv.*

genet/ic code/, *n.* the biochemical instructions that translate the genetic information present as a linear sequence of nucleotide triplets in messenger RNA into the correct linear sequence of amino acids for the synthesis of a particular peptide chain or protein.

genet/ic coun/seling, *n.* the counseling of persons with established or potential genetic problems in regard to inheritance patterns and risks to future offspring.

genet/ic drift/, *n.* random changes in the frequency of alleles in a gene pool, usu. of small populations. Compare GENE FLOW.

genet/ic engineer/ing, *n.* **1.** the development and application of scientific methods, procedures, and technologies that permit direct manipulation of genetic material in order to alter the hereditary traits of a cell, organism, or population. **2.** a technique producing unlimited amounts of otherwise unavailable or scarce biological product by introducing DNA from certain living organisms into bacteria and then harvesting the product, as human insulin produced in bacteria by the human insulin gene. Also called **biogenetics.** —**genet/ic engineer/,** *n.*

genet/ic fin/gerprinting, *n.* DNA FINGERPRINTING. —**genet/ic fin/gerprint,** *n.*

ge·net/i·cist (-ə sist), *n.* a specialist in genetics.

genet/ic load/, *n.* the extent to which a population deviates from the theoretically fittest genetic constitution.

genet/ic map/, *n.* an arrangement of genes on a chromosome.

genet/ic mark/er, *n.* any gene or allele that is associated with a specific chromosome and can be used to identify the chromosome or to locate other genes or alleles. Also called **marker, marker gene.**

ge·net/ics, *n.* (*used with a sing. v.*) **1.** the branch of biology that deals with the principles and mechanisms of heredity and with the genetic contribution to similarities and differences among related organisms. **2.** the genetic properties or constitution of an organism or group.

genet/ic screen/ing, *n.* assessment of an individual's genetic makeup to detect defects that may be transmitted to offspring or to try to predict genetic predisposition to certain illnesses.

gene/ trans/fer, *n.* the insertion of copies of a gene into living cells in order to induce synthesis of the gene's product.

gen·ic (jen/ik), *adj.* of, pertaining to, resembling, or arising from a gene or genes.

gen·i·tal (jen/i tl), *adj.* **1.** of or pertaining to the sexual organs. **2.** of or pertaining to the centering of sexual impulses and excitation on the genitalia. **3.** of, pertaining to, or characteristic of the phase of psychosexual development, from about ages three to five, during which the genitals become the focus of sexual pleasure.

gen′ital her′pes, *n.* a sexually transmitted disease caused by a herpes simplex virus, characterized primarily by transient blisters on and around the genitals.

gen·i·ta·li·a (jen′i tāl′ē ə, -tāl′yə), *n.pl.* the organs of reproduction, esp. the external organs. —**gen′i·tal′ic** (-tal′ik), **gen′i·ta′li·al,** *adj.*

gen′i·tals, *n.pl.* GENITALIA.

gen′ital warts′, *n.pl.* warts occurring in the genital and anal areas and spread mainly by sexual contact, sometimes increasing the risk of cervical cancer in women.

gen′i·to·u′ri·nar′y (jen′i tō-), *adj.* of or pertaining to the genital and urinary organs; urogenital. *Abbr.:* GU

gen·o·gram (jen′ə gram′, jē′nə-), *n.* a family tree depicting the histories, personalities, and relationships of family members, constructed esp. as a diagnostic or therapeutic aid.

ge·nome (jē′nōm), *n.* a full haploid set of chromosomes with all its genes; the total genetic constitution of a cell or organism. —**ge·no′mic,** *adj.*

genomic DNA, *n.* a fragment or fragments of DNA produced by restriction enzymes acting on the DNA of a cell or an organism. *Abbr.:* gDNA

gen·o·type (jen′ə tīp′, jē′nə-), *n.* **1.** the genetic makeup of an organism or group of organisms with reference to a single trait, set of traits, or an entire complement of traits. **2.** the sum total of genes transmitted from parent to offspring. Compare PHENOTYPE. —**gen′o·typ′ic** (-tip′ik), **gen′o·typ′i·cal,** *adj.* —**gen′o·typ′i·cal·ly,** *adv.*

ger·i·at·ric (jer′ē a′trik, jēr′-), *adj.* of or pertaining to geriatrics, old age, or aged persons.

ger′i·at′rics, *n.* (*used with a sing. v.*) **1.** the branch of medicine dealing with the diseases, debilities, and care of aged persons. **2.** the study of the physical processes and problems of aging; gerontology. —**ger′i·a·tri′cian** (-ə trish′ən), **ger′i·at′rist,** *n.*

germ (jûrm), *n.* **1.** a microorganism, esp. when disease-producing; microbe. **2.** the rudiment of a living organism; an embryo in its early stages. **3.** the initial stage in development or evolution, as a germ cell or ancestral form. —**germ′like′,** *adj.*

Ger′man mea′sles, *n.* RUBELLA.

germ′ cell′, *n.* a sexual reproductive cell at any stage from the primordial cell to the mature gamete.

germ′free′ (-frē′, -frē′), *adj.* **1.** STERILE (def. 1). **2.** (of experimental animals) born and raised under sterile conditions.

ger·mi·cide (jûr′mə sīd′), *n.* an agent for killing germs or microorganisms. —**ger′mi·cid′al,** *adj.*

ger′mi·nal ves′icle (jûr′mə nl), *n.* the enlarged, vesicular nucleus of an ovum before the polar bodies are formed at the end of meiosis.

germ′ lay′er, *n.* any of the three primary embryonic cell layers. Compare ECTODERM, ENDODERM, MESODERM.

germ′ plasm′, *n.* the substance of reproductive cells that contains chromosomes.

germ′ the′ory, *n.* the theory that infectious diseases are due to the agency of germs or microorganisms.

ge·ron·tic (jə ron′tik), *adj.* of or pertaining to the last phase in the life cycle of an organism or in the life history of a species.

ger·on·tol·o·gy (jer′ən tol′ə jē, jēr′-), *n.* the study of aging and the problems of aged people. **—ge·ron·to·log·i·cal** (jə ront′l oj′i kəl), *adj.* **—ger′on·tol′o·gist,** *n.*

ge·stalt (gə shtält′, -shtôlt′, -stält′, -stôlt′), *n., pl.* **-stalts, -stal·ten** (-shtält′tn, -shtôlt′-, -stäl′-, -stôl′-). *Psychol.* (*sometimes cap.*) a form or configuration having properties that cannot be derived by the summation of its component parts.

Gestalt′ psychol′ogy, *n.* the school or doctrine holding that behavioral and psychological phenomena cannot be fully explained by analysis of their component parts, as reflexes or sensations, but must be studied as wholes.

ges·tate (jes′tāt), *v.,* **-tat·ed, -tat·ing.** *—v.t.* **1.** to carry in the womb during the period from the initiation of the pregnancy to delivery. *—v.i.* **2.** to experience the process of gestating offspring. **—ges·ta′tion,** *n.* **—ges·ta′tion·al, ges·ta·tive** (jes′tə tiv, je stā′-), *adj.*

gesta′tional car′rier, *n.* SURROGATE MOTHER (def. 2a). Also called **gesta′tional moth′er.**

GH, growth hormone.

gi·ant·ism (jī′ən tiz′əm), *n.* GIGANTISM.

gi·ar·di·a·sis (jē′är dī′ə sis, jär-), *n.* an intestinal infection characterized by chronic intermittent diarrhea, caused by a flagellate protozoan, *Giardia lamblia*, common in contaminated streams and ponds.

gi·gan·tism (jī gan′tiz əm, ji-, jī′gan tiz′əm), *n.* great overgrowth in size or stature of the body or developmentally related parts of the body.

gin·gi·va (jin jī′və, jin′jə-), *n., pl.* **-gi·vae** (-jī′vē, -jə vē′). GUM. **—gin·gi′val,** *adj.*

gin′gi·vec′to·my (-jə vek′tə mē), *n., pl.* **-mies.** surgical removal of gum tissue.

gin′gi·vi′tis (-vī′tis), *n.* inflammation of the gums.

GI series, *n.* gastrointestinal series: x-ray examination of the upper or lower gastrointestinal tract after barium sulfate is given orally or rectally as a contrast medium.

gla·bel·la (glə bel′ə), *n., pl.* **-bel·lae** (-bel′ē). the raised area of bone between the eyebrows. **—gla·bel′lar,** *adj.*

gla·bel·lum (glə bel′əm), *n., pl.* **-bel·la** (-bel′ə). GLABELLA.

glan·du·lar (glan′jə lər), *adj.* **1.** consisting of, containing, or bearing glands. **2.** of, pertaining to, or resembling a gland: *a glandular disorder.*

glan′dular fe′ver, *n.* INFECTIOUS MONONUCLEOSIS.

glans (glanz), *n., pl.* **glan·des** (glan′dēz). the head of the penis (**glans′ pe′nis**) or of the clitoris (**glans′ clit′o·ris**).

glau·co·ma (glô kō′mə, glou-), *n.* a condition of elevated fluid pressure within the eyeball, caused by an abnormally narrow angle between the iris and cornea (**closed-angle glaucoma** or **narrow-angle glaucoma**) or by an obstruction within the canal through which the aqueous humor drains (**open-angle glaucoma** or **wide-angle glaucoma**), causing damage to the eye and progressive loss of vision. —glau·co·ma·tous (-kō′mə təs, -kom′ə-), *adj.*

gleet (glēt), *n.* **1.** a thin, morbid discharge, as from a wound. **2.** persistent or chronic gonorrhea.

gli·a (glī′ə, glē′ə), *n.* NEUROGLIA. —**gli′al,** *adj.*

gli·a·din (glī′ə din, -dn), *n.* a simple protein of cereal grains that imparts elastic properties to flour: used as a nutrient in high-protein diets.

gli·o·ma (glī ō′mə), *n., pl.* **-mas, -ma·ta** (-mə tə). a tumor of the brain composed of neuroglia. —**gli·o′ma·tous** (-ō′mə təs, -om′ə-), *adj.*

gli·o′sis (-sis), *n.* an increase in the size and number of astrocytes of the brain.

Gln, glutamine.

glo·bin (glō′bin), *n.* the protein component of hemoglobin, made up of two isomeric chains.

glob·u·lin (glob′yə lin), *n.* any of a group of proteins, as myosin, that occur in plant and animal tissue and are soluble in salt solutions and coagulable by heat: in blood plasma, globulins are separated by electrophoresis into distinct fractions with various properties and designated alpha, beta, gamma, etc.

glo·mer·u·lo·ne·phri·tis (glō mer′yə lō nə frī′tis, glə-), *n.* a kidney disease affecting the capillaries of the glomeruli, characterized by albuminuria, edema, and hypertension.

glo·mer′u·lus (-ləs), *n., pl.* **-li** (-lī′). any compact cluster of nerves or capillaries, esp. a cluster of capillaries in the nephron of the kidney that acts as a filter of the blood. —**glo·mer′u·lar,** *adj.*

glos·si·tis (glo sī′tis, glô-), *n.* inflammation of the tongue. —**glos·sit′ic** (-sit′ik), *adj.*

glos·so·la·li·a (glos′ə lā′lē ə, glô′sə-), *n.* incomprehensible speech sometimes occurring in a hypnotic trance or in an episode of religious ecstasy.

glos·so·pha·ryn·ge·al (glos′ō fə rin′jē əl, -jəl, -far′in-jē′əl, glô′sō-), *adj.* of or pertaining to the tongue and pharynx.

glot·tis (glot′is), *n., pl.* **glot·tis·es, glot·ti·des** (glot′i-dēz′). the opening at the upper part of the larynx, between the vocal cords. —**glot′tal** (-əl), *adj.*

Glu, glutamic acid.

glu·ca·gon (glōō′kə gon′), *n.* a hormone secreted by the pancreas that acts in opposition to insulin in the regulation of blood glucose levels.

glu·co·cor·ti·coid (glōō′kō kôr′ti koid′), *n.* any of a class of steroid hormones that are produced by the adrenal cortex under conditions of stress and that inhibit immunologic reactions.

glu·co·ki′nase (-kī′nās, -nāz), *n.* an enzyme that catalyzes the phosphorylation of glucose.

glu·co·ne′o·gen′e·sis, *n.* glucose formation in animals from a noncarbohydrate source, as from proteins or fats.

glu·co′sa·mine′ (-sə mēn′, -min), *n.* an amino sugar occurring in many polysaccharides of vertebrate tissue.

glu·cose (-kōs), *n.* a simple sugar, $C_6H_{12}O_6$, that is a product of photosynthesis and is the principal source of energy for all living organisms: concentrated in fruits and honey or readily obtainable from starch, other carbohydrates, or glycogen.

glu·co·side′ (-sīd′), *n.* any of an extensive group of glycosides that yield glucose upon hydrolysis. —**glu·co·sid′ic** (-sid′ik), *adj.*

glu·cu·ron′ic ac′id (glōō′kyə ron′ik, glōō′-), *n.* an acid, $C_6H_{10}O_7$, formed by the oxidation of glucose, found combined with other products of metabolism in the blood and urine.

glu·tam′ic ac′id (-tam′ik) also **glu·ta·min′ic ac′id** (glōō′tə min′ik, glōō′-), *n.* a crystalline amino acid, $C_5H_9NO_4$, obtained by hydrolysis from wheat gluten and sugar-beet residues, used commercially as a flavor intensifier. *Abbr.:* Glu; *Symbol:* E

glu·ta·mine′ (-tə mēn′, -min), *n.* a crystalline amino acid, $C_5H_{10}N_2O_3$, related to glutamic acid and found in many plant and animal proteins. *Abbr.:* Gln; *Symbol:* Q

glu·ta·thi·one (-thī′ōn), *n.* a crystalline, water-soluble peptide of glutamic acid, cysteine, and glycine, $C_{10}H_{17}N_3O_6S$, found in blood and in animal and plant tissues, and important in tissue oxidations and in the activation of some enzymes.

glu·te·al (glōō′tē əl, glōō tē′əl), *adj.* pertaining to the buttock muscles or the buttocks.

glu·ten (glōōt′n), *n.* a grayish, sticky component of wheat flour and other grain flours, composed mainly of the proteins gliadin and glutenin. —**glu′ten·ous,** *adj.*

glu·ten·in (-in), *n.* a simple protein of cereal grains that imparts adhesive properties to flour.

glu·te·us (glōō′tē əs, glōō tē′-), *n., pl.* **-te·i** (-tē i′, -tē′ī). any of the three muscles of each buttock, involved in the rotation and extension of the thigh, esp. the gluteus maximus.

glu′teus max′i·mus (mak′sə məs), *n., pl.* **glutei max·i·mi** (mak′sə mī′). the broad, thick, outermost muscle of each buttock.

Gly, glycine.

glyc·er·al·de·hyde (glis′ə ral′də hīd′), *n.* an aldehyde sugar, $C_3H_6O_3$, that is an intermediate in carbohydrate metabolism and yields glycerol on reduction.

glyc′er·ide′ (-ə rīd′, -ər id), *n.* an ester of glycerol and a fatty acid. Compare TRIGLYCERIDE.

glyc·er·in (-ər in) also **glyc·er·ine** (-ər in, -ə rēn′), *n.* GLYCEROL.

glyc′er·ol′ (-ə rôl′, -rol′), *n.* a colorless liquid, $C_3H_8O_3$, used as a sweetener and preservative, and in suppositories and skin emollients.

gly·cine (glī/sēn, glī sēn/), *n.* a sweet crystalline solid, the simplest amino acid, $C_2H_5NO_2$, present in most proteins. *Abbr.:* Gly; *Symbol:* G

gly·co·gen (glī/kə jən, -jen/), *n.* a polysaccharide, $(C_6H_{10}O_5)_n$, composed of glucose isomers, that is the principal carbohydrate stored by the animal body and is readily converted to glucose when needed for energy use.

gly·co·lip·id (-lip/id), *n.* any of a class of lipids that contain a carbohydrate group.

gly·col/y·sis (-kol/ə sis), *n.* the catabolism of carbohydrates, as glucose and glycogen, by enzymes, with the release of energy and the production of lactic or pyruvic acid. —**gly/co·lyt/ic** (-kə lit/ik), *adj.* —**gly/co·lyt/i·cal·ly,** *adv.*

gly·co·pro·tein (glī/kō prō/tēn, -tē in), *n.* any of a group of complex proteins, as mucin, containing a carbohydrate combined with a simple protein. Also called **gly/co·pep/-tide** (-pep/tīd).

gly·cos·a·mi·no·gly·can (glī/kōs ə mē/nō glī/kan), *n.* any of a class of polysaccharides that form mucins when complexed with proteins. Also called **mucopolysaccharide.**

gly/co·side/ (-kə sīd/), *n.* any of the class of compounds that yield a sugar and a noncarbohydrate group upon hydrolysis. —**gly/co·sid/ic** (-sid/ik), *adj.*

gly·cos·u·ri·a (glī/kōs yŏŏ rē/ə), *n.* excretion of glucose in the urine, as in diabetes. —**gly/cos·u/ric** (-yŏŏr/ik), *adj.*

GMP, guanosine monophosphate: a ribonucleotide constituent of ribonucleic acid that is the phosphoric acid ester of the nucleoside guanosine. Also called **guanylic acid.**

gno·to·bi·o·sis (nō/tō bi ō/sis) also **gno/to·bi·ot/ics** (-ot/iks), *n.* the study of organisms or conditions that are free of germs or contaminants or to which a known germ or contaminant has been introduced for purposes of study. —**gno/to·bi·ot/ic,** *adj.* —**gno/to·bi·ot/i·cal·ly,** *adv.*

GnRH, gonadotropin releasing hormone; a hormone, produced by the hypothalamus, that stimulates the pituitary gland to secrete FSH and LH.

Go/a pow/der (gō/ə), *n.* a yellow medicinal powder obtained from the araroba tree: the source of chrysarobin. Also called **araroba.**

goi·ter (goi/tər), *n.* an enlargement of the thyroid gland on the front and sides of the neck. Also, *esp. Brit.,* **goi/tre.** —**goi/trous** (-trəs), *adj.*

go·mer (gō/mər), *n. Slang.* an undesirable hospital patient.

go·nad (gō/nad, gon/ad), *n.* any organ or gland in which gametes are produced; an ovary or testis. —**go·nad/al, go·na/di·al** (-nā/dē əl), **go·nad/ic** (-nad/ik), *adj.*

go·nad·o·trop·ic (gō nad/ə trop/ik, -trō/pik), *adj.* affecting the development or activity of the ovary or testis.

go·nad·o·tro·pin (gō nad/ə trō/pin), *n.* any of several gonadotropic hormones, as FSH and LH, that are produced in the pituitary gland or placenta.

gonadotro′pin releas′ing hor′mone, *n.* See GnRH. Also, **gonadotro′pin-releas′ing hor′mone.**

gon·o·coc·cus (gon′ə kok′əs), *n., pl.* **-coc·ci** (-kok′si, -sē). the bacterium *Neisseria gonorrhoeae,* causing gonorrhea. —**gon′o·coc′cal, gon′o·coc′cic** (-kok′sik), *adj.* —**gon′o·coc′coid,** *adj.*

gon·or·rhe·a (gon′ə rē′ə), *n.* a contagious, purulent inflammation of the urethra or the vagina, caused by the gonococcus. Also, *esp. Brit.,* **gon′or·rhoe′a.** —**gon′or·rhe′al,** *adj.* —**gon′or·rhe′ic,** *adj.*

goof′ball′, *n. Slang.* a pill containing a barbiturate or a tranquilizing drug.

gork (gôrk), *n. Slang.* a person who is severely impaired mentally or physically.

gos·sy·pol (gos′ə pôl′, -pol′), *n.* a pigment, $C_{30}H_{30}O_8$, derived from cottonseed oil, that lowers sperm production and is considered a potential male contraceptive.

gout (gout), *n.* a painful inflammation, esp. of the big toe, characterized by an excess of uric acid in the blood that leads to crystalline deposits in the small joints.

GP or **G.P.,** **1.** General Practitioner. **2.** Graduate in Pharmacy.

gr or **gr.,** gram.

Graaf′i·an fol′licle (grä′fē ən), *n.* (*sometimes l.c.*) one of the small vesicles containing a developing ovum in the ovary of placental mammals.

graft (graft, gräft), *n.* **1.** a portion of living tissue surgically transplanted from one part of an individual to another, or from one individual to another, for its adhesion and growth. —*v.t.* **2.** to transplant (a portion of living tissue, as of skin or bone) as a graft.

graft′-ver′sus-host′ disease′, *n.* a reaction in which the cells of transplanted tissue immunologically attack the cells of the host.

grain (grān), *n.* the smallest unit of weight in the U.S. and British systems, equal to 0.002285 ounce (0.0648 gram).

gram (gram), *n.* a metric unit of mass or weight equal to 15.432 grains; $\frac{1}{1000}$ of a kilogram. *Abbr.:* g, gr, gr. Also, *esp. Brit.,* **gramme.**

gram′ cal′orie, *n.* CALORIE (def. 1a).

Gram′-neg′ative (gram), *adj.* (*often l.c.*) (of bacteria) not retaining the violet dye when stained by Gram's method.

Gram′-pos′itive (gram), *adj.* (*often l.c.*) (of bacteria) retaining the violet dye when stained by Gram's method.

Gram′s′ meth′od (gramz), *n.* (*sometimes l.c.*) a method of characterizing bacteria that involves staining a slide of fixed specimens with gentian violet, washing with alcohol, and applying a counterstain.

grand mal (gran′ mäl′, -mal′, grand′), *n.* See under EPILEPSY.

grand′ rounds′, *n.* a formal hospital meeting at which

an expert lectures on a clinical issue, sometimes including observations of patients at the bedside.

gran·u·la·tion (gran/yə lā/shən), *n.* **1.** the formation of capillary-rich tissue with an irregular surface, as during wound healing. **2.** the tissue so formed.

gran·u·lo·cyte (gran/yə lō sit/), *n.* a circulating white blood cell having prominent granules in the cytoplasm. —**gran/u·lo·cyt/ic** (-sit/ik), *adj.*

gran·u·lo·ma (-lō/mə), *n., pl.* **-mas, -ma·ta** (-mə tə). an inflammatory tumor or growth composed of granulation tissue. —**gran/u·lom/a·tous** (-lom/ə təs), *adj.*

gra·num (grā/nəm), *n., pl.* **-na** (-nə). (in prescriptions) a grain.

grape/ sug/ar, *n.* DEXTROSE.

GRAS (gras), generally recognized as safe: a status label assigned by the FDA to a listing of substances (**GRAS/ list/**) not known to be hazardous to health.

Graves// disease/ (grāvz), *n.* a disease characterized by an enlarged thyroid and increased basal metabolism due to excessive thyroid secretion.

grav·i·da (grav/i də), *n., pl.* **-das, -dae** (-dē/). **1.** a woman's status regarding pregnancy: usu. followed by a roman numeral designating the number of times the woman has been pregnant. **2.** a pregnant woman. Compare PARA.

gray/ mat/ter, *n.* a reddish gray nerve tissue of the brain and spinal cord, consisting chiefly of nerve cell bodies, with few nerve fibers. Compare WHITE MATTER.

great/er omen/tum, *n.* the part of the omentum that attaches to the stomach and colon and hangs over the small intestine. Also called **caul.**

green/ mon/key disease/, *n.* MARBURG DISEASE.

green/sick/ness, *n.* CHLOROSIS. —**green/sick/,** *adj.*

green/stick frac/ture, *n.* an incomplete fracture of a long bone, in which one side is broken and the other side is intact.

GRF, growth hormone releasing factor.

grippe (grip), *n. Older Use.* INFLUENZA.

gross/ anat/omy, *n.* the branch of anatomy that deals with structures that can be seen with the naked eye.

group/ dynam/ics, *n.* (*used with pl. v.*) the interactions that influence the attitudes and behavior of people when they are grouped with others.

group/ prac/tice, *n.* Also called **group/ med/icine.** the practice of medicine by an association of physicians and other health professionals who work together, usu. in one suite of offices.

group/ ther/apy, *n.* psychotherapy in which a group of patients, usu. led by a therapist, discuss, act out, or attempt to solve their problems.

grow/ing pains/, *n.pl.* dull, quasi-rheumatic pains of varying degree in the limbs during childhood and adolescence, often popularly associated with the process of growing.

growth (grōth), *n.* **1.** the act or process or a manner of growing; development; gradual increase. **2.** an abnormal increase in a mass of tissue, as a tumor.

growth′ fac′tor, *n.* any of various proteins that promote the growth, organization, and maintenance of cells and tissues.

growth′ hor′mone, *n.* any substance that stimulates or controls the growth of an organism, esp. a species-specific hormone, as the human hormone somatotropin.

growth′ hor′mone releas′ing fac′tor, *n.* a substance produced inthe hypothalamus that regulates the release of growth hormone. *Abbr.:* GRF

grume (grōōm), *n.* viscous or clotted fluid, esp. blood.

gru·mous (grōō′məs), *adj.* clotted, as blood. —**gru′mous·ness,** *n.*

GTP, guanosine triphosphate: a nucleotide composed of guanosine and three phosphate groups, important in metabolism and protein synthesis.

GU, genitourinary.

gua·nine (gwä′nēn), *n.* a purine base, $C_5H_5N_5O$, that is a fundamental constituent of DNA and RNA, in which it forms base pairs with cytosine. *Symbol:* G

gua′no·sine′ (-nə sēn′, -sin), *n.* a ribonucleoside component of ribonucleic acid, comprising ribose and guanine.

gua′nosine monophos′phate, *n.* See GMP.

gua′nosine triphos′phate, *n.* See GTP.

gua·nyl′ic ac′id (-nil′ik), *n.* See GMP.

Guil·lain′-Bar·ré′ syn′drome (gē yan′bə rā′), *n.* an uncommon, usu. self-limited form of polyneuritis manifested by loss of muscle strength, loss of or altered sensation, and sometimes paralysis.

gum (gum), *n.* Often, **gums.** the firm, fleshy tissue covering the surfaces of the jaws and enveloping the necks of the teeth. Also called **gingiva.**

gum′boil′, *n.* a small abscess on the gum originating in an abscess in the pulp of a tooth.

gum·ma (gum′ə), *n., pl.* **gum·mas, gum·ma·ta** (gum′ə-tə). a rubbery tumorlike lesion associated with tertiary syphilis. —**gum′ma·tous,** *adj.*

GYN or **gyn,** **1.** gynecological. **2.** gynecologist. **3.** gynecology.

gy·nan·dro·morph (gi nan′drə môrf′, ji-), *n.* an individual having morphological characteristics of both sexes. —**gy·nan′dro·mor′phic, gy·nan′dro·mor′phous,** *adj.* —**gy·nan′dro·mor′phism, gy·nan′dro·mor′phy,** *n.*

gynecol., **1.** gynecological. **2.** gynecology.

gy·ne·col·o·gist (gī′ni kol′ə jist, jin′i-), *n.* a physician specializing in gynecology. *Abbr.:* GYN, gyn

gy·ne·col·o·gy, *n.* the branch of medicine that deals with the health maintenance and diseases of women, esp. of the reproductive organs. *Abbr.:* GYN, gyn —**gy′ne·co·log′ic** (-kə loj′ik), **gy′ne·co·log′i·cal,** *adj.*

gy′ne·co·mas′ti·a (-kə mas′tē ə) also **gy′ne·co·mas′ty,** *n.* abnormal enlargement of the breast in a male.

gy/no·gen/e·sis (gī/nə-), *n.* a type of reproduction by parthenogenesis that requires stimulation by a sperm to activate the egg into development but occurs without fusion of sperm and egg nuclei.

H

H, *Slang.* heroin.

H, *Symbol.* **1.** histidine. **2.** hydrogen.

hab·it-form′ing, *adj.* tending to cause addiction, esp. through physiological dependence.

ha·bit·u·a·tion (hə bich′oo ā′shən), *n.* **1.** physiological tolerance to or psychological dependence on a drug, caused by continued use. **2.** reduction of psychological or behavioral response to a stimulus as a result of repeated or prolonged exposure.

hab·i·tus (hab′i təs), *n., pl.* **-tus.** the physical characteristics and constitution of a person, esp. with regard to susceptibility to disease.

hair′ im·plant′, *n.* the insertion of synthetic fibers or human hair into a bald area of the scalp.

hair′ trans·plant′, *n.* the surgical transfer of clumps of skin with hair or of viable hair follicles to a bald area of the scalp.

Hal·ci·on (hal′sē on′), *n. Trademark.* a benzodiazepine, used as a sleeping drug and as an anxiolytic.

half′-life′ or **half′ life′,** *n., pl.* **-lives.** the time required for the activity of a substance taken into the body to lose one half its initial effectiveness.

hal·i·to·sis (hal′i tō′sis), *n.* a condition of having offensive-smelling breath.

hal·lu·ci·nate (hə loo′sə nāt′), *v.,* **-nat·ed, -nat·ing.** —*v.i.* **1.** to have hallucinations. —*v.t.* **2.** to affect with hallucinations. —**hal·lu′ci·na′tor,** *n.*

hal·lu·ci·na′tion, *n.* **1.** a sensory experience of something that does not exist outside the mind, caused by various physical and mental disorders, or by reaction to certain toxic substances, and usu. manifested as visual or auditory images. **2.** the sensation caused by a hallucinatory condition or the object or scene visualized. —**hal·lu′ci·na′tion·al, hal·lu′ci·na′tive** (-nā′tiv, -nə tiv), *adj.*

hal·lu·ci·na·to′ry (-nə tôr′ē, -tōr′ē), *adj.* pertaining to or characterized by hallucination.

hal·lu′ci·no·gen (-jən), *n.* a substance that produces hallucinations. —**hal·lu′ci·no·gen′ic** (-jen′ik), *adj.*

hal·lu·ci·no′sis (-nō′sis), *n.* a mental state characterized by repeated hallucinations.

hal·o·bac·te·ri·a (hal′ō bak tēr′ē ə), *n.pl., sing.* **-te·ri·um** (-tēr′ē əm). rod-shaped archaebacteria, as of the genera *Halobacterium* and *Halococcus,* occurring in saline environments and using the pigment bacteriorhodopsin rather than chlorophyll for photosynthesis.

ha′lo effect′, *n.* a potential inaccuracy in estimation or judgment, esp. of a person, due to a tendency to overgeneralize from a single salient feature or action, usu. in a favorable direction.

hal·o·per·i·dol (hal′ō per′i dôl′, -dol′), *n.* a major antipsychotic agent, $C_{21}H_{23}ClFNO_2$, used esp. in the management of schizophrenia and severe anxiety.

hal·o·thane (hal'ə thān'), n. a colorless liquid, $C_2HBrClF_3$, used as an inhalant for general anesthesia.

ham·mer (ham'ər), n. MALLEUS.

ham'mer·toe', n. 1. a deformity of a toe, usu. the second or third, in which there is a permanent angular flexion of the joints. 2. a toe with such a deformity.

ham·string', n., v., -strung, -string·ing. —n. 1. (in humans) a. any of the tendons in the region behind the knee. b. ACHILLES TENDON. —v.t. 2. to disable by cutting the hamstring or hamstrings; cripple.

hang'nail', n. a small piece of partly detached skin at the side or base of the fingernail.

Han'sen's disease' (han'sənz), n. LEPROSY.

hap·loid (hap'loid), adj. Also, **hap·loi'dic.** 1. pertaining to a single set of chromosomes. —n. 2. an organism or cell having only one complete set of chromosomes, ordinarily half the normal diploid number.

hap'lont (-lont), n. the haploid individual in a life cycle that has a diploid and a haploid phase.

hard (härd), adj. (of an illicit narcotic or drug) known to be physically addictive, as opium, morphine, or cocaine.

hard' drug', n. an addicting drug capable of producing severe physical or psychological dependence, as heroin.

hard' lens', n. a contact lens of rigid plastic or silicon, exerting light pressure on the cornea of the eye. Compare SOFT LENS.

hard' pal'ate, n. See under PALATE.

hare'lip', n. Sometimes Offensive. CLEFT LIP. —**hare'-lipped'**, adj.

Ha·ver'sian canal' (hə vûr'zhən), n. (sometimes l.c.) any of the channels in bone containing blood vessels and nerves.

Haw'thorne effect', n. a positive change in the performance of a group of persons taking part in an experiment or study that is due to their perception of being singled out for special consideration.

hay' fe'ver, n. allergic rhinitis affecting the mucous membranes of the eyes and respiratory tract, caused by pollen of ragweed and certain other plants.

hCG, human chorionic gonadotropin.

HDL, high-density lipoprotein.

head' cold', n. a common cold characterized esp. by nasal congestion and sneezing.

health'care' or **health' care'**, n. any field or enterprise concerned with supplying services, equipment, information, etc., for the maintenance or restoration of health.

health' food', n. any natural food popularly believed to promote or sustain good health, as through its vital nutrients.

health' insur'ance, n. insurance that compensates the insured for the medical expenses of an illness or hospitalization.

health′ main′tenance organiza′tion, *n.* a plan for comprehensive health services, prepaid by an individual or by a company for its employees, that provides treatment, preventive care, and hospitalization to each participating member in a central health center. *Abbr.:* HMO

health′ profes′sional, *n.* a person trained to work in any field of physical or mental health.

hear′ing aid′, *n.* a compact electronic amplifier worn to improve one's hearing and usu. placed in or behind the ear.

hear′ing-impaired′, *adj.* having reduced or deficient hearing ability; hard-of-hearing.

heart (härt), *n.* a muscular organ in vertebrates (four-chambered in mammals and birds, three-chambered in reptiles and amphibians, and two-chambered in fishes) that receives blood from the veins and pumps it through the arteries to oxygenate the blood during its circuit.

heart′ attack′, *n.* **1.** any sudden insufficiency of oxygen supply to the heart that results in heart muscle damage; myocardial infarction. **2.** any sudden disruption of heart function.

heart′beat′, *n.* a pulsation of the heart, including one complete systole and diastole.

heart′ block′, *n.* a defect in the electrical impulses of the heart resulting in any of various arrhythmias or irregularities in the heartbeat.

heart′burn′, *n.* a burning sensation in the stomach, typically extending toward the esophagus, and sometimes associated with the eructation of an acid fluid; pyrosis; cardialgia.

heart′ disease′, *n.* any condition of the heart that impairs its functioning.

heart′ fail′ure, *n.* **1.** a condition in which the heart fatally ceases to function. **2.** a condition in which the heart pumps inadequate amounts of blood, characterized by edema, esp. of the lower legs, and shortness of breath; congestive heart failure.

heart′-lung′ machine′, *n.* a pumping device through which diverted blood is oxygenated and returned to the body during heart surgery, temporarily functioning for the heart and lungs.

heart′ mur′mur, *n.* MURMUR.

heat′ exhaus′tion, *n.* a condition brought on by intense or prolonged exposure to heat, characterized by profuse sweating with loss of fluids and salts, pale and damp skin, rapid pulse, nausea, and dizziness, progressing to collapse.

heat′ prostra′tion, *n.* HEAT EXHAUSTION.

heat′ rash′, *n.* PRICKLY HEAT.

heat′stroke′, *n.* a disturbance of the temperature-regulating mechanisms of the body caused by overexposure to excessive heat, resulting in headache, fever, hot and dry skin, and rapid pulse, sometimes progressing to delirium and coma.

he·be·phre·ni·a (hē/bə frē/nē ə), *n.* a form of schizophrenia characterized by emotionless, incongruous, or silly behavior, intellectual deterioration, and hallucinations. —**he/be·phren/ic** (-fren/ik), *adj., n.*

he·bet·ic (hi bet/ik), *adj.* pertaining to or occurring in puberty.

hec·tic (hek/tik), *adj.* **1.** of or designating a fevered condition, as in tuberculosis, attended by flushed cheeks, hot skin, and emaciation. **2.** affected with such fever; consumptive.

he·don·ics (hē don/iks), *n.* (*used with a sing. v.*) the branch of psychology that deals with pleasurable and unpleasurable states of consciousness.

heel/ spur/, *n.* an injury to the tissue on the bottom of a foot due to overuse, improper shoes, etc.

Heim/lich maneu/ver (him/lik), *n.* an emergency procedure to aid a person choking on food or some other object by applying sudden pressure with an inward and upward thrust of the fist to the victim's upper abdomen in order to force the obstruction from the windpipe.

He/La (or **He/la** or **he/la**) **cell/** (hel/ə), *n.* a vigorous strain of laboratory-cultured cells descended from a human cervical cancer, used widely in research.

he·li·o·ther·a·py (hē/lē ō ther/ə pē), *n.* treatment of disease by means of sunlight.

he·lix (hē/liks), *n., pl.* **hel·i·ces** (hel/ə sēz/), **he·lix·es.** ALPHA HELIX.

hel·minth (hel/minth), *n.* a worm, esp. a parasitic worm.

hel/min·thi/a·sis (-min thi/ə sis), *n.* a disease caused by parasitic worms in the intestines.

hel·min/thic (-thik), *adj.* **1.** of, pertaining to, or caused by helminths. **2.** expelling intestinal worms; anthelmintic.

helper T cell, *n.* any of a group of T cells that activate the immune system either by enhancing the production of antibody and other T cells or by mobilizing macrophages to engulf invading particles.

he·ma·cy·tom·e·ter (hē/mə si tom/i tər), *n.* HEMOCYTOMETER.

he·mag·glu·ti·nate (hē/mə gloōt/n āt/), *v.,* -**nat·ed,** -**nat·ing.** —*v.i.* **1.** (of red blood cells) to clump. —*v.t.* **2.** to cause (red blood cells) to clump. —**he/mag·glu/ti·na/tion,** *n.* —**he/mag·glu/tin·a/tive,** *adj.*

he/mag·glu/ti·nin (-in), *n.* a substance that causes red blood cells to clump.

he·mal (hē/məl), *adj.* of or pertaining to the blood or blood vessels.

he·man·gi·o·ma (hi man/jē ō/mə), *n., pl.* -**mas,** -**ma·ta** (-mə tə). See under ANGIOMA.

he·ma·te·in (hē/mə tē/in), *n.* a reddish brown, crystalline solid, $C_{16}H_{12}O_6$, obtained from logwood: used chiefly as a stain in microscopy.

he·mat·ic (hi mat/ik), *adj.* **1.** of or pertaining to blood; hemic. **2.** acting on the blood, as a medicine.

he·ma·tin (hē′mə tin) also **he′ma·tine** / (-tēn′, -tin), *n.*
1. HEME. **2.** HEMATEIN.

he·ma·tin′ic, *n.* **1.** a medicine, as a compound of iron, that tends to increase the amount of heme or hemoglobin in the blood. —*adj.* **2.** of or obtained from hematin.

he·mat·o·blast (hi mat′ə blast′), *n.* an immature blood cell.

he·mat·o·cele (-sēl′), *n.* **1.** hemorrhage into a cavity, as the cavity surrounding the testis. **2.** such a cavity.

he·mat·o·crit (-krit), *n.* **1.** a centrifuge for separating the cells of the blood from the plasma. **2.** Also called **hemat′ocrit val′ue.** the ratio of the volume of red blood cells to a given volume of blood so centrifuged, expressed as a percentage.

he·ma·tog·e·nous (hē′mə toj′ə nəs), *adj.* **1.** originating in the blood. **2.** blood-producing. **3.** distributed or spread by way of the bloodstream, as in metastases of tumors or in infections.

he·ma·tol·o·gy (-tol′ə jē), *n.* the study of the nature, function, and diseases of the blood and of blood-forming organs. —**he′ma·to·log′ic** (-tl oj′ik), **he′ma·to·log′i·cal,** *adj.* —**he′ma·tol′o·gist,** *n.*

he·ma·to·ma (-tō′mə), *n., pl.* **-mas, -ma·ta** (-mə tə). a circumscribed collection of blood, usu. clotted, in a tissue or organ, caused by a break in a blood vessel.

he·mat·o·poi·e·sis (hi mat′ō poi ē′sis) also **hemopoie-sis,** *n.* the formation of blood. —**he·mat′o·poi·et′ic** (-et′ik), *adj.*

he·ma·to·sis (hē′mə tō′sis), *n.* HEMATOPOIESIS.

he·ma·tu·ri·a (hē′mə tŏŏr′ē ə, -tyŏŏr′-), *n.* the presence of blood in the urine. —**he′ma·tu′ric,** *adj.*

heme (hēm), *n.* an unstable, deep red, iron-containing blood pigment, $C_{34}H_{32}N_4O_4Fe$, obtained from hemoglobin.

hem·er·a·lo·pi·a (hem′ər ə lō′pē ə), *n.* a condition in which vision is normal in the night or in dim light but is abnormally poor or wholly absent in the day or in bright light. Also called **day blindness.** —**hem′er·a·lop′ic** (-lop′ik), *adj.*

he·mic (hē′mik), *adj.* HEMATIC.

hem·i·cra·ni·a (hem′i krā′nē ə), *n.* pain in one side of the head; migraine.

he·min (hē′min), *n.* a crystalline substance, $C_{34}H_{32}N_4O_4FeCl$, that forms when blood is mixed with sodium chloride and glacial acetic acid and heated: used as a test for the presence of blood in stains.

hem·i·ple·gi·a (hem′i plē′jē ə, -jə), *n.* paralysis of one side of the body. —**hem′i·ple′gic,** *adj., n.*

he·mo·chro·ma·to·sis (hē′mə krō′mə tō′sis), *n.* a disorder of iron metabolism manifested by bronzed skin due to excessive iron absorption, leading to joint pain, diabetes, and liver damage if iron concentration is not reduced. Also called **bronze diabetes, iron-storage disease.** —**he′mo·chro′ma·tot′ic** (-tot′ik), *adj.*

he·mo·cy·tom·e·ter or **he·ma·cy·tom·e·ter** (-sī-tom′i tər), *n.* an instrument for counting blood cells.

he·mo·di·al·y·sis (hē′mō-), *n.* dialysis of the blood, esp. with an artificial kidney, for the removal of waste products.

he·mo·flag·el·late (hē′mə flaj′ə lāt′), *n.* a flagellate protozoan, esp. of the genus *Trypanosoma* or *Leishmania*, that is parasitic in the blood.

he·mo·glo·bin (-glō′bin), *n.* a conjugated protein in red blood cells, comprising globin and iron-containing heme, that transports oxygen from the lungs to the tissues of the body. —**he′mo·glo′bic, he′mo·glo′bin·ous,** *adj.*

he·mo·glo·bi·nu·ri·a (hē′mə glō′bə nŏŏr′ē ə, -nyŏŏr′-), *n.* the presence of hemoglobin pigment in the urine. —**he′mo·glo′bi·nu′ric,** *adj.*

he·mol·y·sis (hi mol′ə sis), *n.* the breaking down of red blood cells with liberation of hemoglobin. —**he·mo·lyt·ic** (hē′mə lit′ik), *adj.*

he·mo·lyze (hē′mə līz′), *v.,* **-lyzed, -lyz·ing.** —*v.t.* **1.** to subject (red blood cells) to hemolysis. —*v.i.* **2.** to undergo hemolysis.

he′mo·phil′i·a (-fil′ē ə), *n.* any of several X-linked genetic disorders, symptomatic chiefly in males, in which excessive bleeding occurs from minor injuries owing to the absence or abnormality of a clotting factor in the blood.

he′mo·phil′i·ac′, *n.* a person who has hemophilia.

he′mo·phil′ic, *adj.* **1.** characteristic of or affected by hemophilia. **2.** (of bacteria) developing best in a culture containing blood, or in blood itself.

he·mo·poi·e′sis (-poi ē′sis), *n.* HEMATOPOIESIS. —**he′mo·poi·et′ic** (-et′ik), *adj.*

he·mop·ty·sis (hi mop′tə sis), *n.* the expectoration of blood or bloody mucus.

hem·or·rhage (hem′ər ij, hem′rij), *n., v.,* **-rhaged, -rhag·ing.** —*n.* **1.** a profuse discharge of blood. —*v.i.* **2.** to bleed profusely. —**hem′or·rhag′ic** (-ə raj′ik), *adj.*

hem·or·rhoid (hem′ə roid′, hem′roid), *n.* Usu., **hemorrhoids.** a varicose vein in the region of the anal sphincter, sometimes painful and bleeding. —**hem′or·rhoi′dal,** *adj.*

hem·or·rhoid·ec·to·my (-roi dek′tə mē), *n., pl.* **-mies.** the surgical removal of hemorrhoids.

he·mo·sta·sis (hē′mə stā′sis) also **he′mo·sta′sia** (-stā′-zhə, -zhē ə), *n.* **1.** the stoppage of bleeding. **2.** the stoppage of the circulation of blood in a part of the body. **3.** stagnation of blood in a part.

he′mo·stat′ (-stat′), *n.* an instrument or agent used to compress or treat bleeding vessels in order to arrest hemorrhage.

he′mo·stat′ic, *adj.* **1.** arresting hemorrhage, as a drug; styptic. **2.** pertaining to stagnation of the blood. —*n.* **3.** a hemostatic agent or substance.

Hen′le's loop′ (hen′lēz), *n.* LOOP OF HENLE.

hep·a·rin (hep′ə rin), *n.* a polysaccharide present in animal tissues, esp. the liver, that has anticoagulant properties and is used in medicine to prevent or dissolve blood clots.

hep·a·tec·to·my (hep/ə tek/tə mē), *n., pl.* **-mies.** the surgical excision of part or all of the liver.

he·pat·ic (hi pat/ik), *adj.* of, pertaining to, or acting on the liver.

hep·a·ti·tis (hep/ə tī/tis), *n.* inflammation of the liver, caused by a virus or a toxin and characterized by jaundice, liver enlargement, and fever.

hepatitis A, *n.* a normally minor form of hepatitis caused by an RNA virus that does not persist in the blood: usu. transmitted by ingestion of contaminated food or water. Also called **infectious hepatitis.**

hepatitis B, *n.* a form of hepatitis caused by a DNA virus (**hepatitis B virus**) that persists in the blood and has a long incubation period: usu. transmitted by sexual contact or by injection or ingestion of infected blood or other bodily fluids. Also called **serum hepatitis.**

hepatitis C, *n.* a form of hepatitis with clinical effects similar to those of hepatitis B, caused by a blood-borne retrovirus (**hepatitis C virus**) that may be of the hepatitis non-A, non-B type.

hep/ati/tis del/ta, *n.* a severe form of hepatitis caused by an incomplete virus (**delta virus**) that links to the hepatitis B virus for its replication. Also called **delta hepatitis.**

hepatitis non-A, non-B, *n.* a disease of the liver that is clinically indistinguishable from hepatitis B but is caused by a retrovirus or retroviruslike agent. Also called **non-A, non-B hepatitis.**

hep/a·to/ma (-tō/mə), *n., pl.* **-mas, -ma·ta** (-mə tə). a tumor of the liver.

hep/a·to·meg/a·ly (-meg/ə lē), *n.* an abnormal enlargement of the liver, usu. associated with liver disease or heart failure.

herb·al·ist (hûr/bə list, ûr/-), *n.* **1.** a person who collects or deals in herbs, esp. medicinal herbs. **2.** HERB DOCTOR.

herb/ doc/tor, *n.* a person who practices healing by the use of herbs.

he·red·i·tar·i·an (hə red/i târ/ē ən), *n.* **1.** a person who believes that differences between individuals or groups are predominantly determined by genetic factors. —*adj.* **2.** characteristic of or based on such belief: *hereditarian theories.* —**he·red/i·tar/i·an·ism,** *n.*

he·red·i·tar·y (-ter/ē), *adj.* **1.** passing, or capable of passing, naturally from parent to offspring through the genes. **2.** of or pertaining to inheritance or heredity. —**he·red/i·tar/i·ly** (-târ/ə lē), *adv.* —**he·red/i·tar/i·ness,** *n.*

he·red·i·ty, *n., pl.* **-ties.** **1.** the passing on of characters or traits from parents to offspring as a result of the transmission of genes. **2.** the genetic characters so transmitted. **3.** the characteristics of an individual that are considered to have been passed on by the parents or ancestors.

her·maph·ro·dite (hûr maf/rə dīt/), *n.* an individual in which reproductive organs of both sexes are present.

—**her·maph/ro·dism, her·maph/ro·dit·ism,** *n.* —**her·maph/ro·dit/ic** (-dit/ik) *adj.* —**her·maph/ro·dit/i·cal·ly,** *adv.*

her·ni·a (hûr/nē ə), *n., pl.* **-ni·as, -ni·ae** (-nē ē/). the protrusion of an organ or tissue through an opening in its surrounding walls, esp. in the abdominal region. —**her/ni·al,** *adj.*

her/ni·ate/ (-āt/), *v.i.* **-at·ed, -at·ing.** to protrude abnormally so as to constitute a hernia. —**her/ni·a/tion,** *n.*

her/niated disk/, *n.* an abnormal protrusion of a spinal disk between vertebrae. Also called **ruptured disk, slipped disk.**

her·o·in (her/ō in), *n.* a white crystalline powder, $C_{21}H_{23}NO_5$, derived from morphine, that is narcotic and addictive: manufacture or importation is prohibited in the U.S. and many other nations.

her·pes (hûr/pēz), *n.* **1.** any of several diseases caused by herpesvirus, characterized by eruption of blisters on the skin or mucous membranes. **2.** HERPESVIRUS.

her/pes sim/plex (sim/pleks), *n.* a recurrent herpesvirus infection that produces clusters of small blisters on the mouth, lips, eyes, or genitalia.

her/pes·vi/rus, *n., pl.* **-rus·es.** any DNA-containing virus of the family Herpesviridae, members of which cause several kinds of diseases, as chickenpox and shingles.

her/pes zos/ter (zos/tər), *n.* SHINGLES.

her/pes zos/ter vi/rus, *n.* a type of herpesvirus that causes chickenpox and shingles. Also called **varicella zoster virus.**

her·pet·ic (hər pet/ik), *adj.* of, pertaining to, or caused by herpes.

het·er·o·chro·mat·ic (het/ər ə krō mat/ik, -ō krə-), *adj.* of or pertaining to heterochromatin. Often, **het/er·o·chrome/** (-ə krōm/). —**het/er·o·chro/ma·tism** (-krō/mə·tiz/əm),** *n.*

het·er·o·chro/ma·tin (-krō/mə tin), *n.* the dense, highly stainable part of a chromosome.

het·er·og·a·mous (het/ə rog/ə məs), *adj.* having unlike gametes, or reproducing by the union of such gametes (opposed to *isogamous*). —**het/er·og/a·my,** *n.*

het/er·o·graft/ (het/ər ə-), *n.* XENOGRAFT.

het/er·o·lec/i·thal, *adj.* having an unequal distribution of yolk, as certain eggs or ova.

het·er·ol·o·gous (het/ə rol/ə gəs), *adj.* consisting of dissimilar tissue, as that of another species or that of a tumor. —**het/er·ol/o·gy** (-jē), *n.*

het·er·o·phil (het/ər ə fil), *adj.* reacting with or having an affinity for more than one kind of substance, as an antibody with more than one antigen.

het/er·o·plas/ty (-plas/tē), *n., pl.* **-ties.** the surgical repair of lesions with tissue from another individual or species. —**het/er·o·plas/tic,** *adj.*

het/er·o·sex/u·al, *adj.* **1.** of, pertaining to, or exhibiting heterosexuality. **2.** pertaining to the opposite sex or to both sexes. —*n.* **3.** a heterosexual person.

het·er·o·sex·u·al·i·ty, *n.* sexual desire or behavior directed toward persons of the opposite sex.

het·er·o·sis (het′ə rō′sis), *n.* the increase in growth, size, yield, or other characters in hybrids over those of the parents. Also called **hybrid vigor.**

het·er·o·tax·is (het′ər ə-) also **het′er·o·tax′i·a, het′-er·o·tax′y,** *n.* abnormal or irregular arrangement, as of parts of the body. —**het′er·o·tac′tic** (-tak′tik), **het′er·o·tac′tous, het′er·o·tax′ic,** *adj.*

het·er·o·zy·gote, *n.* a hybrid containing genes for two unlike forms of a characteristic, and therefore not breeding true to type.

het·er·o·zy·gous (-zi′gəs) also **het′er·o·zy·got′ic** (-ə rō zi got′ik), *adj.* **1.** having dissimilar pairs of genes for any hereditary characteristic. **2.** of or pertaining to a heterozygote. —**het′er·o·zy·gos′i·ty** (-ə rō zi gos′i tē), *n.*

hex·a·meth·yl·ene·tet·ra·mine (hek′sə meth′ə lēn te′trə mēn′), *n.* a white, crystalline, water-soluble powder, $C_6H_{12}N_4$, used esp. as a diuretic and urinary antiseptic. Also called **hex′a·mine′** (-mēn′).

hex·a·ploid (hek′sə ploid′), *adj.* **1.** having a chromosome number that is six times the haploid number. —*n.* **2.** a hexaploid cell or organism. —**hex′a·ploi′dy,** *n.*

hex·o·ki′nase, *n.* an enzyme that catalyzes the phosphorylation of hexose sugars.

hex·ose (hek′sōs), *n.* any of a class of sugars, as glucose and fructose, containing six atoms of carbon.

hGH, human growth hormone.

hi·a·tus (hi ā′təs *or* -āt′l), *n.* protrusion of part of the stomach through the esophageal cleft of the diaphragm.

hic·cup *or* **hic·cough** (hik′up, -əp), *n., v.,* **-cuped** *or* **-cupped** *or* **-coughed, -cup·ing** *or* **-cup·ping** *or* **-cough·ing.** —*n.* **1.** a quick, involuntary inhalation that follows a spasm of the diaphragm and is suddenly checked by closure of the glottis, producing a short, relatively sharp sound. **2.** Usu., **hiccups.** the condition of having such spasms. —*v.i.* **3.** to have the hiccups.

hi·dro·sis (hi drō′sis, hi-), *n.* the excessive production of sweat. —**hi·drot′ic** (-drot′ik), *adj.*

high′ blood′ pres′sure, *n.* elevation of the arterial blood pressure or a condition resulting from it; hypertension.

high′-den′sity lipopro′tein, *n.* a circulating lipoprotein that picks up cholesterol in the arteries and deposits it in the liver for reprocessing or excretion. *Abbr.:* HDL.

hind·brain (hind′brān′), *n.* the most posterior of the three embryonic divisions of the vertebrate brain or the parts derived from this tissue, including the medulla oblongata, the pons of mammals, and the cerebellum; rhombencephalon.

hind′gut′, *n.* the posterior part of the embryonic vertebrate alimentary canal, from which the colon develops. Compare FOREGUT, MIDGUT.

HIP (āch/i/pē′; *sometimes*, hip), Health Insurance Plan.

hip′bone′, *n.* **1.** either of the two bones forming the sides of the pelvis, each consisting of three consolidated bones, the ilium, ischium, and pubis; innominate bone. **2.** ILIUM.

hip·po·cam·pus (hip′ə kam′pəs), *n., pl.* **-pi** (-pī, -pē). a curved ridge in the lateral ventricles of the mammalian brain: part of the limbic system. —**hip′po·cam′pal,** *adj.*

Hip′po·crat′ic oath′, *n.* an oath embodying the duties and obligations of physicians, usu. taken by those about to enter upon the practice of medicine. [named after *Hippocrates,* c460–c377, Greek physician, called "Father of Medicine"]

hir·sut·ism (hûr′sōō tiz′əm, hûr sōō′tiz-), *n.* abnormal hairiness.

hir·u·din (hir′yə din, hir′ə-, hi rōōd′n), *n.* a polypeptide obtained from the buccal gland of leeches, used in medicine chiefly as an anticoagulant.

His, histidine.

his·tam·i·nase (his stam′ə nās′, -nāz′), *n.* an enzyme that catalyzes the decomposition of histamine, used in treating allergies.

his·ta·mine (his′tə mēn′, -min), *n.* a histidine-derived amine compound that is released mainly by damaged mast cells in allergic reactions, causing dilation and permeability of blood vessels and lowering blood pressure. —**his′ta·min′ic** (-min′ik), *adj.*

his·ti·dine (his′ti dēn′, -din), *n.* an essential amino acid, $C_3H_5N_2CH_2CH(NH_2)COOH$, that is a constituent of proteins and is important as the iron-binding site in hemoglobin. *Abbr.:* His; *Symbol:* H

his·to·com·pat·i·bil·i·ty (his′tō kəm pat′ə bil′i tē), *n.* the condition of being similar antigenic types such that cells or tissues transplanted from a donor to a recipient are not rejected. —**his′to·com·pat′i·ble,** *adj.*

histocompatibil′ity an′tigen, *n.* any antigen on the surface of tissue or blood cells that provokes an immune response and subsequent rejection of the tissue or cell when transplanted to an individual of a different antigenic type.

his·to·gen·e·sis (his′tə jen′ə sis), *n.* the origin and development of living tissues. —**his′to·ge·net′ic** (-jə net′ik), *adj.* —**his′to·ge·net′i·cal·ly,** *adv.*

his·tol·y·sis (hi stol′ə sis), *n.* disintegration or dissolution of organic tissues. —**his·to·lyt′ic** (his′tl it′ik), *adj.*

his·tone (his′tōn), *n.* any of a group of five small basic proteins, occurring in the nucleus of eukaryotic cells, that organize DNA strands into nucleosomes by forming molecular complexes around which the DNA winds.

his·to·pa·thol·o·gy (his′tō pə thol′ə jē), *n.* the branch of pathology dealing with the structure of abnormal or diseased tissue. —**his′to·path′o·log′ic** (his′tə-), **his′to·path′o·log′i·cal,** *adj.* —**his′to·pa·thol′o·gist,** *n.*

his·to·phys·i·ol·o·gy (his/tə-), *n.* the branch of physiology dealing with tissues. —**his/to·phys/i·o·log/i·cal,** *adj.*

his·to·plas·mo·sis (his/tō plaz mō/sis), *n.* an infectious disease of the reticuloendothelial system, caused by the fungus *Histoplasma capsulatum* and characterized by fever, anemia, and emaciation.

HIV, *n.* AIDS virus. [*h(uman) i(mmunodeficiency) v(irus)*]

hives (hīvz), *n.* (*used with a sing. or pl. v.*) a transient eruption of large, itchy wheals on the skin usu. caused by an allergic reaction; urticaria.

HLA, human leukocyte antigen: any of a complex of genetically determined antigens, occurring on the surface of almost every human cell, by which one person's cells can be distinguished from another's and histocompatibility established.

HMO, health maintenance organization.

Hodg/kin's disease/ (hoj/kinz), *n.* a malignant disorder characterized by enlargement of the lymph nodes and spleen and by lymphoid infiltration along the blood vessels.

hol·an·dric (ho lan/drik, hō-), *adj.* of or pertaining to a heritable trait appearing only in males (opposed to *hologynic*).

ho·lism (hō/liz əm), *n.* an approach to healing or health care, often involving therapies outside the mainstream of medicine, in which isolated symptoms or conditions are considered secondary to one's total physical and psychological state. —**ho/list,** *n.*

ho·lis/tic (-lis/tik), *adj.* pertaining to or using therapies outside the mainstream of orthodox medicine, as chiropractic, homeopathy, or naturopathy. —**ho·lis/ti·cal·ly,** *adv.*

hol·o·blas·tic (hol/ə blas/tik, hō/lə-), *adj.* undergoing total cleavage in which the whole egg separates into equal blastomeres. —**ho/lo·blas/ti·cal·ly,** *adv.*

hol/o·crine (-ə krin, -krin/), *adj.* **1.** (of a gland) releasing a secretion that is a product of disintegrating cells. **2.** (of a secretion) released by such a gland.

hol·o·en·zyme (hol/ō en/zīm), *n.* an enzyme complete in both its apoenzyme and coenzyme components.

ho·log·a·mous (hə log/ə məs), *adj.* of or pertaining to an organism having reproductive cells similar in size and structure to the somatic cells.

hol·o·gyn·ic (hol/ə jin/ik, -gī/nik, hō/lə-), *adj.* of or pertaining to a heritable trait appearing only in females (opposed to *holandric*).

Hol/ter (or **hol/ter**) **mon/i·tor** (hōl/tər), *n.* a portable electrocardiograph worn by a patient over an extended period of time, usu. for 24 hours, to record on a cassette tape the effect of daily activities on the heart.

ho/me·o·box gene/ (hō/mē ə boks/), *n.* any of a group of genes whose function is to divide the early embryo into bands of cells with the potential to become specific organs or tissues.

ho·me·o·path·ic (-path′ik), *adj.* **1.** of, pertaining to, or according to the principles of homeopathy. **2.** practicing or advocating homeopathy. —**ho′me·o·path′i·cal·ly,** *adv.*

ho·me·op·a·thy (-op′ə thē), *n.* a method of treating disease by minute doses of drugs that in a healthy person would produce symptoms similar to those of the disease (opposed to *allopathy*). —**ho′me·o·path′** (-ə path′), **ho′-me·op′a·thist,** *n.*

ho·me·o·sta·sis (-ə stā′sis), *n.* **1.** the tendency of a system, esp. the physiological system of higher animals, to maintain internal stability, owing to the coordinated response of its parts to any situation or stimulus tending to disturb its normal condition or function. **2.** a state of psychological equilibrium obtained when tension or a drive has been reduced or eliminated. —**ho′me·o·stat′ic** (-stat′ik), *adj.* —**ho′me·o·stat′i·cal·ly,** *adv.*

ho·mog·a·mous (hō mog′ə məs), *adj.* pertaining to the interbreeding of individuals with like characteristics.

ho·mo·graft (hō′mə graft′, -gräft′, hom′ə-), *n.* ALLOGRAFT.

ho·mo·lec·i·thal (hō′mə les′ə thəl), *adj.* (of an egg) having a fairly uniform distribution of yolk.

ho·mo·log·i·cal (hō′mə loj′i kəl, hom′ə-) also **ho′mo·log′ic,** *adj.* HOMOLOGOUS. —**ho′mo·log′i·cal·ly,** *adv.*

ho·mol·o·gous (hə mol′ə gəs, hō-), *adj.* having the same alleles or genes in the same order of arrangement.

ho·mo·logue or **ho·mo·log** (hō′mə lôg′, -log′, hom′ə-), *n.* something homologous.

ho·mo·pho·bi·a (hō′mə fō′bē ə), *n.* unreasoning fear of or antipathy toward homosexuals and homosexuality. —**ho′mo·phobe′,** *n.* —**ho′mo·pho′bic,** *adj.*

ho·mo·sex·u·al (-al), *adj.* **1.** attracted sexually to members of one's own sex. **2.** of or pertaining to homosexuality. —*n.* **3.** a homosexual person.

ho·mo·sex·u·al·i·ty, *n.* sexual desire or behavior directed toward persons of one's own sex.

ho·mo·trans·plant (hō′mō trans′plant′, -plänt′, hom′ō-), *n.* ALLOGRAFT.

ho·mo·zy·gote (hō′mə-, hom′ə-), *n.* an organism with a pair of identical alleles for a given hereditary character, therefore breeding true for that character.

ho·mo·zy′gous (-zī′gəs) also **ho·mo·zy·got·ic** (-zi-got′ik), *adj.* **1.** having a pair of identical alleles at corresponding chromosomal loci. **2.** of or pertaining to a homozygote. —**ho′mo·zy·gos′i·ty** (-gos′i tē), *n.*

ho·mun·cu·lus (hə mung′kyə ləs, hō-), *n., pl.* **-li** (-lī′). a graphic projection of the human image onto the surface of the motor cortex of the brain, depicting the extent of the area activating each part of the body subject to voluntary control. —**ho·mun′cu·lar,** *adj.*

hook′worm′, *n.* **1.** any intestinal bloodsucking nematode worm with hooks around the mouth, belonging to the superfamily Ancylostomatoidea and parasitic in humans and other animals. **2.** a disease caused by hookworms, causing abdominal pain and, if untreated, severe anemia.

hop/head/, *n. Older Slang.* a narcotics addict, esp. an opium addict.

hor·de·o·lum (hôr dē/ə ləm), *n., pl.* **-la** (-lə). STY.

hor·mone (hôr/mōn), *n.* **1.** any of various internally secreted compounds that are formed in endocrine glands and that affect the functions of specifically receptive organs or tissues when transported to them by the body fluids. **2.** a synthetic substance that acts like such a compound when introduced into the body. —**hor·mo/nal, hor·mon/ic** (-mon/ik, -mō/nik), *adj.*

horse/radish per·ox/i·dase (pə rok/si dās/, -dāz/), *n.* an enzyme extracted from horseradish that is used as a tracer in mapping motor neurons in a living organism.

hos·pice (hos/pis), *n.* a health care facility, or a system of professional home visits and supervision, for supportive care of the terminally ill.

host (hōst), *n.* **1.** a living animal or plant from which a parasite obtains nutrition. **2.** the recipient of a graft.

host/-specif/ic, *adj.* capable of living solely on or in one species of host.

hot/ flash/, *n.* a sudden, temporary sensation of heat experienced by some women during menopause. Also called **hot/ flush/.**

hot/ spot/ or **hot/spot/,** *n.* a chromosome site or a section of DNA having a high frequency of mutation.

house/maid's knee/, *n.* inflammation of the bursa over the front of the kneecap.

HPV, human papillomavirus.

h.s., (in prescriptions) at bedtime. [Latin, *hōrā somni* at the hour of sleep]

HTLV, human T-cell lymphotrophic virus: any of a family of retroviruses associated with certain leukemias and immune system deficiencies.

hu/man chorion/ic gonadotro/pin, *n.* **1.** a gonadotropic hormone that stimulates the production of estrogen and progesterone: its presence in blood or urine is an indication of pregnancy. **2.** a commercial form of this substance, used in the treatment of testicular or ovarian disorders. *Abbr.:* hCG

Hu/man Ge/nome Proj/ect, *n.* a federally funded U.S. scientific project to identify both the genes and the entire sequence of DNA base pairs that make up the human genome.

hu/man growth/ hor/mone, *n.* SOMATOTROPIN. *Abbr.:* hGH

hu/man papillo/mavirus, *n.* the virus that causes genital warts. *Abbr.:* HPV

hu/man poten/tial move/ment, *n.* a movement in psychotherapy, esp. in the 1960s, emphasizing the development of each individual's potential through such techniques as group therapy, sensitivity training, and primal therapy.

hu/man rela/tions, *n.* (*usu. with a sing. v.*) the study of group behavior for the purpose of improving interpersonal relationships, as among employees.

human T-cell lymphotrophic virus, *n.* See HTLV.

hu·mer·us (hyōō′mər əs; *often* yōō′-), *n., pl.* **-mer·i** (-mə-rī′). **1.** the long upper bone of the vertebrate arm or fore-limb, extending from the shoulder to the elbow. **2.** BRACHIUM (def. 1).

hu·mor·al (hyōō′mər əl; *often* yōō′-), *adj.* of, pertaining to, or proceeding from a fluid of the body.

Hun′ting·ton′s chore′a (hun′ting tənz), *n.* a hereditary chorea, appearing in middle age, characterized by gradual deterioration of the brain and gradual loss of voluntary movement.

hy·a·line (hī′ə lēn′, -lin), *n.* **1.** a horny substance found in hydatid cysts, closely resembling chitin. **2.** a structure-less, transparent substance found in cartilage, the eye, etc., resulting from the pathological degeneration of tissue.

hy′a·loid′ (-loid′), *n.* HYALOID MEMBRANE.

hy′aloid mem′brane, *n.* the delicate, pellucid, and nearly structureless membrane enclosing the vitreous humor.

hy′a·lu·ron′ic ac′id (hī′ə lōō ron′ik, hī′-), *n.* a mucopolysaccharide serving as a viscous medium in the tissues of the body and as a lubricant in joints.

hy′a·lu·ron′i·dase′ (-i dās′, -dāz′), *n.* an enzyme that decreases viscosity in the tissue spaces of the body by breaking down hyaluronic acid: used as an ingredient for diffusing injected drugs.

HY antigen (āch′wī′), *n.* an antigen encoded by a gene on the Y (male) chromosome, active in the development of male structures. [*H*(*uman*) *Y* (*chromosome*)]

hy·brid (hī′brid), *n.* **1.** the offspring of two animals or plants of different breeds, varieties, or species, esp. as produced through human manipulation for specific genetic characteristics. —*adj.* **2.** bred from two distinct races, breeds, varieties, or species. —**hy′brid·ism, hy·brid′i·ty** (-i tē) *n.*

hy′brid·ize′, *v.,* **-ized, -iz·ing.** —*v.t.* **1.** to cause to produce hybrids; cross. **2.** to breed or cause the production of (a hybrid). —*v.i.* **3.** to produce or cause the production of hybrids. **4.** to form a double-stranded nucleic acid of two single strands of DNA or RNA, or one of each, by allowing the base pairs of the separate strands to form complementary bonds. **5.** to fuse two cells of different genotypes into a hybrid cell. —**hy′brid·iz′a·ble,** *adj.* —**hy′brid·i·za′tion,** *n.*

hy·brid·o′ma (-dō′mə), *n., pl.* **-mas.** a hybrid cell made in the laboratory by fusing a normal cell with a cancer cell, usu. a myeloma or lymphoma, in order to combine desired features of each, such as the ability of the cancer cell to multiply rapidly with the ability of the normal cell to dictate the production of a specific antibody.

hy′brid vig′or, *n.* HETEROSIS.

hy·da·tid (hī′də tid), *n.* **1.** a cyst with watery contents that is produced by a tapeworm larva, esp. of the genus *Echinococcus.* **2.** a cystic vestige of an embryonic feature. —*adj.* **3.** Also, **hy·da·tid/i·nous.** of or pertaining to a hydatid. **4.** containing or affected by hydatids.

hy·dro·cele (hī′drə sēl′), *n.* an accumulation of serous fluid, usu. about the testis.

hy·dro·ceph·a·lus (-sef′ə ləs) also **hy·dro·ceph/a·ly,** *n.* an accumulation of serous fluid within the cranium, esp. in infancy, due to obstruction of the movement of cerebrospinal fluid, often causing great enlargement of the head; water on the brain. —**hy′dro·ce·phal′ic** (hī′drō-), *adj.*, *n.* —**hy′dro·ceph/a·lous,** *adj.*

hy·dro·chlo·ric ac′id (-klôr′ik, -klor′-), *n.* a colorless corrosive fuming liquid, HCl: the acid in gastric juice.

hy·dro·cor′ti·sone′, *n.* a steroid hormone, $C_{21}H_{30}O_5$, of the adrenal cortex, active in carbohydrate and protein metabolism, similar to cortisone in effect.

hy·dro·cy·an·ic ac′id (hī′drō sī an′ik, hī′-), *n.* a colorless, highly poisonous liquid, HCN, an aqueous solution of hydrogen cyanide. Also called **prussic acid.**

hy·dro·gen (hī′drə jən), *n.* a colorless, odorless, flammable gas, the lightest of the elements, that combines chemically with oxygen to form water. *Symbol:* H; *at. wt.:* 1. 00797; *at. no.:* 1; *density:* 0.0899 g/l at 0°C and 760 mm pressure.

hy′drogen per·ox′ide (pə rok′sīd), *n.* a colorless, unstable, oily liquid, H_2O_2, an aqueous solution of which is used chiefly as an antiseptic and a bleaching agent.

hy·dro·lase (hī′drə lās′, -lāz′), *n.* an enzyme that catalyzes hydrolysis.

hy·drol·y·sis (hī drol′ə sis), *n.*, *pl.* **-ses** (-sēz′). chemical decomposition in which a compound is split into other compounds by reacting with water.

hy·dro·lyt·ic (hī′drə lit′ik), *adj.* of, producing, or resulting in hydrolysis.

hy·dro·lyze′ (-līz′), *v.t.*, *v.i.*, **-lyzed, -lyz·ing.** to subject or be subjected to hydrolysis. —**hy′dro·lyz/a·ble,** *adj.* —**hy′dro·ly·za/tion,** *n.* —**hy′dro·lyz/er,** *n.*

hy·drolyzed veg/etable pro′tein, *n.* a vegetable protein broken down into amino acids and used as a food additive to enhance flavor.

hy·drom·e·ter (hī drom′i tər), *n.* an instrument for determining the specific gravity of a liquid, commonly consisting of a graduated tube weighted to float upright in the liquid. —**hy′dro·met′ric** (-drə me′trik), **hy′dro·met/ri·cal,** *adj.* —**hy·drom/e·try,** *n.*

hy·dro·ne·phro·sis (hī′drō nə frō′sis), *n.* dilation of the branches and pelvic cavity of the kidney, caused by an accumulation of urine resulting from obstruction of normal outflow.

hy·drop·a·thy (hī drop′ə thē), *n.* a method of treating disease by immersing the body or body part in water, by taking water internally, or both. —**hy·dro·path·ic** (hī′drə-path′ik), **hy·dro·path′i·cal,** *adj.* —**hy·drop′a·thist, hy′-dro·path′,** *n.*

hy·dro·phil·ic (hī′drə fil′ik), *adj.* having a strong affinity for water; readily absorbing water.

hy′dro·pho′bi·a (-fō′bē ə), *n.* RABIES.

hy′dro·pho′bic, *adj.* pertaining to or affected with hydrophobia.

hy·dro·ther·a·peu·tics (hī′drō ther′ə pyōō′tiks), *n.* (*used with a sing. v.*) HYDROTHERAPY. —**hy′dro·ther′a·peu′tic,** *adj.*

hy·dro·ther′a·py (hī′drə-), *n.* the use of water in the treatment of disease or injury, as with soothing baths or sprays for wounds or heated pools for stiffened joints. —**hy′dro·ther′a·pist,** *n.*

hy·dro·tho′rax, *n.* the presence of serous fluid in one or both pleural cavities. —**hy′dro·tho·rac′ic** (hī′drō-), *adj.*

hy·drox′y ac′id (hī drok′sē), *n.* an organic acid containing both a carboxyl and a hydroxyl group.

hy·drox′y·bu·tyr′ic ac′id (hī drok′sē byōō tir′ik, -drok′-), *n.* one of several volatile liquids of the form $C_4H_8O_3$, soluble in water, alcohol, and ether, found in the urine of diabetics and made synthetically.

hy·drox′yl (-səl), *n.* the univalent group OH, found in both organic compounds, as ethyl alcohol, C_2H_5OH, and inorganic compounds, as sodium hydroxide, NaOH. —**hy′-drox·yl′ic** (-sil′ik), *adj.*

hy·drox·y·pro·line (hī drok′si prō′lēn, -lin), *n.* a nutritionally nonessential amino acid, $C_5H_9NO_3$, found chiefly in collagen.

hy·giene (hī′jēn), *n.* the application of scientific knowledge to the preservation of health and prevention of the spread of disease.

hy·gi·en·ics (hī′jē en′iks, hi jen′-, -jē′niks), *n.* (*used with a sing. v.*) HYGIENE.

hy·men (hī′mən), *n.* a fold of mucous membrane partly closing the external orifice of the vagina in a virgin. —**hy′men·al,** *adj.*

hy·oid (hī′oid), *adj.* **1.** Also, **hy·oi′dal, hy·oi′de·an.** of or designating a bony or cartilaginous structure at the base of the vertebrate tongue, U-shaped in humans. —*n.* **2.** the hyoid bone or structure.

hy·os·cine (hī′ə sēn′, -sin), *n.* SCOPOLAMINE.

hy·os·cy·a·mine (hī′ə sī′ə mēn′, -min), *n.* a poisonous alkaloid, $C_{17}H_{23}NO_3$, obtained from henbane and other plants of the nightshade family, used as a sedative, analgesic, mydriatic, and antispasmodic.

hy·os·cy·a·mus (-məs), *n.* the dried leaves of the henbane, *Hyoscyamus niger,* containing the alkaloids hyoscyamine and scopolamine, used in medicine.

hyp·al·ge·si·a (hip′al jē′zē ə, -sē ə, hi′pal-) also **hy·pal′gia** (-jə, -jē ə), *n.* decreased sensitivity to pain (opposed to *hyperalgesia*). —**hyp′al·ge′sic,** *adj.*

hype (hip), *n.* *Slang.* a hypodermic needle.

hy·per·a·cid·i·ty (hī/pər ə sid/i tē), *n.* excessive acidity, as of the gastric juice. —**hy/per·ac/id,** *adj.*

hy/per·ac/tive, *adj.* (of children) displaying excessive physical activity sometimes associated with neurological or psychological causes. —**hy/per·ac/tive·ly,** *adv.* —**hy/per·ac·tiv/i·ty,** *n.*

hy·per·ae/mi·a (-ē/mē ə), *n.* HYPEREMIA.

hy·per·aes·the·sia (-əs thē/zhə, -zhē ə, -zē ə), *n.* HYPERESTHESIA.

hy·per·al·ge/si·a (-al jē/zē ə, -sē ə) also **hy·per·al·gi·a** (-al/jē ə, -jə) *n.* an exaggerated sense of pain (opposed to *hypalgesia*). —**hy/per·al·ge/sic, hy/per·al·get/ic** (-jet/ik), *adj.*

hy/per·al·i/men·ta/tion, *n.* **1.** overfeeding. **2.** TOTAL PARENTERAL NUTRITION.

hy/per·bar/ic (-bar/ik), *adj.* **1.** (of an anesthetic) having a specific gravity greater than that of cerebrospinal fluid. **2.** pertaining to or utilizing gaseous pressure greater than normal, esp. for administering oxygen in the treatment of certain diseases.

hy/perbar/ic cham/ber, *n.* a steel vessel in which atmospheric pressure can be raised or lowered by air compressors, used to treat aeroembolism and to provide high-oxygen environments for certain medical procedures.

hy/per·cal·ce/mi·a (-kal sē/mē ə), *n.* an abnormally large amount of calcium in the blood.

hy/per·cap/ni·a (-kap/nē ə), *n.* the presence of an excessive amount of carbon dioxide in the blood.

hy·per·cho·les·ter·ol·e/mi·a (-kə les/tər ə lē/mē ə) also **hy·per·cho·les·ter·e·mi·a** (-les/tə rē/-), *n.* the presence of an excessive amount of cholesterol in the blood.

hy·per·e/mi·a (-ē/mē ə), *n.* an abnormally large amount of blood in any part of the body. —**hy/per·e/mic,** *adj.*

hy·per·es·the·sia (-əs thē/zhə, -zhē ə, -zē ə), *n.* an abnormally acute sense of pain, heat, cold, or touch (opposed to *hypesthesia*). —**hy/per·es·thet/ic** (-thet/ik), *adj.*

hy/per·func/tion, *n.* abnormally increased function, esp. of glands or other organs. —**hy/per·func/tion·ing,** *n., adj.*

hy·per·gly·ce/mi·a (-gli sē/mē ə), *n.* an abnormally high level of glucose in the blood. —**hy/per·gly·ce/mic,** *adj.*

hy/per·hi·dro/sis also **hy/per·i·dro/sis** (-i drō/-), *n.* abnormally excessive sweating.

hy/per·in/su·lin·ism (-in/sə li niz/əm, -ins/yə-), *n.* the presence of excessive insulin in the blood, resulting in hypoglycemia.

hy/per·ir/ri·ta·bil/i·ty, *n.* extreme irritability or sensitivity. —**hy/per·ir/ri·ta·ble,** *adj.*

hy/per·ka·le/mi·a (-kə lē/mē ə), *n.* an abnormally high concentration of potassium in the blood. —**hy/per·ka·le/mic,** *adj.*

hy/per·ker/a·to/sis, *n.* **1.** proliferation of the cells of the

cornea. **2.** a thickening of the horny layer of the skin.
—**hy′per·ker′a·tot′ic,** *adj.*

hy′per·ki·ne′sia (-ki nē′zhə, -zhē ə, -zē ə, -ki-) also
hy′per·ki·ne′sis, *n.* **1.** an abnormal amount of uncontrolled muscular action; spasm. **2.** a hyperactive condition.
—**hy′per·ki·net′ic** (-net′ik), *adj.*

hy′per·li·pe′mi·a, also **hy′per·lip′i·de′mi·a** (-lip′i dē′-
-, -li/pi-), *n.* the presence of excessive amounts of fat and
fatty substances in the blood; lipemia. —**hy′per·li·pe′mic,
hy′per·lip′i·de′mic,** *adj.*

hy′per·lip′o·pro′tein·e′mi·a (-lip′ə prō′tē nē′mē ə,
-prō′tē ə-, -li/pə-), *n.* any of various disorders of lipoprotein metabolism, usu. characterized by abnormally high
levels of cholesterol and certain lipoproteins in the blood.

hy′per·mne′sia (hī′pərm nē′zhə), *n.* the condition of
having an unusually vivid or precise memory. —**hy′perm·
ne′sic** (-nē′sik, -zik), *adj.*

hy′per·o·pi·a (hī′pər ō′pē ə), *n.* a condition of the eye in
which parallel rays are focused behind the retina, distant
objects being seen more distinctly than near ones; farsightedness (opposed to *myopia*). Also called **hy′per·me·
tro′pi·a** (-mi trō′pē ə). —**hy′per·op′ic** (-op′ik, -ō′pik),
adj.

hy′per·os·mo′lar co′ma (-oz mō′lər), *n.* loss of consciousness resulting from high levels of blood sugar.

hy′per·os·to′sis (-o stō′sis), *n.* excessive growth of bony
tissue. —**hy′per·os·tot′ic** (-o stot′ik), *adj.*

hy′per·par′a·thy′roid·ism (-par′ə thī′roi diz′əm), *n.*
overactivity of the parathyroid gland, characterized by muscular weakness and softening of the bones.

hy′per·pha′gi·a (-fā′jē ə, -jə), *n.* BULIMIA (def. 2). —**hy′·
per·phag′ic** (-faj′ik, -fā′jik), *adj.*

hy′per·pi·tu′i·ta·rism (-pi tōō′i tə riz′əm, -tyōō′-), *n.* **1.**
overactivity of the pituitary gland. **2.** a resultant condition,
as gigantism or acromegaly.

hy′per·pla′sia (-plā′zhə, -zhē ə, -zē ə), *n.* **1.** abnormal
multiplication of cells. **2.** enlargement of a part due to an
abnormal numerical increase of its cells. —**hy′per·plas′·
tic** (-plas′tik), *adj.*

hy′per·ploid′ (-ploid′), *adj.* having a chromosome number that is greater than but not a multiple of the diploid
number. —**hy′per·ploid′y,** *n.*

hy′per·pne·a (hī′pərp nē′ə, hī/pər nē′ə), *n.* abnormally
deep or rapid respiration.

hy′per·pot′as·se′mi·a (-pot′ə sē′mē ə), *n.* HYPERKALE-
MIA. —**hy′per·pot′as·se′mic,** *adj.*

hy′per·py·rex′i·a, *n.* an abnormally high fever. —**hy′·
per·py·ret′ic** (-ret′ik), *adj.*

hy′per·sen′si·tive, *adj.* allergic to a substance to which
most people do not normally react. —**hy′per·sen′si·tive·
ness, hy′per·sen·si·tiv′i·ty,** *n.*

hy′per·sex′u·al, *adj.* unusually or excessively active in or
concerned with sexual matters. —**hy′per·sex′u·al′i·ty,** *n.*
—**hy′per·sex′u·al·ly,** *adv.*

hy·per·splen·ism (-splē′niz əm, -splen′iz-) also **hy′per·sple′ni·a** (-splē′nē ə), *n.* enlargement of the spleen with abnormal destruction of blood cells. —**hy′per·sple′nic,** *adj.*

hy′per·ten′sion, *n.* **1.** elevation of the blood pressure, esp. the diastolic pressure. **2.** an arterial disease characterized by this condition. Also called **high blood pressure.**

hy′per·ten′sive, *adj.* **1.** characterized by or causing hypertension. —*n.* **2.** a person who has hypertension.

hy′per·ther′mi·a (-thûr′mē ə) also **hy′per·ther′my,** *n.* **1.** abnormally high fever. **2.** treatment of disease by the induction of fever.

hy′per·thy′roid, *adj.* of, pertaining to, or having hyperthyroidism.

hy′per·thy′roid·ism, *n.* **1.** overactivity of the thyroid gland. **2.** a condition resulting from this, characterized by increased metabolism and exophthalmos.

hy′per·to′ni·a (-tō′nē ə), *n.* increased rigidity, tension, and spasticity of the muscles.

hy′per·ton′ic (-ton′ik), *adj.* pertaining to or affected with hypertonia. —**hy′per·to·nic′i·ty** (-tō nis′i tē), *n.*

hy·per·tro·phy (hī pûr′trə fē), *n., pl.* **-phies.** abnormal enlargement of a part or organ due to an increase in the size of its cells; excessive growth. —**hy·per·troph·ic** (hī′-pər trof′ik, -trō′fik), *adj.*

hy′per·u·ri·ce′mi·a (-yŏŏr′ə sē′mē ə), *n.* an excess of uric acid in the blood, often producing gout. —**hy′per·u′ri·ce′mic,** *adj.*

hy′per·ven′ti·late′, *v.t.,* **-lat·ed, -lat·ing.** to cause (a patient) to breathe more rapidly and deeply than normal.

hy′per·ven′ti·la′tion, *n.* prolonged rapid or deep breathing, resulting in excessive oxygen levels in the blood often with accompanying dizziness, chest pain, and tingling of extremities.

hy′per·vi′ta·mi·no′sis (-vī′tə mə nō′sis), *n.* an abnormal condition caused by an excessive intake of vitamins.

hyp·es·the·sia (hip′əs thē′zhə, -zhē ə, -zē ə, hī′pəs-), *n.* an abnormally weak sense of pain, heat, cold, or touch (opposed to *hyperesthesia*). —**hyp′es·the′sic** (-thē′zik, -sik), *adj.*

hyp·na·gog·ic (hip′nə goj′ik, -gō′jik), *adj.* **1.** of or pertaining to the period of drowsiness between wakefulness and sleep: *hypnagogic hallucinations.* Compare HYPNOPOMPIC. **2.** inducing drowsiness.

hyp·no·a·nal·y·sis (hip′nō ə nal′ə sis), *n.* psychoanalysis with the aid of hypnosis or hypnotic drugs. —**hyp′no·an′a·lyt′ic,** *adj.*

hyp·no·gen·e·sis (hip′nə jen′ə sis), *n.* the induction of a hypnotic state. —**hyp′no·ge·net′ic,** *adj.*

hyp·noi·dal (hip noid′l) also **hyp′noid,** *adj.* characterizing a state that resembles mild hypnosis but that is usu. induced by other than hypnotic means.

hyp·nol·o·gy (hip nol′ə jē), *n.* the science dealing with the phenomena of sleep. —**hyp′no·log′ic** (-nl ŏj′ĭk), **hyp′no·log′i·cal**, *adj.* —**hyp·nol′o·gist**, *n.*

hyp·no·pom·pic (hĭp′nə pŏm′pĭk), *adj.* of or pertaining to the semiconscious state prior to complete wakefulness. Compare HYPNAGOGIC.

hyp·no·sis (hĭp nō′sĭs), *n., pl.* **-ses** (-sēz). **1.** an artificially induced trance state resembling sleep, characterized by heightened susceptibility to suggestion. **2.** HYPNOTISM (defs. 1, 2).

hyp′no·ther′a·py, *n.* treatment of a symptom, disease, or addiction by means of hypnotism. —**hyp′no·ther′a·pist**, *n.*

hyp·not′ic (-nŏt′ĭk), *adj.* **1.** of, pertaining to, or resembling hypnosis or hypnotism. **2.** inducing hypnosis. **3.** inducing sleep; soporific. —*n.* **4.** an agent or drug that induces sleep; soporific. **5.** a person who is hypnotized or susceptible to hypnosis. —**hyp·not′i·cal·ly**, *adv.*

hyp′no·tism (-nə tĭz′əm), *n.* **1.** the study or process of inducing hypnosis. **2.** the act of hypnotizing. **3.** HYPNOSIS (def. 1). —**hyp′no·tist**, *n.*

hy·po (hī′pō), *n., pl.* **-pos.** *Informal.* a hypodermic syringe or injection.

hy·po·al·ler·gen·ic (hī′pō al′ər jen′ĭk), *adj.* designed to minimize the likelihood of an allergic response, as by containing few or no potentially irritating substances: *hypoallergenic cosmetics.*

hy·po·bar·ic (hī′pə bar′ĭk), *adj.* (of an anesthetic) having a specific gravity lower than that of cerebrospinal fluid.

hy′po·blast (-blăst′), *n.* **1.** the endoderm of an embryo. **2.** the cells entering into the inner layer of a young gastrula, capable of becoming endoderm and, to some extent, mesoderm. —**hy′po·blas′tic**, *adj.*

hy·po·cal·ce·mi·a (-kăl sē′mē ə), *n.* an abnormally small amount of calcium in the blood.

hy·po·chon·dri·a (hī′pə kŏn′drē ə) also **hy′po·chon·dri′a·sis** (-pō kən drī′ə sĭs), *n.* an excessive preoccupation with one's health, usu. focusing on some particular symptom, as cardiac or gastric problems; excessive worry or talk about one's health.

hy′po·chon′dri·ac′, *adj.* **1.** Also, **hy′po·chon·dri′a·cal** (-kən drī′ə kəl). —*n.* **2.** a person who has or is subject to hypochondria. —**hy′po·chon·dri′a·cal·ly**, *adv.*

hy′po·der′mic (-dûr′mĭk), *adj.* **1.** of or characterized by the introduction of medicine or drugs under the skin: *a hypodermic injection.* **2.** introduced under the skin: *a hypodermic medication.* —*n.* **3.** a hypodermic injection. **4.** a hypodermic syringe or needle. —**hy′po·der′mi·cal·ly**, *adv.*

hypoder′mic syringe′, *n.* a small piston syringe having a detachable hollow needle (**hypoder′mic nee′dle**) for use in injecting solutions subcutaneously.

hy·po·glos·sal (hī′pə glŏs′əl, -glō′səl), *adj.* **1.** situated under the tongue. —*n.* **2.** HYPOGLOSSAL NERVE.

hy′poglos′sal nerve′, *n.* either one of the twelfth pair of cranial nerves, consisting of motor fibers that innervate the muscles of the tongue.

hy·po·gly·ce·mi·a (hī/pō glī sē/mē ə), *n.* an abnormally low level of glucose in the blood. —**hy/po·gly·ce/mic,** *adj.*

hy·po·ka·le/mi·a (-kā lē/mē ə), *n.* an abnormally low concentration of potassium in the blood. —**hy/po·ka·le/mic,** *adj.*

hy·poph·y·sec·to·my (hī pof/ə sek/tə mē, hi-), *n., pl.* **-mies.** surgical excision of the pituitary gland.

hy·poph·y·sis (hī pof/ə sis, hi-), *n., pl.* **-ses** (-sēz/). PITUI-TARY GLAND. —**hy/poph/y·se/al, hy/poph/y·si/al** (-sē/əl, -zē/-), *adj.*

hy·po·pi·tu·i·ta·rism (hī/pō pi tōō/i tə riz/əm, -tyōō/-), *n.* **1.** deficient activity of the pituitary gland, esp. of the anterior lobe. **2.** the condition produced by this, characterized by obesity, retention of adolescent traits, sterility, amenorrhea, and, in extreme cases, dwarfism.

hy·po·pla·sia (hī/pə plā/zhə, -zhē ə) also **hy/po·plas/ty** (-plas/tē), *n.* abnormal deficiency of cells or structural elements. —**hy/po·plas/tic,** *adj.*

hy/po·ploid/ (-ploid/), *adj.* having a chromosome number that is less than the diploid number. —**hy/po·ploid/y,** *n.*

hy·po·py·on (hī pō/pē on/), *n.* an effusion of pus into the anterior chamber of the eye.

hy·po·sen·si·tize (hī/pə sen/si tīz/), *v.t.* **-tized, -tiz·ing.** to cause (a person) to become less sensitive to (a substance producing an allergic reaction); desensitize. —**hy/po·sen/si·ti·za/tion,** *n.*

hy·pos·ta·sis (hī pos/tə sis, hi-), *n., pl.* **-ses** (-sēz/). **1.** the accumulation of blood or its solid components in parts of an organ or body due to poor circulation. **2.** sedimentation, as in a test tube. —**hy·po·stat·ic** (hī/pə stat/ik), **hy/po·stat/i·cal,** *adj.* —**hy/po·stat/i·cal·ly,** *adv.*

hy·po·ten·sion (hī/pə ten/shən), *n.* **1.** decreased or lowered blood pressure. **2.** a disease or condition characterized by this symptom.

hy·po·ten·sive (hī/pō ten/siv), *adj.* characterized by or causing low blood pressure, as shock.

hy/po·thal/a·mus (-thal/ə məs), *n., pl.* **-mi** (-mī/). a region of the diencephalon of the brain that is the regulating center for visceral functions, as sleep cycles, body temperature, and the activity of the pituitary gland. —**hy/po·tha·lam/ic** (-thə lam/ik), *adj.*

hy·po·ther·mi·a (hī/pə thûr/mē ə), *n.* **1.** subnormal body temperature. **2.** the artificial reduction of body temperature to slow down metabolic processes, as for facilitating heart surgery. —**hy/po·ther/mic,** *adj.*

hy/po·thy/roid·ism (-thī/roi diz/əm), *n.* **1.** deficient activity of the thyroid gland. **2.** the condition produced by a deficiency of thyroid secretion, resulting in goiter, myxedema, and, in children, cretinism. —**hy/po·thy/roid,** *adj.*

hy/po·ton/ic (-ton/ik), *adj.* having less than the normal tone, as a muscle. —**hy/po·to·nic/i·ty** (-tō nis/i tē), *n.*

hy·pox·e·mi·a (hi/pok sē/mē ə), *n.* inadequate oxygenation of the blood. —**hy/pox·e/mic**, *adj.*

hy·pox/i·a (-sē ə), *n.* an abnormal condition of the body in which oxygen intake or use is inadequate. —**hy/pox/ic**, *adj.*

hys·ter·ec·to·my (his/tə rek/tə mē), *n., pl.* **-mies.** surgical excision of the uterus. —**hys/ter·ec/to·mize/**, *v.t.*, **-mized, -miz·ing.**

hys·te·ri·a (hi ster/ē ə, -stēr/-), *n.* a psychoneurotic disorder characterized by violent emotional outbreaks, disturbances of sensory and motor functions, and various abnormal effects due to autosuggestion.

hys·ter·o·gen·ic (his/tər ə jen/ik), *adj.* inducing hysteria. —**hys/ter·og/e·ny** (-tə roj/ə nē), *n.*

hys·ter·ot·o·my (his/tə rot/ə mē), *n., pl.* **-mies.** the operation of cutting into the uterus, as in a Cesarean.

I

I, *Symbol.* **1.** iodine. **2.** isoleucine.

i·at·ric (i a′trik, ē a′-) also **i·at′ri·cal,** *adj.* of or pertaining to a physician or to medicine; medical.

i·at′ro·gen′ic (-trə jen′ik), *adj.* induced unintentionally by the medical treatment of a physician: *iatrogenic symptoms.* —**i·at′ro·gen/e·sis,** *n.* —**i·at/ro·ge·nic/i·ty,** *n.*

IBD, inflammatory bowel disease.

i·bu·pro·fen (i′byōō prō′fən), *n.* a nonsteroidal anti-inflammatory drug, $C_{13}H_{18}O_2$, used esp. for reducing local pain and swelling, as of the joints.

ice (is), *n. Slang.* methamphetamine prepared illicitly as crystals for smoking.

ice′ bag′, *n.* a waterproof bag filled with ice and applied to a part of the body, as to reduce pain or swelling.

ice′ pack′, *n.* ICE BAG.

i·chor (i′kôr, i′kər), *n.* the watery ooze of an abrasion, sore, or wound. —**i·chor·ous** (i′kər əs), *adj.*

ich·thy·o·sis (ik′thē ō′sis), *n.* a hereditary disorder of the outermost horny tissue, characterized by dry, scaly skin with, in severe cases, hardened plaques. —**ich′thy·ot′ic** (-ot′ik), *adj.*

ICSH, interstitial-cell-stimulating hormone: a pituitary hormone that stimulates testosterone production in the interstitial cells of the testes: chemically identical with luteinizing hormone.

ic·ter·ic (ik ter′ik) also **ic·ter′i·cal,** *adj.* pertaining to or affected with icterus; jaundiced.

ic·ter·us (ik′tər əs), *n.* JAUNDICE.

ic·tus (ik′təs), *n., pl.* **-tus·es, -tus. 1.** an epileptic seizure. **2.** a stroke, esp. a cerebrovascular accident. —**ic′tic,** *adj.*

ICU, intensive care unit.

id (id), *n. Psychoanal.* the part of the psyche that is the source of unconscious and instinctive impulses that seek satisfaction in accordance with the pleasure principle. Compare EGO, SUPEREGO.

i·dée fixe (ē dā fēks′), *n., pl.* **i·dées fixes** (ē dā fēks′), a persistent or obsessing idea, often delusional, that in extreme form can be a symptom of psychosis. Also called **fixed idea.**

iden·ti·cal twin′, *n.* one of a pair of twins who develop from a single fertilized ovum and therefore have the same genotype, are of the same sex, and usu. resemble each other closely. Compare FRATERNAL TWIN.

i·de·o·mo·tor (i′dē ə mō′tər, id′ē ə-), *adj.* of or pertaining to an involuntary body movement evoked by an idea or thought process rather than by sensory stimulation. —**i′-de·o·mo′tion,** *n.*

id·i·o·path·ic (id′ē ə path′ik), *adj.* of unknown cause, as a disease. —**id′i·o·path′i·cal·ly,** *adv.*

id·i·op′a·thy (-op′ə thē), *n., pl.* **-thies.** a disease not preceded or occasioned by any known pathological condition.

id·i·o·syn′cra·sy (-ə sing′krə sē, -sin′-), *n., pl.* **-sies.** a peculiarity of the physical or mental constitution, esp. a sensitivity to drugs, food, etc. —**id′i·o·syn·crat′ic** (-ō sin-krat′ik, -sing-), *adj.* —**id′i·o·syn·crat′i·cal·ly,** *adv.*

id·i·ot (id′ē ət), *n.* a person of the lowest order in a former classification of mental retardation, having a mental age of less than three years and an intelligence quotient under 25.

id·i·ot sa·vant (id′ē ət sə vänt′, sa-; *Fr.* ē dyō sa vän′), *n., pl.* **idiot savants,** *Fr.* **id·i·ots sa·vants** (ē dyō sa vän′). a mentally defective person with an exceptional skill or talent in a special field, as a highly developed ability to play music or to do arithmetic calculations.

Ig, immunoglobulin.

IL, interleukin.

IL-2, interleukin 2.

Ile, isoleucine.

il·e·ac¹ (il′ē ak′), *adj.* of or pertaining to the ileum.

il·e·ac² (il′ē ak′), *adj.* of or pertaining to ileus.

il′e·i′tis (-ī′tis), *n.* **1.** inflammation of the ileum. **2.** CROHN'S DISEASE.

il′e·os′to·my (-os′tə mē), *n., pl.* **-mies. 1.** a surgical opening from the ileum through the abdominal wall for drainage of contents of the small intestine. **2.** the opening so constructed.

il′e·um (-əm), *n.* the third and lowest division of the small intestine, extending from the jejunum to the large intestine. —**il′e·al,** *adj.*

il′e·us, *n.* intestinal obstruction characterized by lack of peristalsis and leading to severe colicky pain and vomiting.

il′i·ac′ (-ak′), *adj.* of, pertaining to, or situated near the ilium.

il′i·um (-ē əm), *n., pl.* **-i·a** (-ē ə). the uppermost of the three bones of each half of the vertebrate pelvic girdle; in humans, the broad upper portion of each hipbone.

il·lu·sion (i lōō′zhən), *n.* a perception, as of visual stimuli (**optical illusion**), that represents what is perceived in a way different from the way it is in reality. —**il·lu′sion·al, il·lu′sion·ar′y,** *adj.*

im·age (im′ij), *n. Psychol.* a mental representation of something previously perceived, in the absence of the original stimulus.

im′ag·ing, *n.* **1.** *Psychol.* a technique using mental images to control bodily processes and ease pain or to accomplish something one has visualized in advance. **2.** the use of computerized axial tomography, sonography, or other techniques and instruments to obtain pictures of the interior of the body.

i·ma·go (i mā′gō, i mä′-), *n., pl.* **-goes, -gi·nes** (-gə nēz′). *Psychoanal.* an idealized concept of a loved one, formed in childhood and retained unaltered in adult life.

im·be·cile (im′bə sil, -səl; *esp. Brit.* -sēl′), *n.* a person of the second order in a former classification of mental retardation, above the level of idiocy, having a mental age of seven or eight years and an intelligence quotient of 25 to 50. —*adj.* —**im/be·cile·ly,** *adv.*

im·mo·bi·lize (i mō/bə līz/), *v.t.*, **-lized, -liz·ing.** to prevent, restrict, or reduce normal movement in (the body, a limb, or a joint), as by a splint, cast, or prescribed bed rest. —**im/mo/bi·li·za/tion,** *n.* —**im/mo/bi·liz/er,** *n.*

im·mune (i myōon/), *adj.* of or pertaining to the production of antibodies or lymphocytes that can react with a specific antigen: *immune reaction.*

immune/ com/plex, *n.* an aggregate of an antigen and its specific antibody.

immune/ response/, *n.* any of the body's immunologic reactions to an antigen.

im·mu/ni·ty, *n., pl.* **-ties.** **1.** the state of being immune from or insusceptible to a particular disease or the like. **2.** the condition that permits either natural or acquired resistance to disease. **3.** the ability of a cell to react immunologically in the presence of an antigen.

im·mu·ni·za·tion (im/yə nə zā/shən, i myōo/-), *n.* the fact or process of becoming immune, as against a disease.

im/mu·nize/, *v.t.,* **-nized, -niz·ing.** to make immune. —**im/mu·niz/er,** *n.*

im·mu·no·as·say (im/yə nō ə sā/, -as/ā, i myōo/-), *n.* a laboratory method for detecting a substance by using an antibody reactive with it. —**im/mu·no·as·say/a·ble,** *adj.*

im/mu·no·bi·ol/o·gy, *n.* the study of the immune response and the biological aspects of immunity to disease. —**im/mu·no·bi/o·log/ic, im/mu·no·bi/o·log/i·cal,** *adj.* —**im/mu·no·bi·ol/o·gist,** *n.*

im/mu·no·chem/is·try, *n.* the study of the chemistry of immunologic substances and reactions. —**im/mu·no·chem/i·cal,** *adj.* —**im/mu·no·chem/i·cal·ly,** *adv.* —**im/mu·no·chem/ist,** *n.*

im/mu·no·de·fi/cien·cy, *n., pl.* **-cies.** impairment of the immune response, predisposing to infection, certain chronic diseases, and cancer. —**im/mu·no·de·fi/cient,** *adj.*

im/mu·no·di·ag·no/sis, *n., pl.* **-ses** (-sēz). SERODIAGNOSIS.

im/mu·no·dif·fu/sion, *n.* any of various analytical techniques that involve antigen and antibody solutions diffusing toward each other in a gel until antibody binds specifically to antigen to form a precipitate.

im/mu·no·gen (i myōo/nə jən, -jen/), *n.* any substance introduced into the body in order to generate an immune response.

im·mu·no·gen·ic (im/yə nō jen/ik, i myōo/nə-), *adj.* causing or capable of producing an immune response. —**im/mu·no·gen/i·cal·ly,** *adv.* —**im/mu·no·ge·nic/i·ty** (-jə nis/i tē), *n.*

im/mu·no·glob/u·lin, *n.* **1.** any of several classes of globulin proteins that function as antibodies. **2.** the frac-tion of the blood serum containing antibodies. **3.** ANTIBODY. *Abbr.:* Ig

im·mu·no·he·ma·tol·o·gy, *n.* the study of blood and blood-forming tissue in relation to the immune response. —**im·mu·no·he·ma·to·log·ic, im·mu·no·he·ma·to·log·i·cal,** *adj.*

im·mu·no·his·tol·o·gy, *n.* the application of the methods of immunology to the study of tissues. —**im·mu·no·his·to·log·ic, im·mu·no·his·to·log·i·cal,** *adj.* —**im·mu·no·his·to·log·i·cal·ly,** *adv.*

im·mu·nol·o·gy (im′yə nol′ə jē), *n.* the branch of science dealing with the components of the immune system, immunity from disease, the immune response, and immunologic techniques of analysis. —**im′mu·no·log′ic** (-nl oj′ik), **im′mu·no·log′i·cal,** *adj.* —**im′mu·no·log′i·cal·ly,** *adv.* —**im′mu·nol′o·gist,** *n.*

im·mu·no·pa·thol·o·gy (im′yə nō-), *n.* the study of diseases having an immunologic or allergic basis. —**im′mu·no·path′o·log′i·cal, im′mu·no·path′o·log′ic,** *adj.* —**im′mu·no·path′o·log′i·cal·ly,** *adv.* —**im′mu·no·pa·thol′o·gist,** *n.*

im·mu·no·pre·cip·i·ta′tion, *n.* the separation of an antigen from a solution by the formation of a large complex with its specific antibody.

im·mu·no·sup·pres′sion, *n.* the inhibition of the normal immune response because of disease, the administration of drugs, or surgery. —**im′mu·no·sup·press′,** *v.t.*

im·mu·no·sup·pres′sive, *adj.* **1.** capable of causing immunosuppression. —*n.* **2.** Also, **im′mu·no·sup·pres′sor.** any substance that results in or effects immunosuppression.

im·mu·no·ther′a·py, *n., pl.* **-pies.** treatment designed to produce immunity to a disease or enhance the resistance of the immune system to an active disease process, as cancer. —**im′mu·no·ther′a·peu′tic,** *adj.*

im·mu·no·tox′in, *n.* a monoclonal antibody linked to a toxin with the intention of destroying a specific target cell while leaving adjacent cells intact.

im·pe·ti·go (im′pi ti′gō), *n.* a contagious skin infection, usu. streptococcal, characterized by pustules that erupt and form crusts. —**im′pe·tig′i·nous** (-tij′ə nəs), *adj.*

im·plant (*v.* im plant′, -plänt′; *n.* im′plant′, -plänt′), *v.t.* **1.** to insert or graft (a tissue, organ, or inert substance) into the body. —*n.* **2. a.** a device or material used for repairing or replacing part of the body. **b.** medication or radioactive material inserted into tissue for sustained therapy. **3. a.** a frame or support inserted permanently into the bone or tissue of the jaw to hold artificial teeth. **b.** an artificial tooth or bridge attached to such a device. —**im·plant′a·ble,** *adj.*

im·plan·ta′tion, *n.* **1.** the act of implanting. **2.** the state of being implanted. **3.** the attachment of the early embryo to the lining of the uterus.

im·po·tent (im′pə tənt), *adj.* (of a male) unable to attain or sustain a penile erection. —**im′po·tence,** *n.*

im·preg·na·ble (im preg′nə bəl), *adj.* susceptible to impregnation.

im·preg·nate (-nāt), *v.t.,* -**nat·ed, -nat·ing. 1.** to make pregnant. **2.** to fertilize. —**im′preg·na′tion,** *n.*

im·pulse (im′puls), *n.* a progressive wave of excitation over a nerve or muscle fiber having a stimulating or inhibitory effect.

in·breed (in′brēd′, in brēd′), *v.,* -**bred, -breed·ing.** —*v.t.* **1.** to breed (individuals of a closely related group) repeatedly. **2.** to breed within; engender. —*v.i.* **3.** to engage in or undergo such breeding.

in·cised (in sizd′), *adj.* made or cut cleanly: *an incised wound.*

in·ci·sion (-sizh′ən), *n.* a surgical cut into a tissue or organ.

in·com·pat·i·ble (in′kəm pat′ə bəl), *adj.* unable to be mixed together in the body effectively or without causing harm: *incompatible drugs.* —**in′com·pat′i·bil′i·ty,** *n.* —**in′com·pat′i·bly,** *adv.*

in·con·ti·nent (in kon′tn ənt), *adj.* unable to restrain natural discharges or evacuations of urine or feces. —**in·con′ti·nence, in·con′ti·nen·cy,** *n.*

in·cu·ba·tion (in′kyə bā′shən, ing′-), *n.* the period between the initial infection and the appearance of symptoms of a disease. —**in′cu·ba′tion·al, in·cu·ba·to·ry** (in′kyə bə tôr′ē, -tōr′ē, ing′-), *adj.*

in′cu·ba′tor, *n.* **1.** an enclosed apparatus in which prematurely born infants are kept and cared for in controlled conditions. **2.** an apparatus in which media inoculated with microorganisms are cultivated at a constant temperature.

in·cus (ing′kəs), *n., pl.* **in·cu·des** (in kyŏŏ′dēz). the middle bone of the chain of three small bones in the middle ear of mammals. Also called **anvil.** —**in′cu·date′** (-kyə dāt′, -dit), **in′cu·dal,** *adj.*

IND, investigative new drug.

in·di·can (in′di kən), *n.* indoxyl potassium sulfate, $C_8H_6NO_4SK$, a component of urine.

in·di·ges·tion (in′di jes′chən, -di-), *n.* a feeling of discomfort after eating, as of heartburn, nausea, or bloating; dyspepsia.

in·do·lent (in′dl ənt), *adj.* inactive or relatively benign: *indolent ulcer.*

in·do·meth·a·cin (in′dō meth′ə sin), *n.* a substance, $C_{19}H_{16}ClNO_4$, with anti-inflammatory, antipyretic, and analgesic properties.

in·duce (in dōōs′, -dyōōs′), *v.t.,* -**duced, -duc·ing. 1.** *Genetics.* to increase expression of (a gene) by inactivating a negative control system or activating a positive control system. **2.** *Biochem.* to stimulate the synthesis of (a protein, esp. an enzyme) by increasing gene transcription. —**in·duc′i·ble,** *adj.*

in·duc′er, *n.* **1.** *Biochem.* a substance that has the capability of activating genes within a cell. **2.** a part of an embryo that influences differentiation of another part.

in·duc·tion (in duk/shən), *n.* **1.** the process or principle by which one part of an embryo influences the differentiation of another part. **2.** *Biochem.* the synthesis of an enzyme in response to an increased concentration of its substrate in the cell.

in·duc/tive (-tiv), *adj.* capable of bringing about embryonic induction. —**in·duc/tive·ly,** *adv.* —**in·duc/tive·ness,** *n.*

in·du·ra·tion (in/dōō rā/shən, -dyōō-), *n.* an abnormal hardening of an area of the body. —**in·du·ra/tive,** *adj.*

in·ert (in ûrt/, i nûrt/), *adj.* having no pharmacological action, as the excipient of a pill. —**in·ert/ly,** *adv.* —**in·ert/ness,** *n.*

in/fan·tile paral/ysis (in/fən til/, -til), *n.* POLIOMYELITIS.

in·fan·ti·lism (in/fən tl iz/əm, -ti liz/-, in fan/tl iz/əm), *n.* the persistence in an adult of markedly childish anatomical, physiological, or psychological characteristics.

in·farct (in/färkt/, in färkt/), *n.* an area of tissue, as in the heart or kidney, that is dying or dead, having been deprived of its blood supply. —**in·farct/ed,** *adj.*

in·farc/tion, *n.* **1.** the formation of an infarct. **2.** an infarct.

in·fect (in fekt/), *v.t.* to affect or contaminate with disease-producing germs.

in·fec/tion, *n.* **1.** the act of infecting or the state of being infected. **2.** an infecting agency or influence. **3.** an infectious disease. **4.** the condition of suffering an infection.

in·fec/tious, *adj.* **1.** communicable by infection, as from one individual to another or from one part of the body to another. **2.** causing or communicating infection. —**in·fec/tious·ly,** *adv.* —**in·fec/tious·ness,** *n.*

infec/tious hepati/tis, *n.* HEPATITIS A.

infec/tious mononucleo/sis, *n.* an acute infectious form of mononucleosis associated with Epstein-Barr virus and characterized by sudden fever and a benign swelling of lymph nodes. Also called **glandular fever.**

inferior/ity com/plex, *n.* an intense feeling of inferiority, producing a personality characterized either by extreme reticence or, as a result of overcompensation, by extreme aggressiveness.

in·fer·tile (in fûr/tl; *esp. Brit.* -til), *adj.* not fertile; unproductive; sterile. —**in/fer·til/i·ty,** *n.*

in·fil·trate (in fil/trāt, in/fil trāt/), *v.,* **-trat·ed, -trat·ing,** *n.* *Pathol.* —*v.i.* **1.** to penetrate tissue spaces or cells. —*n.* **2.** any substance penetrating tissues or cells and forming a morbid accumulation. —**in/fil·tra/tion,** *n.* —**in/fil·tra/tive,** *adj.* —**in/fil·tra/tor,** *n.*

in·flam·ma·tion (in/flə mā/shən), *n.* redness, swelling, and fever in a local area of the body, often with pain and disturbed function, in reaction to an infection or to a physical or chemical injury.

in·flam·ma·to·ry (in flam′ə tôr′ē, -tōr′ē), *adj.* of or caused by inflammation. —**in·flam′ma·to′ri·ly,** *adv.*

in·flu·en·za (in′flōō en′zə), *n.* an acute, commonly epidemic disease occurring in several forms, caused by numerous rapidly mutating viral strains and characterized by respiratory symptoms and general prostration. —**in′flu·en′zal,** *adj.*

informed′ consent′, *n.* a patient's consent to a medical or surgical procedure or to participation in a clinical study after being properly advised of the relevant medical facts and the risks involved.

in·fu·sion (in fyōō′zhən), *n.* **1.** the introduction of a saline, or other solution into a vein. **2.** the solution used.

In·fu·so·ri·a (in′fyōō sôr′ē ə, -sōr′-), *n.pl.* **1.** protozoans of the phylum Ciliophora (or class Ciliata). **2.** (formerly) various microscopic organisms found in infusions of decaying organic matter. —**in′fu·so′ri·al, in′fu·so′ri·an,** *adj.*

in·gest (in jest′), *v.t.* to take into the body, as food or liquid (opposed to *egest*). —**in·gest′i·ble,** *adj.* —**in·ges′-tion,** *n.* —**in·ges′tive,** *adj.*

in′grown′, *adj.* having grown into the flesh: *an ingrown toenail.*

in·gui·nal (ing′gwə nl), *adj.* of, pertaining to, or situated in the groin.

in·hal·ant (in hā′lənt), *n.* a volatile medicine or other substance that is inhaled for the effect of its vapor.

in·ha·la·tor (in′hə lā′tər), *n.* an apparatus used to help inhale air, anesthetics, medicinal vapors, etc.

in·hib·in (in hib′in), *n.* a male hormone that acts on the pituitary gland to limit the secretion of FSH.

in·hib·it (in hib′it), *v.t.,* **-it·ed, -it·ing.** to suppress or restrain from free expression, as of psychologically or socially unacceptable behavior. —**in·hib′i·to′ry** (-tôr′ē, -tōr′ē), *adj.* —**in·hib′i·tive,** *adj.*

in·hib′it·ed, *adj.* suffering from psychological inhibition.

in·hi·bi·tion (in′i bish′ən, in′hi-), *n.* **1. a.** the conscious or unconscious restraint or suppression of behavior, impulses, etc., often due to guilt or fear produced by past punishment. **b.** the blocking or holding back of one psychological process by another. **2. a.** a restraining, arresting, or checking of the action of an organ or cell. **b.** the reduction of a reflex or other activity as the result of an antagonistic stimulation.

in·ject (in jekt′), *v.t.* to force (a fluid) into a passage, cavity, or tissue. —**in·ject′a·ble,** *adj.* —**in·jec′tor,** *n.*

in·jec′tion, *n.* a liquid injected into the body, esp. for medicinal purposes.

ink′blot test′ (ink′blot′), *n.* any psychological test in which varied patterns formed by inkblots are interpreted by the subject. Compare RORSCHACH TEST.

in′ner ear′, *n.* the inner, liquid-filled, membranous portion of the ear, involved in hearing and balance.

in·ner·vate (i nûr′vāt, in′ər vāt′), *v.t.,* **-vat·ed, -vat·ing.**

to furnish (an organ or tissue) with nerves; grow nerves into. —**in′ner·va′tion,** *n.*

in·nom′i·nate bone′ (i nom′ə nit), *n.* HIPBONE (def. 1).

in·oc·u·late (i nok′yə lāt′), *v.t.,* **-lat·ed, -lat·ing.** to introduce (microorganisms) into surroundings suited to their growth, as a culture medium. —**in·oc′u·la′tive** (-lā′tiv, -lə-), *adj.* —**in·oc′u·la′tor,** *n.*

in·oc′u·la′tion, *n.* **1.** the act or process of inoculating. **2.** an instance of inoculating. **3.** INOCULUM.

in·oc′u·lum (-ləm), *n., pl.* **-la** (-lə). the substance used to make an inoculation.

in·op·er·a·ble (in op′ər ə bəl, -op′rə bəl), *adj.* not admitting of a surgical operation without undue risk; incapable of being treated or cured by surgery: *an inoperable tumor.*

in·o·si·tol (i nō′si tôl′, -tōl′, i nō′-), *n.* a compound, $C_6H_{12}O_6$, occurring in animal tissue, plants, and many seeds, and functioning as a growth factor.

i·no·trop·ic (ē′nə trop′ik, -trō′pik, i′nə-), *adj.* influencing the contractility of muscular tissue.

in·san·i·ty (in san′i tē), *n., pl.* **-ties.** (*not in technical use*) the condition of being insane; mental illness or disorder.

in·sem·i·nate (in sem′ə nāt′), *v.t.,* **-nat·ed, -nat·ing.** to inject semen into (the female reproductive tract); impregnate. —**in·sem′i·na′tion,** *n.*

in′sight′, *n. Psychol.* **1.** an understanding of the motivations behind one's thoughts or behavior. **2.** (in psychotherapy) a recognition of the sources of one's emotional or mental problem.

in·so·la·tion (in′sō lā′shən), *n.* **1.** exposure to the sun's rays, esp. as a process of treatment. **2.** SUNSTROKE.

in·som·ni·a (in som′nē ə), *n.* difficulty in falling or staying asleep, esp. when chronic. —**in·som′ni·ac′,** *n., adj.* —**in·som′ni·ous,** *adj.*

in·suf·fi·cien·cy (in′sə fish′ən sē), *n., pl.* **-cies.** inability of an organ or other body part to function normally: *cardiac insufficiency.*

in·suf·flate (in suf′lāt, in′sə flāt′), *v.t.,* **-flat·ed, -flat·ing.** to blow (air or a medicinal substance) into some opening or upon some part of the body. —**in′suf·fla′tion,** *n.* —**in′suf·fla′tor,** *n.*

in·su·lin (in′sə lin, ins′yə-), *n.* **1.** a hormone, produced by the beta cells of the islets of Langerhans of the pancreas, that regulates the metabolism of glucose and other nutrients. **2.** any of several commercial preparations of this substance, each absorbed into the body at a particular rate: used for treating diabetes.

in′sulin-co′ma ther′apy, *n.* a former treatment for mental illness, esp. schizophrenia, employing insulin-induced hypoglycemia as a method for producing convulsive seizures. Also called **in′sulin-shock′ ther′apy.**

in′sulin shock′, *n.* a state of collapse caused by a decrease in blood sugar resulting from the administration of excessive insulin.

in·te·gra·tion (in′ti grā′shən), *n.* **1.** *Psychol.* the organization of the constituent elements of the personality into a coordinated, harmonious whole. **2. COADAPTATION.**

intel'ligence quo'tient, *n.* an intelligence test score that is obtained by dividing mental age, which reflects the age-graded level of performance as derived from population norms, by chronological age and multiplying by 100: a score of 100 thus indicates a performance at exactly the normal level for that age group. *Abbr.:* IQ

intel'ligence test', *n.* any of various tests designed to measure the relative intellectual capacity of a person.

inten'sive care', *n.* the use of specialized equipment and personnel for continuous monitoring and care of the critically ill, usu. in a special center in a hospital (**inten'sive care' u'nit**).

in·ten'siv·ist, *n.* a medical specialist in intensive care.

in·ter·cel·lu·lar (in'tər sel'yə lər), *adj.* situated between or among cells.

in'ter·cos'tal (-kos'tl, -kô'stl), *adj.* **1.** pertaining to muscles, parts, or intervals between the ribs. **2.** situated between the ribs. —**in'ter·cos'tal·ly,** *adv.*

in'ter·course', *n.* sexual relations or a sexual coupling, esp. coitus.

in'ter·cur'rent, *adj.* (of a disease) occurring while another disease is in progress. —**in'ter·cur'rence,** *n.*

in·ter·fer·ence (in'tər fēr'əns), *n.* the distorting or inhibiting effect of previously learned behavior on subsequent learning. —**in'ter·fe·ren'tial** (-fə ren'shəl), *adj.*

in·ter·fer·on (in'tər fēr'on), *n.* any of various proteins, produced by virus-infected cells, that inhibit reproduction of the invading virus and induce resistance to further infection.

in·ter·leu·kin (in'tər lōō'kin), *n.* any of a family of small proteins that participate in the body's defense system, esp. by promoting the growth and activation of white blood cells. *Abbr.:* IL

interleukin 2, *n.* a T-cell protein that stimulates the production of more T cells and other immune defenses: used experimentally in immunotherapy. *Abbr.:* IL-2

in·ter·mit·tent (in'tər mit'nt), *adj.* stopping or ceasing for a time; alternately ceasing and beginning again: *an intermittent pain.* —**in'ter·mit'tence,** *n.* —**in'ter·mit'tent·ly,** *adv.*

in·ter·mo·lec·u·lar (in'tər mə lek'yə lər, -mō-), *adj.* existing or occurring between molecules.

in·tern (in'tûrn), *n.* **1.** Also, **in'terne,** a resident member of the medical staff of a hospital, usu. a recent medical school graduate serving under supervision. —*v.i.* **2.** to serve as an intern.

inter'nal med'icine, *n.* the branch of medicine dealing with the diagnosis and nonsurgical treatment of diseases, esp. of internal organ systems.

in'terna'tional u'nit, *n.* **1.** an internationally accepted standard, derived by bioassay, to which samples of a pharmaceutical substance are compared for ascertaining their relative potency. **2.** the specific biologically effective quantity of such a substance. Abbr.: IU

in·tern·ist (in'tûr nist, in tûr'nist), *n.* a physician specializing in the diagnosis and nonsurgical treatment of diseases, esp. of adults.

in·ter·o·cep·tor (in'tə rō sep'tər), *n.* a sensory receptor or nerve ending that responds to stimuli originating from within the body. —**in'ter·o·cep'tive,** *adj.*

in·ter·phase (in'tər fāz'), *n.* the period of the cell cycle during which the nucleus is not undergoing division.

in'ter·sex', *n.* an individual displaying both male and female sexual characteristics.

in'ter·sex'u·al, *adj.* pertaining to or having the characteristics of an intersex. —**in'ter·sex'u·al'i·ty, in'ter·sex'u·al·ism,** *n.* —**in'ter·sex'u·al·ly,** *adv.*

in'ter·sti'tial (-stish'əl), *adj.* situated in the interstices of a tissue or organ. —**in'ter·sti'tial·ly,** *adv.*

in'tersti'tial-cell'-stim'ulating hor'mone, *n.* See ICSH.

in'ter·ver'te·bral, *adj.* situated between the vertebrae. —**in'ter·ver'te·bral·ly,** *adv.*

in'terver'tebral disk', *n.* the plate of fibrocartilage between the bodies of adjacent vertebrae.

in·tes·ti·nal (in tes'tə nl), *adj.* of, pertaining to, being in, or affecting the intestines: *intestinal obstruction.* —**in·tes'ti·nal·ly,** *adv.*

in·tes'tine (-tin), *n.* **1.** Usu., **intestines.** the lower part of the alimentary canal, extending from the pylorus to the anus. **2.** Also called **small intestine.** the narrow, longer part of the intestines, comprising the duodenum, jejunum, and ileum, that serves to digest and absorb nutrients. **3.** Also called **large intestine.** the broad, shorter part of the intestines, comprising the cecum, colon, and rectum, that absorbs water from and eliminates the residues of digestion.

in·tox·i·cate (in tok'si kāt'), *v.t.,* **-cat·ed, -cat·ing. 1.** to affect temporarily with diminished physical and mental control by means of alcoholic liquor, a drug, or another substance, esp. to excite or stupefy with liquor. **2.** *Pathol.* to poison.

in·tox'i·ca'tion, *n.* **1.** inebriation; drunkenness. **2.** *Pathol.* poisoning.

in·tra·cel·lu·lar (in'trə sel'yə lər), *adj.* within a cell or cells. —**in'tra·cel'lu·lar·ly,** *adv.*

in'tra·cra'ni·al, *adj.* being or occurring within the skull.

in'tra·cu·ta'ne·ous, *adj.* INTRADERMAL (def. 2). —**in'tra·cu·ta'ne·ous·ly,** *adv.*

in'tracuta'neous test', *n.* a test for sensitivity to an antigen by observing whether a small amount injected into the skin produces a local reaction. Also called **in'trader'mal test'.**

in'tra·der'mal also **in'tra·der'mic,** *adj.* **1.** being, occurring, or located within the dermis. **2.** going between the layers of the skin, as an injection. —**in'tra·der'mal·ly, in'tra·der'mi·cal·ly,** *adv.*

in'tra·mo·lec'u·lar, *adj.* existing or occurring within a molecule.

in'tra·oc'u·lar, *adj.* located or occurring within or or administered through the eye. —**in'tra·oc'u·lar·ly,** *adv.*

in'traoc'ular lens', *n.* a plastic lens implanted surgically to replace the eye's natural lens.

in'tra·psy'chic, *adj.* existing or occurring within the mind or psyche. —**in'tra·psy'chi·cal·ly,** *adv.*

in·tra·u·ter·ine (in'trə yōō'tər in, -tə rin'), *adj.* located or occurring within the uterus.

intrau'terine device', *n.* any of various contrivances, as a loop or coil, for insertion into the uterus as a contraceptive. *Abbr.:* IUD

in·trav·a·sa·tion (in trav'ə sā'shən), *n.* the entrance of foreign matter into a blood vessel.

in·tra·vas·cu·lar (in'trə vas'kyə lər), *adj.* within the blood vessels.

in·tra·ve·nous (in'trə vē'nəs), *adj.* **1.** of, pertaining to, employed in, or administered by injection into a vein. —*n.* **2.** an intravenous injection or feeding. *Abbr.:* IV —**in'tra·ve'nous·ly,** *adv.*

intrin'sic fac'tor, *n.* a gastric glycoprotein involved in the absorption of vitamin B$_{12}$.

in·tro·jec·tion (in'trə jek'shən), *n.* an unconscious psychic process by which a person incorporates into his or her own psychic apparatus the characteristics of another person or object.

in·tron (in'tron), *n.* a noncoding segment in DNA that interrupts a gene-coding sequence or nontranslated sequence. Compare EXON.

in·tro·ver·sion (in'trə vûr'zhən, -shən, in'trə vûr'-), *n.* the act or state of being concerned primarily with one's own thoughts and feelings rather than with the external environment. Compare EXTROVERSION. —**in'tro·ver'sive, in'tro·ver'tive,** *adj.*

in'tro·vert' (-vûrt'), *n.* **1.** a person who exhibits introversion. —*adj.* **2.** Also, **in'tro·vert'ed.** marked by introversion.

in·tu·bate (in'tōō bāt', -tyōō-), *v.t.,* **-bat·ed, -bat·ing.** to insert a tube into (a hollow anatomical structure, as the larynx), esp. for admitting air or a fluid. —**in'tu·ba'tion,** *n.*

in·tu·mes·cence (in'tōō mes'əns, -tyōō-), *n.* **1.** a swelling up, as with congestion. **2.** a swollen mass. —**in'tu·mes'cent,** *adj.*

in·tus·sus·cept (in'təs sə sept'), *v.t.* to take within, as one part of the intestine into an adjacent part; invaginate. —**in'tus·sus·cep'tive,** *adj.*

in'tus·sus·cep'tion, *n.* Also called **invagination.** the slipping of one part within another, as of the intestine.

in·u·lase (in'yə lās', -lāz'), *n.* an enzyme that converts insulin to levulose.

in·u·lin (in'yə lin), *n.* a starchlike polysaccharide,

$(C_6H_{10}O_5)_n$, of many plant roots and tubers, that yields a form of fructose on hydrolysis.

in u·ter·o (in yōō'tə rō'), *adv., adj.* in the uterus; unborn.

in·vag·i·nate (in vaj'ə nāt'), *v.t.* **-nat·ed, -nat·ing.** to fold or draw (a tubular anatomical structure) back within itself; intussuscept.

in·vag'i·na'tion, *n.* **1.** *Embryol.* the inward movement of a portion of the wall of a blastula in the formation of a gastrula. **2.** *Pathol.* INTUSSUSCEPTION

in·va·lid·ism (in'və li diz'əm), *n.* prolonged ill health.

in·va·sive (in vā'siv), *adj.* requiring the entry of a needle, catheter, or other medical and esp. surgical instrument into a part of the body.

in·ver·sion (in vûr'zhən, -shən), *n.* **1.** the turning inward of an anatomical part, as the foot. **2.** a reversal of the linear order of genes on a chromosome. —**in·ver'sive,** *adj.*

in·vert·ase (in vûr'tās, -tāz) also **in·ver'tin,** *n.* an enzyme that causes the inversion of cane sugar into invert sugar. Also called **sucrase.**

in'vert sug'ar, *n.* a mixture of the dextrorotatory forms of glucose and fructose formed naturally in fruits and produced artificially by treating cane sugar with acids.

inves'tigative new' drug', *n.* an unproven drug that is approved by the Food and Drug Administration for restricted use in clinical trials. *Abbr.:* IND

in·vi·a·ble (in vī'ə bəl), *adj.* (of an organism) incapable of sustaining its own life. —**in·vi'a·bil'i·ty,** *n.*

in vi·tro (in vē'trō), *adj.* (of a biological entity or process) developed or maintained in a controlled, nonliving environment, as a laboratory vessel. Compare IN VIVO.

in vi'tro fertiliza'tion, *n.* a technique by which an ovum is fertilized with sperm in a laboratory dish and subsequently implanted in a uterus for gestation. *Abbr.:* IVF

in vi·vo (in vē'vō), *adj.* (of a biological entity or process) being or occurring within a living organism or in a natural setting. Compare IN VITRO.

in·vol·un·tar·y (in vol'ən ter'ē), *adj. Physiol.* acting or functioning without volition: *involuntary muscles.* —**in·vol·un·tar·i·ly** (in vol'ən ter'ə lē, -vol'ən târ'-), *adv.* —**in·vol'un·tar'i·ness,** *n.*

in·vo·lu·tion (in'və lōō'shən), *n. Physiol.* the regressive changes in the body occurring with old age. —**in'vo·lu'tion·al,** *adj.*

i·o·dine (ī'ə dīn', -din; *in Chem. also* -dēn'), *n.* a nonmetallic halogen element occurring as a grayish-black crystalline solid that sublimes to a dense violet vapor when heated: used as an antiseptic, as a nutritional supplement, and in radiolabeling. Compare RADIOIODINE. *Symbol:* I; *at. wt.:* 126.904; *at. no.:* 53; *sp. gr.:* (solid) 4.93 at 20°C.

i·o·dize (ī'ə dīz'), *v.t.,* **-dized, -diz·ing.** to treat, impregnate, or affect with iodine or an iodide. —**i'o·di·za'tion,** *n.* —**i'o·diz'er,** *n.*

i·o·do·form (ī ō'də fôrm', ī od'ə-), *n.* a yellowish, crystalline, water-insoluble solid, CHI₃, having a penetrating odor: used chiefly as an antiseptic.

i·o·dop·sin (ī′ə dop′sin), *n.* a photosensitive violet pigment in the cones of the retina.

i·on·o·phore (ī on′ə fôr′, -fōr′), *n.* any of a group of lipid-soluble substances that can transport an ion through a cell membrane.

i·on·to·pho·re·sis (ī on′tə fə rē′sis), *n.* the method of administering an ionized solution, as of a drug, through intact skin by stimulation with a weak electric current. —**i·on′to·pho·ret′ic** (-ret′ik), *adj.*

ip·e·cac (ip′i kak′), *n.* **1.** a tropical South American shrubby plant, *Cephaelis ipecacuanha*, of the madder family. **2.** the dried root of this plant, used as an emetic.

IQ, intelligence quotient.

ir·i·dec·to·my (ir′i dek′tə mē, ī′ri-), *n.*, *pl.* **-mies.** excision of part of the iris.

ir′i·dol·o·gy (-dol′ə jē), *n.*, *pl.* **-gies.** examination of the iris of the eye as a primary diagnostic aid. —**ir′i·dol′o·gist,** *n.*

i·ris (ī′ris), *n.*, *pl.* **i·ris·es, ir·i·des** (ir′i dēz′, ī′ri-). the contractile, circular diaphragm forming the colored portion of the eye and containing an opening, the pupil, in its center.

i·ri·tis (ī rī′tis), *n.* inflammation of the iris. —**i·rit·ic** (ī rit′ik), *adj.*

i′ron lung′, *n.* a rigid respirator that encloses the whole body except the head and in which alternate pulsations of high and low pressure induce normal breathing movements or force air into and out of the lungs.

i′ron-stor′age disease′, *n.* HEMOCHROMATOSIS.

ir·ra·di·a·tion (i rā′dē ā′shən), *n.* the use of x-rays or other forms of radiation for treatment of disease, manufacture of vitamin D, etc.

ir·reg·u·lar·i·ty (i reg′yə lar′i tē), *n.*, *pl.* **-ties.** occasional mild constipation.

ir·ri·gate (ir′i gāt′), *v.t.*, **-gat·ed, -gat·ing.** to supply or wash (an orifice, wound, etc.) with a spray or a flow of some liquid. —**ir′ri·ga·ble,** *adj.* —**ir′ri·ga·bly,** *adv.* —**ir′ri·ga′tion,** *n.* —**ir′ri·ga′tion·al,** *adj.*

ir·ri·ta·ble (ir′i tə bəl), *adj.* **1.** *Biol.* able to be excited to a characteristic action or function by the application of a stimulus. **2.** *Pathol.* abnormally excitable or sensitive to stimulation. —**ir′ri·ta·bil′i·ty,** *n.* —**ir′ri·ta·bly,** *adv.*

ir′ri·tant (-tnt), *n.* a biological, chemical, or physical agent that stimulates a characteristic action or function or elicits an inflammatory response, esp. an inflammatory response. —**ir′ri·tan·cy,** *n.*

ir′ri·tate′ (-tāt′), *v.t.*, **-tat·ed, -tat·ing. 1.** *Biol.* to excite (a living system) to some characteristic action or function. **2.** *Pathol.* to bring (a body part) to an abnormally excited or sensitive condition.

ir′ri·ta′tion, *n.* **1.** *Pathol.* the bringing of a bodily part or organ to an abnormally excited or sensitive condition. **2.** the condition itself.

ir·ri·ta′tive, *adj.* *Pathol.* characterized or produced by irritation of some body part: *an irritative fever.* —**ir′ri·ta′-tive·ness,** *n.*

is·che·mi·a or **is·chae·mi·a** (i skē′mē ə), *n.* local deficiency of blood supply produced by vasoconstriction or local obstacles to the arterial flow. —**is·che′mic,** *adj.*

is·chi·um (is′kē əm), *n.,* *pl.* **-chi·a** (-kē ə). **1.** the backward-facing lower bone of each half of the vertebrate pelvis; the lower portion of either innominate bone in humans. **2.** either of the bones on which the body rests when sitting.

is′let of Lang′er·hans (läng′ər häns′, -hänz′), *n.* any of the clusters of endocrine cells in the pancreas that are specialized to secrete insulin, somatostatin, or glucagon. Also called **is′land of Lang′erhans.**

i·so·ag·glu·ti·na·tion (ī′sō ə glōōt′n ā′shən), *n.* the clumping of the red blood cells by a transfusion of the blood or serum of a genetically different individual of the same species. —**i′so·ag·glu′ti·na′tive,** *adj.*

i′so·en′zyme, *n.* ISOZYME.

i·sog·a·mous (ī sog′ə məs), *adj.* having or reproducing by two morphologically indistinguishable gametes (opposed to *heterogamous*). —**i·sog′a·my,** *n.*

i·sog·e·nous (ī soj′ə nəs), *adj.* (of bodily organs or parts) having the same or a similar origin. —**i·sog′e·ny,** *n.*

I·so·lette (ī′sə let′), *Trademark.* a brand of incubator for premature or other newborn infants.

i·so·leu·cine (ī′sə lōō′sēn, -sin), *n.* a crystalline amino acid, $C_6H_{13}O_2$, found in most proteins. *Abbr.:* Ile; *Symbol:* I

i·som·er·ase (i som′ə rās′, -rāz′), *n.* any of a class of enzymes that catalyze reactions involving intramolecular rearrangements.

i·so·met·ric (ī′sə me′trik), *adj.* **1.** Also, **i′so·met′ri·cal.** of or pertaining to isometric exercise. —*n.* **2.** isometrics, ISOMETRIC EXERCISE (def. 1). —**i′so·met′ri·cal·ly,** *adv.*

i′somet′ric ex′ercise, *n.* **1.** a program of exercises in which a muscle group is tensed against another muscle group or an immovable object so that the muscles may contract without shortening. **2.** any specific exercise of this type.

i·so·me·tro·pi·a (ī′sō mi trō′pē ə), *n.* equality of refraction in the left and right eyes.

i·so·ni·a·zid (ī′sə nī′ə zid), *n.* a water-soluble solid, $C_6H_7N_3O$, used in the treatment of tuberculosis.

i·so·pro·ter·e·nol (ī′sə prō ter′ə nôl′, -nol′), *n.* a beta-receptor agonist, $C_{11}H_{17}NO_3$, used as a bronchodilator.

i·so·ton·ic (ī′sə ton′ik), *adj.* *Physiol.* of or pertaining to a muscular contraction in which the muscle shortens while tension increases, as in continuous lifting. —**i′so·ton′ic·i·ty** (-tə nis′i tē), *n.*

i·so·zyme (ī′sə zīm′), *n.* a variant form of certain enzymes that catalyzes the same reaction as other forms. Also called **isoenzyme.**

is·sue (ish′ōō; *esp. Brit.* is′yōō), *n.,* *v.,* **-sued, -su·ing.** —*n.*

1. a discharge of blood, pus, or the like. **2.** an incision, ulcer, or the like, emitting such a discharge. —*v.t.* **3.** to send out; discharge; emit.

IU, international unit.

IUD, intrauterine device.

IV (ī/vē/), *n., pl.* **IVs, IV's.** an apparatus for intravenous delivery of electrolyte solutions, medicines, and nutrients.

IV, 1. intravenous. **2.** intravenous injection.

IVF, in vitro fertilization.

J

jake (jāk), *n. Slang.* **1.** a homemade or bootleg liquor made with Jamaica ginger. **2.** Also called **jake′ leg′, jake′-leg′ paral′ysis.** paralysis caused by drinking this or other liquor made with denatured alcohol.

Ja′kob-Creutz′feldt disease′ (yä′kəb), *n.* CREUTZFELDT-JAKOB DISEASE.

jaun·dice (jôn′dis, jän′-), *n.* Also called **icterus.** yellow discoloration of the skin, whites of the eyes, etc., due to an increase of bile pigments in the blood.

je·ju·num (ji jōō′nəm), *n.* the middle portion of the small intestine, between the duodenum and the ileum. —**je·ju′nal,** *adj.*

jet′ gun′, *n.* a small, pressurized device that injects a vaccine at sufficient velocity to penetrate the skin. Also called **jet′ injec′tor.**

jet′ lag′ or **jet′lag′,** *n.* a temporary disruption of the body's normal biological rhythms after high-speed air travel through several time zones. —**jet′-lagged′,** *adj.*

jock′ itch′, *n.* a ringworm of the groin area, caused by any of several fungi.

joint (joint), *n.* **1.** the place of union between two bones or elements of a skeleton, whether fixed or permitting movement. **2.** the mechanical form of such a union: *the ball-and-socket joint of the hip; the hinge joint of the elbow.*

jug·u·lar (jug′yə lər, jōō′gyə-), *adj.* **1.** of or pertaining to the throat or neck. **2.** of or designating any of several veins of the neck that convey blood from the head to the heart. —*n.* **3.** a jugular vein.

jump′ing gene′, *n.* TRANSPOSON.

Jung·i·an (yŏŏng′ē ən), *adj.* **1.** of or pertaining to Carl G. Jung or his psychological theories. —*n.* **2.** an advocate or follower of Jung's theories.

jun′gle fe′ver, *n.* a severe variety of malaria common in the East Indies.

ju′venile-on′set diabe′tes, *n.* See under DIABETES MELLITUS.

K

K, *Symbol.* lysine.

ka·la·a·zar (kä′lə ə zär′), *n.* a tropical parasitic disease marked by irregular fevers, enlarged spleen, and anemia, caused by the protozoan *Leishmania donovani,* and transmitted by sand flies.

Ka·po·si's sarco·ma (kä′pə sēz, kap′ə-), *n.* a cancer of connective tissue characterized by painless purplish red blotches appearing on the skin.

kar·y·o·type (kar′ē ə tip′), *n.* the chromosomes of a cell, usu. displayed as a systematized arrangement of chromosome pairs in descending order of size. —**kar′y·o·typ′ic** (-tip′ik), **kar′y·o·typ′i·cal,** *adj.*

kar′y·o·typ′ing, *n.* the analysis of chromosomes.

kcal, kilocalorie.

ke·loid (kē′loid), *n.* an abnormal proliferation of scar tissue, as on the site of a surgical incision. —**ke·loi′dal,** *adj.*

ker·a·tec·to·my (ker′ə tek′tə mē), *n., pl.* **-mies.** excision of part of the cornea.

ker·a·tin (ker′ə tin), *n.* a tough, insoluble protein that is the main constituent of hair, nails, horn, hoofs, etc., and of the outermost layer of skin. —**ker′a·tin·ize′,** *v.t., v.i.,* -ized, -iz·ing. —**ke·rat′i·nous** (kə rat′n əs), *adj.*

ker′a·ti′tis (-ti′tis), *n.* inflammation of the cornea.

ker′a·toid′ (-toid′), *adj.* resembling corneal tissue.

ker′a·to′ma (-tō′mə), *n., pl.* **-mas, -ma·ta** (-mə tə). KERATOSIS (def. 2).

ker′a·to·plas′ty (-plas′tē), *n., pl.* **-ties.** plastic surgery performed upon the cornea, esp. a corneal transplantation. —**ker′a·to·plas′tic,** *adj.*

ker′a·to′sis (-tō′sis), *n., pl.* **-ses** (-sēz). **1.** any skin disease characterized by a horny growth, as a wart. **2.** Also, **keratoma.** any horny growth. —**ker′a·to′sic, ker′a·tot′ic** (-tot′ik), *adj.*

ke′tone bod′y (kē′tōn), *n.* any of several compounds that are intermediate in the metabolism of fatty acids and are produced in excessive amounts under certain abnormal conditions, as in diabetes mellitus.

ke′to·nu′ri·a (-tō nŏŏr′ē ə, -nyŏŏr′-), *n.* the presence of ketone bodies in the urine.

ke′tose (-tōs), *n.* a monosaccharide that contains a ketone group.

ke·to′sis, *n.* the accumulation of excessive ketone bodies in the blood and urine.

ke·tos·ter·oid (ki tos′tə roid′), *n.* any of a group of steroids containing a ketone group.

kg, kilogram.

kid·ney (kid′nē), *n., pl.* **-neys.** one of a pair of organs in the rear of the upper abdominal cavity of vertebrates that filter waste from the blood, excrete uric acid or urea, and maintain water and electrolyte balance.

kid′ney stone′, *n.* a stony mineral concretion formed abnormally in the kidney.

kill′er cell′, *n.* any of several types of lymphocyte or leukocyte capable of destroying cells that have acquired foreign characteristics.

killer T cell, *n.* a killer cell that destroys target cells only when specifically activated by helper T cells. Compare NATURAL KILLER CELL.

kil·o·cal·o·rie (kil′ə kal′ə rē), *n.* 1000 small calories. *Abbr.:* kcal

kil·o·gram (kil′ə gram′), *n.* a unit of mass equal to 1000 grams. *Abbr.:* kg

ki·nase (ki′nās, -nāz, kin′ās, -āz), *n.* an enzyme that effects the transfer of a phosphate group from ATP to another molecule.

ki·ne·sis (ki nē′sis, ki-), *n.* the movement of an organism in response to a stimulus, as light. —**ki·net·ic** (ki·net′ik), *adj.*

kin·es·the·sia (kin′əs thē′zhə, -zhē ə, ki′nəs-) also **kin′es·the′sis** (-thē′sis), *n.* the sensation in the body of the movement of muscles, tendons, and joints. —**kin′es·thet′ic** (-thet′ik), *adj.*

king′s′ e′vil, *n.* scrofula: so called because it was supposed to be curable by the touch of the reigning sovereign.

ki·nin (ki′nin, kin′in), *n.* any of a group of hormones, formed in body tissues, that cause dilation of blood vessels.

Kline·fel·ter's syn′drome (klin′fel tərz), *n.* a male genetic abnormality in which an extra X chromosome is present, causing small testicles and reduced sperm production.

knee′cap′, *n.* the patella.

knee′ jerk′, *n.* a reflex extension of the leg resulting from a sharp tap on the patellar tendon.

Krause′′s cor′puscle (krou′siz), *n.* any of numerous encapsulated nerve endings in the skin and mucous membranes, sensing cold.

Krebs′ cy′cle (krebz), *n.* the metabolic sequence of enzyme-driven reactions by which carbohydrates, proteins, and fatty acids produce carbon dioxide, water, and ATP.

ku·ru (kŏŏr′ōō), *n.* a fatal disease of the nervous system, resembling scrapie in sheep, reported among highland New Guinea peoples who ritually eat the brains of their dead kin.

kwash·i·or·kor (kwä′shē ôr′kôr, -kər), *n.* a disease, chiefly of children, caused by severe protein and vitamin deficiency and characterized by retarded growth, potbelly, and anemia.

ky·mo·gram (ki′mə gram′), *n.* the graphic record produced by a diagnostic kymograph.

ky′mo·graph′, *n.* an instrument for measuring and

graphically recording variations in fluid pressure, as those of the human pulse. —**ky′mo·graph′ic,** *adj.*

ky·pho·sis (ki fō′sis), *n.* an abnormal convex curvature of the spine, with a resultant bulge at the upper back. —**ky·phot′ic** (-fot′ik), *adj.*

L

L, *Symbol.* leucine.

l-, *Symbol.* levorotatory.

la·bel (lā′bəl), *n., v.,* **-beled, -bel·ing** or (*esp. Brit.*) **-belled, -bel·ling.** —*n.* **1.** a radioactive or heavy isotope incorporated into a molecule for use as a tracer. —*v.t.* **2.** to incorporate a radioactive or heavy isotope into a (molecule) in order to make traceable. —**la′bel·er,** *n.*

la·bi·al (lā′bē əl), *adj.* **1.** of, pertaining to, or resembling a labium. **2.** of or pertaining to the lips. **3.** of or designating the surface of a tooth facing the lips. Compare BUCCAL (def. 3), LINGUAL (def. 2). —**la·bi·al·i·ty,** *n.* —**la′bi·al·ly,** *adv.*

la·bi·a ma·jo·ra (lā′bē ə mə jôr′ə, -jōr′ə), *n.pl., sing.* **la·bi·um ma·jus** (lā′bē əm mā′jəs). the outer folds of skin of the external female genitalia.

la′bia mi·no′ra (mi nôr′ə, -nōr′ə), *n.pl., sing.* **labium mi·nus** (mi′nəs). the inner folds of skin of the external female genitalia.

la·bi·um (lā′bē əm), *n., pl.* **-bi·a** (-bē ə). **1.** a lip or liplike structure or part. **2.** any of the folds of skin bordering the vulva.

la·bor (lā′bər), *n.* **1. a.** the uterine contractions of childbirth. **b.** the interval from the onset of these contractions to childbirth. —*v.i.* **2.** to undergo childbirth. —**la′bor·ing·ly,** *adv.*

lab·y·rinth (lab′ə rinth), *n.* **1.** the bony cavity or membranous part of the inner ear. **2.** the aggregate of air chambers in the ethmoid bone, between the eye and the upper part of the nose.

lab′y·rin·thi′tis (-rin thī′tis), *n.* inflammation of the inner ear often causing motion sickness from disturbed balance.

lac·er·a·tion (las′ə rā′shən), *n.* a rough, jagged tear or wound.

lach·ry·ma·tor or **lac·ri·ma·tor** (lak′rə mā′tər), *n.* a chemical substance that causes the shedding of tears, as tear gas.

lac·ri·mal (lak′rə məl), *adj.* **1.** Also, **lach′ry·mal.** of, pertaining to, situated near, or constituting the glands that secrete tears. —*n.* **2.** LACRIMAL BONE.

lac′rimal bone′, *n.* a skull bone extending from each orbit to the nasal region, greatly reduced in mammals.

lac′rimal gland′, *n.* either of two tear-secreting glands situated in the outer angle of the orbit in mammals.

lac·ri·ma·tion, *n.* the secretion of tears, esp. in abnormal abundance.

lac′ri·ma′tor, *n.* LACHRYMATOR.

lac′tal·bu·min (-təl byoo′min), *n.* the albumin of milk.

lac·tase (-tās, -tāz′), *n.* an enzyme capable of breaking down lactose into glucose and galactose.

lac′tate (-tāt), *v.i.,* **-tat·ed, -tat·ing.** to secrete milk.

lac′tate dehy′drogenase, *n.* an enzyme of carbohydrate metabolism that interchanges lactate and pyruvate: elevated blood levels indicate injury to kidney, heart, or muscles. *Abbr.:* LDH

lac·ta′tion, *n.* **1.** the secretion of milk. **2.** the period of milk production. —**lac·ta′tion·al,** *adj.* —**lac·ta′tion·al·ly,** *adv.*

lac·te·al (-tē əl), *adj.* **1.** pertaining to, consisting of, or resembling milk; milky. **2.** conveying or containing chyle. —*n.* **3.** any of the minute lymphatic vessels that convey chyle from the small intestine to the thoracic duct. —**lac′·te·al·ly,** *adv.*

lac′tic ac′id, *n.* a syrupy liquid, $C_3H_6O_3$, produced by anaerobic metabolism, as in the fermentation of milk or carbohydrates.

lac′to·ba·cil′lus (lak/tō-), *n., pl.* **-cil·li.** any of various anaerobic bacteria of the genus *Lactobacillus,* capable of breaking down carbohydrates to form lactic acid: cultured for use in fermenting milk into yogurt or other milk products.

lac·to·gen·ic (lak/tə jen/ik), *adj.* stimulating lactation.

lac·tor·rhe·a (lak/tə rē′ə), *n.* GALACTORRHEA.

lac·tose (lak/tōs), *n.* a disaccharide, $C_{12}H_{22}O_{11}$, present in milk, that upon hydrolysis yields glucose and galactose.

la·e·trile (lā/i tril), *n.* a controversial drug prepared chiefly from apricot pits and purported to cure cancer.

La·maze′ meth′od, *n.* a method by which an expectant mother is prepared for childbirth by education, psychological and physical conditioning, and breathing exercises.

lam·i·nec·to·my (lam/ə nek/tə mē), *n., pl.* **-mies.** the surgical removal of part of the posterior arch of a vertebra.

lan·cet (lan/sit, län′-), *n.* a sharp-pointed surgical instrument, usu. with two edges, for making small incisions.

la·nu·go (lə nōō/gō, -nyōō′-), *n., pl.* **-gos.** a coat of delicate, downy hairs, esp. that with which the human fetus is covered.

lap·a·ro·scope (lap/ər ə skōp′), *n.* an endoscope equipped for viewing the abdominal cavity through a small incision and for performing local surgery. —**lap/a·ro·scop/ic** (-skop/ik), *adj.* —**lap/a·ros/co·pist** (-ə ros/kə-pist), *n.* —**lap/a·ros/co·py,** *n., pl.* **-pies.**

lap·a·rot·o·my (-rot/ə mē), *n., pl.* **-mies.** a surgical incision through the abdominal wall.

large′ intes′tine, *n.* INTESTINE (def. 3).

la·ryn·ge·al (lə rin/jē əl, lar/ən jē′ən) also **la·ryn′gal** (-ring/gəl), *adj.* of, pertaining to, or located in the larynx. —**la·ryn′ge·al·ly,** *adv.*

lar·yn·gec·to·my (lar/ən jek/tə mē), *n., pl.* **-mies.** surgical excision of part or all of the larynx.

lar·yn·gi·tis (-ji/tis), *n.* inflammation of the larynx, often with accompanying sore throat, hoarseness or loss of voice, and dry cough. —**lar′yn·git/ic** (-jit/ik), *adj.*

lar·yn·gol·o·gy (lar/ing gol/ə jē), *n.* the branch of medicine dealing with the larynx. —**la·ryn·go·log/i·cal** (lə-ring′gə loj′i kəl), **la·ryn′go·log′ic,** *adj.* —**lar′yn·gol′o·gist,** *n.*

la·ryn·go·scope (lə ring′gə skōp′), *n.* an endoscope equipped for viewing the larynx through the mouth and for performing local surgery. —**la·ryn′go·scop′ic** (-skōp′ik), *adj.* —**la·ryn·gos·co·pist** (lar′ing gos′kə pist), *n.* —**lar′-yn·gos′co·py,** *n., pl.* **-pies.**

lar·ynx (lar′ingks), *n., pl.* **la·ryn·ges** (lə rin′jēz), **lar-ynx·es.** a muscular and cartilaginous structure at the upper part of the vertebrate trachea, in which the vocal cords are located.

Las′sa fe′ver (lä′sə), *n.* an infectious, often fatal disease characterized by fever and pharyngitis, caused by an arenavirus.

la′tency pe′riod, *n.* **1.** the stage of personality development, extending from about four or five years of age to the beginning of puberty, during which sexual urges appear to lie dormant. **2.** LATENT PERIOD (def. 1).

la·tent (lāt′nt), *adj.* (of an infectious agent or disease) remaining in an inactive or hidden phase; dormant. —**la′tent·ly,** *adv.*

la′tent pe′riod, *n.* **1.** Also, **latency period.** the interval between exposure to a carcinogen, toxin, or disease-causing organism and development of a consequent disease. **2.** the interval between a stimulus and response. Also called **latency.**

lat·er·al·i·za·tion (lat′ər ə lə zā′shən), *n.* functional specialization of the brain, with some skills, as language, occurring primarily in the left hemisphere and others, as the perception of visual and spatial relationships, occurring primarily in the right hemisphere.

lath·y·rism (lath′ə riz′əm), *n.* a painful disorder esp. of domestic animals caused by ingestion of a poison found in certain legumes of the genus *Lathyrus* and marked by spastic paralysis. —**lath′y·rit′ic** (-rit′ik), *adj.*

la·tis·si·mus dor·si (lə tis′ə məs dôr′sī), *n., pl.* **la·tis·si·mi dorsi** (lə tis′ə mī′). a broad, flat muscle on each side of the middle of the back, the action of which draws the arm backward and downward.

lats (lats), *n.pl. Informal.* latissimus dorsi muscles.

lau·da·num (lôd′n əm, lôd′nəm), *n.* a tincture of opium.

laugh′ing gas′, *n.* NITROUS OXIDE.

la·vage (lə väzh′, lav′ij), *n.* the cleansing of a bodily organ, as the stomach, by irrigation.

law′ of dom′inance, *n.* MENDEL'S LAW (def. 3).

law′ of independ′ent assort′ment, *n.* MENDEL'S LAW (def. 2).

law′ of segrega′tion, *n.* MENDEL'S LAW (def. 1).

lax·a·tive (lak′sə tiv), *n.* **1.** a medicine or agent for relieving constipation. —*adj.* **2.** of, pertaining to, or constituting a laxative; purgative. —**lax′a·tive·ly,** *adv.* —**lax′a·tive·ness,** *n.*

laz·ar (laz′ər, lā′zər), *n.* a person infected with a disease, esp. leprosy.

laz·a·ret·to (laz/ə ret/ō) also **laz/a·ret/, laz/a·rette/,** *n., pl.* **-ret·tos** also **-rets, -rettes.** a hospital for those affected with contagious diseases, esp. leprosy.

la/zy eye/, *n.* **1.** the deviating eye in strabismus. **2.** an amblyopic eye. **3.** STRABISMUS. **4.** AMBLYOPIA.

LD, lethal dose.

LD$_{50}$, median lethal dose.

LDH, lactate dehydrogenase.

LDL, low-density lipoprotein.

L-do·pa (el/dō/pə), *n.* the levorotatory isomer of dopa, converted in the brain to dopamine: used in synthetic form chiefly for treating Parkinson's disease. Also called **levo-dopa**.

lead/ col/ic (led), *n.* PAINTER'S COLIC.

lead/ poi/son·ing (led), *n.* a toxic condition produced by ingestion, inhalation, or skin absorption of lead or lead compounds, resulting in various dose-related symptoms including anemia, nausea, muscle weakness, confusion, blindness, and coma.

learn/ing disabil/ity, *n.* any of several conditions characterized in school-aged children by difficulty in accomplishing specific tasks, esp. reading and writing, and associated with impaired development of a part of the central nervous system.

learn/ing-disa/bled, *adj.* pertaining to or having a learning disability.

lec·i·thal (les/ə thəl) also **lec/i·thic** (-thik), *adj.* having a yolk, as certain eggs or ova.

lec/i·thin (-thin), *n.* any of a group of phospholipids, containing choline and fatty acids, that are a component of cell membranes and are abundant in nerve tissue and egg yolk.

lec·tin (lek/tin), *n.* any of a group of proteins that bind to specific carbohydrates and act as an agglutinin.

left/ brain/, *n.* the left cerebral hemisphere, controlling activity on the right side of the body: in humans, usu. showing some degree of specialization for language and calculation. Compare RIGHT BRAIN.

le·gion·naires/ disease/ (lē/jə nârz/), *n.* a form of pneumonia caused by bacteria of the genus *Legionella,* esp. *L. pneumophila,* typically acquired by inhaling airborne droplets from a contaminated water supply.

lei·o·my·o·ma (lī/ō mī ō/mə), *n., pl.* **-mas, -ma·ta** (-mə-tə). a benign tumor composed of nonstriated muscular tissue. Compare RHABDOMYOMA. —**lei·o·my·om·a·tous** (lī/ō-mī om/ə təs, -ō/mə təs), *adj.*

leish·man·i·a·sis (lēsh/mə nī/ə sis, lish/-) also **leish/-man·i·o/sis** (-man ē ō/sis, -mā nē-), *n.* any infection caused by a parasitic flagellate protozoan of the genus *Leishmania.* Compare KALA-AZAR.

lens (lenz), *n.* Also called **crystalline lens.** a doubly convex, transparent body in the eye, behind the pupil, that focuses incident light on the retina. —**lens/less,** *adj.* —**lens/like/,** *adj.*

len·ti·vi·rus (len/tə vī/rəs), *n., pl.* **-rus·es.** any slow virus of the genus *Lentivirus,* of the retrovirus family, causing brain disease in sheep and other animals.

lep·er (lep/ər), *n.* a person who has leprosy.

lep·ro·sar·i·um (lep/rə sâr/ē əm), *n., pl.* **-sar·i·a** (-sâr/ē ə). a hospital for the treatment of lepers.

lep·ro·sy (lep/rə sē), *n.* a chronic, slowly progressing, usu. mildly infectious disease caused by the bacillus *Mycobacterium leprae,* marked by destruction of tissue and loss of sensation and characterized in persons with poor resistance by numerous inflamed skin nodules and in persons with better resistance by local areas of firm, dry patches. Also called **Hansen's disease.** —**lep·rot·ic** (le prot/ik), *adj.*

lep/rous (-rəs), *adj.* **1.** affected with leprosy. **2.** of or resembling leprosy. —**lep/rous·ly,** *adv.* —**lep/rous·ness,** *n.*

lep·to·spi·ro·sis (lep/tō spī rō/sis), *n.* an infectious disease of humans and domestic animals, caused by the spirochete *Leptospira interrogans* and characterized by fever, muscle pain, and jaundice.

lep·to·tene (lep/tə tēn/), *n.* a stage of cell division during the prophase of meiosis, in which the chromosomes emerge as a mass of tangled threads.

le·sion (lē/zhən), *n.* any localized, usu. well-defined area of diseased or injured tissue or of abnormal structural change.

less/er omen/tum, *n.* the part of the omentum that attaches to the stomach, duodenum, and liver.

le/thal gene/, *n.* a gene that under certain conditions causes the death of an organism. Also called **le/thal fac/·tor, le/thal muta/tion.**

Leu, leucine.

leu·cine (lōō/sēn, -sin), *n.* one of the essential amino acids, $(CH_3)_2CHCH_2CH(NH_2)COOH$, present in most proteins. *Abbr.:* Leu; *Symbol.:* L

leu·ke·mi·a (lōō kē/mē ə), *n.* any of several cancers of the bone marrow characterized by an abnormal increase of white blood cells in the tissues, resulting in anemia, increased susceptibility to infection, and impaired blood clotting. —**leu·ke/mic,** *adj.*

leu·ko·cyte or **leu·co·cyte** (lōō/kə sīt/), *n.* WHITE BLOOD CELL. —**leu/ko·cyt/ic** (-sit/ik), *adj.*

leu·ko·cy·to·sis or **leu/co·cy·to/sis** (-kō si tō/sis), *n.* an increase in the number of white blood cells in the blood. —**leu/ko·cy·tot/ic** (-tot/ik), *adj.*

leu·ko·der·ma or **leu·co·der/ma** (-kə dûr/mə), *n.* VITILIGO.

leu·ko/ma or **leu·co/ma** (-kō/mə), *n.* a dense white opacity of the cornea.

leu·ko·pe·ni·a or **leu/co·pe/ni·a** (-kə pē/nē ə) also **leu/ko·cy/to·pe/ni·a** (-sī/tə-), *n.* a decrease in the number of white blood cells in the blood. —**leu/ko·pe/nic,** *adj.*

leu·ko·pla·ki·a or **leu/co·pla/ki·a** (-plā/kē ə), also **leu/ko·pla/sia, leu/co·pla/sia** (-plā/zhə, -zhē ə), *n.* a condition marked by one or more white patches on a mucous membrane, as of the tongue or cheek, usu. benign but occasionally precancerous.

leu·ko·poi·e·sis or **leu·co·poi·e·sis** (-kō poi ē/sis), *n.* the formation and development of white blood cells. —**leu·ko·poi·et/ic** (-et/ik), *adj.*

leu·ko·tri·ene or **leu·co·tri·ene** (-kə trī/ēn), *n.* a lipid, $C_{20}H_{30}O_3$, produced by white blood cells in an immune response to antigens, that contributes to allergic asthma and inflammatory reactions.

le·va·tor (li vā/tər, -tôr), *n., pl.* **lev·a·to·res** (lev/ə tôr/ēz, -tōr/-). **1.** a muscle that raises a part of the body. Compare DEPRESSOR. **2.** a surgical instrument used to raise a depressed part of the skull.

le·vo·do·pa (lē/və dō/pə), *n.* L-DOPA.

le·vo·ro·ta·to·ry (lē/və rō/tə tôr/ē, -tōr/ē) also **le/vo·ro/ta·ry** (-rō/tə rē), *adj.* turning to the left, esp. rotating to the left of the plane of polarization of light: *levorotatory crystals.* Symbol: *l*-

lev·u·lose (lev/yə lōs/), *n.* FRUCTOSE.

LH, luteinizing hormone: a pituitary hormone that acts in the ovary to stimulate ripening of the follicle and formation of the corpus luteum: chemically identical with ICSH of the male.

LHRH, luteinizing hormone releasing hormone: a hormone, produced in the hypothalamus, that regulates the release of luteinizing hormone.

li·bi·do (li bē/dō), *n., pl.* **-dos. 1.** *Psychoanal.* all of the instinctual energies and desires that are derived from the id. **2.** sexual instinct or drive. —**li·bid/i·nal** (-bid/n l), *adj.* —**li·bid/i·nal·ly,** *adv.*

Lib·ri·um (lib/rē əm), *Trademark.* a brand of chlordiazepoxide.

li/censed prac/tical nurse/, *n.* a person who has completed a program in nursing and is licensed to provide basic nursing care under the supervision of a physician or registered nurse. *Abbr.:* LPN

li·chen (lī/kən), *n.* any of various eruptive skin diseases. —**li/chen·ous,** *adj.*

li·do·caine (lī/də kān/), *n.* a synthetic crystalline powder, $C_{14}H_{22}N_2O$, used in the form of its hydrochloride as a local anesthetic and to treat certain arrhythmias.

life/-care/ or **life/ care/,** *adj.* designed to provide for the basic needs of elderly residents, usu. in return for an initial fee and monthly service payments: *a life-care facility; life-care communities.*

life/ cy/cle, *n.* the sequence of developmental changes undergone by an organism from one primary form, as a gamete, to the recurrence of the same form in the next generation.

life/ expect/ancy, *n.* the number of years an individual is expected to live, according to statistical estimates taking into account sex, physical condition, occupation, etc.

life/ his/tory, *n.* **1.** the history of developmental changes undergone by an organism from inception to death. **2.** LIFE CYCLE.

life′ in′stinct, *n.* See under DEATH INSTINCT.

life′ span′, *n.* **1.** the longest period over which the life of any organism or species may extend. **2.** the longevity of an individual.

life′-support′, *adj.* of or pertaining to equipment or measures that sustain or artificially substitute for essential body functions, as breathing, or that allow humans to function within a hostile environment, as outer space or ocean depths.

lig·a·ment (lig′ə mənt), *n.* a band of strong connective tissue serving to connect bones or hold organs in place.

li·gand (li′gənd, lig′ənd), *n.* a molecule, as an antibody, hormone, or drug, that binds to a receptor.

li·gase (li′gās, -gāz), *n.* an enzyme that catalyzes the joining of two molecules by forming a covalent bond accompanied by the hydrolysis of ATP. Also called **synthetase.**

li·ga·tion (li gā′shən), *n.* the act of surgically tying up a bleeding artery, tumor, etc. —**lig·a·tive** (lig′ə tiv), *adj.*

lig·a·ture (lig′ə chər, -chŏŏr′), *n.* a thread or wire for surgical constriction of blood vessels or for removing tumors by strangulation.

light′ adapta′tion, *n.* the reflex adjustment of the eye to bright light, consisting of a constriction of the pupil, an increase in the number of functioning cones, and a decrease in the number of functioning rods. —**light′-a·dapt′ed,** *adj.*

lim′bic sys′tem, *n.* a group of structures in the brain that include the hippocampus, olfactory bulbs, hypothalamus, and amygdala and are associated with emotion and homeostasis.

li·men (li′mən), *n., pl.* **li·mens, lim·i·na** (lim′ə nə). THRESHOLD.

lime′wa′ter, *n.* an aqueous solution of slaked lime, used in medicine, antacids, and lotions, and to absorb carbon dioxide from the air.

lim·i·na (lim′ə nə), *n.* a pl. of LIMEN.

lim·i·nal (lim′ə nl, li′mə-), *adj.* of, pertaining to, or situated at the limen.

lin·gual (ling′gwəl), *adj.* **1.** of or pertaining to the tongue or some tonguelike part. **2.** of or designating the surface of a tooth facing the tongue. Compare BUCCAL (def. 3), LABIAL (def. 3). —**lin′gual·ly,** *adv.*

lin·i·ment (lin′ə mənt), *n.* a liquid or semiliquid, usu. medicated preparation for rubbing on the skin, esp. to relieve soreness, inflammation, or sprain.

link·age (ling′kij), *n.* an association of two or more genes, usu. on the same chromosome, that tend to be inherited as a unit (**link′age group′**) and to express a set of characteristic traits.

link′age map′, *n.* a genetic map that depicts linkage groups.

linked, *adj.* (of a gene) exhibiting linkage.

li·pase (li′pās, lip′ās), *n.* any of a class of enzymes that break down fats, produced by the liver, pancreas, and other digestive organs or by certain plants.

lip·ec·to·my (li pek′tə mē, li-), *n., pl.* **-mies.** the surgical removal of fatty tissue. Compare LIPOSUCTION.

li·pe·mi·a (li pē′mē ə, li-), *n.* HYPERLIPEMIA. —**li·pe′mic,** *adj.*

lip·id (lip′id, li′pid) also **lip·ide** (-id, -id; -pid, -pid), *n.* any of a group of organic compounds comprising fats, waxes, and similar substances that are greasy, insoluble in water, and soluble in alcohol: one of the chief structural components of the living cell.

lip′id bi′layer, *n.* PHOSPHOLIPID BILAYER.

lip·o·chrome (lip′ə krōm′, li′pə-), *n.* any of the naturally occurring pigments that contain a lipid, as carotene. —**lip′o·chro′mic,** *adj.*

lip′o·cyte′ (-sit′), *n.* FAT CELL.

lip·o·fill·ing (-fil′ing), *n.* the surgical transfer of fat removed by liposuction to areas of the body that need filling out.

lip′oid, *n.* LIPID.

li·pol·y·sis (li pol′ə sis, li-), *n.* the hydrolysis of fats into fatty acids and glycerol, as by lipase. —**lip·o·lit·ic** (lip′ə-lit′ik, li′pə-), *adj.*

li·po·ma (-pō′mə), *n., pl.* **-mas, -ma·ta** (-mə tə). a benign tumor consisting of fat tissue. —**li·pom′a·tous** (-pom′ə təs, -pō′mə-), *adj.*

lip·o·phil·ic (lip′ə fil′ik, li′pə-), *adj.* **1.** having a strong affinity for lipids. **2.** promoting the dissolvability or absorbability of lipids.

lip′o·pol′y·sac′cha·ride′, *n.* any of a class of polysaccharides to which lipids are attached.

lip·o·pro·tein (lip′ə- li′pə-), *n.* any of the class of proteins that contain a lipid combined with a simple protein.

lip′o·some, (-sōm′), *n.* an artificial vesicle composed of a phospholipid outer layer and an inner core of a drug or other matter to be transported into a cell. —**lip′o·so′mal,** *adj.*

lip′o·suc′tion, *n.* the surgical withdrawal of excess fat from local areas under the skin by means of a small incision and vacuum suctioning.

lip·o·trop·ic (-trop′ik, -trō′pik), *adj.* having an affinity for lipids and thus preventing or correcting excess accumulation of fat in the liver. —**li·pot·ro·pism** (li po′trə piz′əm, li-), *n.*

lip′o·tro′pin (-trō′pin), *n.* a pituitary hormone that regulates fat in body tissue and is the precursor of endorphins.

lis·te·ri·o·sis (li stēr′ē ō′sis) also **lis·te·ri′a·sis** (lis′tə-rē′ə-), *n., pl.* **-ses** (-sēz). an infectious disease of animals and birds, esp. attacking the brainstem in ruminants, caused by the bacterium *Listeria monocytogenes* and transmissible to humans by contact with contaminated tissue.

li·thi·a·sis (li thī′ə sis), *n.* the formation or presence of stony concretions in the body.

lith·i·um (lith′ē əm), *n.* LITHIUM CARBONATE.

lith′ium car′bonate, *n.* a colorless crystalline compound, Li$_2$CO$_3$, slightly soluble in water: used in medicine for treating bipolar disorder or mania.

li·thot·o·my (li thot′ə mē), *n., pl.* **-mies.** surgery to remove one or more stones from an organ or duct. —**lith·o·tom·ic** (lith′ə tom′ik), **lith′o·tom′i·cal,** *adj.* —**li·thot′o·mist,** *n.*

lith·o·trip·sy (lith′ə trip′sē), *n., pl.* **-sies.** the pulverization of one or more stones in the body by means of a lithotripter.

lith′o·trip′ter, *n.* a device that employs ultrasound to pulverize stones in the body. —**lith′o·trip′tic,** *adj.*

li·thot·ri·ty (li thot′ri tē), *n., pl.* **-ties.** the operation of crushing stone in the urinary bladder into particles small enough to be voided. —**li·thot′ri·tist,** *n.*

liv·er (liv′ər), *n.* a large, reddish brown, glandular organ in vertebrates, located in the upper abdominal cavity and functioning in the secretion of bile and in essential metabolic processes.

liv·er·ish, *adj.* having a liver disorder; bilious. —**liv′er·ish·ness,** *n.*

liv′er spots′, *n.pl.* CHLOASMA.

liv′ing will′, *n.* a document in which a person stipulates that no extraordinary measures are to be used to prolong his or her life in the event of a terminal illness.

LMP, last menstrual period.

lo·bar (lō′bər, -bär), *adj.* of or pertaining to a lobe, as of the lungs.

lo·bec·to·my (lō bek′tə mē), *n., pl.* **-mies.** the surgical removal of a lobe, esp. of the lung.

lo·bot·o·mize (lə bot′ə mīz′, lō-), *v.t.,* **-mized, -miz·ing.** to perform a lobotomy on. —**lo·bot′o·mist,** *n.* —**lo·bot′o·mi·za′tion,** *n.*

lo·bot·o·my (-mē), *n., pl.* **-mies.** a surgical incision into or across a lobe, esp. the prefrontal lobe, of the brain to sever nerves for the purpose of relieving a mental disorder or treating psychotic behavior.

lo·cal (lō′kəl), *adj.* **1.** (of anesthesia or an anesthetic) affecting only a particular part or area of the body without concomitant loss of consciousness. —*n.* **2.** a local anesthetic. —**lo′cal·ly,** *adv.*

lock′jaw′, *n.* tetanus in which the jaws become firmly locked together; trismus.

lo·co·ism (lō′kō iz′əm), *n.* a disease chiefly of sheep, horses, and cattle, caused by the eating of locoweed and characterized by weakness, impaired vision, irregular behavior, and paralysis. Also called **lo′co, lo′co disease′,**

lo·co·mo·tor atax′ia (lō′kə mō′tər), *n.* TABES DORSALIS.

lo·cus (lō′kəs), *n., pl.* **-ci** (-sī, -kē, -kī). the position of a gene on a chromosome.

loop (lōōp), *n.* INTRAUTERINE DEVICE.

loop′ of Hen′le (hen′lē), *n.* the part of a kidney tubule that loops from the cortex into the medulla of the kidney.

lor·do·sis (lôr dō′sis), *n.* an abnormal forward curvature of the spine in the lumbar region, resulting in a sway-backed posture. Compare KYPHOSIS, SCOLIOSIS. —**lor·dot′ic** (-dot′ik), *adj.*

lo·tion (lō′shən), *n.* a liquid preparation containing insoluble material in suspension or emulsion for medicinal, cleansing, protective, or soothing application to the skin.

Lou′ Gehr′ig's disease (lōō ger′igz), *n.* AMYOTROPHIC LATERAL SCLEROSIS.

louse (lous), *n., pl.* **lice.** any of various small, flat, wingless insects of the order Anoplura, with sucking mouthparts, that are parasitic on humans and other mammals, as *Pediculus humanus capitis* (**head louse**) and *P. humanus corporis* (**body louse**).

lo·va·stat·in (lō′və stat′n), *n.* a drug that reduces the levels of fats in the blood by altering the enzyme activity in the liver that produces lipids.

low′ blood′ pres′sure, *n.* HYPOTENSION.

low′-den′sity lipopro′tein, *n.* a plasma protein that is the major carrier of cholesterol in the blood, with high levels being associated with atherosclerosis. *Abbr.:* LDL

LPN, licensed practical nurse.

LSD (el′es′dē′), *n.* lysergic acid diethylamide: a crystalline solid, $C_{20}H_{25}N_3O$, a powerful psychedelic drug that produces temporary hallucinations and a psychotic state.

L.S.S., life-support system.

LTH, luteotropic hormone.

lu·es (lōō′ēz), *n.* SYPHILIS. —**lu·et′ic** (-et′ik), *adj.*

lum·ba·go (lum bā′gō), *n.* chronic or recurrent pain in the lumbar region of the back.

lum·bar (lum′bər, -bär), *adj.* **1.** of or pertaining to the loin or loins. —*n.* **2.** a lumbar vertebra, artery, or the like.

lum·bri·cal (lum′bri kəl), *n. Anat.* any of four wormlike muscles in the palm of the hand and in the sole of the foot.

lu·men (lōō′mən), *n., pl.* **-mens, -mi·na** (-mə nə) *Anat.* the canal, duct, or cavity of a tubular organ.

Lu·mi·nal (lōō′mə nl), *Trademark.* a brand of phenobarbital.

lump·ec·to·my (lum pek′tə mē), *n., pl.* **-mies.** the surgical removal of a cyst or tumor from the breast.

lump′y jaw′, *n.* ACTINOMYCOSIS.

lu′nar caus′tic, *n.* silver nitrate formed as a stick, used in medicine for cauterizing tissue.

lung (lung), *n.* either of the two saclike respiratory organs in the thorax of humans and other air-breathing vertebrates.

lu·pus (lōō′pəs), *n.* SYSTEMIC LUPUS ERYTHEMATOSUS. —**lu′pous,** *adj.*

lu′pus er·y·the·ma·to′sus (er′ə thē′mə tō′səs, -them′ə-), *n.* any of several autoimmune diseases, esp.

systemic lupus erythematosus, characterized by red, scaly skin patches.

lu·pus vul·ga·ris (vul gâr′əs), *n.* a rare form of tuberculosis of the skin, characterized by brownish tubercles that often heal slowly and leave scars.

lu·te·al (lo͞o′tē əl), *adj.* of or involving the corpus luteum.

lu·te·in (lo͞o′tē in), *n.* a carotenoid yellow pigment that is abundant in egg yolk and the corpus luteum.

lu′te·in·iz·ing hor′mone (lo͞o′tē ə ni′zing), *n.* See LH.

lu·te·o·trop·ic (lo͞o′tē ə trop′ik, -trō′pik) also **lu′te·o·troph′ic** (-trof′ik, -trō′fik), *adj.* affecting the corpus luteum.

lu′teotrop′ic hor′mone, *n.* PROLACTIN.

lu′te·o·tro′pin (-trō′pin), *n.* PROLACTIN.

lux·ate (luk′sāt), *v.t.,* **-at·ed, -at·ing.** to put out of joint; dislocate: *to luxate the left shoulder.* —**lux·a′tion,** *n.*

ly·can·thrope (lī′kən thrōp′, lī kan′thrōp), *n.* a person affected with lycanthropy.

ly·can·thro·py (lī kan′thrə pē), *n.* a delusion in which one imagines oneself to be a wolf or other wild animal. —**ly·can·throp·ic** (lī′kən throp′ik), *adj.*

ly·co·pene (lī′kə pēn′), *n.* a carotenoid red pigment that is abundant in various ripe fruits, as the tomato.

ly·ing-in′, *n., pl.* **ly·ings-in, ly·ing-ins,** *adj.* —*n.* **1.** the state of being in childbed; confinement. —*adj.* **2.** pertaining to or providing facilities for childbirth: *a lying-in hospital.*

Lyme′ disease′ (līm), *n.* a chronic, recurrent inflammatory disease characterized by joint pains, fatigue, and sometimes neurological disturbances, caused by a tick-borne spirochete, *Borrelia burgdorferi,* that often induces a transient bull's-eye reddening of the skin at the site of infection.

lymph (limf), *n.* a clear, yellowish, coagulable fluid, circulated by the lymphatic system, that resembles blood plasma but contains mainly lymphocytes and fats.

lym·phad·e·ni·tis (lim fad′n ī′tis), *n.* inflammation of a lymph node. Also called **adenitis.**

lym·phad′e·nop′a·thy (-op′ə thē), *n.* chronically swollen lymph nodes.

lym·phan·gi·og·ra·phy (lim fan′jē og′rə fē), *n.* x-ray visualization of lymph vessels and nodes following injection of a contrast medium. Also called **lymphography.** —**lym·phan′gio·gram′** (-ə gram′), *n.*

lym·phan′gi·o′ma (-ō′mə), *n., pl.* **-mas, -ma·ta** (-mə-tə). See under ANGIOMA. —**lym·phan′gi·om′a·tous** (-om′-ə təs), *adj.*

lym·phat′ic (-fat′ik), *adj.* **1.** pertaining to, containing, or conveying lymph. —*n.* **2.** a lymphatic vessel. —**lym·phat′·i·cal·ly,** *adv.*

lymphat′ic sys′tem, *n.* the system of glands, tissues, and passages involved in generating lymphocytes and circulating them through the body in the medium of lymph:

includes the lymph vessels, lymph nodes, thymus, and spleen.

lymph′ node′, *n.* any of the glandlike masses of tissue in the lymph vessels containing cells that become lymphocytes. Also called **lymph′ gland′.**

lym•pho•cyte′ (-fə sīt′), *n.* a type of nongranular white blood cell important in the production of antibodies. Compare B CELL (def. 1), T CELL. **—lym′pho•cyt′ic** (-sĭt′ĭk), *adj.*

lym′pho•cy•to′sis (-sī tō′sĭs), *n.* an abnormal increase in the number of lymphocytes in the blood. **—lym′pho•cy•tot′ic** (-tŏt′ĭk), *adj.*

lym′pho•gran′u•lo′ma, *n., pl.* **-mas, -ma•ta. 1.** any of certain diseases characterized by granulomatous lesions of lymph nodes. **2.** Also called **lym′phogran′ulo′ma ve•ne′re•um** (və nēr′ē əm). a venereal form of lymphogranuloma, caused by the bacterium *Chlamydia trachomatis* and characterized initially by a lesion on the genitals.

lym•phog′ra•phy (-fŏg′rə fē), *n.* LYMPHANGIOGRAPHY.

lym′phoid, *adj.* **1.** of, pertaining to, or resembling lymph. **2.** of or pertaining to the tissue **(lym′phoid tis′sue)** that occurs in the lymph nodes, thymus, tonsils, and spleen and produces lymphocytes.

lym•pho′ma (-fō′mə), *n., pl.* **-mas, -ma•ta** (-mə tə). a tumor arising from any of the cellular elements of lymph nodes. **—lym•pho′ma•toid′,** *adj.*

lym′pho•ma•to′sis (-tō′sĭs), *n.* lymphoma spread throughout the body.

lym′pho•poi•e′sis (-poi ē′sĭs), *n.* the formation of lymphocytes. **—lym′pho•poi•et′ic** (-et′ĭk), *adj.*

lym′pho•sar•co′ma, *n.* a malignant tumor in lymphoid tissue, caused by the growth of abnormal lymphocytes.

lym′pho•troph′ic (-fə trŏf′ĭk, -trō′fĭk), *adj.* carrying nutrients from the lymph to the tissues.

Lys, lysine.

lyse (līs), *v.,* **lysed, lys•ing. —v.t. 1.** to cause dissolution or destruction of cells by lysins. **—v.i. 2.** to undergo lysis.

Ly•sen•ko•ism (li seng′kō iz′əm), *n.* a genetic doctrine formulated by the Russian biologist Trofim D. Lysenko (1898-1976), asserting that acquired characteristics are inheritable.

lyser′gic ac′id di•eth•yl•am′ide (li sûr′jik, lī-; di eth′ə-lam′īd, -eth′ə lə mīd′), *n.* See LSD.

ly•sin (lī′sĭn), *n.* an antibody causing the disintegration of red blood cells or bacterial cells.

ly′sine (-sēn, -sĭn), *n.* a crystalline, basic, essential amino acid, $H_2N(CH_2)_4CH(NH_2)COOH$, produced chiefly from many proteins by hydrolysis. *Abbr.:* Lys; *Symbol:* K

ly′sis (-sĭs), *n.* **1.** the dissolution or destruction of cells by lysins. **2.** the gradual recession of a disease. Compare CRISIS.

ly•so•gen (lī′sə jən, -jen′), *n.* a bacterial cell or strain that has been infected with a temperate virus.

ly′so•gen′e•sis, *n.* production of a lysogen.

ly/so·gen/ic, *adj.* harboring a temperate virus, as a pro-
phage or plasmid. —**ly·sog/e·ny** (-soj/ə nē), *n.*

ly·sog·e·nize (li soj/ə niz/), *v.t.,* **-nized, -niz·ing.** to cause
to be lysogenic.

ly·so·zyme (li/sə zim/), *n.* an enzyme that is destructive
of bacteria and functions as an antiseptic, found in tears,
white blood cells, mucus, and egg albumin.

M, married.

M, *Symbol.* methionine.

MAb, monoclonal antibody.

mac·ro·bi·ot·ic (mak′rō bī ot′ik), *adj.* of or pertaining to macrobiotics. —**mac′ro·bi·ot′i·cal·ly**, *adv.*

mac′ro·bi·ot′ics, *n.* (*used with a sing. v.*) a program emphasizing harmony with nature, esp. through a restricted, primarily vegetarian diet.

mac·ro·ceph·a·ly (-sef′ə lē), *n.* disproportionate largeness of the skull or head. —**mac′ro·ce·phal′ic** (-sə fal′ik), *adj.*

mac′ro·cyte′ (-rə sīt′), *n.* an abnormally large red blood cell. —**mac′ro·cyt′ic** (-sit′ik), *adj.*

mac′ro·gam′ete (mak′rō-), *n.* the larger cell, considered as the female, in the reproduction by conjugation of unlike gametes.

mac′ro·mere′ (-rə mēr′), *n.* one of the large blastomeres that form toward the vegetal pole in embryos undergoing unequal cleavage.

mac′ro·mol′e·cule′, *n.* a very large molecule, as a colloidal particle, protein, or esp. a polymer, composed of hundreds or thousands of atoms. —**mac′ro·mo·lec′u·lar** (mak′rō-), *adj.*

mac′ro·mu′tant (mak′rō-), *adj.* **1.** undergoing macromutation. **2.** resulting from macromutation. —*n.* **3.** an organism resulting from macromutation.

mac′ro·mu·ta′tion, *n.* a mutation that results in a profound change in an organism, as a change in a regulator gene that controls the expression of many structural genes.

mac′ro·nu′tri·ent, *n.* any of the nutritional components required in relatively large amounts: protein, carbohydrate, fat, and the essential minerals.

mac′ro·phage (mak′rə fāj′), *n.* a large white blood cell, occurring principally in connective tissue and in the bloodstream, that ingests foreign particles and infectious microorganisms by phagocytosis. —**mac′ro·phag′ic** (-faj′ik), *adj.*

mac·u·la (mak′yə lə), *n., pl.* **-lae** (-lē′), **-las. 1.** a spot, esp. on the skin. **2. a.** an opaque spot on the cornea. **b.** Also called **yellow spot.** an irregularly oval, yellow-pigmented area on the central retina over color-sensitive rods and the central point of sharpest vision. —**mac′u·lar**, *adj.*

mac·u·la lu·te·a (mak′yə lə lōō′tē ə), *n., pl.* **mac·u·lae lu·te·ae** (mak′yə lē′ lōō′tē ē′, mak′yə lī′ lōō′tē ī′). MACULA (def. 2b).

mac′u·la′tion (-lā′shən), *n.* a spotted condition.

mac·ule (-yōōl), *n.* MACULA.

mag·ne·sia (mag nē′zhə, -shə), *n.* a white tasteless substance, magnesium oxide, MgO, used in medicine as an antacid and laxative. Compare MILK OF MAGNESIA. —**mag·ne'sian,** *adj.*

magnet'ic res'onance im'aging, *n.* a process of producing images of the body regardless of intervening bone by means of a strong magnetic field and low-energy radio waves. *Abbr.:* MRI

magnet'ic res'onance scan'ner, *n.* a diagnostic scanner used in magnetic resonance imaging.

ma'jor his'tocompatibil'ity com'plex, *n.* MHC.

ma'jor tran'quilizer, *n.* ANTIPSYCHOTIC (def. 2).

mal·ab·sorp·tion (mal'əb sôrp'shən, -zôrp'-), *n.* faulty absorption of nutritive material from the intestine.

ma·la·cia (mə lā'shə, -shē ə), *n.* **1.** softening or loss of consistency of an organ or tissue. **2.** an abnormal craving for highly spiced food. —**mal·a·coid** (mal'ə koid'), *adj.* —**mal·a·cot'ic** (-kot'ik), *adj.*

ma·laise (ma lāz', -lez', mə-), *n.* a vague feeling of discomfort or unease without signs of a particular illness or disorder.

ma·lar·i·a (mə lâr'ē ə), *n.* any of a group of usu. intermittent or remittent diseases characterized by attacks of chills, fever, and sweating and caused by a parasitic protozoan transferred to the human bloodstream by an anopheles mosquito. —**ma·lar'i·al, ma·lar'i·an, ma·lar'i·ous,** *adj.*

male (māl), *n.* **1.** a person bearing an X and Y chromosome pair in the cell nuclei and normally having a penis, scrotum, and testicles and developing hair on the face at adolescence. **2.** an organism of the sex or sexual phase that normally produces sperm cells.

mal·for·ma·tion (mal'fôr mā'shən, -fər-), *n.* faulty or anomalous formation or structure: *malformation of the teeth.*

mal·formed', *adj.* faultily or anomalously formed.

mal'ic ac'id (mal'ik, mā'lik), *n.* a colorless, crystalline, water-soluble solid, $C_4H_6O_5$, occurring in apples and other fruits.

ma·lig·nan·cy (mə lig'nən sē), *n., pl.* **-cies. 1.** the quality or condition of being malignant. **2.** a malignant tumor.

ma·lig·nant, *adj.* **1.** tending to produce death, as bubonic plague. **2.** (of a tumor) characterized by uncontrolled growth; cancerous or metastatic. —**ma·lig'nant·ly,** *adv.*

mal·le·us (mal'ē əs), *n., pl.* **mal·le·i** (mal'ē ī'). the outermost of the chain of three small bones in the middle ear of mammals. Also called **hammer.**

mal·nour·ished (mal nûr'isht, -nur'-), *adj.* poorly or improperly nourished; suffering from malnutrition.

mal'nu·tri'tion, *n.* lack of proper nutrition; inadequate or unbalanced nutrition.

Mal·pigh'i·an cor'puscle (mal pig'ē ən), *n.* **1.** Also called **Malpigh'ian bod'y.** the structure at the beginning of a vertebrate nephron consisting of a glomerulus and its surrounding Bowman's capsule. **2.** a lymph nodule of the spleen.

mal·po·si·tion, *n.* faulty or wrong position, esp. of a fetus in the uterus.

Mal·ta fe·ver, *n.* BRUCELLOSIS.

malt·ase (môl′tās, -tāz), *n.* an enzyme that converts maltose to glucose.

malt·ose (-tōs), *n.* a white, crystalline, water-soluble sugar, $C_{12}H_{22}O_{11} \cdot H_2O$, formed by the action of diastase, esp. from malt, or on starch: used chiefly as a nutrient or sweetener, and in culture media. Also called **malt′ sug′ar.**

mam·ma (mam′ə), *n., pl.* **mam·mae** (mam′ē). a structure of mammals comprising one or more mammary glands with an associated nipple or teat, activated for the secretion of milk in the female after the birth of young.

mam·mal (mam′əl), *n.* any warm-blooded vertebrate of the class Mammalia, characterized by a covering of hair on some or most of the body, a four-chambered heart, and nourishment of the newborn with milk from maternal mammary glands.

mam·ma·ry (-ə rē), *adj.* of or pertaining to mammae or mammary glands.

mam′mary gland′, *n.* any of the accessory reproductive organs of female mammals that occur in pairs on the chest or ventral surface and contain milk-producing lobes with ducts that empty into a nipple.

mam·mo·gram (mam′ə gram′), *n.* an x-ray photograph obtained by mammography.

mam·mog·ra·phy (ma mog′rə fē), *n.* x-ray photography of a breast, esp. for detection of tumors.

mam·mo·plas·ty (mam′ə plas′tē), *n.* surgical reconstruction or alteration in size or contour of a woman's breast.

man·di·ble (man′də bəl), *n.* the bone or bony composite comprising the lower jaw of vertebrates. —**man·dib′u·lar** (-dib′yə lər), **man·dib′u·late** (-lit), *adj.*

mange (mānj), *n.* any of various skin diseases caused by parasitic mites, affecting animals and sometimes humans and characterized by loss of hair and scabby eruptions.

ma·ni·a (mā′nē ə, mān′yə), *n., pl.* **-ni·as.** a pathological state characterized by euphoric mood, excessive activity and talkativeness, impaired judgment, and sometimes psychotic symptoms. —**man·ic** (man′ik), *adj.*

man′ic-depres′sive, *adj.* **1.** affected with bipolar disorder. —*n.* **2.** a manic-depressive person.

man′ic disor′der, *n.* an affective disorder characterized by euphoric mood, excessive activity and talkativeness, impaired judgment, and sometimes psychotic symptoms, as grandiose delusions.

ma·nip·u·late (mə nip′yə lāt′), *v.t.,* **-lat·ed, -lat·ing.** to examine or treat by skillful use of the hands, as in palpation, reduction of dislocations, or changing the position of a fetus. —**ma·nip′u·lat′a·ble,** *adj.* —**ma·nip′u·la′tion,** *n.* —**ma·nip′u·la·to′ry** (-lə tôr′ē, -tōr′ē), *adj.*

man·ni·tol (man′i tôl′, -tol′), *n.* a hexahydric sugar alcohol, $C_6H_{14}O_6$, present in many plants or synthesized, used in dietetic foods and in medicine.

ma·nom·e·ter (mə nom′i tər), *n.* an instrument for measuring the pressure of a fluid, consisting of a tube filled with a liquid, the level of the liquid being determined by the fluid pressure. —**man·o·met·ric** (man′ə me′trik), **man′o·met′ri·cal,** *adj.* —**man′o·met′ri·cal·ly,** *adv.* —**ma·nom′e·try,** *n.*

Man·toux′ test′ (man tōō′, măn-, man′tōō), *n.* a test for tuberculosis in which a hypersensitive reaction to an intracutaneous injection of tuberculin indicates a previous or current infection.

ma·nu·bri·um (mə nōō′brē əm, -nyōō′-), *n., pl.* **-bri·a** (-brē ə), **-bri·ums.** a bone or segment resembling a handle, esp. the uppermost part of the mammalian sternum. —**ma·nu′bri·al,** *adj.*

MAO, monoamine oxidase.

ma·ras·mus (mə raz′məs), *n.* malnutrition occurring in infants and young children, caused by insufficient intake of calories or protein and characterized by thinness, dry skin, poor muscle development, and irritability. —**ma·ras′mic,** *adj.* —**ma·ras′moid,** *adj.*

Mar′burg disease′ (mär′bûrg), *n.* a viral disease producing a severe and often fatal illness with fever, rash, diarrhea, vomiting, and gastrointestinal bleeding, transmitted to humans through contact with infected green monkeys. Also called **green monkey disease, Mar′burg-Eb′o·la disease′** (eb′ə lə).

Mar′fan syn′drome (mär′fan, mär fan′), *n.* a hereditary disorder characterized by abnormally elongated bones, excessive motility of the joints, and circulatory and eye abnormalities.

ma·ri·jua·na or **ma·ri·hua·na** (mar′ə wä′nə), *n.* the dried leaves and female flowers of the hemp plant used esp. in cigarette form as an intoxicant.

mark·er (mär′kər), *n.* GENETIC MARKER.

mark′er gene′, *n.* GENETIC MARKER.

mar·row (mar′ō), *n.* the soft fatty vascular tissue in the cavities of bones: a major site of blood cell production.

mask·ing (mas′king, mä′sking), *n.* the obscuring or blocking of one sensory process by another.

mas·och·ism (mas′ə kiz′əm, maz′-), *n.* gratification, esp. of a sexual nature, derived from pain, degradation, etc., inflicted by another on oneself. Compare SADISM. —**mas′och·ist,** *n.* —**mas′och·is′tic,** *adj.* —**mas′och·is′ti·cal·ly,** *adv.*

mas·se·ter (mə sē′tər), *n.* a short thick masticatory muscle, assisting in closing the jaws by raising the mandible or lower jaw.

mas·tec·to·my (ma stek′tə mē), *n., pl.* **-mies.** the surgical removal of all or part of a woman's breast, usu. to prevent the spread of cancer.

mas·ti·tis (-stī′tis), *n.* inflammation of the breast or udder. —**mas·stit′ic** (-stit′ik), *adj.*

mas′toid (-toid), *adj.* **1.** of or pertaining to the mastoid process. **2.** resembling a breast or nipple. —*n.* **3.** the mastoid process.

mas′toid·ec′to·my (-toi dek′tə mē), *n., pl.* **-mies.** the surgical removal of part of a mastoid process.

mas′toid·i′tis (-dī′tis), *n.* inflammation of the mastoid process.

mas′toid proc′ess, *n.* a large bony prominence on the base of the skull behind the ear containing air spaces that connect with the middle ear cavity.

mas·tur·ba·tion (mas′tər bā′shən), *n.* the stimulation or manipulation of one's own or another's genitals, esp. to orgasm. —**mas′tur·ba′tion·al,** *adj.*

ma·te·ri·a me·di·ca (mə tēr′ē ə med′i kə), *n.* **1.** (*used with a pl. v.*) remedial substances used in medicine. **2.** (*used with a sing. v.*) the study of or a treatise on the sources, characteristics, and uses of drugs.

mat·ter (mat′ər), *n.* a substance discharged by a living body, esp. pus.

max·il·la (mak sil′ə), *n., pl.* **max·il·lae** (mak sil′ē). an upper jaw or jawbone.

max·il·lar·y (mak′sə ler′ē, mak sil′ə rē), *adj., n., pl.* **-lar·ies.** —*adj.* **1.** of or pertaining to a maxilla. —*n.* **2.** one of a pair of bones constituting the upper jaw.

mcg, microgram.

MD, Doctor of Medicine. [New Latin, *Medicinae Doctor*]

MDA, methylene dioxyamphetamine: an amphetamine derivative, $C_{10}H_{13}NO_2$, having hallucinogenic and stimulant properties.

MDMA, methylene dioxymethamphetamine: an amphetamine derivative, $C_{11}H_{15}NO_2$, that reduces inhibitions and that was used in psychotherapy until it was banned in the U.S. in 1985.

MDR, 1. minimum daily requirement. **2.** minimum dietary requirement.

M.E., Medical Examiner.

mea·sles (mē′zəlz), *n.* **1.** (*used with a sing. or pl. v.*) **a.** an acute infectious disease caused by a paramyxovirus, characterized by a small red spots, fever, and coldlike symptoms, usu. occurring in childhood: rubeola. **b.** any of certain other eruptive diseases, esp. rubella. **2. a.** a disease mostly of domestic swine caused by tapeworm larvae in the flesh. **b.** the larvae.

mech·an·ism (mek′ə niz′əm), *n.* a mode of behavior that helps an individual deal with the physical or psychological environment. Compare DEFENSE MECHANISM, ESCAPE MECHANISM.

mech·a·no·re·cep·tor (mek′ə nō ri sep′tər), *n.* any of the neuronal receptors that respond to vibration, stretching, pressure, or other mechanical stimuli.

me·co·ni·um (mi kō′nē əm), *n.* the first fecal excretion of a newborn child, composed chiefly of bile, mucus, and epithelial cells.

med (med), *adj.* medical: *med school.*

med., 1. medical. 2. medicine.

me·di·a (mē′dē ə), *n., pl.* **-di·ae** (-dē ē′). 1. a pl. of ME-DIUM. 2. the middle layer of an artery or lymphatic vessel.

me′dian le′thal dose′, *n.* the quantity of a lethal substance, as a poison or pathogen, or of ionizing radiation that will kill 50 percent of the organisms subjected to it in a specified time period. *Symbol:* LD$_{50}$

me·di·as·ti·num (mē′dē a stī′nəm), *n., pl.* **-na** (-nə). 1. a median septum or partition between two parts of an organ or paired cavities of the body. 2. the area in the chest that lies between the lungs, is bounded by the sternum, the spinal column, and the diaphragm, and contains the heart, esophagus, trachea, and other thoracic structures. —**me′di·as·ti′nal,** *adj.*

med·ic (med′ik), *n.* a medical doctor or intern.

med·i·cal, *adj.* 1. of or pertaining to the science or practice of medicine. 2. curative; medicinal; *medical properties.* 3. pertaining to or requiring treatment by other than surgical means. 4. pertaining to or indicating the state of one's health: *a medical leave.* —*n.* 5. a medical examination. —**med′i·cal·ly,** *adv.*

med′ical exam′iner, *n.* 1. a government official who performs postmortem examinations of bodies to determine the cause of death. 2. a physician retained by an insurance company, industrial firm, or the like, to give medical examinations to its clients or employees. *Abbr:* M.E.

me·dic·a·ment (mə dik′ə mənt, med′i kə-), *n.* a healing substance; medicine; remedy. —**med′i·ca·men′tal** (-men′tl), *adj.*

Med·i·care (med′i kâr′), *n.* (*sometimes l.c.*) a U.S. government program of medical insurance for aged or disabled persons.

med·i·cate (-kāt′), *v.t.,* **-cat·ed, -cat·ing.** 1. to treat with medicine or medicaments. 2. to impregnate with a medicine: *medicated cough drops.*

med·i·ca·tion, *n.* 1. the use or application of medicine. 2. a medicinal substance; medicament.

me·dic·i·nal (mə dis′ə nl), *adj.* 1. of, pertaining to, or having the properties of a medicine; curative; remedial. —*n.* 2. a medicinal preparation or product. —**me·dic′i·nal·ly,** *adv.*

med·i·cine (med′ə sin), *n.* 1. any substance used in treating disease or illness. 2. the art, science, or profession of preserving health and of curing or alleviating disease.

med′i·co′ (-kō′), *n., pl.* **-cos.** *Informal.* 1. a physician; doctor. 2. a medical student.

med·i·co·le′gal, *adj.* pertaining to medicine and law or to forensic medicine.

med·i·gap′ (-gap′), *n.* (*sometimes cap.*) a supplemental health insurance that provides coverage for people whose government insurance benefits are insufficient.

Med'iterra'nean fe'ver, *n.* BRUCELLOSIS.

me·di·um (mē'dē əm), *n., pl.* **-di·a** (-dē ə), **-di·ums.** Also called **culture medium.** a nutrient material suitable for the cultivation of microorganisms, tissues, etc.

me·dul·la (mə dul'ə), *n., pl.* **-dul·las, -dul·lae** (-dul'ē). **1.** bone marrow. **2.** the soft marrowlike center of an organ, as the kidney or adrenal gland. **3.** MEDULLA OBLONGATA. —**med·ul·lar·y** (med'l er'ē, mej'ə ler'ē, mə dul'ə rē), *adj.*

medul'la ob·long·a'ta (ob'lông gä'tə, -long-), *n., pl.* **medulla oblongatas.** the lowest or hindmost part of the vertebrate brain, continuous with the spinal cord.

med'ullary sheath', *n.* MYELIN SHEATH.

med·ul·lat·ed (med'l ā'tid, mej'ə lā'-, mə dul'ā tid), *adj.* myelinated.

meg·a·dose (meg'ə dōs'), *n.* a very large dose, as of a vitamin.

meg'a·ga·mete', *n.* MACROGAMETE.

meg·a·lo·blast (meg'ə lə blast'), *n.* an abnormally large immature dysfunctional red blood cell found in the blood esp. of persons with pernicious anemia. —**meg'a·lo·blas'tic,** *adj.*

meg'a·lo·car'di·a (-kär'dē ə), *n.* hypertrophy of the heart.

meg'a·lo·ma'ni·a (-mā'nē ə), *n.* a highly exaggerated or delusional concept of one's own importance. —**meg'a·lo·ma'ni·ac',** *n.* —**meg'a·lo·ma·ni'a·cal, meg'a·lo·man'ic,** *adj.*

meg·a·vi·ta·min (meg'ə vī'tə min; *Brit. also* -vit'ə-), *adj.* of, pertaining to, or using very large amounts of vitamins: *megavitamin therapy.*

mei·o·sis (mī ō'sis), *n.* part of the process of gamete formation in sexual reproduction consisting of chromosome conjugation and two cell divisions after which the chromosome number is reduced by half. Compare MITOSIS. —**mei·ot·ic** (mī ot'ik), *adj.*

mel (mel), *n.* (in prescriptions) honey.

mel·an·cho·li·a (mel'ən kō'lē ə, -kōl'yə), *n.* a severe form of depression characterized typically by weight loss, insomnia, and an inability to experience pleasure. —**mel'an·cho'li·ac,** *n.*

mel'an·chol'ic (-kol'ik), *adj.* of, pertaining to, or affected with melancholia.

me·lan·ic (mə lan'ik), *adj.* melanotic.

mel·a·nin (mel'ə nin), *n.* any of a class of insoluble pigments that are found in all forms of animal life and account for the dark color of skin and hair.

me·lan·o·cyte (mə lan'ə sīt', mel'ə nə-), *n.* a cell that produces the dark pigment melanin.

melan'ocyte-stim'ulating hor'mone, *n.* See MSH.

mel·a·noid (mel'ə noid'), *adj.* **1.** of or characterized by melanosis. **2.** resembling melanin; darkish.

mel·a·no·ma (-nō'mə), *n., pl.* **-mas, -ma·ta** (-mə tə). any of several types of skin tumors characterized by the malignant growth of melanocytes.

mel·a·no·sis (-sis), *n.*, *pl.* **-ses** (-sēz). **1.** abnormal deposition or development of black or dark pigment in the tissues. **2.** a discoloration caused by this.

mel·a·not·ic (-not′ik), *adj.* of or affected with melanosis.

mel·a·to·nin (mel′ə tō′nin), *n.* a hormone secreted by the pineal gland in inverse proportion to the amount of light received by the retina, important in regulating biorhythms.

mem′ory trace′, *n.* ENGRAM.

men·a·di·one (men′ə di′ōn), *n.* a synthetic yellow crystalline powder, $C_{11}H_8O_2$, insoluble in water, used as a vitamin K supplement. Also called **vitamin K$_3$.**

men·ar·che (mə när′kē, men′är-), *n.* the first menstrual period; the establishment of menstruation. —**men·ar′-che·al, men·ar′chi·al,** *adj.*

Men·de·li·an (men dē′lē ən, -dēl′yən), *adj.* **1.** of or pertaining to Gregor Mendel or Mendelism. —*n.* **2.** a follower of Mendelism.

Men·del·ism (men′dl iz′əm) *n.* the theories of heredity advanced by Gregor Mendel.

Men′del's law′, *n.* **1.** Also called **law of segregation.** the principle that during the production of gametes the two copies of each hereditary factor segregate so that offspring acquire one factor from each parent. **2.** Also called **law of independent assortment.** the principle that the laws of chance govern the particular characteristics of the parental pairs that will occur in each individual offspring. **3.** Also called **law of dominance.** the principle that one factor in a pair of traits dominates the other in inheritance unless both factors in the pair are recessive.

Mé·nière's′ disease′ (mān yârz′), *n.* a disease of the labyrinth of the ear, characterized by deafness, ringing in the ears, dizziness, and nausea. Also called **Ménière's′ syn′drome.**

me·nin·ges (mə nin′jēz), *n.pl.*, *sing.* **me·ninx** (mē′-ningks). the three membranes covering the brain and spinal cord. Compare ARACHNOID, DURA MATER, PIA MATER. —**me·nin′ge·al** (-jē əl), *adj.*

me·nin·gi·o·ma (-jē ō′mə), *n.*, *pl.* **-mas, -ma·ta** (-mə tə). a hard, encapsulated tumor that grows slowly along the meninges.

men·in·gi·tis (men′in ji′tis), *n.* inflammation of the meninges, esp. of the pia mater and arachnoid, caused by a bacterial or viral infection and characterized by high fever, severe headache, and stiff neck or back muscles. —**men′-in·git′ic** (-jit′ik), *adj.*

me·nin·go·coc·cus (mə ning′gō kok′əs), *n.*, *pl.* **-coc·ci** (-kok′si, -sē). a spherical or kidney-shaped bacterium, *Neisseria meningitidis,* that causes cerebrospinal meningitis. —**me·nin′go·coc′cal, me·nin′go·coc′cic** (-kok′ik, -kok′sik), *adj.*

me·nis·cus (mi nis′kəs), *n.*, *pl.* **-nis·ci** (-nis′ī, -nis′ki, -kē),

-nis·cus·es. a wedge of cartilage between the articulating ends of the bones in certain joints. —**me·nis′coid,** *adj.*

men·o·pause (men′ə pôz′), *n.* the period of natural cessation of menstruation, usu. occurring between the ages of 45 and 55. —**men′o·pau′sal,** *adj.*

men′or·rha′gi·a (-ə rā′jē ə, -jə), *n.* excessive menstrual discharge. —**men′or·rhag′ic** (-raj′ik), *adj.*

men′or·rhe′a or **men′or·rhoe′a** (-rē′ə), *n.* menstrual flow. —**men′or·rhe′al, men′or·rhe′ic,** *adj.*

men·ses (men′sēz), *n.* (*used with a sing. or pl. v.*) the periodic flow of blood and mucosal tissue from the uterus; menstrual flow.

men′stru·al (-strōō əl, -strəl), *adj.* of or pertaining to menstruation or to the menses.

men′stru·ate′ (-strōō āt′, -strāt′), *v.i.,* **-at·ed, -at·ing.** to undergo menstruation.

men′stru·a′tion, *n.* **1.** the periodic discharge of blood and mucosal tissue from the uterus, occurring approximately monthly from puberty to menopause in nonpregnant women and females of other primate species. **2.** the period of menstruating.

men·tal (men′tl), *adj.* **1.** of, pertaining to, or affected by a disorder of the mind: *a mental patient.* **2.** for persons with a psychiatric disorder: *a mental hospital.* —**men·tal·ly,** *adv.*

men′tal age′, *n.* the level of mental ability of an individual, usu. a child, expressed as the chronological age of the average individual at this level of ability, as determined by an intelligence test.

men′tal health′, *n.* psychological well-being and satisfactory adjustment to society and to the ordinary demands of life.

men′tal ill′ness, *n.* any of the various forms of psychosis or severe neurosis. Also called **men′tal disor′der, men′tal disease′.**

men′tal retarda′tion, *n.* a developmental disorder characterized in varying degrees by a subnormal ability to learn, a substantially low IQ, and impaired social adjustment.

men·ta′tion (-tā′shən), *n.* mental activity.

me·per·i·dine (mə per′i dēn′, -din), *n.* a narcotic compound, $C_{15}H_{21}NO_2$, used as an analgesic and as a sedative.

me·pro·ba·mate (mə prō′bə māt′, mep′rō bam′āt), *n.* a white powder, $C_9H_{18}N_2O_4$, used chiefly as a tranquilizer for treating anxiety, tension, and skeletal muscle spasm.

mer·bro·min (mər brō′min), *n.* an iridescent green, water-soluble powder, $C_{20}H_8Br_2HgNa_2O_6$, that forms a red solution in water: used as an antiseptic and as a germicide.

Mer·cu·ro·chrome (mər kyoor′ə krōm′), *Trademark.* a brand of merbromin.

mer·cu′rous chlo′ride (mər kyoor′əs, mûr′kyər əs), *n.* CALOMEL.

mer·cu·ry (mûr′kyə rē), *n., pl.* **-ries. 1.** a heavy, silverwhite, toxic metallic element, liquid at room temperature:

used in barometers, thermometers, pesticides, pharmaceuticals, mirror surfaces, and as laboratory catalyst: quicksilver. **2.** this metal as used in medicine, in the form of various organic and inorganic compounds, usu. for skin infections.

mer′cy kill′ing, *n.* EUTHANASIA..

mer·o·blas·tic (mer′ə blas′tik), *adj.* Embryol. undergoing partial cleavage, resulting in unequal blastomeres: characteristic of yolky eggs. —**mer′o·blas′ti·cal·ly,** *adv.*

me·rog·o·ny (mə rog′ə nē), *n.* the development of an embryo from egg fragments lacking the egg nucleus but having an introduced male nucleus. —**mer·o·gon·ic** (mer′ə gon′ik), **me·rog′o·nous,** *adj.*

Mer·thi·o·late (mər thī′ə lāt′), *Trademark.* a brand of thimerosal.

mes·cal (me skal′), *n.* **1.** Also called **peyote.** a species of spineless, dome-shaped cactus, Lophophora williamsii, of Texas and N Mexico. **2.** MESCAL BUTTON.

mescal′ but′ton, *n.* one of the dried tops of the mescal cactus, containing the hallucinogen mescaline. Also called **peyote.**

mes·ca·line (mes′kə lēn′, -lin), *n.* a white, water-soluble, crystalline powder, $C_{11}H_{17}NO_3$, obtained from mescal buttons, that produces hallucinations.

mes·en·ceph·a·lon (mes′en sef′ə lon′, -lən, mez′-), *n.,* pl. **-lons, -la** (-lə). the midbrain. —**mes′en·ce·phal′ic** (-sə fal′ik), *adj.*

mes·en·chyme (mes′eng kim, mez′-), *n.* cells of mesodermal origin that are capable of developing into connective tissues, blood, and lymphatic and blood vessels. —**mes′en·chy′mal** (-kə məl), **mes′en·chym′a·tous** (-ki′mə təs), *adj.*

mes·en·ter·on (mes en′tə ron′, mez-), *n.,* pl. **-ter·a** (-tər ə). MIDGUT. —**mes′en·ter·on′ic,** *adj.*

mes·en·ter·y (mes′ən ter′ē, mez′-), *n.,* pl. **-ter·ies.** any peritoneal membrane that enfolds an internal vertebrate organ and attaches it to the body wall, esp. the membrane investing the intestines. —**mes′en·ter′ic,** *adj.*

mes·o·blast (mez′ə blast′, mes′-, mē′zə-, -sə-), *n.* the middle layer of the early embryo, which becomes the mesoderm after separation of the germ layers. —**mes′o·blas′tic,** *adj.*

mes′o·derm′ (-dûrm′), *n.* the middle embryonic germ layer, between the ectoderm and endoderm, from which connective tissue, muscles, and blood vessels develop. —**mes′o·der′mal, mes′o·der′mic,** *adj.*

mes′o·mere′ (-mēr′), *n.* **1.** a blastomere of intermediate size between a micromere and a macromere. **2.** the intermediate zone of the mesoderm.

mes′o·mor′phic (-môr′fik), *adj.* pertaining to or having a muscular or sturdy body build characterized by the relative prominence of structures developed from the embryonic mesoderm (contrasted with ectomorphic, endomorphic). —**mes′o·mor′phism,** *n.* —**mes′o·mor′phy,** *n.*

mes·o·neph·ros (-nef′ros), *n., pl.* **-roi** (-roi). an excretory organ of vertebrate embryos, developing into part of the ducts and tubules of the reproductive system in mammals. —**mes′o·neph′ric**, *adj.*

mes·o·the·li·o·ma (-thē′lē ō′mə), *n., pl.* **-mas, -ma·ta** (-mə tə). a malignant tumor of the covering of the lung or the lining of the pleural and abdominal cavities, often associated with exposure to asbestos.

mes·o·the·li·um (-lē əm), *n., pl.* **-li·a** (-lē ə). an epithelium of mesodermal origin that lines the body cavities. —**mes′o·the′li·al**, *adj.*

messenger RNA, *n.* a molecule of RNA that is synthesized in the nucleus from a DNA template and then enters the cytoplasm, where its genetic code specifies the amino acid sequence for protein synthesis. *Abbr.:* mRNA

Met, methionine.

me·tab·o·lism (mə tab′ə liz′əm), *n.* the sum of the physical and chemical processes in an organism by which its substance is produced, maintained, and destroyed, and by which energy is made available. Compare ANABOLISM, CATABOLISM. —**met·a·bol·ic** (met′ə bol′ik), *adj.* —**met′a·bol′i·cal·ly,** *adv.*

me·tab′o·lite′ (-līt′), *n.* a product of metabolism.

me·tab′o·lize′ (-līz′), *v.,* **-lized, -liz·ing.** —*v.t.* **1.** to subject to or change by metabolism. —*v.i.* **2.** to effect metabolism. —**me·tab′o·liz′a·ble,** *adj.*

met·a·car·pal (met′ə kär′pəl), *adj.* **1.** of or pertaining to the metacarpus. —*n.* **2.** a metacarpal bone.

met·a·car·pus (-pəs), *n., pl.* **-pi** (-pī). the bones of a vertebrate forelimb between the wrist, or carpus, and the fingers, or phalanges.

met·a·cen·tric (-sen′trik), *adj.* (of a chromosome) having the centromere positioned at the center and thereby having the two arms of equal length. —**met′a·cen·tric′i·ty** (-tris′i tē), *n.*

met·a·chro·mat·ic (-krə mat′ik), *adj.* **1.** capable of changing or varying in color, esp. with variation of temperature or other physical condition. **2.** (of a laboratory dye) capable of producing contrasting stains in different components of a tissue. —**met′a·chro·ma·tism** (-krō′mə tiz′əm), *n.*

met·a·neph·ros (-nef′ros), *n., pl.* **-roi** (-roi). an embryonic excretory organ that develops into the functional kidney. —**met′a·neph′ric**, *adj.*

met·a·phase′ (-fāz′), *n.* the stage in mitosis or meiosis in which the duplicated chromosomes line up along the equatorial plate of the spindle.

met·a·pla·sia (-plā′zhə, -zhē ə), *n.* the transformation of one type of cellular tissue into another. —**met′a·plas′tic** (-plas′tik), *adj.*

met·a·plasm (-plaz′əm), *n.* the nonliving matter or inclusions, as starch or pigments, within a cell. —**met′a·plas′mic,** *adj.*

me·tas·ta·sis (mə tas′tə sis), *n., pl.* **-ses** (-sēz′). the spread of disease-producing organisms or of cancerous cells to other parts of the body by way of the blood or lymphatic vessels or membranous surfaces. —**met·a·stat·ic** (met′ə stat′ik), adj. —**met′a·stat′i·cal·ly**, adv.

me·tas′ta·size, v.i., **-sized, -siz·ing.** to spread by metastasis.

met·a·tar·sal (met′ə tär′səl), adj. **1.** of or pertaining to the metatarsus. —**n. 2.** a bone in the metatarsus. —**met′a·tar′sal·ly**, adv.

met′a·tar′sus (-səs), n., pl. **-si** (-sī). the bones of a vertebrate hind limb between the tarsus and the toes, or phalanges.

met·en·ceph·a·lon (met′en sef′ə lon′), n., pl. **-lons, -la** (-lə). the anterior section of the hindbrain developing into the cerebellum and the pons. —**met′en·ce·phal′ic** (-səfal′ik), adj.

met·es·trus (met es′trəs), n. the luteal phase of the reproductive cycle.

meth (meth), n. Slang. methamphetamine; Methedrine.

meth·a·done (meth′ə dōn′) also **meth′a·don′** (-don′), n. a synthetic narcotic, $C_{21}H_{28}ClNO$, similar to morphine but effective orally, used in the relief of pain and as a heroin substitute in the treatment of heroin addiction.

meth·am·phet·a·mine (meth′am fet′ə mēn′, -min), n. a central nervous system stimulant, $C_{10}H_{15}N$, used in treating narcolepsy, hyperkinesia, and for blood pressure maintenance in hypotensive states.

meth·an·o·gen (me than′ə jən, -jen′), n. any of a group of archaebacteria that occur in diverse anaerobic environments and are capable of producing methane from a limited number of chemical sources, as carbon dioxide and hydrogen. —**meth·an′o·gen′ic**, adj.

me·tha·qua·lone (mə thak′wə lōn′, meth′ə kwā′lōn, -kwol′ōn), n. a nonbarbiturate substance, $C_{16}H_{14}N_2O$, used to induce sleep.

Meth·e·drine (meth′ə drēn′, -drin), Trademark. a brand of methamphetamine.

met·he·mo·glo·bin (met hē′mə glō′bin, -hem′ə-), n. a form of hemoglobin in which iron has been oxidized, resulting in brownish blood that transports less oxygen.

me·thi·o·nine (me thī′ə nēn′, -nin), n. an essential amino acid, $C_5H_{11}NO_2S$, occurring in casein, yeast, and other proteins. Abbr.: Met; Symbol: M

meth·o·trex·ate (meth′ō trek′sāt), n. a toxic folic acid analogue, $C_{20}H_{22}N_8O_5$, that inhibits cellular reproduction and is used in the treatment of psoriasis and certain cancers.

meth·yl·do·pa (meth′əl dō′pə), n. a white powder, $C_{10}H_{13}NO_4$, used in the treatment of hypertension.

meth′yl·ene blue′ (meth′ə lēn′), n. a dark green, crystalline compound, $C_{16}H_{18}ClN_3S$, that dissolves in water to form a deep blue solution: used chiefly as a dye, as a biological stain, and as an antidote for cyanide poisoning.

meth′y·lene di·ox′y·am·phet′a·mine (dī ok′sē am fet′ə mēn′, -min, -ok′sē-), *n.* See MDA.

meth′yl·phen′i·date′ (-fen′i dāt′, -fē′ni-), *n.* a central nervous system stimulant, $C_{14}H_{19}NO_2$, used in the control of hyperkinetic syndromes and narcolepsy.

meth′yl·tes·tos′ter·one′, *n.* a synthetic androgenic steroid drug, $C_{20}H_{30}O_2$, used for its anabolic properties in males in the treatment of androgen-deficiency disease states, and in females in the treatment of breast cancer.

me·tri·tis (mi trī′tis), *n.* inflammation of the uterus.

me·tror·rha·gi·a (mē′trə rā′jē ə, -jə, me′-), *n.* nonmenstrual discharge of blood from the uterus; uterine hemorrhage. —**me′tror·rhag′ic** (-raj′ik), *adj.*

mg, milligram.

MHC, major histocompatibility complex: a group of genes that determine histocompatibility antigens, located in humans on the sixth chromosome. Compare HLA.

MI, myocardial infarction.

mi·crobe (mi′krōb), *n.* a microorganism, esp. a disease-causing bacterium. —**mi·cro′bi·al, mi·cro′bic,** *adj.*

mi·cro′bi·cide′ (-krō′bə sīd′), *n.* a substance or preparation for killing microbes. —**mi·cro′bi·cid′al,** *adj.*

mi′cro·bi·ol′o·gy, *n.* the branch of biology dealing with microscopic organisms. —**mi′cro·bi′o·log′i·cal, mi′cro·bi′o·log′ic,** *adj.* —**mi′cro·bi·ol′o·gist,** *n.*

mi′cro·cap′sule, *n.* a tiny capsule, 20–150 microns in diameter, used for slow-release application of drugs, pesticides, flavors, etc.

mi′cro·ceph′a·ly (-sef′ə lē), *n.* abnormal smallness of the head or braincase. —**mi′cro·ce·phal′ic** (-sə fal′ik), *adj.,* *n.*

mi′cro·coc′cus, *n.,* pl. **-coc·ci.** any spherical bacterium of the genus *Micrococcus,* occurring in irregular masses, many species of which are pigmented and are saprophytic or parasitic. —**mi′cro·coc′cal, mi′cro·coc′cic,** *adj.*

mi′cro·fi·lar′i·a, *n., pl.* **-lar·i·ae** (-lâr′ē ē′). the embryonic larva of the nematode parasite *Filaria* or of related genera, esp. of those species that cause elephantiasis in humans.

mi′cro·gam′ete, *n.* the smaller cell, considered as the male, in the reproduction by conjugation of unlike gametes.

mi·cro·gram (mi′krə gram′), *n.* a unit of mass or weight equal to one millionth of a gram. *Abbr.:* mcg; *Symbol:* µg

mi′cro·in·jec′tion, *n.* injection performed under a microscope, esp. into a single cell or cell part. —**mi′cro·in·ject′,** *v.t.*

mi′cro·mere (mi′krə mēr′), *n.* one of the small blastomeres that form toward the animal pole in embryos that undergo unequal cleavage.

mi·cro·me·ter (mi′krō mē′tər), *n.* MICRON.

mi·cron (mi′kron), *n., pl.* **-crons, -cra** (-krə). the millionth part of a meter. Also called **micrometer.** *Symbol:* µ, mu

mi·cro·nu·tri·ent (mī/krō-), *n.* an essential nutrient, as a trace mineral, that is required in minute amounts.

mi·cro·or·gan·ism, *n.* any organism too small to be viewed by the unaided eye, as bacteria or some fungi and algae. —**mi/cro·or·gan/ic, mi/cro·or/gan·is/mal,** *adj.*

mi·cro·phage (mī/krə fāj/), *n.* a small phagocyte, present in blood and lymph, that migrates to tissues in the inflammatory immune response.

mi·cro·pi·pette or **mi·cro·pi·pet** (mī/krō pi pet/, -pi-), *n.* a very slender pipette for transferring or measuring minute amounts of fluid, microorganisms, etc.

mi·cro·probe (mī/krə prōb/), *n.* a miniature probe for use in microsurgery.

mi·cro·pump/, *n.* a tiny pump implanted under the skin for the timed administration of medication.

mi/cro·pyle/ (-pīl/), *n.* the surface area of the membrane through which a sperm is transported to the ovum in fertilization. —**mi/cro·py/lar,** *adj.*

mi·cro·some (-sōm/), *n.* a small vesicle containing fragments of ribosomes and other organelles, formed during cell breakage by centrifugation. —**mi/cro·so/mal,** *adj.*

mi·cro·sur·ger·y (mī/krō sûr/jə rē, mī/krō sûr/-), *n.* any of various surgical procedures performed under magnification and with small specialized instruments. —**mi/cro·sur/geon,** *n.* —**mi/cro·sur/gi·cal,** *adj.*

mi·cro·tome (mī/krə tōm/), *n.* an instrument for cutting very thin sections of organic tissue for microscopic examination. —**mi·crot·o·mic** (-tom/ik), **mi·crot/o·mist** (-krot/ə mist), —**mi·crot/o·my,** *n.*

mic·tu·rate (mik/chə rāt/), *v.i.,* **-rat·ed, -rat·ing.** to pass urine; urinate. —**mic/tu·ri/tion** (-rish/ən), *n.*

mid/brain/, *n.* the middle of the three primary divisions of the brain in the embryo of a vertebrate or the part of the adult brain derived from this tissue; mesencephalon.

mid/dle ear/, *n.* the middle portion of the ear consisting of the eardrum and an air-filled chamber lined with mucous membrane that contains the malleus, incus, and stapes.

mid/gut/, *n.* the middle part of the embryonic alimentary canal, from which the intestines develop. Compare FORE-GUT, HINDGUT.

mid/life cri/sis, *n.* a period of stress and self-doubt occurring in middle age.

mid/wife/, *n., pl.* **-wives,** *v.,* **-wifed** or **-wived, -wif·ing** or **wiv·ing.** —*n.* **1.** a person who assists women in childbirth. —*v.t.* **2.** to assist in the birth of (a baby).

mid·wife·ry (mid wīf/ə rē, -wīf/rē, mid/wī/fə rē, -wīf/rē), *n.* the technique or practice of a midwife.

mi·graine (mī/grān *or, Brit.,* mē/-), *n.* a severe, recurrent headache characterized by pressure or throbbing beginning on one side of the head and accompanied by nausea and other disturbances. —**mi·grain/ous,** *adj.*

mil·i·ar·i·a (mil/ē âr/ē ə), *n.* an inflammatory disease of the skin, located about the sweat glands, marked by the formation of vesicles or papules resembling millet seeds; prickly heat.

mil·i·ar·y (mil′ē er′ē, mil′yə rē), *adj.* marked or accompanied by vesicles resembling millet seeds: *miliary tuberculosis.*

mil·i·um (mil′ē əm), *n., pl.* **-i·a** (-ē ə). a small white or yellowish nodule resembling a millet seed, produced in the skin by the retention of sebaceous secretion.

milk (milk), *n.* the opaque white or bluish-white liquid secreted by the mammary glands of female mammals, serving for the nourishment of their young. Compare COLOSTRUM.

milk′ fe′ver, *n.* fever coinciding with the beginning of lactation, formerly believed to be due to lactation but really due to infection.

milk′ leg′, *n.* a painful swelling of the leg soon after childbirth, due to thrombosis of the large veins.

milk′ of magne′sia, *n.* a milky white suspension in water of magnesium hydroxide, Mg (OH)$_2$, used as an antacid or laxative.

milk′ sick′ness, *n.* a disease of humans caused by consuming milk from cattle that have eaten poisonous weeds.

mil·li·gram (mil′i gram′), *n.* a unit of mass or weight equal to $\frac{1}{1000}$ of a gram, and equivalent to 0.0154 grain. *Abbr.:* mg

Min·a·ma·ta disease′ (min′ə mä′tə), *n.* a severe form of poisoning by ingestion of mercury, as from fish caught in polluted water: characterized by neurological degeneration.

mind′-al′tering, *adj.* causing marked changes in patterns of mood, perception, and behavior, as a hallucinogenic drug.

min·er·al (min′ər əl, min′rəl), *n.* any of the inorganic elements, as calcium, iron, magnesium, potassium, or sodium, that are essential to the functioning of the human body and are obtained from foods.

min·er·al·o·cor·ti·coid (min′ər ə lō kôr′ti koid′), *n.* any of a group of corticosteroid hormones, synthesized by the adrenal cortex, that regulate the excretion or reabsorption of sodium and potassium by the kidneys, salivary glands, and sweat glands.

min′eral oil′, *n.* a colorless, oily, almost tasteless oil obtained from petroleum by distillation and used chiefly as a lubricant and laxative.

min·i·pill (min′ē pil′), *n.* a birth control pill that contains only a progestin and is to be taken daily without monthly cessation.

mi′nor tran′quilizer, *n.* TRANQUILIZER (def. 1).

min·ox·i·dil (mi nok′si dil′), *n.* a vasodilative drug used for treating severe hypertension and also applied topically to promote hair growth in some types of baldness.

mi·o·sis or **my·o·sis** (mi ō′sis), *n.* excessive constriction of the pupil of the eye. Compare MYDRIASIS.

mi·ot·ic or **my·ot·ic** (-ot′ik), *adj.* **1.** pertaining to or producing miosis. —*n.* **2.** a miotic drug.

mir′acle drug′, *n.* WONDER DRUG.

mis·car·riage (mis kar′ij, mis′kar′ij), *n.* the expulsion of a fetus before it is viable, esp. between the third and seventh months of pregnancy; spontaneous abortion.

mis·car·ry (mis kar′ē, mis′kar′ē), *v.i.,* **-ried, -ry·ing.** to have a miscarriage.

mis′sionary posi′tion, *n.* a position for sexual intercourse in which the couple lies face to face with the male on top.

mith·ri·date (mith′ri dāt′), *n.* a sweetened medicinal preparation believed to contain an antidote to every poison.

mi·to·chon·dri·on (mī′tə kon′drē ən), *n., pl.* **-dri·a** (-drē ə). an organelle in the cell cytoplasm that has its own DNA, inherited solely from the maternal line, and that produces enzymes essential for energy metabolism. *Abbr.:* mt —**mi′to·chon′dri·al,** *adj.*

mi·to·gen (mī′tə jən, -jen′), *n.* any substance or agent that stimulates mitosis. —**mi′to·gen′ic** (-jen′ik), *adj.*

mi·to·sis (mi tō′sis), *n.* the usual method of cell division, characterized by the resolving of the chromatin of the nucleus into a threadlike form that condenses into chromosomes, each of which separates longitudinally into two parts, one part of each chromosome being retained in each of the two new daughter cells. Compare MEIOSIS. —**mi·tot′ic** (-tot′ik), *adj.* —**mi·tot′i·cal·ly,** *adv.*

mi′tral valve′ (mī′trəl), *n.* the valve between the left atrium and left ventricle of the heart, consisting of two triangular flaps of tissue, that prevents blood from flowing back into the atrium when the ventricle contracts. Also called **bicuspid valve.** Compare TRICUSPID VALVE.

MLD, 1. median lethal dose. **2.** minimum lethal dose.

mo·dal·i·ty (mō dal′i tē), *n., pl.* **-ties.** a therapeutic method.

mo·lar (mō′lər), *n.* **1.** Also called **mo′lar tooth′.** a tooth having a broad biting surface adapted for grinding, being one of 12 in humans, with 3 on each side of the upper and lower jaws. —*adj.* **2.** adapted for grinding, as teeth. **3.** pertaining to such teeth.

mole (mōl), *n.* **1.** a small, congenital spot or blemish on the human skin, usu. of a dark color, slightly elevated, and sometimes hairy; nevus. **2.** a mass in the uterus formed by malformed embryonic or placental tissue.

mo·lec′u·lar biol′ogy, *n.* the branch of biology that deals with the nature of biological phenomena at the molecular level through the study of DNA and RNA, proteins, and other macromolecules involved in genetic information and cell function.

molec′ular clock′, *n.* the changes over time that take place in the amino acid sequences of proteins, from which approximate ages and relationships of life forms can be deduced.

molec/ular genet/ics, *n.* a subdivision of genetics concerned with the structure and function of genes at the molecular level.

mon·gol·ism (mong/gə liz/əm, mon/-), *n.* (*sometimes cap.*) no longer in technical use) DOWN SYNDROME.

Mon/gol·oid/ (-loid/), *adj.* **1.** (*often l.c.*) (no longer in technical use) of, affected with, or characteristic of Down syndrome. —*n.* **2.** (*usu. l.c.*) (no longer in technical use) a person affected with Down syndrome.

mon·i·li·a·sis (mon/ə lī/ə sis, mō/nə-), *n.* CANDIDIASIS.

mon·o·a·mine (mon/ō ə mēn/, -am/in), *n.* an amine that has a single amino group, as the neurotransmitters dopamine, epinephrine, and norepinephrine.

mon/oamine/ ox/idase, *n.* a copper-containing enzyme that catalyzes the breakdown of monoamines. *Abbr.:* MAO

mon/oamine/ ox/idase inhib/itor, *n.* any of various substances that block enzymatic breakdown of certain monoamine neurotransmitters and that are used to treat severe depression. *Abbr.:* MAOI

mon·o·chro·mat·ic (mon/ə krō mat/ik, -ō krə-), *adj.* of or pertaining to monochromatism. —**mon/o·chro·mat/i·cal·ly,** *adv.* —**mon/o·chro·ma·tic/i·ty** (-mə tis/i tē), *n.*

mon·o·chro·ma·tism (-krō/mə tiz/əm), *n.* a defect of vision in which the retina fails to perceive color.

mon·o·clo·nal (mon/ə klōn/l), *adj.* **1.** pertaining to cells or cell products derived from a single biological clone. —*n.* **2.** a monoclonal antibody or other monoclonal product.

mon/oclo/nal an/tibody, *n.* any antibody produced by a laboratory-grown cell clone, either of a hybridoma or a virus-transformed lymphocyte, in order to achieve greater abundance and uniformity than provided by a natural antibody. *Abbr.* MAb

mon/o·clo·nal/i·ty, *n.* the state or condition of having one specific type of antibody.

mon·o·cyte (-sīt/), *n.* a large white blood cell that is formed in bone marrow and spleen and circulates in the blood and may enter tissue to become a macrophage. —**mon/o·cyt/ic** (-sit/ik), *adj.* —**mon/o·cy/toid,** *adj.*

mon·o·gen·ic, *adj.* pertaining to or being controlled by a single gene. —**mon/o·gen/i·cal·ly,** *adv.*

mon·o·nu·cle·ar also **mon/o·nu/cle·ate** (-klē it, -āt/), *adj.* having only one nucleus.

mon·o·nu·cle·o·sis (-ō/sis), *n.* **1.** the presence of an abnormally large number of mononuclear leukocytes, or monocytes, in the blood. **2.** INFECTIOUS MONONUCLEOSIS.

mon·o·pho·bi·a, *n., pl.* -**bi·as.** an abnormal fear of being alone.

mon·o·ple·gi·a (-plē/jē ə, -plē/jə), *n.* paralysis of one extremity or muscle. —**mon/o·ple/gic** (-plē/jik, -plej/ik), *adj.*

mon·o·ploid (-ploid/), *adj.* **1.** having the basic or haploid number of chromosomes. —*n.* **2.** a monoploid cell or organism.

mon·o·sac/cha·ride/ (-sak/ə rid/, -ər id), *n.* a carbohydrate that does not hydrolyze, as glucose or fructose.

monoso/dium glu/ta·mate (glōō/tə māt/), *n.* a white, crystalline, water-soluble powder, $C_5H_8NNaO_4 \cdot H_2O$, used to intensify the flavor of foods. Also called **MSG.** See also **Chinese-restaurant syndrome.**

mon/o·some/ (-sōm/), *n.* **1.** a chromosome having no homologue, esp. an unpaired X chromosome. **2.** a protein-synthetic complex involving the translation of a messenger RNA molecule by a single ribosome.

mon/o·so/mic, *adj.* having one less than the usual diploid number of chromosomes.

mon·o·un·sat·u·rate (mon/ō un sach/ər it), *n.* a monounsaturated fat or fatty acid, as olive oil.

mon/o·un·sat/u·rat/ed (-ə rā/tid), *adj.* (of an organic compound) lacking a hydrogen bond at one point on the carbon chain.

mon/o·zy·got/ic (-zi got/ik) also **mon/o·zy/gous** (-zi/gəs), *adj.* developed from a single fertilized ovum, as identical twins.

mons (monz), *n., pl.* **mon·tes** (mon/tēz). **1.** MONS PUBIS. **2.** MONS VENERIS.

mons/ pu/bis (pyōō/bis), *n., pl.* **montes pubis.** a rounded prominence of fatty tissue over the pubic symphysis, covered with hair after puberty. Also called **mons.** Compare MONS VENERIS.

mons/ ve/ne·ris (ven/ər is), *n., pl.* **montes veneris.** the mons pubis, esp. of the human female. Also called **mons.**

Mon/te·zu/ma's revenge/ (mon/tə zōō/məz), *n. Slang.* traveler's diarrhea, esp. as experienced by some visitors to Mexico.

mor·bid·i·ty (môr bid/i tē), *n.* the proportion of a specific disease in a geographical locality.

morn/ing-af/ter pill/, *n.* a contraceptive pill containing only an estrogen and used by women within a few hours after sexual intercourse.

morn/ing sick/ness, *n.* nausea occurring in the early part of the day during the first months of pregnancy.

mo·ron (môr/on, mōr/-), *n.* a person of borderline intelligence in a former classification of mental retardation, having an intelligence quotient of 50 to 69. **—mo·ron·ic** (mə-ron/ik), *adj.*

mor·phal·lax·is (môr/fə lak/sis), *n., pl.* **-lax·es** (-lak/sēz). the regeneration of a lost body part by the reorganization and growth of remaining or adjacent tissue.

mor·phine (môr/fēn) also **mor·phi·a** (-fē ə), *n.* a white, bitter, crystalline alkaloid, $C_{17}H_{19}NO_3 \cdot H_2O$, the most important narcotic and addictive principle of opium, obtained by extraction and crystallization and used in medicine as a pain reliever and sedative. **—mor·phin/ic** (-fin/ik), *adj.*

mor/pho·gen/e·sis (môr/fə-), *n.* the development of structural features of an organism or part. **—mor/pho·ge·net/ic, mor/pho·gen/ic,** *adj.*

mor·pho·sis (-fō/sis), *n., pl.* **-ses** (-sēz). the sequence or manner of development in an organism or any of its parts. —**mor·phot′ic** (-fot′ik), *adj.*

mor·ti·fi·ca·tion (môr′tə fi kā′shən), *n.* the death of one part of a live body; gangrene; necrosis.

mor′ti·fy′, *v.,* **-fied, -fy·ing.** —*v.t.* **1.** to affect with gangrene or necrosis. —*v.i.* **2.** to become gangrened or necrosed.

mor·u·la (môr′ŏŏ lə, -yŏŏ-), *n., pl.* **-las, -lae** (-lē′). the mass of cells resulting from the cleavage of an ovum before the formation of a blastula. —**mor′u·lar,** *adj.*

mo·sa·ic (mō zā′ik), *n.* an organism exhibiting mosaicism.

mo·sa·i·cism (-ə siz′əm), *n.* a condition in which an organism or part is composed of two or more genetically distinct tissues.

mo′tion sick′ness, *n.* nausea and dizziness resulting from the effect of motion on the semicircular canals of the ear, as during car or plane travel.

mo·tor (mō′tər), *adj.* **1.** conveying an impulse that results or tends to result in motion: *a motor nerve cell.* **2.** of, pertaining to, or involving muscular movement: *a motor response.*

mo′tor neu′ron or **motoneuron,** *n.* a nerve cell that conducts impulses to a muscle, gland, or other effector.

moun′tain sick′ness, *n.* ALTITUDE SICKNESS.

mouth′-to-mouth′ resuscita′tion, *n.* a method of artificial respiration in which a person rhythmically blows air into the victim's lungs.

move (mŏŏv), *v.t.,* **moved, mov·ing.** to cause (the bowels) to discharge feces; evacuate.

move′ment (-mənt), *n.* BOWEL MOVEMENT.

MRI, magnetic resonance imaging.

mRNA, messenger RNA.

MS, multiple sclerosis.

M.S., Master of Surgery.

MSG, monosodium glutamate.

MSH, melanocyte-stimulating hormone: a pituitary gland hormone that causes darkening of the skin by increasing the production of melanin from melanocytes.

mtDNA, mitochondrial DNA.

mu, *Symbol.* micron.

mu·cif·er·ous (myŏŏ sif′ər əs), *adj.* secreting or containing mucus.

mu′cin (-sin), *n.* any of a class of mucoproteins abundant in saliva, gastric juices, and other mucous secretions of the body. —**mu′ci·nous,** *adj.*

mu′coid (-koid), *n.* any of a group of substances resembling the mucins, occurring in connective tissue, cysts, etc.

mu·co·lyt·ic (-kə lit′ik), *adj.* denoting or pertaining to enzymes that break down mucus.

mu′co·pol′y·sac′cha·ride′ (myŏŏ′kō-), *n.* GLYCOSAMINO-GLYCAN.

mu·co·pro·tein (myōō′kə-), *n.* a protein that yields carbohydrates as well as amino acids on hydrolysis.

mu·co·pu·ru·lent, *adj.* containing or composed of mucus and pus.

mu·co·sa (-kō′sə, -zə), *n., pl.* **-sae** (-sē, -zē). MUCOUS MEMBRANE. —**mu·co′sal**, *adj.*

mu·cous (-kəs), *adj.* **1.** of, consisting of, or resembling mucus. **2.** containing or secreting mucus. —**mu·cos′i·ty** (-kos′i tē), *n.*

mu′cous mem′brane, *n.* a mucus-secreting membrane lining all bodily passages that are open to the air, as parts of the digestive and respiratory tracts.

mu′cus (-kəs), *n.* a viscous solution of mucins, water, electrolytes, and white blood cells that is secreted by mucous membranes and serves to protect and lubricate the internal surfaces of the body.

mul·tip·a·ra (mul tip′ər ə), *n., pl.* **-a·ras**, **-a·rae** (-ə rē′). a woman who has borne two or more children or is parturient for the second time.

mul·tip·a·rous, *adj.* **1.** pertaining to a multipara. **2.** producing more than one at a birth. —**mul′ti·par′i·ty** (-ti-par′i tē), *n.*

mul′tiple alleles′, *n.* a series of three or more alternative or allelic forms of a gene, only two of which can exist in any normal, diploid individual. —**mul′tiple allel′ism**, *n.*

mul′tiple fac′tors, *n.* a series of two or more pairs of genes responsible for the development of complex, quantitative characters.

mul′tiple myelo′ma, *n.* a malignant plasma cell tumor of the bone marrow that destroys bone tissue.

mul′tiple personal′ity, *n.* a mental disorder in which a person acquires several personalities that function independently.

mul′tiple sclero′sis, *n.* a chronic degenerative disease marked by patchy destruction of the myelin that surrounds and insulates nerve fibers and mild to severe neural and muscular impairments.

mul·ti·vi·ta·min (mul′ti vī′tə min, mul′tī vī′-), *adj.* **1.** containing or consisting of several vitamins. —*n.* **2.** a compound of several vitamins.

mumps (mumps), *n. (used with a sing. v.)* an infectious disease characterized by inflammatory swelling of the parotid and usu. other salivary glands, and sometimes by inflammation of the testes or ovaries, caused by a paramyxovirus.

mur·mur (mûr′mər), *n.* an abnormal continuous or periodic sound heard within the body by auscultation, esp. one originating in the heart valves.

mus·cle (mus′əl), *n.* **1.** a tissue composed of elongated cells, the contraction of which produces movement in the body. **2.** a specific bundle of such tissue. —**mus′cu·lar** (-kyə lər), —**mus′cu·lar′i·ty**, *n.*

mus′cle fi′ber, *n.* one of the structural cells of a muscle.

mus′cle spin′dle, *n.* a proprioceptor in skeletal muscle, composed of muscle fibers and sensory nerve endings, that conveys information on the state of muscle stretch. Also called **stretch receptor.**

mus′cular dys′trophy, *n.* a hereditary disease characterized by gradual wasting of the muscles.

mus·cu·lo·skel′e·tal (mus/kyə lō-), *adj.* concerning, involving, or made up of both the muscles and the bones.

mus′tard plas′ter, *n.* a preparation of powdered mustard placed on a cloth and applied to the skin as a counterirritant.

mu·ta·gen (myōō′tə jən, -jen′), *n.* a substance or preparation capable of inducing or accelerating mutation. —**mu′ta·gen′ic,** *adj.* —**mu′ta·gen′i·cal·ly,** *adv.* —**mu′ta·ge·nic′i·ty,** *n.*

mu·ta·gen′e·sis, *n.* the origin and development of a mutation. —**mu′ta·ge·net′ic,** *adj.*

mu·tant (myōō′tnt), *n.* **1.** a new type of organism produced as the result of mutation. —*adj.* **2.** undergoing or resulting from mutation.

mu·tate (myōō′tāt), *v.i., v.t.* **-tat·ed, -tat·ing.** to undergo or cause to undergo mutation.

mu·ta·tion, *n.* **1.** a sudden departure from the parent type in one or more heritable characteristics, caused by a change in a gene or a chromosome. **2.** an individual, species, or the like resulting from such a departure. —**mu·ta′tion·al,** *adj.* —**mu·ta′tion·al·ly,** *adv.*

mut′ism, *n.* an inability to speak, due to a physical defect, conscious refusal, or psychogenic inhibition.

my·al·gi·a (mi al′jē ə, -jə), *n.* pain in the muscles; muscular rheumatism. —**my·al′gic,** *adj.*

my·as·the·ni·a (mi/əs thē′nē ə), *n.* muscle weakness. —**my·as·then′ic** (-then/ik), *adj.*

myasthe′nia gra′vis (grav′is, grä′vis), *n.* a disease of impaired transmission of motor nerve impulses, characterized by episodic weakness and fatigability of the muscles, caused by autoimmune destruction of acetylcholine receptors.

my·ce·to·ma (mi/si tō′mə), *n., pl.* **-mas, -ma·ta** (-mə tə) a chronic tumorous infection caused by any of various soil-dwelling fungi, usu. affecting the foot. —**my′ce·to′ma·tous,** *adj.*

my·co·bac·te·ri·um (mi/kō bak tēr′ē əm), *n., pl.* **-te·ri·a** (-tēr′ē ə) any of several rod-shaped aerobic bacteria of the genus *Mycobacterium*, certain species of which, as *M. tuberculosis,* are pathogenic.

my′co·plas′ma (-plaz′mə), *n., pl.* **-mas.** any of a group of very small microorganisms without cell walls, of the prokaryote class Mollicutes, that are a common cause of pneumonia and urinary tract infections.

my·co·sis (mi kō′sis), *n.* **1.** the presence of parasitic fungi in or on any part of the body. **2.** the condition caused by the presence of such fungi. —**my·cot′ic** (-kot/ik), *adj.*

my′co·tox′in, *n.* a toxin produced by a fungus.

my′co·vi′rus. *n., pl.* **-rus·es.** any fungus-infecting virus.

my·dri·a·sis (mi drī'ə sis, mi-), *n.* excessive or prolonged dilatation of the pupil of the eye, as the result of disease or the administration of a drug. Compare MIOSIS.

myd·ri·at·ic (mid'rē at'ik), *adj.* **1.** pertaining to or producing mydriasis. —*n.* **2.** a mydriatic drug.

my·el·en·ceph·a·lon (mī'ə len sef'ə lon'), *n., pl.* **-lons, -la** (-lə). the posterior section of the hindbrain, which develops into the medulla oblongata. —**my'el·en'ce·phal'ic** (-sə fal'ik), *adj.*

my·e·lin (mī'ə lin), *n.* a soft, white, fatty material in the membrane of Schwann cells and certain neuroglial cells of the nervous system: the substance of the myelin sheath. —**my·e·lin'ic**, *adj.*

my'e·li·nat'ed (-lə nā'tid), *adj.* (of a nerve) having a myelin sheath; medullated.

my'e·li·na'tion also **my'e·lin·i·za'tion**, *n.* the formation of a myelin sheath.

my'elin sheath', *n.* a discontinuous wrapping of myelin around certain nerve axons, serving to speed nerve impulses to muscles and other effectors.

my'e·li'tis (-lī'tis), *n.* **1.** inflammation of the substance of the spinal cord. **2.** inflammation of the bone marrow; osteomyelitis.

my'e·lo·cyte' (-lə sīt'), *n.* a cell of the bone marrow, esp. one developing into a granulocyte. —**my'e·lo·cyt'ic** (-sit'ik), *adj.*

my'e·lo·fi·bro'sis (mī'ə lō-), *n.* the replacement of bone marrow by fibrous tissue, characteristic of leukemia and certain other diseases.

my'e·log'e·nous (-loj'ə nəs) also **my'e·lo·gen'ic** (-lə jen'ik), *adj.* produced in the bone marrow.

my'e·lo·gram' (-lə gram'), *n.* an x-ray photograph of the spinal cord, following administration of a radiopaque substance into the space below the spinal arachnoid. —**my'e·log'ra·phy** (-log'rə fē), *n.*

my'e·lo'ma (-lō'mə), *n., pl.* **-mas, -ma·ta** (-mə tə). a tumor of plasma cells, arising in bone marrow and often occurring at multiple sites.

my'e·lop'a·thy (-lop'ə thē), *n., pl.* **-thies.** any disorder of the spinal cord or of bone marrow. —**my'e·lo·path'ic** (-lə path'ik), *adj.*

my·i·a·sis (mī'ə sis), *n., pl.* **-ses** (-sēz'). any disease that results from the infestation of tissues or cavities of the body by larvae of flies.

my·o·car'di·al infarc'tion (or **in'farct**) (mī'ə kär'dē-əl), *n.* HEART ATTACK. *Abbr.:* MI

my'o·car'di·o·graph', *n.* an instrument for recording the movements of the heart.

my'o·car·di'tis (mī'ō-), *n.* inflammation of the myocardium.

my'o·car'di·um (mī'ə kär'dē əm), *n., pl.* **-di·a** (-dē ə). the muscular substance of the heart. —**my'o·car'di·al**, *adj.*

my·oc·lo·nus (mī ok'lə nəs), *n.* an abrupt spasm or

twitch of a muscle or muscles, occurring in some neurological diseases. —**my·o·clon·ic** (mī'ə klon'ik), *adj.*

my·o·e·lec·tric (mī·ō-), *adj.* of or pertaining to electrical impulses generated by muscles of the body, which may be amplified and used esp. to control artificial limbs.

my·o·gen·ic (mī'ə-), *adj.* **1.** originating in muscle, as an impulse or sensation. **2.** producing muscle tissue.

my·o·glo·bin (mī'ə glō'bin, mī'ə glō'-) also **my·o·he·mo·glo·bin**, *n.* hemoglobin of muscle, weighing less and carrying more oxygen and less carbon monoxide than blood hemoglobin.

my·o·graph', *n.* an instrument for recording the contractions and relaxations of muscles. —**my·o·graph·ic**, *adj.* —**my·og·ra·phy** (-og'rə fē), *n.*

my·ol·o·gy (mī ol'ə jē), *n.* the science or branch of anatomy dealing with muscles. —**my·o·log·ic** (-ə loj'ik), **my·o·log·i·cal**, *adj.* —**my·ol·o·gist**, *n.*

my·o·ma (-ō'mə), *n., pl.* **-mas, -ma·ta** (-mə tə). a tumor composed of muscle tissue. —**my·om·a·tous** (-om'ə təs, -ō'mə-), *adj.*

my·op·a·thy (-op'ə thē), *n., pl.* **-thies.** any abnormality or disease of muscle tissue. —**my·o·path·ic** (-ə path'ik), *adj.*

my·o·pi·a (-ō'pē ə), *n.* a condition of the eye in which parallel rays are focused in front of the retina, objects being seen distinctly only when near to the eye; nearsightedness (opposed to *hyperopia*). —**my·op·ic** (-op'ik, -ō'pik), *adj.* —**my·op·i·cal·ly**, *adv.*

my·o·sin (-ə sin), *n.* the principal contractile protein of muscle.

my·o·sis (-ō'sis), *n.* MIOSIS. —**my·ot·ic** (-ot'ik), *adj., n.*

my·o·si·tis (-ə sī'tis), *n.* inflammation of muscle tissue. —**my·o·sit·ic** (-sit'ik), *adj.*

my·o·to·ni·a (-tō'nē ə), *n.* tonic muscle spasm or muscular rigidity. —**my·o·ton·ic** (-ton'ik), *adj.*

myth·o·ma·ni·a (mith'ə mā'nē ə), *n.* lying or exaggerating to an abnormal degree. —**myth'o·ma'ni·ac'**, *n., adj.*

myx·e·de·ma (mik'si dē'mə), *n.* a condition characterized by thickening of the skin, blunting of the senses and intellect, and labored speech, associated with hypothyroidism. —**myx'e·dem'a·tous** (-dem'ə təs, -dē'mə-), *adj.*

myx·o·ma (-sō'mə), *n., pl.* **-mas, -ma·ta** (-mə tə). a soft tumor composed of connective and mucoid tissue. —**myx·om'a·tous** (-som'ə təs), *adj.*

myx·o·ma·to·sis (-sə mə tō'sis), *n.* **1.** a condition characterized by the presence of many myxomas. **2.** a highly infectious viral disease of rabbits, artificially introduced into Great Britain and Australia to reduce the rabbit population.

myx·o·vi·rus (mik'sə vī'rəs, mik'sō vī'-), *n., pl.* **-rus·es. 1.** ORTHOMYXOVIRUS. **2.** PARAMYXOVIRUS.

N

N, *Symbol.* **1.** asparagine. **2.** nitrogen.

Na, *Symbol.* sodium.

NAD, nicotinamide adenine dinucleotide: a coenzyme, $C_{21}H_{27}N_7O_{14}P_2$, involved in many cellular oxidation-reduction reactions.

NADH, an abbreviation for the reduced form of NAD in electron transport reactions. [NAD + *H,* for hydrogen]

NADP, nicotinamide adenine dinucleotide phosphate: a coenzyme, $C_{21}H_{28}N_7O_{17}P_3$, similar in function to NAD in many oxidation-reduction reactions.

na·ive or **na·ïve** (nä ēv′), *adj.* not having previously been the subject of a scientific experiment, as an animal. —**na·ive′ly,** *adv.* —**na·ive′ness,** *n.*

nal·ox·one (nə lok′sōn, nal′ək sōn′), *n.* an analgesic narcotic antagonist, $C_{19}H_{21}NO_4$, used chiefly to counteract overdose.

nal·trex·one (nal trek′sōn), *n.* a nonaddictive substance, $C_{20}H_{23}NO_4$, used in the treatment of heroin addiction and opiate overdose.

nan·o·me·ter (nan′ə mē′tər, nā′nə-), *n.* a unit of measure equal to one billionth of a meter. *Abbr.:* nm

na·prox·en (nə prok′sən), *n.* a nonsteroidal anti-inflammatory substance, $C_{14}H_{14}O_3$.

nar·co·a·nal·y·sis (när′kō ə nal′ə sis), *n.* the treatment of a psychological disorder while the patient is under the influence of a barbiturate. Also called **nar′co·ther′a·py** (-ther′ə pē).

nar·co·lep·sy (när′kə lep′sē), *n.* a disorder characterized by frequent and uncontrollable attacks of deep sleep. —**nar′co·lep′tic,** *adj., n.*

nar·co·ma (-kō′mə), *n., pl.* **-mas, -ma·ta** (-mə tə). stupor produced by narcotics. —**nar·com′a·tous** (-kom′ə-təs), *adj.*

nar·co·sis (-sis), *n.* a state of drowsiness or stupor.

nar·cot·ic (-kot′ik), *n.* **1.** any of a class of habituating or addictive substances that blunt the senses and in increasing doses cause confusion, stupor, coma, and death: some are used in medicine to relieve intractable pain or induce anesthesia. —*adj.* **2.** of or pertaining to narcotics or their use. **3.** used by, or in the treatment of, narcotic addicts. —**nar·cot′i·cal·ly,** *adv.*

nar′row-an′gle glauco′ma, *n.* See under GLAUCOMA.

na·sal (nā′zəl), *adj.* of or pertaining to the nose.

na′so·lac′ri·mal duct′ (nā′zō lak′rə məl, nā′-), *n.* a membranous canal extending from the lacrimal sac to the nasal cavity, through which tears are discharged into the nose.

na′so·phar′ynx, *n., pl.* **-pha·ryn·ges, -phar·ynx·es.** the part of the pharynx behind and above the soft palate, directly continuous with the nasal passages. —**na′so·pha·ryn′ge·al,** *adj.*

na·tiv·ism (nā′ti viz′əm), *n.* the doctrine that certain knowledge, ideas, behavior, or capacities exist innately. —**na′tiv·ist,** *n., adj.* —**na′tiv·is′tic,** *adj.,*

na·tri·u·re·sis (nā′trə yŏŏ rē′sis), *n.* excretion of sodium in the urine. —**na′tri·u·ret′ic** (-ret′ik), *adj., n.*

nat·u·ral (nach′ər əl, nach′rəl), *adj.* having undergone little or no processing and containing no chemical additives: *natural food.*

nat′ural child′birth, *n.* childbirth involving little or no use of drugs or anesthesia and usu. involving a program in which the mother is psychologically and physically prepared for the birth process.

nat′ural kill′er cell′, *n.* a small killer cell that destroys virus-infected cells or tumor cells without activation by an immune system or antibody. Compare KILLER T CELL.

na·tur·op·a·thy (nā′chə rop′ə thē, nach′ə-), *n.* a method of treating disease that employs no surgery or synthetic drugs but uses fasting, special diets, massage, etc., to assist the natural healing processes. —**na′tur·o·path′** (-ə path′), *n.* —**na′tur·o·path′ic,** *adj.*

nau·se·a (nô′zē ə, -zhə, -sē ə, -shə), *n.* sickness at the stomach, esp. when accompanied by a loathing for food and an involuntary impulse to vomit.

nau·se·ant (-ənt), *adj.* **1.** producing nausea. —*n.* **2.** a nauseant agent.

nau·se·ate (-āt′), *v.t.,* **-at·ed, -at·ing.** to affect with nausea; sicken.

nau·se·at′ing, *adj.* causing sickness of the stomach; nauseous. —**nau′se·at′ing·ly,** *adv.*

nau·seous (-shəs, -zē əs), *adj.* **1.** affected with nausea; nauseated. **2.** causing nausea; sickening; nauseating. —**nau′seous·ly,** *adv.* —**nau′seous·ness,** *n.*

na·vel (nā′vəl), *n.* the depression in the surface of the abdomen where the umbilical cord was connected with the fetus; umbilicus.

na·vic·u·lar (nə vik′yə lər), *adj.* **1.** boat-shaped, as certain bones. —*n.* **2.** the bone at the radial end of the proximal row of the bones of the carpus. **3.** the bone in front of the talus on the inner side of the foot.

near′-point′, *n.* the point nearest the eye at which an object is clearly focused on the retina when accommodation of the eye is at a maximum. Compare FAR-POINT.

near′sight′ed, *adj.* seeing distinctly at a short distance only; myopic. —**near′sight′ed·ness,** *n.*

neb·u·la (neb′yə lə), *n., pl.* **-lae** (-lē′, -li′), **-las.** *Pathol.* **1.** a faint opacity in the cornea. **2.** cloudiness in the urine.

nec·ro·bi·o·sis (nek′rō bi ō′sis), *n.* the death of cells or tissue caused by aging or disease. —**nec′ro·bi·ot′ic** (-ot′ik), *adj.*

nec·ro·phil·i·a (nek′rə fil′ē ə), *n.* an erotic attraction to corpses. —**nec′ro·phile′** (-fīl′), *n.* —**nec′ro·phil′i·ac,** **nec′ro·phil′ic,** *adj., n.*

ne·croph·il·ism (nə krof′ə liz/əm), *n.* NECROPHILIA.

nec·ro·pho·bi·a (nek′rə fō′bē ə), *n.* an abnormal fear of dead bodies. **—nec′ro·pho′bic,** *adj.*

nec·rop·sy (nek′rop sē), *n., pl.* **-sies.** the examination of a body after death; autopsy.

ne·crose (nə krōs′, ne-, nek′rōs), *v.t., v.i.,* **-crosed, -cros·ing.** to affect or be affected with necrosis.

ne·cro·sis (nə krō′sis), *n.* death of a circumscribed portion of animal or plant tissue. **—ne·crot′ic** (-krot′ik), *adj.* **—nec·ro·tize** (nek′rə tiz′), *v.i., v.t.,* **-tized, -tiz·ing.**

nee·dle (nēd′l), *n.* **1.** a slender, pointed, steel instrument used in sewing or piercing tissues, as in suturing. **2.** a hypodermic needle. **3.** *Med.* an injection of a drug or medicine; shot.

nee′dle bi′opsy, *n.* the removal for diagnostic study of a small amount of tissue by means of a long, hollow needle.

neg·a·tive (neg′ə tiv), *adj.* failing to show a positive result in a diagnostic test.

neg′ative trans′fer, *n.* interference with new learning because of an established pattern of previous learning.

neg·a·tiv·ism (neg′ə tiv iz′əm), *n. Psychol.* a tendency to resist external commands, suggestions, or expectations, or internal stimuli, as hunger, by doing nothing or something contrary or unrelated to the stimulus. **—neg′a·tiv·ist,** *n.* **—neg′a·tiv·is′tic,** *adj.*

nem·a·tode (nem′ə tōd′), *n.* any unsegmented worm of the phylum Nematoda, having an elongated, cylindrical body and often parasitic on animals and plants; a roundworm.

Nem·bu·tal (nem′byə tôl′, -tal′), *Trademark.* a brand of pentobarbital.

ne·o·cor·tex (nē′ō kôr′teks), *n., pl.* **-ti·ces** (-tə sēz′). the outermost portion of the cerebral cortex, highly developed in mammals. **—ne′o·cor′ti·cal** (-ti kəl), *adj.*

ne·o·Freu·di·an (nē′ō froi′dē ən), *adj.* **1.** of or pertaining to a group of psychoanalytic thinkers whose modifications of Freudian analytic theory emphasize ego functions and interpersonal relationships. **—** *n.* **2.** a psychoanalyst advocating such a view.

ne·o·gen·e·sis, *n.* the regeneration of tissue.

ne·ol·o·gism (nē ol′ə jiz′əm), *n.* a word invented and understood only by the speaker, occurring most often in the speech of schizophrenics. **—ne·ol′o·gis′tic,** *adj.* **—ne·ol′o·gize′,** *v.i.,* **-gized, -giz·ing.**

ne·ol·o·gy, *n., pl.* **-gies.** NEOLOGISM. **—ne′o·log′i·cal** (-ə loj′i kəl), *adj.* **—ne′o·log′ic,** *adj.* **—ne′o·log′i·cal·ly,** *adv.*

ne·o·nate (nē′ə nāt′), *n.* a newborn child, or one in its first 28 days. **—ne′o·na′tal,** *adj.*

ne·o·na·tol·o·gy (nē′ō nā tol′ə jē), *n.* the study of the development and disorders of newborn children. **—ne′o·na·tol′o·gist,** *n.*

ne·o·pla·sia (-plā′zhə, -zhē ə, -zē ə), *n.* the formation and growth of neoplasms.

ne·o·plasm (nē′ə plaz′əm), *n.* a new, often uncontrolled growth of abnormal tissue; tumor. —**ne'o·plas'tic** (-plas'-tik), *adj.*

ne·o·stig·mine (nē'ō stig'mēn, -min), *n.* a synthetic anticholinesterase, $C_{12}H_{19}N_2O_2$, used in the treatment of myasthenia gravis, glaucoma, and postoperative urinary bladder distention.

Ne·o·Sy·neph·rine (nē'ō si nef'rin, -rēn), *Trademark.* a brand of phenylephrine.

ne·o·vas·cu·lar·i·za'tion, *n.* the development of new blood vessels, esp. in tissues where circulation has been impaired by trauma or disease.

ne·phrec·to·my (nə frek'tə mē), *n., pl.* **-mies.** the surgical excision of a kidney.

ne·phri'tis (-frī'tis), *n.* inflammation of the kidneys, esp. in Bright's disease. —**ne·phrit'ic** (-frit'ik), *adj.*

ne·phrol·o·gy (-frol'ə jē), *n.* the branch of medical science that deals with the kidney. —**ne·phrol'o·gist,** *n.*

neph·ron (nef'ron), *n.* the filtering and excretory unit of the kidney, consisting of the glomerulus and convoluted tubule.

ne·phrop·a·thy (nə frop'ə thē), *n.* any disease of the kidney. —**neph·ro·path·ic** (nef'rə path'ik), *adj.*

ne·phro'sis (-frō'sis), *n.* kidney disease, esp. marked by noninflammatory degeneration of the tubular system. —**ne·phrot'ic** (-frot'ik), *adj.*

ne·phrot'o·my (-frot'ə mē), *n., pl.* **-mies.** surgical incision into the kidney.

nerve (nûrv), *n.* one or more bundles of fibers forming part of a system that conveys impulses of sensation, motion, etc., between the brain or spinal cord and other parts of the body.

nerve' cell', *n.* NEURON.

nerve' cord', *n.* the hollow dorsal tract of nervous tissue that constitutes the central nervous system of all chordates and that developed as the spinal cord and brain of vertebrates.

nerve' fi'ber, *n.* an axon or dendrite of a neuron.

nerve' growth' fac'tor, *n.* a protein that promotes the growth, organization, and maintenance of sympathetic and some sensory nerve cells. *Abbr.:* NGF

nerve' im'pulse, *n.* a progressive wave of electric and chemical activity along a nerve fiber, stimulating or inhibiting action.

nerv'ous break'down, *n.* (not in technical use) any disabling mental or emotional disorder requiring treatment.

nerv'ous sys'tem, *n.* the system of neurons, neurochemicals, and allied structures involved in receiving sensory stimuli, generating and coordinating responses, and controlling bodily activities: in vertebrates it includes the brain, spinal cord, nerves, and ganglia.

net'tle rash', *n.* hives caused by contact with various plants.

neu·ral (nŏor'əl, nyŏor'-), *adj.* of or pertaining to a nerve or the nervous system. —**neu'ral·ly,** *adv.*

neu·ral crest′, *n.* a group of ectodermal cells of the embryo that develop into a variety of tissues, including spinal and autonomic ganglia, connective tissue around the brain and spinal cord, and parts of the facial bones.

neu·ral·gia (nŏŏ ral′jə, nyŏŏ-), *n.* sharp and paroxysmal pain along the course of a nerve. **—neu·ral′gic,** *adj.*

neu·ral tube′, *n.* a tube formed in the early embryo by the closure of ectodermal tissue and later developing into the spinal cord and brain.

neur·as·the·ni·a (nŏŏr′əs thē′nē ə, nyŏŏr′-), *n.* a pattern of symptoms including chronic fatigue, sleep disturbances, and persistent aches, often linked with depression. **—neur·as·then′ic** (-then′ik), *adj., n.* **—neur′as·then′i·cal·ly,** *adv.*

neu·rec·to·my (nŏŏ rek′tə mē, nyŏŏ-), *n., pl.* **-mies.** the surgical removal of part or all of a nerve.

neu·ri·lem·ma (nŏŏr′ə lem′ə, nyŏŏr′-), *n., pl.* **-mas.** the thin outer membrane of the myelin sheath of a myelinated nerve fiber or of the axon of some unmyelinated nerve fibers. **—neu·ri·lem′mal,** *adj.*

neu·ri·tis (nŏŏ rī′tis, nyŏŏ-), *n.* inflammation of a nerve, often marked by pain, numbness or tingling, or paralysis. **—neu·rit′ic** (-rit′ik), *adj.*

neu·ro·a·nat·o·my (nŏŏr′ō ə nat′ə mē, nyŏŏr′-), *n., pl.* **-mies.** the branch of anatomy that deals with the nervous system. **—neu·ro·a·nat′o·mist,** *n.* **—neu·ro·an′a·tom′i·cal** (-an′ə tom′i kəl), **neu·ro·an′a·tom′ic,** *adj.*

neu·ro·blas·to′ma (-bla stō′mə), *n., pl.* **-mas, -ma·ta** (-mə tə). a malignant tumor of immature nerve cells, most often affecting the young.

neu·ro·chem′i·cal, *adj.* **1.** of or pertaining to neurochemistry. **—n. 2.** a substance that affects the nervous system.

neu·ro·chem·is·try, *n.* the study of the chemistry of the nervous system. **—neu·ro·chem′ist,** *n.*

neu·ro·en′do·crine, *adj.* of or pertaining to the interactions between the nervous and endocrine systems, esp. in relation to hormones.

neu·ro·en′do·cri·nol′o·gy, *n.* the study of the anatomical and physiological interactions between the nervous and endocrine systems. **—neu·ro·en′do·crin′o·log′i·cal,** *adj.* **—neu·ro·en′do·cri·nol′o·gist,** *n.*

neu·ro·fi·bril (nŏŏr′ə fī′brəl, -fib′rəl, nyŏŏr′-), *n.* a fibril of a nerve cell. **—neu·ro·fi·bril·lar, neu·ro·fi′bril·lar′y,** *adj.*

neu·ro·fi·bro′ma, *n., pl.* **-mas, -ma·ta** (-mə tə). a benign neoplasm composed of the fibrous elements of a nerve.

neu·ro·fi·bro·ma·to′sis (-tō′sis), *n.* a genetic disorder characterized by brown patches on the skin, neurofibromas of the skin and internal organs, and in some cases skeletal deformity.

neu·ro·gen·ic (nŏŏr′ə jen′ik, nyŏŏr′-) also **neu·rog·e·nous** (nŏŏ roj′ə nəs, nyŏŏ-), *adj.* **1.** originating in a nerve or nerve tissue. **2.** caused by disease or abnormality of the nervous system.

neu·rog·li·a (noŏ rog/lē ə, nyoŏ-), *n.* a class of cells in the brain and spinal cord that form a supporting and insulating structure for the neurons. Also called **glia.** —**neu·rog/li·al,** *adj.*

neu·ro·hor·mo/nal (noŏr/ō-, nyoŏr/-), *adj.* **1.** pertaining to or controlled by a neurohormone. **2.** pertaining to, affecting, or controlled by hormones and either neurotransmitters or neurons.

neu/ro·hor/mone, *n.* any of various substances, as antidiuretic hormone, formed in the nervous system and delivered to an effector organ through blood circulation.

neu·ro·hy·poph/y·sis (-hi pof/ə sis, -hi-), *n., pl.* **-ses** (-sēz/). POSTERIOR PITUITARY. —**neu/ro·hy·poph/y·se/al** (-sē/əl), *adj.*

neu·ro·im/mu·nol/o·gy, *n.* a branch of immunology concerned with the interactions between immunological and nervous system functions, esp. as they apply to various autoimmune diseases.

neurol., **1.** neurological. **2.** neurology.

neu·ro·lep/tic (noŏr/ə lep/tik, nyoŏr/-), *adj., n.* ANTIPSYCHOTIC.

neu·rol·o·gy (noŏ rol/ə jē, nyoŏ-), *n.* the branch of medicine dealing with the nervous system. —**neu/ro·log/i·cal** (-ə loj/i kəl), *adj.* —**neu·ro·log/i·cal·ly,** *adv.* —**neu·rol/o·gist,** *n.*

neu·ro·ma (-rō/mə), *n., pl.* **-mas, -ma·ta** (-mə tə). a tumor formed of nerve tissue. —**neu·rom/a·tous** (-rom/ə-təs), *adj.*

neu·ro·mod/u·la/tor (-moj/ə lā/tər), *n.* any of various substances, as certain hormones and amino acids, that influence the function of neurons but do not act as neurotransmitters.

neu/ro·mo/tor, *adj.* **1.** NEUROMUSCULAR. **2.** of or pertaining to the effects of nerve impulses on muscles.

neu·ro·mus/cu·lar, *adj.* pertaining to or affecting both nerves and muscles.

neu·ron (noŏr/on, nyoŏr/-), *n.* a specialized, impulse-conducting cell that is the functional unit of the nervous system, consisting of the cell body and its processes, the axon and dendrites. Also called **nerve cell.** Also, *esp. Brit.,* **neu·rone** (-ōn). —**neu·ron·al** (noŏr/ə nl, nyoŏr/-, noŏ-rōn/l, nyoŏ-), *adj.*

neu·ro·pa·thol/o·gy (noŏr/ō-, nyoŏr/-), *n.* the pathology of the nervous system. —**neu/ro·path/o·log/i·cal,** *adj.* —**neu/ro·pa·thol/o·gist,** *n.*

neu·rop·a·thy (noŏ rop/ə thē, nyoŏ-), *n.* any diseased condition of the nervous system. —**neu·ro·path/ic** (noŏr/-ə path/ik, nyoŏr/-), *adj.* —**neu/ro·path/i·cal·ly,** *adv.*

neu·ro·pep/tide (noŏr/ō pep/tid, nyoŏr/-), *n.* any of various short-chain peptides, as endorphins, that function as neuromodulators in the nervous system and as hormones in the endocrine system.

neu·ro·phar·ma·col·o·gy, *n.* the branch of pharmacology concerned with the nervous system. —**neu·ro·phar·ma·co·log·i·cal**, *adj.* —**neu·ro·phar·ma·col·o·gist**, *n.*

neu·ro·phys·i·ol·o·gy, *n.* the branch of physiology dealing with the nervous system. —**neu·ro·phys·i·o·log·i·cal**, *adj.* —**neu·ro·phys·i·ol·o·gist**, *n.*

neu·ro·psy·chi·a·try, *n.* the branch of medicine dealing with diseases involving the mind and nervous system. —**neu·ro·psy·chi·at·ric**, *adj.* —**neu·ro·psy·chi·a·trist**, *n.*

neu·ro·sci·ence, *n.* the field of study encompassing the various scientific disciplines dealing with all the aspects of the nervous system. —**neu·ro·sci·en·tif·ic**, *adj.* —**neu·ro·sci·en·tist**, *n.*

neu·ro·sen·so·ry, *adj.* of or pertaining to the sensory role of the nervous system.

neu·ro·sis (nŏŏ rō′sis, nyŏŏ-), *n., pl.* **-ses** (-sēz). **1.** Also called **psychoneurosis.** a functional disorder in which feelings of anxiety, obsessional thoughts, compulsive acts, and physical complaints without objective evidence of disease, occurring in various degrees and patterns, dominate the personality. **2.** a relatively mild personality disorder typified by excessive anxiety or indecision and a degree of social maladjustment.

neu·ro·sur·ger·y, *n.* surgery of the brain or other nerve tissue. —**neu·ro·sur·geon** (-jən), *n.* —**neu·ro·sur·gi·cal**, *adj.*

neu·rot·ic (nŏŏ rot′ik, nyŏŏ-), *adj.* **1.** of, pertaining to, or characteristic of neurosis. —*n.* **2.** a neurotic person. —**neu·rot·ic·al·ly**, *adv.* —**neu·rot′i·cism** (-ə siz′əm), *n.*

neu·rot·o·my (-rot′ə mē), *n., pl.* **-mies.** the surgical cutting of a nerve.

neu·ro·tox·ic (nŏŏr′ō tok′sik, nyŏŏr′-), *adj.* poisonous to nerve tissue. —**neu·ro·tox·ic·i·ty** (-sis′i tē), *n.*

neu·ro·tox·in, *n.* a neurotoxic substance, as rattlesnake venom.

neu·ro·trans·mis·sion, *n.* the transmission of a nerve impulse across a synapse.

neu·ro·trans·mit·ter, *n.* any of several chemical substances, as epinephrine or acetylcholine, that transmit nerve impulses across a synapse.

neu·ro·trop·ic (nŏŏr′ə trop′ik, -trō′pik, nyŏŏr′-), *adj.* having an affinity for nerve cells or tissue: *a neurotropic virus.*

neu·ru·la (nŏŏr′ə lə, nyŏŏr′-), *n., pl.* **-las, -lae** (-lē′, -li′). an embryo in the stage from the development of neural tissue to the formation of the neural tube. —**neu′ru·lar**, *adj.* —**neu′ru·la′tion**, *n.*

neu·tro·pe·ni·a (nŏŏ′trə pē′nē ə, nyŏŏ′-), *n.* an abnormal decline of neutrophils in the blood.

neu·tro·phil (nŏŏ′trə fil, nyŏŏ′-) also **neu·tro·phile** (-fil′), *adj.* **1.** (of a cell or cell fragment) easily stained with neutral dyes. —*n.* **2.** a phagocytic white blood cell that contains neutrophil granules.

ne·vus (nē′vəs), *n., pl.* **-vi** (-vī). any congenital anomaly of

the skin, including moles and various types of birthmarks.
—**ne′void,** *adj.*

NGF, nerve growth factor.

NGU, nongonococcal urethritis.

ni·a·cin (nī′ə sin), *n.* NICOTINIC ACID.

ni′a·cin′a·mide′ (-ə mid′), *n.* NICOTINAMIDE.

nick (nik), *n.* a break in a strand of a DNA or RNA molecule.

nic·o·tin·a·mide (nik′ə tin′ə mid′, -mid, -tē′nə-), *n.* a soluble crystal amide of nicotinic acid that is a component of the vitamin B complex and is present in most foods. Also called **niacinamide.**

nicotin′amide ad′enine di·nu′cle·o·tide (dī nōō′klē-ə tīd′, -nyōō′-), *n.* See NAD.

nicotin′amide ad′enine dinu′cleotide phos′phate, *n.* See NADP.

nic·o·tine (nik′ə tēn′, -tin, nik′ə tēn′), *n.* a colorless, oily, water-soluble, highly toxic liquid alkaloid, $C_{10}H_{14}N_2$, found in tobacco. —**nic′o·tined′,** *adj.* —**nic′o·tine·less,** *adj.*

nic·o·tin·ic (nik′ə tin′ik, -tē′nik), *adj.* **1.** of, pertaining to, or containing nicotine. **2.** related to or imitating the effects of nicotine.

nic′otin′ic ac′id, *n.* a crystalline acid, $C_6H_5NO_2$, that is a component of the vitamin B complex, occurring in animal products, yeast, etc. Also called **niacin, vitamin B₃.**

nic·o·tin·ism (nik′ə tē niz′əm, -ti-, nik′ə tīn′iz-), *n.* a pathological condition caused by excessive use of tobacco; nicotine poisoning.

ni·da·tion (nī dā′shən), *n.* implantation of an embryo in the lining of the uterus.

ni·dus (nī′dəs), *n., pl.* **-di** (-dī). any focal point in the body where bacteria or other infectious organisms tend to thrive. —**ni′dal,** *adj.*

night′ blind′ness, *n.* a condition in which vision is normal in daylight but abnormally poor in dim light. —**night′-blind′,** *adj.*

night′ ter′ror, *n.* a sudden feeling of extreme fear that awakens a sleeping person and is not associated with a dream.

NIH, National Institutes of Health.

ni·trite (nī′trīt), *n.* SODIUM NITRITE.

ni·tro·gen (nī′trə jən), *n.* a colorless, odorless, gaseous element that constitutes about four-fifths of the volume of the atmosphere and is present in combined form in animal and vegetable tissues, esp. in proteins. *Symbol:* N; *at. wt.:* 14.0067; *at. no.:* 7; *density:* 1.2506 g/l at 0°C and 760 mm pressure.

ni·trog·en·ase (nī troj′ə nās′, -nāz′, nī′trə jə-), *n.* an enzyme complex that catalyzes the reduction of molecular nitrogen in the nitrogen-fixation process of bacteria.

ni′trogen bal′ance, *n.* the difference between the amount of nitrogen taken in and the amount excreted or lost.

ni′trogen mus′tard, *n.* any of the class of poisonous,

blistering compounds, as $C_5H_{11}Cl_2N$, analogous in composition to mustard gas but containing nitrogen instead of sulfur: used in the treatment of cancer and similar diseases.

ni'trogen narco'sis, *n.* a stupor or euphoria induced in deep-sea divers when nitrogen from air enters the blood at higher than atmospheric pressure. Also called **rapture of the deep.**

ni·tro·glyc·er·in (nī'trə glis'ər in) also **ni'tro·glyc'er·ine** (-ər in, -ə rēn'), *n.* an oily liquid, $C_3H_5N_3O_9$, used in medicine as a vasodilator, esp. in tablet form.

ni'trous ox'ide (nī'trəs), *n.* a colorless, sweet-smelling gas, N_2O, that may induce euphoria when inhaled: used for mild anesthesia.

nm, nanometer.

noc·tam·bu·lism (nok tam'byə liz'əm) *n.* sleepwalking; somnambulism. —**noc·tam'bu·list,** *n.*

noc·tu·ri·a (nok tŏŏr'ē ə, -tyŏŏr'-), *n.* nighttime urination.

noc·tur'nal emis'sion, *n.* involuntary ejaculation of semen during sleep.

node (nōd), *n. Pathol.* circumscribed swelling.

nod·ule (noj'ōōl), *n.* a small, rounded mass or lump. —**nod'u·lar,** *adj.*

no·ma (nō'mə), *n., pl.* **-mas.** a gangrenous ulceration of the mouth or genitalia, occurring mainly in debilitated children.

non-A, non-B hepatitis (non'ā' non'bē'), *n.* HEPATITIS NON-A, NON-B.

non·com·pli·ance (non'kəm plī'əns), *n.* failure or refusal to comply, as with a prescribed medical regimen. —**non'com·pli'ant, non'com·ply'ing,** *adj., adv.*

non·gon·o·coc'cal urethri'tis (non gon'ə kok'əl), *n.* a sexually transmitted infection of the urethra caused by the parasite *Chlamydia trachomatis,* or the mycoplasma *Ureaplasma urealyticum. Abbr.:* NGU

non'in·va'sive, *adj.* **1.** not invading adjacent cells, vessels, or tissues; localized: *a noninvasive tumor.* **2.** not entering or penetrating the body. —**non'in·va'sive·ly,** *adv.*

non'pre·scrip'tion, *adj.* (of drugs) legally purchasable without a doctor's prescription; over-the-counter.

non·self', *n.* any antigen-bearing foreign material that enters the body and normally stimulates an attack by the body's immune system (disting. from *self*).

non·sense (non'sens, -səns), *n.* a DNA sequence that does not code for an amino acid and is not transcribed (disting. from *sense*). —**non·sen'si·cal,** *adj.* —**non·sen'si·cal·ly,** *adv.* —**non·sen'si·cal·ness, non'sen·si·cal'i·ty,** *n.*

non·ste·roi·dal (non'ste roid'l, -sti-), *adj.* **1.** of or pertaining to a substance that is not a steroid but has similar effects. —*n.* **2.** any such substance, esp. an anti-inflammatory drug, as ibuprofen.

non·vi·a·ble (non vī'ə bəl), *adj.* not capable of living, growing, and developing, as an embryo or seed. —**non'vi·a·bil'i·ty,** *n.*

nor·a·dren·a·line (nôr′ə dren′l in, -ēn′) also **nor·a·dren·a·lin** (-in), *n.* NOREPINEPHRINE.

nor·ep·i·neph·rine (nôr′ep ə nef′rin, -rēn), *n.* a neurotransmitter that is similar to epinephrine, acts to constrict blood vessels and dilate bronchi, and is used esp. in medical emergencies to raise blood pressure.

nor·eth·in·drone (nôr eth′in drōn′), *n.* a progestin, $C_{20}H_{26}O_2$, used esp. as an oral contraceptive in combination with an estrogen.

nor·mo·ten·sive (nôr′mō ten′siv), *adj.* **1.** characterized by normal arterial blood pressure. —*n.* **2.** a normotensive person.

Nor′plant (nôr′plant′, -plänt′), *Trademark.* a long-term contraceptive for women, usu. effective for 5 years, consisting of several small slow-release capsules of progestin implanted under the skin.

North′ern blot′, *n.* a test for the presence of a specific gene in a sample, as in testing blood for a hereditary defect, by separating RNA fragments from the sample and observing whether they bind with labeled DNA or RNA from a copy of the gene in question.

nose′bleed′, *n.* bleeding from the nostril; epistaxis.

nose′ job′, *n. Informal.* RHINOPLASTY.

nos·o·co·mi·al (nos′ə kō′mē əl), *adj.* (of infections) contracted in a hospital.

no·sog·ra·phy (nō sog′rə fē), *n.* the systematic description of diseases. —**no·sog′ra·pher,** *n.* —**nos·o·graph·ic** (nos′ə graf′ik), **nos′o·graph′i·cal,** *adj.* —**nos′o·graph′i·cal·ly,** *adv.*

no·sol·o·gy (nō sol′ə jē), *n.* **1.** the branch of medicine dealing with the systematic classification of diseases. **2.** a list or classification of diseases. —**nos·o·log·i·cal** (nos′ə·loj′i kəl), *adj.* —**no·sol′o·gist,** *n.*

nos·trum (nos′trəm), *n.* a medicine sold with false or exaggerated claims; quack medicine.

no·to·chord (nō′tə kôrd′), *n.* a long, flexible, rod-shaped structure that supports the vertical axis of the body in chordates and vertebrate embryos, in the latter developing into the spinal column. —**no′to·chord′al,** *adj.*

No·vo·caine (nō′və kān′), *Trademark.* a brand of procaine.

NP, nurse-practitioner.

nu′clear med′icine, *n.* diagnostic and therapeutic medical techniques using radionuclides or radioisotopes.

nu·cle·ase (nōō′klē ās′, -āz′, nyōō′-), *n.* any enzyme that catalyzes the hydrolysis of nucleic acids.

nu·cle′ic ac′id (nōō klē′ik, -klā′-, nyōō-), *n.* any of a group of long, linear macromolecules, either DNA or various types of RNA, that carry genetic information directing all cellular functions: composed of linked nucleotides.

nu·cle·o·cap·sid (nōō′klē ə kap′sid), *n.* the nucleic acid core and surrounding capsid of a virus; the basic viral structure.

nu·cle·oid′, *n.* **1.** the central region in a prokaryotic cell, as a bacterium, that contains the chromosomes and that has no surrounding membrane. —*adj.* **2.** resembling a nucleus.

nu·cle·o·pro·tein (nōō′klē ō prō′tēn, -tē in, nyōō′-), *n.* any of the class of conjugated proteins occurring in cells and consisting of a protein combined with a nucleic acid, essential for cell division and reproduction.

nu′cle·o·side′ (-ə sīd′), *n.* any of the class of compounds derived by the hydrolysis of nucleic acids or nucleotides, consisting typically of deoxyribose or ribose combined with adenine, guanine, cytosine, uracil, or thymine.

nu′cle·o·some′ (-sōm′), *n.* any of the repeating subunits of chromatin occurring at intervals along a strand of DNA, consisting of DNA coiled around histone.

nu′cle·o·tide′ (-tīd′), *n.* any of a group of molecules that, when linked together, form the building blocks of DNA or RNA: in DNA the group comprises a phosphate group, the bases adenine, cytosine, guanine, and thymine, and a pentose sugar; in RNA the thymine base is replaced by uracil.

nude′ mouse′, *n.* a hairless mutant laboratory-bred mouse having an immune system deficiency and able to accept grafts of foreign tissue.

nul·lip·a·ra (nu lip′ər ə), *n., pl.* **-a·rae** (-ə rē′). a woman who has never borne a child. —**nul·lip·a·ri·ty** (nul′ə par′i-tē), *n.* —**nul·lip′a·rous,** *adj.*

nurse (nûrs), *n.* a person formally educated and trained in the care of the sick or infirm, esp. a registered nurse.

nurse′-prac·ti′tion·er or **nurse′ prac·ti′tion·er,** *n.* a registered nurse qualified to diagnose and treat common or minor ailments. *Abbr.:* NP

nu·tri·ent (nōō′trē ənt, nyōō′-), *adj.* **1.** nourishing; providing nourishment or nutriment. **2.** containing or conveying nutriment, as solutions or vessels of the body. —*n.* **3.** a nutrient substance.

nu′tri·ment (-trə mənt), *n.* **1.** any substance that, taken into a living organism, serves to sustain it, promoting growth, replacing loss, and providing energy. **2.** anything that nourishes; nourishment; food. —**nu′tri·men′tal** (-men′tl), *adj.*

nu·tri′tion (nōō trish′ən, nyōō-), *n.* **1.** the act or process of nourishing or of being nourished. **2.** the study or science of the dietary requirements of humans and animals for proper health and development. **3.** the process by which organisms take in and utilize food material. **4.** food; nutriment. —**nu·tri′tion·al, nu·tri′tion·ar′y,** *adj.* —**nu·tri′tion·al·ly,** *adv.*

nu·tri′tion·ist, *n.* a person who is trained or expert in the science of nutrition.

nu·tri′tious, *adj.* providing nourishment, esp. to a high degree; nourishing; healthful. —**nu·tri′tious·ly,** *adv.* —**nu·tri′tious·ness,** *n.*

nu·tri·tive, *adj.* **1.** serving to nourish; nutritious. **2.** of, pertaining to, or concerned with nutrition. —*n.* **3.** an item of nourishing food. —**nu′tri·tive·ly,** *adv.* —**nu′tri·tive·ness,** *n.*

nyc·ta·lo·pi·a (nik/tl ō/pē ə), *n.* **1.** NIGHT BLINDNESS. **2.** HEMERALOPIA. —**nyc/ta·lop/ic** (-op/ik), *adj.*

nym·pho·ma·ni·a (nim/fə mā/nē ə, -mān/yə), *n.* abnormal, uncontrollable sexual desire in a female. Compare SATYRIASIS. —**nym/pho·ma/ni·ac/**, *n., adj.* —**nym/pho·ma·ni/a·cal**, *adj.*

nys·tag·mus (ni stag/məs), *n.* a persistent, rapid, involuntary side-to-side eye movement. —**nys·tag/mic**, *adj.*

O, *Symbol.* **1.** a major blood group. Compare ABO SYSTEM. **2.** oxygen.

OB, 1. Also, **ob** obstetrical. **2.** obstetrician. **3.** obstetrics.

ob-gyn or **ob/gyn** (ō′bē′jē′wi′en′; *sometimes* ob′gin′), **1.** obstetrics and gynecology. **2.** obstetrician-gynecologist. **3.** obstetrical-gynecological.

ob·li·gate (ob′li git, -gāt′), *adj.* restricted to a particular condition of life, as certain organisms that can survive only in the absence of oxygen (opposed to *facultative*).

obses′sive-compul′sive, *adj.* **1.** of, pertaining to, or characterized by the persistent intrusion of unwanted thoughts accompanied by ritualistic actions, regarded as a form of neurosis. —*n.* **2.** a person with obsessive-compulsive characteristics.

ob·so·lete (ob′sə lēt′, ob′sə lēt′), *adj.* rudimentary in comparison with the corresponding part or trait in related species or in individuals of the opposite sex.

obstet., 1. obstetric. **2.** obstetrics.

ob·stet·ri·cal (əb ste′tri kəl) *also* **ob·stet′ric,** *adj.* **1.** of or pertaining to the care and treatment of women in childbirth and during the period before and after delivery. **2.** of or pertaining to childbirth or obstetrics. —**ob·stet′ri·cal·ly,** *adv.*

ob·ste·tri·cian (ob′sti trish′ən), *n.* a physician who specializes in obstetrics.

ob·stet·rics (əb ste′triks), *n.* (*used with a sing. v.*) the branch of medical science concerned with childbirth and caring for and treating women in or in connection with childbirth.

oc·cip·i·tal (ok sip′i tl), *adj.* **1.** of, pertaining to, or situated near the occiput or the occipital bone. —*n.* **2.** any of several parts of the occiput, esp. the occipital bone. —**oc·cip′i·tal·ly,** *adv.*

occip′ital bone′, *n.* a curved, compound bone forming the back and part of the base of the skull.

occip′ital lobe′, *n.* the most posterior lobe of each cerebral hemisphere, behind the parietal and temporal lobes.

oc·ci·put (ok′sə put′, -pət), *n.*, *pl.* **oc·ci·puts, oc·cip·i·ta** (ok sip′i tə). the back part of the head or skull.

oc·cult (ə kult′, ok′ult), *adj.* not readily detectable, esp. at the place of origin: *occult blood.* —**oc·cult′ly,** *adv.* —**oc·cult′ness,** *n.*

occupa′tional ther′apy, *n.* therapy that utilizes useful and creative activities to facilitate psychological or physical rehabilitation. —**occupa′tional ther′apist,** *n.*

och·lo·pho·bi·a (ok′lə fō′bē ə), *n.* an abnormal fear of crowds. —**och′lo·pho′bist,** *n.*

oc·u·list (ok′yə list), *n.* (formerly) **1.** OPHTHALMOLOGIST. **2.** OPTOMETRIST.

oc·u·lo·mo·tor (ok/yə lō mō/tər), *adj.* moving the eyeball.

oculomo/tor nerve/, *n.* either one of the third pair of cranial nerves, which innervate most of the muscles of the eyeball.

OD (ō/dē/), *n., pl.* **ODs** or **OD's**, *v.*, **OD'd** or **ODed, OD'·ing.** —*n.* **1.** an overdose of a drug, esp. a fatal one. **2.** a person who has become seriously ill or has died from a drug overdose. —*v.i.* **3.** to take a drug overdose. **4.** to die from a drug overdose.

O.D. or **OD, 1.** (in prescriptions) the right eye. [Latin, *oculus dexter*] **2.** overdose.

oe·de·ma (i dē/mə), *n., pl.* **-ma·ta** (-mə tə). EDEMA.

oed·i·pal (ed/ə pəl, ē/də-), *adj.* (*often cap.*) of, characterized by, or resulting from the Oedipus complex.

Oed/i·pus com/plex (ed/ə pəs, ē/də-), *n.* libidinous feelings toward the parent of the opposite sex, often also involving rivalry with the parent of the same sex: esp. applied to males and considered normal in young children. Compare ELECTRA COMPLEX.

of·fic·i·nal (ə fis/ə nl), *adj.* **1.** kept in stock by apothecaries, as a drug. **2.** recognized by a pharmacopoeia. —**offic/i·nal·ly,** *adv.*

oint·ment (oint/mənt), *n.* a soft, unctuous preparation, often medicated, for application to the skin; unguent; salve.

ol·fac·tom·e·ter (ol/fak tom/i tər, ōl/-), *n.* a device for estimating the keenness of the sense of smell.

ol·fac·to·ry (ol fak/tə rē, -trē, ōl-), *adj., n., pl.* **-ries.** —*adj.* **1.** of or pertaining to the sense of smell. —*n.* **2.** Usu., **olfactories.** an olfactory organ. **3.** OLFACTORY NERVE.

olfac/tory bulb/, *n.* the anterior swelling of each olfactory lobe, in which the fibers of the olfactory nerve terminate.

olfac/tory lobe/, *n.* the anterior part of each cerebral hemisphere, involved with olfactory functions.

olfac/tory nerve/, *n.* either one of the first pair of cranial nerves, consisting of sensory fibers that conduct to the brain the impulses from the mucous membranes of the nose.

ol·i·go·gene (ol/i gō jēn/, ə lig/ə-), *n.* a gene that produces or significantly affects the expression of a qualitative heritable characteristic, acting either alone or with a few other genes.

ol·i·go·nu·cle·o·tide (ol/i gō nōo/klē ə tīd/, -nyōo/-), *n.* a chain of a few nucleotides.

ol·i·go·phre·ni·a (ol/i gō frē/nē ə, ə lig/ə-), *n.* less than normal mental development.

o·me·ga-3 fat/ty ac/id (ō mē/gə thrē/, ō mā/-, ō meg/ə-), *n.* a fatty acid found esp. in fish oil and valuable in reducing cholesterol levels in the blood.

o·men·tum (ō men/təm), *n., pl.* **-ta** (-tə). a fold of the peritoneum connecting the stomach and other abdominal viscera and forming a protective and supportive covering. Compare GREATER OMENTUM, LESSER OMENTUM.

o·nan·ism (ō′nə niz′əm), *n.* **1.** withdrawal of the penis in sexual intercourse so that ejaculation takes place outside the vagina; coitus interruptus. **2.** MASTURBATION. —**o′nan·ist,** *n.* —**o′nan·is′tic,** *adj.*

on·cho·cer·ci·a·sis (ong′kō sər kī′ə sis) also **on′cho·cer·co′sis** (-kō′sis), *n.* an infestation with filarial worms of the genus *Onchocerca,* common in tropical America and Africa, transmitted by black flies, and characterized by nodules under the skin, an itchy rash, eye lesions, and in severe cases, elephantiasis. Also called **river blindness.**

on·co·gene (ong′kə jēn′), *n.* any gene that is a causative factor in the initiation of cancerous growth.

on′co·gen′e·sis (-jen′ə sis), *n.* the generation of tumors. —**on′co·gen′ic, on′co·ge·net′ic,** *adj.*

on′co·ge·nic′i·ty, *n.* the capability of inducing tumor formation.

on·col·o·gy (ong kol′ə jē), *n.* the branch of medical science dealing with tumors, including the origin, development, diagnosis, and treatment of cancer. —**on′co·log′ic** (-kə loj′ik), **on′co·log′i·cal,** *adj.* —**on·col′o·gist,** *n.*

on·co·na·vi·rus (ong′kə vī′rəs) also **on·cor·na·vi·rus** (ong-kôr′nə-), *n., pl.* **-rus·es.** any retrovirus of the subfamily Oncovirinae, capable of producing tumors.

on·tog·e·ny (on toj′ə nē) also **on′to·gen′e·sis** (-tə jen′ə sis), *n.* the development or developmental history of an individual organism. Compare PHYLOGENY. —**on′to·ge·net′ic** (-jə net′ik), **on′to·gen′ic,** *adj.* —**on′to·ge·net′i·cal·ly, on′to·gen′i·cal·ly,** *adv.* —**on′to·ge·net′i·cist,** *n.*

o·o·cyte (ō′ə sīt′), *n.* an immature egg cell of the animal ovary: in humans, one oocyte matures during the menstrual cycle while several others partially mature and disintegrate.

o′o·gen′e·sis, *n.* the formation and development of the ovum. —**o′o·ge·net′ic,** *adj.*

o·o·pho·rec·to·my (ō′ə fə rek′tə mē), *n., pl.* **-mies.** surgical removal of the ovary. Also called **ovariectomy.**

o·o·pho·ri·tis (ō′ə fə rī′tis), *n.* inflammation of an ovary. Also called **ovaritis.**

o·o·tid (ō′ə tid), *n.* an intermediate ovarian egg cell that results from oocyte division and matures into an ovum under certain conditions.

OPD, Outpatient Department.

o′pen-an′gle glauco′ma, *n.* See under GLAUCOMA.

o′pen-heart′ sur′gery, *n.* surgery performed on the exposed heart with the aid of a heart-lung machine.

op·er·a·ble (op′ər ə bəl, op′rə-), *adj.* treatable by a surgical operation. Compare INOPERABLE. —**op′er·a·bil′i·ty,** *n.* —**op′er·a·bly,** *adv.*

op·er·ate (op′ə rāt′), *v.i.,* **-at·ed, -at·ing.** to perform a surgical procedure.

op·er·a·tion, *n.* a procedure aimed at restoring or improving the health of a patient, as by correcting a malformation, removing diseased parts, implanting new parts, etc.

op·er·a·tive (op′ər ə tiv, op′rə tiv, op′ə rā′tiv), *adj.* concerned with, involving, or pertaining to surgical operations. —**op′er·a·tive·ly,** *adv.*

op′er·a′tor, *n.* a segment of DNA that interacts with a regulatory molecule, preventing transcription of the adjacent region.

op′er·on′ (-ə ron′), *n.* a set of two or more adjacent cistrons whose transcription is under the coordinated control of a promoter, an operator, and a regulator gene.

oph·thal·mi·a (of thal′mē ə, op-), *n.* inflammation of the eye, esp.. of its membranes or external structures.

oph·thal′mic, *adj.* of or pertaining to the eye.

oph′thal·mol′o·gist (-thəl mol′ə jist, -thə-, -thal-), *n.* a physician specializing in ophthalmology.

oph′thal·mol′o·gy, *n.* the branch of medicine dealing with the anatomy, functions, and diseases of the eye. —**oph·thal·mo·log′i·cal** (-mə loj′i kəl), **oph·thal′mo·log′ic,** *adj.*

oph′thal·mo·scope′ (-thal′mə skōp′), *n.* an instrument for viewing the interior of the eye and esp. the retina. —**oph′thal·mos·cop′ic** (-skop′ik), *adj.* —**oph′thal·mos′-co·py** (-mos′kə pē), *n.*

o·pi·ate (ō′pē it, -āt′), *n.* **1.** a drug containing opium or its derivatives. **2.** any sedative, soporific, or narcotic. —*adj.* **3.** pertaining to the eye.

o′pi·oid′, *n.* **1.** any opiumlike substance, as the endorphins produced by the body or the synthetic compound methadone. —*adj.* **2.** pertaining to such a substance.

o′pi·um, *n.* the dried, condensed juice of the seed capsules of a poppy, *Papaver somniferum,* that has a narcotic effect and contains morphine, codeine, papaverine, and other alkaloids.

op·por·tun·is·tic (op′ər tōō nis′tik, -tyōō-), *adj.* **1.** (of a microorganism) causing disease only under certain conditions, as when a person's immune system is impaired. **2.** (of a disease or infection) caused by such an organism, as pneumocystis pneumonia in a person with AIDS. —**op′por·tun·is′ti·cal·ly,** *adv.*

op·sin (op′sin), *n.* any of several compounds that form the protein component of the light-sensitive pigment rhodopsin.

op·tic (op′tik), *adj.* of or pertaining to the eye or sight.

op·ti·cal, *adj.* **1.** of or pertaining to the eye or sight. **2.** constructed to assist sight. —**op′ti·cal·ly,** *adv.*

op′tical illu·sion, *n.* See under ILLUSION.

op′tic chias′ma (or **chi′asm**), *n.* a site at the base of the forebrain where the inner half of the fibers of the left and right optic nerves cross to the opposite side of the brain.

op·ti·cian (op tish′ən), *n.* **1.** a person who makes or sells eyeglasses and contact lenses in accordance with the prescriptions of ophthalmologists and optometrists. **2.** a maker or seller of optical glass and instruments.

op′tic nerve′, *n.* either of a pair of cranial nerves consisting of sensory fibers that conduct impulses from the retina to the brain.

op·tom·e·trist (op tom′i trist), *n.* a licensed professional who practices optometry.

op·tom′e·try, *n.* the practice or profession of examining the eyes for defects of vision and eye disorders in order to prescribe corrective lenses or other appropriate treatment. —**op·to·met·ri·cal** (op′tə me′tri kəl), *adj.*

OR, operating room.

o·ral (ôr′əl, ōr′-), *adj.* of or pertaining to a group of adult behaviors and personality traits including eating, talking, feeding, and being friendly and generous. —**o·ral′i·ty,** *n.* —**o′ral·ly,** *adv.*

o′ral contracep′tive, *n.* BIRTH-CONTROL PILL.

o′ral her′pes, *n.* a disease caused by a herpes simplex virus, characterized chiefly by a cluster of small, transient blisters (**cold sore**) at the edge of the lip or nostril.

or·bit (ôr′bit), *n.* the bony cavity of the skull that contains the eye; eye socket.

or·bit·al (ôr′bi tl), *adj.* of or pertaining to an orbit.

or·gan (ôr′gən), *n.* a grouping of tissues into a distinct structure, as a heart or kidney, that performs a specialized task or tasks.

or·gan·elle (ôr′gə nel′, ôr′gə nel′), *n.* a specialized cell structure that has a specific function; a cell organ.

or·gan·ic (ôr gan′ik), *adj.* **1.** noting or pertaining to a class of chemical compounds contaning carbon and forming the chemical basis of all living things. **2.** pertaining to, characteristic of, or derived from living organisms. —**or·gan′i·cal·ly,** *adv.* —**or′gan·ic′i·ty** (-gə nis′i tē), *n.*

or·gan·ism (ôr′gə niz′əm), *n.* any individual life form considered as an entity; an animal, plant, fungus, protozoan, alga, bacterium, or the like.

or·gan·iz·er (ôr′gə nī′zər), *n.* any part of an embryo that stimulates the development and differentiation of another part.

or′gan of Cor′ti (kôr′tē), *n.* a structure in the cochlea of the ear consisting of hair cells that serve as receptors for sound waves.

or·ga·no·gen·e·sis (ôr′gə nō jen′ə sis, ôr gan′ō-), *n.* the development of bodily organs. —**or′ga·no·ge·net′ic** (-jə net′ik), *adj.*

or·ga·no·lep·tic (ôr′gə nl ep′tik, ôr gan′l ep′-), *adj.* **1.** perceived by a sense organ. **2.** capable of detecting a sensory stimulus.

or′ga·no·phos′phate (ôr′gə nō-, ôr gan′ə-), *n.* any of a variety of organic compounds that contain phosphorus and often have intense neurotoxic activity: orig. developed as nerve gases.

or·ga·not·ro·pism (ôr′gə no′trə piz′əm), *n.* the attraction of microorganisms or chemical substances to particular organs or tissues of the body. —**or·ga·no·trop·ic** (ôr′gə nə trop′ik, -trō′pik, ôr gan′ə-), *adj.*

or·gasm (ôr′gaz əm), *n.* **1.** the intense physical and emotional sensation experienced at the peak of sexual excitation, usually accompanied in the male by ejaculation; climax. —*v.i.* **2.** to have an orgasm. —**or·gas′mic, or·gas′-tic** (-gas′-), *adj.*

o·ri·en·ta·tion (ôr′ē ən tā′shən, -en-, ōr′-), *n.* the ability to locate oneself in one's environment with reference to time, place, and people. —**o′ri·en·ta′tive,** *adj.*

or·ni·thine (ôr′nə thēn′), *n.* an amino acid, $H_2N(CH_2)_3CH(NH_2)COOH$, obtained by the hydrolysis of arginine and occurring as an intermediate compound in the urea cycle of mammals.

or·ni·tho·sis (-thō′sis), *n.* psittacosis, esp. of birds other than those of the parrot family.

or·tho·gen·ic (ôr′thə jen′ik), *adj.* of, concerned with, or providing corrective treatment for mentally retarded or seriously disturbed children.

or·tho·mo·lec·u·lar (ôr′thō mə lek′yə lər), *adj.* being or pertaining to the treatment of disease by increasing, decreasing, or otherwise controlling the intake of natural substances, esp. vitamins.

or·tho·myx·o·vi·rus (ôr′thə mik′sə vī′rəs, -mik′sə vī′-), *n., pl.* **-rus·es.** any of several RNA-containing viruses of the family Orthomyxoviridae that are spherical or oval and have an envelope: includes viruses that cause influenza. Also called **myxovirus.**

or′tho·pe′dics or **or′tho·pae′dics** (-pē′diks), *n.* (*used with a sing. v.*) the medical specialty concerned with correction of deformities or functional impairments of the skeletal system, esp. the spine, and associated structures, as muscles and ligaments. —**or′-tho·pe′dic,** *adj.* —**or′tho·pe·di·cal·ly,** *adv.* —**or′tho·pe′-dist,** *n.*

or·tho·psy·chi·a·try (ôr′thō sī kī′ə trē, -sī-), *n.* an approach to psychiatry that is concerned with the prophylactic treatment of behavioral disorders, esp. in young people. —**or′tho·psy′chi·at′ric** (-sī′kē a′trik), *adj.* —**or′tho·psy·chi′a·trist,** *n.*

or·thop·tic (ôr thop′tik), *adj.* pertaining to or producing normal binocular vision.

or·tho·scop·ic (ôr′thə skop′ik), *adj.* pertaining to or characteristic of normal vision.

or′tho·stat′ic (-stat′ik), *adj.* caused by standing upright: *orthostatic hypotension.*

or·thot·ic (ôr thot′ik), *n.* **1.** a device or support used to relieve or correct an orthopedic problem, esp. of the foot. —*adj.* **2.** of or pertaining to orthotics.

or·thot′ics, *n.* (*used with a sing. v.*) a branch of medicine dealing with the making and fitting of orthotic devices. —**or·thot·ist** (ôr thot′ist, ôr′thə tist), *n.*

O.S., (in prescriptions) the left eye. [Latin, *oculus sinister*]

os·mo·sis (oz mō′sis, os-), *n.* **1.** the tendency of a fluid, usu. water, to pass through a semipermeable membrane into a solution where the solvent concentration is higher, thus equalizing the concentrations of materials on either side of the membrane. **2.** the diffusion of fluids through membranes or porous partitions. —**os·mot/ic** (-mot/ik), *adj.* —**os·mot/i·cal·ly**, *adv.*

os·se·in (os/ē in), *n.* the collagen of bone.

os/se·ous, *adj.* composed of, containing, or resembling bone; bony.

os·te·i·tis (os/tē i/tis), *n.* inflammation of bone. —**os/te·it/ic** (-it/ik), *adj.*

os/te·o·ar·thri/tis (os/tē ō-), *n.* arthritis marked by chronic breakdown of cartilage in the joints leading to pain, stiffness, and swelling. Also called **degenerative joint disease.**

os/te·o·ar·thro/sis (-är thrō/sis), *n.* chronic, noninflammatory arthritis.

os/te·o·blast (os/tē ə blast/), *n.* a bone-forming cell. —**os/te·o·blas/tic**, *adj.*

os/te·oc/la·sis (-ok/lə sis), *n.* **1.** the breaking down or absorption of osseous tissue. **2.** the fracturing of a bone to correct deformity.

os/te·o·clast (os/tē ə klast/), *n.* **1.** a skeletal cell that functions in bone formation. **2.** a surgical instrument for effecting osteoclasis. —**os/te·o·clas/tic**, *adj.*

os/te·o·gen/e·sis, *n.* the formation of bone.

os/te·o·gen/ic, *adj.* **1.** derived from or made up of bone-forming tissue. **2.** of or pertaining to osteogenesis.

os/te·ol/o·gy (-ol/ə jē), *n.* the branch of anatomy dealing with the skeleton. —**os/te·o·log/i·cal** (-ə loj/i kəl), **os/te·o·log/ic**, *adj.* —**os/te·ol/o·gist**, *n.*

os/te·o·ma (-ō/mə), *n., pl.* **-mas, -ma·ta** (-mə tə). a benign tumor composed of osseous tissue.

os/te·o·ma·la·cia (os/tē ō mə lā/shə, -shē ə), *n.* a condition characterized by softening of the bones with resultant pain, weakness, and bone fragility. —**os/te·o·ma·la/cial**, **os/te·o·ma·lac/ic** (-mə las/ik), *adj.*

os/te·o·my/e·li/tis, *n.* an inflammation of bone and bone marrow, usu. caused by bacterial infection.

os/te·o·path (os/tē ə path/) also **os/te·op/a·thist** (-op/ə thist), *n.* a practitioner of osteopathy.

os/te·op/a·thy (-op/ə thē), *n.* a system of medical practice emphasizing the manipulation of muscles and bones to promote structural integrity and the relief of certain disorders. —**os/te·o·path/ic** (-ə path/ik), *adj.* —**os/te·o·path/i·cal·ly**, *adv.*

os/te·o·phyte (os/tē ə fīt/), *n.* a small, abnormal outgrowth of bone, usu. near damaged cartilage. —**os/te·o·phyt/ic** (-fit/ik), *adj.*

os/te·o·plas/tic, *adj.* **1.** pertaining to osteoplasty. **2.** pertaining to bone formation.

os/te·o·plas/ty, *n., pl.* **-ties.** plastic surgery on a bone to repair a defect or loss.

os/te·o·po·ro/sis (os/tē ō pə rō/sis), *n.* a disorder in which the bones become increasingly porous, brittle, and subject to fracture, owing to loss of calcium and other mineral components. —**os′te·o·po·rot′ic** (-rot′ik), adj.

os·te·o·sar·co·ma (ŏs′tē ō sär kō mə), n., pl. **-mas, -ma·ta** (-mə tə). a malignant tumor of the bone.

os·te·ot·o·my (ŏs′tē ŏt′ə mē), n., pl. **-mies. 1.** the surgical division of a bone to reposition the ends. **2.** the excision of part of a bone. —**os′te·ot′o·mist,** n.

os·to·my (ŏs′tə mē), n., pl. **-mies.** any of various surgical procedures in which an artificial opening is made for the drainage of waste products.

OT, occupational therapy.

o·tal·gi·a (ō tal′jē ə, -jə), n. EARACHE. —**o·tal′gic,** adj.

OTC, over-the-counter.

o·ti·tis (ō tī′tis), n. inflammation of the ear.

oti′tis me′di·a (mē′dē ə), n. inflammation of the middle ear, characterized by pain, dizziness, and impaired hearing.

o·to·cyst (ō′tə sist), n. one of a pair of pouches that form in the front part of the embryo by the infolding of a thickened area of ectoderm, later developing into an internal ear. —**o′to·cys′tic,** adj.

o·to·lar·yn·gol·o·gy (ō′tō lar′ing gol′ə jē), n. OTORHINO-LARYNGOLOGY. —**o·to·la·ryn′go·log′i·cal** (-lə ring′gə loj′i-kəl), adj. —**o·to·lar′yn·gol′o·gist,** n.

o·tol·o·gy (ō tol′ə jē), n. the study and treatment of diseases of the ear. —**o·to·log′i·cal** (ōt′l oj′i kəl), adj. —**o·tol′o·gist,** n.

o·to·rhi·no·lar·yn·gol·o·gy (ō′tō rī′nō lar′ing gol′ə jē) also **otolaryngology,** n. the study and treatment of diseases of the ear, nose, and throat. —**o′to·rhi′no·la·ryn′go·log′i·cal** (-lə ring′gə loj′i kəl), adj. —**o′to·rhi′no·la·ryn·gol′o·gist,** n.

o·to·scle·ro·sis (ō′tə skli rō′sis), n. formation of new bone about the stapes or cochlea, resulting in hearing loss.

o′to·tox′ic, adj. having a harmful effect on the organs or nerves concerned with hearing and balance. —**o′to·tox·ic′i·ty,** n.

out′-of-bod′y, adj. of, pertaining to, or characterized by the dissociative sensation of perceiving oneself from an external vantage point, as though the mind or soul has left the body and is acting on its own: *an out-of-body experience.*

out·pa′tient or **out′-pa′tient,** n. a person who receives treatment at a hospital but is not hospitalized.

ov·al·bu·min (ov′al byōō′min, ō′val-), n. the principal protein of egg white.

o·var·i·an (ō vâr′ē ən) also **o·var′i·al,** adj. of or pertaining to an ovary.

o·var′i·ec·to·my (-ek′tə mē), n., pl. **-mies.** OOPHOREC-TOMY.

o·var′i·ot·o·my (-ot′ə mē), n., pl. **-mies.** surgical incision into or removal of an ovary.

o·va·ri·tis (ō′və rī′tis), n. OOPHORITIS.

o·va·ry (ō′və rē), *n., pl.* **-ries.** the female gonad or reproductive gland, in which the ova and the female sex hormones develop.

o′ver·com·pen·sa′tion, *n. Psychoanal.* a pronounced striving to overcome a trait perceived as unacceptable by substituting an opposite trait.

o·ver·dose (*n.* ō′vər dōs′; *v.* ō′vər dōs′, ō′vər dōs′), *n., v.,* **-dosed, -dos·ing.** —*n.* **1.** an excessive dose of a drug. —*v.i.* **2.** to take an excessive dose, esp. of a narcotic.

o′ver·fa·tigue′, *n.* excessive tiredness from which recuperation is difficult. —**o′ver·fa·tigued′,** *adj.*

o′ver·sexed′, *adj.* having an unusually strong sexual drive.

o′ver-the-count′er, *adj.* sold legally without a prescription: *over-the-counter drugs.*

ov·u·lar (ov′yə lər, ō′vyə-), *adj.* pertaining to or of the nature of an ovule.

ov·u·late′ (-lāt′), *v.i.,* **-lat·ed, -lat·ing.** to produce and discharge eggs from an ovary or ovarian follicle. —**ov′u·la′tion,** *n.* (-lə tôr′ē, -tōr′ē), *adj.*

ov·ule (ov′yōōl, ō′vyōōl), *n.* a small egg.

o·vum (ō′vəm), *n., pl.* **o·va** (ō′və). the female reproductive cell, developed in the ovary; female gamete; egg cell.

ox′a·lo·a·ce′tic ac′id (ok′sə lō ə sē′tik, ok′-, ok sal′ō-, -sal′-), *n.* a crystalline organic acid, $C_4H_4O_5$, an important intermediate in the Krebs cycle, where it is formed by the oxidation of malic acid and is acetylated to form citric acid.

ox·i·dase (ok′si dās′, -dāz′), *n.* any of a class of enzymes that catalyze oxidation by molecular oxygen and, in most cases, form hydrogen peroxide. —**ox′i·da′sic,** *adj.*

oxida′tion-reduc′tion, *n.* a chemical reaction between two substances in which one substance is oxidized and the other reduced. Also called **redox.**

ox′idative phosphoryla′tion, *n.* the aerobic synthesis, coupled to electron transport, of ATP from phosphate and ADP.

ox·i·do·re·duc·tase or **ox·i·do·re·duc·tase** (ok′si dō-ri duk′tās, -tāz′), *n.* any of a class of enzymes that act as a catalyst, some of them conjointly, causing the oxidation and reduction of compounds.

ox·y·ceph·a·ly (ok′si sef′ə lē), *n.* a malformation in which the head is somewhat pointed, caused by premature closure of the skull sutures. Also called **acrocephaly.** —**ox·y·ce·phal·ic** (ok′sē sə fal′ik), **ox′y·ceph′a·lous,** *adj.*

ox·y·gen (ok′si jən), *n.* a colorless, odorless, gaseous element constituting about one-fifth of the volume of the atmosphere and present in a combined state in nature. *Symbol:* O; *at. wt.:* 15.9994; *at. no.:* 8; *density:* 1.4290 g/l at 0°C and 760 mm pressure. —**ox′y·gen′ic** (-jen′ik), **ox·yg′e·nous** (-sij′ə nəs), *adj.*

ox·y·gen·ase (ok′si jə nās′, -nāz′), *n.* an oxidoreductase enzyme that catalyzes the introduction of molecular oxygen into an organic substance.

ox′y·gen·ate′ (-nāt′), *v.t.,* **-at·ed, -at·ing.** to treat, combine, or enrich with oxygen: *to oxygenate the blood.* —**ox′y·gen·a′tion,** *n.* —**ox′y·gen·a′tor,** *n.*

ox′ygen debt′, *n.* the body's oxygen deficiency resulting from strenuous physical activity.

ox′ygen mask′, *n.* a masklike device placed or worn over the nose and mouth when inhaling supplementary oxygen from an attached tank.

ox′ygen tent′, *n.* a small transparent canopy placed over a patient for delivering an increased concentration of oxygen.

ox′y·he′mo·glo′bin (ok'si-), *n.* a chemical compound of hemoglobin and oxygen that gives arterial blood its bright red color.

ox′y·to′cic (-tō′sik, -tos′ik), *adj.* **1.** of or causing the stimulation of the involuntary muscle of the uterus. **2.** promoting or accelerating childbirth. —*n.* **3.** an oxytocic substance or drug.

ox′y·to′cin, *n.* a pituitary hormone that stimulates contraction of the smooth muscles of the uterus, used in obstetrics to induce labor.

ox·y·u·ri·a·sis (ok'sē yŏŏ rī′ə sis), *n.* infection with pinworms of the family Oxyuridae.

P

P¹, parental.

P², *Symbol.* **1.** phosphorus. **2.** proline.

PA, physician's assistant.

PABA (pä′bə), *n.* para-aminobenzoic acid.

pab·u·lum (pab′yə ləm), *n.* **1.** something that nourishes; food. **2.** a soft, bland cereal for infants.

pace′mak′er, *n.* **1.** an electronic device surgically implanted beneath the skin to provide a normal heartbeat by electrical stimulation of the heart muscle. **2.** any specialized body tissue governing a rhythmic physiological activity, esp. the sinoatrial mode of the heart that regulates heartbeat. **—pace′mak′ing,** *adj.*

pach·y·tene (pak′i tēn), *n.* the third stage of prophase in meiosis, during which each chromosome pair separates into sister chromatids with some breakage and crossing over of genes.

Pa·cin′i·an cor′puscle (pə sin′ē ən), *n.* (*sometimes l.c.*) a microscopic, onionlike body consisting of layers of connective tissue wrapped around a nerve ending, located in the deep layers of skin, tendons, etc., and functioning as a sensory receptor of pressure and vibration.

Pag′et's disease′ (paj′its), *n.* **1.** a chronic disease characterized by episodic accelerated bone resorption and growth of abnormal replacement bone. **2.** an inflammatory condition of the nipple associated with breast cancer.

pain′kill′er, *n.* something, as a drug or treatment, that relieves pain, esp. an analgesic. **—pain′kill′ing,** *adj.*

paint′er's col′ic, *n.* lead poisoning causing intense intestinal pain.

pal·a·tal (pal′ə tl), *adj.* of or pertaining to the palate.

pal·ate (pal′it), *n.* the roof of the mouth in mammals, consisting of an anterior bony portion (**hard palate**) and a posterior fleshy portion (**soft palate**) that separate the oral cavity from the nasal cavity.

pal·a·tine (pal′ə tīn′, -tin), *adj.* of, near, or in the palate; palatal: *the palatine bones.*

pal·li·ate (pal′ē āt′), *v.t.,* **-at·ed, -at·ing.** to relieve without curing; mitigate; alleviate: *to palliate a chronic disease.* **—pal′li·a′tion,** *n.* **—pal′li·a·tor,** *n.*

pal·li·a·tive (pal′ē ā′tiv, -ē ə tiv), *adj.* serving to palliate: *a palliative medicine.* **—pal′li·a·tive·ly,** *adv.*

pal·pate (pal′pāt), *v.t.,* **-pat·ed, -pat·ing.** to examine by touch, esp. for the purpose of diagnosing disease or illness. **—pal·pa′tion,** *n.* **—pal′pa·to·ry** (-pə tôr′ē, -tōr′ē), *adj.*

pal·pe·bral (pal′pə brəl, pal pē′brəl, -peb′rəl), *adj.* of or pertaining to the eyelids.

pal·pi·tate (pal′pi tāt′), *v.i.,* **-tat·ed, -tat·ing.** to pulsate, as the heart, with unusual rapidity; flutter.

pal·pi·ta'tion, *n.* **1.** the act of palpitating. **2.** an unusually or abnormally rapid or violent beating of the heart.

pal·sy (pôl'zē), *n., pl.* **-sies. 1.** any of several conditions characterized by paralysis, as Bell's palsy. **2.** any of a variety of atonal muscular conditions characterized by tremors of the body parts or of the entire body.

pal·u·dism (pal'yə diz'əm), *n.* MALARIA.

pan·cre·as (pan'krē əs, pang'-), *n.* a large compound gland, situated near the stomach, that secretes digestive enzymes into the intestine and glucagon and insulin into the bloodstream. —**pan'cre·at'ic** (-at'ik), *adj.*

pan'creat'ic juice', *n.* a colorless alkaline fluid secreted by the pancreas, containing enzymes that break down protein, fat, and starch.

pan·cre·a·tin (pan'krē ə tin, pang'-), *n.* a mixture of the pancreatic enzymes trypsin, amylase, and lipase, used to promote digestion.

pan·cre·a·ti·tis (pan'krē ə tī'tis, pang'-), *n.* inflammation of the pancreas.

pan·dem·ic (pan dem'ik), *adj.* **1.** (of a disease) prevalent throughout an entire country, continent, or the whole world; epidemic over a large area. —*n.* **2.** a pandemic disease.

pan·ic (pan'ik), *n.* an anxiety disorder characterized by feelings of impending doom and physical symptoms such as trembling and hyperventilation.

pan·op·tic (pan op'tik) also **pan·op'ti·cal,** *adj.* permitting the viewing of all parts or elements: *a panoptic tissue stain for microscopic viewing.*

pan·sex'u·al, *adj.* expressing or involving sexuality in many different forms. —**pan'sex·u·al'i·ty,** *n.*

pan'to·then'ic ac'id (pan'tə then'ik, pan'-), *n.* a hydroxy acid, $C_9H_{17}O_5N$, that is a component of the vitamin B complex, abundant in liver, yeast, and bran.

pan·trop·ic (pan trop'ik, -trō'pik), *adj.* attracted to or affecting many types of body tissue: *pantropic viruses.*

pa·pa·in (pə pā'in, -pī'in), *n.* a proteolytic enzyme present in papaya, used as a meat tenderizer and as a digestant.

Pa·pa·ni·co·laou' test' (pä'pə nē'kə lou', pap'ə nik'-əlou'), *n.* PAP TEST.

pa·pav·er·ine (pə pav'ə rēn', -ər in, pə pā'və rēn', -vər-in), *n.* a white, crystalline alkaloid, $C_{20}H_{21}NO_4$, used as a smooth-muscle relaxant.

pap·il·lo·ma (pap'ə lō'mə), *n., pl.* **-ma·ta** (-mə tə), **-mas.** a benign tumor of the skin or mucous membrane consisting of hypertrophied epithelial tissue, as a wart or corn. —**pap'il·lo·ma·to'sis** (-lō'mə təs, -lom'ə-), *n.* —**pap'il·lo·ma·tous** (-lō'mə təs, -lom'ə-), *adj.*

pap'il·lo'ma·vi'rus, *n., pl.* **-rus·es.** a type of papovavirus, containing circular DNA, that causes papillomas, including genital warts.

pa·po'va·vi'rus (pə pō'və-), *n., pl.* **-rus·es.** any of a group of small DNA-containing viruses of the family Papovaviridae, most of which produce tumors.

Pap′ (or **pap′**) **test′** (pap), *n.* **1.** a test for cancer of the cervix, consisting of the staining of cells taken in a cervical or vaginal smear (**Pap′** (or **pap′**) **smear′**) for examination of exfoliated cells. **2.** a vaginal Pap smear used to evaluate estrogen levels. **3.** an examination of exfoliated cells in any body fluid, as sputum or urine, for cancer cells. Also called **Papanicolaou test.**

pap·ule (pap′yōōl), *n.* a small, somewhat pointed, usu. inflammatory elevation of the skin. —**pap′u·lar** (-yə lər), *adj.* —**pap′u·lose′** (-yə lōs′), *adj.*

par·a (par′ə), *n., pl.* **par·as, par·ae** (par′ē). **1.** Also called **parity.** a woman's status regarding the bearing of offspring: usu. followed by a numeral designating the number of times the woman has given birth. **2.** the woman herself. Compare GRAVIDA.

par′a·a·mi·no·ben·zo′ic ac′id (par′ə ə mē′nō ben-zō′ik, -am′ə nō-), *n.* a yellowish, crystalline solid, $C_7H_7NO_2$, that is a component of the vitamin B complex: used in pharmaceuticals and dyes. *Abbr.:* PABA

par·a·bi·o·sis (par′ə bi ō′sis, -bē-), *n.* the physiological or anatomical union of two individuals. —**par′a·bi·ot′ic** (-ot′ik), *adj.*

par·aes·the·sia (par′əs thē′zhə, -zhē ə, -zē ə), *n.* PARESTHESIA. —**par′aes·thet′ic** (-thet′ik), *adj.*

par′a·in′flu·en′za (par′ə-), *n.* an influenzalike respiratory infection, caused by any of several paramyxoviruses.

par·al·de·hyde (pə ral′də hīd′), *n.* a colorless liquid compound, $C_6H_{12}O_3$, produced by polymerization of acetaldehyde, used in medicine as a rapidly acting sedative and hypnotic.

pa·ral·y·sis (pə ral′ə sis), *n., pl.* **-ses** (-sēz′). **1.** a loss or impairment of movement or sensation in a body part, caused by injury or disease of the nerves, brain, or spinal cord. **2.** a disease characterized by this, esp. palsy.

paral′ysis ag′i·tans (aj′i tanz′), *n.* PARKINSON'S DISEASE.

par·a·lyt·ic (par′ə lit′ik), *n.* **1.** a person affected with paralysis. —*adj.* **2.** affected with or subject to paralysis. —**par′a·lyt′i·cal·ly,** *adv.*

par·a·me·ci·um (par′ə mē′shē əm, -shəm, -sē əm), *n., pl.* **-ci·a** (-shē ə, -sē ə). a freshwater protozoan of the genus *Paramecium,* having an oval body with a long, deep oral groove and a fringe of cilia.

par·a·med·ic[1] (par′ə med′ik), *n.* a person who is trained to assist a physician or to give first aid or other health care in the absence of a physician.

par·a·med·ic[2] (par′ə med′ik, par′ə med′-), *n.* **1.** a medic in the paratroops. **2.** a physician who parachutes into remote areas to give medical care.

par′a·med′i·cal, *adj.* related to the medical profession in a secondary or supplementary capacity.

par·am·ne·sia (par′am nē′zhə), *n.* **1.** a distortion of memory in which fact and fantasy are confused. **2.** the inability to recall the correct meanings of words.

par·a·myx·o·vi·rus (par/ə mik/sə vī/rəs, -mik/sə vī/-), *n., pl.* **-rus·es.** any of various RNA-containing viruses of the family Paramyxoviridae, distinguished by a helical nucleocapsid surrounded by an envelope: includes viruses causing measles and mumps. Also called **myxovirus.**

par·a·noi·a (par/ə noi/ə), *n.* a mental disorder characterized by systematized delusions ascribing hostile intentions to other persons, often linked with a sense of mission.

par/a·noid/, *adj.* **1.** Also, **par/a·noi/dal.** of, like, or suffering from paranoia. —*n.* **2.** a person suffering from paranoia.

par/a·nor/mal, *adj.* of or pertaining to events or perceptions occurring without scientific explanation, as clairvoyance or extrasensory perception. —**par/a·nor/mal·ly,** *adv.*

par·a·pa·re·sis (par/ə pə rē/sis, -par/ə sis), *n.* partial paralysis, esp. of the lower limbs.

par·a·phil·i·a (par/ə fil/ē ə), *n.* a mental disorder characterized by a preference for or obsession with unusual sexual practices, as pedophilia, sadomasochism, or exhibitionism. —**par/a·phil/ic,** *adj.*

par·a·ple·gi·a (par/ə plē/jē ə, -jə), *n.* paralysis of both lower limbs due to spinal disease or injury. —**par/a·ple/gic** (-plē/jik, -plej/ik), *adj., n.*

par·a·prax·is (par/ə prak/sis) also **par·a·prax·i·a** (-prak/sē ə), *n., pl.* **-prax·es** (-prak/sēz) also **-prax·i·as.** a slip of the tongue, misplacement of objects, or other error thought to reveal unconscious wishes or attitudes.

par/a·sex/u·al, *adj.* of or pertaining to reproduction by recombination of DNA from genetically distinct individuals without the fusion of nuclei within a multinucleate fungal cell. —**par/a·sex/u·al/i·ty,** *n.*

par·a·site (par/ə sīt/), *n.* an organism that lives on or within an organism of another species, from which it obtains nutrients (opposed to *host*).

par·a·sit·ic (par/ə sit/ik) also **par/a·sit/i·cal,** *adj.* (of diseases) due to parasites. —**par/a·sit/i·cal·ly,** *adv.*

par·a·sit·ism (par/ə si tiz/əm, -si-), *n.* a diseased condition due to parasites.

par·a·si·tize (par/ə si tīz/, -sī-), *v.t.,* **-tized, -tiz·ing.** to live on (a host) as a parasite. —**par/a·sit·i·za/tion,** *n.*

par·a·si·to·sis (par/ə sī tō/sis, -si-), *n.* PARASITISM.

par/a·sym/pa·thet/ic, *adj.* pertaining to that part of the autonomic nervous system consisting of nerves and ganglia that arise from the cranial and sacral regions and generally function in regulatory opposition to the sympathetic system, as in slowing heartbeat or contracting the pupil of the eye.

par·athy/roid gland/ (par/ə thī/roid), *n.* any of several small paired glands in vertebrates, usu. lying near or embedded in the thyroid gland, that secrete parathyroid hormone.

parathy′roid hor′mone, *n.* a polypeptide hormone, produced in the parathyroid glands, that helps regulate the blood levels of calcium and phosphate. *Abbr.:* PTH

par·a·ty·phoid (par′ə ti′foid), *n.* **1.** Also called **par′aty′-phoid fe′ver.** an infectious disease, similar in some of its symptoms to typhoid fever but usu. milder, caused by any of several bacilli of the genus *Salmonella* other than *S. typhi.* —*adj.* **2.** of or pertaining to paratyphoid. **3.** resembling typhoid.

par·e·gor·ic (par′i gôr′ik, -gor′-), *n.* an opium derivative used as a mild sedative and to treat diarrhea.

pa·ren·tal (pə ren′tl), *adj. Genetics.* pertaining to the sequence of generations preceding the filial generation, each generation being designated by a P followed by a subscript number indicating its place in the sequence. —**pa·ren′tal·ly,** *adv.*

par·en·ter·al (pə ren′tər əl), *adj.* **1.** taken into the body in a manner other than through the digestive canal. **2.** inside the body but outside the intestine. —**par·en′ter·al·ly,** *adv.*

pa·re·sis (pə rē′sis, par′ə sis), *n.* partial motor paralysis. —**pa·ret′ic** (-ret′ik, -rē′tik), *n., adj.*

par·es·the·sia or **par·aes·the·sia** (par′əs thē′zhə, -zhē ə, -zē ə), *n.* an abnormal tingling or prickling sensation. —**par·es·thet′ic** (-thet′ik), *adj.*

pa·ri·e·tal (pə rī′i tl), *adj.* **1.** of or pertaining to the wall of an organ or cavity. **2.** of, pertaining to, or situated near the parietal bones of the skull. —*n.* **3.** any of several parts in the parietal region of the skull, esp. the parietal bone.

pari′etal bone′, *n.* either of a pair of bones forming, by their union at the sagittal suture, part of the sides and top of the skull.

pari′etal lobe′, *n.* the middle part of each cerebral hemisphere behind the central sulcus.

par·i·ty (par′i tē), *n.* **1.** the condition of having borne offspring. **2.** PARA (def. 1).

par·kin·so·ni·an (pär′kin sō′nē ən), *adj.* of, related to, or resembling Parkinson's disease.

Par′kin·son's disease′ (pär′kin səns), *n.* a neurologic disease believed to be caused by deterioration of the brain cells that produce dopamine, occurring primarily after the age of 60, and characterized by tremors, esp. of the fingers and hands, muscle rigidity, and a shuffling gait. Also called **par′kin·son·ism** (-sə niz′əm), **paralysis agitans.**

par·o·nych·i·a (par′ə nik′ē ə), *n.* inflammation of the folds of skin bordering a nail of a finger or toe; felon. —**par′o·nych′i·al,** *adj.*

pa·rot·id (pə rot′id), *n.* **1.** Also called **parot′id gland′.** a salivary gland situated below the ear. —*adj.* **2.** of, pertaining to, or situated near the ear. —**pa·rot′i·de·an,** *adj.*

par·o·ti·tis (par′ə tī′tis) also **pa·rot·i·di·tis** (pə rot′i di′-tis), *n.* **1.** inflammation of a parotid. **2.** MUMPS.

par·ox·ysm (par′ok siz′əm), *n.* a severe attack or a sudden increase in intensity of a disease, usu. recurring periodically. —**par·ox·ys′mal, par′ox·ys′mic,** adj. —**par′ox·ys′mal·ly,** adv.

par′rot fe′ver, n. PSITTACOSIS.

par·the·no·gen·e·sis (pär′thə nō jen′ə sis), n. development of an egg without fertilization. —**par′the·no·ge·net′ic** (-jə net′ik), adj. —**par′the·no·ge·net′i·cal·ly,** adv.

par·tu·ri·ent (pär tŏŏr′ē ənt, -tyŏŏr′-), adj. **1.** bearing or about to bear young. **2.** pertaining to parturition. —**par·tu′ri·en·cy,** n.

par·tu·ri·fa·cient (pär tŏŏr′ə fā′shənt, -tyŏŏr′-), adj. **1.** accelerating labor or childbirth; oxytocic. —n. **2.** a parturifacient agent.

par·tu·ri·tion (pär′tŏŏ rish′ən, -tyŏŏ-, -chŏŏ-), n. the act or process of bringing forth young; childbirth.

par·vo (pär′vō), n., pl. **-vos.** PARVOVIRUS.

par·vo·vi·rus (pär′vō vī′rəs), n., pl. **-rus·es. 1.** a contagious, often fatal viral disease of dogs, characterized by vomiting, diarrhea, and a high fever. **2.** any of several small, DNA-containing viruses of the family Parvoviridae, esp. the virus causing parvovirus disease in dogs and distemper in cats.

pas′sive immu′nity, n. immunity that results from an external source, as injected antibody, or in infants from maternal antibody that has passed through the placenta or been received from breast milk.

pas′sive smok′ing, n. the inhaling of the cigarette, cigar, or pipe smoke of others, esp. by a nonsmoker in an enclosed area.

pas·teur·ize (pas′chə rīz′, pas′tə-), v.t., **-ized, -iz·ing.** to expose (a food, as milk, cheese, yogurt, beer, or wine) to an elevated temperature for a period of time sufficient to destroy harmful or undesirable microorganisms without radically altering taste or quality. —**pas′teur·i·za′tion,** n. —**pas′teur·iz′er,** n.

pas·tille (pa stēl′, -stil′) also **pas·til** (pas′til), n. a flavored or medicated lozenge; troche.

patch (pach), n. a piece of material used to cover or protect a wound, an injured part, etc., or as an adhesive containing medication for absorption into the bloodstream.

patch′ test′, n. a test for suspected allergy in which a patch impregnated with an allergen is applied to the skin.

pa·tel·la (pə tel′ə), n., pl. **-tel·las, -tel·lae** (-tel′ē). **1.** the flat, movable bone at the front of the knee; kneecap. **2.** any other disklike or pan-shaped anatomical structure. —**pa·tel′lar,** adj.

pa·ten·cy (pāt′n sē, pat′-), n. the state of being patent.

pat·ent (pat′nt), adj. open; unobstructed, as a bodily passage.

pat′ent med′icine, n. **1.** a nonprescription drug that is protected by the trademark of a company that owns the patent on its manufacture or is licensed to distribute it. **2.** any proprietary drug.

pa·ter·ni·ty (pə tûr′ni tē), n. the state of being a father; fatherhood.

pater′ni·ty test′, *n.* an assessment of possible paternity based on a comparison of the genetic markers of the offspring and those of the putative father.

path., 1. pathological. 2. pathology.

path·o·gen (path′ə jən, -jen′), *n.* any disease-producing agent, esp. a virus, bacterium, or other microorganism.

path·o·gen·e·sis, also **pa·thog·e·ny** (pə thoj′ə nē), *n.* the production and development of disease. —**path′o·ge·net′ic**, *adj.*

path·o·gen′ic, *adj.* capable of producing disease. —**path′o·ge·nic′i·ty** (-ō jə nis′i tē), *n.*

pa·thog·no·mon·ic (pə thog′nə mon′ik), *adj.* characteristic or diagnostic of a specific disease.

pathol., 1. pathological. 2. pathology.

path·o·log·i·cal (path′ə loj′i kəl) also **path′o·log′ic**, *adj.* 1. of or pertaining to pathology. 2. caused or affected by disease. 3. characterized by an unhealthy compulsion: *a pathological liar.* —**path′o·log′i·cal·ly**, *adv.*

pa·thol·o·gy (pə thol′ə jē), *n., pl.* **-gies** 1. the science or the study of the origin, nature, and course of diseases. 2. the conditions and processes of a disease. 3. any deviation from a healthy, normal, or efficient condition. —**pa·thol′o·gist,** *n.*

path·o·phys·i·ol·o·gy (path′ō fiz′ē ol′ə jē), *n.* the physiology of abnormal or diseased organisms or their parts; the functional changes associated with a disease or syndrome.

path′way′, *n.* a sequence of reactions, usu. controlled and catalyzed by enzymes, by which one organic substance is converted to another.

pa·tient (pā′shənt), *n.* a person who is under medical care or treatment.

Pav·lov′ian condi′tioning (pav lō′vē ən, -lô′-, -lov′ē-), *n.* CONDITIONING (def. 2).

PCP, 1. phencyclidine. 2. pneumocystis pneumonia.

PCR, polymerase chain reaction.

pecs (peks), *n.pl. Informal.* pectoral muscles.

pec·to·ral (pek′tər əl), *adj.* 1. of, in, on, or pertaining to the chest or breast; thoracic. —*n.* 2. a pectoral body part or organ. —**pec′to·ral·ly**, *adv.*

pec′toral mus′cle, *n.* any of four muscles, two on each side, originating in the chest wall and extending to the shoulders and upper arms.

ped·er·ast (ped′ə rast′, pē′də-), *n.* a man who engages in pederasty.

ped·er·as·ty (ped′ə ras′tē, pē′də-), *n.* sexual relations between a man and a boy. —**ped′er·as′tic,** *adj.* —**ped′er·as′ti·cal·ly,** *adv.*

pe·di·at·rics (pē′dē a′triks), *n.* (*used with a sing. v.*) the branch of medicine concerned with the development, care, and diseases of babies and children. —**pe′di·at′ric,** *adj.*

pe·dic·u·lo·sis (pə dik′yə lō′sis), *n.* infestation with lice of the genus *Pediculus* or *Pthirus.* —**pe·dic′u·lous** (-ləs), *adj.*

pe·dol·o·gy (pi dol′ə jē), *n.* 1. the scientific study of the nature and development of children. **2.** PEDIATRICS. —**pe·do·log·i·cal** (pĕd′l oj′i kəl), **pe′do·log′ic,** adj. —**pe·dol′o·gist,** n.

pe·do·phil·i·a (pē′də fil′ē ə), n. sexual desire in an adult for a child. —**pe′do·phile′** (-fīl′), n. —**pe′do·phil′i·ac,** adj., n. —**pe′do·phil′ic,** adj.

pel·la·gra (pə lag′rə, -lā′grə, -grə-), n. a disease caused by a deficiency of nicotinic acid in the diet, characterized by skin changes, severe nerve dysfunction, mental symptoms, and diarrhea. —**pel·la′grose, pel·la′grous,** adj.

pel·la·grin, n. a person affected with pellagra.

pel′vic gir′dle, n. the compound bony or cartilaginous arch supporting the hind limbs or analogous parts in vertebrates.

pel′vic inflam′matory disease′, n. an inflammation of the female pelvic organs, most commonly the fallopian tubes, usu. as a result of bacterial infection. Abbr.: PID

pel·vis (pel′vis), n., pl. **-vis·es, -ves** (-vēz). **1. a.** the basinlike cavity in the lower trunk of the body, formed by the sacrum, ilium, ischium, and pubis. **b.** the bones forming this cavity. **2.** the cavity of the kidney that receives the urine before it is passed into the ureter. —**pel′vic,** adj.

pem·phi·gus (pem′fi gəs, pem fī′-), n. a skin disease characterized by blisters and ulcerations.

pen·e·trance (pen′i trəns), n. the frequency, expressed as a percentage, with which a particular gene produces its effect in a group of organisms. Compare EXPRESSIVITY.

pen·i·cil·la·mine (pen′ə sil′ə mēn′, -min), n. a substance produced by the degradation of penicillin, used esp. to treat rheumatoid arthritis and heavy-metal poisoning.

pen·i·cil·lin (pen′ə sil′in), n. any of several antibiotics produced naturally or semisynthetically from molds of the genus *Penicillium,* widely used to prevent and treat bacterial infection and other diseases.

pe·nis (pē′nis), n., pl. **-nis·es, -nes** (-nēz). the male organ of copulation and, in mammals, of urinary excretion. —**pe·nile** (pēn′l, pē′nil), adj.

pen·tam·i·dine (pen tam′i dēn′, -din), n. an antiprotozoal substance, $C_{19}H_{24}N_4O_2$, used in treating pneumocystis pneumonia, leishmaniasis, and trypanosomiasis.

pen·tane (pen′tān), n. a hydrocarbon having three liquid isomers, the most important of which, C_5H_{12}, is a highly volatile petroleum distillate used as a solvent and an anesthetic.

pen·ta·ploid (pen′tə ploid′), adj. **1.** having a chromosome number that is five times the haploid number. —n. **2.** a pentaploid cell or organism. —**pen′ta·ploi′dy,** n.

pen·taz·o·cine (pen taz′ə sēn′), n. a synthetic narcotic analgesic, $C_{19}H_{27}NO.$

pen·to·bar·bi·tal (pen′tə bär′bi tôl′, -tal′), n. a barbiturate, $C_{11}H_{17}N_2O_3$, used as a hypnotic and as a sedative.

pen·tose (pen′tōs), n. a monosaccharide containing five atoms of carbon, as xylose, $C_5H_{10}O_5.$

Pen·to·thal (pen′tə thôl′), *Trademark.* a brand of thiopental sodium.

pep′ pill′, *n.* a pill, tablet, or capsule that contains a stimulant drug, esp. amphetamine.

pep·sin (pep′sin), *n.* **1.** an enzyme, produced in the stomach, that splits proteins into proteoses and peptones. **2.** a commercial preparation containing pepsin, obtained from hog stomachs, used chiefly as a digestive and as a ferment in making cheese.

pep·sin·o·gen (pep sin′ə jən, -jen′), *n.* a crystalline zymogen of the gastric glands that is converted to pepsin during digestion.

pep·tic (pep′tik), *adj.* **1.** pertaining to or associated with digestion; digestive. **2.** promoting digestion. **3.** of or pertaining to pepsin. —*n.* **4.** a substance promoting digestion.

pep′tic ul′cer, *n.* an erosion of the mucous membrane of the lower esophagus, stomach, or duodenum, caused in part by the corrosive action of the gastric juice.

pep·ti·dase (pep′ti dās′, -dāz′), *n.* any of the class of enzymes that catalyze the hydrolysis of peptides or peptones to amino acids.

pep·tide (pep′tīd), *n.* a compound containing two or more amino acids in which the carboxyl group of one acid is linked to the amino group of the other.

pep′tide bond′, *n.* a covalent bond formed by joining the carboxyl group of one amino acid to the amino group of another, with the removal of a molecule of water.

pep·tone (pep′tōn), *n.* any of a class of diffusible, soluble substances into which proteins are converted by partial hydrolysis. —**pep·ton′ic** (-ton′ik), *adj.*

per·cuss (pər kus′), *v.t.* to use percussion for diagnosis or therapy.

per·cus·sion, *n.* the striking or tapping of the surface of a part of the body for diagnostic or therapeutic purposes. —**per·cus′sion·al,** *adj.*

per·cu·ta·ne·ous (pûr′kyoo tā′nē əs), *adj.* administered, removed, or absorbed by way of the skin, as an injection or needle biopsy.

per·fuse (pər fyooz′), *v.t.,* **-fused, -fus·ing.** to pass (fluid) through blood vessels or the lymphatic system to an organ or tissue. —**per·fu′sion** (-fyoo′zhən), *n.* —**per·fu′sive** (-siv), *adj.*

per·i·car·di·tis (per′i kär dī′tis), *n.* inflammation of the pericardium. —**per′i·car·dit′ic** (-dit′ik), *adj.*

per·i·car·di·um (per′i kär′dē əm), *n., pl.* **-di·a** (-dē ə). the membranous sac enclosing the heart.

per·i·chon·dri·um (per′i kon′drē əm), *n., pl.* **-dri·a** (-drē ə). the membrane of fibrous connective tissue covering the surface of cartilages except at the joints. —**per′i·chon′dral, per′i·chon′dri·al,** *adj.*

per·i·derm (per′i dûrm′), *n.* the outermost layer of epidermal skin in most mammalian fetuses, usu. disappearing before birth. Also called **epitrichium.** —**per′i·der′mal, per′i·der′mic,** *adj.*

per·i·lymph (per′i limf′), *n.* the fluid between the bony and membranous labyrinths of the ear. —**per′i·lym·phat′ic,** *adj.*

pe·rim·e·ter (pə rim′i tər), *n.* an instrument for determining the peripheral field of vision.

per·i·my·si·um (per′ə miz′ē əm, -mizh′-), *n.,* pl. **-my·si·a** (-miz′ē ə, -mizh′-). the connective tissue surrounding bundles of skeletal muscle fibers. —**per′i·my′si·al,** *adj.*

per·i·na·tal (per′ə nāt′l), *adj.* occurring during or pertaining to the phase surrounding the time of birth, from the 20th week of gestation to the 28th day of newborn life. —**per′i·na′tal·ly,** *adv.*

per·i·ne·um (per′ə nē′əm), *n.,* pl. **-ne·a** (-nē′ə). the area in front of the anus extending to the fourchette of the vulva in the female and to the scrotum in the male. —**per′i·ne′al,** *adj.*

pe·ri·od (pēr′ē əd), *n.* **1.** an occurrence of menstruation. **2.** a time of the month during which menstruation occurs.

periodon′tal disease′, *n.* PYORRHEA (def. 2).

per·i·o·don·tics (per′ē ə don′tiks) also **per·i·o·don·tia** (-don′shə, -shē ə), *n.* (*used with a sing. v.*) the branch of dentistry dealing with the study and treatment of diseases of the periodontium. —**per′i·o·don′tal, per′i·o·don′tic,** *adj.* —**per′i·o·don′tist,** *n.*

per·i·o·don·ti·tis (per′ē ō don tī′tis), *n.* **1.** inflammatory disease of the periodontium. **2.** PYORRHEA (def. 2).

per·i·o·don·tium (per′ē ə don′shəm, -shē əm), *n.,* pl. **-ti·a** (-shə, -shē ə). the bone, connective tissue, and gum surrounding and supporting a tooth.

per·i·os·te·um (per′ē os′tē əm), *n.,* pl. **-te·a** (-tē ə). the dense, fibrous connective layer of tissue covering all bones except where ligaments attach and on the surfaces of joints. —**per′i·os′te·al, per′i·os′te·ous,** *adj.* —**per′i·os′te·al·ly,** *adv.*

per·i·os·ti·tis (per′ē o stī′tis), *n.* inflammation of the periosteum. —**per′i·os·tit′ic** (-stit′ik), *adj.*

periph′eral nerv′ous sys′tem, *n.* the portion of the nervous system lying outside the brain and spinal cord.

periph′eral vi′sion, *n.* all that is visible to the eye outside the central area of focus; side vision.

per·i·stal·sis (per′ə stôl′sis, -stal′-), *n.,* pl. **-ses** (-sēz). progressive waves of involuntary muscle contractions and relaxations that move matter along certain tubelike structures of the body, as ingested food along the alimentary canal. —**per′i·stal′tic,** *adj.* —**per′i·stal′ti·cal·ly,** *adv.*

per·i·to·ne·um (per′i tn ē′əm), *n.,* pl. **-to·ne·ums, -to·ne·a** (-tn ē′ə). the serous membrane lining the abdominal cavity and investing its viscera. —**per′i·to·ne′al,** *adj.* —**per′i·to·ne′al·ly,** *adv.*

per′i·to·ni′tis (-tn i′tis), *n.* inflammation of the peritoneum. —**per′i·to·nit′ic** (-it′ik), *adj.* —**per′i·to·nit′al,** *adj.*

per·me·ase (pûr′mē ās′, -āz′), *n.* any protein of the cell membrane that functions as a channel for specific molecular substances to enter or leave the cell.

per·mis·sive (pər mis/iv), *adj. Genetics.* (of a cell) permitting replication of a strand of DNA that could be lethal, as a viral segment or mutant gene.

per·ni·cious ane/mia (pər nish/əs), *n.* a severe anemia associated with inadequate intake or absorption of vitamin B_{12}, characterized by defective production of red blood cells.

per·ni·o (pûr/nē ō/), *n., pl.* **per·ni·o·nes** (pûr/nē ō/nēz). CHILBLAIN.

per·o·ne·al (per/ə nē/əl), *adj.* pertaining to or situated near the fibula.

per·o·ral (pə rôr/əl, -rōr/-), *adj.* administered or performed through the mouth, as surgery or administration of a drug. —**per·o/ral·ly,** *adv.*

per·phen·a·zine (pər fen/ə zēn/, -zin), *n.* a crystalline, water-insoluble powder, $C_{21}H_{26}ClN_3OS$, used chiefly as a tranquilizer and in treating intractable hiccups and nausea.

per·so·na (pər sō/nə), *n., pl.* **-nae** (-nē), **-nas.** (in the psychology of C. G. Jung) the public role or personality a person assumes or is perceived to assume (contrasted with *anima*).

per·tus·sis (pər tus/is), *n.* WHOOPING COUGH. —**per·tus/-sal,** *adj.*

pes·sa·ry (pes/ə rē), *n., pl.* **-ries. 1.** a device worn in the vagina to support a displaced uterus. **2.** a vaginal suppository. **3.** DIAPHRAGM (def. 3).

pes·ti·lence (pes/tl əns), *n.* **1.** a deadly or virulent epidemic disease. **2.** BUBONIC PLAGUE.

pes·ti·lent, *adj.* producing or tending to produce infectious or contagious, often epidemic, disease; pestilential.

pes·ti·len/tial (-en/shəl), *adj.* **1.** producing or tending to produce pestilence. **2.** pertaining to or of the nature of pestilence, esp. bubonic plague.

PET (pet), *n.* positron emission tomography: a technique for revealing active areas of the brain while information is being processed by detecting radiolabeled glucose in the cerebral blood flow. Compare PET SCANNER.

pe·te·chi·a (pi tē/kē ə, -tek/ē ə), *n., pl.* **-te·chi·ae** (-tē/-kē ē/, -tek/ē ē/). a minute, round, nonraised hemorrhage in the skin or in a mucous or serous membrane. —**pe·te/chi·al,** *adj.*

pe·tit mal (pet/ē mäl/, mal/, pə tē/), *n.* See under EPILEPSY.

PET/ scan/, *n.* **1.** an examination performed with a PET scanner. **2.** an x-ray image obtained by examination with a PET scanner.

PET/ scan/ner, *n.* a tomographic device that produces computerized cross-sectional images of biochemical activity in the brain or other organ through the use of radioactive tracers.

pe·yo·te (pā ō/tē), *n., pl.* **-tes. 1.** MESCAL (def. 1). **2.** MESCAL BUTTON. **3.** MESCALINE.

pH, the symbol for the logarithm of the reciprocal of hydrogen ion concentration in gram atoms per liter, used to describe the acidity or alkalinity of a chemical solution on a scale of 0 (more acidic) to 14 (more alkaline).

phac·o·e·mul·si·fi·ca·tion (fak′ō i mul′sə fi kā′shən), *n.* the removal of a cataract by first liquefying the affected lens with ultrasonic vibrations and then extracting it by suction.

phage (fāj), *n.* BACTERIOPHAGE.

phag·o·cyte (fag′ə sit′), *n.* any cell, as a macrophage, that ingests foreign particles, bacteria, or cell debris. —**phag′o·cyt′ic** (-sit′ik), *adj.*

phag′ocyt′ic in′dex, *n.* the average number of bacteria ingested per phagocyte in an incubated mixture of bacteria, phagocytes, and blood serum.

phag·o·cy·to·sis (fag′ə si tō′sis), *n.* the ingestion by a cell of a microorganism, cell particle, or other matter surrounded and engulfed by the cell. Compare ENDOCYTOSIS. —**phag′o·cy·tot′ic** (-tot′ik), *adj.*

pha·lanx (fā′langks, fal′angks), *n., pl.* **pha·lan·ges.** any of the bones of the fingers or toes.

phal·lic (fal′ik), *adj.* **1.** of or pertaining to a phallus. **2.** GENITAL (def. 3).

phal·lus (fal′əs), *n., pl.* **phal·li** (fal′ī), **phal·lus·es.** **1.** PENIS. **2.** the undifferentiated embryonic organ out of which either the penis or the clitoris develops.

phan′tom limb′ pain′, *Pathol.* a phenomenon characterized by the experience of pain, discomfort, or other sensation in the area of a missing limb or other body part, as a breast. Also called **pseudesthesia.**

Phar. or **phar.,** pharmacy.

pharm., **1.** pharmaceutical. **2.** pharmacology. **3.** pharmacopoeia. **4.** pharmacy.

phar·ma·ceu·ti·cal (fär′mə sōō′ti kəl) also **phar′ma·ceu′tic,** *adj.* **1.** pertaining to pharmacy or pharmacists. —*n.* **2.** a pharmaceutical preparation or product. —**phar′ma·ceu′ti·cal·ly,** *adv.*

phar·ma·ceu·tics, *n.* (*used with a sing. v.*) PHARMACY (def. 2).

phar·ma·cist (-sist), *n.* a person licensed to prepare and dispense drugs and medicines; druggist.

phar·ma·cog·no·sy (-kog′nə sē), *n.* MATERIA MEDICA (def. 2). —**phar′ma·cog′no·sist,** *n.* —**phar′ma·cog·nos′tic** (-nos′tik), *adj.*

phar·ma·co·ki·net·ics (-kō ki net′iks, -ki-), *n.* **1.** (*used with a pl. v.*) the actions of drugs within the body, as their absorption, distribution, metabolism, and elimination. **2.** (*used with a sing. v.*) the study of such actions.

phar·ma·col·o·gy (-kol′ə jē), *n.* the science dealing with the preparation, uses, and esp. the effects of drugs. —**phar′ma·co·log′i·cal** (-kə loj′i kəl), **phar′ma·co·log′ic,** *adj.* —**phar′ma·co·log′i·cal·ly,** *adv.* —**phar′ma·col′o·gist,** *n.*

phar·ma·co·poe·ia or **phar·ma·co·pe·ia** (-kə pē′ə), *n., pl.* **-ias. 1.** a book published usu. under the jurisdiction of the government and containing a list of drugs, their formulas, methods for making medicinal preparations, and other related information. **2.** a stock of drugs. —**phar·ma·co·poe·ial, phar·ma·co·poe·ic,** *adj.* —**phar·ma·co·poe·ist,** *n.*

phar·ma·cy (fär′mə sē), *n., pl.* **-cies. 1.** a place where drugs and medicines are prepared and dispensed. **2.** the art and science of preparing and dispensing drugs and medicines. Also called **pharmaceutics.**

pha·ryn·ge·al (fə rin′jē əl, -jəl, far′in jē′əl) also **pha·ryn·gal** (fə ring′gəl), *adj.* of, pertaining to, or situated near the pharynx.

phar·yn·gi·tis (far′in jī′tis), *n.* inflammation of the mucous membrane of the pharynx; sore throat.

pha·ryn·go·scope (fə ring′gə skōp′), *n.* an instrument for inspecting the pharynx. —**pha·ryn′go·scop′ic** (-skop′ik), *adj.* —**phar·yn·gos·co·pist** (far′ing gos′kə pist), *n.* —**phar′yn·gos′co·py,** *n.*

phar·ynx (far′ingks), *n., pl.* **pha·ryn·ges** (fə rin′jēz), **phar·ynx·es.** the portion of the alimentary canal, with its membranes and muscles, that connects the mouth and nasal passages with the larynx.

Phe, phenylalanine.

phe·nac·e·tin (fə nas′i tin), *n.* a white, crystalline solid, $C_{10}H_{13}NO_2$, formerly used to relieve pain and fever: withdrawn because of unfavorable side effects.

phen·cy·cli·dine (fen sī′kli dēn′, -sik′li-), *n.* an anesthetic drug, $C_{17}H_{25}N$, used as an animal tranquilizer: also widely used in several forms as an illicit hallucinogen. Also called **PCP.**

phene (fēn), *n.* any characteristic of an individual organism that is genetically determined.

phen·met·ra·zine (fen me′trə zēn′), *n.* a compound, $C_{11}H_{15}NO$, used chiefly to control the appetite in the treatment of obesity.

phe·no·bar·bi·tal (fē′nō bär′bi tôl′, -tal′, -nə-), *n.* a white, crystalline powder, $C_{12}H_{12}N_2O_3$, used as a sedative, a hypnotic, and as an antispasmodic in epilepsy.

phe·no·cop·y (fē′nə kop′ē), *n., pl.* **-cop·ies.** a trait or condition that resembles a known genetic defect but is externally caused and not inheritable.

phe·nol (fē′nôl, -nol), *n.* a white, crystalline, water-soluble, poisonous substance, C_6H_5OH, used chiefly as a disinfectant, as an antiseptic, and in organic synthesis. —**phe·nol·ic** (fi nō′lik, -nol′ik), *adj.*

phe·nol·phthal·ein (-thal′ēn, -ē in, -fthal′-), *n.* a white, crystalline compound, $C_{20}H_{14}O_4$, used as a laxative.

phe·nol·sul·fone·phthal·ein (-sul′fōn-), *n.* a bright to dark red crystalline compound, $C_{19}H_{14}O_5S$, slightly soluble in water, alcohol, and acetone: used as a diagnostic reagent in medicine. Also called **phe′nol red′.**

phe·no·thi·a·zine (fē′nə thī′ə zēn′, -zin), *n.* any of a class of medications used principally to treat psychotic symptoms, as hallucinations, and excessive excitability.

phe·no·type (fē′nə tīp′), *n.* **1.** the observable constitution of an organism. **2.** the appearance of an organism resulting from the interaction of the genotype and the environment. Compare GENOTYPE. —**phe/no·typ/ic** (-tip/ik), **phe/no·typ/i·cal**, *adj.* —**phe/no·typ/i·cal·ly**, *adv.*

phen·yl·al·a·nine (fen/l al/ə nēn′, -nin, fēn/-), *n.* a crystalline, water-soluble, essential amino acid, $C_6H_5CH_2CH-(NH_2)COOH$, necessary to the nutrition of humans and most other animals, occurring in egg white and skim milk. *Abbr.:* Phe; *Symbol:* F

phen/yl·bu/ta·zone (-byōō/tə zōn′), *n.* a potent substance, $C_{19}H_{20}N_2O_2$, used to reduce pain and inflammation in rheumatic diseases and gout, and used in veterinary medicine for musculoskeletal disorders.

phen/yl·eph/rine (-ef/rēn, -rin), *n.* an alpha-adrenergic stimulant, $C_{19}H_{13}NO_2$, used chiefly as a nasal decongestant.

phen/yl·ke/to·nu/ri·a (-kē/tō nŏŏr/ē ə, -nyŏŏr/-), *n.* an inherited defect of the ability to metabolize phenylalanine, requiring a diet free of or low in phenylalanine to avoid eczema, mental retardation, and other effects.

phen/yl·pro/pan·ol/a·mine (-prō/pə nol/ə mēn′, -min), *n.* a substance, $C_9H_{13}NO$, related to ephedrine and amphetamine, available in various nonprescription diet aids as an appetite suppressant.

phen/yl·thi/o·car/ba·mide (-thī/ō kär/bə mīd′, -mid, -kär bam/īd, -id), *n.* a crystalline, slightly water-soluble solid, $C_6H_5NHCSNH_2$, that is either tasteless or bitter, depending upon the heredity of the taster, used in medical genetics and as a diagnostic. *Abbr.:* PTC Also called **phen/yl·thi/o·u·re/a** (-yōō rē/ə, -yŏŏr/ē ə).

phen·y·to·in (fen/i tō/in, fə nit/ō-), *n.* a barbiturate-related substance, $C_{15}H_{12}N_2O_2$, used as an anticonvulsant in the treatment of epilepsy.

phi·mo·sis (fī mō/sis, fi-), *n., pl.* **-ses** (-sēz) a constriction of the opening of the prepuce, preventing the foreskin from being drawn back to uncover the glans penis. —**phi·mot/ic** (-mot/ik), *adj.*

phi/ phenom/enon/, *n.* the perception of movement when stationary stimuli are presented as a series in an ordered progression.

phle·bi·tis (flə bī/tis), *n.* inflammation of a vein, often occurring in the legs and involving the formation of a thrombus, characterized by swelling, pain, and change of skin color. —**phle·bit/ic** (-bit/ik), *adj.*

phle·bol·o·gy (flə bol/ə jē), *n.* the study of the anatomy, physiology, and diseases of veins. Also called **venology**. —**phle·bol/o·gist**, *n.*

phle·bot·o·mist (flə bot/ə mist) *n.* a nurse or other health worker trained in drawing venous blood for testing or donation.

phle·bot·o·my, *n., pl.* **-mies.** the act or practice of opening a vein to let or draw blood as a therapeutic or diagnostic measure. Also called **venesection**. —**phleb·o·tom·ic** (fleb/ə tom/ik), *adj.* —**phle·bot/o·mize′**, *v.t.*, **-mized**, **-miz·ing.**

phlegm (flem), *n.* the thick mucus secreted in the respiratory passages and discharged through the mouth, esp. that occurring in the lungs and throat passages, as during a cold.

phlo·gis·tic (flō jis′tik), *adj. Pathol.* inflammatory.

phlyc·te·na (flik tē′nə), *n., pl.* **-nae** (-nē). a small vesicle, blister, or pustule.

pho·bi·a (fō′bē ə), *n., pl.* **-bi·as.** a persistent, irrational fear of a specific object, activity, or situation that leads to a compelling desire to avoid it. —**pho′bic,** *adj., n.*

pho·no·car·di·o·gram (fō′nə kär′dē ə gram′), *n.* the graphic record produced by a phonocardiograph.

pho′no·car′di·o·graph′ (-graf′, -gräf′), *n.* an instrument for graphically recording the sound of the heartbeat. —**pho′no·car′di·og′ra·phy** (-og′rə fē), *n.*

phos·phate (fos′fāt), *n.* a salt or ester of phosphoric acid, essential to growth. —**phos·phat′ic** (-fat′ik, -fā′tik), *adj.*

phos·pha·tide (fos′fə tid′, -tid), *n.* PHOSPHOLIPID.

phos·pha·tu·ri·a (fos′fə tŏŏr′ē ə, -tyŏŏr′-), *n.* the presence of an excessive quantity of phosphates in the urine. —**phos′pha·tu′ric,** *adj.*

phos·phene (fos′fēn), *n.* a luminous visual image produced by mechanical stimulation of the retina, as when pressing on closed eyelids.

phos·pho·cre·a·tine (fos′fō krē′ə tēn′, -tin), *n.* a compound, $C_4H_{10}O_5N_3P$, occurring in muscle, formed by the enzymatic interaction of an organic phosphate and creatine, the breakdown of which provides energy for muscle contraction. Also called **creatine phosphate.**

phos′pho·lip′id (-lip′id), *n.* any of a group of fatty compounds, composed of phosphoric esters, present in living cells.

phos′pho·lip′id bi′lay·er, *n.* a two-layered arrangement of phosphate and lipid molecules that form a cell membrane, the hydrophobic lipid ends facing inward and the hydrophilic phosphate ends facing outward. Also called **lipid bilayer.**

phos·pho·pro·tein, *n.* a protein, as casein or ovalbumin, having phosphate groups attached to the side chain of its amino acids.

phos·phor·ic (fos fôr′ik, -for′-), *adj.* of or containing phosphorus, esp. in the pentavalent state.

phos·pho·rism (fos′fə riz′əm), *n.* chronic phosphorus poisoning.

phos·pho·rus (fos′fər əs), *n., pl.* **-pho·ri** (-fə rī′). a nonmetallic element existing in yellow, red, and black allotropic forms and an essential constituent of plant and animal tissue: used, in combined form, in matches and fertilizers. Symbol: P; *at. wt.:* 30.974; *at. no.:* 15; *sp. gr.:* (yellow) 1.82 at 20°C, (red) 2.20 at 20°C, (black) 2.25–2.69 at 20°C. s

phos·pho·ryl·ase (fos′fər ə lās′, -lāz′, fos fôr′ə-, -for′-), *n.* any enzyme, occurring widely in animal and plant tissue, that in the presence of an inorganic phosphate catalyzes the conversion of glycogen into sugar phosphate.

phos′pho•ryl•ate′, *v.t.,* **-at•ed, -at•ing.** to introduce the trivalent group =P=O into an organic compound. —**phos′pho•ryl•a′tion,** *n.*

pho•to•ag•ing (fō′tō ā′jing), *n.* damage to the skin, as wrinkles or discoloration, caused by prolonged exposure to sunlight.

pho•to•co•ag′u•la′tion (-kō ag′yə lā′shən), *n.* a surgical technique that uses an intense beam of light, as from a laser, to seal blood vessels or coagulate tissue. —**pho′to•co•ag′u•late′,** *v.t.,* **-lat•ed, -lat•ing.** —**pho′to•co•ag′u•la′tive** (-lā′tiv, -lə tiv), *adj.*

pho′to•fluor′o•gram′ (-flŏŏr′ə gram′, -flôr′-, -flōr′-), *n.* a recording on photographic film of images produced by a fluoroscopic examination.

pho′to•fluo•rog′ra•phy (-flŏŏ rog′rə fē, -flô-, -flō-), *n.* photography of images produced by a fluoroscopic examination, used in x-ray examination of the lungs of large groups of people. Also called **fluorography.**

pho•to•gen•ic (fō′tə jen′ik), *adj.* **1.** producing or emitting light, as certain bacteria; luminiferous; phosphorescent. **2.** produced or caused by light, as a skin condition. —**pho′to•gen′i•cal•ly,** *adv.*

pho•to•pho′bi•a (-fō′bē ə), *n.* **1.** an abnormal sensitivity to or intolerance of light, as in iritis. **2.** an abnormal fear of light. —**pho•to•pho′bic,** *adj.*

pho•to•pi•a (fō tō′pē ə), *n.* vision in bright light (opposed to *scotopia*). —**pho•top′ic** (-top′ik, -tō′pik), *adj.*

pho•to•re•cep•tion (fō′tō ri sep′shən), *n.* the physiological perception of light. —**pho•to•re•cep′tive,** *adj.*

pho′to•re•cep′tor, *n.* a membrane protein or end organ that is stimulated by light.

pho•to•scan (fō′tə skan′), *v.t.,* **-scanned, -scan•ning.** to study the distribution of a radioactive isotope or radiopaque dye in (a body organ or part) through the use of x-rays.

pho′to•sen′si•tive (-sen′si tiv), *adj.* sensitive to light or similar radiation.

pho′to•sen′si•tiv′i•ty, *n.* **1.** the quality of being photosensitive. **2.** abnormal sensitivity of the skin to ultraviolet light, usu. following exposure to certain drugs or other sensitizing chemicals.

pho′to•ther′a•py (-ther′ə pē), *n.* the treatment of disease by means of exposure to light.

pho′to•tox′in (-tok′sin), *n.* a plant toxin that causes an allergic reaction in a susceptible person who touches or ingests it and is subsequently exposed to sunlight.

phthi•ri•a•sis (thi ri′ə sis, thi-), *n.* infestation of pubic hair or other body hair by crab lice.

phyl•lo•qui•none (fil′ō kwi nōn′, -kwin′ōn), *n.* VITAMIN K₁.

phy•log•e•ny (fī loj′ə nē), *n.* **1.** the development or evolution of a particular group of organisms. **2.** the evolutionary history of a group of organisms, esp. as depicted in a family tree. Compare ONTOGENY. —**phy·log/e·nist,** *n.*

phys·i·at·rics (fiz/ē a/triks), *n.* (used with a sing. v.) **1.** PHYSIATRY. **2.** PHYSICAL THERAPY. —**phys/i·at/ric, phys/i·at/ri·cal,** *adj.*

phy·si·a·try (fi zī/ə trē, fīz/ē a/-) also **physiatrics,** *n.* the medical specialty for the treatment of disease and injury by physical agents, as exercise, manipulation, or heat therapy. Also called **physical medicine.** —**phy·si/a·trist,** *n.*

phys/ical examina/tion, *n.* an examination, usu. by a physician, of a person's body in order to determine his or her state of health or physical fitness.

phys·i·cal·i·ty (fiz/i kal/i tē), *n., pl.* **-ties.** preoccupation with one's physical needs, or appetites.

phys/ical med/icine, *n.* PHYSIATRY.

phys/ical ther/apy, *n.* the treatment or management of physical disability, malfunction, or pain by physical techniques, as exercise, massage, hydrotherapy, etc. —**phys/ical ther/apist,** *n.*

phy·si·cian (fi zish/ən), *n.* **1.** a person who is legally qualified to practice medicine; doctor of medicine. **2.** a person engaged in general medical practice, as distinguished from a surgeon. —**phy·si/cian·ly,** *adj.*

physi/cian assis/tant or **physi/cian's assis/tant,** *n.* a person trained and certified to perform many clinical procedures under the supervision of a physician. *Abbr.:* PA

phys·i·o·log·i·cal (fiz/ē ə loj/i kəl) also **phys/i·o·log/ic,** *adj.* **1.** of or pertaining to physiology. **2.** consistent with the normal functioning of an organism. —**phys/i·o·log/i·cal·ly,** *adv.*

physiolog/ical psychol/ogy, *n.* the branch of psychology concerned with the relationship between the physical functioning of an organism and its behavior.

phys/i·ol·o·gy (-ol/ə jē), *n.* **1.** the branch of biology dealing with the functions and activities of living organisms and their parts. **2.** the organic processes or functions in an organism or in any of its parts.

phy·so·stig·mine (fī/sō stig/mēn, -min), *n.* an alkaloid, $C_{15}H_{21}N_3O_2$, used in the treatment of Alzheimer's disease to raise the level of the neurotransmitter acetylcholine. Also called **eserine.**

phy·to·a·lex·in (fī/tō ə lek/sin), *n.* any of a class of plant compounds that accumulate at the site of invading microorganisms and confer resistance to disease.

phy·to·na·di·one (fī/tō nə dī/ōn), *n.* VITAMIN K₁.

pi·a ma·ter (pī/ə mā/tər, pē/ə), *n.* the delicate, fibrous, and highly vascular membrane forming the innermost of the three coverings of the brain and spinal cord. Compare ARACHNOID, DURA MATER, MENINGES.

pi·ca (pī/kə), *n.* an abnormal appetite or craving for substances that are not fit to eat, as chalk or clay.

pi·cor·na·vi·rus (pi kôr/nə vī/rəs, -kôr/nə vī/-), *n., pl.* **-rus·es.** any of several small, RNA-containing viruses of the family Picornaviridae, including poliovirus and the rhinoviruses that cause the common cold.

pic·ro·tox·in (pik'rə tok'sin), *n.* a poisonous stimulant, $C_{30}H_{34}O_{13}$, obtained from the seeds of *Anamirta cocculus*, used chiefly in the treatment of barbiturate poisoning. —**pic'ro·tox'ic,** *adj.*

PID, pelvic inflammatory disease.

pi'geon breast', *n.* CHICKEN BREAST.

pi'geon-toed', *adj.* having the toes or feet turned inward.

pig·ment (pig'mənt), *n.* any of various biological substances, as chlorophyll and melanin, that produce color in the tissues of organisms.

pile (pīl), *n.* Usu., **piles. 1.** HEMORRHOID. **2.** the condition of having hemorrhoids.

pill (pil), *n.* **the pill,** (*sometimes cap.*) BIRTH-CONTROL PILL.

pi·lo·car·pine (pī'lə kär'pēn, -pin, pil'ə-), *n.* an oil or crystalline alkaloid, $C_{11}H_{16}N_2O_2$, obtained from the South American plant jaborandi, used chiefly to promote the flow of saliva or contract the pupil of the eye.

pil·ule (pil'yōol), *n.* a small pill (contrasted with *bolus*).

pim·ple (pim'pəl), *n.* a small, usu. inflammatory swelling or elevation of the skin; papule or pustule.

pin·e·al (pin'ē əl, pī'nē-, pi nē'-), *adj.* of or pertaining to the pineal gland.

pin'eal gland', *n.* a small, cone-shaped endocrine organ in the posterior forebrain, secreting melatonin and involved in biorhythms and gonadal development. Also called **epiphysis.**

pink'eye', *n.* a contagious, epidemic form of acute conjunctivitis occurring in humans and certain animals: so called from the color of the inflamed eye.

pin·na (pin'ə), *n., pl.* **pin·nae** (pin'ē), **pin·nas.** the visible portion of the ear that projects from the head. —**pin'nal,** *adj.*

pin·ta (pin'tə, -tä) *n.* an infectious disease occurring chiefly in Central and South America, caused by *Treponema carateum*, characterized by spots of various colors on the skin.

pin·worm (pin'wûrm'), *n.* a small nematode worm, *Enterobius vermicularis*, infesting the intestine and migrating to the anus, esp. in children.

pi·tu·i·tar·y (pi tōō'i ter'ē, -tyōō'-), *n., pl.* **-tar·ies,** *adj.* —*n.* **1.** a hormonal extract obtained from pituitary glands for use as a medicine. —*adj.* **2.** noting an abnormal physical type resulting from excessive pituitary secretion.

pitu'itary gland', *n.* a small, somewhat cherry-shaped double-lobed structure attached to the base of the brain, constituting the master endocrine gland affecting all hormonal functions of the body. Compare ANTERIOR PITUITARY, POSTERIOR PITUITARY.

pit·y·ri·a·sis (pit'ə rī'ə sis), *n.* any of several skin diseases marked by the shedding of branlike scales.

PKU, phenylketonuria

pla·ce·bo (plə sē'bō), *n., pl.* **-bos, -boes. 1.** a substance having no pharmacological effect but given to placate a patient who supposes it to be a medicine. **2.** a pharmacologically inactive substance or a sham procedure administered as a control in testing the efficacy of a drug or course of action.

pla·ce′bo effect′, *n.* a reaction to a placebo manifested by a lessening of symptoms or the production of anticipated side effects.

plague (plāg), *n.* **1.** an epidemic disease that causes high mortality. **2.** an infectious, epidemic disease caused by a bacterium, *Yersinia pestis,* characterized by fever, chills, and prostration, transmitted to humans from rats by means of the bites of fleas. Compare BUBONIC PLAGUE.

pla·ni·graph (plā′ni graf′, -gräf′, plan′i-) also **pla·ni·gram** (-gram′), *n.* an x-ray photograph focused on a given plane of the body, leaving those above and below out of focus. **—pla·nig·ra·phy** (plə nig′rə fē), *n.*

plan·tar (plan′tər), *adj.* of or pertaining to the sole of the foot.

plaque (plak), *n.* **1.** a flat, often raised patch on any external or internal body surface. **2.** an abnormal hardened deposit on the inner wall of an artery. **3.** a soft, sticky, whitish film formed on tooth surfaces, composed of bacteria, mucin, and other matter. **4.** a clear area in a laboratory dish of a bacterial culture, indicating dead bacteria.

plas·ma (plaz′mə), *n.* **1.** the fluid part of blood or lymph, as distinguished from the cellular components. **2.** PROTOPLASM. Also, **plasm** (plaz′əm). **—plas·mat·ic** (-mat′ik), **plas′mic,** *adj.*

plas′ma cell′, *n.* an antibody-secreting cell, derived from B cells, that plays a major role in antibody-mediated immunity. Also called **plas·ma·cyte** (plaz′mə sīt′).

plas′ma·pher·e·sis (-fə rē′sis), *n.* a type of apheresis in which blood cells are returned to the bloodstream of the donor and the plasma is used, as for transfusion.

plas·mid (plaz′mid), *n.* a strand or loop of DNA that exists independently of the chromosome in bacteria and yeast and that is capable of genetic replication: used in recombinant DNA procedures as a vehicle of gene transfer.

plas·min (plaz′min), *n.* an enzyme in the blood that dissolves blood clots by breaking down fibrin. Also called **fibrinolysin.**

plas·min′o·gen (-ə jən, -jen′), *n.* a substance in the blood that forms plasmin when activated.

plas·ter (plas′tər, plä′stər), *n.* a solid or semisolid preparation spread upon cloth or other material and applied to the body, esp. for some healing purpose.

plas′tic sur′gery, *n.* the surgical repair, replacement, or reshaping of malformed, injured, or lost parts of the body. **—plas′tic sur′geon,** *n.*

plate·let (plāt′lit), *n.* a small platelike body, esp. a blood platelet.

pleas′ure prin′ciple, *n. Psychoanal.* an automatic mental drive or instinct seeking to avoid pain and to obtain pleasure.

pledg·et (plej′it), *n.* a small, flat mass of lint, absorbent cotton, or the like, for use on a wound, sore, etc.

plei·ot·ro·py (pli o′trə pē), *n.* the phenomenon of one gene affecting more than one phenotypic characteristic. —**plei′o·trop′ic** (-ə trop′ik, -trō′pik), *adj.* —**plei′o·trop′i·cal·ly,** *adv.*

ples·sor (ples′ər), *n.* PLEXOR.

ple·thys·mo·gram (plə thiz′mə gram′), *n.* the recording of a plethysmograph.

ple·thys′mo·graph′, *n.* a device for measuring and recording changes in the volume of the body or of a body part or organ. —**ple·thys′mo·graph′ic,** *adj.* —**pleth·ys·mog·ra·phy** (pleth′iz mog′rə fē), *n.*

pleu·ra (plŏŏr′ə), *n., pl.* **pleu·rae** (plŏŏr′ē). one of a pair of serous membranes each of which covers a lung and folds back to line the corresponding side of the chest wall.

pleu′ral, *adj.* of or pertaining to the pleura.

pleu·ri·sy (plŏŏr′ə sē), *n.* inflammation of the pleura, with or without a liquid effusion in the pleural cavity, characterized by a dry cough and pain in the affected side. —**pleu·rit·ic** (plŏŏ rit′ik), *adj.*

pleu·ro·pneu·mo·nia (plŏŏr′ō nŏŏ mōn′yə, -mō′nē ə, -nyŏŏ-), *n.* pleurisy conjoined with pneumonia. —**pleu′ro·pneu·mon′ic** (-nŏŏ mon′ik, -nyŏŏ-), *adj.*

plex·or (plek′sər) also **plessor,** *n.* a small hammer with a soft head, used in medicine for diagnostic percussion.

plex·us (-səs), *n., pl.* **-us·es, -us.** a network, as of nerves or blood vessels. —**plex′al,** *adj.*

ploi·dy (ploi′dē), *n.* the number of chromosome sets in the nucleus of a cell.

plum·bism (plum′biz əm), *n.* LEAD POISONING.

PMS, premenstrual syndrome.

pneu·mec·to·my (nŏŏ mek′tə mē, nyŏŏ-), *n., pl.* **-mies.** PNEUMONECTOMY.

pneu·mo·ba·cil·lus (nŏŏ′mō bə sil′əs, nyŏŏ′-), *n., pl.* **-cil·li** (-sil′ī). an enterobacterium, *Klebsiella pneumoniae,* that is a cause of pneumonia and urinary tract infection.

pneu′mo·coc′cus (nŏŏ′mə-), *n., pl.* **-coc·ci.** a bacterium, *Streptococcus (Diplococcus) pneumoniae,* that invades the respiratory tract and is a major cause of pneumonia. —**pneu′mo·coc′cal,** *adj.*

pneu′mo·co·ni·o′sis (-kō′nē ō′sis), *n.* any chronic lung disease, including anthracosis, asbestosis, and silicosis, caused by the inhalation of particles of coal, asbestos, silica, or similar substances and leading to fibrosis and loss of lung function.

pneu·mo·cys′tis pneumo′nia (nŏŏ′mə sis′tis, nyŏŏ′-), *n.* a rare form of pulmonary infection caused by the protozoan *Pneumocystis carinii,* occurring as an opportunistic disease in persons with impaired immune systems, as persons with AIDS. *Abbr.:* PCP Also called **pneumocys′tis ca·ri′ni·i pneumo′nia** (kə ri′nē ī′).

pneu'mo·graph', *n.* a device for recording graphically the respiratory movements of the thorax. —**pneu'mo·graph'ic**, *adj.*

pneu'mo·nec'to·my (-nek/tə mē) also **pneumonectomy**, *n., pl.* **-mies.** surgical excision of all or part of a lung.

pneu·mo·nia (nŏŏ mōn/yə, -mō/nē ə, nyŏŏ-), *n.* **1.** inflammation of the lungs with congestion. **2.** an acute infection of the lungs caused by the bacterium *Streptococcus pneumoniae.*

pneu·mon·ic (nŏŏ mon/ik, nyŏŏ-), *adj.* **1.** of, pertaining to, or affecting the lungs; pulmonary. **2.** pertaining to or affected with pneumonia.

pneu·mo·ni·tis (nŏŏ/mə ni/tis, nyŏŏ'-), *n.* inflammation of the lung.

pneu'mo·tho'rax, *n.* the presence of air or gas in the pleural cavity.

p.o., (in prescriptions) by mouth. [Latin, *per os*]

pock (pok), *n.* a pockmark.

pocked, *adj.* having pustules, pockmarks, or pits.

pock'mark', *n.* a scar or pit on the skin left by a pustule of smallpox, chickenpox, acne, etc.

po·dag·ra (pō dag/rə, pod/ə grə), *n.* gouty inflammation of the great toe. —**po·dag'ral, po·dag'ric, po·dag'rous,** *adj.*

po·di·a·trist (pə di/ə trist, pō-), *n.* a person qualified to diagnose and treat foot disorders. Also called **chiropodist.**

po·di·a·try, *n.* the care of the human foot, esp. the diagnosis and treatment of foot disorders. Also called **chiropody.**

pod·o·phyl·lin (pod/ə fil/in), *n.* a light brown to greenish dried resin used in an ointment for the removal of warts. —**pod/o·phyl/lic,** *adj.*

poi'son i'vy, *n.* **1.** a vine or shrub, *Rhus radicans*, of the cashew family, with trifoliate leaves and whitish berries: may cause allergic dermatitis when touched. **2.** POISON OAK. **3.** the rash caused by touching poison ivy.

poi'son oak', *n.* either of two North American shrubs of the cashew family, *Rhus toxicodendron*, of the eastern U.S., or *R. diversiloba*, of the Pacific coastal area, with leaves resembling those of poison ivy: may cause allergic dermatitis when touched.

po'lar bod'y, *n.* one of the minute cells arising from the unequal meiotic divisions of the ovum at or near the time of fertilization.

po·li·o (pō/lē ō'), *n.* POLIOMYELITIS.

po'li·o·my·e·li'tis (-mi/ə li/tis), *n.* an acute infectious disease of motor nerves of the spinal cord and brain stem, caused by a poliovirus and sometimes resulting in muscular atrophy and skeletal deformity: formerly epidemic in children and young adults, now controlled by vaccination.

po·li·o·vi·rus (pō/lē ō vi/rəs, pō/lē ō vi/-), *n., pl.* **-rus·es.** any of three picornaviruses of the genus *Enterovirus* that cause poliomyelitis.

pol·li·no·sis or **pol·le·no·sis** (pol/ə nō/sis), *n.* HAY FEVER.

pol·y A (pol/ē ā/), n. POLYADENYLIC ACID.

pol/y·ad·e·nyl/ic ac/id (pol/ē ad/n il/ik, pol/-), n. a segment of nucleotides composed of adenylic acid residues, appearing at the tail end of messenger RNA after transcription and inducing stability: added to DNA fragments in certain genetic engineering procedures.

pol/y·dac/tyl (-dak/til) also **pol/y·dac/tyl·ous,** adj. having more than the normal number of fingers or toes. —**pol/y·dac/ty·ly, pol/y·dac/tyl·ism,** n.

pol/y·dip/si·a (-dip/sē ə), n. excessive thirst.

pol/y·em/bry·o·ny (-em/brē ə nē, -ō/nē, -em brī/ə nē), n. the production of more than one embryo from one egg.

pol/y·gene/, n. any of a group of genes that act together cumulatively to produce a trait, as stature or skin pigmentation. —**pol/y·gen/ic,** adj.

pol/y·mer·ase (pol/ə mə rās/, -rāz/), n. any of several enzymes that catalyze the formation of a long-chain molecule by linking smaller molecular units.

pol/ymerase chain/ reac/tion, n. the laboratory production of numerous copies of a gene by separating the two strands of the DNA containing the gene segment, marking its location with a primer, and using a DNA polymerase to assemble a copy alongside each segment and continuously copy the copies. Abbr.: PCR

pol/y·mor·phism (pol/ē môr/fiz əm), n. **1.** the state or condition of being polymorphous. **2. a.** a genetic variation that produces differing characteristics in individuals of the same population or species. **b.** the occurence of different castes or types within the same sex, as in social ants. —**pol/y·mor/phic,** adj.

pol/y·mor/phous, adj. having, assuming, or passing through many or various forms, stages, or the like; polymorphic.

polymor/phous perverse/, adj. Psychoanal. pertaining to or manifesting the diffuse and nonspecific forms of eroticism found in infant sexuality.

pol/y·neu·ri/tis, n. an inflammation or inflammatory disease of peripheral nerves. —**pol/y·neu·rit/ic,** adj.

pol/y·nu/cle·o·tide/, n. a sequence of nucleotides, as in DNA or RNA, bound into a chain.

pol·yp (pol/ip), n. a projecting growth from a mucous surface, as of the nose, being either a tumor or a hypertrophy of the mucous membrane. —**pol/yp·ous,** adj.

pol/y·pep/tide, n. a chain of amino acids linked together by peptide bonds and having a molecular weight of up to about 10,000.

pol/y·pha/gi·a (-fā/jē ə, -jə), n. excessive desire to eat.

pol/y·ploid/ (-ploid/), adj. **1.** having a chromosome number that is more than double the basic or haploid number. —**n. 2.** a polyploid cell or organism. —**pol/y·ploi/dic,** adj. —**pol/y·ploi/dy,** n.

pol·yp·ne·a (pol/ip nē/ə), n. rapid breathing; panting.

pol·y·ri·bo·some (pol/ē rī/bə sōm/), n. POLYSOME.

pol/y·sac/cha·ride/ (-sak/ə rīd/, -rid), n. a complex carbohydrate, as starch, inulin, or cellulose, formed by the combination of nine or more monosaccharides and capable of hydrolyzing to these simpler sugars. Also, **pol′y·sac′cha·rose′** (-rōs′).

pol′y·some′ (-sōm′), *n.* a complex of ribosomes that lines up along a strand of messenger RNA and translates the genetic code during protein synthesis.

pol′y·un·sat′u·rate (-un sach′ər it, -ə rāt′), *n.* a type of fat found in vegetable oils that tends to lower cholesterol levels in the blood when substituted for saturated fats. —**pol′y·un·sat′u·rat′ed,** *adj.*

pol′y·u·ri·a (-yŏŏr′ē ə), *n.* the passing of an excessive quantity of urine. —**pol′y·u′ric,** *adj.*

pons (ponz), *n., pl.* **pon·tes** (pon′tēz). **1.** a band of nerve fibers forming the part of the brainstem that lies between the medulla oblongata and the midbrain. **2.** any tissue connecting two parts of a body organ or structure.

pons Va·ro·li·i (ponz′ və rō′lē i′), *n., pl.* **pon·tes Varolii** (pon′tēz). **pons** (def. 1).

por·phyr·i·a (pôr fēr′ē ə, -fī′rē ə), *n.* a hereditary defect of blood pigment metabolism marked by an excess of porphyrins in the urine and an extreme sensitivity to sunlight.

por·phy·rin (pôr′fə rin), *n.* a dark red, photosensitive pigment: a component of chlorophyll, heme, and vitamin B_{12}.

por′tal circula′tion, *Physiol.* blood flow in a portal system.

por′tal vein′, *n.* a large vein conveying blood to the liver from the veins of the stomach, intestine, spleen, and pancreas.

port′-wine′ stain′, *n.* a large birthmark of purplish color, usu. on the face or neck.

pos·i·tive (poz′i tiv), *adj.* **1.** (of blood, affected tissue, etc.) showing the presence of disease. **2.** (of a diagnostic test) indicating the presence of the disease, condition, etc., tested for.

pos′i·tron emis′sion tomog′raphy (poz′i tron′), *n.* the process of producing a PET scan. Compare PET SCAN-NER.

po·sol·o·gy (pə sol′ə jē, pō-), *n.* the branch of pharmacology that deals with the determination of dosage. —**pos·o·log·ic** (pos′ə loj′ik), **pos′o·log′i·cal,** *adj.* —**po·sol′o·gist,** *n.*

poste′rior pitu′itary, *n.* the posterior region of the pituitary gland, which develops embryologically from the forebrain and secretes the hormones vasopressin and oxytocin. Also called **neurohypophysis.**

post·hyp·not·ic (pōst′hip not′ik), *adj.* **1.** of or pertaining to the period after hypnosis. **2.** (of a suggestion) made during hypnosis so as to be effective after awakening. —**post′hyp·not′i·cal·ly,** *adv.*

post·mor·tem (-môr′təm), *adj.* **1.** of or pertaining to examination of the body after death. —*n.* **2.** a postmortem examination; autopsy.

post′nasal drip′, *n.* a trickling of mucus onto the pharyngeal surface from the posterior portion of the nasal cavity.

post·na·tal (-nāt′l), *adj.* subsequent to childbirth.

post·op′er·a·tive (-op′ər ə tiv, -ə rā′tiv, -op′rə tiv), *adj.* occurring after a surgical operation. —**post·op′er·a·tive·ly,** *adv.*

post·par′tum (-pär′təm), *adj.* following childbirth.

post·sy·nap′tic (-si nap′tik), *adj.* being or occurring on the receiving end of a discharge across a synapse.

post′trau·mat′ic, *adj.* occurring after physical or psychological trauma.

post′traumat′ic stress′ disor′der, *n.* a mental disorder occurring after a traumatic event, characterized by generalized anxiety, nightmares or intrusive recollections, and emotional detachment.

po·tas·si·um (pə tas′ē əm), *n.* a silvery white metallic element: essential in metabolism and for maintenance of normal fluid balance. *Symbol:* K; *at. wt.:* 39.102; *at. no.:* 19; *sp. gr.:* 0.86 at 20°C.

potas′sium bro′mide, *n.* a white, crystalline, water-soluble powder, KBr, used as a sedative.

potas′sium i′odide, *n.* a white, crystalline, water-soluble powder, KI, used as a laboratory reagent, in biological staining, and to treat thyroid conditions.

Pott′s′ disease′ (pots), *n.* caries of the bodies of the vertebrae, often resulting in marked curvature of the spine.

poul·tice (pōl′tis), *n., v.,* **-ticed, -tic·ing.** —*n.* **1.** a soft, moist mass of cloth, bread, meal, herbs, etc., applied hot as a medicament to the body. —*v.t.* **2.** to apply a poultice to.

pox (poks), *n.* **1.** a disease characterized by multiple skin pustules, as smallpox. **2.** syphilis.

pox′vi′rus, *n. pl.* **-rus·es.** any of various large, brick-shaped or ovoid viruses of the family Poxviridae, including the viruses that cause smallpox and other pox diseases.

pre·an·es·thet·ic (prē an′əs thet′ik, prē′an-), *n.* **1.** a substance that produces a preliminary or light anesthesia. —*adj.* **2.** given prior to an anesthetic that induces total insensibility.

pre·can′cer·ous, *adj.* showing pathological changes that may be preliminary to malignancy.

pre·cip·i·tate (*v.* pri sip′i tāt′; *n.* -tit, -tāt′), *v.,* **-tat·ed, -tat·ing,** *n.* —*v.t.* **1.** to separate (a substance) in solid form from a solution, as by means of a reagent. —*n.* **2.** a substance precipitated from a solution.

pre·cip·i·tin (pri sip′i tin), *n.* an antibody that reacts with an antigen to form a precipitate.

pre·clin·i·cal (prē klin′i kəl), *adj.* of or pertaining to the period prior to the appearance of symptoms. —**pre·clin′i·cal·ly,** *adv.*

pre·con′scious, *adj.* **1.** capable of being readily brought into consciousness. **2.** occurring prior to the development of consciousness. —*n.* **3.** the complex of memories and emotions that may influence or readily be brought into consciousness.

pre·cur·sor (pri kûr′sər, prē′kûr-), *n.* **1.** a chemical that is transformed into another compound, as in the course of a chemical reaction, and therefore precedes that compound in the synthetic pathway: *Cholesterol is a precursor of testosterone.* **2.** a cell or tissue that gives rise to a variant, specialized, or more mature form.

pre/di·gest′, *v.t.* to treat (food) by an artificial process analogous to digestion so that, when taken into the body, it is more easily digestible. —**pre/di·ges′tion,** *n.*

pred·nis·o·lone (pred nis′ə lōn′), *n.* an analog of cortisone, $C_{21}H_{28}O_5$, used topically and in various other forms for treating eye and skin inflammations, allergies, and autoimmune diseases.

pred·ni·sone (pred′nə sōn′, -zōn′), *n.* an analog of cortisone, $C_{21}H_{26}O_5$, used in tablet form chiefly for treating allergies, autoimmune diseases, and certain cancers.

pre·e·clamp·si·a or **pre·e·clamp·si·a** (prē′i klamp′sē ə), *n.* a form of toxemia of pregnancy characterized by hypertension, fluid retention, and albuminuria, sometimes progressing to eclampsia.

pree·mie (prē′mē), *n.* an infant born prematurely; a preterm.

pre·fron·tal (prē frun′tl), *adj.* anterior to, situated in, or pertaining to the anterior part of a frontal structure.

pre/frontal lobe′, *n.* the anterior region of the frontal lobe of the brain.

Prem·a·rin (prem′ə rin), *Trademark.* a brand name for a mixture of conjugated natural estrogens used chiefly for estrogen replacement therapy.

pre·ma·ture (prē′mə chŏŏr′, -tŏŏr′, -tyŏŏr′; *esp. Brit.* prem′ə-), *adj.* born before gestation is complete; preterm. —**pre/ma·ture′ly,** *adv.* —**pre/ma·tu′ri·ty, pre/ma·ture′ness,** *n.*

pre·med (prē med′), *adj.* **1.** premedical. —*n.* **2.** a program of premedical study or training. **3.** a student enrolled in such a program.

pre·med/i·cal, *adj.* of, pertaining to, or engaged in studies in preparation for the formal study of medicine.

premen′strual syn′drome, *n.* a complex of physical and emotional changes, as depression, irritability, bloating, and soreness of the breasts, one or more of which may be experienced in the several days before the onset of menstrual flow. *Abbr.:* PMS

pre·mo/lar, *adj.* **1.** situated in front of the molar teeth. —*n.* **2.** a premolar tooth. **3.** Also called **bicuspid.** (in humans) any of eight teeth located in pairs on each side of the upper and lower jaws between the cuspids and the molar teeth.

pre·na/tal (-nāt′l), *adj.* previous to birth or to giving birth; antenatal: *prenatal care for mothers.* —**pre·na/tal·ly,** *adv.*

pre·op or **pre-op** (prē'op'), *adj.* **1.** preoperative. —*adv.* **2.** preoperatively.

pre·op·er·a·tive (-op'ər ə tiv, -ə rā'tiv, -op'rə tiv), *adj.* occurring or related to the period or preparations before a surgical operation. —**pre·op'er·a·tive·ly,** *adv.*

prep (prep), *n., adj., v.,* **prepped, prep·ping.** —*n.* **1.** the act of preparing a patient for a medical or surgical procedure. —*adj.* **2.** involving or used for preparation: *prep room.* —*v.t.* **3.** to prepare (a patient) for a medical or surgical procedure.

pre·po·ten·cy (prē pōt'n sē), *n.* the ability of one parent to impress its hereditary characters on its progeny because it possesses more homozygous, dominant, or epistatic genes.

pre·po'tent, *adj.* pertaining to or having prepotency. —**pre·po'tent·ly,** *adv.*

pre·pu·ber·ty, *n.* the period of life just before sexual maturation. —**pre·pu'ber·tal,** *adj.*

pre·pu·bes'cence, *n.* PREPUBERTY. —**pre·pu·bes'cent,** *adj., n.*

pre·puce (prē'pyo͞os), *n.* **1.** the fold of skin that covers the head of the penis; foreskin. **2.** a similar covering of the clitoris. —**pre·pu·tial** (pri pyo͞o'shəl), *adj.*

pres·by·o·pi·a (prez'bē ō'pē ə, pres'-), *n.* farsightedness due to ciliary muscle weakness and loss of elasticity in the crystalline lens, usu. associated with aging. —**pres'by·op·ic** (-op'ik), *adj.*

pre·scribe (pri skrīb'), *v.,* **-scribed, -scrib·ing.** —*v.t.* **1.** to designate or order the use of (a medicine, remedy, treatment, etc.). —*v.i.* **2.** to order a treatment or medicine. —**pre·scrib'a·ble,** *adj.* —**pre·scrib'er,** *n.*

pre·scrip·tion (pri skrip'shən), *n.* **1.** a written direction by a physician for the preparation and use of a medicine or remedy. **2.** an act of prescribing. **3.** something prescribed. —*adj.* **4.** (of drugs) sold only upon medical prescription.

pres·en·ta·tion (prez'ən tā'shən, prē'zen-), *n.* the position of the fetus in the uterus during labor, esp. in relation to its appearance at the cervix: *a breech presentation.*

pre·serv·a·tive (pri zûr'və tiv), *n.* a chemical substance used to preserve foods or other organic materials from decomposition or fermentation.

pres·sor (pres'ər), *adj.* **1.** causing an increase in blood pressure; causing vasoconstriction. —*n.* **2.** a substance or nerve that causes an increase in blood pressure; vasoconstrictor.

pres·sure (presh'ər), *n.* BLOOD PRESSURE.

pres'sure sore', *n.* BEDSORE.

pre·sump·tive (pri zump'tiv), *adj.* pertaining to the part of an embryo that, in the course of normal development, will predictably become a particular structure or region. —**pre·sump'tive·ly,** *adv.*

pre·syn·ap·tic (prē'si nap'tik), *adj.* being or occurring on the transmitting end of a discharge across a synapse. —**pre′syn·ap′ti·cal·ly**, *adv.*

pre·term′, *adj.* **1.** occurring earlier in pregnancy than expected. —*n.* **2.** a baby born before the 37th week of pregnancy, esp. when undersized.

pre·ven·tive (pri ven′tiv) also **pre·vent·a·tive** (-tə tiv), *n.* a drug or other substance for preventing disease.

pri·ap·ic (pri ap′ik), *adj.* exaggeratedly concerned with masculinity and male sexuality.

pri·a·pism (prī′ə piz′əm), *n.* continuous, usu. nonsexual erection of the penis, esp. due to disease. —**pri′a·pis′mic,** *adj.*

prick′ly heat′, *n.* a cutaneous eruption accompanied by a prickling and itching sensation, due to an inflammation of the sweat glands. Also called **heat rash.**

pri′mal scream′, *n.* a scream uttered by a person undergoing primal therapy.

pri′mal ther′apy, *n.* a form of psychotherapy in which the patient is encouraged to relive traumatic events, often screaming or crying, in order to achieve catharsis.

pri·ma·quine (prī′mə kwēn′), *n.* a viscous liquid, $C_{15}H_{21}N_3O$, used in the treatment of malaria.

pri′mary sex′ characteris′tic, *n. Anat.* any of the body structures directly concerned in reproduction, as the testes, ovaries, and external genitalia. Also called **pri′mary sex′ char′acter.**

pri·mip·a·ra (prī mip′ər ə), *n., pl.* **-a·ras, -a·rae** (-ə rē′). a woman who has borne only one child or who is to give birth for the first time. —**pri′mi·par′i·ty** (-par′i tē), *n.* —**pri·mip′a·rous,** *adj.*

pri·mor·di·um (prī môr′dē əm), *n., pl.* **-di·a** (-dē ə). the first recognizable, histologically differentiated stage in the development of an organ.

pri·mus (prī′məs), *adj.* (in prescriptions) first.

pri·on (prē′on, prī′-), *n.* a hypothetical infectious particle composed solely of protein and likened to viruses and viroids but having no genetic component.

p.r.n., (in prescriptions) as the occasion arises; as needed. [Latin, *pro re nata*]

Pro, proline.

pro·band (prō′band), *n.* a person who is the initial member of a family to come under study for an inheritable trait or disease.

probe (prōb), *n.* **1.** a slender surgical instrument for exploring the depth or direction of a wound, sinus, or the like. **2. a.** DNA PROBE. **b.** any labeled or otherwise identifiable substance that is used to detect or isolate another substance in a biological system or specimen.

pro·caine (prō kān′, prō′kān), *n.* a compound, $C_{13}H_{20}N_2O_2$, used chiefly as a local and spinal anesthetic.

procaine′ am′ide, *n.* a white, crystalline compound, $C_{13}H_{21}N_3O_3$, used in the treatment of arrhythmia.

proc·ess (pros′es; *esp. Brit.* prō′ses), *n. Anat.* a natural outgrowth, projection, or appendage: *a process of a bone.*

proc·tol·o·gy (prok tol/ə jē), *n.* the branch of medicine dealing with the rectum and anus. —**proc·to·log/ic** (-tl-oj/ik), **proc/to·log/i·cal**, *adj.* —**proc·tol/o·gist**, *n.*

proc·to·scope (prok/tə skōp/), *n.* an instrument for visual examination of the interior of the rectum. —**proc/to·scop/ic** (-skop/ik), *adj.* —**proc·tos/co·py** (-tos/kə pē), *n.*

pro·drome (prō/drōm), *n.* a premonitory symptom. —**prod·ro·mal** (prod/rə məl, prə drō/-), *adj.*

pro·drug (prō/drug/), *n.* an inactive substance that is converted to a drug within the body by the action of enzymes or other chemicals.

pro·en/zyme, *n.* ZYMOGEN.

pro·gen/i·tive, *adj.* capable of having offspring; reproductive. —**pro·gen/i·tive·ness**, *n.*

pro·gen/i·tor, *n.* a biologically related ancestor. —**pro·gen/i·tor·ship/**, *n.*

pro·ge·ri·a (prō jēr/ē ə), *n.* a rare congenital abnormality characterized by premature and rapid aging, the affected individual appearing in childhood as an aged person.

pro/ges·ta/tion·al, *adj.* **1.** prepared for pregnancy, as the lining of the uterus prior to menstruation or in the early stages of gestation itself. **2.** of, noting, or characteristic of the action of progesterone.

pro·ges·ter·one (prō jes/tə rōn/), *n.* a female hormone, synthesized chiefly in the corpus luteum of the ovary, that functions in the menstrual cycle to prepare the lining of the uterus for a fertilized ovum.

pro·ges/tin (-tin) also **pro·ges·to·gen** (-jes/tə jən), *n.* any substance having progesteronelike activity.

prog·na·thous (prog/nə thəs, prog nā/-) also **prog·nath/ic** (-nath/ik), *adj.* having protrusive jaws. —**prog/na·thism**, **prog/na·thy**, *n.*

prog·no·sis (prog nō/sis), *n., pl.* **-ses** (-sēz). a forecasting of the probable course and outcome of a disease, esp. of the chances of recovery.

prog·nos/tic (-nos/tik), *adj.* of or pertaining to prognosis. —**prog·nos/ti·cal·ly**, *adv.*

pro·jec·tive (prə jek/tiv), *adj.* of or pertaining to a psychological test or technique for probing a person's thoughts, feelings, attitudes, etc., by eliciting his or her responses to ambiguous test materials, as ink blots or cartoons. —**pro·jec/tive·ly**, *adv.* —**pro·jec·tiv·i·ty** (prō/jek·tiv/i tē), *n.*

pro·lac·tin (prō lak/tin), *n.* a pituitary hormone that in mammals stimulates milk production at parturition. Also called **luteotropin.**

pro·lam·in (prō lam/in, prō/lə min), *n.* any of a class of simple proteins, as gliadin, that are insoluble in water but soluble in dilute acids, alkalis, and alcohols.

pro·lapse (prō laps/, prō/laps), *n.* a falling down of an organ or part, as the uterus, from its normal position.

pro·line (prō/lēn, -lin), *n.* an alcohol-soluble amino acid, $C_4H_8NHCOOH$, occurring in high concentration in collagen. *Abbr.:* Pro; *Symbol:* P

pro·mot·er (prə mō′tər), *n.* **1.** a site on a DNA molecule at which RNA polymerase binds and initiates transcription. **2.** a gene sequence that activates transcription.

pro·na·tion (prō nā′shən), *n.* **1.** an everting motion of the foot so as to turn the sole outward. **2.** the position assumed as the result of this rotation. —**pro′nate,** *v.t., v.i.,* **-nat·ed, -nat·ing.**

pro·na·tor (prō′nā tər, prō nā′-), *n.* any of several muscles that permit pronation of the hand, forelimb, or foot.

pro·phage (prō′fāj′), *n.* a stable, inherited form of bacteriophage in which the genetic material of the virus is integrated into, replicated, and expressed with the genetic material of the bacterial host.

pro·phase (prō′fāz′), *n.* the first stage of mitosis or meiosis in cell division, during which the nuclear envelope breaks down and strands of chromatin form into chromosomes.

pro·phy·lac·tic (prō′fə lak′tik, prof′ə-), *adj.* **1.** preventive or protective, esp. from disease or infection. —*n.* **2.** a prophylactic medicine or measure. **3.** a device used to prevent conception or venereal infection, esp. a condom. —**pro′phy·lac′ti·cal·ly,** *adv.*

pro′phy·lax′is (-lak′sis), *n., pl.* **-lax·es.** the prevention of disease, as by protective measures.

pro′pi·on′ic ac′id (prō′pē on′ik, prō′-), *n.* a colorless, oily, water-soluble liquid, $C_3H_6O_2$, having a pungent odor: used as a topical fungicide.

pro·pos·i·tus (prə poz′i təs), *n., pl.* **-ti** (-tī′). PROBAND.

pro·pox·y·phene (prō pok′sə fēn′), *n.* a nonnarcotic analgesic, $C_{22}H_{29}NO_2$.

pro·pran·o·lol (prō pran′ə lôl′, -lol′), *n.* a beta-blocking drug, $C_{16}H_{21}NO_2$, used in the treatment of hypertension, angina pectoris, and arrhythmia.

pro·pri·e·tar·y (prə prī′i ter′ē), *adj., n., pl.* **-tar·ies.** —*adj.* **1.** manufactured and sold only by the owner of the patent, trademark, etc.: *proprietary medicine.* —*n.* **2.** a proprietary drug or medicine. —**pro·pri′e·tar′i·ly** (-târ′i-lē), *adv.*

pro·pri·o·cep·tion (prō′prē ə sep′shən), *n.* perception governed by proprioceptors, as awareness of the position of one's body.

pro′pri·o·cep′tive, *adj.* pertaining to proprioceptors, the stimuli acting upon them, or the nerve impulses initiated by them.

pro′pri·o·cep′tor, *n.* a sensory nerve ending, located in a muscle, tendon, or the inner ear, that provides a sense of the position of the body.

prop·to·sis (prop tō′sis), *n.* **1.** the forward displacement of an organ. **2.** EXOPHTHALMOS.

pro·sect (prō sekt′), *v.t.* to dissect (a cadaver or part) for anatomical demonstration or to establish the cause of death. —**pro·sec′tor,** *n.*

pros·en·ceph·a·lon (pros′en sef′ə lon′, -lən), *n., pl.*

-lons, -la (-lə). the forebrain. —**pros′en·ce·phal′ic** (-sə-fal′ik), *adj.*

pros·ta·cy·clin (pros′tə si′klin), *n.* a prostaglandin, $C_{20}H_{32}O_5$, that specifically inhibits the formation of blood clots.

pros·ta·glan·din (-glan′din), *n.* any of a class of fatty acids with hormonelike functions, that are involved in the contraction of smooth muscle, the control of inflammation and body temperature, and many other physiological functions.

pros·tate (pros′tāt), *adj.* **1.** Also, **pros·tat·ic** (pro stat′ik). of or pertaining to the prostate gland. —*n.* **2.** PROSTATE GLAND.

pros·ta·tec·to·my (pros′tə tek′tə mē), *n., pl.* **-mies.** excision of part or all of the prostate gland.

pros′tate gland′, *n.* a partly muscular gland that surrounds the urethra of males at the base of the bladder and secretes an alkaline fluid that makes up part of the semen.

pros·ta·tism (pros′tə tiz′əm), *n.* symptoms of prostate disorder, esp. obstructed urination, as from enlargement of the gland.

pros·ta·ti·tis (-tī′tis), *n.* inflammation of the prostate gland.

pros·the·sis (pros thē′sis), *n., pl.* **-ses** (-sēz). a device, either external or implanted, that substitutes for or supplements a missing or defective part of the body. —**pros·thet′ic** (-thet′ik), *adj.* —**pros·thet′i·cal·ly,** *adv.*

prosthet′ic group′, *n.* the portion of a conjugated protein that is not composed of amino acids.

pros·thet·ics (pros thet′iks), *n.* (*used with a sing. v.*) **1.** the branch of surgery or of dentistry that deals with the replacement of missing parts with artificial structures. **2.** the fabrication and fitting of prosthetic devices, esp. artificial limbs. —**pros′the·tist** (-thə tist), *n.*

pros·tho·don·tics (pros′thə don′tiks) also **pros·tho·don·tia** (-don′shə, -shē ə), *n.* (*used with a sing. v.*) the branch of dentistry that deals with the replacement of missing teeth and related oral structures by artificial devices.

pros·trate (pros′trāt), *v.t.,* **-trat·ed, -trat·ing.** to reduce to physical weakness or exhaustion. —**pros·tra′tion,** *n.*

pro·tag·o·nist (prō tag′ə nist), *n.* AGONIST (def. 1). —**pro·tag′o·nism,** *n.*

prot·a·mine (prō′tə mēn′, pro tam′in), *n.* any of a group of arginine-rich, strongly basic proteins that are not coagulated by heat.

pro·ta·no·pi·a (prōt′n ō′pē ə), *n.* a type of color blindness in which the retina fails to respond to red or green or confuses the two. —**pro′ta·nop′ic** (-op′ik), *adj.*

pro·te·ase (prō′tē ās′, -āz′), *n.* any of a group of enzymes that catalyze the hydrolytic degradation of proteins or polypeptides to smaller amino acid polymers.

pro·tein (prō′tēn, -tē in), *n.* **1.** any of numerous organic molecules constituting a large portion of the mass of every life form, composed of 20 or more amino acids linked in one or more long chains, the final shape and other properties of each protein being determined by the side chains of the amino acids and their chemical attachments. **2.** plant or animal tissue rich in such molecules, considered as a food source. —**pro·tein·a′ceous** (-tē nā′shəs, -tē i-nā′-), **pro·tein′ic**, **pro·tein′ous**, *adj.*

pro·tein·ase (prō′tē nās′, -nāz′, -tē i-), *n.* any of a group of enzymes that are capable of hydrolyzing proteins.

pro′tein coat′, *n.* CAPSID.

pro′tein syn′thesis, *n.* the process by which amino acids are linearly arranged into proteins through the involvement of ribosomal RNA, transfer RNA, messenger RNA, and various enzymes.

pro·tein·u·ri·a (prō′tē nŏŏr′ē ə, -nyŏŏr′-, -tē ə-), *n.* excessive protein in the urine, as from kidney disease.

pro·te·ol·y·sis (prō′tē ol′ə sis), *n.* the breaking down of proteins into simpler compounds, as in digestion. —**pro′te·o·lyt′ic** (-ə lit′ik), *adj.*

pro′te·ose′, *n.* any of a class of soluble compounds derived from proteins by the action of the gastric juices, pancreatic juices, etc.

Pro·te·us (prō′tē əs, -tyŏŏs), *n.* (*l.c.*) any of several rod-shaped, aerobic bacteria of the genus *Proteus,* sometimes found as pathogens in the gastrointestinal and genitourinary tracts of humans.

pro·throm·bin (prō throm′bin), *n.* a plasma protein involved in blood coagulation that is converted to thrombin.

pro·to·col (prō′tə kôl′, -kol′, -kōl′), *n.* a plan for carrying out a scientific study or a patient's treatment regimen.

pro·to·path·ic (prō′tə path′ik), *adj.* of or pertaining to neurons that sense only general areas of pain, heat, or cold. —**pro·top·a·thy** (prə top′ə thē), *n.*

pro·to·plasm (prō′tə plaz′əm), *n.* the colloidal and liquid substance of which cells are formed, excluding horny, chitinous, and other structural material; the cytoplasm and nucleus. —**pro′to·plas′mic**, *adj.*

pro·to·troph·ic (prō′tə trof′ik, -trō′fik), *adj.* **1.** having the same nutritional requirements as the normal or wild type. **2.** capable of synthesizing nutrients from inorganic matter: *prototrophic bacteria.* —**pro′to·troph′** (-trof′, -trōf′), *n.*

pro·to·zo·an (prō′tə zō′ən), *n., pl.* **-zo·ans,** (*esp. collectively*) **-zo·a** (-zō′ə), *adj.* —*n.* **1.** any of various one-celled organisms that usu. obtain nourishment by ingesting food particles rather than by photosynthesis: classified as the superphylum Protozoa encompassing separate phyla according to means of movement, as by pseudopodia, flagella, or cilia. —*adj.* **2.** of, pertaining to, or characteristic of a protozoan.

pro·to·zo·on (-zō′on, -ən), *n., pl.* **-zo·a** (-zō′ə). PROTOZOAN.

proud′ flesh′, *n.* GRANULATION (def. 2).

pro·vi·rus (prō′vī′rəs, prō vī′-), *n., pl.* **-rus·es.** a viral form that is incorporated into the genetic material of a host cell.

pro·vi·ta·min, *n.* a substance that an organism can transform into a vitamin, as carotene, which is converted to vitamin A in the liver.

provitamin A, *n.* CAROTENE.

Pro·zac (prō′zak), *Trademark.* a drug that inhibits the release of serotonin and is used chiefly as an antidepressant.

pru·ri·go (prŏŏ ri′gō), *n.* a chronic skin disease characterized by pale, itching papules.

pru·ri·tus (-təs), *n.* itching. —**pru·rit′ic** (-rit′ik), *adj.*

prus′sic ac′id (prus′ik), *n.* HYDROCYANIC ACID.

psel·lism (sel′iz əm), *n.* stuttering; stammering.

pseud·es·the·sia (sŏŏ′dəs thē′zhə, -zhē ə, -zē ə), *n.* PHANTOM LIMB PAIN.

pseu·do·cy·e·sis (sŏŏ′dō si ē′sis), *n.*, *pl.* **-ses** (-sēz). FALSE PREGNANCY.

pseu·do·po·di·um (sŏŏ′də pō′dē əm), *n.*, *pl.* **-di·a** (-dē ə). a temporary protrusion of the protoplasm, as of certain protozoans, usu. serving as an organ of locomotion or prehension.

pseu·do·preg·nan·cy (sŏŏ′dō preg′nən sē), *n.*, *pl.* **-cies.** FALSE PREGNANCY. —**pseu′do·preg′nant,** *adj.*

psi·lo·cin (sil′ə sin, sī′lə-), *n.* a psilocybin metabolite with strong hallucinogenic potency produced after ingestion of the mushroom *Psilocybe mexicana.*

psil′o·cy′bin (-si′bin), *n.* a hallucinogenic crystalline solid, $C_{12}H_{17}N_2O_4P$, obtained from the mushroom *Psilocybe mexicana.*

psit·ta·co·sis (sit′ə kō′sis), *n.* a rickettsial disease affecting birds of the parrot family, pigeons, and domestic fowl, caused by the chlamydia *Chlamydia psittaci* and transmissible to humans. Also called **parrot fever.**

pso·as (sō′əs), *n.*, *pl.* **pso·ai** (sō′ī), **pso·ae** (sō′ē). either of a pair of deep loin muscles extending from the sides of the spine to the femur. —**pso·at′ic** (-at′ik), *adj.*

pso·ra·len (sôr′ə lən, sōr′-), *n.* a toxic substance, $C_{11}H_6O_3$, present in certain plants, as parsnips, used to increase the response to ultraviolet light in the treatment of severe cases of acne and psoriasis.

pso·ri·a·sis (sə rī′ə sis), *n.* a common chronic, inflammatory skin disease characterized by scaly patches. —**pso·ri·at·ic** (sôr′ē at′ik, sōr′-), *adj.*

psych., **1.** psychological. **2.** psychologist. **3.** psychology.

psy·che (sī′kē), *n.* the mental or psychological structure of a person, esp. as a motive force.

psych·e·del·ic (sī′ki del′ik), *adj.* **1.** of or noting a mental state of intensified sensory perception. **2.** of or pertaining to any of various drugs that produce this state. —*n.* **3.** a psychedelic drug. **4.** a person who uses such a substance. —**psych′e·del′i·cal·ly,** *adv.*

psy·chi·a·try (si kī′ə trē, sī-), *n.* the branch of medicine concerned with the study, diagnosis, and treatment of mental disorders. —**psy·chi·at·ric** (si′kē a/trik), *adj.* —**psy′chi·at′ri·cal·ly,** *adv.* —**psy·chi′a·trist,** *n.*

psy·chic (si′kik), *adj.* **1.** *Psychol.* pertaining to or noting mental phenomena. **2.** sensitive to influences or forces of a nonphysical or supernatural nature. —**psy′chi·cal·ly,** *adv.*

psy·cho (si′kō), *n., pl.* **-chos,** *adj. Informal.* —*n.* **1.** a psychopathic person; psychopath. —*adj.* **2.** psychopathic.

psy′cho·ac′tive, *adj.* of or pertaining to a substance that has a significant effect on mood or mental state.

psy′cho·a·nal′y·sis, *n.* **1.** a systematic structure of theories concerning the relation of conscious and unconscious psychological processes. **2.** a technical procedure for investigating unconscious mental processes and for treating mental illness. —**psy′cho·an′a·lyst,** *n.* —**psy′cho·an′a·lyt′ic, psy′cho·an′a·lyt′i·cal,** *adj.* —**psy′cho·an′a·lyt′i·cal·ly,** *adv.*

psy′cho·an′a·lyze′, *v.t.,* **-lyzed, -lyz·ing.** to investigate or treat by psychoanalysis.

psy·cho·dra·ma (si′kō drä′mə, -dram′ə, si′kō drä′mə, -dram′ə), *n.* a method of group psychotherapy in which participants take roles in improvisational dramatizations of emotionally charged situations. —**psy′cho·dra·mat′ic** (-drə mat/ik), *adj.*

psy′cho·dy·nam′ics, *n.* **1.** (*used with a pl. v.*) the motivational forces, both conscious and unconscious, that determine human behavior and attitudes. **2.** (*used with a sing. v.*) any branch of psychology or method of clinical treatment that views personality as the result of an interplay between conscious and unconscious factors. —**psy′cho·dy·nam′ic,** *adj.* —**psy′cho·dy·nam′i·cal·ly,** *adv.*

psy′cho·gen′e·sis, *n.* **1.** the origin and development of a psychological or behavioral state. **2.** the emotional cause of or contribution to symptoms of a disorder. —**psy′cho·ge·net′ic,** *adj.*

psy·cho·gen·ic (si′kə jen′ik), *adj.* having origin in the mind or in a mental condition or process: *a psychogenic disorder.*

psy′cho·graph′, *n.* a graph indicating the relative strength of the personality traits of an individual. —**psy′cho·graph′ic,** *adj.*

psychol., **1.** psychological. **2.** psychology.

psy·cho·log·i·cal (si′kə loj′i kəl) also **psy′cho·log′ic,** *adj.* **1.** of pertaining to psychology. **2.** pertaining to the mind or to mental phenomena as the subject matter of psychology. **3.** pertaining to, dealing with, or affecting the mind, esp. as a function of awareness, feeling, or motivation. —**psy′cho·log′i·cal·ly,** *adv.*

psy·chol·o·gy (si kol′ə jē), *n., pl.* **-gies. 1.** the science of the mind or of mental states and processes. **2.** the science of human and animal behavior. **3.** the sum of the mental states and processes characteristic of a person or class of persons.

psy·cho·met·rics (si′kə me′triks), *n.* (*used with a sing.*

v.) the measurement of mental traits, abilities, and processes.

psy·chom·e·try (sī kom′i trē), *n.* PSYCHOMETRICS. —**psy**′**-
cho·met**′**ric**, **psy**′**cho·met**′**ri·cal**, *adj.* —**psy·chom**′**e·
trist**, *n.*

psy·cho·mi·met·ic (sī′kō mi met′ik, -mī-), *adj.* PSYCHOT-
OMIMETIC.

psy·cho·mo·tor, *adj.* of or pertaining to a response involving both the brain and motor activity.

psy·cho·neu·ro·sis, *n.*, *pl.* -**ses** (-sēz). NEUROSIS (def. 1).
—**psy**′**cho·neu·rot**′**ic**, *adj.*

psy·cho·path (sī′kə path′), *n.* a person having a character disorder distinguished by amoral or antisocial behavior
without feelings of remorse; psychopathic person.

psy·cho·path′**ic**, *adj.* of, pertaining to, or affected with
psychopathy; engaging in amoral or antisocial acts without
feeling remorse. —**psy·cho·path**′**i·cal·ly**, *adv.*

psy·cho·pa·thol·o·gy (sī′kō pə thol′ə jē), *n.*, *pl.* -**gies**.
1. the study of the causes, conditions, and processes of
mental disorders. **2.** the systematic description of a mental
disorder. **3.** PSYCHOSIS. —**psy**′**cho·path**′**o·log**′**i·cal**
(-path′ə loj′i kəl), **psy**′**cho·path**′**o·log**′**ic**, *adj.* —**psy**′**cho·
pa·thol**′**o·gist**, *n.*

psy·chop·a·thy (sī kop′ə thē), *n.*, *pl.* -**thies**. **1.** a character or personality disorder distinguished by chronic amoral
or antisocial behavior without feelings of remorse. **2.** any
mental disease.

psy·cho·phar·ma·col·o·gy (sī′kō fär′mə kol′ə jē), *n.*
the branch of pharmacology dealing with the psychological
effects of drugs. —**psy**′**cho·phar**′**ma·co·log**′**ic** (-kə-
loj′ik), **psy**′**cho·phar**′**ma·co·log**′**i·cal**, *adj.*

psy·cho·phys·ics, *n.* (*used with a sing. v.*) the branch of
psychology that deals with the relationships between physical stimuli and resulting sensations and mental states.
—**psy**′**cho·phys**′**i·cal**, **psy**′**cho·phys**′**ic**, *adj.* —**psy**′**cho·
phys**′**i·cist**, *n.*

psy′**cho·phys·i·ol**′**o·gy**, *n.* the branch of physiology that
deals with the interrelation of mental and physical phe-
nomena. —**psy**′**cho·phys**′**i·o·log**′**i·cal**, **psy**′**cho·phys**′**i·
o·log**′**ic**, *adj.* —**psy**′**cho·phys**′**i·ol**′**o·gist**, *n.*

psy·cho·sex·u·al, *adj.* of or pertaining to the relationship of psychological and sexual phenomena. —**psy**′**cho·
sex**′**u·al**′**i·ty**, *n.* —**psy**′**cho·sex**′**u·al·ly**, *adv.*

psy·cho·sis (sī kō′sis), *n.*, *pl.* -**ses** (-sēz). **1.** a mental disorder characterized by symptoms, as delusions or hallucinations, that indicate impaired contact with reality. **2.** any
severe form of mental disorder, as schizophrenia or paranoia.

psy·cho·so′**cial**, *adj.* of or pertaining to the interaction
between social and psychological factors.

psy·cho·so·mat′**ic**, *adj.* **1.** of or pertaining to a physical
disorder that is caused or notably influenced by emotional
factors. **2.** pertaining to or involving both the mind and the
body. —**psy**′**cho·so·mat**′**i·cal·ly**, *adv.*

psy·cho·sur·ger·y, *n.* treatment of mental disorders by means of brain surgery. —**psy'cho·sur'geon,** *n.* —**psy'cho·sur'gi·cal,** *adj.*

psy·cho·syn'the·sis, *n.* a theoretical effort to reconcile components of the unconscious with the rest of the personality.

psy·cho·ther'a·peu'tics, *n.* (*used with a sing. v.*) PSYCHOTHERAPY. —**psy'cho·ther'a·peu'tic,** *adj.* —**psy'cho·ther'a·peu'ti·cal·ly,** *adv.*

psy·cho·ther'a·py, *n., pl.* **-pies.** the treatment of psychological disorders or maladjustments by a professional technique, as psychoanalysis, group therapy, or behavioral therapy. —**psy'cho·ther'a·pist,** *n.*

psy·chot·ic (sī kot'ik), *adj.* **1.** characterized by or afflicted with psychosis. —*n.* **2.** a person afflicted with psychosis. —**psy·chot'i·cal·ly,** *adv.*

psy·chot/o·mi·met'ic (-ō mə met'ik, -mi-) also **psy·chomimetic,** *adj.* (of a substance or drug) tending to produce symptoms like those of a psychosis; hallucinatory.

psy·cho·tro·pic (sī/kō trō'pik), *adj.* **1.** affecting mental activity, behavior, or perception, as a mood-altering drug. —*n.* **2.** a psychotropic drug, as a tranquilizer, sedative, or antidepressant.

psyl·li·um (sil'ē əm), *n.* the seeds of the fleawort, used as a mild laxative esp. in breakfast cereals.

PT, precipitin test.

PTC, phenylthiocarbamide.

pte·ryg·i·um (tə rij'ē əm), *n., pl.* **-ryg·i·ums, -ryg·i·a** (-rij'ē ə). an abnormal triangular mass of thickened conjunctiva extending over the cornea and interfering with vision. —**pte·ryg'i·al,** *adj.*

PTH, parathyroid hormone.

pto·maine (tō'mān, tō mān'), *n.* any of a class of foul-smelling nitrogenous substances produced by bacteria during putrefaction of animal or plant protein: formerly thought to cause food poisoning (**ptomaine' poi'soning**). —**pto·main'ic,** *adj.*

pto·sis (tō'sis), *n., pl.* **-ses** (-sēz). prolapse or drooping of an organ or part, esp. a drooping of the upper eyelid. —**pto·tic** (tō'tik), *adj.*

PTSD, posttraumatic stress disorder.

pty·a·lin (tī'ə lin), *n.* an enzyme in the saliva that converts starch into dextrin and maltose.

pty'a·lism, *n.* excessive secretion of saliva.

pu·ber·ty (pyoō'bər tē), *n.* the period of life during which the genital organs mature, secondary sex characteristics develop, and the individual becomes capable of sexual reproduction. —**pu'ber·tal, pu'ber·al,** *adj.*

pu·bes·cent (pyoō bes'ənt), *adj.* arriving or arrived at puberty. —**pu·bes'cence,** *n.*

pu·bic (pyoō'bik), *adj.* of, pertaining to, or situated near the pubes or the pubis.

pu·bis (pyoō'bis), *n., pl.* **-bes** (-bēz). one of the paired anterior bones of the vertebrate pelvic girdle, forming the front of each innominate bone in humans.

pub′lic health′, *n.* health services to improve and protect community health, esp. preventive medicine, immunization, and sanitation.

pu·den·dum (pyōō den′dəm) *n., pl.* **-da** (-də). Usu. **pudenda.** the external genital organs, esp. those of the female; vulva.

pu·er·il·ism (pyōō′ər ə liz′əm, pyōōr′ə-), *n. Psychiatry.* childishness in the behavior of an adult.

pu·er·per·a (pyōō ûr′pər ə), *n., pl.* **-per·ae** (-pə rē′). a woman who has recently given birth to a child.

pu·er′per·al, *adj.* **1.** of or pertaining to a woman in childbirth. **2.** pertaining to or connected with childbirth.

puer′peral fe′ver, *n.* a bacterial infection of the endometrium occurring in women after childbirth or abortion, usu. as the result of unsterile obstetric practices.

pu′er·pe′ri·um (-pēr′ē əm), *n.* the four-week period following childbirth.

PUFA, polyunsaturated fatty acid.

pull′-up′, *n.* CHIN-UP.

pul·mo·nar·y (pul′mə ner′ē, pōōl′-), *adj.* of or affecting the lungs.

pul′monary ar′tery, *n.* one of a pair of arteries conveying venous blood from the right ventricle of the heart to the lungs.

pul′monary vein′, *n.* one of the veins conveying oxygenated blood from the lungs to the left atrium of the heart.

pulp (pulp), *n.* the inner substance of the tooth, containing arteries, veins, and lymphatic and nerve tissue. Also called **dental pulp.**

pulp′ cav′ity, *n.* the entire space occupied by the pulp of a tooth.

pul·sate (pul′sāt), *v.i.,* **-sat·ed, -sat·ing.** to expand and contract rhythmically, as the heart; beat; throb.

pul·sa′tion, *n.* the act of pulsating; beating or throbbing.

pulse (puls), *n.* **1.** the regular throbbing of the arteries, caused by the successive contractions of the heart, esp. as may be felt at an artery, as at the wrist. **2.** a single pulsation of the arteries or heart.

pu·pil (pyōō′pəl), *n.* the expanding and contracting opening in the iris of the eye, through which light passes to the retina.

pur·ga·tion (pûr gā′shən), *n.* **1.** the act of purging. **2.** the result of purging.

pur·ga·tive (pûr′gə tiv), *adj.* **1.** purging or cleansing, esp. by causing evacuation of the bowels. —*n.* **2.** a purgative medicine or agent; cathartic. —**pur′ga·tive·ly,** *adv.*

purge (pûrj), *v.,* **purged, purg·ing.** *n.* —*v.t.* **1.** to clear or empty (the stomach or intestines) by inducing vomiting or evacuation. —*v.i.* **2.** to undergo or cause emptying of the stomach or intestines. —*n.* **3.** something that purges, as a purgative medicine.

pu·rine (pyŏŏr′ēn, -in), *n.* **1.** a white, crystalline compound, $C_5H_4N_4$, from which is derived a group of compounds including uric acid, xanthine, and caffeine. **2.** one of several purine derivatives, esp. the bases adenine and guanine, which are fundamental constituents of nucleic acids.

Pur·kin·je cell′ (pər kin′jē), *n.* a large, densely branching neuron in the cerebellar cortex of the brain.

pur·pu·ra (pûr′pyŏŏr ə), *n.* a skin rash of purple or brownish red spots resulting from the bleeding into the skin of subcutaneous capillaries. —**pur·pu′ric**, *adj.*

pu·ru·lence (pyŏŏr′ə ləns, pyŏŏr′yə-) also **pu′ru·len·cy**, *n.* **1.** the condition of containing or forming pus. **2.** pus.

pu′ru·lent, *adj.* **1.** full of, containing, forming, or discharging pus; suppurating. **2.** attended with suppuration: *purulent appendicitis.* **3.** of the nature of or like pus. —**pu′ru·lent·ly**, *adv.*

pus (pus), *n.* a yellow-white, more or less viscid substance found in abscesses, sores, etc., consisting of a liquid plasma in which white blood cells are suspended.

push′-up′, *n.* an exercise in which a person lies in a prone position with the hands palms down under the shoulders and raises and lowers the body using only the arms.

pus·tu·lant (pus′chə lənt), *adj.* causing the formation of pustules.

pus·tu·lar, *adj.* **1.** of, pertaining to, or of the nature of pustules. **2.** characterized by or covered with pustules.

pus·tule (-chŏŏl), *n.* **1.** a small elevation of the skin containing pus. **2.** any pimplelike or blisterlike swelling or elevation. —**pus′tuled**, *adj.*

pu·tre·fac·tion (pyŏŏ′trə fak′shən), *n.* **1.** bacterial or fungal decomposition of organic matter with resulting obnoxious odors; rotting. **2.** the state of being putrefied; decay. —**pu′tre·fac′tive**, **pu′tre·fa′cient** (-fā′shənt), *adj.*

pu′tre·fy′, *v.*, **-fied, -fy·ing.** —*v.i.* **1.** to become putrid; rot. **2.** to become gangrenous. —*v.t.* **3.** to render putrid; cause to rot or decay with an offensive odor.

PWA, person with AIDS.

py·e·li·tis (pī′ə lī′tis), *n.* inflammation of the renal pelvis. —**py′e·lit′ic** (-lit′ik), *adj.*

py·e·lo·gram (pī′ə lə gram′, pī el′ə-) also **py·e·lo·graph** (-graf′, -gräf′), *n.* an x-ray produced by pyelography.

py·e·log·ra·phy (pī′ə log′rə fē), *n.* the science or technique of x-raying the kidneys, renal pelves, and ureters after administering a contrast solution. —**py′e·lo·graph′ic** (-lə graf′ik), *adj.*

py·e·lo·ne·phri·tis (pī′ə lō-), *n.* inflammation of the kidney and its pelvis, caused by a bacterial infection. —**py′e·lo·ne·phrit′ic**, *adj.*

py·e·mi·a (pī ē′mē ə), *n.* a diseased state in which pyogenic bacteria are circulating in the blood, characterized by the development of abscesses in various organs. —**py·e′·mic,** *adj.*

pyk·nic (pik′nik), *adj.* **1.** (of a physical type) having a fat, rounded build or body structure. —*n.* **2.** a person of the pyknic type.

py·lo·rus (pī lôr′əs, -lōr′-, pi-), *n., pl.* **-lo·ri** (-lôr′ī, -lōr′ī). the opening between the stomach and the start of the intestine in most vertebrates. —**py·lor′ic** (-lôr′ik, -lor′-), *adj.*

py·o·gen·ic (pī′ə jen′ik), *adj.* **1.** producing or generating pus. **2.** attended with or pertaining to the formation of pus. —**py′o·gen′e·sis** (-ə sis), *n.*

py′or·rhe′a or **py′or·rhoe′a** (-rē′ə), *n.* **1.** a discharge of pus. **2.** Also called **pyorrhe′a al·ve·o·lar′is** (al vē′ə-lar′is), **Riggs′ disease.** severe periodontitis, characterized by bleeding and suppuration of the gums and often loosening of the teeth. —**py′or·rhe′al, py′or·rhe′ic,** *adj.*

py·o·sis (pī ō′sis), *n.* the formation of pus; suppuration.

py·ram′i·dal tract′ (pi ram′i dl), *n.* any of the massed bundles of motor fibers extending from the cerebral hemispheres into the medulla and spinal cord.

py·ret·ic (pī ret′ik), *adj.* of, pertaining to, affected by, or producing fever.

py·rex·i·a (pī rek′sē ə), *n.* FEVER. —**py·rex′i·al, py·rex′ic,** *adj.*

pyr·i·dine (pir′i dēn′, -din), *n.* a colorless, flammable, liquid organic base, C_5H_5N, used chiefly as a solvent and in organic synthesis. —**py·rid′ic** (pi rid′ik), *adj.*

pyr·i·dox·ine (pir′i dok′sēn, -sin) also **pyr·i·dox·in** (-sin), *n.* a derivative of pyridine, required for the formation of hemoglobin and the prevention of pellagra; vitamin B_6.

py·rim·i·dine (pī rim′i dēn′, pi-), *n.* **1.** a cyclic compound, $C_4H_4N_2$, that is the basis of several important biochemical substances. **2.** one of several pyrimidine derivatives, esp. the bases cytosine, thymine, and uracil, which are fundamental constituents of nucleic acids.

py·ro·gen (pī′rə jən, -jen′), *n.* a substance, as a bacterial toxin, that produces a rise in body temperature.

py′ro·gen′ic, *adj.* producing or produced by heat or fever.

py·ro·sis (pī rō′sis), *n.* HEARTBURN.

pyr·u·vate (pī rōō′vāt, pi-), *n.* an ester or salt of pyruvic acid.

py·ru′vic ac′id, a water-soluble liquid, $C_3H_4O_3$, important in many metabolic and fermentative processes, used chiefly in biochemical research.

py·u·ri·a (pī yŏŏr′ē ə), *n.* the presence of pus in the urine.

Q

Q, *Symbol.* glutamine.

q.d., (in prescriptions) every day. [Latin, *quaque die*]

Q fever, *n.* an acute, influenzalike disease transmitted to humans by contact with infected cattle, sheep, and goats, caused by the rickettsia *Coxiella burnetii.*

q.h., (in prescriptions) each hour; every hour. [Latin, *quaque hora*]

q.i.d., (in prescriptions) four times a day. [Latin, *quater in die*]

Quaa·lude (kwā′lōōd), *Trademark.* a brand of methaqualone.

quad (kwod), *n.* a quadruplet.

quad·ri·ple·gi·a (kwod′rə plē′jē ə, -jə), *n.* paralysis of all four limbs or of the entire body below the neck. —**quad′-ri·ple′gic,** *n., adj.*

quad·ru·plet (kwo drup′lit, -drōō′plit, kwod′rōō plit), *n.* **1.** quadruplets, four children or offspring born of one pregnancy. **2.** one of four such children or offspring.

quan′titative inher′itance, *n.* the process in which the additive action of a group of genes results in a trait, as height or shape, showing continuous variability.

quar·an·tine (kwôr′ən tēn′, kwor′-, kwôr′ən tēn′, kwor′-), *n., v.,* **-tined, -tin·ing.** —*n.* **1.** a strict isolation imposed to prevent the spread of disease. **2.** a period, orig. 40 days, of detention or isolation imposed upon ships, people, animals, or plants on arrival at a port or place, when suspected of carrying a contagious disease. **3.** the place, as a hospital, where people are detained. —*v.t.* **4.** to put in or subject to quarantine. —**quar′an·tin′a·ble,** *adj.* —**quar′-an·tin′er,** *n.*

quar·tan (kwôr′tn), *adj.* **1.** recurring every fourth day, both days of consecutive occurrence being counted: *quar-tan fevers.* —*n.* **2.** a quartan fever, ague, etc.

quick·en (kwik′ən), *v.i.* **1.** to enter that stage of pregnancy in which the fetus gives indications of life. **2.** (of a fetus in the womb) to begin to manifest signs of life.

quin·a·crine (kwin′ə krēn′), *n.* an alkaloid, $C_{23}H_{30}ClN_3O$, used in the treatment of malaria.

quin·i·dine (-i dēn′, -din), *n.* a colorless, crystalline alkaloid, isomeric with quinine, obtained from cinchona bark and used for treating malaria and arrhythmia.

qui·nine (kwī′nīn, kwin′īn; *esp. Brit.* kwi nēn′), *n.* a white crystalline alkaloid, $C_{20}H_{24}N_2O_2$, obtained from cinchona bark, used chiefly for treating resistant forms of malaria.

quin·sy (kwin′zē), *n.* an abscess located between the tonsil and the pharynx accompanied by a severe sore throat and fever. —**quin′sied,** *adj.*

quint (kwint), *n.* a quintuplet.

quin·tu·plet (kwin tup′lit, -tōō′plit, -tyōō′-, kwin′tōō plit,

-tyŏŏ-), *n.* **quintuplets,** five children or offspring born of one pregnancy.

quo·tid·i·an (kwō tid′ē ən), *adj.* **1.** recurring daily: *quotidian fever.* —*n.* **2.** a quotidian fever or ague.

R

R, *Symbol.* arginine.

R., **1.** Roentgen. **2.** Also, **R** (in prescriptions) take. [Latin, *recipe*]

rab′bit fe′ver, *n.* TULAREMIA.

rab·id (rab′id), *adj.* affected with or pertaining to rabies: *a rabid dog.* —**rab·id·i·ty** (rə bid′i tē, ra-), **rab′id·ness,** *n.* —**rab′id·ly,** *adv.*

ra·bies (rā′bēz), *n.* an infectious, usu. fatal disease of dogs, cats, and other warm-blooded animals, caused by a rhabdovirus and transmitted to humans by the bite of a rabid animal: characterized by fever, extreme irritability, and inability to swallow water and saliva. Also called **hydrophobia.**

ra·chi·tis (rə kī′tis), *n.* RICKETS. —**ra·chit′ic** (-kit′ik), *adj.*

ra·di·al (rā′dē əl), *adj.* of, pertaining to, or situated near the radius of the forearm. —**ra′di·al·ly,** *adv.*

ra′dial ker·a·tot′o·my (ker′ə tot′ə mē), *n.* a surgical technique for correcting nearsightedness by making a series of spokelike incisions in the cornea to change its shape and focusing properties.

ra′dial sym′metry, *n.* a basic body plan in which the organism can be divided into similar halves by passing a plane at any angle along a central axis. Compare BILATERAL SYMMETRY.

radia′tion sick′ness, *n.* sickness caused by irradiation with x-rays or radioactive materials, characterized by nausea and vomiting, headache, diarrhea, loss of hair and teeth, destruction of white blood cells, and hemorrhage.

ra·di·o·graph (rā′dē ō graf′, -gräf′), *n.* **1.** a photographic image produced by the action of x-rays or nuclear radiation. —*v.t.* **2.** to make a radiograph of. —**ra′di·og′ra·phy** (-og′rə fē), *n.* —**ra·di·o·graph′ic** (-graf′ik), *adj.* —**ra′di·o·graph′i·cal·ly,** *adv.*

ra·di·o·im′mu·no·as′say (-im′yə nō as′ā, -a sā′, -i myoō′-), *n.* a test procedure that integrates immunologic and radiolabeling techniques to measure minute quantities of a substance, as a protein, hormone, or drug, in a given sample of body fluid or tissue.

ra′di·o·i′o·dine′, *n.* any of nine radioisotopes of iodine, esp. iodine 131 and iodine 125, used as radioactive tracers in research and clinical diagnosis and treatment.

ra′di·o·i′so·tope′, *n.* a radioactive isotope, usu. artificially produced: used in physical and biological research and therapeutics. —**ra′di·o·i′so·top′ic,** *adj.*

ra·di·o·la·bel (rā′dē ō lā′bəl), *n., v.t.* LABEL (defs. 1, 2).

ra·di·o·log′i·cal (rā′dē ə loj′i kəl) also **ra′di·o·log′ic,** *adj.* of or pertaining to radiology. —**ra′di·o·log′i·cal·ly,** *adv.*

ra·di·ol·o·gy (rā dē ol′ə jē), *n.* the branch of medicine dealing with x-rays, other forms of radiation, and various imaging techniques for diagnosis and treatment. —**ra′di·ol′o·gist,** *n.*

ra·di·o·lu·cent (rā′dē ō lōō′sənt), *adj.* almost entirely transparent to radiation; almost entirely invisible in x-ray photographs and under fluoroscopy. —**ra′di·o·lu′cence, ra′di·o·lu′cen·cy,** *n.*

ra·di·o·paque (rā′dē ō pāk′), *adj.* opaque to radiation; visible in x-ray photographs and under fluoroscopy. —**ra′di·o·pac′i·ty** (-pas′i tē), *n.*

ra·di·o·phar′ma·ceu′ti·cal, *n.* a radioactive drug used diagnostically or therapeutically.

ra·di·os·co·py (rā′dē os′kə pē), *n.* the examination of objects opaque to light by means of another form of radiation, usu. x-rays. —**ra′di·o·scop′ic** (-ō skop′ik), **ra′di·o·scop′i·cal,** *adj.*

ra·di·o·sen′si·tive, *adj.* (of certain tissues or organisms) sensitive to or destructible by various types of radiant energy, as x-rays. —**ra′di·o·sen′si·tiv′i·ty,** *n.*

ra·di·o·ther′a·py, *n.* the treatment of disease, as cancer, by means of x-rays or radioactive substances. —**ra′di·o·ther′a·pist,** *n.*

ra·di·o·trans·par′ent, *adj.* transparent to radiation; invisible in x-ray photographs and under fluoroscopy. —**ra′di·o·trans·par′en·cy,** *n.*

ra·di·us (rā′dē əs), *n., pl.* **-di·i** (-dē ī′), **-di·us·es.** the bone of the forearm on the thumb side.

raf·fi·nose (raf′ə nōs′), *n.* a colorless, crystalline sugar, $C_{18}H_{32}O_{16} \cdot 5H_2O$, with little or no sweetness, obtained from cottonseed and sugar beets and breaking down to fructose, glucose, and galactose on hydrolysis.

rale (ral, räl), *n.* an abnormal rattling sound made while breathing.

ran·u·la (ran′yə lə), *n., pl.* **-las.** a cystic growth on the underside of the tongue. —**ran′u·lar,** *adj.*

rap′id eye′ move′ment, *n.* rapidly shifting movements of the eyes under closed lids, associated with the dreaming phase of the sleep cycle. Compare REM SLEEP.

rap′ture of the deep′, *n.* NITROGEN NARCOSIS.

rat′bite fe′ver, *n.* either of two relapsing febrile diseases, widely distributed geographically, caused by infection with *Streptobacillus moniliformis* or *Spirillum minor* and transmitted by rats.

ra′tional-emo′tive ther′apy, *n.* a form of psychotherapy in which a patient is asked to reject irrational attitudes and assumptions in order to deal effectively with stressful situations.

Ray·naud′s′ disease′ (rā nōz′), *n.* a vascular disorder characterized by blanching and numbness of the fingers or toes upon exposure to cold or stress.

RBC, red blood cell.

RDA or **R.D.A., 1.** recommended daily allowance. **2.** recommended dietary allowance.

RDS, respiratory distress syndrome.

re·ac·tion (rē ak′shən), *n.* **1.** a physiological response to an action or condition. **2.** a physiological change indicating sensitivity to foreign matter: *an allergic reaction.* —**re·ac′-tion·al,** *adj.*

reac′tion time′, *n.* the interval between a stimulus and response.

re·a·gent (rē ā′jənt), *n.* a substance that, because of the reactions it causes, is used in analysis and synthesis.

re·a·gin (rē ā′jin, -gin), *n.* **1.** an antibody formed in response to syphilis and reactive with cardiolipin in various blood tests for the disease. **2.** an antibody found in certain human allergies, as hay fever and asthma.

real′ity prin′ciple, *n. Psychoanal.* the realization that gratification must sometimes be deferred or forgone.

re·can·al·i·za·tion (rē kan′l ə zā′shən, rē′kə nal′-), *n.* the surgical reopening of an occluded passageway in a blood vessel.

re·ca·pit·u·late (rē′kə pich′ə lāt′), *v.t.* to repeat (ancestral evolutionary stages) during embryonic development or during a life cycle.

re′ca·pit′u·la′tion, *n.* the theory that the evolutionary history of a species is made evident in the developmental stages of each of its representative organisms. —**re′ca·pit′u·la′tive, re′ca·pit′u·la·to′ry,** *adj.*

re·cep·tor (ri sep′tər), *n.* a sensory nerve ending or sense organ that is sensitive to stimuli.

re·ces·sive (ri ses′iv), *Genetics.* —*adj.* **1.** of or pertaining to that allele of a gene pair whose effect is masked by the second allele when both are present in the same cell or organism. **2.** of or pertaining to the hereditary trait determined by such an allele. —*n.* **3.** the recessive allele of a gene pair. **4.** the individual carrying such an allele. **5.** a recessive trait. Compare DOMINANT. —**re·ces′sive·ness,** *n.*

rec·og·ni·tion (rek′əg nish′ən), *n. Biochem.* the responsiveness of one substance to another based on the reciprocal fit of a portion of their molecular shapes.

rec′og·nize′ (-nīz′), *v.t.,* **-nized, -niz·ing.** *Biochem.* to bind with, cleave, or otherwise react to (another substance) as a result of fitting its molecular shape or a portion of this shape.

re·com·bi·nant (rē kom′bə nənt), *adj.* **1.** of or resulting from new combinations of genetic material: *recombinant cells.* —*n.* **2.** a cell or organism whose genetic material results from recombination. **3.** the genetic material produced when segments of DNA from different sources are joined to produce recombinant DNA.

recombinant DNA, *n.* DNA in which one or more segments or genes have been inserted, either naturally or by laboratory manipulation, from a different molecule or from another part of the same molecule, resulting in a new genetic combination.

re′com·bi·na′tion, *n.* the formation of new combinations of genes, either naturally or in the laboratory.

recov′ery room′, *n.* a room in a hospital in which postoperative and postpartum patients recover from anesthesia.

rec·tal (rek′tl), *adj.* of, pertaining to, or for the rectum. —**rec′tal·ly**, *adv.*

rec·to·cele (rek′tə sēl′), *n.* a hernia of the rectum into the vagina.

rec·tum (rek′təm), *n., pl.* **-tums, -ta** (-tə) the terminal section of the large intestine, ending in the anus.

rec′tus, *n., pl.* **-ti** (-tī) any of several straight muscles, esp. of the abdomen, thigh, or eye.

red (red), *n. Slang.* a red capsule containing secobarbital.

red′ blood′ cell′, *n.* any of the cells of the blood that in mammals are enucleate disks concave on both sides, contain hemoglobin, and carry oxygen to the cells and tissues and carbon dioxide back to the respiratory organs. Also called **erythrocyte, red′ blood′ cor′puscle.** *Abbr.:* RBC

red·in·te·gra·tion (red in′ti grā′shən, ri din′-), *n. Psychol.* **1.** the recalling of an entire memory from a partial cue. **2.** the repeating of the response to a complex stimulus on experiencing any part of that stimulus.

red′out′, *n.* a condition experienced by pilots and astronauts in which rapid deceleration or a negative gravity force drives blood to the head, reddening the field of vision.

re·dox (rē′doks), *n.* OXIDATION-REDUCTION.

re·duce (ri dōōs′, -dyōōs′), *v.t.,* **-duced, -duc·ing. 1.** to deoxidize. **2.** to add hydrogen to. **3.** to decrease the positive charge on (an ion) by adding electrons.

reduc′ing a′gent, *n.* a substance that causes another substance to undergo reduction and that is oxidized in the process.

re·duc·tase (ri duk′tās, -tāz), *n.* any enzyme acting as a reducing agent.

re·duc′tion (-shən), *n.* **1.** meiosis, esp. the first meiotic cell division in which the chromosome number is reduced by half. **2.** the process or result of reducing a chemical substance.

re·duc′tion·ism, *n.* the theory that every complex phenomenon, esp. in biology or psychology, can be explained by analyzing the simplest, most basic physical mechanisms that are in operation during the phenomenon. —**re·duc′tion·ist,** *n., adj.*

referred′ pain′, *n.* pain felt in an area remote from the site of origin.

re·flex (rē′fleks), *adj.* **1.** noting or pertaining to an involuntary response to a stimulus, the nerve impulse from a receptor being transmitted inward to a nerve center that in turn transmits it outward to an effector. —*n.* **2. a.** Also called **re′flex act′.** movement caused by a reflex response. **b.** Also called **re′flex ac′tion.** the entire physiological process activating such movement.

re′flex arc′, *n.* the nerve pathways followed by an impulse during a reflex.

re·flex·ol·o·gy (rē′flek sol′ə jē), *n.* **1.** a system of massaging specific areas of the foot or sometimes the hand in order to promote healing, relieve stress, etc., in other parts of the body. **2.** the study of reflex movements and processes. —**re·flex·ol·o·gist,** n.

re·fract (ri frakt′), v.t. **1.** to subject to refraction. **2.** to determine the refractive condition of (an eye).

re·frac′tion, n. **1.** the ability of the eye to refract light that enters it so as to form an image on the retina. **2.** the determining of the refractive condition of the eye. —**re·frac′tion·al,** adj.

re·frac′tive (-tiv), adj. **1.** of or pertaining to refraction. **2.** having power to refract. —**re·frac′tive·ly,** adv. —**re·frac′tive·ness,** n.

refrac′tory pe′riod, n. a short period after a nerve or muscle cell responds during which the cell cannot respond to additional stimulation.

re·gen·er·ate (ri jen′ə rāt′), v.t., **-at·ed, -at·ing.** to restore or revive (a lost, removed, or injured body part) by the growth of new tissue. —**re·gen′er·a·ble,** adj. —**re·gen′er·a′tion,** n.

re·gime or **ré·gime** (rə zhēm′, rā-; sometimes -jēm′), n. REGIMEN.

reg·i·men (rej′ə mən, -men′, rezh′-), n. a regulated course, as of diet, exercise, or manner of living, to preserve or restore health or to attain some result.

reg′istered nurse′, n. a graduate nurse who has passed a state board examination and been registered and licensed to practice nursing. Abbr.: RN, R.N.

re·gres·sion (ri gresh′ən), n. **1.** Biol. reversion to an earlier or less advanced state or form or to a general type. **2.** Psychoanal. reversion to an earlier, less adaptive emotional state or behavior pattern. **3.** the subsidence of a disease or its symptoms.

reg′ulator gene′, n. any gene that exercises control over the expression of another gene or genes.

re·gur·gi·tate (ri gûr′ji tāt′), v.i. to surge or rush back, as liquids, gases, or undigested food. —**re·gur′gi·tant** (-tənt), n.

re·gur·gi·ta′tion, n. **1.** voluntary or involuntary return of partly digested food from the stomach to the mouth. **2.** the reflux of blood through defective heart valves.

re·in·force or **re·en·force** (rē′in fôrs′, -fōrs′), v.t., **-forced, -forc·ing.** to strengthen the probability of (a desired behavior) by giving or withholding a reward. —**re′in·forc′er,** n.

re′in·force′ment, n. a procedure, as a reward or punishment, that alters a behavioral response.

re·ject (ri jekt′), v.t. to have an immunological reaction against (a transplanted organ or grafted tissue). Compare ACCEPT. —**re·jec′tion,** n.

re·lapse (v. ri laps′; n. also rē′laps), v., **-lapsed, -laps·ing,** n. —v.i. **1.** to fall back into illness after convalescence or apparent recovery. —n. **2.** a return of a disease after partial recovery from it.

relaps′ing fe′ver, *n.* one of a group of tropical fevers characterized by relapses, caused by spirochetes of the genus *Borrelia* and spread by ticks and lice.

re·lax·ant (ri lak′sənt), *n.* a drug that causes a body or organ to relax, esp. one that lessens strain in muscle.

re·lax′in (-sin), *n.* a polypeptide hormone, produced by the corpus luteum during pregnancy, that causes the pelvic ligaments and cervix to relax during pregnancy and delivery.

releas′ing fac′tor, *n.* a substance usu. of hypothalamic origin that triggers the release of a hormone from an endocrine gland.

rem (rem), *n.* the quantity of ionizing radiation whose biological effect is equal to that produced by one roentgen of x-rays.

REM (rem), *n.* RAPID EYE MOVEMENT.

rem·e·dy (rem′i dē), *n., pl.* **-dies.** something, as a medicine, that cures or relieves a disease or bodily disorder.

re·mis·sion (ri mish′ən), *n.* **1.** a temporary or permanent decrease or subsidence of manifestatiosn of a disease. **2.** a period during which such a decrease or subsidence occurs. —**re·mis′sive** (-mis′iv), *adj.*

re·mit·tent (ri mit′nt), *adj.* abating and relapsing in cycles: *remittent fever.* —**re·mit′tence, re·mit′ten·cy,** *n.* —**re·mit′tent·ly,** *adv.*

REM′ sleep′, *n.* rapid eye movement sleep: a recurrent sleep pattern during which dreaming occurs while the eyes rapidly shift under closed lids. Compare SLOW-WAVE SLEEP.

re·nal (rēn′l), *adj.* of or pertaining to the kidneys or the surrounding regions.

re·o·vi·rus (rē′ō vī′rəs, rē′ō vī′-), *n., pl.* **-rus·es.** any of several large viruses of the family Reoviridae having double-stranded RNA and a polyhedral capsid: includes viruses that cause gastroenteritis.

re·plant′, *v.t.* to reattach, as a severed finger, esp. with the use of microsurgery. —**re′plan·ta′tion,** *n.*

rep·li·case (rep′li kās′, -kāz′), *n.* RNA SYNTHETASE.

rep·li·ca·tion, *n.* the process by which double-stranded DNA makes copies of itself, each strand, as it separates, synthesizing a complementary strand.

rep′li·ca′tive, *adj.* characterized by or capable of replication, esp. of an experiment.

rep′li·con′ (-kon′), *n.* any genetic element that can regulate and effect its own replication from initiation to completion.

re·po·si·tion (rē′pə zish′ən, rep′ə-), *n.* replacement, as of a bone.

re·press (ri pres′), *v.t.* **1.** to check or inhibit (actions or desires). **2.** to suppress (memories, emotions, or impulses) unconsciously.

re·pressed (ri prest′), *adj.* subjected to, affected by, or characteristic of psychological repression.

re·pres′sion, *n.* the suppression from consciousness of distressing or disagreeable ideas, memories, feelings, or impulses.

re·pres'sor, *n.* a protein that binds DNA at an operator site and thereby prevents transcription of one or more adjacent genes.

re·pro·duce (rē'prə dōōs', -dyōōs'), *v.,* **-duced, -duc·ing.** —*v.t.* **1.** to produce one or more other individuals of (a given kind of organism) by some process of generation or propagation, sexual or asexual. **2.** to cause or foster the reproduction of (organisms). —*v.i.* **3.** to reproduce one's kind, as an organism; propagate; bear offspring.

re'pro·duc'tion (-duk'shən), *n.* the process among organisms by which new individuals of the same kind are generated.

re·sect (ri sekt'), *v.t.* to do a resection on. —**re·sect'a·ble,** *adj.* —**re·sect'a·bil'i·ty,** *n.*

re·sec·tion (ri sek'shən), *n.* the surgical excision of all or part of an organ or tissue. —**re·sec'tion·al,** *adj.*

res·er·pine (res'ər pin, -pēn', rə sûr'-), *n.* an alkaloid, $C_{33}H_{40}N_2O_9$, obtained from the root of the rauwolfia, *Rauwolfia serpentina,* used in the treatment of hypertension.

res·i·den·cy (rez'i dən sē), *n., pl.* **-cies.** the position or tenure of a medical resident.

res'i·dent, *n.* a physician employed by a hospital while receiving specialized training there. —**res'i·dent·ship',** *n.*

re·sist·ance (ri zis'təns), *n.* **1.** the body's capacity to withstand the action or effect of pathogenic microorganisms. **2.** *Psychoanal.* opposition to an attempt to bring repressed thoughts or feelings into consciousness.

res·o·lu·tion (rez'ə lōō'shən), *n.* the reduction or disappearance of a swelling or inflammation without suppuration.

re·solve (ri zolv'), *v.t.,* **-solved, -solv·ing.** to cause (swellings, inflammation, etc.) to disappear without suppuration.

res·o·nance (rez'ə nəns), *n.* (in percussing for diagnostic purposes) a sound produced when air is present.

res'o·nate' (-nāt'), *v.i.,* **-nat·ed, -nat·ing.** to amplify vocal sound by the sympathetic vibration of air in certain cavities and bony structures. —**res'o·na'tion,** *n.*

re·sorb (ri sôrb', -zôrb'), *v.t.* to absorb again, as an exudation. —**re·sorb'ence,** *n.* —**re·sorb'ent,** *adj.*

res·or·cin·ol (ri zôr'sə nôl', -nol', rez ôr'-) also **res·or'cin,** *n.* a white, needlelike, water-soluble solid, $C_6H_6O_2$, used chiefly in making dyes, as a reagent, and as a skin medication.

re·sorp·tion (ri sôrp'shən, -zôrp'-), *n.* the dissolution or assimilation of a substance, as bone tissue, by biochemical activity. —**re·sorp'tive** (-tiv), *adj.*

res·pi·ra·tion (res'pə rā'shən), *n.* **1.** inhalation and exhalation of air; breathing. **2. a.** the sum total of the physical and chemical processes by which oxygen is conveyed to tissues and cells and the oxidation products, carbon dioxide and water, are given off. **b.** the oxidation of organic compounds occurring within cells and producing energy for cellular processes. —**res′pi·ra′tion·al**, *adj.*

res′pi·ra′tor, *n.* **1.** an apparatus to produce artificial respiration. **2.** a filtering device worn over the nose and mouth to prevent inhalation of noxious substances.

res·pi·ra·to·ry (res′pər ə tôr′ē, -tōr′ē, ri spīr′ə-), *adj.* pertaining to or serving for respiration.

res′piratory dis·tress′ syn′drome, *n.* **1.** an acute lung disease of newborn, esp. premature, infants, caused by a deficiency of the surface-active substance that keeps the alveoli of the lungs expanded. **2.** extreme shortness of breath caused by an acute illness or injury. *Abbr.:* RDS

res′piratory quo′tient, *n.* the ratio of the amount of carbon dioxide released by the lungs to the amount of oxygen taken in during a given period.

res′piratory sys′tem, *n.* the system of organs and tissues involved in drawing oxygen into the body and removing carbon dioxide: in mammals, includes the nasal cavity, pharynx, trachea, bronchi, lungs, and the diaphragm.

re·spire (ri spīr′), *v.i.,* **-spired, -spir·ing. 1.** to inhale and exhale air for the purpose of maintaining life; breathe. **2.** (of a living system) to exchange oxygen for carbon dioxide and other products.

res·pi·rom·e·ter (res′pə rom′i tər), *n.* an instrument for measuring oxygen consumption or carbon dioxide production.

re·spond (ri spond′), *v.i. Physiol.* to exhibit some action or effect; react: *Nerves respond to a stimulus.*

re·sponse (ri spons′), *n.* any behavior of a living organism that results from an external or internal stimulus. —**re·sponse′less,** *adj.*

response′ time′, *n.* REACTION TIME.

rest′ home′, *n.* a residential establishment that provides special care for convalescents and aged or infirm persons.

restric′tion en′zyme, *n.* any of a group of enzymes that are capable of cutting DNA at specific sites along its strand.

restric′tion frag′ment, *n.* a length of DNA cut from the strand by a restriction enzyme.

restric′tion site′, *n.* the place on a DNA molecule where a restriction enzyme acts.

re·sus·ci·tate (ri sus′i tāt′), *v.t.,* **-tat·ed, -tat·ing.** to revive, esp. from apparent death or from unconsciousness. —**re·sus′ci·ta·ble** (-tə bəl), *adj.* —**re·sus′ci·ta′tion,** *n.* —**re·sus′ci·ta′tive,** *adj.*

re·sus′ci·ta′tor, *n.* a device used in the treatment of asphyxiation that, by forcing oxygen or a mixture of oxygen and carbon dioxide into the lungs, initiates respiration.

re·te (rē′tē), *n., pl.* **re·ti·a** (rē′shē ə, -shə, -tē ə). a network, as of fibers, nerves, or blood vessels. —**re′ti·al** (-shē əl), *adj.*

re·tic·u·lar (ri tik′yə lər), *adj.* **1.** having the form of a net; netlike. **2.** of or pertaining to a reticulum. —**re·tic′u·lar·ly,** *adv.*

retic′ular forma′tion, *n.* a network of neurons in the brainstem involved in consciousness, breathing, and the transmission of sensory stimuli to higher brain centers.

re·tic·u·lo·cyte (ri tik′yə lə sit′), *n.* an immature red blood cell, containing a network of filaments.

re·tic′u·lo·en·do·the′li·al, *adj.* **1.** having the qualities of both reticular and endothelial cells; netlike and smooth-walled. **2.** of, pertaining to, or involving cells of the reticuloendothelial system.

reticuloendothe′lial sys′tem, *n.* the aggregate of the phagocytic cells that have reticular and endothelial characteristics and function in the immune system's defense against foreign bodies. *Abbr.:* RES

re·tic′u·lum (-ləm), *n., pl.* **-la** (-lə). **1.** a network of intercellular fibers in certain tissues. **2.** a network of structures in the endoplasm or nucleus of certain cells.

ret·i·na (ret′n ə, ret′nə), *n., pl.* **ret·i·nas, ret·i·nae** (ret′-n ē′). the innermost coat of the posterior part of the eyeball that receives the image produced by the lens, is continuous with the optic nerve, and consists of several layers, one of which contains the rods and cones that are sensitive to light.

Ret·in-A (ret′n ā′), *Trademark.* a brand of tretinoin, used esp. to reduce wrinkles caused by overexposure to the sun.

ret·i·nal¹ (ret′n əl), *adj.* of or pertaining to the retina of the eye.

ret·i·nal² (ret′n al′, -ôl′), *n.* an orange visual pigment, $C_{20}H_{28}O$, the active component of rhodopsin and iodopsin, that is liberated upon the absorption of light in the vision cycle.

ret′i·nene′ (-ēn′), *n.* RETINAL².

ret′i·ni′tis (-i′tis), *n.* inflammation of the retina.

retini′tis pig·men·to′sa (pig′men tō′sə, -mən-), *n.* degeneration of the retina manifested by night blindness and gradual loss of peripheral vision, eventually resulting in tunnel vision or total blindness.

ret·i·no·blas·to·ma (ret′n ō bla stō′mə), *n., pl.* **-mas, -ma·ta** (-mə tə). an inheritable tumor of the eye.

ret′i·noid′, *n.* any of a group of substances related to and functioning like vitamin A in the body.

ret′i·nol′ (-ôl′, -ol′), *n.* VITAMIN A.

ret′i·nop′a·thy (-op′ə thē), *n.* any diseased condition of the retina, esp. one that is noninflammatory.

ret′i·no·scope′ (-ə skōp′), *n.* an apparatus that determines the refractive power of the eye by observing the lights and shadows on the pupil when a mirror illumines the retina. **—ret′i·nos′co·py** (-os′kə pē), *n.*

re·trac·tor (ri trak′tər), *n. Surg.* an instrument for drawing the edges of an incision.

ret·ro·flex·ion or **ret·ro·flec·tion** (re′trə flek′shən), *n.* the folding backward of an organ, esp. of the uterus in relation to its cervix.

ret·ro·ver·sion (-vûr′zhən, -shən), *n.* the tilting backward of an organ, esp. of the uterus.

Ret·ro·vir (re′trō vēr′), *Trademark.* the international brand name for azidothymidine. Compare AZT, ZIDOVUDINE.

ret·ro·vi·rus (re′trə vī′rəs, re′trə vī′-), *n., pl.* **-rus·es.** any of various single-stranded RNA-containing viruses, of the family Retroviridae, that have a helical envelope and contain the enzyme reverse transcriptase, which enables genetic information from viral RNA to become part of host DNA. —**ret′ro·vi′ral,** *adj.*

re·vas·cu·lar·ize (rē vas′kyə lə rīz′), *v.t.,* **-ized, -iz·ing.** to improve the blood circulation of (an organ or area of the body) by surgical means. —**re·vas′cu·lar·i·za′tion,** *n.*

reverse′ transcrip′tase, *n.* a retrovirus enzyme that synthesizes DNA from viral RNA, the reverse of the usual DNA-to-RNA replication: used in genetic engineering.

Reye′s′ syn′drome (riz, rāz), *n.* a rare disorder occurring primarily in children after a viral illness and associated with aspirin usage, characterized by vomiting, swelling of the brain, and liver dysfunction.

R factor, *n.* a genetic component of some bacteria that provides resistance to antibiotics and can be transferred from one bacterium to another by conjugation.

RFLP (rif′lip′), *n.* restriction fragment length polymorphism: a fragment of DNA, cut by a restriction enzyme, that is different in length for each genetically related group and is used to trace family relationships. Also called **riflip.**

Rh, RH FACTOR.

rhab·do·my·o·ma (rab′dō mi ō′mə), *n., pl.* **-mas, -ma·ta** (-mə tə). a benign tumor made up of striated muscular tissue. Compare LEIOMYOMA.

rhab′do·my′o·sar·co′ma (-mi′ō sär kō′mə), *n., pl.* **-mas, -ma·ta** (-mə tə). a malignant tumor made up of striated muscle tissue.

rhab·do·vi′rus, *n., pl.* **-rus·es.** any of numerous bullet-shaped or oblong RNA-containing viruses, of the family Rhabdoviridae, that have spikes protruding from their envelope: includes the virus that causes rabies.

rham·nose (ram′nōs, -nōz), *n.* a crystalline sugar, $C_6H_{12}O_5$, that is an important component of the polysaccharides of plant cell walls.

rhe·om·e·ter (rē om′i tər), *n.* an instrument for measuring the flow of fluids, esp. blood. —**rhe′o·met′ric** (-ə-me′trik), *adj.* —**rhe·om′e·try,** *n.*

Rhe′sus fac′tor (rē′səs), *n.* RH FACTOR.

rhe′sus mon′key (rē′səs), *n.* a macaque, *Macaca mulatta,* of India, used in biological and medical research. Also called **rhe′sus.**

rheum (rōōm), *n.* **1.** a thin discharge of the mucous membranes, esp. during a cold. **2.** catarrh; cold. —**rheum′ic,** *adj.*

rheu·mat·ic (rōō mat′ik), *adj.* **1.** pertaining to or of the nature of rheumatism. **2.** affected with or subject to rheumatism. —*n.* **3.** a person affected with rheumatism. —**rheu·mat/i·cal·ly,** *adv.*

rheumat/ic fe/ver, *n.* an acute complication of certain streptococcal infections, usu. affecting children, characterized by fever, arthritis, chorea, and heart disturbances.

rheumat/ic heart/ disease/, *n.* damage to the myocardium or valves of the heart as a result of rheumatic fever.

rheu·ma·tism (rōō/mə tiz/əm), *n.* **1.** any of several disorders characterized by pain and stiffness in the joints or muscles. **2.** RHEUMATIC FEVER.

rheu·ma·toid/ also **rheu/ma·toi/dal,** *adj.* **1.** resembling rheumatism. **2.** RHEUMATIC. —**rheu/ma·toi/dal·ly,** *adv.*

rheu/matoid arthri/tis, *n.* a chronic autoimmune disease characterized by inflammation and progressive deformity of the joints.

rheu/matoid fac/tor, *n.* an antibody that is found in the blood of many persons afflicted with rheumatoid arthritis and that reacts against globulins in the blood.

rheu·ma·tol·o·gy (-tol/ə jē), *n.* the study and treatment of rheumatic disorders. —**rheu/ma·tol/o·gist,** *n.*

rheum/y, *adj.,* **-i·er, -i·est.** pertaining to, causing, full of, or affected with rheum.

rhex·is (rek/sis), *n., pl.* **rhex·es** (rek/sēz). rupture of a blood vessel or an organ.

Rh factor (är/āch/), *n.* any of a group of antigens present on the surface of the red blood cells, those having inherited such antigens being designated Rh+ (**Rh positive**) and those lacking them, a much smaller group, being designated Rh− (**Rh negative**): transfused or fetal Rh+ blood may induce a severe reaction in an Rh− individual.

rhi·ni·tis (rī nī/tis), *n.* inflammation of the nose or its mucous membrane.

rhi·nol·o·gy (rī nol/ə jē), *n.* the branch of medicine dealing with the nose and its diseases. —**rhi·no·log·ic** (rīn/l oj/ik), **rhi/no·log/i·cal,** *adj.* —**rhi·nol/o·gist,** *n.*

rhi·no·plas·ty (rī/nō plas/tē), *n., pl.* **-ties.** plastic surgery of the nose. —**rhi/no·plas/tic,** *adj.*

rhi·nos·co·py (rī nos/kə pē), *n., pl.* **-pies.** medical examination of the nasal passages. —**rhi/no·scop/ic** (-nə skop/ik), *adj.*

rhi·no·vi·rus (rī/nō vī/rəs, rī/nō vī/-), *n., pl.* **-rus·es.** any of a varied and widespread group of picornaviruses responsible for many respiratory diseases, including the common cold.

rhi·zot·o·my (rī zot/ə mē), *n., pl.* **-mies.** the surgical cutting of a spinal nerve root.

Rh negative (är/āch/), *adj.* See under RH FACTOR.

rho·dop·sin (rō dop/sin), *n.* a bright red photosensitive pigment found in the rod-shaped cells of the retina of certain fishes and most higher vertebrates: it is broken down by the action of dim light into retinal and opsin.

rhom·ben·ceph·a·lon (rom/ben sef/ə lon/, -lən), *n., pl.* **-lons, -la** (-lə). the hindbrain.

rhon·chus (rong′kəs), *n., pl.* **-chi** (-kī). an abnormal wheezing or snoring sound made while breathing. —**rhon′chi·al** (-kē əl), **rhon′chal** (-kəl), *adj.*

Rh positive (är′āch′), *adj.* See under Rh FACTOR.

rhythm′ meth′od, *n.* a method of birth control by abstaining from sexual intercourse when ovulation is most likely to occur.

ri·ba·vi·rin (rī′bə vī′rin), *n.* a synthetic compound, $C_8H_{12}N_4O_5$, active against several DNA and RNA viruses.

ri·bo·fla·vin (rī′bō flā′vin, rī′bō flā′-, -bə-), *n.* a vitamin B complex factor essential for growth, occurring as a yellow crystalline compound, $C_{17}H_{20}N_4O_6$, abundant in milk, meat, eggs, and leafy vegetables and produced synthetically. Also called **vitamin B₂**.

ri·bo·nu·cle·ase (rī′bō nōō′klē ās′, -āz′, -nyōō′-), *n.* any of a class of enzymes that catalyze the hydrolysis of RNA. Also called **RNase, RNAase.**

ri′bo·nu·cle′ic ac′id, *n.* See RNA.

ri′bo·nu′cle·o·pro′tein, *n.* a substance composed of RNA in close association with protein; a nucleoprotein containing RNA. *Abbr.:* RNP

ri′bo·nu′cle·o·side′, *n.* a ribonucleotide precursor containing ribose and a purine or pyrimidine base.

ri′bo·nu′cle·o·tide′, *n.* an ester, composed of a ribonucleoside and phosphoric acid, that is a constituent of ribonucleic acid.

ri·bose (rī′bōs), *n.* a white, crystalline, water-soluble, slightly sweet solid, $C_5H_{10}O_5$, a pentose sugar obtained by the hydrolysis of RNA.

ri·bo·so·mal RNA (rī′bə sō′məl), *n.* a type of RNA, distinguished by its length and abundance, that functions in protein synthesis as a component of ribosomes. *Abbr.:* rRNA

ri·bo·zyme (rī′bə zim′), *n.* a segment of RNA that can act as a catalyst. —**ri′bo·zy′mal**, *adj.*

ri·cin (rī′sin, ris′in), *n.* a white, poisonous, protein powder from the bean of the castor-oil plant.

rick·ets (rik′its), *n.* (*used with a sing. v.*) a childhood disease in which the bones soften from an inadequate intake of vitamin D and insufficient exposure to sunlight. Also called **rachitis.**

rick·ett·si·a (ri ket′sē ə), *n., pl.* **-si·as, -si·ae** (-sē ē′). any of various rod-shaped infectious microorganisms of the heterogeneous group Rickettsieae, formerly classified with the bacteria but markedly smaller and reproducing only inside a living cell: parasitic in fleas, ticks, mites, or lice and transmitted by bite. —**rick·ett′si·al**, *adj.*

ric·tus (rik′təs), *n., pl.* **-tus, -tus·es.** the gaping or opening of the mouth. —**ric′tal**, *adj.*

rif·lip (rif′lip′), *n.* See RFLP.

Riggs′ disease′ (rigz), *n.* PYORRHEA (def. 2).

right′ brain′, *n.* the right brain hemisphere, controlling activity on the left side of the body: in humans, usu.

showing specialization for spatial and nonverbal concepts. Compare LEFT BRAIN.

rig·or (rig′ər), *n.* **1.** a sudden coldness, as that preceding certain fevers; chill. **2.** muscular rigidity.

rig′or mor′tis (môr′tis), *n.* the stiffening of the body after death.

Ring′er's solu′tion (ring′ərz), *n.* an aqueous solution of the chlorides of sodium, potassium, and calcium in the same concentrations as normal body fluids, used chiefly in the laboratory for sustaining tissue.

ring′worm′, *n.* any of a number of contagious skin diseases caused by certain parasitic fungi and characterized by the formation of ring-shaped eruptive patches.

Rit·a·lin (rit′l in), *Trademark.* a brand of methylphenidate in its hydrochloride form.

rit·u·al (rich′ōō əl), *n. Psychiatry.* a specific act, as handwashing, performed repetitively to a pathological degree.

riv′er blind′ness, *n.* see ONCHOCERCIASIS.

RN or **R.N.,** registered nurse.

RNA, ribonucleic acid: any of a class of single-stranded nucleic acid molecules composed of ribose and uracil, found chiefly in the cytoplasm of cells and in certain viruses, and important in protein synthesis and in the transmission of genetic information transcribed from DNA. Compare MESSENGER RNA, RIBOSOMAL RNA, TRANSFER RNA.

RNA polymerase, *n.* an enzyme that synthesizes the formation of RNA from a DNA template during transcription.

RNase (är′en/ās, -āz) also **RNAase** (är′en/ā′ās, -āz), *n.* RIBONUCLEASE.

RNA synthetase, *n.* an enzyme that catalyzes the synthesis of RNA in cells infected with RNA viruses, allowing production of copies of the viral RNA. Also called **replicase.**

RNA virus, *n.* any virus containing RNA; retrovirus.

RNP, ribonucleoprotein.

Ro·chelle′ salt′ (rə shel′, rō-), *n.* potassium sodium tartrate: a colorless or white, water-soluble solid, $KNaC_4H_4O_6·4H_2O$, used as an ingredient in baking powder and laxatives.

Rock′y Moun′tain spot′ted fe′ver, *n.* an acute infectious disease caused by a rickettsia and transmitted by the bite of a wood tick, characterized by high fever, joint and muscle pain, and a rash.

rod (rod), *n.* one of the rodlike cells in the retina of the eye, sensitive to low intensities of light. Compare CONE.

roent·gen or **rönt·gen** (rent′gən, -jən, runt′-), *n.* a unit of radiation dosage equal to the amount of ionizing radiation required to produce one electrostatic unit of charge per cubic centimeter of air. *Abbr.:* r, R

roent·gen·ol·o·gy (rent′gə nol′ə jē, -jə-, runt′-), *n.* the branch of medicine dealing with diagnosis and therapy through x-rays. —**roent′gen·o·log′ic** (-nl oj′ik), **roent′-gen·o·log′i·cal,** *adj.* —**roent·gen·ol′o·gist,** *n.*

Rolf·ing (rôl′fing, rol′-), *Trademark.* a type of massage therapy involving sometimes intensive manipulation of the fascia of the muscles and internal organs. —**Rolf,** *v.t.,* **Rolfed, Rolf·ing.** —**Rolf′er,** *n.*

room′ing-in′, *n.* an arrangement in some hospitals that enables postpartum mothers to keep their babies with them in their rooms rather than in a separate nursery.

root′ ca·nal′, *n.* **1.** the root portion of the pulp cavity of a tooth. **2.** ROOT CANAL THERAPY (def. 2).

root′ ca·nal′ ther′a·py, *n.* **1.** the branch of endodontics that treats disease of the dental pulp. **2.** a treatment for such disease in which the pulp is removed from the pulp cavity and replaced by filling material.

Ror′schach test′ (rôr′shäk, rōr′-), *n.* a diagnostic test of personality and intellect based on the viewer's interpretations of a standard series of inkblot designs. Compare INK-BLOT TEST.

ro·sa·ce·a (rō zā′shē ə), *n.* a chronic form of acne affecting the nose, forehead, and cheeks, characterized by red pustular lesions. Also called **acne rosacea.**

rose′ fe′ver, *n.* a form of hay fever caused by rose pollen, characterized by nasal discharge and lacrimation.

ro·se·o·la (rō zē′ə lə, rō′zē ō′lə), *n.* **1.** a rose-colored rash occurring in various febrile diseases. **2.** RUBELLA. —**ro·se′o·lar,** *adj.*

ro·ta·vi·rus (rō′tə vī′rəs), *n., pl.* **-rus·es.** a double-stranded RNA virus of the genus *Rotavirus,* family Reoviridae, that is a major cause of infant diarrhea.

rough·age (ruf′ij), *n.* FIBER (def. 2).

round′worm′, *n.* any nematode, esp. *Ascaris lumbricoides,* that infests the intestine of humans and other mammals.

RQ, respiratory quotient.

rRNA, ribosomal RNA.

RU 486, *n.* a drug in pill form that prevents pregnancy: it stops a fertilized egg from attaching to the uterine wall by blocking the action of progesterone.

rub′ber room′, *n. Informal.* a room padded with foam rubber for the confinement of a violent mentally ill person.

rub′bing al′cohol, *n.* a poisonous solution of about 70 percent isopropyl or denatured ethyl alcohol, used in massaging.

ru·be·fa·cient (rōō′bə fā′shənt), *adj.* **1.** causing redness of the skin, as a medicinal application. —*n.* **2.** a rubefacient application, as a mustard plaster.

ru·bel·la (rōō bel′ə), *n.* a usu. mild infection caused by a togavirus of the genus *Rubivirus,* characterized by fever, cough, and a fine red rash: may cause fetal damage if contracted during pregnancy. Also called **German measles.**

ru·be·o·la (rōō bē′ə lə, rōō′bē ō′lə), *n.* MEASLES (def. 1a). —**ru·be′o·lar,** *adj.*

ru·di·ment (rōō′də mənt), *n.* an incompletely developed organ or part.

run′ner's knee′, *n.* pain under the kneecap or patella

caused by wear of the cartilage in the knee, as in cycling or running.

run·ning (run′ing), *adj.* discharging pus or other matter: *a running sore.*

rup·ture (rup′chər), *n.* hernia, esp. abdominal hernia. —**rup′tur·a·ble,** *adj.*

rup′tured disk′, *n.* HERNIATED DISK.

S

S, *Symbol.* serine.

S., (in prescriptions) mark; label. [Latin, *signa*]

Sa·bin vaccine (sā′bin), *n.* an orally administered vaccine of live viruses for immunization against poliomyelitis.

sac·cade (sa kād′), *n.* a rapid, irregular eye movement that occurs when changing focus from one point to another, as while reading or looking out from a moving train. —**sac·cad·ic**, *adj.*

sac·char·i·fy (sə kar′ə fī′), *v.t.*, **-fied, -fy·ing.** to convert (starch) into sugar. —**sac·char·i·fi·ca·tion**, *n.* —**sac·char·i·fi·er**, *n.*

sa·cral (sā′krəl, sak′rəl), *adj.* of or pertaining to the sacrum.

sa·crum (sak′rəm, sā′krəm), *n., pl.* **sac·ra** (sak′rə, sā′krə). a bone between the lumbar vertebrae and tail vertebrae, in humans composed usu. of five fused vertebrae and forming the posterior wall of the pelvis.

SAD, seasonal affective disorder.

sa·dism (sā′diz əm, sad′iz-), *n.* sexual gratification gained by causing pain or degradation to others. Compare MASOCHISM. —**sa·dist**, *n., adj.* —**sa·dis·tic** (sə dis′tik), *adj.* —**sa·dis·ti·cal·ly**, *adv.*

sa·do·mas·o·chism (sā′dō mas′ə kiz′əm, -maz′-, sad′ō-), *n.* gratification, esp. sexual, gained through inflicting or receiving pain. —**sa·do·mas·o·chist**, *n., adj.* —**sa·do·mas·o·chis·tic**, *adj.*

safe′ sex′, *n.* sexual activity in which precautions are taken to prevent diseases transmitted by sexual contact.

Saint′ An′thony's fire′, *n.* any of certain skin conditions that are of an inflammatory or gangrenous nature, as erysipelas.

Saint′ Vi′tus's (or **Vi′tus'**) **dance′** (vī′tə siz), *n.* CHOREA (def. 2).

sal (sal), *n. Pharm.* salt.

sal·i·cin (sal′ə sin), *n.* a colorless, crystalline, water-soluble glucoside, $C_{13}H_{18}O_7$, obtained from the bark of the American aspen: used in medicine chiefly as an antipyretic and analgesic.

sal′i·cyl′ic ac′id (sal′ə sil′ik), *n.* a white crystalline substance, $C_7H_6O_3$, used as a food preservative and in the manufacture of aspirin.

sa·line (sā′lēn, -lin), *adj.* **1.** of, containing, or tasting of common salt; salty: *a saline solution.* **2.** of or pertaining to a chemical salt, esp. of sodium, potassium, or magnesium, used as a cathartic. —*n.* **3.** a saline solution. —**sa·lin·i·ty** (sə lin′i tē), *n.*

sa·li·va (sə lī′və), *n.* a viscid, watery fluid, secreted into the mouth by the salivary glands, that functions in the tasting, chewing, and swallowing of food, moistens the mouth, and starts the digestion of starches. —**sal·i·var·y** (sal′ə-ver′ē), *adj.*

sal′ivary gland′, *n.* any of several glands of the mouth and jaw that secrete saliva.

sal·i·vate (sal′ə vāt′), *v.i.* **-vat·ed, -vat·ing.** to produce saliva.

sal·i·va′tion, *n.* **1.** the act or process of salivating. **2.** an abnormally abundant flow of saliva; ptyalism.

Salk′ vaccine′ (sôk), *n.* a vaccine that contains three types of inactivated poliomyelitis viruses and induces immunity against the disease.

sal·mo·nel·la (sal′mə nel′ə), *n., pl.* **-nel·lae** (-nel′ē), **-nel·las. 1.** any of several rod-shaped bacteria of the genus *Salmonella* that enter the digestive tract in contaminated food, causing food poisoning. **2. SALMONELLOSIS.**

sal·mo·nel·lo·sis (-nl ō′sis), *n.* food poisoning, esp. violent diarrhea and cramps, caused by consumption of food contaminated with salmonella bacteria.

sal·pin·gec·to·my (sal′pin jek′tə mē), *n., pl.* **-mies.** excision of the fallopian tube.

sal·pin·gi·tis (-ji′tis), *n.* inflammation of a salpinx. —**sal·pin·git′ic** (-jit′ik), *adj.*

sal·pinx (sal′pingks), *n., pl.* **sal·pin·ges** (sal pin′jēz). a trumpet-shaped tube, as a fallopian or Eustachian tube. —**sal·pin′gi·an** (-pin′jē ən), *adj.*

salt (sôlt), *n.* **1.** a crystalline compound, sodium chloride, NaCl, occurring chiefly as a mineral or a constituent of seawater, and used for seasoning food and as a preservative. **2.** any of a class of chemical compounds formed by neutralization of an acid by a base.

san·a·to·ri·um (san′ə tôr′ē əm, -tōr′-), *n., pl.* **-to·ri·ums, -to·ri·a** (-tôr′ē ə, -tōr′ē ə). **1.** a hospital for the treatment of chronic diseases, as tuberculosis or various nervous or mental disorders. **2. SANITARIUM.**

sand′fly fe′ver, *n.* a usu. mild viral disease occurring in hot, dry areas, transmitted by sandflies of the genus *Phlebotomus.*

sa·ni·es (sā′nē ēz′), *n.* a thin, often greenish, serous fluid discharged from an ulcer or wound. —**sa′ni·ous,** *adj.*

san·i·tar·i·um (san′i târ′ē əm) also **sanatorium,** *n., pl.* **-tar·i·ums, -tar·i·a** (-târ′ē ə). an institution for the preservation of health; health resort.

san′itary nap′kin, *n.* a disposable pad of absorbent material, as cotton, worn by women during menstruation to absorb the uterine flow.

san·ton·i·ca (san ton′i kə), *n., pl.* **-cas.** dried wormwood flower heads, used as a vermifuge.

sa·phe′nous vein′ (sə fē′nəs), *n.* either of two large veins near the surface of the leg from thigh to foot, one along the inner side and the other outer and posterior.

sa·pre·mi·a (sə prē′mē ə), *n.* blood poisoning caused by bacterial putrefaction, as in gangrene. —**sa·pre′mic,** *adj.*

sap·ro·gen·ic (sap′rō jen′ik) also **sa·prog·e·nous** (sə-proj/ə nəs), *adj.* **1.** producing putrefaction or decay, as certain bacteria. **2.** formed by putrefaction.

sap·ro·phyte (sap/rə fīt/), *n.* any organism that lives on dead organic matter, as certain bacteria. —**sap/ro·phyt/ic** (-fit/ik), *adj.*

sar·coid (sär/koid), *n.* **1.** a growth resembling a sarcoma. **2.** a lesion of sarcoidosis. **3.** SARCOIDOSIS. —*adj.* **4.** resembling a sarcoma.

sar/coid·o/sis (-koi dō/sis), *n.* a disease of unknown cause, characterized by granulomatous tubercles of the skin, lymph nodes, lungs, or other structures.

sar·co·ma (-kō/mə), *n., pl.* **-mas, -ma·ta** (-mə tə). any of various malignant tumors composed of neoplastic cells resembling embryonic connective tissue. —**sar·co/ma·toid/, sar·co/ma·tous** (-kō/mə təs, -kom/ə-), *adj.*

sar·co/ma·to/sis (-tō/sis), *n.* a condition marked by the presence of multiple sarcomas.

sat·u·rate (sach/ ər it, -ə rāt/), *n.* a saturated fat or fatty acid.

sat/urated fat/, *n.* any animal or vegetable fat, abundant in fatty meats, dairy products, coconut oil, and palm oil, tending to raise cholesterol levels in the blood.

sat·ur·nine (sat/ər nīn/), *adj.* **1.** suffering from lead poisoning. **2.** due to absorption of lead, as bodily disorders.

sat/ur·nism (-niz/əm), *n.* LEAD POISONING.

sa·ty·ri·a·sis (sā/tə rī/ə sis, sat/ə-), *n.* abnormal, uncontrollable sexual desire in a male. Also called **Don Juanism.** Compare NYMPHOMANIA.

sax·i·tox·in (sak/si tok/sin), *n.* a neurotoxin produced by the dinoflagellate *Gonyaulax catenella.*

scab (skab), *n., v.,* **scabbed, scab·bing.** —*n.* **1.** the incrustation that forms over a sore or wound during healing. —*v.i.* **2.** to become covered with a scab.

sca·bies (skā/bēz, -bē ēz/), *n. (used with a sing. v.)* a form of mange caused by the itch mite, *Sarcoptes scabiei,* which burrows into the skin. —**sca/bi·et/ic** (-bē et/ik), *adj.*

sca/bi·ous (-bē əs), *adj.* pertaining to or of the nature of scabies.

scall (skôl), *n.* DANDRUFF.

scal·o·gram (skā/lə gram/), *n. Psychol.* a test so arranged that responses to several items can be correlated to define or measure a person's attitudes.

scal·pel (skal/pəl), *n.* a small, light, usu. straight knife used in surgical and anatomical operations and dissections. —**scal·pel/lic** (-pel/ik), *adj.*

scan (skan), *v.,* **scanned, scan·ning,** *n.* —*v.t.* **1.** to examine (a body or body part) with a scanner. —*n.* **2.** an examination of the body or a body part using a scanner. —**scan/na·ble,** *adj.*

scan/ner, *n.* a device for examining a body, organ, or tissue. Compare CAT SCANNER, PET SCANNER.

scap·u·la (skap/yə lə), *n., pl.* **-las, -lae** (-lē/). either of two flat triangular bones each forming the back part of a shoulder; shoulder blade.

scap'u·lar, *adj.* of or pertaining to the shoulders or the scapula or scapulas.

scar·i·fy (skar'ə fī/), *v.t.,* **-fied, -fy·ing.** to make scratches or superficial incisions in, as in vaccination. **—scar·i·fi·ca'tion,** *n.*

scar·la·ti·na (skär/lə tē/nə), *n.* **1.** SCARLET FEVER. **2.** a mild form of scarlet fever. **—scar·la·ti/nal, scar·la·ti·nous** (skär/lə tē/nəs, skär lat/n əs), *adj.*

scar/let fe/ver, *n.* a contagious febrile disease caused by streptococci and characterized by a red rash.

scar/ tis/sue, *n.* connective tissue that has contracted and become dense and fibrous, forming a scar.

Schick/ test/ (shik), *n.* a diphtheria immunity test in which diphtheria toxoid is injected intracutaneously, immunity being indicated by an inflammation at the injection site.

schis·to·some (shis/tə sōm/), *n.* **1.** Also called **bilharzia.** any trematode of the genus *Schistosoma,* parasitic in the blood of birds and mammals, including humans; a blood fluke. **—adj. 2.** Also, **schis/to·so/mal.** pertaining to or caused by schistosomes.

schis/to·so·mi/a·sis (-sō mī/ə sis), *n.* a chronic anemia and organ infection caused by parasitic flukes of the genus *Schistosoma,* transmitted through feces-contaminated water or river snails. Also called **bilharziasis, snail fever.**

schiz·oid (skit/soid), *adj.* **1.** of or pertaining to a personality disorder marked by dissociation, passivity, and indifference to praise or criticism. **2.** of or pertaining to schizophrenia or to multiple personality. **—n. 3.** a schizoid person.

schiz·o·my·cete (skiz/ō mī/sēt, -mi sēt/, skit/sō-), *n.* any of numerous microorganisms of the subkingdom (or phylum) Schizophyta, kingdom Monera, comprising the bacteria. **—schiz/o·my·ce/tous,** *adj.*

schiz·o·phre·ni·a (skit/sə frē/nē ə), *n.* a severe mental disorder associated with brain abnormalities and typically evidenced by disorganized speech and behavior, delusions, and hallucinations. **—schiz/o·phren/ic** (-fren/ik), *adj., n.* **—schiz/o·phren/i·cal·ly,** *adv.*

Schwann/ cell/ (shwän, shvän), *n.* a cell of the peripheral nervous system that wraps around a nerve fiber, jelly-roll fashion, forming the myelin sheath.

sci·at·ic (si at/ik), *adj.* of, pertaining to, situated near, or affecting the ischium or back of the hip or the sciatic nerves. **—sci·at/i·cal·ly,** *adv.*

sci·at/i·ca (-i kə), *n.* pain involving the sacral plexus or sciatic nerve, often felt in the lower back and along the back of the thigh.

sciat/ic nerve/, *n.* either of a pair of nerves that originate in the sacral plexus of the lower back and extend down the buttocks to the back of the knees, where they divide into other nerves.

scin·tig·ra·phy (sin tig/rə fē), *n.* the production of a record of the intensity and distribution of radioactivity in tissues after administration of a radioactive tracer.

scir·rhous (skir′əs, sir′-), *adj. Pathol.* **1.** of a hard, fibrous consistency. **2.** of, relating to, or constituting a scirrhus. —**scir·rhos·i·ty** (ski ros′i tē), *n.*

scir·rhus (skir′əs, sir′-), *n., pl.* **scir·rhi** (skir′ī, sir′ī), **scir·rhus·es.** a firm, densely collagenous cancer.

scle·ra (sklēr′ə), *n., pl.* **-ras.** a dense, white, fibrous membrane that, with the cornea, forms the external covering of the eyeball. —**scle′ral,** *adj.*

scle·rec·to·my (skli rek′tə mē), *n., pl.* **-mies. 1.** surgical excision of part of the sclera. **2.** removal of the adhesions formed in the middle ear during chronic otitis media.

scle·ri·tis (-rī′tis), *n.* inflammation of the sclera.

scle·ro·der·ma (sklēr′ə dûr′mə, sklēr′-), *n.* a disease in which connective tissue anywhere in the body becomes hardened and rigid. —**scle′ro·der′ma·tous,** *adj.*

scle·ro·ma (skli rō′mə), *n., pl.* **-mas, -ma·ta** (-mə tə). a tumorlike hardening of tissue.

scle·rosed (skli rōst′, sklēr′ōzd, sklēr′-), *adj.* hardened or indurated, as by sclerosis.

scle·ro·sis (skli rō′sis), *n., pl.* **-ses** (-sēz). a hardening of a body tissue or part, or an increase of connective tissue or the like at the expense of more active tissue. —**scle·ro′sal,** *adj.*

scle·ro·ther·a·py (sklēr′ə ther′ə pē, sklēr′-), *n.* a treatment for varicose veins, hemorrhoids, and excessive bleeding in which blood flow is diverted and the veins collapsed by injection of a hardening solution.

scle·rot·ic (skli rot′ik), *adj.* **1.** of or pertaining to the sclera. **2.** pertaining to or affected with sclerosis.

scle·rot′o·my (-ə mē), *n., pl.* **-mies.** incision into the sclera, as to extract foreign bodies.

sco·li·o·sis (skō′lē ō′sis, skol′ē-), *n.* an abnormal lateral curvature of the spine. Compare KYPHOSIS, LORDOSIS. —**sco′li·ot′ic** (-ot′ik), *adj.*

sco·pol·a·mine (skə pol′ə mēn′, -min, skō′pə lam′in), *n.* a colorless, syrupy, water-soluble alkaloid, $C_{17}H_{21}NO_4$, obtained from certain plants of the nightshade family, used chiefly as a sedative and antinauseant and to dilate the pupils.

scor·bu·tic (skôr byōō′tik) also **scor·bu′ti·cal,** *adj.* pertaining to, of the nature of, or having scurvy. —**scor·bu′ti·cal·ly,** *adv.*

sco·to·ma (skō tō′mə), *n., pl.* **-mas, -ma·ta** (-mə tə). loss of vision in a part of the visual field. Compare BLIND SPOT. —**sco·tom′a·tous** (-tom′ə təs), *adj.*

sco·to·pi·a (skə tō′pē ə, skō-), *n.* vision in dim light (opposed to *photopia*). Compare DARK ADAPTATION. —**sco·top′ic** (-top′ik), *adj.*

scratch′ test′, *n.* a test for an allergy in which the skin is scratched and an allergen applied to the area.

scrof·u·la (skrof′yə lə), *n.* primary tuberculosis of the lymphatic glands, esp. of the neck. Also called **king's evil.**

scrof′u·lous, *adj.* pertaining to, resembling, of the nature of, or affected with scrofula.

scro·tum (skrō′təm), *n., pl.* **-ta** (-tə), **-tums.** the pouch of skin that contains the testes. **—scro′tal,** *adj.*

scrub′ suit′, *n.* a loose-fitting, two-piece garment, often of green cotton, worn by surgeons.

scrub′ ty·phus′, *n.* an infectious disease occurring chiefly in Japan and southeast Asia, caused by the organism *Rickettsia tsutsugamushi,* transmitted by mites through biting.

scurf (skûrf), *n.* the scales or small shreds of epidermis that are continually exfoliated from the skin.

scurf′y, *adj.,* **-i·er, -i·est.** resembling, producing, or covered with or as if with scurf.

scur·vy (skûr′vē), *n., adj.,* **-vi·er, -vi·est.** **—n.** a disease marked by swollen and bleeding gums, livid spots on the skin, and prostration, caused by a lack of vitamin C.

sea′ salt′, *n.* table salt produced through the evaporation of seawater.

sea′sick′, *adj.* afflicted with seasickness.

sea′sick′ness, *n.* nausea and dizziness, often accompanied by vomiting, induced by the motion of a vessel at sea.

sea′sonal affec′tive disor′der, *n.* recurrent winter depression characterized by oversleeping, overeating, and irritability and relieved by the arrival of spring or by light therapy. *Abbr.:* SAD

se·ba·ceous (si bā′shəs), *adj.* **1.** pertaining to, of the nature of, or resembling tallow or fat; fatty; greasy. **2.** secreting a fatty substance.

seba′ceous gland′, *n.* any of the cutaneous glands that secrete oily matter for lubricating hair and skin.

seb·or·rhe·a (seb′ə rē′ə), *n.* abnormally heavy discharge from the sebaceous glands. **—seb′or·rhe′al, seb′or·rhe′ic,** *adj.*

se·bum (sē′bəm), *n.* the fatty secretion of the sebaceous glands.

sec·o·bar·bi·tal (sek′ō bär′bi tôl′, -tal′), *n.* a white, odorless, slightly bitter powder, $C_{12}H_{18}N_2O_3$, used as a sedative and hypnotic.

Sec·o·nal (sek′ə nôl′, -nal′, -nl), *Trademark.* a brand of secobarbital.

sec′ondary sex′ characteris′tic, *n.* any of a number of manifestations, as breasts or a beard, specific to each sex and incipient at puberty but not essential to reproduction.

sec′ond-degree′ burn′, *n.* See under BURN.

sec′ondhand smoke′, *n.* smoke from a cigarette, cigar, or pipe that is involuntarily inhaled, esp. by nonsmokers.

se·cre·ta·gog or **se·cre·ta·gogue** (si krē′tə gog′, -gôg′), *n. Physiol.* a substance or situation that promotes secretion.

se·crete (si krēt′), *v.t.,* **-cret·ed, -cret·ing.** to discharge, generate, or release by secretion.

se·cre·tin (si krē′tin), *n.* a polypeptide hormone, produced in the small intestine, that activates the pancreas to secrete pancreatic juice.

se·cre'tion, *n.* **1.** (in a cell or gland) the process of separating, elaborating, and releasing a substance that fulfills some function within the organism or undergoes excretion. **2.** the product of this process. —**se·cre'tion·ar'y** (-shə-ner′ē), *adj.*

se·cre'to·ry (-tə rē) *adj.* **1.** pertaining to secretion. **2.** performing the process of secretion.

sec·tion (sek′shən), *n.* **1.** a thin slice of a tissue, mineral, or the like, as for microscopic examination. —*v.t.* **2.** to make a surgical incision.

se·date (si dāt′), *v.t.,* **-dat·ed, -dat·ing.** to put under sedation.

se·da'tion, *n.* **1.** the bringing about of mental or physiological relaxation, esp. by the use of a drug. **2.** the state so induced.

sed·a·tive (sed′ə tiv), *adj.* **1.** assuaging pain or allaying irritability or excitement. —*n.* **2.** a sedative drug or agent.

seg·re·gate (seg′ri gāt′), *v.i.,* **-gat·ed, -gat·ing.** (of allelic genes) to separate during meiosis.

seg're·ga'tion, *n.* the separation of allelic genes into different gametes during meiosis. —**seg're·ga'tion·al,** *adj.*

Seid'litz pow'ders (sed′lits), *n.pl.* a mild laxative consisting of tartaric acid, sodium bicarbonate, and Rochelle salt dissolved separately, mixed, and drunk after effervescence.

sei·zure (sē′zhər), *n.* a sudden attack, as of epilepsy.

se·le·ni·um (si lē′nē əm), *n.* a nonmetallic element occurring in several allotropic forms and having an electrical resistance that varies under the influence of light. *Symbol:* Se; *at. wt.:* 78.96; *at. no.:* 34; *sp. gr.:* (gray) 4.80 at 25°C, (red) 4.50 at 25°C.

self (self), *n., pl.* **selves.** any of the natural constituents of the body that are normally not subject to attack by components of the immune system (disting. from *nonself*).

self'-actualiza'tion, *n.* the achievement of one's full potential through creativity, independence, spontaneity, and a grasp of the real world. —**self'-ac'tualize,** *v.i.,* **-ized, -iz·ing.**

self'-anal'ysis, *n.* the application of psychoanalytic techniques to an analysis of one's own personality and behavior without the aid of another person.

self'-an'tigen or **self' an'tigen,** *n.* AUTOANTIGEN.

self'-examina'tion, *n.* examination of one's body for signs of illness or disease. —**self'-exam'ining,** *adj.*

self'-hypno'sis, *n.* AUTOHYPNOSIS. —**self'-hypnot'ic,** *adj.* —**self'-hyp'notism,** *n.*

self'-lim'iting or **self'-lim'ited,** *adj.* (of a disease) running a definite and limited course. —**self'-limita'tion,** *n.*

self'-medica'tion, *n.* the use of medicine without medical supervision to treat one's own ailment.

self'-rep'licating, *adj.* making an exact copy or copies of itself, as a strand of DNA. —**self'-replica'tion,** *n.*

se·men (sē′mən), *n.* a viscid, whitish fluid produced in the male reproductive organs, containing sperm. —**sem·i·nal** (sem′ə nl), *adj.*

semicir′cular canal′, *n.* any of the three curved tubular canals in the inner ear, associated with the sense of equilibrium.

sem′inal flu′id, *n.* the fluid component of semen, excluding the sperm.

sem′inal ves′icle, *n.* either of two small saclike glands, located on each side of the bladder in males, that add nutrient fluid to semen during ejaculation.

sem·i·nif′er·ous tu′bule (sem′ə nif′ər əs), *n.* any of the coiled tubules of the testis in which spermatozoa are produced.

se·mi·ot·ic (sē′mē ot′ik, sem′ē, sē′mi-), *adj.* Also, **se′mi·ot′i·cal.** of or pertaining to symptoms of disease; symptomatic.

sem·i·syn·thet·ic (sem′ē sin thet′ik, sem′i-), *adj.* derived synthetically from one or more substances of natural origin. —**sem′i·syn·thet′i·cal·ly,** *adv.*

Sen′dai′ vi′rus (sen′dī′), *n.* a paramyxovirus that tends to cause cell fusion: in inactive form, used in biological research to produce cells with multiple nuclei of different genetic constitutions.

se·nile (sē′nil, sen′il), *adj.* **1.** showing a decline or deterioration of physical strength or mental functioning, esp. short-term memory and alertness, as a result of old age or disease. **2.** of or belonging to old age or aged persons; gerontological; geriatric.

se′nile demen′tia, *n.* a syndrome of progressive, irreversible impairment of cognitive function, caused by organic factors and having its onset late in life.

se·nil·i·ty (si nil′i tē), *n.* the state of being senile, esp. the weakness or mental infirmity of old age.

sen·sa·tion (sen sā′shən), *n.* the faculty of perception of stimuli.

sense (sens), *n.* **1.** any of the faculties, as sight, hearing, smell, taste, or touch, by which humans and animals perceive stimuli originating from outside or inside the body. **2.** these faculties collectively. **3.** their operation or function; sensation. **4.** a DNA sequence that is capable of coding for an amino acid (disting. from *nonsense*).

sense′ da′tum, *n.* the basic unit of an experience resulting from the stimulation of a sense organ; a stimulus or an object of perception or sensation.

sense′ percep′tion, *n.* perception by one or more of the senses rather than by the intellect.

sen·si·tive (sen′si tiv), *adj. Physiol.* having a low threshold of sensation or feeling. —**sen′si·tive·ly,** *adv.* —**sen′si·tive·ness,** *n.*

sen·si·tiv·i·ty (sen′si tiv′i·tē), *n., pl.* **-ties. 1.** the ability of an organism or part of an organism to react to stimuli; irritability. **2.** degree of susceptibility to stimulation.

sensitiv′ity train′ing, *n.* a form of group therapy designed to develop understanding of oneself and others through free, unstructured discussion.

sen'si·ti·za'tion (-tə zā'shən), *n.* the process of becoming susceptible to a given stimulus that previously had no effect or significance.

sen·so·ri·mo·tor (sen'sə rē mō'tər), *adj.* of, pertaining to, or having both sensory and motor functions, as certain areas of the brain.

sen'so·ri·neu'ral, *adj.* related to or affecting a sensory nerve or a sensory mechanism together with its neural circuitry.

sen'so·ry also **sen·so'ri·al** (-sôr'ē əl, -sōr'-), *adj.* of or noting a physiological structure for receiving or conveying an external stimulus.

sen'sory depriva'tion, *n.* extreme reduction of environmental stimuli, often leading to cognitive, perceptual, or behavioral disorientation or, in infants, developmental damage.

sen'sory neu'ron (or **nerve'**), *n.* a nerve cell that conducts impulses from the periphery of the body to the central nervous system.

sep·sis (sep'sis), *n.* local or generalized invasion of the body by pathogenic microorganisms or their toxins: *dental sepsis; wound sepsis.*

sep'tic (-tik), *adj.* **1.** pertaining to or of the nature of sepsis; infected. **2.** putrefactive. **—sep'ti·cal·ly**, *adv.* **—sep·tic'i·ty** (-tis'i tē), *n.*

sep'ti·ce'mi·a (-tə sē'mē ə), *n.* the presence of pathogenic bacteria in the bloodstream. **—sep'ti·ce'mic**, *adj.*

sep'tic sore' throat', *n.* an acute toxic streptococcus infection of the throat producing fever, tonsillitis, and other serious effects.

sep·tum (sep'təm), *n., pl.* **-ta** (-tə). a dividing wall, membrane, or the like in an animal structure; dissepiment.

se·que·la (si kwē'lə), *n., pl.* **-lae** (-lē). an abnormal condition resulting from a previous disease.

se·quence (sē'kwəns), *n., v.,* **-quenced, -quenc·ing. —***n.* **1.** the linear order of nucleotides in DNA or RNA or amino acids in a protein. **—***v.t.* **2.** to determine the order of (nucleotides in DNA or RNA or amino acids in a protein).

se'quenc·er, *n.* a device that can sequence nucleic acids or protein.

Ser, serine.

ser·ine (ser'ēn, -in, sēr'-), *n.* a crystalline amino acid, HOCH₂CH(NH₂)COOH, found in many proteins. *Abbr.:* Ser; *Symbol:* S

se·ro·di·ag·no·sis (sēr'ō dī'əg nō'sis), *n., pl.* **-ses** (-sēz). a diagnosis involving tests on blood serum or other serous fluid of the body. Also called **immunodiagnosis. —se'ro·di'ag·nos'tic** (-nos'tik), *adj.*

se·rol·o·gy (si rol'ə jē), *n.* the science dealing with the immunological properties and actions of serum. **—se·ro·log'ic** (sēr'ə loj'ik), **se'ro·log'i·cal,** *adj.* **—se'ro·log'i·cal·ly,** *adv.* **—se·rol'o·gist,** *n.*

se·ro·neg·a·tive (sēr′ō neg′ə tiv), *adj.* showing no significant level of serum antibodies, or other immunologic marker in the serum, that would indicate previous exposure to the infectious agent being tested. —**se′ro·neg′a·tiv′i·ty**, *n.*

se′ro·pos′i·tive, *adj.* showing a significant level of serum antibodies, or other immunologic marker in the serum, indicating previous exposure to the infectious agent being tested. —**se′ro·pos′i·tiv′i·ty**, *n.*

ser·o·to·nin (ser′ə tō′nin, sēr′-), *n.* an amine, $C_{10}H_{12}N_2O$, that occurs esp. in blood and nervous tissue and functions as a vasoconstrictor and neurotransmitter.

se·ro·type (sēr′ə tip′, ser′-), *n., v.,* **-typed, -typ·ing.** —*n.* **1.** a group of organisms, microorganisms, or cells distinguished by their shared specific antigens as determined by serologic testing. **2.** the set of antigens that characterizes the group. —*v.t.* **3.** to classify by serotype.

se·rous (sēr′əs), *adj.* of, pertaining to, or characterized by serum: *serous fluid.* —**se·ros·i·ty** (si ros′i tē), **se′rous·ness,** *n.*

se′rous mem′brane, *n.* any of various thin membranes, as the peritoneum, that line certain cavities of the body and exude a serous fluid. Also called **serosa.**

se·rum (sēr′əm), *n., pl.* **se·rums, se·ra** (sēr′ə). **1.** the clear, pale yellow liquid that separates from the clot in the coagulation of blood; blood serum. **2.** any watery animal fluid. —**se′rum·al,** *adj.*

se′rum albu′min, *n.* the principal protein of blood plasma, important in osmotic regulation of the blood and transport of metabolites: used in the treatment of shock.

se′rum glob′ulin, *n.* the globulin in blood serum containing most of the blood's antibodies.

se′rum hepati′tis, *n.* HEPATITIS B.

sex (seks), *n.* **1.** either the female or male division of a species, esp. as differentiated with reference to the reproductive functions. **2.** the sum of the structural and functional differences by which the female and male are distinguished, or the phenomena or behavior dependent on these differences. **3.** SEXUAL INTERCOURSE.

sex′ change′, *n.* the alteration, by surgery and hormone treatments, of a person's morphological sex characteristics to approximate those of the opposite sex.

sex′ chro′matin, *n.* BARR BODY.

sex′ chro′mosome, *n.* a chromosome, differing in shape or function from other chromosomes, that determines the sex of an individual.

sex′ hor′mone, *n.* any of a class of steroid hormones that regulate the growth and function of the reproductive organs or stimulate the development of the secondary sexual characteristics.

sex′-lim′ited, *adj.* (of a gene character) expressed in one sex only.

sex′-link′age, *n.* an association between genes in sex chromosomes such that the characteristics determined by these genes appear more frequently in one sex than in the other.

sex′-linked′, *adj.* **1.** (of a gene) located in a sex chromosome. **2.** (of a character) determined by a sex-linked gene.

sex·ol·o·gy (sek sol′ə jē), *n.* the study of sexual behavior. —**sex′o·log′i·cal** (-sə loj′i kəl), *adj.* —**sex·ol′o·gist,** *n.*

sex′ ther′apy, *n.* treatment of sexual disorders that have psychological causes, as by psychiatric counseling.

sex·tu·plet (seks tup′lit, -too′plit, -tyoo′-, seks′too plit, -too-), *n.* **sextuplets,** six children or offspring born of one pregnancy.

sex·u·al (sek′shoo əl), *adj.* **1.** of or pertaining to sex. **2.** occurring between or involving the sexes: *sexual relations.* **3.** having sexual organs, or reproducing by processes involving both sexes. —**sex′u·al·ly,** *adv.*

sex′ual in′tercourse, *n.* genital contact or coupling between individuals, esp. one involving penetration of the penis into the vagina.

sex′u·al′i·ty, *n.* sexual character; possession of the structural and functional traits of sex.

sex′ually transmit′ted disease′, *n.* any disease characteristically transmitted by sexual contact, as gonorrhea, syphilis, genital herpes, and chlamydia. *Abbr.:* STD Also called **venereal disease.**

SGO, Surgeon General's Office.

shak′en ba′by syn′drome, *n.* a usu. fatal condition of abused infants brought on by violent shaking by the arms or shoulders that causes severe internal bleeding, esp. around the brain and in the eyes.

shell′ shock′, *n.* BATTLE FATIGUE. —**shell′-shocked′,** *adj.*

shi·at·su or **shi·at·zu** (shē ät′soo), *n.* (*sometimes cap.*) a Japanese massage technique that includes the use of acupressure.

shi·gel·la (shi gel′ə), *n., pl.* **-gel·lae** (-gel′ē), **-gel·las.** any of several rod-shaped aerobic bacteria of the genus *Shigella,* certain species of which are pathogenic.

shig·el·lo·sis (shig′ə lō′sis), *n.* dysentery caused by shigellae.

shin′bone′, *n.* the tibia.

shin·gles (shing′gəlz), *n.* (*used with a sing. or pl. v.*) a disease caused by the herpes zoster virus, characterized by skin eruptions and pain along the course of involved sensory nerves. Also called **herpes zoster.**

shin′ splints′, *n.* (*used with a pl. v.*) a painful condition of the front lower leg associated with muscle strain or stress of the tibia from strenuous activity.

shock (shok), *n.* **1.** gravely diminished blood circulation caused by severe injury or pain, blood loss, or certain diseases and characterized by pallor, weak pulse, and very low blood pressure. **2.** the physiological effect produced by the passage of an electric current through the body. —**shock′a·ble,** *adj.* —**shock′a·bil′i·ty,** *n.*

shock′ ther′apy, *n.* any of various therapies, as insulin shock therapy or electroconvulsive therapy, that induce convulsions or unconsciousness and are used for symptomatic relief in certain mental disorders. Also called **shock/ treat/ment.**

shoul/der blade/, *n.* SCAPULA.

show (shō), *v.* **n. 1.** the first appearance of blood at the onset of menstruation. **2.** a blood-tinged mucous discharge from the vagina that indicates the onset of labor.

shunt (shunt), *n.* **1.** a channel through which blood or other bodily fluid is diverted from its normal path by surgical reconstruction or by a synthetic tube. —*v.t.* **2.** to divert (blood or other fluid) by means of a shunt. —**shunt/er,** *n.*

si·al·a·gogue or **si·al·o·gogue** (sī al/ə gôg/, -gog/), *n.* an agent or medicine that increases salivary flow. —**si/a·la·gog/ic, si/a·lo·gog/ic** (-ə lə goj/ik), *adj.*

sick/ build/ing syn/drome, *n.* an illness caused by exposure to pollutants or germs inside an airtight building. Also called **building sickness.**

sick/ head/ache, *n.* MIGRAINE.

sick/le cell/ (sik/əl), *n.* an elongated, often sickle-shaped red blood cell, caused by defective hemoglobin.

sick/le cell/ ane/mia, *n.* a chronic hereditary blood disease, primarily affecting indigenous Africans and their descendants, in which an accumulation of oxygen-deficient sickle cells results in anemia, blood clotting, and joint pain. Also called **sicklemia.**

sick/le cell/ trait/, *n.* the usu. asymptomatic hereditary condition that occurs when a person inherits from only one parent the abnormal hemoglobin gene characteristic of sickle cell anemia.

sick·le·mi·a (sik/ə lē/mē ə, sik lē/-), *n.* SICKLE CELL ANEMIA. —**sick/le/mic,** *adj.*

sick/out/, *n.* an organized absence from work by employees on the pretext of sickness.

sid·er·o·phile (sid/ər ə fīl/), *adj.* **1.** having an affinity for metallic iron. —*n.* **2.** a siderophile element, tissue, or cell.

sid/er·o/sis (-ə rō/sis), *n.* a disease of the lungs caused by inhaling iron or other metallic particles. —**sid/er·ot/ic** (-rot/ik), *adj.*

SIDS, sudden infant death syndrome.

sig·moid (sig/moid) also **sig·moi/dal,** *adj.* of, pertaining to, or situated near the sigmoid flexure of the large intestine. —**sig·moi/dal·ly,** *adv.*

sig/moid flex/ure, *n.* **1.** an S-shaped curve in a body part. **2.** Also called **sig/moid co/lon.** the S-shaped curve of the large intestine where the descending colon joins the rectum in humans.

sig·moid/o·scope/ (-moi/də skōp/), *n.* a rigid or flexible endoscope for visual examination of the rectum and sigmoid colon. —**sig·moid/o·scop/ic** (-skop/ik), *adj.* —**sig/moid·os/co·pist** (-dos/kə pist), *n.*

sig·na·ture (sig/nə chər, -chŏŏr/), *n.* **1.** that part of a physician's prescription that specifies directions for use. **2.** a distinctive characteristic or set of characteristics by which a biological structure or medical condition is recognized.

si·lent (sī'lənt), *adj.* producing no detectable symptoms: *a silent heart attack.*

sil·i·co·sis (sil'i kō'sis), *n.* a disease of the lungs caused by the inhaling of siliceous particles, as by stonecutters. —**sil'i·cot'ic** (-kot'ik), *adj.*

sil'ver ni'trate, *n.* a corrosive, poisonous powder, AgNO₃, used as a laboratory reagent and as an antiseptic and astringent.

si·meth·i·cone (si meth'i kōn'), *n.* an active ingredient in many antacid preparations that causes small mucus-entrapped air bubbles in the intestines to coalesce into larger bubbles that are more easily passed.

simian virus 40, *n.* See SV 40.

sim'ple frac'ture, *n.* a fracture in which the bone does not pierce the skin.

sim'ple sug'ar, *n.* a monosaccharide.

sim·u·la·tion (sim'yə lā'shən), *n.* a conscious attempt to feign some mental or physical disorder.

sin·a·pism (sin'ə piz'əm), *n.* MUSTARD PLASTER.

sin'gle-blind', *adj.* of or pertaining to an experiment or clinical trial in which the researchers but not the subjects know which subjects are receiving the active treatment, medication, etc., so as to eliminate subject bias. Compare DOUBLE-BLIND.

si'no·a'tri·al node' (sī'nō ā'trē əl, sī'-), *n.* a small mass of tissue in the right atrium functioning as pacemaker of the heart by giving rise to the electric impulses that initiate heart contractions.

sin·se·mil·la (sin'sə mil'ə), *n.* marijuana from seedless female hemp plants that contain very high levels of THC.

si·nus (sī'nəs), *n., pl.* **-nus·es. 1. a.** any of various cavities, recesses, or passages in the body, as a hollow in a bone or a reservoir or channel for venous blood. **b.** one of the hollow cavities in the skull connecting with the nasal cavities. **c.** an expanded area in a canal or tube. **2.** a narrow passage leading to an abscess or the like. —**si'nus·like'**, *adj.*

si·nus·i·tis (sī'nə sī'tis), *n.* inflammation of a sinus or the sinuses of the skull.

sit'-up', *n.* an exercise in which a person lies flat on the back, lifts the torso to a sitting position, and then lies flat again without changing the position of the legs: formerly done with the legs straight but now usu. done with the knees bent.

sitz' bath' (sits, zits), *n.* **1.** a chairlike bathtub in which the thighs and hips are immersed in warm water. **2.** a therapeutic bath so taken.

skel·e·tal (skel'i tl), *adj.* of, pertaining to, or like a skeleton. —**skel'e·tal·ly,** *adv.*

skel'etal mus'cle, *n.* VOLUNTARY MUSCLE.

skel·e·ton (skel'i tn), *n.* the bones of a vertebrate considered as a whole, together forming the internal framework of the body.

skin′ graft′, *n.* surgically transplanted skin, used for covering a burn or extensive wound.

skin′ graft′ing, *n.* the surgical process of transplanting skin to a wound or burn in order to form new skin; dermatoplasty.

Skin·ner·i·an (ski nēr′ē ən), *n.* **1.** a psychologist who follows the behaviorist theories of B. F. Skinner. —*adj.* **2.** of or pertaining to these theories, esp. concerning operant conditioning.

skin′-pop′, *v.,* **-popped, -pop·ping.** —*v.t.* **1.** to inject (a drug) under the skin rather than into a vein. —*v.i.* **2.** to inject a drug under the skin.

sleep′ ap′ne·a, *n.* a brief suspension of breathing occurring repeatedly during sleep.

sleep′ing pill′, *n.* a pill or capsule containing a drug for inducing sleep.

sleep′ing sick′ness, *n.* **1.** Also called **trypanosomiasis.** an infectious, usu. fatal disease of Africa, characterized by wasting and progressive lethargy, and caused by a trypanosome carried by the tsetse fly. **2.** Also called **encephalitis.** a viral disease affecting the brain, characterized by apathy, sleepiness, extreme muscular weakness, and impairment of vision.

sleep′walk′ing, *n.* the act or state of walking while asleep; somnambulism. —**sleep′walk′,** *v.i.* —**sleep′walk′er,** *n.*

slim′ disease′, *n.* a form of AIDS common in Africa, marked by emaciation and fever.

slipped′ disk′, *n.* HERNIATED DISK.

slough (sluf), *n.* **1.** a mass or layer of dead tissue separated from the surrounding or underlying tissue. —*v.i.* **2.** to separate from the sound flesh, as a slough.

slow′-release′, *adj.* (of a drug) capable of gradual release of an active agent, allowing for a sustained effect; sustained-release.

slow′ vi′rus, *n.* a virus or viruslike agent that remains dormant in the body for a long time before producing symptoms.

slow′-wave′ sleep′, *n.* a recurrent period of deep sleep distinguished by the presence of slow brain waves and by very little dreaming. Also called **S sleep.** Compare REM SLEEP.

small′ cal′orie, *n.* CALORIE (def. 1a).

small′ intes′tine, *n.* INTESTINE (def. 2).

small·pox (smôl′poks′), *n.* an acute, highly contagious, febrile disease, caused by the variola virus and characterized by a pustular eruption that often leaves permanent pits or scars: eradicated worldwide by vaccination programs.

smeg·ma (smeg′mə), *n.* a thick, cheeselike, sebaceous secretion that collects beneath the foreskin or around the clitoris.

smooth′ mus′cle, *n.* involuntary muscle tissue in the

walls of viscera and blood vessels, consisting of nonstriated, spindle-shaped cells.

snail/ fe/ver, *n.* SCHISTOSOMIASIS.

snort (snôrt), *Slang.* —*v.i.* **1.** to take a drug by inhaling. —*v.t.* **2.** to take (a drug) by inhaling: *to snort cocaine.* —**snort/er,** *n.*

snow (snō), *n. Slang.* cocaine or heroin.

snow/bird/, *n. Slang.* a cocaine addict or habitual user.

snow/ blind/ness, *n.* the usu. temporary dimming of the sight caused by the glare of reflected sunlight on snow. —**snow/-blind/,** *adj.*

so/cial disease/, *n.* a venereal disease.

so/cialized med/icine, *n.* any of various systems designed to provide a nation with complete medical care through government subsidization and regularization of medical and health services.

so/cial psychol/ogy, *n.* the psychological study of social behavior, esp. of the reciprocal influence of the individual and the group with which the individual interacts.

so·ci·o·path (sō/sē ə path′, sō/shē-), *n.* a person, as a psychopath, whose behavior is antisocial and who lacks a sense of moral responsibility or social conscience. —**so/ci·o·path/ic,** *adj.* —**so/ci·op/a·thy** (-op/ə thē), *n.*

so·di·um (sō/dē əm), *n.* **1.** a soft, silver-white, chemically active metallic element that occurs naturally only in combination: a necessary element in the body for the maintenance of normal fluid balance and other physiological functions. *Symbol:* NA; *at. wt.:* 22.9898; *at. no.:* 11; *sp. gr.:* 0.97 at 20ºC. **2.** any salt of sodium, as sodium chloride or sodium bicarbonate.

so/dium ben/zoate, *n.* a white, water-soluble powder, $C_7H_5NaO_2$, used chiefly as a food preservative.

so/dium bicar/bonate, *n.* a white water-soluble powder, $NaHCO_3$, used as an antacid. Also called **bicarbonate of soda, baking soda.**

so/dium chlo/ride, *n.* SALT¹ (def. 1).

so/dium ni/trite, *n.* a yellowish or white crystalline compound, $NaNO_2$, used as a color fixative and in food as a flavoring and preservative.

so/dium pump/, *n.* an energy-consuming mechanism in cell membranes that transports sodium ions across the membrane, in exchange for potassium ions or other substances.

soft/ chan/cre, *n.* CHANCROID.

soft/ drug/, *n.* a drug, usu. illicit, that does not produce significant psychological or physical dependence.

soft/ lens/, *n.* a nonrigid contact lens made of porous plastic, having a high water content that is replenished from eye surface moisture. Compare HARD LENS.

soft/ pal/ate, *n.* See under PALATE.

so/lar plex/us, *n.* **1.** a network of nerves at the upper part of the abdomen, behind the stomach and in front of the aorta. **2.** a point on the stomach wall just below the sternum where a blow will affect this network.

so·mat·ic (sō matʹik, sə-), *adj.* **1.** of the body; bodily; physical. **2.** of or pertaining to the body walls, as distinguished from the inner organs. **3.** of or pertaining to a somatic cell. —**so·matʹi·cal·ly**, *adv.*

somatʹic cellʹ, *n.* **1.** one of the cells that take part in the formation of the body, becoming differentiated into the various tissues, organs, etc. **2.** any cell of the body that is not a sexually reproductive cell (opposed to *germ cell*).

so·mat·o·me·din (sə matʹə mēdʹn), *n.* any of various liver hormones that enhance the activity of a variety of other hormones, as somatotropin.

so·mat·o·plasm (-plazʹəm), *n.* the cytoplasm of a somatic cell, esp. as distinguished from germ plasm. —**soʹma·to·plasʹtic**, *adj.*

so·mat·o·pleure (-plŏŏrʹ), *n.* the double layer formed by the association of the upper layer of the lateral plate of mesoderm with the overlying ectoderm. —**so·matʹo·pleuʹral, so·matʹo·pleuʹric**, *adj.*

so·mat·o·stat·in (-statʹn), *n.* a polypeptide hormone, produced in the brain and pancreas, that inhibits secretion of somatotropin from the hypothalamus and inhibits insulin production by the pancreas.

so·mat·o·tro·pin (-trōʹpin), *n.* a polypeptide growth hormone of humans, secreted by the anterior pituitary gland. Also called **human growth hormone.**

so·mat·o·type (sō matʹə tīpʹ), *n.* bodily structure, proportions, and development; physique.

so·mite (sōʹmīt), *n.* one of the thickened segments of tissue that occur in pairs along the back of the vertebrate embryo. —**soʹmi·tal** (-mi tl), **so·mitʹic** (-mitʹik), *adj.*

som·nam·bu·late (som namʹbyə lātʹ, səm-), *v.i.*, **-lat·ed, -lat·ing.** to walk during sleep; sleepwalk. —**som·namʹbu·lant,** *adj., n.* —**som·namʹbu·laʹtion,** *n.*

som·nam·bu·lism, *n.* SLEEPWALKING. —**som·namʹbu·list,** *n.* —**som·namʹbu·lisʹtic,** *adj.*

som·ni·fa·cient (som'nə fāʹshənt), *n.* a drug or other agent that induces or tends to induce sleep.

son·o·gram (sonʹə gram', sōʹnə-), *n.* the visual image produced by reflected sound waves in a diagnostic ultrasound examination.

sop·o·rif·ic (sop'ə rifʹik, sōʹpə-), *adj.* **1.** causing or tending to cause sleep. —*n.* **2.** something that causes sleep, as a medicine or drug. —**sop'o·rifʹi·cal·ly,** *adv.*

sor·bi·tol (sôrʹbi tôlʹ, -tolʹ), *n.* a sugar alcohol, $C_6H_{14}O_6$, naturally occurring in many fruits or synthesized, used as a sugar substitute and in the manufacture of vitamin C.

soreʹ throatʹ, *n.* **1.** a painful or sensitive condition of the throat due to pharyngitis. **2.** PHARYNGITIS.

Southʹern blotʹ, *n.* a test for the presence of a specific DNA segment in a sample by observing whether single strands of DNA from the sample will bond with labeled strands from a known segment of the DNA in question.

spaceʹ medʹicine, *n.* the branch of medicine dealing

with the effects on humans of flying outside the earth's atmosphere.

spar·te·ine (spär′tē ēn′, -in), *n.* a bitter, poisonous, liquid alkaloid, $C_{15}H_{26}N_2$, obtained from certain species of broom, esp. *Cytisus scoparius,* used in medicine to stimulate the heart and also the uterine muscles in childbirth.

spasm (spaz′əm), *n.* a sudden, abnormal, involuntary muscular contraction, consisting of a continued muscular contraction or of a series of alternating muscular contractions and relaxations.

spas·mod·ic (spaz mod′ik) also **spas·mod′i·cal,** *adj.* pertaining to or of the nature of a spasm; characterized by spasms. —**spas·mod′i·cal·ly,** *adv.*

spas·tic (spas′tik), *adj.* **1.** pertaining to, of the nature of, characterized by, or afflicted with spasm or spastic paralysis. —*n.* **2.** a person exhibiting or afflicted with spasms or spastic paralysis. —**spas′ti·cal·ly,** *adv.* —**spas·tic·i·ty** (spa stis′i tē), *n.*

spas′tic paral′ysis, *n.* a condition in which the muscles affected are marked by continued, or tonic, spasm and increased tendon reflexes.

spe·cif·ic (spi sif′ik), *adj.* **1. a.** (of a disease) produced by a special cause or infection. **b.** (of a remedy) having special effect in the prevention or cure of a certain disease. **2.** (of an antibody or antigen) having a particular effect on only one antibody or affecting it in only one way. —**spe·cif′i·cal·ly,** *adv.*

specif′ic grav′ity, *n.* the ratio of the density of any substance to the density of a standard substance, water being the standard for liquids and solids. —**spe·cif′ic-grav′i·ty,** *adj.*

spec·i·fic·i·ty (spes′ə fis′i tē), *n.* **1.** the quality or state of being specific. **2.** the selective attachment or influence of one substance on another, as of an antibiotic on its target organism.

spec·i·men (spes′ə mən), *n.* a sample of a substance or material for examination or study.

SPECT (spekt), *n.* single photon emission computed tomography: a technique for measuring brain function similar to PET.

spec·u·lum (spek′yə ləm), *n., pl.* **-la** (-lə), **-lums.** a medical instrument for rendering a part accessible to observation, as by enlarging an orifice.

speed (spēd), *n. Slang.* a stimulating drug, esp. methamphetamine or amphetamine.

speed′ball′, *n. Slang.* any combination of a stimulant and a depressant taken together, esp. a mixture of heroin and cocaine or heroin and methamphetamine injected into the bloodstream.

sperm (spûrm), *n., pl.* **sperm, sperms** for 1. **1.** a male reproductive cell; spermatozoon. **2.** semen. —**sper′mous,** *adj.*

sper·mat·ic cord′ (spûr mat′ik), *n.* the cord by which a testis is suspended in the scrotum, containing the vas deferens.

sper'ma·tid (-mə tid), *n.* one of the cells that result from the meiotic divisions of a spermatocyte and that mature into spermatozoa.

sper·mat·o·cyte (spûr mat'ə sīt'), *n.* a male sex cell that gives rise by meiosis to a pair of haploid cells, which become the reproductive cells.

sper·mat·o·gen·e·sis (-jen'ə sis), *n.* the origin and development of spermatozoa.

sper·mat·or·rhe·a (-rē'ə), *n.* abnormally frequent and involuntary nonorgasmic emission of semen.

sper·mat·o·zo·on (spûr mat'ə zō'ən, -on), *n., pl.* **-zo·a** (-zō'ə). the mature male reproductive cell, actively motile in semen and serving to fertilize the ovum. —**sper·mat'o·zo'al, sper·mat'o·zo'an, sper·mat'o·zo'ic,** *adj.*

sperm' bank', *n.* a repository for storing sperm and keeping it viable under scientifically controlled conditions prior to its use in artificial insemination.

sperm' cell', *n.* **1.** SPERMATOZOON. **2.** any male gamete.

sper·mi·cide (spûr'mə sīd'), *n.* a sperm-killing agent, esp. a commercial birth-control preparation, usu. a cream or jelly. —**sper'mi·cid'al,** *adj.* —**sper'mi·cid'al·ly,** *adv.*

sper·mi·o·gen·e·sis (spûr'mē ō jen'ə sis), *n.* the development of a spermatozoon from a spermatid.

SPF, sun protection factor: the effectiveness of suntanning preparations in protecting the skin from ultraviolet radiation.

sphe·noid (sfē'noid), *adj.* Also, **sphe·noi'dal.** of or pertaining to a compound bone at the base of the skull.

sphe·ro·plast (sfēr'ə plast', sfer'-), *n.* a Gram-negative bacterial cell with a cell wall that has been altered or is partly missing, resulting in a spherical shape.

sphinc·ter (sfingk'tər), *n.* a circular band of voluntary or involuntary muscle that encircles and closes an orifice of the body or one of its hollow organs. —**sphinc'ter·al,** *adj.*

sphyg·mic (sfig'mik), *adj.* of or pertaining to the pulse.

sphyg·mo·graph (sfig'mə graf', -gräf'), *n.* an instrument for recording the strength, and uniformity of the arterial pulse. —**sphyg'mo·graph'ic** (-graf'ik), *adj.* —**sphyg·mog'ra·phy** (-mog'rə fē), *n.*

sphyg·mo·ma·nom·e·ter (sfig'mō mə nom'i tər), *n.* an instrument, often attached to an inflatable cuff and used with a stethoscope, for measuring blood pressure in an artery. —**sphyg'mo·man'o·met'ric** (-man'ə me'trik), *adj.* —**sphyg'mo·ma·nom'e·try,** *n.*

sphyg·mus (sfig'məs), *n.* the pulse.

spi·na bif·i·da (spī'nə bif'i də), *n.* a congenital defect in which part of the meninges or spinal cord protrudes through the spinal column, often resulting in neurological impairment.

spi·nal (spīn'l), *adj.* **1.** of, pertaining to, or belonging to a spine or thronlike structure, esp. the backbone. —*n.* **2.** a spinal anesthetic. —**spi'nal·ly,** *adv.*

spi′nal anesthe′sia, *n.* injection of an anesthetic into the lumbar region of the spinal canal to reduce sensitivity to pain in the lower body. Also called **spi′nal block′.**

spi′nal canal′, *n.* the tube formed by the vertebrae in which the spinal cord and its membranes are located.

spi′nal col′umn, *n.* the series of vertebrae forming the axis of the skeleton in vertebrate animals; spine; backbone.

spi′nal cord′, *n.* the cord of nerve tissue extending through the spinal canal of the spinal column.

spi′nal nerve′, *n.* any of a series of paired nerves that originate in the nerve roots of the spinal cord and emerge from the vertebrae on both sides of the spinal column, each branching out to innervate a specific region of the neck, trunk, or limbs.

spine (spīn), *n.* SPINAL COLUMN. —**spined,** *adj.* —**spine′-like′,** *adj.*

spi·ril·lum (spī ril′əm), *n., pl.* **-ril·la** (-ril′ə). any of various spirally twisted bacteria of the genus *Spirillum,* certain species of which are pathogenic.

spir·it (spir′it), *n.* a solution in alcohol of an essential or volatile principle; essence.

spi·ro·chete (spī′rə kēt′), *n.* any of various mobile, very slender, tightly to loosely coiled bacteria of the family Spirochaetaceae, including pathogenic species that are the cause of syphilis, leptospirosis, or relapsing fever.

spi·rom·e·ter (spī rom′i tər), *n.* an instrument for determining lung capacity. —**spi′ro·met′ric** (-rə met′trik), spi′-ro·met′ri·cal,** *adj.* —**spi·rom′e·try,** *n.*

splay′foot′ (splā′fŏŏt′), *n., pl.* **-feet.** FLATFOOT (def. 1).

spleen (splēn), *n.* a highly vascular, glandular, ductless organ, situated in humans at the cardiac end of the stomach, serving chiefly in the formation of mature lymphocytes, in the destruction of worn-out red blood cells, and as a reservoir for blood. —**spleen′ish,** *adj.*

sple·nec·to·my (spli nek′tə mē), *n., pl.* **-mies.** surgical excision or removal of the spleen.

sple·no·meg·a·ly (splē′nō meg′ə lē, splen′ō-) also **sple·no·me·ga·li·a** (-mə gā′lē ə, -gāl′yə), *n.* enlargement of the spleen.

splice (splīs), *v.t.,* **spliced, splic·ing.** to join (segments of DNA or RNA) together.

splint (splint), *n.* a thin piece of wood or other rigid material used to immobilize a fractured or dislocated bone, or to maintain any part of the body in a fixed position.

split′-brain′, *adj.* having, involving, or pertaining to the separation of the cerebral hemispheres by severing the corpus callosum.

spon·dy·li·tis (spon′dl ī′tis), *n.* inflammation of the vertebrae. —**spon′dy·lit′ic** (-it′ik), *adj.*

spon·dy·lo·sis (spon′dl ō′sis), *n.* immobility and fusion of vertebral joints.

sponge (spunj), *n.* **1.** a piece of any of various absorbent materials, as a block of porous cellulose or a surgical gauze pad. **2.** a disposable piece of polyurethane foam impregnated with a spermicide for insertion into the vagina as a contraceptive.

spon·gin (spun′jin), *n.* a fibrous protein that is the main constituent of the skeleton in certain sponges.

sponta′neous abor′tion, *n.* MISCARRIAGE.

spore (spôr, spōr), *n.* the resting or dormant stage of a bacterium or other microorganism. —**spo·ra·ceous** (spə-rā′shəs), *adj.*

spo·ro·cyst (spôr′ə sist′, spōr′-), *n.* **1. 2.** a resting or dormant cell that produces spores. **3.** the first, saclike stage of many trematode worms, giving rise to cercariae by budding.

spo′ro·cyte′ (-sit′), *n.* a cell from which a spore or spores are produced.

spo·ro·gen′e·sis, *n.* **1.** the production of spores. **2.** reproduction by means of spores.

spo·rog·o·ny (spə rog′ə nē), *n.* (in certain sporozoans) the multiple fission of an encysted zygote or oocyte, resulting in the formation of sporozoites.

spo·ro·zo·an (spôr′ə zō′ən, spōr′-), *n.* any parasitic spore-forming protozoan of the class Sporozoa, several species of which, as plasmodia, cause malaria.

spo′ro·zo′ite, *n.* one of the minute, active bodies into which the spore of certain sporozoans divides, each developing into an adult individual.

sports′ med′icine, *n.* a field of medicine concerned with the functioning of the human body during physical activity and with the prevention and treatment of athletic injuries.

spot′ted fe′ver, *n.* **1.** any of several fevers characterized by spots on the skin, as Rocky Mountain spotted fever or typhus fever. **2.** TICK FEVER.

sprain (sprān), *v.t.* **1.** to overstrain or wrench (the ligaments around a joint) so as to injure without fracture or dislocation. —*n.* **2.** a wrenching injury to ligaments around a joint. **3.** the condition of being sprained.

sprue (sprōō), *n.* a chronic tropical disease of intestinal malabsorption characterized by ulceration, diarrhea, and a smooth tongue.

spur (spûr), *n.* an abnormal bony growth or projection.

spu·tum (spyōō′təm), *n.*, *pl.* **-ta** (-tə) matter, as saliva mixed with mucus or pus, expectorated from the lungs and respiratory passages.

squa·lene (skwā′lēn), *n.* an oil, $C_{30}H_{50}$, intermediate in the synthesis of cholesterol, obtained for use in manufacturing pharmaceuticals.

squa·ma (skwā′mə), *n.*, *pl.* **-mae** (-mē) a scale or scale-like part, as of epidermis or bone. —**squa′mous**, *adj.*

SQUID (skwid), *n.* superconducting quantum interference device: a device which senses minute changes in magnetic fields, used to indicate neural activity in the brain.

squint (skwint), *v.i.* **1.** to be affected with strabismus; be cross-eyed. —*v.t.* **2.** to cause to squint.

squint′-eyed′, *adj.* affected with or characterized by strabismus.

ss or **ss.**, (in prescriptions) a half. [Latin, *semis*]

S sleep, *n.* SLOW-WAVE SLEEP.

stage (stāj), *v.t.*, **staged, stag·ing.** to classify the natural progression of (a disease, esp. cancer).

stain (stān), *v.t.* to dye (a microscopic specimen) in order to give distinctness, produce contrast of tissues, etc. —**stain′a·ble**, *adj.*

stanch (stônch, stanch, stänch) also **staunch** (stônch), *v.t.* **1.** to stop the flow of (a liquid, esp. blood). **2.** to stop the flow of blood or other liquid from (a wound, leak, etc.). —*v.i.* **3.** to stop flowing, as blood; be stanched. —**stanch′a·ble**, *adj.* —**stanch′er**, *n.*

Stan′ford-Bi·net′ test′ (stan′fərd) any of several revised versions of the Binet-Simon scale for testing intelligence.

sta·pe·dec·to·my (stā′pi dek′tə mē), *n., pl.* **-mies.** a microsurgical procedure to relieve deafness by replacing the stapes in the middle ear with a prosthetic device. —**sta′pe·dec′to·mize′**, *v.t.*, **-mized, -miz·ing.**

sta·pes (stā′pēz), *n., pl.* **sta·pes, sta·pe·des** (stə pē′dēz). a small, stirrup-shaped bone, the innermost of the chain of three small bones of the middle ear. Also called **stirrup.** —**sta·pe′di·al** (-dē əl), *adj.*

staph (staf), *n.* STAPHYLOCOCCUS.

staph·y·lo·coc·cus (staf′ə lə kok′əs), *n., pl.* **-coc·ci** (-kok′sī). any of several spherical bacteria of the genus *Staphylococcus*, occurring in pairs, tetrads, and irregular clusters, certain species of which, as *S. aureus*, are pathogenic. —**staph′y·lo·coc′cal** (-kok′əl), **staph′y·lo·coc′cic** (-kok′sik), *adj.*

starch′ block′er or **starch/block′**, *n.* a substance ingested in the belief that it inhibits the body's ability to metabolize starch and thereby promotes weight loss: declared illegal in the U.S. by the FDA. —**starch′-block′ing**, *adj.*

sta·sis (stā′sis, stas′is), *n., pl.* **sta·ses** (stā′sēz, stas′ēz). stagnation in the flow of any of the fluids of the body. —**stat′ic** (stat′ik), *adj.*

stat (stat), *adv.* immediately.

stat., (in prescriptions) immediately. [Latin, *statim*]

STD, sexually transmitted disease.

ste·ap·sin (stē ap′sin), *n.* the lipase present in pancreatic juice.

ste·ar·ic (stē ar′ik, stēr′ik), *adj.* **1.** of or pertaining to suet or fat. **2.** of or derived from stearic acid.

stear′ic ac′id, *n.* a colorless, waxlike, sparingly water-soluble fatty acid, $C_{18}H_{36}O_2$, occurring in animal fats and some vegetable oils.

ste·a·rin (stē′ər in, stēr′in) also **ste·a·rine** (*also* stē′ə-rēn′), *n.* any of the three glyceryl esters of stearic acid, esp. $C_3H_5(C_{18}H_{35}O_2)_3$, a soft, white, odorless solid found in many natural fats.

ste·a·to·py·gi·a (stē at′ə pī′jē ə), *n.* extreme accumulation of fat on and about the buttocks. —**ste·at'o·pyg'ic** (-pij'ik), **ste·at·o·py·gous** (-pi'gəs), *adj.*

ste·at·or·rhe·a or **ste·at·or·rhoe·a** (-rē'ə), *n.* the presence of excess fat in the stools.

ste·nosed (sti nōst', -nōzd'), *adj.* characterized by stenosis; abnormally narrowed.

ste·no·sis (sti nō'sis), *n.* a narrowing or stricture of a passage or vessel of the body. —**ste·not'ic** (-not'ik), *adj.*

stent (stent), *n.* a small, expandable tube used for inserting in a blocked vessel or other part.

ster·co·ra·ceous (stûr'kə rā'shəs) also **ster·co·rous** (stûr'kər əs), *adj.* consisting of, resembling, or pertaining to dung or feces.

ster·e·op·sis (ster'ē op'sis, stēr'-), *n.* stereoscopic vision; the ability to see in three dimensions.

ster·e·os·co·py (ster'ē os'kə pē, stēr'-), *n.* three-dimensional vision. —**ster·e·os'co·pist,** *n.*

ster·e·o·tax·ic (ster'ē ə tak'sik, stēr'-), *adj.* of or pertaining to precise measurements in three dimensions of a place in the brain, esp. as an adjunct to surgery or radiation.

ster·e·o·typ·y (ster'ē ə ti'pē, stēr'-), *n.* persistent mechanical repetition of speech or movement, sometimes occurring as a symptom of schizophrenia, autism, or other mental disorder.

ster·ile (ster'il; *esp. Brit.* -īl), *adj.* **1.** free from living germs or microorganisms; aseptic. **2.** incapable of producing offspring; infertile. —**ster'ile·ly,** *adv.* —**ste·ril·i·ty** (stə ril'i tē), *n.*

ster·i·lize (ster'ə līz'), *v.t.* **-lized, -liz·ing. 1.** to cleanse by destroying microorganisms, parasites, etc., usu. by bringing to a high temperature. **2.** to render (a person or animal) infertile by removing or inhibiting the sex organs. —**ster'i·li·za'tion,** *n.*

ster·nal (stûr'nl), *adj.* of or pertaining to the sternum.

ster·num (stûr'nəm), *n., pl.* **-na** (-nə) **-nums.** the bony plate or series of bones to which the ribs are attached anteriorly or ventrally in most vertebrates; breastbone.

ster·nu·ta·tion (stûr'nyə tā'shən), *n.* the act of sneezing.

ster·nu·ta·to·ry (stər nōō'tə tôr'ē, -tōr'ē, -nyōō'-), *adj., n., pl.* **-ries.** —*adj.* **1.** Also, **ster·nu'ta·tive.** causing or tending to cause sneezing. —*n.* **2.** a sternutatory substance.

ste·roid (stēr'oid, ster'-), *n.* any of a large group of fat-soluble organic compounds, as the sterols, bile acids, and sex hormones, most of which have specific physiological action. Compare ANABOLIC STEROID, CORTICOSTEROID. —**ste·roi'dal** (sti roid'l, ste-), *adj.*

ste·roi·do·gen·e·sis (sti roi'də jen'ə sis, ste-), *n.* the formation of steroids, as by the adrenal cortex, testes, and ovaries.

ste·rol (stēr'ôl, -ol, ster'-), *n.* any of a group of solid, mostly unsaturated, polycyclic alcohols, as cholesterol and ergosterol, derived from plants or animals.

ster·tor (stûr′tər), *n.* an abnormal snoring sound accompanying breathing.

steth·o·scope (steth′ə skōp′), *n.* an instrument used in auscultation to detect sounds in the chest or other parts of the body. —**ste·thos·co·py** (ste thos′kə pē, steth′ə skō′-), *n.* —**steth′o·scop′ic** (-skop′ik), *adj.*

stick′y end′, *n.* a single-stranded end of a DNA or RNA molecule, produced in the laboratory for connecting with another molecule by base-pairing.

stil·bes·trol (stil bes′trōl, -trol), *n.* DIETHYLSTILBESTROL.

stim·u·lant (stim′yə lənt), *n.* a drug or other agent that temporarily quickens some vital process or the functional activity of some organ or part: *a heart stimulant.*

stim·u·late′, *v.t.,* **-lat·ed, -lat·ing.** to excite (a nerve, gland, etc.) to its functional activity. —**stim′u·la′tion,** *n.* —**stim′u·la′tor,** *n.*

stim·u·lus (stim′yə ləs), *n., pl.* **-li** (-lī′) something that excites an organism or part to functional activity.

stir·rup (stûr′əp, stir′-, stur′-), *n.* **1.** STAPES. **2.** stirrups, apparatus in which a patient places the feet during a gynecological examination.

sto·ma (stō′mə), *n., pl.* **sto·ma·ta** (stō′mə tə, stom′ə-, stō mä′tə), **sto·mas.** a surgical opening in an organ constructed to permit passage of fluids or waste products to another organ or to the outside of the body. —**sto′mal,** *adj.*

stom·ach (stum′ək), *n.* a saclike enlargement of the vertebrate alimentary canal, forming an organ for storing and partially digesting food.

stom′ach·ache′, *n.* pain in the stomach or abdomen.

sto·mach·ic (stō mak′ik), *adj.* **1.** of or pertaining to the stomach; gastric. **2.** beneficial to the stomach; stimulating gastric digestion; sharpening the appetite. —*n.* **3.** a stomachic agent or drug.

stom′ach pump′, *n.* a suction pump for removing the contents of the stomach, used esp. in cases of poisoning.

sto·ma·ta (stō′mə tə, stom′ə-, stō mä′tə), *n.* a pl. of STOMA.

stom·a·tal (stom′ə tl, stō′mə-), *adj.* **1.** of, pertaining to, or of the nature of a stoma. **2.** having stomata.

sto·mat·ic (stō mat′ik), *adj.* **1.** of or pertaining to the mouth. **2.** STOMATAL.

sto·ma·ti·tis (stō′mə tī′tis, stom′ə-), *n.* inflammation of the mouth. —**sto′ma·tit′ic** (-tit′ik), *adj.*

sto·ma·to·plas·ty (stō mat′ə plas′tē), *n., pl.* **-ties.** plastic surgery of the mouth or the cervix. —**sto·mat′o·plas′tic,** *adj.*

sto·ma·tot·o·my (stō′mə tot′ə mē, stom′ə-), *n., pl.* **-mies.** surgical incision of the cervix to facilitate labor.

sto·mo·de·um (stō′mə dē′əm, stom′ə-), *n., pl.* **-de·a** (-dē′ə). a depression in the ectoderm of the oral region of a young embryo, which develops into the mouth and oral cavity. —**sto′mo·de′al,** *adj.*

stone (stōn), *n.* a calculous concretion in the body, as in the kidney, gallbladder, or urinary bladder.

stool (stōol), *n.* the fecal matter evacuated at each movement of the bowels.

stra·bis·mus (strə biz′məs), *n.* a deviation from normal orientation of one or both eyes so that both cannot be directed at the same object at the same time; squint; crossed eyes. —**stra·bis′mal, stra·bis′mic, stra·bis′mi·cal,** *adj.* —**stra·bis′mal·ly,** *adv.*

strain (strān), *n.* **1.** the body of descendants of a common ancestor, as a family or stock. **2.** any of the different lines of ancestry united in a family or an individual. **3.** a variety, esp. of microorganisms. **4.** hereditary or natural character, tendency, or trait.

stra·mo·ni·um (strə mō′nē əm), *n.* the dried leaves of the jimsonweed, formerly used in medicine as an antispasmodic.

stran·gu·late (strang′gyə lāt′), *v.t.,* **-lat·ed, -lat·ing. 1.** to compress or constrict (a duct, intestine, vessel, etc.) so as to prevent circulation or suppress function. **2.** to strangle. —**stran′gu·la′tion,** *n.*

stran·gu·ry (strang′gyə rē), *n.* painful urination in which the urine is emitted drop by drop.

straw′ber·ry mark′, *n.* a small, reddish, slightly raised birthmark.

stream′ of con′sciousness, *n.* thought regarded as a succession of ideas and images constantly moving forward in time. —**stream′-of-con′sciousness,** *adj.*

strep (strep), *n.* **1.** streptococcus. —*adj.* **2.** streptococcal.

strep′ throat′, *n.* an acute sore throat caused by hemolytic streptococcus.

strep·to·ba·cil·lus (strep′tō bə sil′əs), *n., pl.* **-cil·li** (-sil′-ī). any of various bacilli that form in chains.

strep·to·coc·cus (strep′tə kok′əs), *n., pl.* **-coc·ci** (-kok′sī, -sē). any of several spherical bacteria of the genus *Streptococcus*, occurring in pairs or chains, species of which cause such diseases as tonsillitis, pneumonia, and scarlet fever. —**strep′to·coc′cal** (-kok′əl), **strep′to·coc′cic** (-kok′sik), *adj.*

strep·to·ki·nase (strep′tō ki′nās, -nāz, -kin′ās, -āz), *n.* an enzyme used to dissolve blood clots.

strep·to·my·ces (strep′tə mi′sēz), *n., pl.* **-ces.** any of several aerobic bacteria of the genus *Streptomyces*, certain species of which produce antibiotics.

strep·to·my·cin (strep′tə mi′sin), *n.* an antibiotic, $C_{21}H_{39}N_7O_{12}$, produced by a streptomyces and used chiefly to treat tuberculosis.

stress (stres), *n.* **1.** a specific response by the body to a stimulus, as fear or pain, that disturbs or interferes with the normal physiological equilibrium. **2.** physical, mental, or emotional strain or tension. —*v.t.* **3.** to subject to stress. —**stress′ful,** *adj.* —**stress′ful·ly,** *adv.*

stress′ frac′ture, *n.* a hairline crack in the foot or

lower leg due to repetitive motion, like running: common among athletes.

stres·sor (stres′ər, -ôr), *n.* a stimulus causing stress.

stress′ test′, *n.* a test of cardiovascular health made by recording heart rate, blood pressure, electrocardiogram, and other parameters while a person undergoes physical exertion.

stretch′ mark′, *n.* a silvery streak occurring typically on the abdomen or thighs and caused by stretching of the skin over a short period of time, as during pregnancy or rapid weight gain.

stretch′ recep′tor, *n.* MUSCLE SPINDLE.

stri·a (strī′ə), *n., pl.* **stri·ae** (strī′ē). a slight or narrow furrow, ridge, stripe, or streak, esp. one of a number in parallel arrangement: *striae of muscle fiber.*

stri·at·ed (strī′ā tid), *adj.* marked with striae; furrowed; streaked.

stri·a·tion (strī ā′shən), *n.* any of the alternating light and dark crossbands that are visible in certain muscle fibers.

stric·ture (strik′chər), *n.* an abnormal contraction of any passage or duct of the body. —**stric′tured,** *adj.*

stri·dor (strī′dər), *n.* a harsh respiratory sound due to obstruction of the breathing passages. —**strid·u·lous** (strij′ə-ləs), **strid′u·lant,** *adj.*

stro·bi·la (strō bī′lə), *n., pl.* **-lae** (-lē). the body of a tapeworm composed of the head and neck region.

stroke (strōk), *n.* a blockage or hemorrhage of a blood vessel leading to the brain, causing an inadequate oxygen supply and often long-term impairment of sensation, movement, or functioning of part of the body; apoplexy.

stron·gyle or **stron·gyl** (stron′jil), *n.* any nematode of the family Strongylidae, parasitic as an adult in the intestine of mammals, esp. horses. —**stron′gy·late** (-jə lāt′), *adj.*

stroph·u·lus (strof′yə ləs), *n.* a papular eruption of the skin, esp. in infants, occurring in several forms and usu. harmless.

struc′tural gene′, *n.* CISTRON.

struc·tur·al·ism (struk′chər ə liz′əm), *n.* a school of psychology that analyzes conscious mental activity by studying the hierarchical association of structures, or complex ideas, with simpler ideas, perceptions, and sensations. —**struc′tur·al·ist,** *n., adj.* —**struc′tur·al·is′tic,** *adj.*

struc′tural psychol′ogy, *n.* STRUCTURALISM.

stru·ma (strōō′mə), *n., pl.,* **-mae** (-mē). GOITER. —**stru′mose, stru′mous,** *adj.*

strych·nine (strik′nin, -nēn, -nin), *n.* a colorless, crystalline poison, $C_{21}H_{22}N_2O_2$, obtained chiefly by extraction from the seeds of nux vomica, formerly used as a central nervous system stimulant. —**strych′nic,** *adj.*

stu·pe·fa·cient (stōō′pə fā′shənt, styōō′-), *n.* a drug or agent that produces stupor.

stu·por (stōō′pər, styōō′-), *n.* suspension or great diminution of sensibility, as in disease or as caused by narcotics, intoxicants, etc.

St. Vi·tus's dance (vī′təs siz) also **St. Vi·tus dance** (vī′təs), **St. Vi·tus' dance** (vī′təs, -tə siz), *n.* CHOREA (def. 2).

sty or **stye** (stī), *n., pl.* **sties** or **styes.** a circumscribed abscess caused by bacterial infection of the glands on the edge of the eyelid; hordeolum.

sty·let (stī′lit), *n.* **1.** a surgical probe. **2.** a wire run through the length of a catheter, cannula, or needle to make it rigid or to clear it.

styp·sis (stip′sis), *n.* the action or application of a styptic.

styp·tic (stip′tik), *adj.* Also, **styp′ti·cal. 1.** serving to contract organic tissue; astringent; binding. **2.** serving to check hemorrhage or bleeding, as a drug; hemostatic. **—n. 3.** a styptic agent or substance. **—styp·tic′i·ty** (-tis′i tē), *n.*

styp′tic pen′cil, *n.* a pencil-shaped stick of alum or a similar styptic agent, used to stanch the bleeding of minor cuts.

sub·a·cute (sub′ə kyōōt′), *adj.* somewhat or moderately acute: *a subacute fever.* **—sub′a·cute′ly,** *adv.*

sub·acute scle·ros·ing pan′en·ceph·a·li′tis (sklī rō′sing pan′en sef′ə li′tis, pan′-), *n.* an infection of the central nervous system caused by the measles virus, occurring in children and adolescents several years after a measles attack and characterized by progressive personality changes, seizures, and muscular incoordination.

sub·cla·vi·an (sub klā′vē ən), *adj.* situated behind or under the clavicle.

subcla′vian ar′tery, *n.* either of a pair of large arteries that supply blood to the neck and arms.

subcla′vian vein′, *n.* either of a pair of large veins that return blood from the arms.

sub·clin·i·cal, *adj.* pertaining to an early stage of a disease; having no noticeable clinical symptoms.

sub·con′scious, *adj.* **1.** existing or operating in the mind beneath or beyond consciousness. **—n. 2.** the totality of mental processes of which the individual is not aware. **—sub·con′scious·ly,** *adv.* **—sub·con′scious·ness,** *n.*

sub·cul·ture (n. sub′kul′chər; v. sub kul′chər), *n., v.,* **-tured, -tur·ing. —n. 1.** a bacterial culture derived from a strain that has been recultivated on a different medium. **—v.t. 2.** to cultivate (a bacterial strain) again on a different medium.

sub·cu·ta·ne·ous (sub′kyōō tā′nē əs), *adj.* situated or introduced under the skin; subdermal. **—sub′cu·ta·ne·ous·ly,** *adv.*

sub·der·mal (sub dûr′məl), *adj.* SUBCUTANEOUS.

sub·le′thal, *adj.* almost lethal or fatal: *a sublethal dose of poison.*

sub·li·mate (sub′lə māt′), *v.t.,* **-mat·ed, -mat·ing.** to divert the energy of (a sexual or other biological impulse) from its immediate goal to one of a more acceptable social, moral, or aesthetic nature or use. **—sub′li·ma′tion,** *n.* **—sub′li·ma′tion·al,** *adj.*

sub·lim·i·nal (sub lim′ə nl), *adj.* existing or operating below the threshold of consciousness; insufficiently intense to produce a discrete sensation but influencing or designed to influence mental processes or behavior. —**sub·lim′i·nal·ly,** *adv.*

sub·lin·gual (sub ling′gwəl), *adj.* situated under the tongue, or on the underside of the tongue. —**sub·lin′·gual·ly,** *adv.*

sub·lux·a·tion (sub′luk sā′shən), *n.* **1.** partial dislocation, as of a joint. **2.** (in chiropractic) misalignment of one or more vertebrae.

sub′stance abuse′, *n.* long-term use of an addictive or behavior-altering drug when not needed for medical treatment.

substance P, *n.* a small peptide released upon stimulation in the nervous system and involved in regulation of the pain threshold.

sub·strate (sub′strāt), *n.* **1.** the surface or medium on which an organism lives or grows. **2.** the substance acted upon by an enzyme.

sub·vi·ral (sub vī′rəl), *adj.* **1.** of or pertaining to any macromolecule smaller in size or possessing a lesser degree of organization than a comparable intact viral particle. **2.** of or pertaining to a component or precursor particle of an intact infective virus.

suc·ci·nyl·cho·line chlo·ride (suk′sə nil kō′lēn, -kol′ēn, -sə nl-), *n.* a crystalline compound, $C_{14}H_{30}Cl_2N_2O_4$, used as a skeletal muscle relaxant in surgical procedures.

su·crase (soo′krās, -krāz), *n.* INVERTASE.

su·crose (soo′krōs), *n.* SUGAR (def. 1).

su·da·to·ry (soo′də tôr′ē, -tōr′ē), *adj.* pertaining to or causing sweating.

sud′den in′fant death′ syn′drome, *n.* death from cessation of breathing in a seemingly healthy infant, almost always during sleep. *Abbr.:* SIDS Also called **crib death.**

su·dor·if·er·ous (soo′də rif′ər əs), *adj.* secreting sweat.

su·dor·if·ic, *adj.* causing sweat.

sug·ar (shŏŏg′ər), *n.* **1.** a sweet, crystalline substance, $C_{12}H_{22}O_{11}$, obtained from the juice or sap of many plants, esp. commercially from sugarcane and the sugar beet; sucrose. **2.** any other plant or animal substance of the same class of carbohydrates, as fructose or glucose.

sul·cus (sul′kəs), *n., pl.* **-ci** (-sī). a groove or fissure, esp. a fissure between two convolutions of the brain.

sul·fa (sul′fə), *adj.* **1.** related chemically to sulfanilamide. **2.** pertaining to, consisting of, or involving a sulfa drug or drugs.

sul′fa drug′, *n.* any of a group of drugs closely related in chemical structure to sulfanilamide, having a bacteriostatic effect: used in the treatment of various wounds, burns, and infections. Also called **sulfonamide.**

sul′fa·meth·ox′a·zole (-meth ok′sə zōl′), *n.* an antimicrobial substance, $C_{10}H_{11}N_3O_3S$, used to treat urinary-tract and skin infections.

sul′fa·nil′a·mide′ (-nil′ə mid′, -mid), *n.* a white, crystalline amide of sulfanilic acid, $C_6H_8N_2O_2S$, formerly used in the treatment of bacterial infections: replaced by its derivatives and by antibiotics.

sul·fite (sul′fīt), *n.* any sulfite-containing compound, esp. one that is used in foods or drug products as a preservative. **—sul·fit′ic** (-fit′ik), *adj.*

sul·fon′a·mide (sul fon′ə mid′, -mid, sul′fə nam′id, -id), *n.* SULFA DRUG.

sul·fur (sul′fər), *n.* Also, *esp. Brit.,* **sulphur.** a nonmetallic element, ordinarily a flammable yellow solid, of widespread occurrence in combined form, as in sulfide and sulfate compounds and cellular protein. Symbol: S; *at. wt.:* 32.064; *at. no.:* 16; *sp. gr.:* 2.07 at 20° C.

sul′fur bacte′ria, *n.pl.* several species of bacteria, esp. of the genera *Beggiatoa* and *Thiobacillus*, that have the ability to utilize sulfur or inorganic sulfur compounds as an energy source.

sum·ma·tion (sə mā′shən), *n.* the arousal of nerve impulses by a rapid succession of sensory stimuli. **—sum·ma′tion·al,** *adj.*

sun′block′ or **sun′ block′,** *n.* a substance that provides a high degree of protection against sunburn, often preventing most tanning or sunburn.

sun′burn′, *n., v.,* **-burned** or **-burnt, -burn·ing. —n. 1.** inflammation of the skin caused by overexposure to the sun or a sunlamp. **—v.i., v.t. 2.** to become or cause to become sunburned.

sun·down (sun′doun′), *v.i.* to experience nighttime confusion, esp. as a result of strange surroundings, drug effects, or decreased sensory input.

sun′lamp′, *n.* a lamp that generates ultraviolet rays, used therapeutically or for suntanning.

sun′ protec′tion fac′tor, *n.* See SPF.

sun′screen′ or **sun′ screen′,** *n.* a substance that protects the skin from excessive exposure to the ultraviolet radiation of the sun.

sun′stroke′, *n.* a sudden and sometimes fatal condition caused by overexposure to the sun's rays, marked by prostration with or without fever, convulsion, and coma; insolation. **—sun′struck′,** *adj.*

su·per·coil (sōō′pər koil′), *n.* a twist formed by intertwining strands of DNA or by protein chains. **—su′per·coiled′,** *adj.*

su·per·e·go (-ē′gō, -eg′ō), *n., pl.* **-gos.** *Psychoanal.* the part of the psyche representing the conscience, formed in early life by internalization of the standards of parents and other models of behavior. Compare EGO, ID.

su·per·fe·cun·da·tion (-fē′kən dā′shən, -fek′ən-), *n.* the fertilization of two or more ova discharged at the same ovulation.

su·per·fe·ta·tion (-fē tā′shən), *n.* the fertilization of an ovum in a female mammal already pregnant. —**su′per·fe′tate,** *adj.*

su′per·gene′, *n.* a portion of a chromosome consisting of linked genes that act as a single unit of inheritance.

su′per·he·lix (-hē′liks), *n., pl.* **-hel·i·ces** (-hel′ə sēz′), **-he·lix·es.** SUPERCOIL. —**su′per·hel′i·cal** (-hel′i kəl, -hē′li-), *adj.*

su′per·in·fec′tion, *n.* infection by a parasitic microorganism during treatment for another infection.

superior′ity com′plex, *n.* an exaggerated feeling of one's own importance.

su′per·ov′u·late′ (-ov′yə lāt′, -ō′vyə-), *v.i.,* **-lat·ed, -lat·ing.** (of humans, domestic animals, etc.) to produce more than the normal number of ova at one time. —**su′per·ov′·u·la′tion,** *n.*

su′per·scrip′tion (-skrip′shən), *n.* (in prescriptions) the sign ℞, meaning "take."

support′ group′, *n.* a group of people who meet regularly to support or sustain each other by discussing problems affecting them in common, as alcoholism or bereavement.

sup·pos·i·to·ry (sə poz′i tôr′ē, -tōr′ē), *n., pl.* **-ries.** a solid mass of medicinal substance that melts upon insertion into the rectum or vagina.

sup·press (sə pres′), *v.t.* to inhibit (an impulse or action) consciously. —**sup·pres′sive,** *adj.* —**sup·pres′sive·ly,** *adv.* —**sup·pres′sor, sup·press′er,** *n.*

sup·pres′sant, *n.* a substance that suppresses an undesirable action or condition: *a cough suppressant.*

sup·pres′sion, *n. Psychoanal.* **1.** conscious or unconscious inhibition of a painful memory or idea. **2.** conscious inhibition of an impulse.

suppressor T cell, *n.* a T cell capable of inhibiting the activity of B cells and other T cells. Also called **T suppressor cell.**

sup·pu·rate (sup′yə rāt′), *v.i.,* **-rat·ed, -rat·ing.** to produce or discharge pus. —**sup′pu·ra′tion,** *n.* —**sup′pu·ra′tive,** *n., adj.*

su·pra·lim·i·nal (sōō′prə lim′ə nl), *adj.* (of a stimulus) above the threshold of perception. —**su′pra·lim′i·nal·ly,** *adv.*

su·pra·mo·lec′u·lar (-mə lek′yə lər), *adj.* **1.** more complex in organization than a molecule. **2.** composed of an aggregate of molecules.

su′pra·or′bit·al (-ôr′bi tl), *adj.* situated above the eye socket.

su·pra·re·nal (-rēn′l), *adj.* **1.** situated above or on the kidney. —*n.* **2.** a suprarenal part, esp. the adrenal gland.

suprare′nal gland′, *n.* ADRENAL GLAND.

su′pra·vi′tal (-vit′l), *adj.* pertaining to or involving a staining method for a preparation of living cells.

surg., **1.** surgeon. **2.** surgery. **3.** surgical.

sur·geon (sûr′jən), *n.* a physician who specializes in surgery.

sur′geon gen′eral, *n., pl.,* **surgeons general. 1.** the chief of medical services in one of the armed forces. **2.** (*caps.*) the head of the U.S. Bureau of Public Health or, in some states, of a state health agency.

sur′geon's knot′, *n.* a knot resembling a reef knot, used by surgeons for tying ligatures and the like.

sur·ger·y (sûr′jə rē), *n., pl.* **-ger·ies** for 3–5. **1.** the art, practice, or work of treating diseases, injuries, or deformities by manual or operative procedures. **2.** the branch of medicine concerned with such treatment. **3.** treatment, as an operation, performed by a surgeon. **4.** a room or place for surgical operations. **5.** *Brit.* a doctor's office.

sur·gi·cal (sûr′ji kəl), *adj.* **1.** pertaining to or involving surgery or surgeons. **2.** used in surgery. —**sur′gi·cal·ly,** *adv.*

sur·gi·cen·ter (sûr′jə sen′tər), *n.* a surgical facility, not based in a hospital, where minor surgery is performed on an outpatient basis.

sur′rogate moth′er, *n.* **1.** a person who acts in the place of another person's biological mother. **2. a.** a woman who helps a couple to have a child by carrying to term an embryo conceived by the couple and transferred to her uterus; gestational carrier. **b.** a woman who helps a couple to have a child by being inseminated with the man's sperm and either donating the embryo for transfer to the woman's uterus or carrying it to term.

surviv′al curve′, *n.* a line or curve plotted on a graph indicating survival rates of a specific population, as breast-cancer patients, over a period of time.

suspend′ed anima′tion, *n.* a state of temporary cessation of the vital functions.

sus·pen·sor (sə spen′sər), *n.* SUSPENSORY.

sus·pen·so·ry (sə spen′sə rē), *n., pl.* **-ries,** *adj.* —*n.* **1.** a supporting bandage, muscle, ligament, etc. —*adj.* **2.** serving as a suspensory.

suspen′sory lig′ament, *n.* any ligament that suspends an organ of the body, esp. the transparent ligament supporting the lens of the eye.

sustained′-release′, *adj.* SLOW-RELEASE.

su·ture (sōō′chər), *n., v.,* **-tured, -tur·ing.** —*n.* **1.** a. a joining of the edges of a wound or the like by stitching or some similar process. **b.** a particular method of doing this. **c.** one of the stitches or fastenings employed. —*v.t.* **2.** to unite by or as is by a suture. —**su′tur·al,** *adj.*

SV 40, simian virus 40: a virus of the Papovaviridae family, orig. isolated from monkeys and used in research and genetic engineering.

swab or **swob** (swob), *n.* a bit of cotton, sponge, or the like, often fixed to a stick, for applying medicaments, cleansing the mouth, etc.

Swed′ish massage′, *n.* a massage employing techniques systematized in Sweden in the 19th century.

swell·ing (swel′ing), *n.* an abnormal enlargement or protuberance, as that resulting from edema.

swim·mer's ear′, *n.* an ear infection contracted by swimming in unclean water.

swim·mer's itch′, *n.* intense itching caused by penetration of the skin by cercariae.

swob (swob), *n.* SWAB.

sy·co·sis (si kō′sis), *n.* an inflammatory disease of the hair follicles, characterized by a pustular eruption.

syco·sis bar′bae (bär′bē, -bī), *n.* BARBER'S ITCH.

sym·pa·thec·to·my (sim′pə thek′tə mē), *n., pl.* -mies. surgery that interrupts a nerve pathway of the sympathetic or involuntary nervous system.

sym·pa·thet·ic (sim′pə thet′ik), *adj.* pertaining to that part of the autonomic nervous system that originates in the thoracic and lumbar region of the spinal cord and that regulates involuntary reactions to stress, stimulating the heartbeat, breathing rate, sweating, and other physiological processes. —**sym′pa·thet′i·cal·ly**, *adv.*

sym′pa·tho·lyt′ic (-thō lit′ik), *adj.* opposing the effects of stimulation of the sympathetic nervous system.

sym′pa·tho·mi·met′ic (-thō mi met′ik, -mi-), *adj.* mimicking stimulation of the sympathetic nervous system.

sym·pa·thy (sim′pə thē), *n., pl.* -thies. *Physiol.* the relation between parts or organs whereby a condition or disorder of one part induces some effect in another.

symp·tom (simp′təm), *n.* a phenomenon that arises from and accompanies a particular disease or disorder and serves as an indication of it.

symp·to·mat·ic (simp′tə mat′ik) also **symp′to·mat′i·cal**, *adj.* **1.** pertaining to a symptom or symptoms. **2.** of the nature of or constituting a symptom; indicative (often fol. by *of*): *a condition symptomatic of cholera.* **3.** according to symptoms: *a symptomatic classification of disease.* —**symp′to·mat′i·cal·ly**, *adv.*

symp·tom·a·tol·o·gy (simp′tə mə tol′ə jē), *n.* **1.** the branch of medical science dealing with symptoms. **2.** the collective symptoms of a patient or disease.

syn·apse (sin′aps, si naps′), *n., v.,* -apsed, -aps·ing. —*n.* **1. a.** a region where nerve impulses are transmitted across a small gap from an axon terminal to an adjacent structure, as another axon or the end plate of a muscle. **b.** Also called **synap′tic gap′**. the gap itself. —*v.i.* **2.** to form a synapse or a synapsis.

syn·ap·sis (si nap′sis), *n., pl.* -ses (-sēz). **1.** the pairing of homologous chromosomes, one from each parent, during early meiosis. **2.** SYNAPSE. —**syn·ap′tic** (-tik), *adj.* —**syn·ap′ti·cal·ly**, *adv.*

syn·ar·thro·sis (sin′är thrō′sis), *n., pl.* -ses (-sēz). *Anat.* an immovable joint or articulation.

syn·chro·nic·i·ty (sing′krə nis′i tē), *n.* synchronism of events that appear to be connected but have no demonstrable causal relationship.

syn·co·pe (sing′kə pē′, sin′-), *n.* brief loss of consciousness associated with an inadequate flow of oxygenated blood to the brain. —**syn·cop·ic** (sin kop′ik), **syn′co·pal,** *adj.*

syn·cy·tium (sin sish′əm, -ē əm), *n., pl.* **-cy·tia** (-sish′ə, -ē ə). a multinucleate mass of cytoplasm that is not separated into cells. —**syn·cy′tial** (-sish′əl), *adj.*

syn·des·mo·sis (sin′dez mō′sis, -des-), *n., pl.* **-ses** (-sēz). a joining of bones by ligaments or other fibrous tissue. —**syn′des·mot′ic** (-mot′ik), *adj.*

syn·drome (sin′drōm, -drəm), *n.* a group of symptoms that together are characteristic of a specific disorder, disease, or the like. —**syn·drom′ic** (-drom′ik), *adj.*

syn·ech·i·a (si nek′ē ə, -nē′kē ə, sin′i ki′ə), *n., pl.* **syn·ech·i·ae** (si nek′ē ē′, -nē′kē ē′, sin′i ki′ē). any adhesion of parts of the eye, as of the iris to the cornea.

syn·er·gism (sin′ər jiz′əm, si nûr′jiz-), *n.* the joint action of agents, as drugs, that when taken together increase each other's effectiveness (contrasted with *antagonism*). —**syn′er·gis′tic,** *adj.*

syn·er·gist (sin′ər jist), *n.* a drug, organ, etc., that combines or co-operates with another or others to enhance an effect.

syn·er·gy (sin′ər jē), *n., pl.* **-gies.** combined action or functioning; synergism. —**syn·er·gic** (si nûr′jik), *adj.*

syn·es·the·sia or **syn·aes·the·sia** (sin′əs thē′zhə, -zhē ə), *n.* a sensation produced in one modality when a stimulus is applied to another modality, as when the hearing of a certain sound induces the visualization of a certain color. —**syn′es·thete′** (-thēt′), *n.* —**syn′es·thet′ic** (-thet′ik), *adj.*

syn·kar·y·on (sin kar′ē on′, -ən), *n., pl.* **-kar·y·a** (-kar′ē ə). a nucleus formed by the fusion of two preexisting nuclei.

syn·o·vi·a (si nō′vē ə), *n.* a clear, viscous lubricating fluid secreted by membranes that surround the body's joints. —**syn·o′vi·al,** *adj.* —**syn·o′vi·al·ly,** *adv.*

syn·o·vi·tis (sin′ə vī′tis), *n.* inflammation of a synovial membrane. —**syn′o·vit′ic** (-vit′ik), *adj.*

syn·the·tase (sin′thə tās′, -tāz′), *n.* **1.** LIGASE. **2.** Also called **tRNA synthetase.** a ligase that assists in translating the genetic code into protein by linking a transfer RNA with a specific amino acid.

syph·i·lis (sif′ə lis), *n.* a chronic infectious disease caused by a spirochete, *Treponema pallidum,* usu. venereal in origin but often congenital, affecting almost any body organ, esp. the genitals, skin, brain, and nervous tissue.

syph′i·lit′ic, *adj.* **1.** pertaining to, noting, or affected with syphilis. —*n.* **2.** a person affected with syphilis. —**syph′i·lit′i·cal·ly,** *adv.*

sy·ringe (sə rinj′, sir′inj), *n., v.,* **-ringed, -ring·ing.** —*n.* **1.** a small tube with a narrow outlet and fitted with a piston or rubber bulb for drawing in or ejecting fluid. —*v.t.* **2.** to cleanse, wash, inject, etc., by means of a syringe.

sy·rin·go·my·e·li·a (sə ring′gō mi ē′lē ə), *n.* a disease of the spinal cord in which the nerve tissue is replaced by a fluid-filled cavity. —**sy·rin′go·my·el′ic** (-el′ik), *adj.*

sys·tal·tic (si stôl′tik, -stal′-), *adj.* rhythmically contracting, as the heart.

sys·tem·ic (si stem′ik), *adj.* pertaining to, affecting, or circulating through the entire body: *systemic disease; systemic pesticide.* —**sys·tem′i·cal·ly,** *adv.*

system′ic lu′pus er·y·the·ma·to′sus (er′ə thē′mə-tō′səs, -them′ə-), *n.* an autoimmune inflammatory disease of the connective tissues, chiefly characterized by skin eruptions, joint pain, recurrent pleurisy, and kidney disease.

sys·to·le (sis′tə lē′, -lē), *n.* the normal rhythmical contraction of the heart, during which the blood in the chambers is forced onward. Compare DIASTOLE. —**sys·tol·ic** (si-stol′ik), *adj.*

T

T, *Symbol.* **1.** threonine. **2.** thymine.

TA, transactional analysis.

tab (tab), *n. Informal.* a tablet, as of a drug.

tab., (in prescriptions) tablet. [Latin, *tabella*]

ta·bes (tā′bēz), *n.* **1.** a gradually progressive emaciation. **2.** TABES DORSALIS. —**ta·bet·ic** (tə bet′ik), *adj., n.* —**tab·id** (tab′id), *adj.*

ta′bes dor·sal′is (dôr sal′is, -sā′lis), *n.* progressive degeneration of the spinal cord and nerve roots, esp. as a consequence of syphilis. Also called **locomotor ataxia.**

tab·let (tab′lit), *n.* a small, flattish cake or piece of some solid or solidified substance, as a drug.

ta·chis·to·scope (tə kis′tə skōp′), *n.* an apparatus that exposes visual stimuli, as words, very briefly, used to test perception or to increase reading speed. —**ta·chis′to·scop′ic** (-skop′ik), *adj.*

tach·y·car·di·a (tak′i kär′dē ə), *n.* excessively rapid heartbeat.

tac′tile cor′puscle, *n.* an oval sense organ made of flattened cells and encapsulated nerve endings, occurring in hairless skin, as the tips of the fingers and toes, and functioning as a touch receptor.

tae·ni·a·sis or **te·ni·a·sis** (tē nī′ə sis), *n.* infestation with tapeworms.

tail·bone (tāl′bōn′), *n.* COCCYX.

tal·i·ped (tal′ə ped′), *adj.* (of a foot) twisted or distorted out of shape or position.

tal·i·pes (tal′ə pēz′), *n.* CLUBFOOT.

tam·pon (tam′pon), *n.* **1.** a plug of cotton or the like for insertion into a wound, body cavity, etc., chiefly for absorbing blood or stopping hemorrhages. —*v.t.* **2.** to fill or plug with a tampon.

tan·ta·lum (tan′tl əm), *n.* a hard, gray, rare metallic element that resists corrosion by most acids: used for chemical, dental, and surgical instruments. *Symbol:* Ta; *at. wt.:* 180.948; *at. no.:* 73; *sp. gr.:* 16.6.

tap (tap), *n.* the surgical withdrawal of fluid: *spinal tap.*

tape′worm′, *n.* any of various flat, ribbony worms of the class Cestoda, parasitic in the digestive system of humans and other vertebrates.

ta·pote·ment (tə pōt′mənt), *n.* the use of various light, quick, chopping, slapping, or beating strokes on the body during massage.

tar·dive (tär′div), *adj.* appearing or tending to appear late, as in human development or in the treatment of a disease.

tar′dive dyskine′sia, *n.* nerve damage resulting in involuntary rolling of the tongue or twitching of facial or other small muscles, usu. associated with long-term use of antipsychotic drugs.

tar·sal (tär′səl), *adj.* **1.** of or pertaining to the tarsus of the foot. **2.** pertaining to the tarsi of the eyelids. —*n.* **3.** a tarsal bone, joint, or the like.

tar·sus (tär′səs), *n., pl.* **-si** (-sī, -sē). **1.** the bones between the tibia and metatarsus of the foot, forming the ankle joint. **2.** the small plate of connective tissue along the border of an eyelid.

tar′tar emet′ic (tär′tər), *n.* a poisonous powder, $C_4H_4KO_7Sb$, used in medicine as an expectorant, emetic, etc.

TAT, Thematic Apperception Test.

tax·is (tak′sis), *n., pl.* **tax·es** (tak′sēz). the repositioning of a displaced body part by manipulation without cutting. —**tac·tic** (tak′tik), *adj.*

tax′ol (tak′sôl, -sōl), *n.* a chemical substance derived from the bark, needles, and roots of a yew tree: used experimentally as a drug in the treatment of ovarian, breast, and lung cancer.

Tay′-Sachs′ disease′ (tā′saks′), *n.* a degenerative brain disorder caused by lack of or deficiency in an essential enzyme, usu. resulting in mental and physical deterioration and death in early childhood.

TB or **tb,** **1.** tubercle bacillus. **2.** tuberculosis.

TCDD, dioxin.

T cell, *n.* any of several closely related lymphocytes, developed in the thymus, which circulate in the blood and lymph and regulate the immune system's response to infected or malignant cells. Also called **T lymphocyte.**

teach′ing hos′pital, *n.* a hospital associated with a medical college and offering practical experience to medical students, interns, and residents.

tel·an·gi·ec·ta·sis (tel an′jē ek′tə sis), *n., pl.* **-ses** (-sēz′). chronic dilatation of the capillaries and other small blood vessels. —**tel·an′gi·ec·tat′ic** (-tat′ik), *adj.*

tel·en·ceph·a·lon (tel′en sef′ə lon′, -lən), *n., pl.* **-lons, -la** (-lə). the anterior section of the forebrain comprising the cerebrum and olfactory lobes. —**tel′en·ce·phal′ic** (-sə fal′ik), *adj.*

tel·e·ther·a·py (tel′ə ther′ə pē), *n.* **1.** treatment in which the source of therapy is some distance from the body, as certain radiation therapies. **2.** psychological counseling by telephone.

tel·o·cen·tric (tel′ə sen′trik, tē′lə-), *adj.* (of a chromosome) having the centromere positioned at one end and thereby having the shape of a rod.

tel·o·lec·i·thal (tel′ō les′ə thəl, tē′lō-), *adj.* having an accumulation of yolk near the vegetal pole.

tel·o·mere (tel′ə mēr′, tē′lə-), *n.* the segment of DNA that occurs at the ends of chromosomes.

tel·o·phase (tel′ə fāz′, tē′lə-), *n.* the final stage of meiosis or mitosis in cell division, during which the two sets of chromosomes reach opposite poles and nuclei form around them as the cell divides in midsection. —**tel′o·pha′sic,** *adj.*

tem·per·ate (tem′pər it, tem′prit), *adj.* (of a virus) existing in infected host cells but rarely causing lysis. —**tem′per·ate·ly,** *adv.* —**tem′per·ate·ness,** *n.*

tem·per·a·ture (tem′pər ə chər, -chŏŏr′, -prə-, -pər-chər, -chŏŏr′), *n.* **1.** the degree of heat in a living body, normally about 98.6°F (37°C) in humans. **2.** a level of such heat above normal; fever: *running a temperature.*

tem·plate or **tem·plet** (tem′plit), *n.* a strand of DNA that serves as pattern for the formation of a complementary strand.

tem·po·ral (tem′pər əl, tem′prəl), *adj.* **1.** of, pertaining to, or situated near the temple or a temporal bone. —*n.* **2.** any of several parts in the temporal region, esp. the temporal bone.

tem′poral bone′, *n.* either of a pair of compound bones forming the sides of the primate skull.

tem′poral lobe′, *n.* the lateral lobe of each cerebral hemisphere, in front of the occipital lobe.

tem·po·ro·man·dib·u·lar (tem′pə rō man dib′yə lər), *adj.* of, pertaining to, or situated near the hinge joint formed by the lower jaw and the temporal bone.

tem′poromandib′ular joint′ syn′drome, *n.* a group of symptoms stemming from tension in or faulty articulation of the temporomandibular joint, including pain in the head or neck region, dizziness, and tinnitus. *Abbr.:* TMJ

te·nac·u·lum (tə nak′yə ləm), *n., pl.* **-la** (-lə). a small, sharp-pointed hook set in a handle, used for seizing and picking up parts in surgical operations and dissections.

ten·di·ni·tis or **ten·do·ni·tis** (ten′də nī′tis), *n.* inflammation of a tendon.

te·nes·mus (tə nez′məs, -nes′-), *n.* a straining to urinate or defecate, without the ability to do so.

te·ni·a·sis (tē nī′ə sis), *n.* TAENIASIS.

ten′nis el′bow, *n.* inflammation and pain at the elbow caused by strong, repetitive movements of the forearm and wrist, as while playing tennis.

te·nor·rha·phy (tə nôr′ə fē, -nor′-), *n., pl.* **-phies.** suture of a tendon.

ten·o·syn·o·vi·tis (ten′ō sin′ə vī′tis), *n.* inflammation of a tendon sheath, as from trauma, repeated strain, or systemic disease.

te·not·o·my (tə not′ə mē), *n., pl.* **-mies.** the surgical cutting of a tendon.

TENS (tenz), *n.* a self-operated portable device used to treat chronic pain by sending electrical impulses through electrodes placed over the painful area. [t(*ranscutaneous*) e(*lectrical*) n(*erve*) s(*timulator*)]

tent (tent), *n.* **1.** a surgical probe. **2.** a roll or pledget, usu. of soft absorbent material, as lint or gauze, for dilating an orifice, keeping a wound open, etc. —*v.t.* **3.** to keep (a wound) open with a tent.

te·rat·o·gen (tə rat′ə jən, -jen′), *n.* a drug or other substance capable of interfering with the development of a fetus, causing birth defects. —**te·rat′o·gen′ic,** *adj.*

te·rat·o·gen'e·sis also **ter·a·tog·e·ny** (ter′ə toj′ə nē), **te·rat·o·ge·nic·i·ty** (tə rat′ō jə nis′i tē), *n.* the production or induction of malformations or monstrosities, esp. in an embryo or fetus. —**te·rat′o·ge·net′ic,** *adj.*

ter·a·to·ma (ter′ə tō′mə), *n., pl.,* **-mas, -ma·ta** (-mə tə). a tumor made up of different types of tissue.

ter·mi·nal (tûr′mə nl), *adj.* occurring at or causing the end of life; fatal: *terminal cancer.* —**ter′mi·nal·ly,** *adv.*

ter·tian (tûr′shən), *adj.* (of a malarial fever, etc.) characterized by paroxysms that recur every other day.

test′cross′, *n.* a genetic test for heterozygosity in which an organism of dominant phenotype, but unknown genotype, is crossed with an organism recessive for all markers in question. —**test′-cross′,** *v.t.*

tes·ti·cle (tes′ti kəl), *n.* a testis, esp. of a human being.

tes·tic·u·lar (te stik′yə lər), *adj.* of or pertaining to the testes.

tes·tis (tes′tis), *n., pl.* **-tes** (-tēz). the male gonad or reproductive gland, either of two oval glands located in the scrotum.

tes·tos·ter·one (tes tos′tə rōn′), *n.* the sex hormone, $C_{19}H_{28}O_2$, secreted by the testes, that stimulates the development of male sex organs, secondary sexual traits, and sperm: isolated from animal testes or produced synthetically for use in medicine.

test′-tube′ ba′by, *n.* an infant developed from an ovum fertilized in an experimental dish and implanted into a woman's uterus, usu. that of the biological mother.

te·tan·ic (tə tan′ik) also **te·tan′i·cal,** *adj.* **1.** pertaining to, of the nature of, or characterized by tetanus. **2.** capable of producing muscle spasms that are characteristic of tetanus.

tet·a·nize (tet′n īz′), *v.t.,* **-nized, -niz·ing.** to induce tetanic spasms in (a muscle). —**tet′a·ni·za′tion,** *n.*

tet·a·nus (tet′n əs), *n.* **1.** an infectious disease characterized by tonic spasms and rigidity of muscles, esp. of the lower jaw and neck, sometimes leading to respiratory paralysis and death, caused by a bacterium, *Clostridium tetani,* which commonly enters the body through wounds and cuts. Compare LOCKJAW. **2.** sustained contraction of a muscle, esp. when induced experimentally or by a poison. —**tet′a·nal,** *adj.* —**tet′a·noid′,** *adj.*

tet′a·ny, *n.* a condition marked by severe, intermittent tonic contractions and muscular pain, due to abnormal calcium metabolism.

tet·ra·cy·cline (te′trə sī′klēn, -klin), *n.* an antibiotic, $C_{22}H_{24}H_2O_8$, derived from a streptomyces, used in medicine to treat a broad variety of infections.

tet·ra·hy·dro·can·nab·i·nol (te′trə hī′drə kə nab′ə nôl′, -nol′), *n.* a compound, $C_{21}H_{30}O_2$, that is the physiologically active component in cannabis preparations, including marijuana and hashish, derived from the Indian hemp plant or produced synthetically. *Abbr.:* THC

tet·ra·ploid (te′trə ploid′), *adj.* **1.** having a chromosome

number that is four times the basic or haploid number.
—*n.* **2.** a tetraploid cell or organism. —**tet′ra·ploi′dy,** *n.*

te·tro·do·tox·in (te trō′də tok′sin), *n.* a neurotoxin, $C_{11}H_{17}N_3O_8$, occurring in a species of puffer fish: ingestion may be fatal.

tet·ter (tet′ər), *n.* any of various eruptive skin diseases, as herpes or eczema.

thal·a·mus (thal′ə məs), *n.,* pl. **-mi** (-mī′). the middle part of the diencephalon of the brain, serving to transmit and integrate sensory impulses. —**tha·lam·ic** (thə lam′ik), *adj.*

thal·as·se·mi·a (thal′ə sē′mē ə), *n.* a hereditary anemia marked by the abnormal production of hemoglobin, occurring chiefly in people of Mediterranean origin. Also called **Cooley's anemia.**

tha·lid·o·mide (thə lid′ə mīd′), *n.* a crystalline, slightly water-soluble solid, $C_{13}H_{10}N_2O_4$, formerly used as a sedative: if taken during pregnancy, it may cause severe abnormalities in the limbs of the fetus.

thal·li·um (thal′ē əm), *n.* a bluish white metallic element, injected into the bloodstream as a radioisotope, esp. in a stress test, to form an image of blood flowing to the heart. *Symbol:* Tl; *at. wt.:* 204.37; *at. no.:* 81; *sp. gr.:* 11.85 at 20°C.

than·a·tol·o·gy (than′ə tol′ə jē), *n.* the branches of medicine and psychiatry concerned with the terminally ill and their survivors. —**than′a·to·log′i·cal** (-tl oj′i kəl), *adj.* —**than·a·tol′o·gist,** *n.*

than·a·to·pho·bi·a (than′ə tə fō′bē ə), *n.* an abnormal fear of death.

Than·a·tos (than′ə tos′, -tōs), *n. Psychoanal.* (*usu. l.c.*) the death instinct, esp. as expressed in violent aggression. —**Than′a·tot′ic** (-tot′ik), *adj.*

THC, tetrahydrocannabinol.

T helper cell, *n.* HELPER T CELL.

Themat′ic Appercep′tion Test′, *n. Psychol.* a projective technique in which stories told by a subject about each of a series of pictures are assumed to reveal dominant needs or motivations. *Abbr.:* TAT

the·o·bro·mine (thē′ə brō′mēn, -min), *n.* a crystalline alkaloid powder, $C_7H_8N_4O_2$, related to caffeine, obtained from the cacao bean and used chiefly in medicine as a diuretic and stimulant.

the·o·phyl·line (thē′ə fil′ēn, -in), *n.* a crystalline alkaloid, $C_7H_8N_4O_2$, an isomer of theobromine extracted from tea leaves or produced synthetically, used in the treatment of asthma to relieve bronchial spasms.

ther′apeu′tic in′dex, *n.* the ratio between the dosage of a drug that causes a lethal effect and the dosage that causes a therapeutic effect.

ther·a·py (ther′ə pē), *n., pl.* **-pies. 1.** the treatment of disease or disorders, as by some remedial, rehabilitative, or curative process: *speech therapy.* **2.** PSYCHOTHERAPY.

ther·mo·dur·ic (thûr′mə door′ik, -dyoor′ik), *adj.* (of certain microorganisms) able to survive high temperatures, as during pasteurization.

ther·mo·gen·e·sis (thûr′mō jen′ə sis), *n.* the production of heat, esp. in an animal body by physiological processes. —**ther′mo·ge·net′ic** (-jə net′ik), *adj.*

ther·mo·gram (thûr′mə gram′), *n.* a graphic or visual record produced by thermography.

ther·mog·ra·phy (thər mog′rə fē), *n.* a technique for measuring regional skin temperatures, used esp. as a screening method for detection of breast cancer. —**ther′mog′ra·pher**, *n.* —**ther·mo·graph·ic** (thûr′mə graf′ik), *adj.* —**ther′mo·graph′i·cal·ly**, *adv.*

ther·mo·la·bile (thûr′mō lā′bil, -bil), *adj.* subject to destruction or loss of characteristic properties by the action of moderate heat, as certain toxins and enzymes (opposed to *thermostable*). —**ther′mo·la·bil′i·ty**, *n.*

ther·mol·y·sis (thər mol′ə sis), *n.* the dispersion of heat from the body. —**ther·mo·lyt′ic** (thûr′mə lit′ik), *adj.*

ther·mom·e·ter (thər mom′i tər), *n.* an instrument for measuring temperature, often a sealed glass tube containing a column of liquid, as mercury, that expands and contracts with temperature changes, the temperature being read where the top of the column coincides with a calibrated scale on the tube or frame.

ther·mo·phil·ic (thûr′mə fil′ik), *adj.* growing best in a warm environment, as many bacteria.

ther·mo·re·cep·tor (thûr′mō ri sep′tər), *n.* a receptor stimulated by changes in temperature.

ther′mo·reg′u·la′tion, *n.* the regulation of body temperature. —**ther′mo·reg′u·late′**, *v.t.*, **-lat·ed**, **-lat·ing**. —**ther′mo·reg′u·la·to′ry**, *adj.*

ther′mo·sta·ble, *adj.* capable of being subjected to a moderate degree of heat without loss of characteristic properties (opposed to *thermolabile*). —**ther′mo·sta·bil′i·ty**, *n.*

ther·mo·tax·is (thûr′mə tak′sis), *n.* the regulation of body temperature. —**ther′mo·tac′tic** (-tak′tik), **ther′mo·tax′ic**, *adj.*

the′ta rhythm′, *n.* a pattern of brain waves (**the′ta waves**) with a regular frequency of 4 to 7 hertz, occurring during light sleep.

thi·a·mine (thī′ə min, -mēn) also **thi·a·min** (-min), *n.* a crystalline, water-soluble vitamin-B compound, $C_{12}H_{17}ClN_4OS$, abundant in liver, legumes, and cereal grains. Also called **vitamin B₁**.

thi·a·zide (thī′ə zid′, -zid), *n.* any of a class of diuretic substances that promote the excretion of sodium and water.

thigh·bone (thī′bōn′), *n.* FEMUR.

thi·mer·o·sal (thi mûr′ə sal′, -mer′-), *n.* a crystalline, water-soluble powder, $C_9H_9HgNaO_2S$, used as an antiseptic.

thi·o·ba·cil·lus (thī′ō bə sil′əs), *n., pl.* **-cil·li** (-sil′ī). any of several rod-shaped sulfur bacteria, of the genus *Thiobacillus*, that are common in soil and sewage.

thi·o·pen·tal so·di·um (thī′ə pen′tl, -tal, -tôl, thī′-), *n.* a barbiturate, $C_{11}H_{18}N_3NaO_2S$, used as an anesthetic and in narcoanalysis.

third′-degree′ burn′, *n.* See under BURN.

tho·rac·ic (thô ras′ik, thō-), *adj.* of, pertaining to, or involving the thorax.

thorac′ic duct′, *n.* the main trunk of the lymphatic system, passing along the spinal column in the thoracic cavity and conveying a large amount of lymph and chyle into the venous circulation.

tho·ra·cot·o·my (thôr′ə kot′ə mē, thōr′-), *n., pl.* **-mies.** surgical incision into the chest cavity.

tho·rax (thôr′aks, thōr′-), *n., pl.* **tho·rax·es, tho·ra·ces** (thôr′ə sēz′, thōr′-). the part of the trunk between the neck and the abdomen, containing the heart and lungs in a bony cage of vertebrae, ribs, and sternum; chest: in mammals separated from the lower trunk by the diaphragm.

Tho·ra·zine (thôr′ə zēn′, thōr′-), *Trademark.* a brand of chlorpromazine.

Thr, threonine.

thre·o·nine (thrē′ə nēn′, -nin), *n.* an essential amino acid, $CH_3CHOHCH(NH_2)COOH$, obtained by the hydrolysis of proteins. *Abbr.:* Thr; *Symbol:* T

thresh·old (thresh′ōld, thresh′hōld), *n.* Also called **limen.** the point at which a stimulus is of sufficient intensity to begin to produce an effect: *the threshold of consciousness; a low threshold of pain.*

throm·bin (throm′bin), *n.* an enzyme of the blood plasma that catalyzes the conversion of fibrinogen to fibrin, the last step of the blood-clotting process.

throm·bo·cyte (throm′bə sīt′), *n.* **1.** BLOOD PLATELET. **2.** one of the minute, nucleate cells that aid coagulation in the blood of those vertebrates that do not have blood platelets. —**throm·bo·cyt′ic** (-sit′ik), *adj.*

throm·bo·cy·to·pe·ni·a (throm′bō sī′tə pē′nē ə), *n.* an abnormal decrease in the number of blood platelets.

throm′bo·em′bo·lism, *n.* the blockage of a blood vessel by a thrombus carried through the bloodstream from its site of formation. —**throm′bo·em·bol′ic** (-em bol′ik), *adj.*

throm·bo·phle·bi′tis, *n.* the presence of a thrombus in a vein accompanied by inflammation of the vessel wall.

throm·bo·plas·tic (throm′bə plas′tik), *adj.* causing or accelerating blood-clot formation. —**throm′bo·plas′ti·cal·ly,** *adv.*

throm′bo·plas′tin, *n.* a lipoprotein in the blood that converts prothrombin to thrombin. Also called **throm·bo·ki·nase** (throm′bō kī′nās, -kin′ās).

throm·bo·sis (throm bō′sis), *n.* intravascular coagulation of the blood in any part of the circulatory system. —**throm·bot′ic** (-bot′ik), *adj.*

throm·box·ane (throm bok′sān), *n.* a compound, $C_{20}H_{32}O_5$, formed in blood platelets, that constricts blood vessels and promotes clotting.

throm·bus (throm′bəs), *n., pl.* **-bi** (-bī). a fibrinous clot that forms in and obstructs a blood vessel, or that forms in one of the chambers of the heart.

thrush (thrush), *n.* a disease of the mouth characterized by a whitish growth and ulcerations, caused by a fungus of the genus *Candida*, esp. *C albicans*. Compare CANDIDIASIS.

thy·mec·to·my (thī mek′tə mē), *n., pl.* **-mies.** surgical removal of the thymus gland.

thym·ic (thī′mik), *adj.* of or pertaining to the thymus.

thy·mi·dine (thī′mi dēn′), *n.* a nucleoside, $C_{10}H_{14}N_2O_5$, containing thymine and deoxyribose, that is a constituent of DNA.

thy·mine (thī′mēn, -min), *n.* a pyrimidine base, $C_5H_6N_2O_2$, that is one of the principal components of DNA, in which it is paired with adenine. *Symbol:* T

thy·mo·cyte (thī′mə sīt′), *n.* a cell that develops in the thymus and is the precursor of T cells.

thy·mol (thī′mōl, -mōl), *n.* a colorless crystalline compound, $C_{10}H_{14}O$, extracted from oil of thyme or prepared synthetically, used as a preservative of biological specimens and as an antiseptic.

thy·mo·sin (thī′mə sin), *n.* a hormone, produced by the thymus gland, that promotes the development of T cells from stem cells.

thy·mus (thī′məs), *n., pl.* **-mus·es, -mi** (-mī). a ductless, butterfly-shaped gland lying at the base of the neck, formed mostly of lymphatic tissue and aiding in the production of T cells of the immune system: after puberty, the lymphatic tissue gradually degenerates. Also called **thy′mus gland′.**

thy·roid (thī′roid), *adj.* **1.** of or pertaining to the thyroid gland. **2.** of or pertaining to the largest cartilage of the larynx, forming the projection known in humans as the Adam's apple. —*n.* **3.** THYROID GLAND. **4.** the thyroid cartilage. **5.** an artery, vein, etc., in the thyroid region. —**thy·roi′dal,** *adj.* —**thy′roid·less,** *adj.*

thy·roid·ec·to·my (thī′roi dek′tə mē), *n., pl.* **-mies.** surgical excision of all or a part of the thyroid gland.

thy′roid gland′, *n.* a two-lobed endocrine gland located at the base of the neck and secreting two hormones that regulate the rates of metabolism, growth, and development. Compare THYROXINE, TRIIODOTHYRONINE.

thy·roid·i·tis (thī′roi dī′tis), *n.* inflammation of the thyroid gland.

thy′roid-stim′ulating hor′mone, *n.* THYROTROPIN. *Abbr.:* TSH

thy·ro·tox·i·co·sis (thī′rō tok′si kō′sis), *n.* GRAVES′ DISEASE.

thy·ro·troph·ic (thī′rə trof′ik, -trō′fik) also **thy·ro·trop·ic** (-trop′ik, -trō′pik), *adj.* capable of stimulating the thyroid gland.

thy·ro·tro·pin (thī′rə trō′pin, thī rō′trə-) also **thy·ro·tro·phin** (-fin), *n.* an anterior pituitary hormone that regulates the activity of the thyroid gland. Also called **thyroid-stimulating hormone.**

thyrotro/pin-releas/ing hor/mone, *n.* See TRH.

thy·rox·ine (thī rok/sēn, -sin) also **thy·rox·in** (-sin), *n.* a hormone of the thyroid gland that regulates the metabolic rate of the body: preparations of it used for treating hypothyroidism.

TIA, transient ischemic attack.

tib·i·a (tib/ē ə), *n., pl.* **tib·i·ae** (tib/ē ē/), **tib·i·as.** the inner of the two bones of the leg, extending from the knee to the ankle and articulating with the femur and the talus; shinbone. —**tib/i·al,** *adj.*

tic (tik), *n.* **1.** a sudden spasmodic, painless, involuntary muscular contraction, as of the face. **2.** TIC DOULOUREUX.

tic dou·lou·reux (tik/ dōō/lə rōō/; *Fr.* tēk dōō lōō rœ/), *n.* paroxysmal darting pain and muscular twitching in the face, caused by a disorder of the trigeminal nerve and commonly affecting elderly people. Also called **trigeminal neuralgia.**

tick/ fe/ver, *n.* any infectious disease transmitted by ticks, as Rocky Mountain spotted fever.

timed/-release/ also **time-release,** *adj.* SLOW-RELEASE.

tim·o·lol (tim/ə lōl/, -lol/), *n.* a beta blocker, $C_{13}H_{24}N_4O_3S$, used in the treatment of angina, hypertension, and glaucoma.

tinc·ture (tingk/chər), *n.* a solution of alcohol or of alcohol and water, containing animal, vegetable, or chemical drugs.

tin·e·a (tin/ē ə), *n.* any of several fungal infections of the skin, esp. ringworm. —**tin/e·al,** *adj.*

tin/ea bar/bae (bär/bē), *n.* barber's itch caused by any of various fungi.

tin/ea cru/ris (krōōr/is), *n.* JOCK ITCH.

tin·ni·tus (ti nī/təs, tin/i-), *n.* a sensation of sound, as ringing, in the ears.

tis·sue (tish/ōō; *esp. Brit.* tis/yōō), *n.* an aggregate of similar cells and cell products forming one of the structural materials of an organism.

tis/sue cul/ture, *n.* **1.** the technique or process of growing living tissue in a prepared medium outside the body. **2.** the tissue so cultured.

tis/sue plasmin/ogen ac/tivator, *n.* See TPA.

tit·u·ba·tion (tich/ōō bā/shən), *n.* a neurological disturbance of body equilibrium resulting in an uncertain gait and trembling. —**tit/u·bant** (-bənt), *adj.*

T lymphocyte, *n.* T CELL.

TMJ, temporomandibular joint syndrome.

TNF, tumor necrosis factor.

to·coph·er·ol (tō kof/ə rôl/, -rol/), *n.* any of several oils that constitute vitamin E.

to·ga·vi·rus (tō/gə vī/rəs), *n., pl.* **-rus·es.** any of several RNA-containing viruses of the family Togaviridae, typically enveloped in a layer of lipid and including the arboviruses and the rubella virus.

tol·er·ance (tol′ər əns), *n.* **1.** the power of enduring or resisting the action of a drug, poison, etc. **2.** the lack of, or low levels of, immune response to transplanted tissue or other foreign substance.

tol′er·ant, *adj.* **1.** able to endure or resist the action of a drug, poison, etc. **2.** lacking or exhibiting low levels of, immune response to a normally immunogenic substance.

tol′er·ate′ (-rāt′), *v.t.,* **-at·ed, -at·ing.** to endure or resist the action of (a drug, invasive procedure, etc.).

tol·naf·tate (tōl naf′tāt, tol–), *n.* an antifungal substance, $C_{19}H_{17}NOS$, used topically for treating certain skin diseases, as athlete's foot.

to·mo·gram (tō′mə gram′), *n.* the visual record produced by tomography.

to′mo·graph′, *n.* **1.** TOMOGRAM. **2.** an apparatus for making tomograms.

to·mog·ra·phy (tə mog′rə fē), *n.* a method of making x-ray photographs of a selected plane of the body. **—to·mo·graph·ic** (tō′mə graf′ik), *adj.* **—to′mo·graph′i·cal·ly,** *adv.*

tone (tōn), *n., v.,* **toned, ton·ing.** **—n. 1. a.** the normal state of tension or responsiveness of the organs or tissues of the body. **b.** that state of the body or of an organ in which all its functions are performed with healthy vigor. **2. a.** a normal healthy mental condition. **b.** a particular mental state or disposition. **—v.t. 3.** to give or restore physical or mental tone to.

tongue′-tie′, *n.* impeded motion of the tongue caused esp. by shortness of the frenum, which binds it to the floor of the mouth.

tongue′-tied′, *adj.* affected with tongue-tie.

ton·ic (ton′ik), *n.* **1.** a medicine that invigorates or strengthens. **—adj. 2.** pertaining to, maintaining, increasing, or restoring the tone or health of the body or an organ, as a medicine. **—ton′i·cal·ly,** *adv.*

to·nom·e·ter (tō nom′i tər), *n.* any of various instruments for measuring intraocular pressure or blood pressure. **—ton·o·met·ric** (ton′ə me′trik, tō′nə–), *adj.* **—to·nom′e·try,** *n.*

ton·sil (ton′səl), *n.* a prominent oval mass of lymphoid tissue on each side of the throat. **—ton′sil·lar,** *adj.*

ton·sil·lec·to·my (ton′sə lek′tə mē), *n., pl.* **-mies.** the operation of excising or removing one or both tonsils.

ton·sil·li·tis (ton′sə lī′tis), *n.* inflammation of a tonsil or the tonsils. **—ton′sil·lit′ic** (-lit′ik), *adj.*

ton·sil·lot·o·my (ton′sə lot′ə mē), *n., pl.* **-mies.** incision or excision of a portion of a tonsil.

to·nus (tō′nəs), *n.* a normal state of continuous slight tension in muscle tissue that facilitates its response to stimulation.

to·phus (tō′fəs), *n., pl.* **-phi** (-fī). a calcareous concretion formed in the soft tissue about a joint, in the pinna of the ear, etc., esp. in gout. **—to·pha·ceous** (tə fā′shəs), *adj.*

top·i·cal (top′i kəl), *adj.* on the skin or external surface: *a topical ointment.* —**top′i·cal·ly,** *adv.*

tor·ti·col·lis (tôr′ti kol′is), *n.* a condition in which the neck is twisted and the head inclined to one side, caused by spasmodic contraction of the muscles of the neck. Also called **wryneck.**

to·tal paren′teral nutri′tion, *n.* intravenous administration of a solution of essential nutrients to patients unable to ingest food. *Abbr.:* TPN Also called **hyperalimentation.**

to·tip·o·tent (tō tip′ə tənt), *adj.* (of a cell or part) having the potential for developing in various specialized ways. —**to·tip′o·ten·cy,** *n.*

Tourette′s syn′drome (tŏŏ rets′), *n.* a neurological disorder characterized by recurrent involuntary movements, esp. of the neck, and sometimes vocal tics, as grunts or words, esp. obscenities.

tour·is·ta or **tu·ris·ta** (tŏŏ rē′stə), *n.* traveler's diarrhea, esp. as experienced by some visitors to Latin America.

tour·ni·quet (tûr′ni kit, tŏŏr′-), *n.* any device for arresting bleeding by forcibly compressing a blood vessel, as a bandage tightened by twisting.

tox·e·mi·a (tok sē′mē ə), *n.* **1.** blood poisoning resulting from the presence of toxins, as bacterial toxins, in the blood. **2.** an abnormal condition of pregnancy characterized by hypertension, fluid retention, and edema. —**tox·e′mic,** *adj.*

tox·ic (tok′sik), *adj.* **1.** of, pertaining to, affected with, or caused by a toxin or poison: *a toxic condition.* **2.** acting as or having the effect of a poison; poisonous: *a toxic drug.* —**tox′i·cal·ly,** *adv.*

tox·i·cant (tok′si kənt), *adj.* poisonous; toxic.

tox·ic·i·ty (tok sis′i tē), *n., pl.* **-ties.** the quality, relative degree, or specific degree of being toxic or poisonous.

tox·i·co·gen·ic (tok′si kō jen′ik), *adj.* generating or producing toxic products or poisons.

tox·i·col·o·gy (tok′si kol′ə jē), *n.* the branch of pharmacology dealing with the effects, antidotes, detection, etc., of poisons. —**tox′i·co·log′i·cal** (-kə loj′i kəl), **tox′i·co·log′ic,** *adj.* —**tox′i·co·log′i·cal·ly,** *adv.* —**tox′i·col′o·gist,** *n.*

tox′i·co′sis (-kō′sis), *n.* an abnormal condition produced by the action of a poison.

tox′ic shock′ syn′drome, *n.* a rapidly developing toxemia caused by the bacterium *Staphylococcus aureus,* occurring esp. in menstruating women using high-absorbency tampons.

tox·i·gen·ic (tok′si jen′ik), *adj.* (esp. of microorganisms) producing toxins. —**tox′i·ge·nic′i·ty,** *n.*

tox·in (tok′sin), *n.* any poison produced by an organism, including the bacterial toxins that are the causative agents of tetanus, diphtheria, etc., and such plant and animal toxins as ricin and snake venom.

tox·oid (tok′soid), *n.* a bacterial toxin rendered harmless by chemicals and used for inducing immunity.

tox·o·plas·mo·sis (tok′sō plaz mō′sis), *n.* an infection with a protozoan, *Toxoplasma gondii*, commonly transmitted by contaminated meat or cat feces: usu. mild but a cause of fetal damage in pregnant women.

TPA or **tPA**, tissue plasminogen activator: an anticlotting enzyme of the blood, produced in quantity by genetic engineering for use in dissolving blood clots.

TPN, total parenteral nutrition.

trace′ el′ement, *n.* any chemical element that is required in minute quantities for physiological functioning. Also called **trace′ min′eral.**

trac·er (trā′sər), *n.* a substance, esp. a radioactive one, traced through a biological, chemical, or physical system in order to study the system.

tra·che·a (trā′kē ə), *n., pl.* **-che·ae** (-kē ē′), **-che·as.** (in air-breathing vertebrates) a tube that extends from the larynx to the bronchi, serving as the principal passageway of air to and from the lungs; windpipe.

tra′che·al, *adj.* pertaining to or connected with the trachea or tracheae.

tra′che·i′tis (-i′tis), *n.* inflammation of the trachea.

tra′che·o·bron′chi·al, *adj.* of, pertaining to, or affecting the trachea and bronchi.

tra·che·os·to·my (trā′kē os′tə mē), *n., pl.* **-mies. 1.** the construction of an artificial opening through the neck into the trachea, usu. for the relief of difficulty in breathing. **2.** the opening so constructed.

tra′che·ot′o·my, *n., pl.* **-mies.** the operation of cutting into the trachea. —**tra′che·ot′o·mist,** *n.*

tra·cho·ma (trə kō′mə), *n.* a chronic eye infection characterized by granulations and scarring of the cornea and conjunctiva, caused by the bacterium *Chlamydia trachomatis.* —**tra·chom′a·tous** (-kom′ə təs, -kō′mə-), *adj.*

trac·tion (trak′shən), *n.* the deliberate and prolonged pulling of a muscle, organ, or the like, as by weights, to correct dislocation, relieve pressure, etc. —**trac′tion·al,** *adj.*

tran·quil·iz·er or **tran·quil·liz·er** (trang′kwə li′zər), *n.* **1.** Also called **anxiolytic, minor tranquilizer.** any of various drugs, as the benzodiazepines, that have a mildly sedative, calming, or muscle-relaxing effect. **2.** ANTIPSYCHOTIC (def. 2).

trans·ac·tion (tran sak′shən, -zak′-), *n. Psychol.* an interaction of an individual with one or more other persons, esp. as influenced by their assumed relational roles of parent, child, or adult. —**trans·ac′tion·al,** *adj.* —**trans·ac′tion·al·ly,** *adv.*

transac′tional anal′ysis, *n.* a form of psychotherapy focusing on social interactions and analysis of relationships as individuals shift among the roles of parent, child, and adult. *Abbr.:* TA

trans·am·i·nase (trans am′ə nās′, -nāz′, tranz-), *n.* any of a class of enzymes that conduct transamination.

trans·am′i·na′tion (-am′ə nā′shən), *n.* the transfer of an amino group from one compound to another.

tran·scribe (tran skrīb′), *v.t.* **-scribed, -scrib·ing.** to cause to undergo transcription. —**tran·scrib′er,** *n.*

tran·scrip·tase (tran skrip′tās, -tāz), *n.* RNA POLYMERASE.

tran·scrip·tion (tran skrip′shən), *n.* the process by which messenger RNA is synthesized on a template of DNA.

trans·cu·ta·ne·ous (trans′kyoō tā′nē əs, tranz-), *adj.* by way of or through the skin.

trans·der·mal (-dûr′məl), *adj.* **1.** Also, **trans·der′mic.** transcutaneous. **2.** (of a medication) applied to the skin, usu. as part of an adhesive patch, for absorption into the bloodstream.

trans·duce (trans doōs′, -dyoōs′, tranz-), *v.t.* **-duced, -duc·ing.** to cause transduction in (a cell).

trans·duc·tion (-duk′shən), *n.* the transfer of genetic material from one cell to another by means of a virus. —**trans·duc′tant** (-tənt), *n.* —**trans·duc′tion·al,** *adj.*

trans·fec·tion (trans fek′shən), *n.* the insertion into a bacterial cell of a viral nucleic acid in order to cause the cell to produce the virus. —**trans·fect′,** *v.t.* **-fect·ed, -fect·ing.**

trans·fer·ase (trans′fə rās′, -rāz′), *n.* any of a group of enzymes, the transaminases, that effect the transfer of an organic group from one compound to another.

trans·fer·ence (trans fûr′əns, trans′fər əns), *n.* Psychoanal. **1.** the shift of emotions, esp. those experienced in childhood, from one person or object to another, esp. the transfer of feelings about a parent to an analyst. **2.** DISPLACEMENT. —**trans·fer·en′tial** (-fə ren′shəl), *adj.*

trans·fer·rin (trans fer′in), *n.* a plasma glycoprotein that transports dietary iron to the liver, spleen, and bone marrow.

transfer RNA, *n.* any of a class of small, cloverleaf forms of RNA that transfer unattached amino acids in the cell cytoplasm to the ribosomes for protein synthesis. *Abbr.:* tRNA

trans·for·ma·tion (trans′fər mā′shən), *n.* the transfer of genetic material from one cell to another resulting in a genetic change in the recipient cell. —**trans′for·ma′tion·al,** *adj.*

trans·fuse (trans fyoōz′), *v.t.* **-fused, -fus·ing.** to transfer (blood, saline solution, etc.) by injection into a vein or artery. —**trans·fus′i·ble, trans·fus′a·ble,** *adj.* —**trans·fu′sive** (-fyoō′siv, -ziv), *adj.*

trans·fu′sion, *n.* the direct transferring of blood, plasma, etc., into a blood vessel.

trans·gen′ic, *adj.* of, pertaining to, or containing a gene or genes transferred from another species: *transgenic mice.*

tran′sient ische′mic attack′, *n.* a brief vascular

spasm in which a partially blocked artery impedes blood flow to the brain; a minor stroke. *Abbr.*: TIA.

trans·il·lu·mi·nate (trans/i loo̅/mə nāt/, tranz/-), *v.t.*, **-nat·ed, -nat·ing.** to throw a strong light through (an organ or body part) as a means of diagnosis. —**trans/il·lu/mi·na/tion,** *n.* —**trans/il·lu/mi·na/tor,** *n.*

trans·la·tion (trans lā/shən, tranz-), *n.* the process by which messenger RNA specifies the sequence of amino acids that line up on a ribosome for protein synthesis. —**trans·la/tion·al,** *adj.*

trans·lo·ca/tion, *n.* the movement of a gene or set of genes from one chromosome to another.

trans·mem/brane, *adj.* occurring across a membrane, as an electric potential or the transport of ions or gases.

trans·mit (trans mit/, tranz-), *v.t.*, **-mit·ted, -mit·ting. 1.** to pass or spread (disease, infection, etc.) to another. **2.** to pass on (a genetic characteristic) from parent to offspring. —**trans·mit/ta·ble,** *adj.* —**trans·mit/tal,** *n.*

trans·mit/ter, *n.* NEUROTRANSMITTER.

trans·per/son·al, *adj.* being or involving an altered state of consciousness. —**trans·per/son·al·ly,** *adv.*

trans·pla·cen/tal (trans/plə sen/tl), *adj.* across or passing through the placenta.

trans·plant (*v.* trans plant/, -plänt/; *n.* trans/plant/, -plänt/), *v.t.* **1.** to transfer (an organ, tissue, etc.) from one part of the body to another or from one person or animal to another. —*n.* **2.** an organ, tissue, etc., that has been transplanted. —**trans·plant/a·ble,** *adj.* —**trans/plan·ta/tion,** *n.*

trans·po·si·tion (trans/pə zish/ən), *n.* the movement of a gene or set of genes from one DNA site to another. —**trans/po·si/tion·al, trans·pos/i·tive** (-poz/i tiv), *adj.*

trans·po·son (trans pō/zon), *n.* a gene or set of genes capable of inserting copies of itself into other DNA sites within the same cell. Also called **jumping gene.**

trans·sex·u·al (trans sek/shoo əl), *n.* **1.** a person who has undergone surgical and hormonal treatment in order to assume the physical characteristics and gender role of the opposite sex. —*adj.* **2.** of, pertaining to, or characteristic of transsexuals. —**trans·sex/u·al·ism, trans·sex/u·al/i·ty,** *n.*

tran·sude (tran sood/), *v.i.*, **-sud·ed, -sud·ing.** to pass or ooze through pores or interstices, as a fluid.

trans/verse co/lon (kō/lən), *n.* the middle portion of the colon, lying across the upper abdominal cavity between the ascending colon on the right and the descending colon on the left.

transverse/ proc/ess, *n.* a process that projects from the sides of a vertebra.

trans·ves·tite (trans ves/tit, tranz-), *n.* a person, esp. a man, who assumes the dress and often the manner usu. associated with the opposite sex, esp. for psychological gratification. —**trans·ves/tism, trans·ves/ti·tism,** *n.*

tra·pe·zi·us (trə pē′zē əs), *n., pl.* **-us·es.** a broad, flat muscle on each side of the upper back.

trau·ma (trou′mə, trô′-), *n., pl.* **-mas, -ma·ta** (-mə tə). **1. a.** a body wound or shock produced by physical injury, as from violence or an accident. **b.** the condition produced by this; traumatism. **2.** *Psychiatry.* severe distress from experiencing a disastrous event outside the range of usual experience, as rape, military combat, or an airplane crash. —**trau·mat·ic** (trə mat′ik, trô-, trou-), *adj.* —**trau·mat·i·cal·ly,** *adv.*

trau·ma·tism, *n.* **1.** any abnormal condition produced by a trauma. **2.** the trauma or wound itself.

trau·ma·tize′, *v.t.,* **-tized, -tiz·ing. 1.** to cause a trauma in or to. **2.** to injure (tissues) by force or by thermal, chemical, etc., agents. —**trau·ma·ti·za′tion,** *n.*

trau·ma·tol·o·gy, *n.* a branch of medicine dealing with major wounds caused by accidents or violence. —**trau·ma·tol′o·gist,** *n.*

trav′elers′ diarrhe′a, *n.* diarrhea caused by ingestion of local bacteria to which one's digestive system is not adapted.

treat·ment (trēt′mənt), *n.* **1.** the application of medicines, surgery, therapy, etc., in treating a disease or disorder. **2.** a substance, procedure, or course of such substances or procedures used in treating medically. —**treat′a·ble,** *adj.*

tre·ha·lose (trē′hə lōs′, tri hā′lōs), *n.* a white, crystalline disaccharide, $C_{12}H_{22}O_{11}$, occurring in yeast, certain fungi, etc., and used to identify certain bacteria.

trem·a·tode (trem′ə tōd′, trē′mə-), *n.* any of various parasitic flatworms of the class Trematoda, having external suckers. Also called **fluke.**

trem·or (trem′ər, trē′mər), *n.* involuntary shaking of the body or limbs, as from disease. —**trem′or·ous,** *adj.*

trench′ fe′ver, *n.* a recurrent fever and pain in the muscles and joints, often suffered by soldiers serving in trenches, caused by a rickettsia transmitted by the body louse.

trench′ foot′, *n.* injury of the skin, blood vessels, and nerves of the feet due to prolonged exposure to cold and moisture, common among soldiers serving in trenches.

trench′ mouth′, *n.* an acute ulcerating infection of the gums and throat, caused by a combination of bacilli and spirochetes. Also called **Vincent's angina, acute necrotizing gingivitis.**

tre·pan (tri pan′), *v.t.,* **-panned, -pan·ning.** to operate on surgically with a trephine. —**trep·a·na·tion** (trep′ə nā′shən), *n.* —**tre·pan′ner,** *n.*

tre·phine (tri fīn′, -fēn′), *n., v.,* **-phined, -phin·ing.** —*n.* **1.** a small circular saw used in surgery to remove disks of bone, esp. from the skull. —*v.t.* **2.** to operate on with a trephine. —**treph·i·na·tion** (tref′ə nā′shən), *n.*

trep·o·ne·ma (trep′ə nē′mə), *n., pl.* **-mas, -ma·ta** (-mə tə). any of several spirochetes of the genus *Treponema,* certain species of which cause diseases in warm-blooded animals, as the syphilis spirochete in humans. —**trep′o·nem′a·tous** (-nem′ə təs, -nē′mə-), **trep′o·ne′mal**, *adj.*

tre·tin·o·in (trə tin′ō in), *n.* a drug chemically related to vitamin A, used as a topical ointment to treat skin disorders, esp. acne.

TRH, thyrotropin-releasing hormone: a hormone of the hypothalamus that controls the release of thyrotropin by the pituitary gland.

tri·age (trē äzh′), *n., adj., v.,* **-aged, ag·ing.** —*n.* **1.** the process of sorting victims, as of a battle or disaster, to determine priority of medical treatment, with highest priority usu. given to those having the greatest likelihood of survival. **2.** the determination of priorities for action in an emergency. —*adj.* **3.** of, pertaining to, or performing the task of triage: *a triage officer.* —*v.t.* **4.** to act on or in by triage: *to triage a crisis.*

tri·am·cin·o·lone (tri′am sin′ə lōn′), *n.* a synthetic glucocorticoid drug, $C_{21}H_{27}FO_6$, used in the symptomatic treatment of inflammation.

tri·car′box·yl′ic ac′id cy′cle (tri kär′bok sil′ik, -kär′-), *n.* KREBS CYCLE.

tri·ceps (tri′seps), *n., pl.* **-ceps·es** (-sep siz), **-ceps.** any muscle with three heads, esp. the one at the back of the upper arm, extending the forearm when contracted.

tri·chi·a·sis (tri kī′ə sis), *n.* a condition in which the eyelashes grow inwardly.

tri·chi·na (tri kī′nə), *n., pl.* **-nae** (-nē). a nematode, *Trichinella spiralis,* parasitic esp. in humans, pigs, and rats.

trich·i·no·sis (trik′ə nō′sis) also **trich·i·ni·a·sis** (-ni′ə-sis), *n.* infestation of the intestines and muscle tissue with trichinae, usu. by eating infected meat, esp. undercooked pork.

trich·i·nous (trik′ə nəs), *adj.* **1.** infested with trichinae. **2.** having or pertaining to trichinosis.

trich·ome (trik′ōm, tri′kōm), *n.* a microorganism composed of many filamentous cells arranged in strands or chains. —**tri·chom·ic** (tri kom′ik, -kō′mik), *adj.*

trich·o·mo·nad (trik′ə mon′ad, -mō′nad), *n.* any flagellate protozoan of the genus *Trichomonas,* parasitic in humans or animals. —**trich′o·mon′a·dal, trich·o·mon·al** (trik′ə mon′l, -mōn′l, tri kom′ə nl), *adj.*

trich·o·mo·ni·a·sis (-mə nī′ə sis), *n.* **1.** a sexually transmitted disease typically asymptomatic in men and resulting in vaginitis with a copious, frothy discharge and itching in women, caused by a trichomonad, *Trichomonas vaginalis.* **2.** any of various other diseases caused by a trichomonad.

trich′o·san′thin (-san′thin), *n.* COMPOUND Q.

tri·cho·sis (tri kō′sis), *n.* any disease of the hair.

tri·chro·mat·ic (tri′krō mat′ik, -krə-), *adj.* of, pertaining to, or exhibiting normal color vision.

tri·chro·ma·tism (tri krō′mə tiz′əm), *n.* normal color vision.

tri·crot·ic (trī krot′ik), *adj.* **1.** having three arterial beats for one heartbeat, as certain pulses. **2.** pertaining to such a pulse. **—tri·cro·tism** (trī′krə tiz′əm, trik′rə-), *n.*

tri·cus·pid valve′, *n.* a valve of the heart, composed of three flaps, that keeps blood from flowing backward from the right ventricle into the right atrium. Compare MITRAL VALVE.

tri·cy·clic (trī sī′klik, -sik′lik), *n.* any of a group of pharmacologically active substances that share a common three-ring structure, used to treat depression and cocaine abuse. Also called **tricy′clic antidepres′sant.**

tri·fa·cial (trī fā′shəl), *adj.* TRIGEMINAL.

tri·flu·o·per·a·zine (trī floo′ə per′ə zēn′), *n.* a compound, $C_{21}H_{24}F_3N_3S$, used as an antipsychotic drug.

tri·gem·i·nal (trī jem′ə nl), *adj.* of or pertaining to the trigeminal nerve.

trigem′inal nerve′, *n.* either one of the fifth pair of vertebrate cranial nerves that innervate the jaw muscles and head region.

trigem′inal neural′gia, *n.* TIC DOULOUREUX.

tri·glyc·er·ide (trī glis′ə rīd′, -ər id), *n.* an ester obtained from glycerol, forming much of the fats and oils stored in animal and vegetable tissues. Compare GLYCERIDE.

tri·i·o·do·thy·ro·nine (trī′ī ō′dō thī′rə nēn′, -ī od′ō-), *n.* a thyroid hormone, $C_{15}H_{12}I_3NO_4$, similar to thyroxine but more potent: preparations of it used in treating hypothyroidism.

tri·meth·o·prim (trī meth′ə prim), *n.* a synthetic crystalline compound, $C_{11}H_{18}N_4O_3$, usu. combined with a sulfa drug as an antibiotic preparation in the treatment of urinary tract infections and pneumocystis pneumonia.

tri·nu·cle·o·tide (trī noo′klē ə tīd′, -nyoo′-), *n.* three linked nucleotides; triplet.

tri·ose (trī′ōs), *n.* a monosaccharide that has three atoms of carbon.

tri·pha·sic (trī fā′zik), *n.* a combination drug given in three phases and eliciting three physiological effects.

tri·plet (trip′lit), *n.* **1.** one of three children or offspring born at the same birth. **2. triplets,** three offspring born at one birth. **3.** a sequence of three nucleotides; a codon in messenger RNA and an anticodon in transfer RNA.

trip·lo·blas·tic (trip′lō blas′tik), *adj.* (of an animal embryo) differentiating into three primary layers, the ectoderm, endoderm, and mesoderm.

trip′loid, *adj.* **1.** having a chromosome number that is three times the basic or haploid number. **—n. 2.** a triploid cell or organism. **—trip′loi·dy,** *n.*

tris·kai·dek·a·pho·bi·a (tris′kī dek′ə fō′bē ə, tris′kə-), *n.* fear or a phobia concerning the number 13. **—tris′kai·dek′a·pho′bic,** *adj.*

tris·mus (triz′məs, tris′-), *n.,* *pl.* **-mus·es. 1.** a spasm of the jaw muscles that makes it difficult to open the mouth. **2.** LOCKJAW. **—tris′mic,** *adj.*

tri·so·my (trī′sō mē), *n.* a genetic deviation characterized by the presence of three chromosomes where there are usually a pair. —**tri·so′mic,** *adj.*

trisomy 21, *n.* DOWN SYNDROME.

tRNA, TRANSFER RNA.

tRNA synthetase, *n.* SYNTHETASE (def. 2).

tro·car (trō′kär), *n.* a sharp-pointed surgical instrument enclosed in a cannula, used for withdrawing fluid from a cavity, as the abdominal cavity.

tro·che (trō′kē), *n.,* *pl.* **-ches.** a small tablet or lozenge, usu. a circular one, made of medicinal substance worked into a paste with sugar and mucilage or the like and dried.

troch·le·a (trok′lē ə), *n.,* *pl.* **-le·ae** (-lē ē′), **-le·as.** a pulleylike anatomical structure or arrangement of parts.

troch′le·ar, *adj.* **1.** (of a body part or function) pulleylike. —*n.* **2.** Also, **troch′lear nerve′.** either one of the fourth pair of cranial nerves, consisting of motor fibers that innervate certain eye muscles.

trom·bi·di·a·sis (trom/bi di′ə sis), *n.* the condition of being infested with chiggers.

troph·ic (trof′ik, trō′fik), *adj.* of or pertaining to nutrition; involving nutritive processes: *a trophic disease.* —**troph′i·cal·ly,** *adv.*

troph·o·blast (trof′ə blast′, trō′fə-), *n.* the layer of extra-embryonic ectoderm that chiefly nourishes the embryo or develops into fetal membranes with nutritive functions. —**troph′o·blas′tic,** *adj.*

tro·po·nin (trō′pə nin, trop′ə-), *n.* a protein of muscle tissue that binds calcium ions and is involved in contraction.

Trp, tryptophan.

truss (trus), *n.* a device consisting of a pad usu. supported by a belt for maintaining a hernia in a reduced state.

truth′ se·rum, *n.* a drug, as the barbiturate thiopental sodium, considered to induce an inclination to talk freely and to reveal repressed or consciously withheld information. Also called **truth′ drug′.**

try·pan·o·some (tri pan′ə sōm′, trip′ə nə-), *n.* any of various flagellated protozoans of the genus *Trypanosoma,* transmitted by insect bite and parasitic in the blood and tissue of humans, domestic animals, and other vertebrates. —**try·pan′o·so′mal, try·pan′o·som′ic** (-som′ik), *adj.*

try·pan·o·so·mi·a·sis (-sō mi′ə sis), *n.* **1.** SLEEPING SICKNESS (def. 1). **2.** any other infectious disease caused by a trypanosome.

tryp·sin (trip′sin), *n.* an enzyme of the pancreatic juice, capable of converting proteins into peptone. —**tryp′tic** (-tik), *adj.*

tryp·sin·o·gen (trip sin′ə jən, -jen′), *n.* a precursor of trypsin that is secreted by the pancreas and converted to trypsin in the small intestine.

tryp·to·phan (trip′tə fan′) also **tryp·to·phane** (-fān′), *n.* an essential amino acid, $(C_8H_6N)CH_2CH(NH_2)COOH$, released from proteins by the enzyme trypsin during digestion. *Abbr:* Trp; *Symbol:* W

tset′se (or **tzet′ze**) **fly′** (tset′sē, tet′-, tsē′tsē, tē′-), *n.* any of several bloodsucking African flies of the genus *Glossina,* including some that are vectors of trypanosomes that cause sleeping sickness and other diseases. Also called **tset′se.**

TSH, thyroid-stimulating hormone.

TSS, toxic shock syndrome.

tub′al liga′tion, *n.* a method of permanent sterilization for women, involving the surgical sealing of the fallopian tubes to prevent the ovum from passing from the ovary to the uterus.

tube (tōōb, tyōōb), *n.* any hollow, cylindrical vessel or organ: *the bronchial tubes.* —**tube′like′,** *adj.*

tu•ber•cle (tōō′bər kəl, tyōō′-), *n.* **1.** a small rounded projection or excrescence, as on a bone or on the surface of the body. **2. a.** a small, firm, rounded nodule or swelling. **b.** such a swelling as the characteristic lesion of tuberculosis.

tu′bercle bacil′lus, *n.* the bacterium, *Mycobacterium tuberculosis,* causing tuberculosis.

tu•ber•cu•lar (tōō bûr′kyə lər, tyōō-), *adj.* Also, **tuberculous. 1.** pertaining to or infected with tuberculosis. **2.** of, pertaining to, or of the nature of a tubercle or tubercles. —*n.* **3.** a person affected with tuberculosis. —**tu•ber′cu•lar•ly,** *adv.*

tu•ber•cu•late (-lit, -lāt′), *adj.* **1.** Also, **tu•ber′cu•lat′ed.** having tubercles. **2.** TUBERCULAR. —**tu•ber′cu•la′tion,** *n.*

tu•ber•cu•lin, *n.* a sterile liquid prepared from cultures of the tubercle bacillus, used in a scratch test for tuberculosis.

tu•ber•cu•lo•sis, *n.* **1.** an infectious disease that may affect almost any tissue of the body, esp. the lungs, caused by the organism *Mycobacterium tuberculosis,* and characterized by tubercles. **2.** this disease when affecting the lungs. *Abbr.:* TB

tu•ber•cu•lous, *adj.* TUBERCULAR. —**tu•ber′cu•lous•ly,** *adv.*

tu•ber•ous (tōō′bər əs, tyōō′-), *adj.* characterized by the presence of rounded or wartlike prominences or tubers.

tu•bo•cu•ra•rine (tōō′bō kyōō rär′ēn, -in, tyōō′-), *n.* the principal active alkaloid of curare, $C_{38}H_{44}Cl_2N_2O,$ used as a muscle relaxant, esp. as an adjunct to anesthesia.

tu•la•re•mi•a or **tu•la•rae•mi•a** (tōō′lə rē′mē ə), *n.* a plaguelike disease of rabbits, squirrels, etc., caused by a bacterium, *Francisella tularensis,* transmitted to humans by insects or ticks or by the handling of infected animals.

tu•me•fa•cient (tōō′mə fā′shənt, tyōō′-), *adj.* becoming swollen; swelling.

tu•me•fac•tion (tōō′mə fak′shən, tyōō′-), *n.* **1.** a swollen part. **2.** a swelling up of a part.

tum′my tuck′, *n. Informal.* ABDOMINOPLASTY.

tu•mor (tōō′mər, tyōō′-), *n.* **1.** a swollen part; swelling; protuberance. **2.** an uncontrolled, abnormal, circumscribed growth of cells in any animal or plant tissue; neoplasm. Also, *esp. Brit.,* **tu′mour.** —**tu′mor·like′,** *adj.* —**tu′mor·ous,** *adj.*

tu·mor·i·gen·e·sis (tōō′mər i jen′ə sis, tyōō′-), *n.* the production or development of tumors.

tu·mor·i·gen′ic, *adj.* (of cells or a substance) capable of producing tumors. —**tu′mor·i·ge·nic′i·ty,** *n.*

tu′mor necro′sis fac′tor, *n.* a protein, produced in humans and other animals, that is destructive to cells showing abnormally rapid growth. *Abbr.:* TNF

tun′nel vi′sion, *n.* a drastically narrowed field of vision, as in looking through a tube, symptomatic of retinitis pigmentosa. —**tun′nel-vi′sioned,** *adj.*

tu·ris·ta (tōō rē′stə), *n.* TOURISTA.

Tur·ner's syn′drome (tûr′nərz), *n.* an abnormal congenital condition resulting from a defect on or absence of the second sex chromosome, characterized by retarded growth of the gonads.

tus·sive (tus′iv), *adj.* of or pertaining to a cough.

Twelve′ Step′ or **12-step,** *adj.* of or based on a program for recovery from addiction originating with Alcoholics Anonymous and providing 12 progressive levels toward attainment. —**12-stepper,** *n.*

twen′ty-twen′ty or **20-20,** *adj.* having normal visual acuity.

Ty·le·nol (tī′lə nôl′, -nol′), *Trademark.* a brand of acetaminophen.

tym·pan·ic (tim pan′ik), *adj.* pertaining or belonging to a tympanum.

tympan′ic bone′, *n.* (in mammals) a bone of the skull, supporting the tympanic membrane and enclosing part of the middle ear.

tympan′ic mem′brane, *n.* EARDRUM.

tym·pa·ni·tes (tim′pə nī′tēz), *n.* gross distention of the abdominal wall by gas in the peritoneal cavity or intestines. —**tym·pa·nit′ic** (-nit′ik), *adj.*

tym·pa·num (tim′pə nəm), *n., pl.* **-nums, -na** (-nə). **1.** MIDDLE EAR. **2.** EARDRUM.

Type A, *n.* a personality type characterized by competitive, aggressive, and tense behavior, believed to be associated with susceptibility to heart attack.

Type B, *n.* a personality type characterized by amiable, tolerant, and relaxed behavior, believed to be associated with decreased risk of heart attack.

ty·phoid (tī′foid), *n.* **1.** Also called **ty′phoid fe′ver, enteric fever.** an acute infectious disease characterized by high fever and intestinal inflammation, spread by food or water contaminated with the bacillus *Salmonella typhosa.* —*adj.* **2.** resembling typhus; typhous. **3.** typhoidal.

ty·phoi′dal, *adj.* of, pertaining to, or resembling typhoid.

Ty′phoid Mar′y, *n.* a carrier or transmitter of anything undesirable, harmful, or catastrophic.

ty·phus (tī′fəs), *n.* an acute infectious disease caused by several species of rickettsias, esp. *Rickettsia prowazekii,* transmitted by lice and fleas, and characterized by acute prostration, headache, and a peculiar eruption of reddish spots on the body. Also called **ty′phus fe′ver.** —**ty′phous,** *adj.*

Tyr, tyrosine.

ty·ra·mine (tī′rə mēn′), *n.* an amine, $C_8H_{11}NO$, abundant in ripe cheese as a breakdown product of tyrosine.

ty·ro·si·nase (tī′rō si nās′, -nāz′, tir′ō-), *n.* an enzyme of plant and animal tissues that catalyzes the aerobic oxidation of tyrosine into melanin and other pigments.

ty·ro·sine (tī′rə sēn′, -sin, tir′ə-), *n.* a crystalline amino acid, $HOC_6H_4CH_2CH(NH_2)COOH$, abundant in ripe cheese, that acts as a precursor of norepinephrine and dopamine. *Abbr.:* Tyr; *Symbol:* Y

U

U, *Symbol.* uracil.

u·biq·ui·tin (yōō bik′wi tin), *n.* a small protein, present in all eukaryotic cells, that participates in the destruction of defective proteins and in the synthesis of new proteins.

ul·cer (ul′sər), *n.* **1.** a sore on the skin or a mucous membrane, accompanied by the disintegration of tissue, the formation of pus, etc. **2.** PEPTIC ULCER.

ul·cer·ate (ul′sə rāt′), *v.,* **-at·ed, -at·ing.** —*v.i.* **1.** to form an ulcer; become ulcerous. —*v.t.* **2.** to cause an ulcer on or in. —**ul′cer·a′tion,** *n.*

ul·cer·a·tive (ul′sə rā′tiv, -sər ə tiv), *adj.* **1.** causing the formation of ulcers. **2.** of the nature of or affected with ulcers.

ul′cer·ous, *adj.* **1.** of the nature of an ulcer; characterized by the formation of ulcers. **2.** affected with an ulcer.

ul·na (ul′nə), *n., pl.* **-nae** (-nē) **-nas.** the bone of the forearm on the side opposite to the thumb. —**ul′nar,** *adj.*

ul·tra·cen·tri·fuge (ul′trə sen′trə fyōōj′), *n.* a high-speed centrifuge for subjecting solutions to forces many times that of gravity and producing concentration differences depending on the weight of the micelle or molecule.

ul·tra·mi·cro·tome (-mi′krə tōm′), *n.* a microtome capable of producing very fine slices of tissue or cellular specimens for examination by electron microscope.

ul·tra·son·ic (-son′ik), *adj.* of, pertaining to, or utilizing sound with a frequency greater than 20,000 hertz, approximately the upper limit of human hearing. —**ul′tra·son′i·cal·ly,** *adv.*

ul·tra·son′o·gram′, *n.* an image or record produced by ultrasonography.

ul·tra·so·nog·ra·phy (-sə nog′rə fē, -sō-), *n.* a diagnostic imaging technique utilizing reflected ultrasonic waves to delineate, measure, or examine internal body structures or organs.

ul·tra·sound′, *n.* the application of ultrasonic waves to therapy or diagnostics, as in deep-heat treatment of a joint or in ultrasonography.

ul·tra·vi′rus, *n., pl.* **-rus·es.** FILTERABLE VIRUS.

umbil′ical cord′, *n.* a cordlike structure connecting the fetus with the placenta during pregnancy, conveying nourishment from the mother and removing wastes.

um·bil·i·cus (um bil′i kəs, um′bə li′kəs), *n., pl.* **-bil·i·ci** (-bil′ə sī′, -bə li′sī). NAVEL. —**um·bil′i·form′,** *adj.*

un·ci·na·ri·a·sis (un′sə nə rī′ə sis), *n.* HOOKWORM (def. 2).

un·con·di·tioned (un′kən dish′ənd), *adj.* not having been learned or taught: *an unconditioned response.*

un·con·scious (un kon′shəs), *adj.* **1.** not conscious; without awareness, sensation, or cognition. **2.** temporarily devoid of consciousness. —*n.* **3. the unconscious,** *Psychoanal.* the part of the psyche that is rarely accessible to awareness but that has a pronounced influence on behavior. —**un·con′scious·ly,** *adv.* —**un·con′scious·ness,** *n.*

un·der·nour·ished (un′dər nûr′isht, -nur′-), *adj.* not nourished with sufficient or proper food to maintain health or normal growth. —**un′der·nour′ish·ment,** *n.*

un′der·sexed′ (-sekst′), *adj.* having a weaker sexual drive than is considered usual or normal.

un′dulant fe′ver, *n.* BRUCELLOSIS.

un·guent (ung′gwənt), *n.* an ointment or salve, esp. when liquid or semiliquid. —**un′guen·tar′y,** *adj.*

u·ni·cel·lu·lar (yōō′nə sel′yə lər), *adj.* having or consisting of a single cell. —**u′ni·cel′lu·lar′i·ty,** *n.*

u′ni·fac·to′ri·al (-fak tôr′ē əl, -tōr′-), *adj.* **1.** of or pertaining to a single gene. **2.** of a phenotypic character controlled by a single gene.

u′ni·nu·cle·ate (-nōō′klē it, -āt′, -nyōō′-), *adj.* (of a cell) having one nucleus.

u·ni·va·lent (yōō′nə vā′lənt, yōō niv′ə-), *adj.* **1.** having one binding site, as an antibody. **2.** unpaired, as a chromosome.

u′niver′sal do′nor, *n.* a person with blood type O.

up·per (up′ər), *n. Slang.* a stimulant drug, esp. an amphetamine.

up′stream′, *adv.* against or opposite to the direction of transcription, translation, or synthesis of a DNA, RNA, or protein molecule.

u·ra·cil (yōōr′ə sil), *n.* a pyrimidine base, $C_4H_4N_2O_2$, that is one of the fundamental components of RNA, in which it forms base pairs with adenine. *Symbol:* U

u·re·a (yōō rē′ə, yōōr′ē ə), *n.* a compound, $CO(NH_2)_2$, occurring in urine and other body fluids as a product of protein metabolism. —**u·re′al, u·re′ic,** *adj.*

ure′a cy′cle, *n.* a metabolic process by which ammonia derived from amino acids is converted into urea in the liver.

u·re·ase (yōōr′ē ās′, -āz′), *n.* an enzyme that changes urea into ammonium carbonate, occurring in bacteria, fungi, etc.

u·re·do (yōō rē′dō), *n.* skin irritation; hives; urticaria.

u·re·mi·a (yōō rē′mē ə), *n.* the presence in the blood of excessive urea and other products normally excreted in the urine. —**u·re′mic,** *adj.*

u·re·ter (yōō rē′tər), *n.* a duct that conveys urine from the kidney to the bladder. —**u·re′ter·al, u·re·ter·ic** (yōōr′i-ter′ik), *adj.*

u·re·thra (yōō rē′thrə), *n., pl.* **-thrae** (-thrē), **-thras.** a duct that conveys urine from the bladder to the exterior and, in most male mammals, also conveys semen. —**u·re′thral,** *adj.*

u·re·thri·tis (yōōr′ə thrī′tis), *n.* inflammation of the urethra. —**u·re·thrit′ic** (-thrit′ik), *adj.*

u·re·thro·scope (yōō rē′thrə skōp′), *n.* an apparatus for observing the urethra. —**u·re′thro·scop′ic** (-skop′ik), *adj.* —**u·re·thros·co·py** (yōōr′ə thros′kə pē), *n.*

ur·gi·cen·ter (ûr′jə sen′tər), *n.* a clinic or facility where a person can get immediate medical help in an emergency or treatment for a minor illness or injury.

u·ric (yŏŏr′ik), *adj.* of, pertaining to, contained in, or derived from urine.

u′ric ac′id, *n.* a compound, $C_5H_4N_4O_3$, present in mammalian urine in small amounts as the product of the metabolism of purines.

u·ri·dine (yŏŏr′i dēn′, -din), *n.* a ribonucleoside composed of ribose and uracil.

u·ri·nal·y·sis (yŏŏr′ə nal′ə sis), *n., pl.* **-ses** (-sēz′). a diagnostic analysis of urine.

u·ri·nar·y (yŏŏr′ə ner′ē), *adj.* of or pertaining to urine.

u′rinary blad′der, *n.* a distensible, muscular sac in most vertebrates, in which urine is retained until discharged from the body. Also called **bladder.**

u′rinary cal′culus, *n.* a calcareous stone in the urinary tract.

u·rine (yŏŏr′in), *n.* the waste matter excreted by the kidneys in mammals as a slightly acid yellowish liquid.

u·rin·if·er·ous (yŏŏr′ə nif′ər əs), *adj.* conveying urine.

u·ri·no·gen·i·tal (yŏŏr′ə nō jen′i tl), *adj.* GENITOURINARY.

u·ri·nom·e·ter (yŏŏr′ə nom′i tər), *n.* a device for assessing the specific gravity of urine; a hydrometer for use on urine specimens.

u·ro·chrome (yŏŏr′ə krōm′), *n.* a yellow pigment that gives the color to urine.

u·ro·gen·i·tal (yŏŏr′ō jen′i tl), *adj.* GENITOURINARY.

u·ro·ki·nase (yŏŏr′ə kī′nās, -nāz), *n.* an enzyme, present in the blood and urine of mammals, that activates plasminogen and is used medicinally to dissolve blood clots.

u·ro·lith (yŏŏr′ə lith), *n.* URINARY CALCULUS. —**u′ro·lith′ic,** *adj.*

u·ro·li·thi·a·sis (yŏŏr′ō li thī′ə sis), *n.* a diseased condition marked by the formation of stones in the urinary tract.

u·rol·o·gy (yŏŏ rol′ə jē), *n.* the scientific, clinical, and esp. surgical aspects of the study of the urinary and the genitourinary tract. —**u·ro·log·ic** (yŏŏr′ə loj′ik), **u′ro·log′i·cal,** *adj.* —**u·rol′o·gist,** *n.*

u·ron′ic ac′id, *n.* any of a group of organic acids, as glucuronic acid, occurring in urine.

ur·ti·car·i·a (ûr′ti kâr′ē ə), *n.* HIVES.

ur′ti·cate′, *v.i.,* **-cat·ed, -cat·ing.** (of skin) to erupt with hives. —**ur′ti·ca′tion,** *n.*

u·ru·shi·ol (ŏŏ rŏŏ′shē ôl′, -ol′), *n.* a catechol derivative that is the irritant in poison ivy and its allies.

U.S.P., United States Pharmacopeia. Also called **U.S. Pharm.**

U.S.P.H.S., United States Public Health Service.

u·ter·ine (yŏŏ′tər in, -tə rin′), *adj.* of or pertaining to the uterus or womb.

u·ter·us (yŏŏ′tər əs), *n., pl.* **u·ter·i** (yŏŏ′tə rī′), **u·ter·us·es.** a hollow expandable organ of female placental mammals in which the fertilized egg develops during pregnancy; womb.

UTI, urinary tract infection.

u·tri·cle (yōo′tri kəl), *n.* a small baglike body, as an air-filled cavity in a seaweed. —**u·tric′u·lar** (-yə lər), *adj.*

u·ve·a (yōo′vē ə), *n., pl.* **u·ve·as.** the pigmented vascular tunic of the eye, comprising the iris, choroid coat, and ciliary body. —**u′ve·al, u′ve·ous,** *adj.*

u·ve·i·tis (yōo′vē ī′tis), *n.* inflammation of the uvea. —**u′-ve·it′ic** (-it′ik), *adj.*

u·vu·la (yōo′vyə lə), *n., pl.* **-las, -lae** (-lē′). the small, fleshy, conical body projecting downward from the middle of the soft palate.

u′vu·lar, *adj.* of or pertaining to the uvula. —**u′vu·lar·ly,** *adv.*

V

V, *Symbol.* valine.

VA, Also, **V.A.** Veterans Administration.

vac·cine (vak sēn′; *esp. Brit.* vak′sēn), *n.* **1.** any preparation introduced into the body to prevent a disease by stimulating antibodies against it. **2.** the virus of cowpox, used in vaccination, obtained from pox vesicles of a cow or person.

vac·ci·nee (vak′sə nē′), *n.* a person who receives a vaccination.

vac·cin·i·a (vak sin′ē ə), *n., pl.* **-cin·i·as.** a variant of the cowpox virus that became established in vaccines derived from cowpox-inoculated humans. —**vac·cin′i·al,** *adj.*

vac′uum aspira′tion, *n.* a method of sampling or emptying the contents of the uterus.

va·gal (vā′gəl), *adj.* of or pertaining to a vagus nerve.

va′gal block′, *n.* the obstruction of vagus nerve impulses by the administration of drugs, used to reduce secretion of stomach acid.

va·gi·na (və jī′nə), *n., pl.* **-nas, -nae** (-nē). **1.** the passage leading from the uterus to the vulva in female mammals. **2.** a sheathlike part or organ.

vag·i·nal (vaj′ə nl), *adj.* pertaining to or involving the vagina. —**vag′i·nal·ly,** *adv.*

vag·i·nis·mus (vaj′ə niz′məs), *n.* a painful spasm of the vagina.

vag′i·ni′tis (-nī′tis), *n.* inflammation of the vagina.

va·got·o·my (vā got′ə mē), *n., pl.* **-mies.** the surgical severance of vagus nerve fibers, performed to reduce acid secretion by the stomach.

va·go·to·ni·a (vā′gə tō′nē ə), *n.* hyperexcitability of the vagus nerve, producing bradycardia, decreased heart output, and faintness. —**va′go·ton′ic** (-ton′ik), *adj.*

va′go·trop′ic (-trop′ik, -trō′pik), *adj.* affecting the vagus nerve.

va·gus (vā′gəs), *n., pl.* **-gi** (-jī, -gī). either of the tenth pair of cranial nerves, composed of long sensory and motor neurons that innervate the body from the throat to the abdominal viscera and that function in speech, swallowing, breathing, heart rate, and digestion. Also called **va′gus nerve′.**

Val, valine.

va·lence (vā′ləns) also **va′len·cy,** *n.* the number of binding sites on a molecule, as an antibody or antigen.

val·gus (val′gəs), *n., pl.* **-gus·es.** an abnormally turned position of a part of the bone structure of a human being, esp. of the leg.

val·ine (val′ēn, -in, vā′lēn, -lin), *n.* a white, crystalline, water-soluble compound, $(CH_3)_2CHCH(NH_2)COOH$, an essential amino acid present in most plant and animal proteins. *Abbr.:* Val; *Symbol:* V

Val·i·um (val′ē əm), *Trademark.* a brand of diazepam.

val·pro′ic ac/id (val prō′ik), *n.* a carboxylic acid, $C_8H_{16}O_2$, used in the treatment of epilepsy.

Val·sal/va maneu/ver (val sal′və), *n.* an attempt to expel air against a closed glottis or closed lips and nostrils, used for adjusting pressure in the middle ear.

val·vu·li·tis (val′vyə lī′tis), *n.* inflammation of a valve, esp. of the heart.

var·i·cel·la (var′ə sel′ə), *n.* CHICKENPOX. —**var′i·cel/lar,** *adj.*

var/i·cel/ter vi/rus, *n.* HERPES ZOSTER VIRUS.

var·i·ces (vâr′ə sēz′), *n.* pl. of VARIX.

var·i·co·cele (var′i kō sēl′), *n.* a varicose condition of the spermatic veins of the scrotum.

var·i·cose (var′i kōs′), *adj.* **1.** abnormally enlarged or swollen: *a varicose vein.* **2.** pertaining to or affected with varices.

var/i·co/sis, *n.* the formation of a varix or varices.

var·i·cos·i·ty (var′i kos′i tē), *n., pl.* **-ties.** VARIX.

var·i·cot·o·my (-kot′ə mē), *n., pl.* **-mies.** surgical removal of a varicose vein.

va·ri·o·la (və rī′ə lə), *n.* SMALLPOX. —**va·ri/o·lous, va·ri/o·lar,** *adj.*

var·ix (vâr′iks), *n., pl.* **var·i·ces** (vâr′ə sēz′). a varicose vein. Also called **varicosity.**

var·us (vâr′əs), *n.* abnormal angulation of a bone or joint, with the angle pointing away from the midline.

vas·cu·lar (vas′kyə lər), *adj.* pertaining to, composed of, or provided with vessels that convey fluids, as blood. —**vas/cu·lar·i·ty,** *n.*

vas/cu·lar·ize′, *v.,* **-ized, -iz·ing.** —*v.i.* **1.** (of a tissue) to develop or extend blood vessels or other fluid-bearing vessels or ducts. —*v.t.* **2.** to supply (an organ or tissue) with blood vessels. —**vas/cu·lar·i·za/tion,** *n.*

vas de·fe·rens (vas′ def′ə renz′, -ər ənz), *n., pl.* **va·sa de·fe·ren·ti·a** (vā′sə def′ə ren/shē ə, -shə). a duct that transports sperm from the epididymis to the penis.

va·sec·to·my (va sek′tə mē, vā zek′-), *n., pl.* **-mies.** surgical excision of part or all of the vas deferens to effect sterility in men. —**va·sec/to·mize′,** *v.t.,* **-mized, -miz·ing.**

vas·o·ac·tive (vas′ō ak′tiv, vā′zō-), *adj.* of or pertaining to a substance, drug, or event that changes the diameter of a blood vessel.

vas·o·con·stric·tor (vas′ō kən strik′tər, vā′zō-), *n.* any of various agents, as certain nerves or drugs, that narrow blood vessels and thereby maintain or increase blood pressure. —**vas/o·con·stric/tion,** *n.* —**vas/o·con·stric/tive,** *adj.*

vas·o·di·la·tor (vas′ō di lā′tər, -di-, -di′lā-, vā′zō-), *n.* any of various agents, as certain nerves or drugs, that relax or widen blood vessels and thereby maintain or lower blood pressure. —**vas/o·di·la·ta/tion** (-dil/ə tā′shən, -dī/lə-), **vas/o·di·la/tion,** *n.* —**vas/o·di·la/tive,** *adj.*

vas·o·pres·sin (vas′ō pres′in), *n.* a hormone released by the posterior pituitary gland that constricts small blood vessels and increases the absorption of water by the kidney. Also called **antidiuretic hormone, ADH.**

vas·o·pres·sor, *n.* any hormone or drug that acts as a vasoconstrictor and increases blood pressure and heart rate.

vas·o·spasm (vas/ō spaz′əm, vā′zō-), *n.* a sudden constriction of an artery or vein. —**vas·o·spas′tic** (-spas′tik), *adj.*

vas·ot·o·my (va sot/ə mē, vā zot′-), *n., pl.* **-mies.** surgical incision or opening of the vas deferens.

vas·o·va·sos·to·my (vas/ō vā sos′tə mē, vā′zō-), *n., pl.* **-mies.** the reversal of a vasectomy performed by surgical reconnection of the severed ends of the vas deferens.

VD, venereal disease.

vec·tor (vek/tər), *n.* **1.** something or someone, as a person or an insect, that carries and transmits a disease-causing organism. **2.** any agent, as a mutated virus, that acts as a carrier or transporter. —**vec·to′ri·al** (-tôr′ē əl, -tōr′-), *adj.* —**vec·to′ri·al·ly,** *adv.*

ve·gan (vē′gən, vej′ən), *n.* a vegetarian who omits all animal products from the diet. —**ve′gan·ism,** *n.*

veg′e·tal pole′ (vej′i tl), *n.* the relatively inactive part of an ovum opposite the animal pole, containing much yolk and little cytoplasm.

veg·e·tar·i·an (vej/i târ′ē ən), *n.* **1.** a person who does not eat meat, fish, fowl, or, in some cases, any food derived from animals. —*adj.* **2.** of or pertaining to vegetarianism or vegetarians.

veg′e·tar′i·an·ism, *n.* the practices or beliefs of a vegetarian.

ve·hi·cle (vē′i kəl *or, sometimes,* vē′hi-), *n.* a chemically inert substance used as a medium for active remedies.

vein (vān), *n.* one of the system of branching vessels or tubes conveying blood from various parts of the body to the heart.

ve·na ca·va (vē′nə kā′və), *n., pl.* **ve·nae ca·vae** (vē′nē kā′vē). either of two large veins discharging blood into the right atrium of the heart.

ve·ne·re·al (və nēr′ē əl), *adj.* **1.** arising from, connected with, or transmitted through sexual intercourse, as an infection. **2.** pertaining to conditions so arising.

vene′real disease′, *n.* SEXUALLY TRANSMITTED DISEASE. *Abbr.:* VD

vene′real wart′, *n.* a soft, warty nodule of viral origin that occurs on the mucosal surfaces of the genitalia or around the anus.

ven·e·sec·tion (ven′ə sek/shən, vē′nə-), *n.* PHLEBOTOMY.

ven·in (ven/in, vē′nin), *n.* any of several poisonous substances occurring in snake venom.

ven·i·punc·ture (ven/ə pungk/chər, vē′nə-), *n.* the puncture of a vein for surgical or therapeutic purposes or for collecting blood specimens for analysis.

ve·nog·ra·phy (vē nog′rə fē), n. x-ray examination of a vein or veins following injection of a radiopaque substance.

ve·nol·o·gy (vē nol′ə jē), n. PHLEBOLOGY.

ve·nous (vē′nəs), adj. pertaining to or designating the oxygen-poor, dark red blood that is carried back to the heart by the veins and by the pulmonary artery. —**ve′nous·ly,** adv. —**ve′nous·ness, ve·nos·i·ty** (vi nos′i tē), n.

ven·ti·late (ven′tl āt′), v.t., **-lat·ed, -lat·ing. 1.** to oxygenate (blood) by exposure to air in the lungs or gills. **2.** to assist the breathing of (a person), as with a respirator.

ven·tri·cle (ven′tri kəl), n. **1.** any of various hollow organs or parts in an animal body. **2.** either of the two lower chambers of the heart that receive blood from the atria and in turn force it into the arteries. **3.** one of a series of connecting cavities of the brain.

ven·tric·u·lar (ven trik′yə lər), adj. of, pertaining to, or of the nature of a ventricle.

ve·ra·pam·il (vēr′ə pam′əl, ver′-), n. a white, crystalline powder, $C_{27}H_{38}N_2O_4$, used as a calcium blocker in the treatment of angina and certain arrhythmias.

ver·big·er·a·tion (vər bij′ə rā′shən), n. the constant or obsessive repetition of meaningless words or phrases, as in mental illness.

ver·mi·cide (vûr′mə sīd′), n. a substance used to kill worms, esp. a drug for killing intestinal worms. —**ver′mi·cid′al,** adj.

ver·mi·form (vûr′mə fôrm′), adj. resembling a worm in shape; long and slender.

ver′miform appen′dix, n. a wormlike tube, closed at the end, extending from the cecum of the large intestine. Also called **appendix.**

ver·mi·fuge (-fyoōj′), adj. **1.** serving to expel worms or other animal parasites from the intestines, as a medicine. —n. **2.** a vermifuge medicine or agent.

ver·ru·ca (və roō′kə, ve-), n., pl. **-cae** (-sē). a wart or wartlike prominence.

ver·ru·cose (ver′ə kōs′, və roō′kōs′), adj. studded with wartlike protuberances or elevations. —**ver′ru·cos′i·ty** (-kos′i tē), **ver′ru·cose′ness,** n.

ver·sion (vûr′zhən, -shən), n. **1.** the act of turning a fetus in the uterus so as to bring it into a more favorable position for delivery. **2.** an abnormal direction of the axis of the uterus or other organ.

ver·te·bra (vûr′tə brə), n., pl. **-brae** (-brē′, -brā′), **-bras.** any of the bones or segments of the spinal column, consisting in higher vertebrates of a cylindrical body with two projections, forming an arch surrounding the spinal cord.

ver′te·bral, adj. of, pertaining to, or composed of vertebrae; spinal.

ver·te·brate (-brit, -brāt′), adj. **1.** having vertebrae; having a segmented backbone. —n. **2.** a vertebrate animal.

ver·tig·i·nous (vər tij′ə nəs), adj. affected with vertigo. —**ver·tig′i·nous·ly,** adv. —**ver·tig′i·nous·ness,** n.

ver·ti·go (vûr′ti gō′), n., pl. **ver·ti·goes, ver·tig·i·nes**

(vər tij/ə nēz/). a disordered condition in which one feels oneself or one's surroundings whirling about.

ve·si·ca (və si/kə, -sē/-, -ves/i kə), *n., pl.* **-cae** (-sē, -sē/, -kē, -kē/) a bladder.

ves·i·cal (ves/i kəl), *adj.* of or pertaining to a vesica or bladder, esp. the urinary bladder.

ves·i·cant (ves/i kənt), *adj.* **1.** producing a blister or blisters, as a medicinal substance. —*n.* **2.** a vesicant agent or substance.

ves·i·cate/ (-kāt/), *v.t.,* **-cat·ed, -cat·ing.** to raise vesicles or blisters on; blister. —**ves/i·ca/tion,** *n.*

ves·i·cle (ves/i kəl), *n.* **1.** a small sac, cyst, or cavity, esp. one filled with fluid. **2.** BLISTER (def. 1).

ve·sic·u·late (və sik/yə lit, -lāt/), *adj.* **1.** characterized by or covered with vesicles. **2.** of the nature of a vesicle. —**ve·sic/u·la/tion,** *n.*

ves·ti·bule (ves/tə byōōl/), *n.* any hollow part in the body serving as an approach to another hollow part, esp. the front part of the inner ear leading to the cochlea. —**ves·tib·u·lar** (ve stib/yə lər), *adj.*

vi·a·ble (vī/ə bəl), *adj.* (of a fetus) sufficiently developed to be capable of living, under normal conditions, outside the uterus. —**vi/a·bil/i·ty,** *n.* —**vi/a·bly,** *adv.*

vib·ri·o (vib/rē ō/), *n., pl.* **-ri·os.** any of several comma- or S-shaped bacteria of the genus *Vibrio,* certain species of which are pathogenic. —**vib/ri·oid/,** *adj.*

vi·car·i·ous (vī kâr/ē əs, vi-), *adj. Physiol.* noting or pertaining to a situation in which one organ performs part of the functions normally performed by another. —**vi·car/i·ous·ly,** *adv.* —**vi·car/i·ous·ness,** *n.*

Vin·cent's an·gi·na, *n.* TRENCH MOUTH.

vin·cris·tine (vin kris/tēn), *n.* an alkaloid, $C_{46}H_{56}N_4O_{10}$, derived from the periwinkle, *Vinca rosea,* used in treating certain cancers.

vi·ral (vī/rəl), *adj.* of, pertaining to, or caused by a virus.

vi·re·mi·a (vī rē/mē ə), *n.* the presence of a virus in the blood. —**vi·re/mic,** *adj.*

vi·ri·cide (vī/rə sid/), *n.* VIRUCIDE. —**vi/ri·cid/al,** *adj.*

vir·il·ism (vir/ə liz/əm), *n.* the condition in a female of having male secondary sex characteristics.

vi/ril·ize/, *v.t.,* **-ized, -iz·ing.** to induce or promote the development of male secondary sex characteristics in (a female). —**vi/ril·i·za/tion,** *n.*

vi·ri·on (vī/rē on/, vir/ē-), *n.* the infectious form of a virus as it exists outside the host cell, consisting of a core of DNA or RNA, a protein coat, and, in some species, an external envelope.

vi·ru·cide (vī/rə sid/), *n.* an agent for destroying viruses. —**vi/ru·cid/al,** *adj.*

vir·u·lence (vir/yə ləns, vir/ə-) also **vir/u·len·cy,** *n.* **1.** the quality of being virulent. **2.** the relative ability of a microorganism to cause disease; degree of pathogenicity.

vir/u·lent, *adj.* **1.** actively poisonous; intensely noxious.

2. highly infective; malignant or deadly: *a virulent disease.* —**vir′u·lent·ly,** *adv.*

vi·rus (vī′rəs), *n., pl.* **-rus·es. 1.** an ultramicroscopic (20 to 300 nm in diameter), metabolically inert, infectious agent that replicates only within the cells of living hosts, mainly bacteria, plants, and animals: composed of an RNA or DNA core, a protein coat, and, in more complex types, a surrounding envelope. **2.** a disease caused by a virus. —**vi′rus·like′,** *adj.*

vis·cer·a (vis′ər ə), *n.pl., sing.* **vis·cus** (vis′kəs). **1.** the organs in the cavities of the body, esp. those in the abdominal cavity. **2.** (not in technical use) the intestines.

vis′cer·al, *adj.* of, pertaining to, or affecting the viscera. —**vis′cer·al·ly,** *adv.*

vis·cer·o·mo·tor (vis′ə rō mō′tər), *adj.* of or pertaining to the normal movements of the viscera, esp. the digestive tract.

vis′ual acu′ity, *n.* acuteness of the vision as determined by a comparison with the normal ability to identify certain letters at a given distance, usu. 20 ft. (6 m).

vis′ual field′, *n.* FIELD OF VISION.

vis·u·o·spa·tial (vizh′oō ō spā′shəl), *adj.* pertaining to perception of the spatial relationships among objects within the field of vision.

vi′tal capac′ity, *n.* the greatest amount of air that can be forced from the lungs after maximum inhalation.

vi′tal signs′, *n.pl.* essential body functions, comprising pulse rate, body temperature, and respiration.

vi·ta·min (vī′tə min; *Brit. also* vit′ə-), *n.* any of a group of organic substances essential in small quantities to normal metabolism, found in minute amounts in natural foodstuffs and also produced synthetically: deficiencies of vitamins produce specific disorders. —**vi′ta·min′ic,** *adj.*

vitamin A, *n.* a yellow, fat-soluble alcohol, $C_{20}H_{30}O$, obtained from carotene and occurring in green and yellow vegetables, egg yolk, etc.: essential to growth, the protection of epithelial tissue, and the prevention of night blindness. Also called **vitamin A₁, retinol.**

vitamin A₂, *n.* a yellow oil, $C_{20}H_{28}O$, similar to vitamin A, obtained from fish liver.

vitamin B₁, *n.* THIAMINE.

vitamin B₂, *n.* RIBOFLAVIN.

vitamin B₃, *n.* NICOTINIC ACID.

vitamin B₆, *n.* PYRIDOXINE.

vitamin B₁₂, *n.* a complex water-soluble solid, $C_{63}H_{88}N_{14}O_{14}PCo$, obtained from liver, milk, eggs, fish, oysters, and clams: a deficiency causes pernicious anemia and disorders of the nervous system. Also called **cyanocobalamin, cobalamin, extrinsic factor.**

vitamin B complex, *n.* an important group of water-soluble vitamins containing vitamin B₁, vitamin B₂, etc.

vitamin C, *n.* ASCORBIC ACID.

vitamin D, *n.* any of the several fat-soluble vitamins occurring in milk and fish-liver oils, esp. cod and halibut: essential for the formation of normal bones and teeth.

vitamin D₁, *n.* a form of vitamin D obtained by ultraviolet irradiation of ergosterol.

vitamin D₂, *n.* CALCIFEROL.

vitamin D₃, *n.* a form of vitamin D, $C_{27}H_{43}OH$, occurring in fish-liver oils, that differs from vitamin D₂ by slight structural differences in the molecule. Also called **cholecalciferol.**

vitamin E, *n.* a pale yellow, viscous fluid, abundant in vegetable oils, cereal grains, butter, and eggs, important as an antioxidant.

vitamin G, *n.* RIBOFLAVIN.

vitamin H, *n.* BIOTIN.

vitamin K₁, *n.* a yellowish, oily, viscous liquid, $C_{31}H_{46}O_2$, that occurs in leafy vegetables, rice, bran, and hog liver or is obtained esp. from alfalfa or putrefied sardine meat or synthesized and that promotes blood clotting by increasing the prothrombin content of the blood. Also called **phylloquinone, phytonadione.**

vitamin K₂, *n.* a light yellow, crystalline solid, $C_{41}H_{56}O_2$, having properties similar to those of vitamin K₁.

vitamin K₃, *n.* MENADIONE.

vitamin M, *n.* FOLIC ACID.

vitamin P, *n.* BIOFLAVONOID.

vi·tel·lin (vi tel′in, vī-), *n.* a phosphoprotein in the yolk of eggs.

vi·tel·line (vi tel′in, -ēn, vī-), *adj.* of or pertaining to the egg yolk.

vi·tel·lo·gen·e·sis (vi tel′ō jen′ə sis, vī-), *n.* the process by which a yolk is formed and accumulated in the ovum.

vit·i·li·go (vit′l ī′gō, -ē′gō), *n.* a skin disorder, of unknown cause, characterized by patches of unpigmented skin. —**vit′i·li′goid,** *adj.*

vit·rec·to·my (vi trek′tə mē), *n., pl.* **-mies.** the microsurgical procedure of removing the vitreous humor and replacing it with saline solution to improve vision that has been impaired by opaque areas.

vit′reous hu′mor, *n.* the transparent gelatinous substance that fills the eyeball behind the crystalline lens.

viv·i·sect (viv′ə sekt′, viv′ə sekt′), *v.t., v.i.* to subject to or practice vivisection. —**viv′i·sec′tor,** *n.*

viv·i·sec′tion, *n.* **1.** the action of cutting into or dissecting a living body. **2.** the practice of subjecting living animals to cutting operations, esp. in order to advance physiological and pathological knowledge. —**viv′i·sec′tion·al,** *adj.*

VLDL, very-low-density lipoprotein: a plasma lipoprotein with a high lipid content, associated with atherosclerosis.

vo′cal cords′, *n.pl.* either of two pairs of folds of mucous membrane stretched across the larynx, the lower pair of which produces sound or voice as it is made to vibrate by the passage of air from the lungs.

vo′cal folds′, *n.pl.* VOCAL CORDS.

vol′untary mus′cle, *n.* any muscle moved at will and composed of bundles of striated fibers.

vol·vu·lus (vol′vyə ləs), *n., pl.* **-lus·es.** a twisting of the intestine, causing obstruction.

vom·it (vom′it), *v.i.* **1.** to eject the contents of the stomach through the mouth. —*n.* **2.** the matter ejected in vomiting.

vom′i·to·ry (-i tôr′ē, -tōr′ē), *adj.* inducing vomiting; emetic.

vom·i·tus (vom′i təs), *n.* vomited matter. Also called **emesis.**

vor·ti·cel·la (vôr′tə sel′ə), *n., pl.* **-cel·lae** (-sel′ē), **-cel·las.** any ciliated protozoan of the genus *Vorticella,* having a transparent, bell-shaped body with a retractile stalk.

vo·yeur (vwä yûr′, voi ûr′), *n.* a person who obtains sexual gratification by looking at sexual objects or acts, esp. secretively. —**vo·yeur·ism** (vwä yûr′iz əm, voi ûr′-, voi′ə riz′-), *n.* —**voy′eur·is′tic,** *adj.* —**voy′eur·is′ti·cal·ly,** *adv.*

vul·va (vul′və), *n., pl.* **-vae** (-vē), **-vas.** the external female genitalia. —**vul′val, vul′var,** *adj.* —**vul′vi·form′** (-və fôrm′), **vul′vate** (-vāt, -vit), *adj.*

vul·vi·tis (vul vī′tis), *n.* inflammation of the vulva.

vul·vo·vag·i·ni·tis (vul′vō vaj′ə nī′tis), *n.* inflammation of the vulva and vagina.

W

W, *Symbol.* tryptophan.

wall′eye′, *n., pl.* **-eyes. EXOTROPIA.**

wall′eyed′, *adj.* **1.** having exotropia; exotropic. **2.** having a milky whitish eye, as from an opacity of the cornea.

war·fa·rin (wôr′fə rin), *n.* a crystalline anticoagulant, $C_{19}H_{16}O_4$, used in the management of clotting disorders.

warm′-blood′ed or **warm′blood′ed,** *adj.* of or designating animals, as mammals and birds, having a body temperature that is relatively constant and independent of the environment. —**warm′-blood′ed·ness,** *n.*

wart (wôrt), *n.* **1.** a small, often hard growth in the skin, usu. caused by a papillomavirus. **2. VENEREAL WART.** —**wart′ed,** *adj.*

wash (wosh, wôsh), *n.* a lotion or other liquid having medicinal properties (often used in combination): *to apply wash to a skinned knee; mouthwash.*

Was′ser·mann test′ (wä′sər mən), *n.* a diagnostic test for syphilis using the complement fixation by the serum of a syphilitic individual. Also called **Was′sermann reac′tion.**

waste (wāst), *n.* **1.** wastes, excrement. —*adj.* **2.** *Physiol.* pertaining to material unused by or unusable to the organism.

wa′ter blis′ter, *n.* a blister containing a clear, serous fluid.

wa′ter cure′, *n.* **HYDROTHERAPY.**

wa′ter on the brain′, *n.* **HYDROCEPHALUS.**

wa′ter pill′, *n.* a diuretic pill.

wa′ter-sol′uble, *adj.* capable of dissolving in water.

WBC, white blood cell.

weal (wēl), *n.* **WHEAL.**

Wechs′ler Scales′ (weks′lər), *n.pl.* a group of intelligence tests that measure both verbal and performance skills and give separate scores for subtests in vocabulary, arithmetic, assembly of objects, and other abilities.

wen (wen), *n.* a benign encysted tumor of the skin, esp. on the scalp, containing sebaceous matter.

Wer′nick·e-Kor′sa·koff syn′drome (vâr′ni kə kôr′sə kôf′, -kof′), *n.* central nervous system damage caused by thiamine deficiency, characterized by incoordination, memory impairment, and abnormal eye movements.

West′ern blot′, *n.* a test to detect a specific protein, such as that of the AIDS virus, in a blood sample or other extract by introducing a labeled antibody of the protein and observing whether any protein from the sample has bound with it.

wet′ dream′, *n.* an erotic dream accompanied by a nocturnal emission.

wet′ pack′, *n.* a type of bath in which wet sheets are applied to the patient.

wheal (hwēl, wēl) also **weal,** *n.* a small, burning or itching swelling on the skin, as from a mosquito bite or from hives.

whelk (hwelk, welk), *n.* a pimple or pustule.

whip′lash′, *n.* a neck injury caused by a sudden jerking of the head backward, forward, or both.

whip′worm′, *n.* any of several parasitic nematodes of the genus *Trichuris,* having a long, slender, whiplike anterior end.

whirl′pool′, *n.* WHIRLPOOL BATH.

whirl′pool bath′, *n.* **1.** a bath in which the body is immersed in swirling water as therapy or for relaxation. **2.** a device that swirls and often heats the water in such a bath. **3.** a tub or pool containing or equipped with such a device.

white (hwit, wit), *n.* a pellucid, viscous fluid that surrounds the yolk of an egg; albumen.

white′ blood′ cell′, *n.* any of various nearly colorless cells of the immune system that circulate mainly in the blood and lymph, comprising the B cells, T cells, macrophages, monocytes, and granulocytes. Also called **leukocyte, white′ blood′ cor′puscle, white′ cell′.**

white·head (hwit′hed′, wit′-), *n.* MILIUM.

white′ mat′ter, *n.* nerve tissue, esp. of the brain and spinal cord, that primarily contains myelinated fibers and is nearly white in color. Compare GRAY MATTER.

whit·low (hwit′lō, wit′-), *n.* FELON².

WHO, World Health Organization.

whole′ blood′, *n.* blood for transfusion that has not been separated into its components.

who·lism (hō′liz əm), *n.* HOLISM. —**who·lis′tic,** *adj.*

whoop (hwoop, hwŏŏp, woop, wŏŏp, hoop, hŏŏp), *n.* a deep intake of air with a hollow gasping sound, as brought on by choking or rapidly repetitive coughing.

whoop′ing cough′ (hoo′ping, hŏŏp′ing), *n.* an infectious disease of the respiratory mucous membrane caused by the bacterium *Bordetella pertussis* and characterized by a series of short, convulsive coughs followed by a whooping intake of breath. Also called **pertussis.**

wide′-an′gle glauco′ma, *n.* See under GLAUCOMA.

wild′ type′, *n.* **1.** an organism having an appearance that is characteristic of the species in a natural breeding population. **2.** the form or forms of a gene commonly occurring in nature in a given species.

Wil′son's disease′ (wil′sənz), *n.* a rare hereditary disease marked by copper accumulation in the brain and liver, leading to neurological damage and kidney malfunction.

wind′burn′, *n.* an inflammation of the skin caused by overexposure to the wind. —**wind′burned′,** *adj.*

wis′dom tooth′, *n.* the third molar on each side of the upper and lower jaws: the last tooth to erupt.

wish′ fulfill′ment, *n.* the drive to free oneself from the tension caused by a suppressed desire, esp. by symbolizing the desire in dreams, slips of the tongue, etc.

with·draw·al (wiᵺ drô′əl, -drôl′, with-), *n.* **1.** the act or process of ceasing to use an addictive drug. **2.** COITUS INTERRUPTUS.

Wolff′i·an bod′y (vôl′fē ən), *n.* MESONEPHROS.

won′der drug′, *n.* a new drug that is noted for its striking curative effect. Also called **miracle drug.**

word′ blind′ness, *n.* ALEXIA. —**word′-blind′,** *adj.*

word′ deaf′ness, *n.* inability to comprehend the meanings of words though they are heard, caused by lesions of the auditory center of the brain. —**word′-deaf′,** *adj.*

word′ sal′ad, *n.* incoherent speech consisting of both real and imaginary words and lacking comprehensive meaning, occurring in schizophrenic states or other pathological conditions.

work′up′, *n.* a thorough medical diagnostic examination including laboratory tests and x-rays.

worm (wûrm), *n.* **worms,** (*used with a sing. v.*) any disease or disorder arising from the presence of parasitic worms in the intestines or other tissues; helminthiasis.

worm′seed′, *n.* the dried, unexpanded flower heads of a wormwood, *Artemisia cina,* or the fruit of certain goosefoots, esp. *Chenopodium ambrosioides,* used as an anthelmintic drug.

worm′wood′, *n.* any composite plant of the genus *Artemisia,* esp. the bitter, aromatic plant, *A. absinthium,* of Eurasia, used as a vermifuge and a tonic.

wound (wo̅o̅nd), *n.* an injury, usu. involving division of tissue or rupture of the integument or mucous membrane, due to external violence or some mechanical agency rather than disease.

wry·neck (rī′nek′), *n.* **1.** *Informal.* TORTICOLLIS. **2.** a person having torticollis.

X

xan·than (zan′thən), *n.* a gum produced by bacterial fermentation and used commercially as a binder or food stabilizer. Also called **xan′than gum′**.

xan·thine (zan′thēn, -thin), *n.* **1.** a crystalline, nitrogenous compound, $C_5H_4N_4O_2$, related to uric acid, occurring in urine, blood, and certain animal and vegetable tissues. **2.** any derivative of this compound, used esp. as a bronchodilator in the treatment of asthma.

xan·tho·ma (zan thō′mə), *n., pl.* **-mas, -ma·ta** (-mə tə). a yellow papule or nodule in the skin, containing lipid deposits.

X chromosome, *n.* a sex chromosome of humans and most mammals that determines femaleness when paired with another X chromosome and that occurs singly in males. Compare Y CHROMOSOME.

xen·o·bi·ot·ic (zen′ə bī ot′ik, -bē-, zē′nə-), *n.* a chemical or substance that is foreign to an organism or biological system.

xen·o·graft (zen′ə graft′, -gräft′, zē′nə-), *n.* a graft obtained from a member of one species and transplanted to a member of another species. Also called **heterograft**. Compare ALLOGRAFT, AUTOGRAFT.

xe·ro·der·ma (zēr′ə dûr′mə), *n.* a disease in which the skin becomes dry, hard, and scaly.

xe·roph·thal·mi·a (zēr′of thal′mē ə, -op-), *n.* abnormal dryness of the eye caused by a deficiency of tears. —**xe′roph·thal′mic**, *adj.*

xe·ro·sis (zi rō′sis), *n.* abnormal dryness of the skin, eyeballs, or mucous membranes. —**xe·rot′ic** (-rot′ik), *adj.*

X-linked (eks′lingkt′), *adj.* **1.** of or pertaining to a trait controlled by a gene or genes on the X chromosome. **2.** of or pertaining to a gene on an X chromosome.

x-ray or **X-ray** (eks′rā′), *n., v.,* **x-rayed** or **X-rayed**, **x-ray·ing** or **X-ray·ing**. —*n.* Also, **x ray, X ray**. **1.** Often, **x-rays.** electromagnetic radiation having wavelengths in the range of approximately 0.1–10 nm, between ultraviolet radiation and gamma rays, and capable of penetrating solids and of ionizing gases. **2.** a radiograph made by x-rays. —*v.t.* **3.** to photograph, examine, or treat with x-rays. —*adj.* **4.** of or pertaining to x-rays.

x-ray therapy, *n.* treatment of a disease using controlled quantities of x-rays.

xy·li·tol (zī′li tôl′, -tol′), *n.* a naturally occurring pentose sugar alcohol, $C_5H_{12}O_5$, used as a sugar substitute.

xy·lose (zī′lōs), *n.* a colorless pentose sugar, $C_5H_{10}O_5$, used in dyeing, tanning, and diabetic foods.

Y

Y, *Symbol.* tyrosine.

yaw (yô), *n.* one of the lesions of yaws.

yaws (yôz), *n.* (*used with a sing. v.*) an infectious tropical disease, primarily of children, characterized by raspberry-like eruptions of the skin and caused by a spirochete, *Treponema pertenue.* Also called **frambesia.**

Y chromosome, *n.* a sex chromosome of humans and most mammals that is present only in males and is paired with an X chromosome. Compare X CHROMOSOME.

yeast (yēst), *n.* **1.** any of various small, single-celled fungi of the phylum Ascomycota that reproduce by fission or budding, the daughter cells often remaining attached, and that are capable of fermenting carbohydrates into alcohol and carbon dioxide. **2.** any of several yeasts of the genus *Saccharomyces,* used in brewing alcoholic beverages, as a leaven in baking breads, and in pharmacology as a source of vitamins and proteins.

yel·low (yel′ō), *n. Slang.* YELLOW JACKET.

yel′low fe′ver, *n.* an acute, often fatal, infectious febrile disease of warm climates, caused by a togavirus transmitted by a mosquito, esp. *Aedes aegypti,* and characterized by liver damage and jaundice. Also called **yellow jack.**

yel′low jack′, *n.* YELLOW FEVER.

yel′low jack′et, *n. Slang.* a yellow capsule of phenobarbital.

Yellow No. 5, *n.* a yellow dye used in food, drugs, cosmetics, and other products: required by FDA regulations to be identified on food labels because of possible allergic reactions.

yel′low spot′, *n.* MACULA (def. 2b).

yo·ga (yō′gə), *n.* (*sometimes cap.*) a system of physical and mental disciplines practiced to attain control of body and mind, tranquillity, etc., esp. a series of postures and breathing exercises.

yo·him·bine (yō him′bēn), *n.* an extract of the bark of the yohimbe or rauwolfia tree, used as an antiadrenergic drug to oppose the effects of epinephrine.

yolk (yōk, yōlk), *n.* the part of the contents of the egg of an animal that enters directly into the formation of the embryo, together with any material that nourishes the embryo during its formation.

yolk′ sac′, *n.* an extraembryonic membrane that encloses the yolk of eggs.

yolk′ stalk′, *n.* a tubular connection between the yolk sac and the embryonic gut in the developing embryo.

yup′pie flu′, *n. Informal.* CHRONIC FATIGUE SYNDROME.

Z

zi·do·vu·dine (zi dō′vyōō dēn′), *n.* the international generic term for azidothymidine. Compare AZT.

zinc (zingk), *n.* a ductile, bluish white metallic element: essential in minute quantities for physiological functioning. *Symbol:* Zn; *at. wt.:* 65.37; *at. no.:* 30; *sp. gr.:* 7.14 at 20°C.

zinc′ oint′ment, *n.* a ointment composed of mineral oil and zinc oxide, used as a sunblock and to treat skin conditions.

zinc′ ox′ide, *n.* a white powder, ZnO, used as a pigment, in cosmetics and dental cement, and in medicine for treatment of skin conditions.

zo·a (zō′ə), *n.* pl. of ZOON.

zo·an·thro·py (zō an′thrə pē), *n.* a mental disorder in which one believes oneself to be an animal.

zo·na pel·lu·ci·da (zō′nə pə lōō′si də, pel yōō′-), *n., pl.* **zo·nae pel·lu·ci·dae** (zō′nē pə lōō′si dē′, pel yōō′-). a transparent jellylike substance surrounding the ovum of mammals. Also called **zo′na.**

zo·o·gle·a or **zo·o·gloe·a** (zō′ə glē′ə), *n., pl.* **-gle·as** or **-gloe·as, -gle·ae** or **-gloe·ae** (-glē′ē). a jellylike mass of microorganisms. —**zo′o·gle′al,** *adj.*

zo·on (zō′on), *n., pl.* **zo·a** (zō′ə). any individual, or the individuals collectively, produced from a single egg. —**zo′on·al** (-ə nl), *adj.*

zo·on·o·sis (zō on′ə sis, zō′ə nō′sis), *n., pl.* **-ses** (-sēz′, -sēz). any disease of animals communicable to humans.

zo·o·pho·bi·a (zō′ə fō′bē ə), *n.* abnormal fear of animals.

zo′o·plas′ty (-plas′tē), *n., pl.* **-ties.** the transplantation of living tissue to the human body from an animal of another species. —**zo′o·plas′tic,** *adj.*

zos·ter (zos′tər), *n.* SHINGLES.

zy·go·gen·e·sis (zi′gō jen′ə sis, zig′ō-), *n.* **1.** the formation of a zygote. **2.** reproduction by means of gametes. —**zy′go·ge·net′ic** (-jə net′ik), *adj.*

zy·go·ma (zi gō′mə, zi-), *n., pl.* **-ma·ta** (-mə tə), **-mas. 1.** ZYGOMATIC ARCH. **2.** the zygomatic process of the temporal bone. **3.** ZYGOMATIC BONE.

zy·go·mat·ic (zi′gə mat′ik, zig′ə-), *adj.* **1.** of, pertaining to, or situated near the zygoma. **2.** ZYGOMATIC BONE.

zy′gomat′ic arch′, *n.* the bony arch at the outer border of the eye socket, formed by the union of the cheekbone and the zygomatic process of the temporal bone.

zy′gomat′ic bone′, *n.* a bone on each side of the face below the eye, forming the prominence of the cheek; cheekbone.

zygomat′ic proc′ess, *n.* any of several bony processes that articulate with the cheekbone.

zy·go·mor·phism (zi′gə môr′fiz əm, zig′ə-) also **zy·go·**

mor·phy (zi′gə môr′fē, zig′ə-), *n.* BILATERAL SYMMETRY.
—**zy′go·mor′phic, zy′go·mor′phous,** *adj.*

zy·gos·i·ty (zi gos′i tē, zi-), *n.* **1.** the characterization of a
hereditary trait in an individual according to whether the
gene pairs for the trait are homozygous or heterozygous.
2. the characterization of twins, triplets, etc., according to
whether they are monozygotic or dizygotic.

zy·gote (zi′gōt, zig′ōt), *n.* the cell produced by the union
of two gametes, before it undergoes cleavage. —**zy·got·ic**
(zi got′ik, zi-), *adj.* —**zy·got′i·cal·ly,** *adv.*

zy·go·tene (zi′gə tēn′, zig′ə-), *n.* the second stage of
prophase in meiosis, during which corresponding chromosomes become paired.

zy·mase (zi′mās), *n.* an enzyme complex, abundant in
yeast, that acts in alcoholic fermentation and in the production of lactic acid.

zy·mo·gen (zi′mə jən, -jen′), *n.* any of various enzyme
precursor molecules that may change into an enzyme as a
result of catalytic change. Also called **proenzyme.**

zy·mol·o·gy (zi mol′ə jē), *n.* ENZYMOLOGY. —**zy·mo·log′ic**
(-mə loj′ik), *adj.* —**zy·mol′o·gist,** *n.*

zy·mo·sis (zi mō′sis), *n., pl.* **-ses** (-sēz). an infectious or
contagious disease. —**zy·mot′ic** (-mot′ik), *adj.*

Height and Weight Standards

Following are weight tables by height and frame, for people aged 25 to 59, in shoes and wearing 5 pounds of indoor clothing for men, 3 pounds for women.

MEN

Height	Small	Medium	Large
5'2"	128–134	131–141	138–150
5'3"	130–136	133–143	140–153
5'4"	132–138	135–145	142–156
5'5"	134–140	137–148	144–160
5'6"	136–142	139–151	146–164
5'7"	138–145	142–154	149–168
5'8"	140–148	145–157	152–172
5'9"	142–151	148–160	155–176
5'10"	144–154	151–163	158–180
5'11"	146–157	154–166	161–184
6'0"	149–160	157–170	164–188
6'1"	152–164	160–174	168–192
6'2"	155–168	164–178	172–197
6'3"	158–172	167–182	176–202
6'4"	162–176	171–187	181–207

WOMEN

Height	Small	Medium	Large
4'10"	102–111	109–121	118–131
4'11"	103–113	111–123	120–134
5'0"	104–115	113–126	122–137
5'1"	106–118	115–129	125–140
5'2"	108–121	118–132	128–143
5'3"	111–124	121–135	131–147
5'4"	114–127	124–138	134–151
5'5"	117–130	127–141	137–155
5'6"	120–133	130–144	140–159
5'7"	123–136	133–147	143–163
5'8"	126–139	136–150	146–167
5'9"	129–142	139–153	149–170
5'10"	132–145	142–156	152–173
5'11"	135–148	145–159	155–176
6'0"	138–151	148–162	158–179

Reprinted through the courtesy of Metropolitan Life Insurance Company.

Recommended Daily Dietary Allowances

Designed for the maintenance of good nutrition of practically all healthy people in the United States

Category	Age (years) or Condition	Weight (kg)	Weight (lb)	Height (cm)	Height (in)	Protein (g)	Fat-Soluble Vitamins				Water-Soluble Vitamins						
							Vita-min A (mcg)	Vita-min D (mcg)	Vita-min E (mg)	Vita-min K (mcg)	Vita-min C (mg)	Thia-min (mg)	Ribo-flavin (mg)	Niacin (mg)	Vita-min B6 (mg)	Fo-late (mcg)	Vita-min B12 (mcg)
Infants	0.0–0.5	6	13	60	24	13	375	7.5	3	5	30	0.3	0.4	5	0.3	25	0.3
	0.5–1.0	9	20	71	28	14	375	10	4	10	35	0.4	0.5	6	0.6	35	0.5
Children	1–3	13	29	90	35	16	400	10	6	15	40	0.7	0.8	9	1.0	50	0.7
	4–6	20	44	112	44	24	500	10	7	20	45	0.9	1.1	12	1.1	75	1.0
	7–10	28	62	132	52	28	700	10	7	30	45	1.0	1.2	13	1.4	100	1.4
Males	11–14	45	99	157	62	45	1,000	10	10	45	50	1.3	1.5	17	1.7	150	2.0
	15–18	66	145	176	69	59	1,000	10	10	65	60	1.5	1.8	20	2.0	200	2.0
	19–24	72	160	177	70	58	1,000	10	10	70	60	1.5	1.7	19	2.0	200	2.0
	25–50	79	174	176	70	63	1,000	5	10	80	60	1.5	1.7	19	2.0	200	2.0
	51+	77	170	173	68	63	1,000	5	10	80	60	1.2	1.4	15	2.0	200	2.0
Females	11–14	46	101	157	62	46	800	10	8	45	50	1.1	1.3	15	1.4	150	2.0
	15–18	55	120	163	64	44	800	10	8	55	60	1.1	1.3	15	1.5	180	2.0
	19–24	58	128	164	65	46	800	10	8	60	60	1.1	1.3	15	1.6	180	2.0
	25–50	63	138	163	64	50	800	5	8	65	60	1.1	1.3	15	1.6	180	2.0
	51+	65	143	160	63	50	800	5	8	65	60	1.0	1.2	13	1.6	180	2.0
Pregnant						60	800	10	10	65	70	1.5	1.6	17	2.2	400	2.2
Lactating	1st 6 months					65	1,300	10	12	65	95	1.6	1.8	20	2.1	280	2.6
	2nd 6 months					62	1,200	10	11	65	90	1.6	1.7	20	2.1	260	2.6

Category	Age (years) or Condition	Weight (kg)	Weight (lb)	Height (cm)	Height (in)	Minerals Calcium (mg)	Phosphorus (mg)	Magnesium (mg)	Iron (mg)	Zinc (mg)	Iodine (mcg)	Selenium (mcg)
Infants	0.0-0.5	6	13	60	24	400	300	40	6	5	40	10
	0.5-1.0	9	20	71	28	600	500	60	10	5	50	15
Children	1-3	13	29	90	35	800	800	80	10	10	70	20
	4-6	20	44	112	44	800	800	120	10	10	90	20
	7-10	28	62	132	52	800	800	170	10	10	120	30
Males	11-14	45	99	157	62	1,200	1,200	270	12	15	150	40
	15-18	66	145	176	69	1,200	1,200	400	12	15	150	50
	19-24	72	160	177	70	1,200	1,200	350	10	15	150	70
	25-50	79	174	176	70	800	800	350	10	15	150	70
	51+	77	170	173	68	800	800	350	10	15	150	70
Females	11-14	46	101	157	62	1,200	1,200	280	15	12	150	45
	15-18	55	120	163	64	1,200	1,200	300	15	12	150	50
	19-24	58	128	164	65	1,200	1,200	280	15	12	150	55
	25-50	63	138	163	64	800	800	280	15	12	150	55
	51+	65	143	160	63	800	800	280	10	12	150	55
Pregnant						1,200	1,200	320	30	15	175	65
Lactating	1st 6 months					1,200	1,200	355	15	19	200	75
	2nd 6 months					1,200	1,200	340	15	16	200	75

Source: Food and Nutrition Board, National Academy of Sciences

Hormones of the Endocrine Glands

Gland	Hormone
adrenal	epinephrine (adrenaline)
	glucocorticoid
	norepinephrine
ovary	estrogen
	progesterone
pancreas	glucagon
	insulin
parathyroid	parathyroid hormone
pituitary	adrenocorticotropic hormone (ACTH)
	antidiuretic hormone (ADH, vasopressin)
	follicle-stimulating hormone (FSH)
	growth hormone (GH)
	human growth hormone (hGH, somatotropin)
	interstitial-cell-stimulating hormone (ICSH)
	luteinizing hormone (LH)
	malanocyte-stimulating hormone (MSH)
	oxytocin
	prolactin (LTH, luteotropin)
	thyroid-stimulating hormone (TSH, thyrotropin)
testes	testosterone
thyroid	thyroxine

The 20 Amino Acids Required for Protein Synthesis

Amino acid	Abbrev.	Symbol
alanine	Ala	A
arginine	Arg	R
asparagine	Asn	N
aspartic acid	Asp	D
cysteine	Cys	C
glutamic acid	Gtu	E
glutamine	Glu	Q
glycine	Gly	G
histidine	His	H
*isoleucine	Ile	I
*leucine	Leu	L
*lysine	Lys	K
*methionine	Met	M
*phenylalanine	Phe	F
proline	Pro	P
serine	Ser	S
*threonine	Thr	T
*tryptophan	Trp	W
tyrosine	Tyr	Y
*valine	Val	V

*Essential amino acids: Human beings cannot synthesize these amino acids internally and must obtain them in the diet.

Signs and Symbols

*	birth.
†	death.
♂ } □ }	male.
♀ } ○ }	female.
+	1. excess of. 2. acid reaction. 3. positive reaction (to a clinical or diagnostic test).
−	1. deficiency of. 2. alkaline reaction. 3. negative reaction (to a clinical or diagnostic test).
Ⓐ	admitted.
AV	atrioventricular, arteriovenous.
BP	blood pressure.
BUN	blood urea nitrogen (kidney function test).
CBC	complete blood count.
CC	chief complaint.
CNS	central nervous system.
C/O	complained of.
CSF	cerebrospinal fluid.
D&C	dilation and curettage.
D_5W	5% dextrose in water.
D/W	dextrose in water.
Dx	diagnosis.
EKG, ECG	electrocardiogram.
EEG	electroencephalogram.
ESR	erythrocyte sedimentation rate (test for inflammation in the body).
GI	gastrointestinal.
Hct	hematocrit (a measure of red blood cells).
HDL	high density lipoprotein.

HEENT	head, eyes, ears, nose, and throat.
Hx	history.
IM	intramuscular.
IV	intravenous.
Ⓛ	left.
LDL	low density lipoprotein.
NPO	nothing by mouth.
PO	by mouth.
Px	past history, physical examination.
PT, PTT	prothrombin time, partial prothrombin time (measures of blood clotting time).
Ⓡ	right.
R/O	rule out.
SC	subcutaneous.
SGOT	serum glutamic oxaloacetic transaminase (kidney function test).
S_1	first heart sound.
S_2	second heart sound.
S&S, Sx	signs and symptoms.
VLDL	very low density lipoprotein.
$VO_{2\ max}$	maximum ventilation rate of oxygen.
W/V	weight in volume.

Prescriptions

Rx	take (L. *recipe*): presumably based on ♃, the sign of Jupiter, and used to propitiate the god in writing a prescription.
a̅a̅, aa	of each (Gr. *ana*).
a.c.	before meals (L. *ante cibum*).
ad	to (L. *ad*).
ad lib.	as desired (L. *ad libitum*).
ante	before (L. *ante*).
aq	water (L. *aqua*).
b.i.d.	twice a day (L. *bis in die*).
bis	twice (L. *bis*).
c̄, c	with (L. *cum*).
caps.	à capsule (L. *capsula*).
chart.	powder paper (L. *chartula*).
collyr.	an eyewash (L. *collyrium*).
div.	divide (L. *divide*).
d.t.d.	give of such a dose (L. *datur talis dosis*).
elix.	elixir (L., from Arabic, *al iksir*).
enem.	enema (Gr. *enema*).
et	and (L. *et*).
ft. f.	make (L. *fiat*).
ft. pulv.	make a powder (L. *fiat pulvis*).
gtt.	drops (L. *guttae*).
H.	an hour (L. *hora*).
hor.som., H.S.	at bedtime, before going to sleep (L. *hora somni*).
in d.	daily (L. *in dies*).
inf.	infusion (L. *infusio*).
inject.	injection (L. *injectio*).
inter	between (L. *inter*).
liq	a solution (L. *liquor*).
lot.	lotion (L. *lotio*).
M.	mix (L. *misce*).